CANADA'S RMC

ROYAL MILITARY COLLEGE OF CANADA

Presented to
Lieutenant-General Sir Martin Farndale, KCB
Commander, 1 British Corps
BAOR
On the Occasion of His Visit to
The Royal Military College of Canada
7 May 1984

F.J. Norman
COMMANDANT

The Hon. Alexander Mackenzie, prime minister of Canada, 1873–8
From the documentary portrait by Lawren P. Harris, 1964

CANADA'S RMC

A HISTORY OF THE
ROYAL MILITARY COLLEGE

By Richard Arthur Preston

PUBLISHED FOR THE
ROYAL MILITARY COLLEGE CLUB OF CANADA BY
THE UNIVERSITY OF TORONTO PRESS

This history of the Royal Military College of Canada
is respectfully dedicated to the memory of

Number 1557

COLONEL WILLIAM REGINALD SAWYER

O.B.E., E.D., P.S.C., RMC, B.SC., M.SC.,
PH.D., LL.D., D.SC.MIL., F.C.I.C.

Gentleman Cadet, 1920–1924
Associate Professor of Chemistry, 1935–1941
Vice-Commandant and Director of Studies, 1948–1967
Honorary Life Member of the
Royal Military College Club of Canada

GOVERNMENT HOUSE
OTTAWA

The Royal Military College Club of Canada has published this book as its project to mark the centennial anniversary of Canada's Confederation. RMC, which is only nine years younger than Confederation, has been a powerful factor in the growth and security of the country; but this is the first full account of its history. This book is, therefore, a fitting contribution by RMC's ex-cadets to the celebration of Canada's one hundredth birthday.

Too few Canadians realize the significance and importance of the role that RMC has played in the development of their country. This book is designed to fill that deficiency. Even fewer know that Canada's RMC has been a pioneer in military education and that its success was due to the application of the initiative of Canadians and the experience of British regular officers to what was in origin an American model. The story of this unique institution has lessons for military educators everywhere.

Roland Michener

March 1969

PREFACE

The Royal Military College of Canada was from its inception distinctive among military colleges and academies for two reasons: it was the first to be established in a colonial dependency and it had a double function, the preparation of cadets for civilian careers as well as for military commissions.* This dual role did not lead, as sceptics might suspect, to failure to achieve success in either objective. On the contrary, RMC maintained a standard of excellence on both sides that has not been surpassed elsewhere. After World War II, RMC became different from most other military colleges in a third way. Having long produced officers for all the services, it became officially tri-service.† In view of these interesting aspects of RMC's development and the services which it undoubtedly rendered to Canada, empire, and commonwealth, it seems strange that a history of this college which is now approaching its centennial anniversay has hitherto been lacking.

Several abortive starts were in fact made. In 1902, the RMC Club of Canada, with the approval of Sir Frederick Borden, the minister of militia, commissioned a Mr. Alfred Hewett of Toronto to write a college history. In 1904 Hewett's book was destroyed by a fire in the publisher's bindery, but by 1907 he had prepared another manuscript which was expected to be published in May 1908. For some unknown reason the book did not appear and no one has been able to discover why.

When Professor W. R. P. Bridger inaugurated the *R.M.C. Review* in 1920 he wrote to ex-cadets in all parts of the world and began a correspondence that was a fertile source of material about the history of the college. He and his associate, Professor T. F. Gelley, collected information for articles of an historical nature which appeared from time to time in the *Review*. In 1934, as a result of a suggestion from the Advisory Board, the staff-adjutant, Major H. M. Logan, announced that he intended to write the college history and appealed for material. Professor Gelley turned over

*Ecole Polytechnique in Paris, France, founded in 1795, also produces army officers and civilian engineers but the latter are chiefly for the civil service.

†The cadet college in India, opened a few months before Canada's RMC was re-established in 1948, was also tri-service from the outset, but differs in that it gives cadets destined for each of the three services professional training in each one of them.

to him the notes that he had collected, and Logan obtained more documentary material from the Public Archives of Canada. He then wrote one introductory chapter (which is now in the files of the Directorate of History), began to draft a second, but was too busy and subsequently too ill to complete his self-appointed task. Accordingly, Mr. Ronald Way, the director of Fort Henry, was asked to take over his project; Major Logan's notes were sent to him but arrangements had not been completed when the war came and the proposal lapsed.

Early in the war, Professor Bridger began to put together a series of articles about the history of the college, decade by decade. These were factual annals rather than historical narrative or analysis. That covering the first decade seems to have been set only in typescript, but the succeeding articles were published in the *R.M.C. Review*. Professor Bridger's own set of these articles, a volume loosely bound together with ties, is the only extant complete history of the Royal Military College of Canada down to 1942. He gave it to me and it is now deposited in the Massey Library at RMC.

My interest in the history of RMC derives from seventeen happy years spent there as professor of history. Appointed in 1948 when the college was re-opened after the war, I saw the re-establishment from the beginning. It was clear to all who participated that under the leadership of the Director of Studies, Colonel W. R. Sawyer, and a succession of able commandants, we were taking part in a great military and academic experiment that sought to combine the experience and traditions of the past with the changes needed for the future. I wrote several articles about the new developments at RMC and also did considerable research into the early history of Kingston and Point Frederick. Several colleagues suggested at various times that I should write the much needed college history. One suggestion was that a "quick book" should be produced!

Brigadier D. R. Agnew sparked my interest in the history of the college by his own deep concern with it. Air Commodore (now Lieutenant-General) D. A. R. Bradshaw, set me on the way by having me collect pictures for an album illustrative of the history of RMC. Commodore (now Rear-Admiral) D. W. Piers asked me to find out when a broad pennant had last flown on Point Frederick and so initiated an enquiry that revealed that the standard military histories of Canada were quite inaccurate about developments there. Brigadier (now Lieutenant-General) W. A. B. Anderson appointed me as chairman of a committee to tell the history of the college in a museum in Fort Frederick, and Brigadier (now Major-General) G. H. Spencer furthered the development of that museum in its early stages. General Anderson also enthusiastically approved my proposal that I should write a full history of RMC and offered what help the college could give. Air Commodore L. J. Birchall opened doors to official archives in Ottawa. Commodore (Brigadier-General) W. P. Hayes has been most helpful during the process of preparation for the press.

In the early stages of the writing of this history of RMC, material was collected as a byproduct of work on my book *Canada and "Imperial Defense"* which was supported by research grants made by the Canada Council and by the United States Social Science Research Council. While I was still on the faculty at RMC travel assistance was given me to go to the Public Archives. When I was appointed W. K. Boyd Professor of History at Duke University, the Provost, Dr. R. Taylor Cole, encouraged me to complete this work, then in an early stage of preparation. The Duke University Commonwealth Studies Committee and the Duke University Council on Research made generous grants towards the cost of innumerable trips to Ottawa, the purchase of microfilm and xerox copies, and the typing of the manuscript.

To name all those who have helped and encouraged me in this labour would be impossible in the available space, they are so numerous. Some, however, must be picked out for special mention. Colonel T. F. Gelley, the retired RMC Registrar, as the secretary of the RMC Club of Canada was an enthusiastic supporter from the beginning and was instrumental in putting the proposal for the publication of this history up to the club as a centennial project. He read all the manuscript and made innumerable suggestions and corrections from his vast store of knowledge of RMC and also collected material for the appendices and the illustrations. Mr. John W. Spurr, chief librarian at RMC, has similarly been involved at every stage and without his help this book could not have been written. Mr. T. L. Brock, an ex-cadet with an unbounded passion for history and anecdotes of the college, very kindly put at my disposal copies of manuscripts and narratives of interviews which he had collected, and made valuable criticisms of draft chapters of my manuscript. Colonel C. P. Stacey, formerly director of the Canadian Army Historical Section and the integrated forces section, encouraged me from the beginning and obtained access for me to classified material. Jack Pike provided me with RMC Club branch minutes and other material. Mr. Joe Cardillo and his staff of DNDHQ Central Registry helped me to find my way through HQ indexes. Many ex-cadets contributed information, material, advice, criticisms or granted interviews. Four cadets, J. L. Granatstein, K. C. Eyre, A. B. C. Bowles, and G. M. Reay helped by producing indexes of *Sessional Papers* and the *R.M.C. Review*. Among several typists, three helped so much with the deciphering of my rough drafts that they deserve special thanks, Mrs. Dorothy Sapp, Mrs. Martha Love, and Mrs. Elizabeth McConnell.

The library staff at RMC (especially Mr. Clifford Watt), at Queen's University, and at Duke University (in particular the reference librarians Miss Florence Blakeley and Miss Mary W. Canada) were patient and meticulous in seeking answers to my most abstruse questions. Miss Barbara Wilson at the Public Archives helped many times from her great knowledge of military history sources. My gratitude to others in these and other libraries must also be mentioned in general terms though all cannot be named individually.

The manuscript was read in early draft by my former colleague, Sydney F. Wise, now director of History of the Canadian Armed Forces and also by Dr. J. M. Hitsman, of the same Directorate. Both of these good friends saved me from many errors and suggested many new angles. The late Colonel W. R. Sawyer, Colonel L. F. Grant, and Brigadier D. G. Cunningham, as well as those mentioned above, read various parts of the manuscript in draft and verified details or suggested improvements. The late Brigadier D. R. Agnew offered to read proof and made helpful suggestions. Nevertheless the responsibility for what appears, and for what errors remain, is mine alone. As usual, my wife, Marjorie, has patiently accepted my preoccupation with research and writing and has shown even greater charity by offering to undertake the tedious task of reading the proofs.

I am especially indebted to Mrs. Rosemary Shipton of the University of Toronto Press for most skilled editorial assistance.

This book is not "official history". Begun as a personal project by one who aimed only at objective detachment, it is critical as well as laudatory. It has not attempted to name every RMC graduate who was prominent at the college or in after life; to have done so would have made the book unwieldy. Names which appear were included because they serve to illustrate the story of the college itself. In biographical footnotes, an officer is given by the highest rank that he attained. However, the names of officers still serving are shown with the pre-tri-service rank.

Publication by the RMC Club of Canada does not make the club or the college responsible for the material selected for inclusion or for the views expressed.

His Excellency the Governor-General, Mr. Roland E. Michener, honoured the college, the RMC Club, and the author by writing a foreword.

Finally, I wish to express my humble gratitude for the gracious permission of Her Majesty, Queen Elizabeth II, to make use of the Duke of Cambridge's papers in the Royal Archives at Windsor.

RICHARD A. PRESTON,
Duke University,
Durham, North Carolina,
25 December 1968.

PREFACE
to the Second Edition

The author is indebted to the following for perceptive criticism and corrections:-

1118 G. G. M. Carr-Harris
Stanley L. Fall, Industrial College of the Armed Forces,
   Washington, D. C.
1177 D. H. Mackay
490 Brigadier-General F. M. Maynard
Major Warren Perry, Camberwell, Victoria, Australia
Clifford Watt.

RICHARD A. PRESTON
Durham, N.C. 27706

BIBLIOGRAPHICAL NOTE

Documentary sources for the history of RMC are very scattered. The only official records at the college, apart from those of recent date, are the registers of cadets showing personal details, enlistment, promotion, and graduation arranged by college numbers. The RMC Club possesses personnel files showing later careers, arranged by college number, and apparently made up first shortly after World War I. The commandant's office has a card index of all ex-cadets in the prewar college arranged alphabetically.

A few current files on particular subjects go back to the prewar college. The Massey Library at RMC has preserved official files of a few odd topics, as for instance, one containing the papers of the Arnold case. The library also possesses minute books for the reading room and recreation club, a college attestation register, a medical officer's day book, pay lists for staff, and albums of staff photographs.

In addition to these official records the library has accumulated other material relating to the history of RMC, such as scrapbooks made in the college, scrapbooks and photograph albums kept by cadets, and various other collections of documents. Among the latter are General A. B. Perry's diary, the Reverend George Ferguson's letters to his wife (on microfilm) and some letters of General W. T. Bridges. Commodore Robert Barrie's papers throw light on the early history of Point Frederick.

RMC does not possess a complete set of the commandants' annual reports which would be a natural starting point for the preparation of a history. Until 1924 the annual report was printed in full in the *Sessional Papers* and the originals were not preserved. (Fortunately, when I began my work, a set of the *Sessional Papers* had recently been acquired by the RMC library.) After 1924 only selected excerpts from the commandants' reports were printed in the Reports of the Department of National Defence. It was learned that the complete originals had been destroyed at Ottawa on the grounds that whatever was important in the reports had been printed! A fairly complete set of copies of the full reports for the 1920s and 1930s (presumably those which had been originally kept at RMC) was found in the files of the Directorate of History. The reports for the period after 1948 are available at the college.

The reports of the Boards of Visitors and of its successor, the Advisory Board, were not always printed either in whole or in part in the *Sessional Papers*. As these bodies did not necessarily meet every year, it was not easy to discover how many reports there should be. In addition to those that were printed in the *Sessional Papers*, there are some among the commandants' reports in the Directorate of History and some in the Deputy Minister's files. Printed copies of certain important Visitors' reports for 1895, which were not printed in the *Sessional Papers* but were circulated separately, and which cannot now be found at Ottawa where they may have been destroyed in the parliamentary fire in 1917, are fortunately preserved at RMC. The RMC papers in the Public Archives of Canada consist only of examination papers and similar material. Some RMC files from the 1930s are to be found among the records in the Directorate of History. All other earlier RMC records appear to have been destroyed.

For the main thread of the history of RMC it was necessary to turn to the records at the Department of Militia and Defence and its successor the Department of National Defence. The routine supervision of the administration of the college was the work of the adjutant-general until 1904 and even later. His voluminous files therefore contain very many references to RMC but these are mainly of a routine or minor nature. The deputy minister was responsible for policy, and his files are a major source for the history of the college in the nineteenth century. After the re-organization of the militia in the early twentieth century, files dealing with the college and its affairs were kept at headquarters. Because of British interest and concern with the establishment of RMC and with its subsequent operation, there is also much important material in the Governor-General's office in Ottawa (now largely deposited with the Public Archives) and in the Colonial Office and War Office papers in the Public Record Office in London. For the Canadian Services Colleges from 1942 the headquarters' files of all three services as well as of the deputy minister had to be used. But many important decisions do not appear in these official papers. It was therefore necessary to resort to the personal papers of various governors-general, colonial secretaries, prime ministers, ministers of national defence, and service personnel.

The location of the most important material is as follows. In the Public Archives of Canada, the Deputy Ministers' Numbered Files (1867–1903), Reports and Memoranda (1867–1904), and Despatches include material about RMC, especially the first. Also necessary are the minutes of the Militia Council (1904–1920), Returns and Answers to Parliament (1884–1902), Orders-in-Council (1859–1907), the Adjutant-General's Office Letter-Books (1868–1903), Royal Military College Records, and

Pay Lists of the RMC Staff. The Governor-General's Office Papers and the transcripts and microfilm of Colonial Office Papers (CO 42 and CO 537) are invaluable. The files of the Department of Militia and Defence and of the Department of National Defence deposited at the Public Archives (Tunney's Pasture) include the CEF files (especially the Cummins Transcripts) and HQ files. In addition the following papers in the manuscript groups contain RMC material: the papers of Governors-General the Earl of Minto, the Marquis of Dufferin (microfilm) and Earl Grey, of Prime Ministers Alexander Mackenzie (letter-books), Sir John A. Macdonald, Wilfrid Laurier, and Sir Robert Borden, of Militia Minister Sir Adolphe Caron, of the chiefs of the General Staff Major-General Sir James MacBrien and Sir Willoughby Gwatkin, of Acting High Commissioner Sir George Perley, and of Colonial Secretary the Earl of Carnarvon (microfilm).

The Colonial Office Papers microfilmed for the PAC (CO 42 and CO 537) can be consulted at the Public Record Office where War Office Papers (WO 32) also include some RMC material, especially requests for commissions. Also at the PRO are the Carnarvon Papers (Dufferin-Carnarvon Correspondence, PRO 30/6) mentioned above. The Marquis of Dufferin's papers which supplement the above are in the Public Record Office of Northern Ireland at Belfast.

The Deputy Ministers' files of more recent date than those deposited in the Public Archives, and HQ files of the army, navy, and air force, are at DND, Ottawa. The Directorate of History, in addition to RMC files mentioned above, holds General Crerar's Papers and General McNaughton's Papers.

Sir Wilfrid Laurier's Papers were consulted at Queen's University, where they are on microfilm. Queen's also holds Alexander Mackenzie's inletters and some Norman Rogers Papers. Sir Frederick W. Borden's Papers are deposited in the Archives of Nova Scotia in Halifax. Finally, the Papers of the Commander-in-Chief, the Duke of Cambridge, are at Windsor Castle.

CONTENTS

CANADA'S RMC

1

WHY

THE COLLEGE

WAS FOUNDED

One morning in 1874 two gentlemen presented themselves at Fort Henry overlooking Kingston, Ontario, and asked to be shown around. One of them claimed to be the prime minister of Canada. Fort Henry, on a peninsula of the same name close to the place where Lake Ontario empties into the St. Lawrence River, and hard by the entrance to the Rideau Canal which connects the Great Lakes with the Ottawa River, was at that time occupied by "A" Battery of the Canadian Active Militia which doubled as a school of gunnery. As orders had been issued that no one was to be admitted to the fort without express authority, a messenger was sent across the bridge over the Cataraqui River to Tête-de-Pont barracks to inform the Commanding Officer, Major D. T. Irwin, RA.* Consoling himself that any unfortunate delay could be attributed to the lack of forewarning, Irwin rode up to Fort Henry where he found that his unexpected guest was indeed the Prime Minister, the Honourable Alexander Mackenzie.

Mackenzie proved to be "most agreeable" despite the inconvenience caused by the delay. He proceeded to look over the fort and also inspect the buildings on Point Frederick, the next peninsula to the west between Point Henry and Kingston, which had at one time been the site of a royal dockyard. Mackenzie already knew something about the buildings on Point Frederick because he had worked as a stone mason on the construction of the Kingston martello towers soon after he had arrived from Scotland as an immigrant. While the inspection was in progress a messenger

*Colonel de La Cherois Thomas Irwin, C.M.G., RA (1843–1928), a graduate of RMA, Woolwich, and the Staff College, Camberley; assistant inspector of artillery and commandant of "A" Battery, the school of gunnery at Kingston (which he preferred to call The Royal School of Artillery), 1873–82; inspector of artillery, 1882–98.

arrived with a telegram. Mackenzie told Irwin that it was about the construction of a telegraph line to link Ontario with the new province of British Columbia. The officer was surprised to see that, although interrupted by such important official business, the Prime Minister was making careful notes of minor repairs that the unoccupied buildings needed. If Irwin learned why Mackenzie had come in person to inspect the military property in Kingston he kept it to himself.[1] The visit was in fact the first constructive step in a significant development for Canada, the establishment of a military college to educate and train officers.

There had been military colleges in Europe from the end of the sixteenth century. The earliest ones were established to provide for the education of the sons of deceased or impoverished officers and were boys' schools rather than professional colleges for the training of officers. Until the Napoleonic wars it was not thought necessary for officers, other than those in such technical branches as the artillery and the engineers, to have formal training. The establishment at the beginning of the nineteenth century of St Cyr in France, of High Wycombe and Marlow (later Sandhurst) in England, and of West Point in the United States had shown that "the conduct of war had become a recognized 'profession' " and that all officers could benefit by education and training.[2] But in Britain subsequent attempts to require every applicant for a commission in the cavalry and the infantry to pass through Sandhurst (originally set up to provide for officers' sons) and proposals to use university courses for army entrance came to nothing.[3] In 1871, after the abolition of purchase, the Royal Military College at Sandhurst ceased cadet training and was used for some years for training officers who had already been commissioned on the basis of a competitive academic examination.[4] Although the British RMC once again became a cadet college in 1877, British officers learned their business mainly in their regiments during most of the nineteenth century.

Long before 1874 "the neighbourhood of a restless and growing nation" had led to proposals for a military college in Canada. In 1815 the Assembly of Lower Canada decided to establish one, but religious and racial conflicts blocked agreement upon its organization. Thereupon Captain A. G. Douglas,* an officer who had served in the Nova Scotia Regiment of Fencible Infantry, suggested that the governor-in-chief who commanded the troops in British North America at this time should establish a military college by using money collected by public subscription. Douglas

*Captain A. G. Douglas had been born in France of Scottish parents and educated in a French military college. He had served in the French and Spanish artillery in the West Indies and also in the British army in Portugal.

said that the college could be set up at Three Rivers where there was a disused government house and where, incidentally, he lived. He offered himself as superintendent.[5] For nine years Douglas had been the adjutant of the Junior Department of the new British military college at Great Marlow when his father-in-law, General Francis Jarry, was the senior instructor and first commandant of the Senior Department (later the Staff College) at High Wycombe. Douglas argued that a Canadian military college under the governor was preferable to one set up by the Assembly because it would be above religious, political, and mercantile controversies. He wrote: "Colleges as they are generally understood will still be headed in this country by Priests, Philosophers, or Lawyers and occupied by such or such kind of people; so that education will be lost." The surest way to unify the population would be "to begin to work upon young minds of different ... parties and persuasions." The Canadian military college would be the only college or school in the country open to Catholics and Protestants alike; and the cadets would attend divine service according to their persuasion. Douglas professed to believe that, as a result, "old prejudices would vanish not only among the students, but even among their relations, and a common interest would ensue."

The military college which Douglas proposed in 1816 was to have been a boarding school for young boys run on military lines. He wanted to admit boys as soon as they could read and write and knew "the first two rules of arithmetic," that is addition and subtraction. Douglas proposed that the college should teach a great deal of Latin (which he said could be "learned in half the time it formerly was") and also English, French, history, geography, drawing, and mathematics. His college was intended in part to provide an education for the sons of officers who were to be educated free or on a graduated scale according to their means. Douglas noted that the Governor-in-Chief, Sir John Sherbrooke, had shown his concern for the "welfare of meritorious officers" and would therefore probably support the plan.

There were by that time military schools in the United States designed to give boys a disciplined education. Douglas knew that a predominantly military emphasis might not be popular in certain quarters in Canada and he was quite willing that it should be minimized. "If the word *military* sounds too harsh let it be dropped; let the establishment be called by any other name, provided that the plan of the mother country ... be as near as possible followed." He pointed out that graduates of American military schools did not necessarily follow a military career and also that it was well known that "Marlow cadets" (from the Junior Department of the British Royal Military College) "would have joined an University, a

Compting house, or the army of Lord Wellington with the same advantages." Douglas' professed aim was to inculcate a spirit of obedience and respect in young Canadians to make them into "good [British] subjects."

Douglas said that all that the government need provide for the college was accommodation, rations, fuel, and a small drill staff. Fees paid by the sons of ordinary gentlemen would support the professors who, because the cadets would be "officered among themselves," would have "nothing to do but give their lessons." The staff could therefore be expected to carry a heavy teaching load. He expected that money voted by the Assembly of Lower Canada for its military college would be turned over to support one founded by Governor Sherbrooke; and that the Assembly in the upper province, which had not yet considered setting up a college, could be induced to follow the lower province's lead. The Three Rivers college would thus be under the control of the governor-in-chief of British North America but would be supported by the various provinces.

On 20 May 1826 a proposal somewhat similar to Douglas' was made in a petition drawn up by retired British navy and army officers who had settled in Upper Canada in March township near the present city of Ottawa. Fearing the alienation of genuine British feelings in their children who were exposed to a mixed community in this new land "in the vicinity of a republican government," they asked for a subsidized education on naval and military lines in a college situated on the Great Lakes where it could contribute to the maintenance of naval superiority. A year later Lieutenant-Governor Sir Peregrine Maitland, whose opinion had been asked, declared that although there was ample provision for public education in the province already, he would be willing to further any project the Admiralty undertook.[6]

But nothing more was heard of the proposal, no doubt because the provinces of British North America, protected by the Royal Navy and a British garrison, were unwilling to spend much on defence. They believed that all that was necessary was service by the inhabitants in an emergency. From the earliest days of settlement legislation had established the principle of compulsory military service but from the first the training of the militia had been farcical. When the militia organization was revived shortly before the American Civil War it was for all practical purposes voluntary. However, the militia tradition was strong. It held, incorrectly as historical research has shown, that it was Canadian militia that had saved Canada from the Americans during the War of 1812. The belief that it could do so again, even without preliminary training, suited colonials desirous of avoiding taxation for defence.

Commissions in the militia were issued by the lieutenant-governor of a province on the recommendation of local militia colonels who were often politicians. Ex-officers of the British army who had retired to settle in Canada were sometimes appointed but commissions in the militia did not necessarily require previous training and were liable to be used as patronage. Canadian militia officers were therefore frequently inexperienced amateurs. This was, however, not far out of line with contemporary practice elsewhere for, as has been seen, not all regular officers in Britain attended Sandhurst before being commissioned.

The need for a system of training for officers in Canada became more apparent when danger seemed to threaten. During the American Civil War a shortage of officers for proposed "service companies" of the Canadian militia led to the establishment of military schools paid for by Canada but staffed by British officers from the regiments that had been sent out during the *Trent* crisis. Two were established in Toronto and Quebec in 1864 and four more at Montreal, Kingston, London, and Hamilton in 1865. (The two last-named failed to attract enough candidates and were closed within the year.) Although the "service" militia did not get started, the remaining schools flourished and their graduates were soon found as officers in militia units in almost every town and village in Upper and Lower Canada. Colonel Garnet Wolseley, the future field-marshal and commander-in-chief of the British army, who was assistant quartermaster-general of the British army in North America, commanded summer camps of instruction for the militia at Laprairie in 1865 and at Thorold in 1866. The skirmish with Fenian invaders from the United States at Ridgeway, in which the militia was deployed, confirmed its need for unit training. But Wolseley reported that the success of the militia battalions was directly proportional to the number of old army officers and of graduates of the military schools which they included. He said that this proved the value of the schools.[7]

Like officer training courses in twentieth-century wars, these military schools differed from Douglas' projected military college, and also from the future RMC, in that the basic course they gave was short (no more than three months) and strictly military in nature. Although the pre-Confederation militia schools in Nova Scotia were not part of the same scheme, an undated outline of the programme for a school proposed in connection with the Halifax garrison shows the way such schools operated. The "pupils" there were divided into groups of twelve to fifteen for purposes of discipline, with each group in charge of the senior member. They were drilled three to four hours daily on five to five-and-a-half days a week. They were given practice in drilling squads and also had lectures on drill commands, keeping military records, courts martial, the Articles of War, discipline and punishments, promotion of non-commissioned officers, military accounts, and pay and messing. They attended orderly rooms and pay and clothing parades as observers. The cadets lived anywhere in the district. The length of time that a cadet served with this regiment of instruction in Nova Scotia is not stated; but unless he elected to try for the first-class certificate as well, he probably remained only until he received a second-class certificate of military proficiency and with it a gratuity of $50. The province supplemented the pay of the regular officers and drill instructors who staffed the school at rates varying from one shilling a day for a drill instructor to eight shillings a day for the commanding officer.[8] No doubt the Canadian schools were in general run on the same lines. Furthermore, unlike the earlier proposals for military colleges in Canada, the militia schools were for men and not for boys.

At Confederation the four military schools in operation at Quebec, Montreal, Kingston, and Toronto were retained. In that year temporary schools of cavalry and artillery were formed in Toronto, and one for artillery was established in Montreal. These were put on a more permanent basis in 1868 and military schools were opened in Halifax and Saint John after Confederation. Graduates qualified for a commission in the militia. The considerable success of the schools was made possible by the British regulars who staffed them. It came to be believed that "competent officers can now be found, and the question of instructors is no longer an impediment."[9]

The first dominion Militia Act, passed in 1868, was largely modelled on the legislation of the province of Canada and similarly preserved the principle of compulsory enrolment. But only the Active Militia of 40,000 volunteers (this number to be completed if necessary by the enrolment) was required to drill. Sir George-Etienne Cartier's Act had been drafted in the belief that the Canadian militia need only be, as always in the past, a source of auxiliary troops to back up the British garrison. Not organized as a field force, the militia was headed by an adjutant-general on loan from the British army who was a relatively junior officer and whose duties were mainly administrative. It lacked the supporting arms and supply system which would, in the event of war, be provided for it by the British regulars. Furthermore, it was dependent for its limited training upon the services of the British officers and NCOs of the garrison. If Canada were threatened, the militia would be embodied and put at the disposal of the British general commanding the regulars at Halifax. However, without further training, it would be of use only as a source of individual recruits to fill out the ranks of the British army regiments, for transport and garrison duties, for protection of lines of communication, and perhaps for reconnaissance.

In 1870–1 the British regulars were recalled from overseas stations to strengthen British power in Europe without increasing military costs.[10] It was believed that self-governing colonies should make greater contributions to their own defence. But after the Treaty of Washington, even more than before, the Canadian government thought it unnecessary to pick up the financial burden for North American defence that the British were laying down. Lieutenant-General the Honourable James Lindsay,* who was sent to organize the withdrawal of British troops from Ontario and Quebec, proposed that the dominion should establish its own permanent force by taking over the personnel, but not the officers, of the Royal Canadian Rifles, a regiment of veterans established by the British in 1840 for duty in Canada which was now to be disbanded. His proposal was ignored. The Canadian government said that it would enlist no British soldier until after he had been discharged.[11] This opportunity to set up a permanent Canadian force to replace the British garrison was thus rejected. But the withdrawal of the redcoats not only removed Canada's main protection and left the militia with new responsibilities, it also deprived Canada of its chief means of training officers and men. Yet Canada's only defence force, the Active Militia, depended more than ever upon the quality of its officers both for training and for leadership in any operations in which it might become involved. There was therefore a serious vacuum.

The withdrawal of the British garrisons from Toronto, Kingston, and Montreal in 1870 meant that at those places the militia staff had to step in to keep the military schools going. Immediately abuses crept in. Too many unsuitable candidates were admitted and it was necessary to lay down strict instructions for the future administration of the schools throughout the dominion. There were to be six schools, held from December to May, the slack season in a primarily agricultural country, and the months when the militia staff had time to conduct officer training. They were to be for cavalry, infantry, and artillery with a maximum capacity for the whole dominion of five hundred cadets distributed according to population but with fifty extra in the Maritime provinces until such time

---

*Lieutenant-General James Lindsay (1815–1874), second son of the 24th Earl of Crawford, joined the Grenadier Guards at 16; served in Canada, 1838–42, where he distinguished himself as a runner, outdistancing Indians who excelled in that sport; MP for Wigan, 1845; in 1863 he was posted to Canada in command of the Brigade of Guards; returned to England a year later to resume his parliamentary duties; in 1868 he was appointed inspector of the Foot Guards but went back to Canada in 1870 on special service connected with the withdrawal of the British garrison; while there he helped to prepare the Red River expedition, and for these services he received the K.C.M.G.; afterwards he was inspector-general of the Reserve Forces in England and military secretary to the commander-in-chief, the Duke of Cambridge.

as the number of qualified militia officers there had reached the same proportion to population as in the rest of the dominion. Three of the schools, those at Halifax, Saint John, and Quebec, were to be run in connection with the British garrisons at those places; the others were to be operated by the Canadian militia staff with the aid of former British army drill sergeants.[12]

Officers were selected and promoted in the Canadian militia on the recommendation of boards of officers or of militia colonels and, as in the contemporary British army,[13] examinations were often perfunctory.[14] On the other hand the practice of officers taking their qualifying examinations at summer militia camps had been found "very objectionable" because it wasted time that should properly be used for unit training. Because of the Fenian invasion the militia were called out again in 1870. Militia volunteers also accompanied a British force sent to quell the Métis in the Northwest. These crises served to re-emphasize the value of military schools for teaching Canadian militia officers how to train and discipline their men. For the needs of the infantry the militia schools seemed quite adequate; and by 1871, 6,285 candidates had qualified for drill certificates in the seven years since the schools were set up.[15]

But artillery training was too technical to leave entirely to militia instructors; and it was also necessary to employ a permanent staff to care for the guns and stores in the fortresses vacated by the British. "A" and "B" Batteries, at Kingston and Quebec, the first full-time units of the Canadian militia, therefore became gunnery schools on a year-round basis. Courses in these schools lasted from three to twelve months with the possibility of extension. These permanent schools proved so much more effective than the militia schools that Colonel P. Robertson-Ross,* the adjutant-general of the militia, recommended that the infantry and cavalry schools, in which the quality of instruction had already seriously declined, should similarly be put on a permanent basis. He also proposed that all the schools should be organized as tactical brigades of three arms.[16] This advice, which seemed like another proposal for the creation of a small permanent nucleus for a Canadian regular force, was not accepted by the Canadian government.

By this time, however, powerful support for military reorganization

---

*Major-General P. Robertson-Ross (1828–1883) served in the Cape Mounted Rifles during the Kaffir War of 1850–1 and had the local rank of captain when in command of an irregular unit called "Armstrong's Horse"; he was six times thanked in general orders and three times in despatches; he fought in the Crimea where he received further distinctions and was promoted brevet-major; promoted colonel in 1870, he was appointed adjutant-general of the Canadian militia in succession to Major-General P. L. Macdougall; he resigned in 1873.

was forthcoming from a rather more influential source. The Earl of Dufferin,* who had come to Canada as governor-general in April 1872, was an Ulster landlord in the whig tradition whose brilliance had brought him junior ministerial offices and important diplomatic missions at an early age. He was determined to strengthen Canada's connection with Britain and he believed that this could be done best by remedying the weak military state of the country. But he had no professional military experience and the War Office, because of the withdrawal of the troops, had refused to supply him with a military secretary. Dufferin therefore brought to Canada as his private secretary, Colonel Henry C. Fletcher of the Scots Fusilier Guards, who had given testimony before the Royal Commission on Military Education (1868–9), of which Dufferin was chairman, and who had also served as a member in the commission's later stages.

Fletcher was the son of a retired British major-general, now a magistrate in Kent, whose family was connected with the Earls of Romney by marriages in two successive generations. His wife, Harriet, the daughter of an earl, came to Canada as Countess Dufferin's lady companion and the Fletchers participated in the gay social life at Rideau Hall. The colonel was, however, a serious-minded soldier. During the American Civil War, when serving in Canada, he had visited the Union army and had been allowed to pitch his tent close to that of General McClellan "who showed him every courtesy." General Fenwick Williams, the British commander in Montreal, found Fletcher's reports on the war "admirable."[17] After returning to England Fletcher published a *History of the American War* in three volumes[18] which was sound though not marked by any real insight into the revolutionary changes that were taking place. Dufferin said that Fletcher was "not particularly brilliant or quick, but ... sensible and trustworthy... . Everybody here [in Canada] liked him."[19] After leaving Canada in 1875 to rejoin his regiment Fletcher was appointed ADC to the Duke of Cambridge, the commander-in-chief of the British army. He thus had all the personal and social qualities and connections needed for the work he had come to Canada to do.

Immediately upon the arrival of the Governor-General's party in Canada, Colonel Fletcher set to work to urge the reconstruction of the country's defence system. Addressing groups of militia officers, he said that Canada must have a force capable not only of defending the country and of preserving law and order but also "far in the background, to be a

---

*Frederick Temple Hamilton-Temple Blackwood, the first marquis of Dufferin and Ava (1826–1902), had been undersecretary of state for India and then for War in the Gladstone ministry; governor-general of Canada, 1872–8, he later served as ambassador at St. Petersburg and as viceroy of India.

symbol of the state which pertains to all nations aspiring to rank as such among their peers." Because the United States was now peaceful, only a small permanent force was needed for use as a training school and as a standard of comparison for the real army of the country, the Active and Reserve Militia. Fletcher said that Canada would not be content to rely on Britain for trained troops and professional officers. He therefore recommended there should be three permanent officer-training schools. The two schools already established for artillery training at Kingston and Quebec and a third, to be set up in the Maritimes, should be expanded to serve all arms. The commandants of these schools should be from the British regular army and if possible should be Canadians. Candidates for militia commissions should attend the schools for six months, or longer if they needed to. Fletcher realized that after receiving the benefits of a military education the graduates of these schools might refuse to serve in the militia. But he argued that there could be safeguards against this possibility; for instance, the best guarantee would be "good selection [of cadets] for first appointments."[20]

In July the Duke of Cambridge, perhaps as a consequence of the growing military interest which Fletcher was obviously arousing in Canada, sent by way of the Earl of Kimberley, the Colonial Secretary, an offer to help Dufferin with the reorganization of the Canadian militia; but, when he forwarded the proposal, Kimberley attached to the offer in transit a warning that nothing would be done in England until the Canadian government had shown that it approved.[21]

Fletcher's lecture was printed, under the title *Memorandum on the Militia*, and circulated privately in Canada in 1873. Prime Minister John A. Macdonald received a copy,[22] but perhaps not until his days in office were numbered. By this time the Conservative government in Canada was being shaken by the furore over the financing of the Canadian Pacific Railway. In the midst of the parliamentary investigation the Minister of Militia, Cartier, died and Colonel Robertson-Ross, who was his protégé, gave up his appointment as adjutant-general and left the country. This was no time for military innovations. Then in November Macdonald's government resigned.

Macdonald's defence policy had rested entirely upon the principle that the British would provide any regular forces that were needed and that Canada's contribution should be limited to a part-time militia. But his government had not built the permanent defence works west of Quebec that Canadian ministers had tentatively promised in London in 1865 and without which the inexperienced militia force would have been useless. As the British government was concerned only to secure a bridgehead at

Quebec, Canada was able to obtain permission to use the loans for public works of a civil nature. When the British government, which had initiated the navy's withdrawal from the Great Lakes, was unwilling to pay for its redeployment there, Canada would not take the project on. Macdonald's government had protested vigorously against the withdrawal of the regulars but, apart from setting up the two batteries for instructional purposes, it had not replaced them by Canadians. In 1871, when supporting the application of a Canadian who sought a commission in the British army when purchase was abolished, Macdonald had added the suggestion that a certain number of army commissions should, like commissions in the Royal Navy, be reserved annually for Canadians. This proposal, which was rejected by the Secretary of State for War, Edward Cardwell,[23] was apparently all that the Canadian Prime Minister was willing to do at that time for Canadians who wanted to make a career in the army or to provide officers for the defence of Canada. In the two years preceding his resignation, Robertson-Ross's successive proposals for a staff college and for all-arms military schools had been ignored. All these things suggest that it is unlikely that, had he stayed in office, Macdonald would have done anything in the immediate future to produce the professional officers that Canada needed.

The attitude of the new Liberal government seemed no more promising. The Conservatives had found the militia a useful form of relatively cheap patronage. Liberal attacks in the house therefore had often taken the form of attacks on the militia in particular, and military expenditures in general, as examples of Conservative waste and extravagance. However, a few Canadian Liberals, including Mackenzie, the new prime minister, had occasionally echoed the British Liberal doctrine that a self-governing colony ought to shoulder the burden of its own defence.[24] Unlike some British Liberals who believed that this development would further the empire's inevitable disintegration, these Canadian Liberals tended to believe, like Dufferin, that a Canadian defence force would give it strength.

Dufferin sent the new Liberal cabinet a copy of Fletcher's memorandum, and in his first interview with Mackenzie after the December election, he urged that the defence of Canada should be put on a sounder footing.[25] The Prime Minister, although not Macdonald's equal in ability or political finesse, was a man of tremendous industry and great integrity who was possessed of a determination to do his duty. He had always been interested in military affairs and during the Fenian raids had held a militia commission in the 27th Lambton Battalion of Infantry.[26] Therefore, despite his frequently expressed determination to economize by reducing the militia estimates, an expediency made even more necessary by the business slump that occurred as he took office, Mackenzie listened receptively to Dufferin's advice and said he would think it over. The Duke of Cambridge, who had been "fearful that the subject would drop for want of interest being taken in it in these peaceful times," was very gratified.[27]

To enable Mackenzie to decide the kind of military organization that he would set up, Dufferin sent him a copy of the *Report ... on Military Education* which he, Dufferin, had drafted in 1868–9 when chairman of the British commission on that subject.[28] This *Report* undoubtedly helped Mackenzie to formulate his views. The commissioners had believed that the prevailing aristocratic social system in England made the abolition of purchase and the introduction of free competition for military commissions impossible; but they had severely criticized the British Royal Military College at Sandhurst. They had reported that the idleness of the majority of cadets who were not likely to qualify for a commission without purchase was encouraged because the governor of the college had inadequate powers of punishment, because the military element predominated over the academic, and because the instructors had less authority than the executive officers. But, though they had recommended more academic competition at Sandhurst, the commissioners had not agreed with an earlier suggestion that the solution for the problem was the amalgamation of Sandhurst with the more efficient Royal Military Academy at Woolwich which trained officers for commissions in the artillery and the engineers where there was no purchase.[29]

Because Sandhurst's graduates were believed to have served the country well since the beginning of the century, the college had built up a "death or glory" tradition. The Dufferin Commission's criticisms of the British Royal Military College were therefore largely ignored by the War Office.[30] The commission did, however, have an incidental but important influence in Canada. When Fletcher had appeared before it as a witness, he had testified that he believed that the basic training of infantry and engineer officers could be on similar lines.[31] The commission, as has been shown, had rejected Fletcher's idea and had come to a different conclusion for adoption by the British army. Nevertheless, Dufferin apparently thought that such a system might be appropriate in different circumstances. Therefore to obtain information for Mackenzie, he sent his secretary to visit and report on the United States Military Academy at West Point where all arms were trained together much in the same way as Fletcher had advocated.[32] Fletcher's convictions about all-arms training were thereby strengthened.

The Department of Militia was already very concerned about the problem of officer training. When Robertson-Ross resigned and left Canada,

Colonel Walker Powell,* a Canadian militia officer, took over as acting adjutant-general. In December 1873 Powell obtained permission to divert some of the appropriation from military schools to the instruction of artillery officers and non-commissioned officers.[33] Then in his annual report he said that although the infantry schools had been most useful in imparting primary instruction to officers and candidates for militia commissions, they had been found inadequate to provide the higher class of instruction that had now become indispensable to maintain the militia's efficiency. "Nor do they supply instruction such as is necessary for the education of those who may be required for the future military necessities of the Dominion." Powell said that for ordinary duties an officer required no special training but "the higher class of duties and the capacity for superior command" could only be reached through a long course of study and preparation. He therefore advised that two alternatives should be considered. Either young Canadians should be sent to England for a military education, or a military school with high standards should be set up in Canada. In view of the distance of the United Kingdom from Canada he thought the latter expedient preferable.[34] This report was presented to the House of Commons after Dufferin had urged Mackenzie to do something for Canada's defences. Powell may have been simply echoing what was already known to be under discussion. However, he had pointed to something different from the permanent militia schools which Fletcher had suggested.

Some of Mackenzie's other supporters were also giving him advice on the subject. Lieutenant-Colonel George T. Denison,† who had stood as a Reform candidate without success, but who claimed that he had done much to get Mackenzie's party elected, stated in his book, *Soldiering in Canada*, that Mackenzie asked him what he wanted by way of reward. Denison asked that the command of the militia should never go to an officer of lower rank than a full colonel (which meant in practice a British officer) and that a military college should be established. According to Denison's story, after considerable delay Mackenzie said that he would

*Colonel Walker Powell (1828–1915), born in Waterford, Upper Canada, was elected to the Legislative Assembly of Canada in 1857; deputy adjutant-general for Upper Canada in 1863, be became deputy adjutant-general of the Canadian militia and in 1875 adjutant-general with the rank of colonel; he retired in 1896.

†George T. Denison (1835–1925), third of the name and a lawyer by profession, was a member of Denison's Horse; in 1866 he became lieutenant-colonel of the Governor-General's Body Guard as his unit had been renamed; he served in the Fenian raids of 1866 and the Northwest campaign of 1885. A leading member of the Canada First movement and of the Imperial Federation League, he was the senior police magistrate in Toronto from 1877 to 1923. One of his books on cavalry won a prize given by the Tsar of Russia.

do both things and kept his word.[35] Denison thus considered that he had been the one to plant the idea of a Canadian military college in the Prime Minister's mind.

But the idea also came from other sources. Another officer who recommended a college in 1874 was Lieutenant-Colonel T. B. Strange,* the British officer lent to Canada to command the gunnery school at Quebec. In a pamphlet called *Artillery Retrospect of the Last Great War, 1870: With Its Lessons for Canadians,* Strange relates that he had come to the conclusion that a college was immediately required for the scientific training of officers and that a permanent artillery corps should be attached to this college and to the "provincial" schools of gunnery, that is to say to "A" and "B" Batteries. In the hope of promoting a military college in Canada, Strange went on his own initiative to West Point. He then offered to send a report about it to the Canadian government. He was hurt and piqued when told that he had been forestalled. Fletcher's report was already in Mackenzie's hands.[36]

Colonel Fletcher's report began by referring to a report on the academy furnished by Colonel P. L. MacDougall† at the request of the Royal Commission on Military Education in 1869 and printed as an appendix to its *Report.* This Mackenzie had already seen. MacDougall had stressed the high moral tone of West Point, which contrasted strongly with the Dufferin Commission's view of Sandhurst. He also commented on West Point's *esprit de corps* and the smartness of its cadets. He had noted that entry was by nomination and by a relatively easy qualifying examination but that rigorous competition commenced immediately thereafter. West Point trained officers for duties in all arms, and there was little postgraduate specialist training elsewhere in the American army. Though normally military, that is, designed to produce army officers, the academy was almost as much a nursery for the education of civil servants. The state did not guarantee military employment to the academy's graduates and many had gone into private civilian occupations.[37]

*Major-General Thomas Bland Strange (1831–1925), born in India, was commissioned in the artillery and fought in the Mutiny; he was appointed inspector of artillery in Canada in 1871 and organized one of the batteries; in 1882 he was placed on reserve but in 1885 was appointed to command the Alberta Field Force in the Northwest Rebellion. His autobiography entitled *Gunner Jingo's Jubilee* was published in 1894.

†General Sir Patrick Leonard MacDougall (1819–1894), was commissioned in 1836, transferred to the Royal Canadian Rifles in 1844 and served for ten years in Toronto and Kingston; in 1854 he went to Sandhurst as superintendent of studies and established a reputation by writing on military matters; adjutant-general in Canada 1865–9; in 1873 he headed the new intelligence branch at the War Office; commanded British forces in North America at Halifax 1877–83 and served when required as administrator of Canada.

Fletcher's report, intended for a somewhat different purpose from that of MacDougall's, gave more information about the organization of the academy and about its value as a model for Canada. He said that there was a considerable analogy between the defensive forces now being organized in the dominion and those raised earlier in the republic. West Point had been associated with the growth of the American army almost from its first beginnings. More than a military school, it was the nucleus of the army to which officers returned for periods of duty and to renew their studies.

West Point was open to all classes of the community. Educational qualifications for entry were low because they must be obtainable at ordinary schools within reach of everyone, whatever his means. The academy therefore began with relatively elementary education and stressed educational work in its curriculum. It had adopted the principle that the training of the mind was more important than knowledge; and mathematics was the basic element of the academic curriculum. Contrary to what Mac-Dougall had reported, Fletcher said that while it was true that in the first half-century of its existence West Point graduates had contributed largely to the development of their country by taking up civilian occupations, often after a period of junior military service, this practice no longer pertained. Civilian engineering colleges had begun to turn out graduates and West Pointers were not needed for civil work. Since the Civil War, therefore, the bulk of the cadets had made careers in the army.

Fletcher argued that, just as in the United States, permanent military institutions would develop in Canada with the growth of the country. He saw the schools of gunnery and the police force then being organized on military lines in the West as the first of these. They, and others to follow them, would need officers. He admitted that it might happen that graduates of a Canadian military college would embrace civilian careers, but that the answer would be to offer them sufficient inducement to take up the military profession. Fletcher thought that, as graduates of a Canadian college would have access to British advanced military training courses that were superior to anything in the United States, a military career would prove to be more attractive to Canadians than to Americans.[38]

Mackenzie was convinced by these arguments, probably most of all by the idea that the West Point plan was the least expensive method of training officers.* He decided that, although he was appointing a British

---

*This is the conclusion of the précis of the Dufferin Commission's reports on foreign military colleges printed in the *Militia Report, 1873*, appendix no. 9, "Memoranda relating to the Military Educational Systems of England, France, Prussia and the United States of America", pp. 218–23.

general officer to command the militia, he would have Canada follow the American type of military college for producing officers. His government therefore proposed to appropriate $50,000 "to be applied to the establishment of a Military School of the character of the West Point Academy in the U.S.,"[39] which meant one for all arms of the service.

Soon afterwards Mackenzie's government granted £80 to Colonel Fletcher as an honorarium for the report on West Point, but that officer politely refused the money. He said that he had merely acted in the course of duty.[40] However Dufferin reported to the Commander-in-Chief and to the Colonial Secretary that Colonel Fletcher had contributed largely to the revival of the military spirit in Canada,[41] and a little later he was decorated with the CMG.[42] Colonel Henry Fletcher, more than any one else, deserves the credit for proposing to Mackenzie the creation of a military college in Canada to help to fill the vacuum left by the departing British regulars and for suggesting the form that the college should take.

But Alexander Mackenzie was the real founder of the college. In spite of the dislike of many of his followers for standing armies, he personally rejected permanent militia schools in favour of a cadet college to produce career officers. He probably regarded this as the first logical step towards providing Canada with an effective military force. At any rate in 1878, when still in office, he wrote to tell Dufferin that

... faith in voluntary organizations was no doubt justified so far as the bravery of the men was concerned, but it was evident that without educated officers it would be impossible to place an Army Corps in the field for serious and continuous operations. This belief led me in 1874 to propose the establishment of a Military College modelled on existing similar institutions in England and the United States, with the expectation that when the first batch of Graduates were leaving the College, means would be found to employ the Graduates in the Canadian Military Service.

The founding of the College was in fact laying the foundation of a future national military system, but a complete change could not be effected in a day or a year .... We have, however, provided for the education of superior officers. The next natural step is to provide for the education of junior and non-commissioned officers ... .[43]

The establishment of RMC was not, as has been suggested, a British plot "to retain real British control over Canadian Military affairs."* Rather it was a Canadian effort to build Canada's own military strength.

*The theory that RMC was established in an attempt "to restore British influence in Canadian military matters" is presented in an article by Adrian Preston entitled "The Founding of the Royal Military College: Gleanings from the Royal Archives," *Queen's Quarterly*, LXXIV (autumn, 1967), 398–412, but is not supported by the evidence which he offers from the Duke of Cambridge's papers. British military aid was necessary for Canada because there was no expertise in the country. But although it was to Britain's advantage that Canada should be able to counter American threats, aid was given rather grudgingly. Cambridge was consulted about the new military college only because, as commander-in-chief, he had had much to do with army promotions and knew who was available to staff the college. He did not make policy. His papers are therefore interesting rather than important. Dr. Preston did not attempt to use the very much more significant material in the Mackenzie Papers in the Public Archives in Ottawa, in the Dufferin and Carnarvon Papers in the Public Record Offices in London and Belfast, and in the Mackenzie Papers in Queen's University library. His further suggestion that British domination of RMC prevented the rise of Canadian military theorists is absurd. A cadet college cannot produce top-level strategists and military philosophers in a country devoid of military institutions and professional personnel. British aid was an essential first step towards providing the necessary technical knowledge and it helped, rather than hindered, Canadian military development.

2

THE ESTABLISHMENT OF THE
MILITARY COLLEGE
IN KINGSTON

When the Minister of Militia and Defence, William Ross,* moved the second reading of the military college bill in the Canadian House of Commons on 15 May 1874, the significance of Mackenzie's decision to follow the West Point model became clearer. Although the United States Military Academy produced officers for all arms, it was primarily a school of engineering. The first paragraph of the bill showed that the new Canadian military college would follow it in that respect. It read: "An institution shall be established for the purpose of imparting a complete education in all branches of military tactics, fortification, engineering and general scientific knowledge in subjects connected with and necessary to a thorough knowledge of the military profession and for qualifying officers for command and staff appointments. Such institution to be known as the Military College, and to be located in some one of the garrison towns of Canada."[1] Ross said that the four-year curriculum of the proposed college, which would be at a higher level than the present schools for the Canadian militia, would adapt the curricula of West Point and of the higher level English military schools to meet Canadian needs. He made it quite evident that the college was intended to turn out officers qualified as engineers as well as for the cavalry, artillery, and infantry.[2]

The phrase about "qualifying officers for command and staff appointments" needs further examination. As early as 1870 Colonel Robertson-Ross had recommended a Canadian staff course like that in England.[3] When he introduced the RMC bill, William Ross stated in the Commons that in addition to the cadets it was intended to admit to the college up to ten militia officers who held first-class certificates.[4] This provision to pre-

*William Ross (1825–1912), MP for Victoria, Nova Scotia, minister of Militia, 1873–4, and a lieutenant-colonel in the militia.

pare militia officers for permanent staff appointments must have helped to win support in parliament: but, though the proposal was raised again by the general officer commanding the militia in 1876,[5] it was not immediately put into effect. The phrase could also have been included to permit the establishment of staff courses attached to the military college. But staff and pre-staff college courses did not come until much later;* and there is a much more satisfactory explanation. In his *Report* for 1873 Colonel Walker Powell had stressed that the short professional training in the military schools was inadequate preparation for senior military appointments for which a long course of study was required.[6] The nature of the proposed college insured that its graduates would receive the necessary broad basic education to fit them not merely to serve as subalterns but also for senior appointments in later life.

The decision to produce engineer officers was particularly significant because as yet the Canadian militia had almost no engineers. Much of the work that it had traditionally done for the British regulars in war had, it is true, consisted of road and fortification building, but these engineering tasks had been performed by sedentary militia under the direction of British officers. Eleven companies of militia engineers had been recruited from civilian artificers and mechanics before Confederation, but they were unsatisfactory and most of them had proved unstable and short-lived. In 1874 only two companies remained in existence, one in Montreal and the other in Saint John, New Brunswick; and these did infantry drill and musketry rather than military engineering work. Qualified civilian engineers and surveyors capable of officering militia units were hard to find and harder to retain in a rapidly developing country where engineers frequently moved from place to place. Colonel Casimir Gzowski,† a distinguished engineer of Polish origin, who had been educated in the Kremenetz Military Engineering College in Volhynia, had been appointed lieutenant-colonel and staff officer in the Canadian militia in 1872. A month before the Military College bill was introduced into the Commons he was gazetted as "specially attached as Staff Officer to the Engineer Force of the Dominion." During 1874 he and another Canadian civil

---

*These staff courses were separate from the cadet college. A Militia officer was posted to RMC as a cadet in 1915. Lieutenant Patterson "collected a lot of salutes" before his classmates noticed he was one of them. (G. G. M. Carr-Harris, "Some Reminiscences of R.M.C.," Brock mss., in the possession of T. L. Brock, Montreal.)

†Sir Casimir Stanislas Gzowski, K.C.M.G. (1813–1898), civil engineer and financier. A Pole by birth, he had joined the Russian army but took part in the Polish revolt in 1830 and was exiled; in 1841 he went to Toronto and entered government service; in 1853 he set up an engineering firm which made great contributions to the expansion of Canadian railroads. He was the first president of the Canadian Society of Civil Engineers.

engineer with Liberal political connections, Thomas C. Scoble,* were active in promoting the establishment of an engineer company of militia in Toronto. There were hopes that eventually every military district in Canada would have one.[7] But these were merely dreams in 1874 and as yet there was no place in the militia for graduates of an engineering college.

Major-General Edward Selby Smyth,† the newly appointed general officer commanding the militia, wrote in his report at the end of 1874 that the course of study proposed for the college was of a higher and more scientific order than the mechanical instruction in the *minutiae* of discipline, drill, and the interior economy of the regiment which was all that cavalry and infantry officers needed.[8] Although the training of artillery officers was similar to that for engineers, and although the artillery was thus a possible outlet for the graduates of the college, the two permanent batteries then in existence would not take many graduates. In fact, as Dufferin told the Duke of Cambridge, the college would produce more qualified officers than Canada would need unless there was to be a permanent force.[9] Ross admitted to the Commons that he personally favoured a small professional army but said he thought one not appropriate at the present stage in Canada's national development. Furthermore, he hoped that the spread of peaceful ideas might mean that Canada would never need one. He therefore noted that the military college would "naturally fit its graduates for civil employment." The elements of discipline and drill in the college course would make the cadets "generally useful as civilians"; if they went to civil occupations "the public would have the advantage of their industry"; and they would always be "ready to place themselves at the service of the Dominion should occasion arise." During the college course they would receive relatively little professional military training except that they would go to camp with the Active Militia. Ross concluded by stressing the moral qualities of West Point. A newspaper reported that as he sat down the house broke into loud cheers.[10] If so, he had apparently touched some responsive chords, probably by his reference to the civil value of the proposed college.

Nevertheless several of the Minister's proposals were attacked by the

---

*Thomas Clarkson Scoble, a Toronto engineer, later became editor of the *Nor'-Wester*, a Winnipeg journal.

†General Sir Edward Selby Smyth, K.C.B. (1819–1897), formerly of the 2nd Foot who had served in India, South Africa, and Mauritius, was appointed adjutant-general of the Canadian militia 1 October 1874 and became its first general officer commanding on 21 April 1875. He left Canada in 1880, the only GOC to serve out his full term and, despite the vigour of his criticisms, to resign voluntarily and on good terms with the Canadian government.

opposition. George Kirkpatrick,* member for Frontenac County (in which Kingston is situated) and Dr. Charles Tupper of Cumberland were afraid that nomination of cadets by the governor-in-council would make entrance to the college a part of the Liberal government's patronage. The Prime Minister answered this himself by pointing out that all that was needed by those to be admitted as cadets was a knowledge of the three Rs. As the course would be rigorous, he thought that few would apply for it and that a competitive examination was therefore unnecessary. When this answer failed to appease the critics, he yielded and agreed that the Act should prescribe entry by competition. A second major criticism concerned the location of the college. The government was urged to announce its intentions. Mackenzie at first said that he was quite willing to let parliament approve the location. On further questioning he stated that he himself would have preferred Ottawa as the location of the college so that members could visit it easily, but as there was no accommodation there he thought that either Quebec or Kingston would be selected. He could not say which one until both had been investigated.

In the debate on the third reading of the bill on the following day (16 May) Tupper deprecated what he called "playing fast and loose" between those two cities, but the government refused to name the location in the Act or even to agree that the selection would be submitted later to parliament for approval. The Prime Minister said that it was enough that control could be exercised through parliament's supervision of appropriations.[11]

Times were hard and the Commons was very hesitant because of the expense of the project. In his opening speech Ross had stressed that the military college would not be costly because public buildings (he meant the military installations vacated by the British) were available. One member objected to spending anything to enable soldiers to be idle. He obtained no support for this extreme view but the Commons cut the salaries to be offered to the commandant and the first two professors. Ross had suggested $3500 and $3000 as maximum rates; the Act prescribed $3000 and $2000 respectively.[12] Another amendment raised the age of entry. Instead of fifteen to twenty years it was to be sixteen to twenty.[13]

Little was said about what was from several points of view the most important provision of the bill, namely Ross's revelation that the government intended to set up a college to produce engineers who might take up

*Sir George Airey Kirkpatrick, K.C.M.G. (1841–1899), a lawyer, succeeded his father as Conservative MP for Frontenac in 1870; he was lieutenant-governor of Ontario, 1892–7.

civil careers. It was apparently accepted as a desirable development. One member asked how the college's graduates would be directed into government departments to further the public works that Canada greatly needed. He was probably thinking more of the potential drain to the United States than of the rival attraction of private employment in Canada. He was told that young Canadians trained in the college would probably prefer to work for their country.[14] Under section 93 of the British North America Act, education was a provincial matter and the registration of professional men also came to be a provincial matter by virtue of sections 92.9 and 92.10, but no one questioned the constitutionality of the military college. The college was established under section 91.7 of the BNA ACT that authorized the dominion parliament to legislate for defence. When parliament had not yet set up permanent forces in which they could serve, it would have been unrealistic to have endeavoured to require that all young men trained under this provision take up a military career. The house was probably pleased to learn that, as a side result of making provision for defence, the college could produce some of the engineers needed for what it thought a more important immediate objective, the development of Canada. The military college would educate engineers for both military and civil careers.

Civil engineering (which originally meant non-military engineering and included all the various branches) had only been distinguished from military engineering early in the nineteenth century.[15] The basic preparation for civil and military engineering was still the same. The rapid development of Canada had created a great need for qualified engineers, but facilities for training engineers in Canada were limited.* Developed in response to a need for facilities for training civil, as well as military, engineers in Canada, the Military College opened in June 1876 and is thus the second oldest existing institution set up in Canada specifically as an engineering college and the third oldest to teach engineering continuously. The enabling bill received the royal assent on 26 May 1874. The Honour-

---

*The University of New Brunswick began to give courses in engineering in 1854, and McGill University had an engineering course in its Faculty of Arts from 1855. However, the McGill department, set up in 1856, closed down in 1870 because of lack of funds; and efforts to set up a Technological Institute in Toronto in 1870 were stalled by political difficulties. King's College, Windsor, which had the right to grant engineering degrees from 1827, did not begin instruction in the field until 1871. (It gave degrees in engineering from 1876 to 1920.) A technological college was started in Montreal in 1873 and it adopted its present name, Ecole Polytechnique, in 1875. The Faculty of Applied Science at McGill and the School of Practical Science which later became part of the University of Toronto date from 1878 (*Encyclopedia Canadiana* [10 vols., Ottawa, 1958], IV, 6).

able Richard Cartwright, finance minister and MP for Lennox and Addington, seized the opportunity to gain political advantage in nearby Kingston. Political bitterness throughout the country had been aggravated by the revelation that prominent Conservatives, including John A. Macdonald (MP for Kingston), had received campaign funds from the promoters of the Canadian Pacific Railway. Feelings in Kingston and district ran particularly high. In 1872 Macdonald had lost his temper on a political platform and had physically assaulted a Liberal opponent, Mr. Carruthers. Cartwright tells in his *Reminiscences* of his own personal feud with the Conservative leader who tried hard to prevent his re-election after he was made a minister.[16] He therefore probably sought to secure the military college for Kingston as part of an attempt to weaken Macdonald's hold on his seat in parliament.

The departure of the British garrison had hit Kingston particularly hard. Therefore on 19 May, the Mayor of Kingston, Michael Sullivan,* who was a Conservative, had to play the Liberal game. He held a public meeting of the citizens which produced a petition asking that the military college be located in the vicinity of the city. The petition listed Kingston's many advantages: its convenient and central location, its "remarkable healthfulness," its population moderate in number and orderly in conduct, its clean and elevated site, its facilities for aquatic and other sports suitable and even desirable for students attending college, its military and naval buildings, drill grounds and rifle ranges, its religious facilities, libraries, and reading rooms, its genial and hospitable society, and the presence of Queen's College with its staff of learned professors, library, and scientific apparatus. The petitioners declared that the Duke of Wellington had considered Kingston to be an important military post; and they noted that it had in fact been one for over a century. Furthermore, Kingston was "not without historical fame in the annals of the country which could render it the more proper site for a military college."[17] The Kingston petition was forwarded to Cartwright. Its phraseology and that of the covering letter suggest that he had been behind the move. Mayor Sullivan wrote, "For the short time at our disposal, I may say that the meeting called in connection with the matter by circular was highly influential."[18]

Early in June Mackenzie and Colonel Fletcher paid that visit to inspect

*Dr. Michael Sullivan (1838–1915), professor of anatomy at Queen's University 1862–70 and of surgery 1870–1904; unsuccessful Conservative candidate for the House of Commons in Kingston, 1882; senator, 1884; purveyor-general during the Northwest rebellion, 1885.

the Kingston military installations mentioned in the first chapter. What they saw there convinced Mackenzie that Kingston would be a satisfactory site for the college. However, since he was a very conscientious man, Mackenzie told the Governor-General that he must also investigate Quebec before making the final decision.[19] He therefore requested Colonel H. W. Montagu, the British commanding royal engineer of the Halifax garrison, to report on the relative merits of Kingston and Quebec. Montagu leaned towards Quebec, chiefly because that city was the most important military post in Canada and had to be held in order to maintain communication between England and Canada. He said that the buildings in the Quebec Citadel could be adapted for use as a college; the presence of large numbers of tourists would be a disadvantage but this did not make the French city entirely unacceptable. A few days later Montagu examined Kingston. He showed that the dockyard and the storehouse known as the Stone Frigate could be altered to provide classrooms, cadet study-bedrooms, a kitchen, and mess halls, but he ruled against it because the stores now kept in it would have to be transferred to less suitable locations further from the pier and therefore from cheap water carriage. He reported that the Fort Henry casemates could be made into classrooms and that if a third story with a tin roof were added to them the fort would be protected more effectively against deterioration and so could be preserved for military use. But because Kingston was vulnerable to attack from the United States he advised against its selection.[20] A few days later, without being asked, Montagu sent in a third report on the advantages of the fort and barracks at Toronto which could house up to a hundred cadets, more than the number that could be accommodated immediately at either Quebec or Kingston.[21]

Montagu's report on Toronto was already too late. Either because Mackenzie was unable to decide between Quebec and Kingston from Montagu's complicated weighing of the pros and cons of both places, or because Montagu's preference for Quebec was not to his liking, the Prime Minister had referred the question to the Acting Adjutant-General of the Militia, Colonel Walker Powell, who replied that the buildings at Quebec were being used by the school of gunnery. Powell said that the danger of an American attack on Kingston was not serious; Fort Henry had the same disadvantages as the casemates at Quebec and was not suitable for a college; Point Frederick could easily be isolated because it was a narrow peninsula and therefore officers' quarters and a fence could be built to control access. The Stone Frigate could be divided into convenient quarters for the accommodation of the first class, but another wing would be indispensable after the first year. Alterations should begin at once so as not to disturb the cadets more than was absolutely necessary after the college opened. It would be necessary to plant trees because the peninsula was quite bare.[22] Powell thus reported in favour of the selection of Kingston.

When Mackenzie's government had been returned to power, Macdonald held his seat in Kingston by only thirty-seven votes compared with one hundred and thirty-one in 1872; and the legality of the election was challenged in the courts. In the new contest in December he won again, but by only seventeen votes.[23] By this time it had become known that the military college was to be in Kingston.[24] Mackenzie's selection of Kingston as the site for the college may have contributed to the Conservative leader's near-defeat.

Despite these political motives for the selection of Kingston, its superior advantages as a site were genuine enough. Not least of these was its historic importance. Count Frontenac had selected Cataraqui (as the Indians and French called it) as the location of a trading post in 1673 and had built there the fort that bore his name. La Salle held it as a seigniory and used it as a base for his western discoveries. The fort was intermittently besieged by the Iroquois in 1687 and 1688 and in 1689 was abandoned. Re-established in 1695, it became an important port for the trans-shipment of furs. During the eighteenth century a small fleet of French war vessels was built at Cataraqui to contest control of the lake with the English at Fort Ontario (Oswego). In 1758, as part of the campaign that eventually led to the English conquest of Canada, Colonel Bradstreet had crossed Lake Ontario from Oswego and had seized Fort Frontenac.[25]

In 1783, when Carleton Island, the British port of trans-shipment at the junction of the St. Lawrence and Lake Ontario which had been established during the War of American Independence, seemed likely to pass to the United States by the terms of the peace treaty, Governor Haldimand sent Major John Ross of the 34th Regiment to set up a new port of trans-shipment at Cataraqui and to prepare for a loyalist settlement there. Ross built barracks on the ruins of old Fort Frontenac on the west bank of the Greater Cataraqui estuary, and constructed a government wharf on Point Frederick on the eastern side of the river. By 1792 transport schooners of the Provincial Marine were being built on the point by the quartermaster-general's department of the army which, up to that time, had a monopoly of shipping on the Lakes. In 1809 a more heavily armed three-masted square-rigged vessel, *Royal George*, was built there and launched in Navy Bay, the first ship to be built on the lakes specifically for fighting. About the same time batteries were set up on Points Mississauga and Frederick on opposite sides of the Greater Cataraqui.[26]

During the War of 1812 Point Frederick became a busy dockyard and naval base from which attacks were launched on the American bases at Sackets Harbor and Oswego. However the Americans attacked Kingston only once – at the beginning of the war – when they pursued *Royal George* into Kingston harbour on 10 November 1812 and were held off by the shore batteries.[27] Faulty strategic planning led them to concentrate their main operational efforts elsewhere.

In 1813 the Royal Navy took over operations on the Great Lakes from the Provincial Marine and sent Commodore Sir James Lucas Yeo, an officer who had had a distinguished fighting career, to take command. Yeo set up his headquarters on shipboard at Kingston. Realizing that the preservation of the use of Lake Ontario was essential to British operations further west, Yeo fought cautiously in order to keep a fleet in being.[28] Ships were frantically built on Point Frederick by the successive commissioners of the Kingston Yard, Captain Richard O'Conor and Sir Robert Hall. The War of 1812 on the lakes has therefore been called a "shipbuilder's war" – and the vessels launched from Point Frederick grew in size until, at the end of the campaigning season of 1814, HMS *St. Lawrence*, a first-rate ship of war with up to a hundred and twelve guns and so bigger than Nelson's *Victory*, sailed Lake Ontario unchallenged.

Two bigger American ships were building at Sackets when hostilities ended at Christmas of 1814. By the time the news of peace reached Kingston some nine weeks later, Yeo and Hall also had two ships, HMS *Wolfe* and HMS *Canada*, which were almost as big, nearing completion on the stocks on Point Frederick. If the war had gone into the next year a naval battle of great moment might have been fought on Lake Ontario. Even so, there is no doubt that, although the actions fought were limited, the dockyard on Point Frederick had played an important role and that it had been used effectively to save Canada.[29]

After the war, when the Rush-Bagot agreement of 1817 restricted the naval forces on Lake Ontario to one small gunboat, the British kept Sir Robert Hall in Kingston to maintain the ships of the fleet "in ordinary," that is, in mothballs. When Hall died in 1818 Captain Robert Barrie, his replacement, built a stone warehouse to store the gear and rigging from the ships lying dismantled and housed over in Navy Bay,[30] an undertaking authorized in Hall's time but not started by him. The wooden barracks on Point Frederick had burned down in 1816.[31] The new warehouse thus became the main building on Point Frederick. The whig government's economy programme in the early 1830s led to the auctioning of the warships which were now merely hulks, to Barrie's recall, and to the closing of the yard.[32] The present Fort Henry, a large and impressive fortification that dominates the landscape, was built between 1832 and 1836 to protect the entrance to the Rideau Canal that linked Lake Ontario with the Ottawa River to enable reinforcements to bypass the section of the St. Lawrence which formed the boundary with the United States. The British garrison in Tête-de-Pont barracks and Fort Henry was an important element in the social life of the city until its recall in 1870.

Rebellions in the Canadas in 1837 led to the re-opening of the Kingston naval yard on a smaller basis only three years after it had been closed. Captain Williams Sandom and a party of sailors took up their residence in the stone warehouse and established their nominal headquarters in one of the 1812 hulks, HMS *Niagara*, which had been repurchased. Small steamships were hired. These transported regulars and militia from Kingston to overwhelm "patriot" invaders at the Battle of the Windmill near Prescott. In the following years the dockyard was again active. Steam warships were operated from it. After the Oregon crisis four stone martello towers were built to defend Kingston, one of them to replace the old wooden blockhouse that protected the battery at the end of Point Frederick.[33] By the 1860s the military and naval installations had decayed but one wharf and some of the buildings including the Stone Frigate were kept in repair.[34] When the British garrison withdrew in 1870, the Ordnance and Admiralty lands in Kingston were transferred to the Canadian government and the dockyard on Point Frederick was handed over on the condition that it should never be used for anything except "naval purposes." The Canadian order-in-council which ratified the agreement of transfer added the phrase "and for the naval defence of Canada."[35]

Thus, when Kingston was selected as the site of the new military college, it not only had a military and naval history that could be considered superior to those of Quebec and Halifax, but there were still on every hand the visible signs of a richly military past. The grey walls of Fort Henry dominated the scene to the east. The four great circular martello towers were strung along the shore, the largest being that on Point Frederick near the old dockyard. The Stone Frigate storehouse and a blacksmith's shop (built in the dockyard in 1823 and now to be used for college purposes) were close to the St. Lawrence pier in Navy Bay. There was a stone building that is said to have been built about 1813 and which was used as a naval hospital during the war. It was now known as the Ordnance storekeeper's quarters. Also probably still standing was the old wooden commodore's house (it is shown on a plan dated 1869–70); and there was a row of artificer's cottages that had been built in 1822, but half of them had recently been destroyed by fire. On the site of the French Fort Frontenac on the Kingston side of the river were the Tête-de-Pont barracks. In Navy Bay itself, and in Deadman Bay to the east, could be seen the skeleton-like frames of the old hulks of the War of 1812, hard aground in the mud and much broken up by the lake's annual freezing and thawing. Running down into Navy Bay were what was left of the heavy timbers of the great slips that had been used for launching and careening warships in these tideless seas. Point Frederick was indeed a worthy site to inspire young men who came to learn the military trade. The use of the dockyard as a military college, while it contravened the letter of the terms of agreement about naval usage made when the Point had been transferred to the dominion, was fully in its spirit.

What was even more important for the future of the college than adequate accommodation and an historical location was the appointment of a good man to set it up. Clearly he must come from the British army. On 9 June 1874 Dufferin wrote to the new Secretary of State for the Colonies, the Earl of Carnarvon, who belonged to the opposite political persuasion but was an old friend, to appeal for special consideration for an official request that was to follow. He declared that the quality of the commandant sought for the college was no less important than that of an officer to hold the recently created post of general officer commanding the militia: "It will entirely depend upon the ability and administrative power of this officer, whether the Institution makes a good start and proves a success or becomes discredited and unpopular." The pay would be about £600 and a house.[36]

Carnarvon asked for more information about the exact nature of the proposed college. Was the intention to prepare only for the "ordinary branches of the army – Infantry and Artillery [*sic*]?" If so an excellent regimental officer was all that was needed and would easily be found. But if the college was to be of a more advanced nature like Woolwich or West Point then a man with high scientific attainments was needed and would be difficult to secure. He said that he felt that it should be made clear to potential appointees that the position had good prospects. As he realized that Dufferin was concerned lest an inferior man be sent out, Carnarvon assured him that when the matter came to his attention officially he would refuse to consent to any arrangement that was not in the best interests of Canada.[37]

Carnarvon was given a memorandum prepared by Colonel Fletcher which he forwarded to General Sir Lintorn Simmons, the governor of the Royal Military Academy, Woolwich, to ask for advice. The Royal Military Academy can claim to trace its origins back to 1721[38] and so was one of the oldest engineering colleges in the world. It enjoyed a high reputation.

Its graduates with higher standing had the option of being commissioned in the Royal Engineers; the remainder went to the Royal Artillery. Simmons said that, although Fletcher had called the proposed course "elementary," a four-year course starting at age sixteen would take the brighter students into advanced mathematics as well as practical mechanics. He said that if the curriculum also included good practical courses in chemistry and physics the cadets would get grounding as civil engineers which would be important for them because there was no Canadian permanent force. The commandant of the Canadian military college should therefore not only know the various arms of the service but also, in view of the small size of the college, should be capable of teaching some of the subjects on the curriculum. He must be a man of tact and of the highest possible military rank; and he should be given a fairly long tenure so that he would have the greatest possible influence. The least that should be offered for a superior man with scientific qualifications was £800 in addition to regimental pay and quarters, with appointment for six years and the possibility of reappointment. He recommended Major Lonsdale A. Hale, RE,* an instructor in tactics, military law, and organization at the School of Military Engineering, Chatham. Although Hale was, despite his twenty-one years of service, rather junior for the appointment, Simmons was sure he possessed the required qualities and qualifications.[39]

Dufferin then sent the official request for transmission to the War Office and Carnarvon wrote personally to the Duke of Cambridge, stating that he had heard that Major Hale and two other officers would be suitable nominees. The salary offered was $3200, or about £640 sterling. Cambridge found that Hale had "misgivings" because he feared to lose connection with the British army. The Duke therefore asked Carnarvon to talk to him personally. Carnarvon managed to persuade Hale to accept, only to have him think the matter over again and withdraw. The Colonial Secretary then approached the next officer on his list who was, he thought, quite as good. But he was unsuccessful and he had to report to Dufferin that he must now try again elsewhere.[40]

The Canadian government pressed for haste in making the appointment in order to get the military college started.[41] It had begun to receive applications from men who wanted to join the staff and from boys who wished to be cadets.[42] It had also received at least two requests from

---

*Later Colonel Sir Lonsdale Augustus Hale, RE, was well known for his military writings which included *The Peoples' War in France, 1870-1871* (London, 1904), *The Army and the Franchise* (London, 1886), and various military lectures and texts.

officers who wanted to be commandant. One was from Major Leonard Griffiths, RA, the deputy governor of the Brixton Convict Establishment in Britain; and the second was from Lieutenant-Colonel Strange, the commandant of its own school of gunnery at Quebec, who had been one of the advocates of a military college for Canada.[43]

The official letter requesting the nomination of a commandant had been forwarded to the War Office before Carnarvon saw it. He thought the letter of transmittal sent by his department "not full enough on a very important matter"; he therefore had it redrafted and sent to the War Office with a request that the new version be substituted.[44] Meanwhile Strange had apparently already applied to the War Office, for on 2 December a War Office clerk wrote to tell the Colonial Office that he had been selected to command the Canadian military college.[45] About the same time, as if in support of this appointment, an article appeared about him in the *Army and Navy Gazette*. The editor had received from Quebec copies of two lectures entitled "Artillery Retrospect of the Last Great War – 1870" which Strange had given to the Literary and Historical Society in that city. The editor commented that the syllabus of the course of instruction in the school of gunnery, which had been enclosed with the lectures, attested to Colonel Strange's valuable efforts to make up for the want of a military college; and he added that he could not doubt that when the time came to establish one the dominion would avail itself of "the gallant author's services."[46]

By the time this article appeared Carnarvon had written to urge Cambridge to cancel Strange's appointment on the grounds that he could not be compared with Hale. He said that any disappointment in Canada might lead to the total abandonment of this worthwhile scheme.[47] Cambridge retorted that Strange was "a fit man and qualified" and had been recommended by General Napier, the director general of military education. In justification of the appointment he forwarded clippings of the leading article on Strange in the *Army and Navy Gazette*.[48] Carnarvon replied that he had information from Canada that suggested that Strange's appointment would not be well received: he was well liked and was no doubt a good artillery officer, but he had not had the experience in tuition that the post required.[49]

Privately the Colonial Secretary told Dufferin, "I have just had a really preposterous attempt to force on me a gentleman who would be unfitted for the post"; and he complained that "the W[ar] O[ffice] – as usual – is anxious to provide for officers at the cost of Canada and with very little regard to the real necessities of the case." With the admonition that the author's identity ought to be concealed, he sent the Governor-General a memorandum drawn up by his secretary, Montagu Ommanney,* to be used as the basis of a memorandum to the Canadian ministers to suggest what should be done in order to make the appointment possible.[50]

Carnarvon then began a long search for new possibilities and at the same time strove to induce Canada and the War Office to make concessions that would allow the appointment of a man of the quality he thought necessary. Rather than appoint one he thought inferior, he was even willing to allow the project to die. There were many difficulties. The Canadian government believed that, as the appointment had advantages for the empire as well as for Canada, the War Office should be prepared to permit the commandant to retain his pay and prospects in the British army in the same manner as the recently appointed GOC. Carnarvon, who saw this college as one of great imperial significance, agreed, but he found that getting money out of the War Office was "like getting water out of flint."[51] The War Office refused to waive the rule that officers who were not on the British active list could not receive full regimental pay. Furthermore, service in Canada not only lacked the glamour and glory of other overseas postings where fighting was possible but also was likely to be difficult and uncertain. British officers feared to put their careers at the mercy of a colonial government which had shown no great interest in military matters and in a place where prospects for military advancement were not large. Many of those officers who accepted appointments in Canada in the last part of the nineteenth century, even as GOC, did so because they had personal reasons for wanting to live in the dominion. Often they were married to Canadian girls who were delighted to be posted home. (Indeed, if it had not been for the large number of troops who were rushed to Canada during the American Civil War and for the large number of impressionable young officers who became attached to attractive colonial girls,† the dominion would probably have not succeeded in obtaining the service of enough British officers for its very small requirements.)

*Captain (later Sir) Montagu F. Ommanney (1867–1925), private secretary to Lord Carnarvon in the Colonial Office; crown agent for the colonies, 1877–1900; permanent undersecretary for the colonies, 1900–7.

†General Sir Fenwick Williams (1800–1883), a Nova Scotian commissioned in the Royal Artillery, was commander-in-chief in Canada (1859–65) during the American Civil War. He was disturbed by the number of his young officers who married Canadian girls; he sent home one young officer named Herbert who had become infatuated with a Canadian girl nicknamed "short horns" who swore like a trooper. Williams' complaint was not the morals of the Canadian brides but that they were not wealthy.

By the end of February 1875 Carnarvon had found two more very good officers for the task, a Colonel Fisher* and a Major Hewett. Cambridge preferred to send the former because Hewett was working on the construction of fortifications at Spithead and could ill be spared. Fisher declined but the Duke found that Sir Frederick Chapman, the inspector general of fortifications, was willing to release Hewett. However, when he was offered the Canadian appointment, Hewett also declined. The Duke told Carnarvon: "The fact is that the place is not well paid and that officers don't think it worth while to give up their professional prospects at home for an uncertain future in Canada."[52] Nevertheless on 11 March Carnarvon was able to write to tell Dufferin that he had not given up hope of either of these officers.[53] Past experience had shown that they were more likely to be persuaded by him than by the Duke. Six days later he reported to Cambridge that he had reason to believe that Hewett, who would be an effective head for the school, was anxious to reconsider his refusal.[54]

Major Edward Osborne Hewett, who needed the appointment because he had a large family to provide for, had Canadian associations and connections. Two of his great uncles had served with Wolfe at Quebec. His father, Lieutenant John Hewett (or Hewitt) of the Royal Marines, had fought in Canada in the War of 1812, had been stationed in Kingston, and had been mentioned in despatches for gallantry at the attack on Oswego in 1814 when he climbed the fort flagstaff under fire to tear down colours that were nailed to the mast. On retirement from the army as a colonel, John Hewett had settled at Tyr Mab Ellis in Glamorgan and was deputy lieutenant of the county and a promoter of the volunteer movement. In these comfortable circumstances, Edward Osborne Hewett was born in 1835. Educated at Cheltenham College and the Royal Military Academy, he had shown early promise, being quickly appointed a cadet NCO and winning prizes for both intellectual and physical work. He had passed through RMA in three years instead of the usual four and had been commissioned in the Royal Engineers in 1854, missing service in the Crimea by a hair's breadth when his draft was cancelled because of the fall of Sebastopol.

Although Hewett lacked operational experience, his promotion had been rapid and he had served in various important capacities. He had worked on the construction of fortifications at Dover and in the creation of the large permanent camp at Shorncliffe. He had served twice in the West Indies and commanded there in the absence of the commanding

*Either Brevet-Colonel Arthur A'Court Fisher, C.B., RE, who was posted home from Bermuda in 1874 or Colonel Edward Henry Fisher, RA, commandant of the school of gunnery at Shoeburyness.

royal engineer. He had also been employed on the construction of land fortifications at Portsmouth. After a term as instructor of military surveying and practical astronomy at Woolwich he had resigned to volunteer for the command of the 18th Royal Engineer Company which was ordered to Canada at the time of the *Trent* incident. Appointed commanding royal engineer of the troops west of Hamilton, Hewett had prepared defensive positions in expectation of an invasion. He had visited the scene of American Civil War operations, spending an equal time with the opposing armies. He had been present at Antietam and Perrysville, his horse had been killed under him, and he had been captured by the Confederates. Hewett had also visited West Point for a week. Before leaving Canada he had been employed on construction work at the Halifax naval base.

On 4 February 1864 in Toronto Hewett had married Catharine Mary Biscoe, daughter of the late Colonel Vincent Joseph Biscoe, RE, who had served in Canada during the rebellions of 1837–8. After her father's death at Hong Kong in 1850 Catharine had lived with her brother, Colonel Vincent Biscoe, said to be an officer of the Loyal North Lancashire Regiment and an adjutant at Halifax who had retired to reside in Toronto. Thus, in addition to his father's connection with Canada and his own tour of duty there, Major Hewett had married into a family which was Canadian by adoption. Undoubtedly these associations helped to influence his decision to accept the unpromising post of commandant of the new military college.

During his service Major Hewett had frequently had command responsibilities. The memorandum of his qualifications sent to Canada emphasized that a commanding royal engineer had the same powers and position as a colonel of infantry without the assistance of an adjutant, rifle instructor, paymaster, or quartermaster. On his return to England in 1867 he had been employed on the construction of four large iron forts far out in the tidal waters of Spithead. He must often have compared his work there with that of the engineers who had built the Shoal Tower in Kingston harbour – but there had been no ice in Spithead waters from which to sink the necessary coffer dams for construction of his forts. Major Hewett, in addition to his engineering and command responsibilities, had been for eight years an inspector of the science and art schools of Great Britain. Lastly he was accomplished as a painter, a skill which had practical as well as aesthetic values for a soldier of his time since field-sketching was still an important military technique.[55] Hewett was a very suitable man for the Kingston appointment.

The Canadian government (despite the terms of the Act) now agreed to increase the salary of the commandant to thirty-five hundred dollars.[56]

Then, on 13 April, the War Office outlined the conditions on which Hewett would accept it. In the first place, he objected to the requirement that he should teach personally.[57] Mackenzie and the new Minister of Militia and Defence, W. B. Vail, agreed that the duties of the commandant would consist chiefly of supervision; in the first two years the college would be small and the commandant would not be expected to teach the junior classes.[58] But the question of his British regimental pay, which Hewett hoped to have in addition to his Canadian salary, was still a stumbling block. The Colonial Office had to remind the War Office that unless the appointments were made soon the Canadian government would become impatient and might withdraw from the scheme altogether.[59] On 23 July official consent was given for Hewett's appointment, but it was only for a two-year term.[60] Ommanney minuted the report in the Colonial office, "a more unfortunate condition could hardly have been attached to the War Office's comment unless, indeed, their object is to prevent any Imperial Officer being appointed." The Colonial Office pressed for a four-year term.[61] Colonel Charles Chesney, the senior engineer officer at Aldershot and a distinguished military instructor and writer, explained that the real difficulty was that an officer going to Canada was liable to lose his place on the half-pay list and unless this was changed nobody worth having would go.[62]

Carnarvon was very apprehensive about the whole project and talked of giving it up if a suitable man could not be found. "I have written and talked on the subject till I fear it has become as distasteful to others as a hopeless question always becomes." All that the War Office would concede was that Hewett, but not necessarily another appointee if Hewett did not go, would receive his regimental pay for two years. Carnarvon was disgusted that "a scheme of very large proportions of great imperial value, and calculated I believe ultimately to save this country money and men," might fail through "technical objections."[63] Cambridge said that it was unreasonable of engineer officers to make difficulties about taking the appointment. Once again he recommended Strange, but he told Carnarvon to speak directly to Colonel Brown, the deputy adjutant-general of the Royal Engineers.[64]

Hewett then attempted to provide for his future by asking Mackenzie, who was in England, for a personal promise that if his regimental pay ceased after two years the Canadian government would pay him the equivalent. Mackenzie replied that, although he accepted Hewett's assurance that he would not divulge a confidential promise, nevertheless he could make no private bargain about public business.[65] Hewett therefore took the appointment without receiving a guarantee of the retention of regimental pay, or of its equivalent from Canada, after two years. Starting from 16 September, the day he sailed for Canada, his Canadian salary was to be £650 sterling and he was to have a house and fuel and free passage to and from Canada for himself and his family.[66]

When Vail had endeavoured to reassure Hewett about the conditions of his appointment in April, he had said that as soon as the commandant arrived in Canada he would meet with the GOC and the Minister of Militia to draw up regulations to be approved by the governor-in-council (that is to say, the cabinet) for the management of the school.[67] General regulations for the military college were authorized by order-in-council on 26 October 1875. This was after Hewett had arrived in Canada, but it is not certain that he took part in the discussions. These regulations were published in the *Canada Gazette* of 30 October 1875. Repeating the objects of the college as laid down in the Act, they stated that the course would be four years. They also set forward detailed admission regulations, awards to be bestowed on selected cadets, and payments and allowances to be exacted. Boards of examiners were to be set up in each military district and admission would be granted to successful candidates in open competition. Age of entry (which was not strictly adhered to) was to be between fifteen and twenty years on the first day of the month following the examination. The maximum entry for the first year was to be twenty-two cadets selected by the governor-in-council from the lists submitted by the examiners "having reference to the order of merit in which the candidates passed the examination." This might seem at first sight to leave loopholes for patronage or discrimination, but it was qualified by a later regulation which said the "successful candidates being those who stand first on the list up to the number of vacancies competed for, if otherwise qualified." Cadets must be British subjects and have resided, or be the children of parents who had resided, in Canada for at least five years. Short periods of absence in Europe for educational purposes would not be a disqualification. Cadets must be single and must remain so while at the college. They must pass medical examinations and meet certain physical standards. They could try the entrance examinations three times only.

There was to be a compulsory preliminary qualifying examination in mathematics, grammar and composition, geography, history, French, German, Latin, and drawing, and further optional examinations in algebra, Euclid, trigonometry, English literature, British and Canadian history, French, German, Latin, and drawing. A sword was to be presented for excellence of conduct to a member of each graduating class; and three outstanding graduates were to receive commissions predated by one year. The fees were to be $200 for the first year and $150 in each succeeding year and cadets were to provide themselves with uniforms, books, instruments, and apparatus as required.[68]

These regulations were referred to the Colonial Office, and Ommanney, assuming, perhaps wrongly, that they had been drawn up by Major Hewett, commented on them critically in the customary fashion of the members of that office who were never deterred by lack of first-hand knowledge of the problems involved from expressing opinions on local matters in the colonies. Ommanney thought the length of the course excessive when the most graduates could receive in return was a militia commission. He recommended that examiners should be reappointed annually and he pointed out that the statement that selection would be made by the governor-in-council was redundant when admission was in order of merit. He thought that the English and history books chosen would encourage cramming, that "too great value appears to be attached to a little Euclid," and that geometrical drawing should replace freehand drawing. Lord Carnarvon was at first inclined to send "Mr. Ommanney's excellent memo" privately to Canada, but he soon wisely thought better of it.[69]

Hewett submitted additional regulations relating to the government of the College and the administration of its affairs. These may be the first of his many contributions to the future well-being of RMC. They included provision for the appointment of the GOC of the militia as *ex officio* president of the college; provision for a board of visitors; restriction of all staff appointments (except modern languages) to British subjects of ten years' standing; power for the commandant to suspend professors and instructors; organization of the college "on a military basis" with the commandant responsible for discipline and for the general superintendence of studies; the commandant to have powers to issue standing orders; establishment of an academy board to assist in the arrangement of studies; an obligation on the part of the commandant to consult the staff regularly on the affairs of their separate "branches"; provision that only the commandant have power of punishment; provision for military officers and the civil staff to report misconduct and to have powers of arrest and, at the discretion of the commandant, provision for the military staff to be authorized to award two days' extra drill; provision for the staff to perform such duties connected with the cadet company as the commandant may assign; provision for the civil and military staff to be liable to assist in other branches when required; appointment of a captain of cadets and a staff officer; and provision that the commandant have a power of rustication and of sentencing offenders to lose places on the list of successful candidates for employment.

The four-year course was to include compulsory courses in mathematics including plane trigonometry and practical mechanics; fortifications; artillery; military drawing, reconnaissance, and surveying; military history, administration, law, strategy, and tactics; French or German; elementary chemistry and geology, "etc."; drawing; drills and exercises; and discipline. In addition there were optional subjects in which a lower standard would be required but which could contribute to a graduate's final standing. These were higher mathematics; higher fortification; higher chemistry and physics; French or German other than that taken compulsorily; architecture, construction, estimating, etc.; hydraulic engineering, "etc. etc." The final examination was to be marked by outside examiners.[70]

On the advice of the Minister of Justice, Edward Blake, Hewett's proposal to restrict appointment on the staff to British subjects was omitted because it was not covered by the Act. General Selby Smyth, the GOC, had amended the proposed regulation about powers of punishment to permit the commandant to delegate the power to military staff to impose up to two days' extra drill. The cabinet apparently altered the regulation about staff members undertaking any duties the commandant might assign them so that it would cover civilians as well as officers. With these revisions the additional regulations were passed by council for the approval of the Governor-General on 17 December 1875.[71]

Before Hewett accepted, Mackenzie had been under heavy pressure to appoint Canadians to the staff of the military college. References were made in the Canadian House of Commons to certain Canadians serving in the British army. The Prime Minister assured his critics that as far as possible qualified Canadian officers would be employed and he said that the names of several distinguished military men had been received. But he said that the commandant must be chosen from the British army and, before making other appointments to the staff, the government would have to consult him. He added that the salaries were fixed by the Act.[72] He seems to have been under some pressure to appoint Canadian militia officers, but the Colonial Office assumed that the senior military professors would be appointed from the British army. However, Carnarvon was unable to persuade the War Office to give any more officers their regimental pay.

On arriving in Canada, Hewett recommended that the military professors should come from England;[73] and he made no attempt to restrict the selection to Canadians which would have severely limited his choice. He wanted one officer from his own corps, the Royal Engineers, and one from the Royal Artillery. He said that in order to secure good men the salaries set down in the Act must be raised. But it proved impossible to get another engineer officer. Through the Colonial Office, Hewett obtained

Captain Edgar Kensington, RA,* an instructor of mathematics at RMA, as professor of mathematics and artillery, at a salary of $2700 and lodging allowance of $300; and, after at least one other officer had refused and Hewett had recommended direct application to the Commander-in-Chief,[74] Captain George Walter Hawkins, RA, was appointed professor of surveying, fortification, field engineering, and drawing at a salary of $2500 and lodging allowance.†

Hewett's amendments to the proposed regulations, designed to strengthen military organization and discipline in the college, had included the establishment of a captain of cadets, an officer who, under the commandant, would be in charge of the cadet body. He wanted to secure for this appointment Captain William Everett‡ of the 33rd (Duke of Wellington's) Regiment, an instructor at Woolwich. However, the minister substituted the name of Captain Joseph Bramley Ridout of the Cameronians (Scottish Rifles).[75] Ridout was a Canadian,§ his father, Thomas Gibbs Ridout, having been a deputy assistant commissary general during the War of 1812 and the cashier of the Bank of Upper Canada from 1822 to 1861. His sister was Lady Edgar, who wrote family history and a biography of Brock; and his brother, John Gibbs Ridout, who had joined the

---

*Colonel Edgar Kensington, RA, p.a.c., professor of mathematics and artillery, RMC, 23 March 1876–20 August 1884, was the son of a fellow of New College, Oxford, and had been educated at RMA, Woolwich; he had served for five years with his regiment in Canada and was instructor in mathematics at RMA in 1875 where he was a tutor of the Prince Imperial, the son of Emperor Napoleon III, who was killed in Zululand in 1878; he retired from the army in 1886 on half-pay and went on to the reserve in 1895; he was re-employed in the Ministry of Munitions during World War I. His wife died in 1941 at the age of 92, probably the last link with those who founded RMC in 1876.

†Major George Walter Hawkins, RA, p.s.c., p.a.c., educated at Addiscombe, Woolwich, and Camberley; professor of surveying, RMC, 8 June 1876–10 September 1877; captain instructor of the Royal Laboratory, a division of the Royal Arsenal at Woolwich, 1882–6. He retired from the army in 1886 but is found in army lists until 1918.

‡Later Sir William Everett, C.M.G., vice-consul at Erzeroum and consul for Kurdistan.

§Ridout had joined the 80th Regiment, and had served in the Bhutan campaign where he earned a medal and clasp. The Bhutan campaign, in very difficult country on the borders of British India, occurred when a British envoy, the Honourable Ashley Eden, was unable to get satisfaction about border raids; a Bhutanese leader rubbed dough on Eden's face, pulled his hair, slapped him on the back, and committed other insolent acts which Eden at first thought were friendly customs of the country. (Surgeon David Field Rennie, *Bhootan and the Story of the Dooar War* [London, 1866], pp. 124–5; Nigel G. Woodyatt, *History of the 3rd Queen Alexandra's Own Ghurka Rifles, 1815–1927* [London, 1929], pp. 35–6.) Three of the British army officers on the RMC staff had served in the Bhutan campaign, Ridout, Oliver, and Cameron. Ridout had also been on the staff of the Hythe School of Musketry and had frequently been concerned with the annual rifle competition at Wimbledon in which the Canadian militia competed.

100th Royal Canadians in 1858 had recently been called to the bar in the province of Ontario. An old Ontario family, the Ridouts were connected by marriage with the Baldwins, the Sullivans, and the Boultons. Although their traditional political interests were tory, they also had a foot in the Liberal political camp. Captain Ridout's appointment was thus not so much "political" as "Canadian." He seemed a good man for the position because of his experience and his personality. He became popular with the cadets who called him "Joe." The selection of a Canadian with British army experience to have direct control of young Canadian cadets was eminently sound.

The need for a professor to teach non-military subjects made possible the appointment of another Canadian. Since November 1874 there had been rumours in Kingston that the military college would be staffed by Queen's professors on a part-time basis. The appointment of the first two British officers scotched the idea that mathematics instructors would be required and it was believed that no arts professors would be needed for a military college. But one man who was particularly interested was Professor the Reverend George Ferguson,* the son of the owner of the *Montreal Herald*. The elder Ferguson had secured the chair of history at Queen's for his son, but the latter was unable to live on his salary. Moreover, his wife and family were living in Germany for cultural and health reasons. Professor Ferguson saw an appointment at the military college as a solution for his financial difficulties. He therefore kept a careful eye on developments. But as he believed that the Liberal government had made all new appointments in other departments on a political basis (this was before the appointment of Hewett) he felt that his own political connections (which were Conservative) would exclude him. He also feared that Richard Cartwright might secure the appointment for Grant Allen, the poet, who was an unpaid instructor at Queen's, or for one of his own brothers or cousins.

It happened that when Hewett arrived in Kingston he at first stayed in the British-American hotel where Ferguson lived while his wife was in Germany. Ferguson promptly called on the commandant who told him that the government wanted to appoint to the college's chair of literature a French Canadian who was willing to teach French, German, and chemistry for $1000 a year. Hewett revealed to Ferguson that he had been so convinced that the man was unsuitable that he had threatened to resign.

---

*The Reverend George Dalrymple Ferguson (1829–1926), historian, was ordained in the Church of Scotland in Canada; professor of history at Queen's University, 1869–1908, and from 1 June 1876–3 October 1883 he also taught French, German, and English at RMC. He was the author of *Lectures on the History of the Middle Ages* (Kingston, 1904). (Katherine Ferguson, "George Dalrymple Ferguson," *Historic Kingston*, No. 14, Jan. 1966, pp. 51–66.)

He said he had informed Mackenzie that either the government must pay enough to get a first-class man from England or they must make use of part-time help by Queen's professors who were already "engaged in such studies." He asked Ferguson whether he had time for the work and if he was interested in a part-time appointment. Ferguson, concealing his eagerness, said that he would not "become a candidate" because he feared that he was politically unacceptable. But Hewett had apparently taken a fancy to him. Some time later he assured Ferguson that he would "bear all his weight on the government" to secure the appointment for him. He also offered to give him leave of absence early in the year so that he could bring his family back from Europe.[76]

Hewett's determination to resist government pressure and to appoint a staff he thought competent for the work brought him into so much disfavour in Canada that Dufferin reported to England that he was "a failure" and implied that he was about to be dismissed. Lord Carnarvon replied: "He [Hewett] had so high a reputation in every way that I thought we were quite safe in him. It cannot be helped and I only hope that this unfortunate 'stumble on the threshold' will not in any way prejudice the future fortunes of the School."[77] The Governor-General had, however, spoken too soon. Ferguson obtained support from the Tory member for Frontenac, George Kirkpatrick, who told Minister of Militia Vail that Ferguson ought to have the appointment. A few days later Ferguson met Sir John A. Macdonald socially in Kingston and revealed to him that he expected to be appointed to the college. Sir John said that if there was any trouble Ferguson should let him know and he would put the "screws" on the government and get it for him. Hewett's determination in fact won through. Ferguson was appointed at $1000 a year with expectation of an early increase. And, as he had support from the opposition, Ferguson was assured that he could expect to keep his job if the government changed.[78]

The appointment of Captain Hawkins, who sailed from England on 8 June 1876 after the college opened, completed the list of senior staff for the first year.[79] As the enrolment was expected to be small at first, a commandant, three professors, and one officer in command of the cadets were considered adequate. A staff-sergeant acted as quartermaster, clerk, paymaster, and librarian.[80] Four college servants and a bombardier and trumpeter attached from the battery in Tête-de-Pont barracks constituted the whole establishment in June 1876.

But the preparation of accommodation and equipment had been found quite as difficult and time-consuming as the collection of this small staff. Even before Hewett arrived, steps had been taken to prepare Point Frederick for the college. The military hospital building on Point Henry had been given to the Stores Department to house the contents of the Stone Frigate.[81] Furthermore, as Colonel Montagu had suggested when searching for a site for the college, stone from the market battery in front of the City Hall in Kingston had been used to build two gatehouses at the entrance to Point Frederick.* These were ready for occupation by March 1876.[82] During the winter of 1874–5, while the sledding was good, the guns lying in the dockyard were removed.[83] During the same winter forty carpenters were set to work to refit the Stone Frigate to make classrooms and cadet rooms; the ground outside was levelled; and a large part of the money appropriated was spent on repairing the fortifications on the Point.[84]

Hewett's first and only assistant at the time of his arrival was a clerk, Staff-Sergeant M. J. Leaden,† a Crimean veteran who had been stationed at Lévis as a commissariat storeman. Leaden reported to Kingston in October 1875 and was officially taken on to the staff of the college on 1 May 1876.[85] Hewett's first act was to submit a paper stating what must be done before the college opened. The existing building, when the reconstruction was completed with certain alterations which he had in mind, would accommodate about twenty-four cadets and would provide temporary quarters for one officer, a dining room and classrooms, servants' quarters, and a hospital. He stressed that care should be given to sanitary arrangements to reduce to a minimum the danger of epidemics which might affect the popularity and prospects of the college; and he urged that long-term planning be immediately undertaken to provide accommodation for a cadet body of the strength authorized by the Act of Parliament (118). "The only strictly *national* educational establishment," he wrote, "should not be behind similar Provincial and Urban institutions, whether public or private, so far at any rate, as fitness for its purpose is concerned." He therefore recommended a second block of cadet barracks, a block to contain classrooms, offices, library, and probably mess rooms, a drill shed and riding school, workshops, a gymnasium and ball courts, quarters for the subordinate staff, quarters for the superior staff and military officers, a "foot parade," and the planting of trees because there was a total absence of shade throughout the entire peninsula. These new buildings should be concentrated not only for convenience of communication, but also for the economical provision of services and drainage. He wrote:

---

*Colonel Montagu had noted that the city of Kingston wished to obtain possession of the site of the market battery and had suggested that an exchange might be worked out. The land became the site of a station for the Pembroke Railway. (PAC, DM 02673, Department of Public Works, 22 March 1826; *British Whig*, 14 March 1876.)

†Sergeant-Major Leaden remained on the RMC staff until the purge in 1897.

"The peculiar, indeed it may fairly be said unique, conditions of the site should be realized and borne in mind in the whole arrangements and requirements of the college."[86]

Eight days later Hewett wrote to the Adjutant-General about his own quarters in Kingston. The building now known as Hewett House, which is located on the site of the quarters built by Commissioner Hall, was apparently being built as a commandant's house. There is a tradition that Hewett refused to accept it because it was too magnificent. The origin of this story seems to be a question in the House of Commons. George Kirkpatrick asked Mackenzie why the commandant's house had been so badly planned that no room in it was large enough to accommodate ten persons. He wished to know who was "the architect of this wonderful edifice." He alleged that the commandant would not live in it. Mackenzie (by profession a building contractor) retorted that he received the rebuke with becoming modesty from one who knew so much more about plans than he did. (Kirkpatrick was a lawyer.) He said that the building had been planned by an able architect under his direction and that he thought it had been done well. He was prepared to defend the building. Kirkpatrick then admitted that he was not speaking on behalf of the commandant but as a consequence of a personal inspection of the house.[87]

It was known in Kingston that officers' quarters were being built on Point Frederick for the use of the instructional staff.[88] When Hewett wrote about his own quarters in October he made no reference to the house then being built for him but only about arrangements by which he could obtain a house in town. (The probable explanation is that as he had a large family he preferred to live in town.) He found the British-American Hotel expensive, but he was unwilling to take on a more permanent commitment in the form of a private lease until he was sure that the college would be properly established. Furthermore he said that cadet barracks and staff quarters must take precedence over the commandant's quarters. He therefore asked that the government lease a house for him in Kingston. The minister replied that Hewett should state how much he would accept from the department in lieu of a house and fuel.[89] The Adjutant-General then recommended that a house in Kingston belonging to Mr. Grant Macdonald should be taken by the government for Hewett's use. In that house on the corner of Barrie and King Streets opposite Murney Tower Hewett lived until 1879. This magnificent structure with portico and columns, later known as the Bermingham House, was thus the first RMC commandant's residence.* Although the rebuilt Commodore's House on Point

*Hewett then bought Edgewater on Emily Street and lived there until he left Kingston.

Frederick may have originally been intended for the commandant, it was occupied by one of his staff, Major Kensington.

Hewett was anxious to make one other important rearrangement in the construction already under way in order to accommodate his senior staff more to his satisfaction. He was convinced that for the sake of discipline it was necessary to have the captain of cadets located in or near the cadet barracks. He therefore recommended that three floors at the south end of the Frigate be converted into an officer's quarters with a separate entrance. To do this the cadet dining room would have to be transferred from the south end of the basement to the north end of the ground floor, service lifts must be installed from the kitchen below, a classroom had to be moved from the south end of the ground floor to the north end of the first floor, and the staircase had to be put in another place. Hewett also wanted two extra baths in place of some urinals and wash-basins. With these alterations Hewett reckoned that the Frigate would accommodate one officer and twenty-four cadets. The estimated cost over and above what had already been spent on the Frigate was $1362.47.[90] When the GOC urged that extra work should be kept to a minimum, Hewett replied that the proposed officer's quarters were essential and that if they were constructed he could then provide all the accommodation needed for the college until such time as a new building was erected. He said that when the new block became available for offices and classrooms, which should be before the end of 1876, the Stone Frigate barracks would accommodate fifty to sixty cadets. A third block should be built in 1877 to provide accommodation for the total number of cadets permitted by the Act.[91]

Hewett had many other things to arrange in preparation for opening the college. Quarters were needed for the college servants and he was promised as many of the naval cottages as he required.[92] Civilians resident on the point had to be evicted and action had to be taken to exclude strangers and civilians from the area. This was unpopular because it interfered with bathing from the point.[93] Hewett also requested that thought be given to the arrangements for heating the Stone Frigate in winter;[94] and he noted that the water supply was close to the cesspits and thus a danger to health.[95] A piece of ground within the college enclosure was levelled and turfed for a cricket pitch; and an iron roller was requisitioned to prepare the wicket.[96] Patterns for furniture were prepared in the Kingston penitentiary and tenders were called for its manufacture.[97] A guard room and area rail, arms racks, and a gunshed were constructed,[98] the latter by the adaptation of the old blacksmith's shop which also served as a gymnasium. Indian clubs, gymnastic apparatus, and a boat were purchased, as well as drawing materials, maps, survey reports, and a gyroscope.[99] Fire extinguishers and fire buckets were needed urgently because the oil lamps used for lighting presented a formidable risk.[100] Uniform was obtained for the college servants and subordinate staff.[101]

A most important decision concerned the uniform the cadets would wear. Authority for it was received from Ottawa at the end of 1875. Derived from the dress of the British army of the time it consisted of a scarlet tunic and blue trousers with a scarlet side strip. The headdress was a four-inch shako* with a gilt chain and gilt cap-plate with a sunburst with the words "Military College of Canada" around a crown. In winter cadets wore a grey greatcoat and a dark grey persian lamb cap with side flap and scarlet top cloth. Cadet sergeant-majors were permitted to wear greatcoats trimmed with grey persian fur and also grey persian fur gauntlets. The undress jacket was blue and the forage cap was a blue pill-box with a scarlet welt around the crown.[102]

By 1 June 1876, when the first cadets were due to report to the commandant, the arrangements on Point Frederick were still not quite finished. Reporters from the Kingston newspapers, the *British Whig* and the *Daily News*, found "the old stone ship to have been worthily utilized." The building was said to be "most admirably laid out," the halls and dormitories exceedingly pleasant, the rooms well lighted, the views of the surrounding country cheery, ... and the atmosphere "free from the slightest impurity." The cadet rooms on the third floor were fitted out plainly but substantially like those at an ordinary hotel with furniture which, it was understood, had been supplied by the penitentiary. The officers' rooms and classrooms were on the second floor and were conveniently fitted out. The captain of cadets was lodged in the building. In the basement and on the ground floor Mr. R. Irwin, who had contracted to mess the cadets, reigned supreme with his "usual geniality" and "excellent management." Tramways to carry the trays from the dining room to the kitchen caught one reporter's eye as a modern innovation and seemed a symbol of the care which had been given to detail and to modern convenience.

The *Whig* reporter, however, felt "taken down" by the abrupt answers of Colonel Hewett who curtly referred his questioners to the Prime Minister in Ottawa for further information and turned away "on his heel." The editor of that paper, normally a supporter of the government, therefore wrote a cryptic sub-editorial about the autocratic behaviour of "Commodore [*sic*]" Hewett. The *News*, an opposition paper, seized the

---

*Between 1878 and 1880, when the shako went out of style in the British army, the RMC headdress became a Wolseley type helmet with a similar helmet plate, and the blue undress jacket was replaced by one in scarlet. In later years the round fur cap gave way to one that was wedge-shaped. After 1878 the helmet plate, etc., bore the words "Royal Military College, Canada."

opportunity to quote the *Whig* to blame Mackenzie for imposing gags on all at the Military College. It also stated that it had heard that orders had been given that all college purchases were to be made only "from Grits so that the youth in training may neither eat bread made by Tory hands nor drink beer supplied by a Tory grocer."

Despite this unfortunate squabble the reporters from both papers were obviously impressed by what they had seen and were aware of its importance. "Last evening," wrote the *Whig* man, "the east and west wings of the College were illuminated [internally by oil lamps] and from the city had a very attractive aspect ... . The opening [of the Military College] though very informal, is considered an event of considerable importance."[103]

3

COLONEL HEWETT AND THE

OLD EIGHTEEN

1876-1880

In 1876 the future of the Canadian Military College was uncertain. Colonel Hewett's reluctance to lease or purchase a house privately to take the place of the official quarters prepared for him on Point Frederick shows his lack of confidence in the success of a college which one newspaperman had called an "experiment for a nation." Most Canadians were not interested in military affairs. The project had succeeded thus far only because a few enthusiasts in both political parties had helped Mackenzie to get the measure through the house despite general apathy. In the event of serious difficulty or breath of scandal, apathy would quickly turn to hostility; and political opposition could bring the project to an end. A suitable location had been found and a competent staff had been collected, but these things were only part of the answer. The college must now attract enough young Canadians qualified to take its courses. To continue to do so it must show that its graduates could go on to enjoy good careers. Above all, it must be of value to the country.

In the first two years of the college's history, Hewett had little room for optimism. The response to the announcement that entrance examinations would be held in February 1876 was disappointing. The college was expected to open with twenty-two cadets in the first year and to admit ninety-six more in the ensuing three years, these later entrants to be drawn equally from the twelve military districts in Canada.[1] However, when the syllabus for the examinations was issued, there were complaints that the standard was unreasonably high – higher, it was alleged, than for any English military college. Some of the complainants blamed the Canadian government for this; others said it was the fault of the British officers on the staff. At least ten potential candidates were reported to have withdrawn in order to become better prepared in another year. Some others enquired what government posts would be available for graduates. The number that eventually wrote the examination was small; and of these only eight qualified.[2] One of the successful candidates, T. L. Reed of Saint John, New Brunswick, reported to Kingston in April without waiting for his joining instructions. He precipitated a minor crisis because the college was not yet ready to receive recruits. Hewett sent Reed home and asked for an authority to pay for official telegrams to cope with future emergencies.[3] The government had in fact decided to await the results of a second entrance examination in order to fill up the first class. This time advertisements were placed in nine newspapers in addition to the official announcement in the *Canada Gazette*;[4] but fewer applicants appeared than before and, although the passing mark was reduced from 50 to 40 per cent, again only eight were successful.[5] A few stragglers applied late; two of these qualified at a further special examination and reported to the college a few days after it opened.[6] The first class was therefore only eighteen strong instead of the twenty-two that had been contemplated.

This poor response led to criticism of the project as a whole. An editorial in the *Toronto Daily Mail* in May said that "if the military college is good for anything, it is good for nothing as at present constituted." The writer declared that young men would not spend five (he meant four) years of their lives in the college when the only inducement was a militia commission; and he recommended a scheme of Dr. Charles Tupper's whereby military college graduates would get preference for government posts in surveying and engineering.[7] An offer like that would undoubtedly have increased interest, but it could hardly be made before the college had proved its quality. The high standards of entrance, about which some critics had complained, were obviously necessary to achieve this end.

One source of trouble was that, as the college had not yet become widely known, candidates had come forward from only a few areas. Of the first eighteen cadets, thirteen were from Ontario, three from New Brunswick where the militia staff officers showed great interest, and two from Bishop's College School in Lennoxville, Quebec. There were no entrants from Nova Scotia or French Canada. Distant British Columbia, new to Confederation, and Prince Edward Island, were also unrepresented.[8]

There were other disparities as well in age. Three of the recruits were not yet sixteen and seemed very young by contrast with L. H. ("Shy") Irving, German-educated and already one month past his twentieth birthday. When he was a senior, Irving was to sport mutton-chop whiskers and an eye glass and have a general appearance of solemnity and sedateness.[9] As a recruit he was much older in appearance and experience than most of his classmates. Even more serious was the very uneven academic preparation of the recruits. The new cadets had passed what amounted to no more than a qualifying examination and some had merely scored marginal marks. The lowest had obtained only 1930 as against an average of 5017 for the class as a whole and the 9534 received by the top man, A. G. G. Wurtele.[10] This great range was only partially explained by the fact that candidates could write extra subjects on a voluntary basis to augment their total. There were great differences in preparation and also in ability.

If the task of Hewett and his academic professors thus seemed likely to be hard, that of Ridout and the military staff was formidable. Few of the recruits had any idea at all what a military life meant. "None of us knew anything whatever of military discipline and we could not understand how it was possible for an officer to be so stern and uncompromising in all affairs of duty and at all other times so kindly, considerate, and genial," "A Graduate of the RMC, one of the old eighteen" wrote about Captain Ridout to the Toronto *Globe* in 1881.[11] One recruit cannot have been quite so green. Septimus Julius Augustus Denison came from an old Toronto military family.* The *British Whig* playfully said that his classical names suggested he must have an adequate academic background, but, as a Denison, he probably had some idea of the nature of military life.[12] Most of the first class, however, were like A. B. Perry of Napanee, one of the youngest, who had seen only one military parade – at the celebration of Confederation on 1 July 1867 when he was eight years old, who had known only one army officer – when he was six, and who had no soldier relatives except his mother's first cousin, an officer in the militia. All that young Perry knew about soldiering came from stories about the British army in *Blackwood's Magazine*. In later life he was unable to recall why he and his parents, after noticing an item in the *Globe*,[13] decided that he should apply for entry to the college. When he and the other recruits reported on 1 June 1876, most of them had no idea how big a change they were making in their lives.

There was no special ceremony for opening day and there were no distinguished visitors. Despite some later reports to the contrary, Mackenzie was not present. He did not visit his new college until 9 July, six weeks later. Most of the recruits had arrived in Kingston before the opening day. They reported individually to Point Frederick between 10 AM and 12 noon on 1 June as instructed. Some found Kingston cabbies who had not heard of the college and who had to be told where it was.[14] On their arrival at the gate they were met by a resplendent figure in the full-dress uniform of

---

*In 1837 his grandfather, George Taylor Denison, had organized a volunteer cavalry unit, Denison's Horse, later known as the Governor-General's Body Guard.

the British army, Regimental Sergeant-Major Mortimer,* an old horse gunner who had served in the Indian Mutiny. At least one nervous young man saluted him in the belief that he was the commandant.[15]

Ordering a college servant to take charge of the luggage, Mortimer led each awed recruit in turn to Captain Ridout who greeted him in a friendly fashion and then conducted him to the commandant. Both men attempted to put the new arrivals at their ease; they talked a little about army life and encouraged them by telling them that in time they would come to love it. Perry recalled in later years that Hewett said to him, "Your back is a little hollow. You will suit the cavalry."[16] Each cadet was given a number based on his standing in the obligatory subjects in the entrance examination.† He then took an oath of allegiance to the Queen before a police magistrate, subscribing to serve as a cadet of the Military College of Canada for the span of four years and to be duly subject to the Mutiny Act, the Articles of War, and the Regulations for the Militia. Unlike his fellows at Sandhurst and Woolwich, who were only subject to the discipline of their college, the Canadian cadet was thus placed under military law and discipline on the same terms as a regular soldier. Hewett had requested authority for the commandant to administer this oath, but the Minister of Militia sought advice from Edward Blake, the Minister of Justice. The presence of the police magistrate at the attestation must have been due to Blake's belief that his drastic contract by Canadian minors ought to have clear backing from the civil authorities.[17]

The recruit was then shown to his room on the second or third floor of the Stone Frigate. Each cadet in this first year had a room to himself. He found it plainly furnished with an iron military cot, a writing table, two chairs, a chest of drawers, and a bookshelf. On the wall was a shelf with hooks for the personal harness "equipment" of the contemporary valise type that the cadet was soon to receive. There may also have been an arms-stand for his Snider-Enfield rifle.[18] His government-issue furniture, simple though it was, was the envy of contemporary militia officers who had to provide their own when they took gunnery courses at neighbouring Tête-de-Pont barracks.[19]

The next day the recruits were lined up by Sergeant-Major Mortimer

*Mortimer was not listed on the pay sheet until 1 September 1876 but two accounts say that he was present when the college opened. He may have been attached from another unit for the first three months. He served at RMC until 1884.

†Henceforward college numbers were issued to all successful candidates in the entrance examinations. As some did not take up cadetships, certain numbers remained vacant. Among ex-cadets college numbers have great significance. It is the custom for ex-cadets to identify themselves to each other by prefixing their number to their name. This practice is not followed in this book except where the number has a particular significance.

for an address by the commandant. Hewett carefully explained the need for discipline, good conduct, and application to studies. Mortimer then commenced elementary drill. As the recruits had plenty of practice, for instance when forming up for their meals, they learned quickly. During June a tailor fitted them for uniforms and they were taught the essentials of military housekeeping – how to make beds in regulation fashion, how to fold uniforms neatly, and how to pipe-clay buckskin belts, equipment, and rifle slings so that they were snow white. When a bed was not properly made, or a uniform not properly folded, one swift stroke of the inspecting officer's cane tore it apart and a new start was necessary. They soon began to compete eagerly with each other, even in the distasteful job of pipe-claying. When off duty they enjoyed lying in the sun to acquire the mark of an old soldier, a white strip across their cheeks like that sported by the sergeant-major where the half-inch chin strap of his forage cap had prevented tanning. Perry says in his memoirs that Denison won that particular competition.[20]

Discipline was at first lightly administered, but the recruits nevertheless found themselves under an unaccustomed restraint. They were not allowed to leave the college grounds until they had received their uniform, which took at least a month. Their condition was brought home to them dramatically when the father of Cadet Fairbank, a wealthy oil magnate from Petrolia, Ontario, dropped in at the college to take his son on a trip to the Centennial Exposition in Philadelphia. The visitor was surprised to find that Charles could not go with him. Rumour said that Colonel Hewett told him that he could take his son to the exposition if, in fairness to all other cadets, he took the whole class! To compensate for the disappointment, the oilman gave his son a piano for his room, which all the cadets greatly enjoyed.[21] The Fairbank story shows how little some Canadians of that day knew about military life.

Hewett was a considerate commandant with a flair for handling men. To make a break in this stern new régime, to give the recruits a taste of another side of military life, and perhaps to get away from the summer heat of treeless Point Frederick, he applied to Ottawa for permission to take the cadets to camp.[22] Boats were hired and on the third of August the whole college moved to St. John's Island* near Gananoque where they did all the duties of a military camp – pitching tents, setting up day

*In the RMC library there is a delightful pencil sketch of a camp on St. Lawrence River island by Colonel Hewett, probably this camp in 1876. St. John's Island has not been identified. There is a St. James Island about five miles from Gananoque but this seems too far away. A later account suggested that the camp was on Howe Island.

and night guards, and working in the cookhouse.[23] In addition to instruction in army camp life, there was time for boating, swimming, and visiting Gananoque. The townsfolk there were kind and sociable, and "the girls seemed to like the new kind of boys, something which Kingston beauties had yet to learn."[24] Cadet Davis recorded that he was appointed camp cook. But when he put a whole bottle of curry powder in the Irish stew so that the duty officer found it "rather hot," Hewett sent for the regular caterer from college and put Davis on night sentry duty. Davis then got his revenge by calling "all's well" into the cook's tent every half-hour from 2 AM to 4 AM.[25] As a relief from the busy life on Point Frederick, this camp interlude loomed so large in the memories of those who enjoyed it that General Perry mistakenly declared in his memoirs that it began at the end of June and lasted through July.[26] It actually came to an end after a glorious eight days.

When the college returned to the city after this refreshing experience, the cadets were finally allowed to visit Kingston, though only when they could show a written invitation from a hostess. On the other hand, discipline was stepped up. Irving, the eldest recruit, had been made lance-corporal on the first day of the term. For the next two years he was regularly promoted until he became the battalion sergeant-major. He had power to award two days' confinement to barracks. The regulations which gave civil and military professors powers of arrest and officers the power to impose two days' extra drill began to be enforced. For more serious offences the commandant could impose up to fifty-six hours of solitary confinement; when the college got its new building, a cell with a barred window was provided for the incarceration of delinquent cadets. Cadets were "bound in honour" to observe all arrests or confinements, but espionage was specifically repudiated. These powers and principles were accompanied by the advice that "authority is more for the purpose of restraining and checking evil than for punishing it." This was laid down in RMC *Standing Orders*, said to have been drafted by Captain Ridout, which were approved by the General Officer Commanding the Militia on 5 December 1876 and printed locally in Kingston for distribution in the college.[27]

The eighteen new recruits soon settled down to their strange new life. Although they had at first believed Captain Ridout an ogre or a devil sent to torment them, they came to respect and admire this "dapper little man," who was only five feet five inches tall but was always immaculately turned out. He was an expert on drill and had "a most perfect word of command." He could modulate his voice so that when he was standing near the gymnasium he could be heard distinctly at Fort Frederick. Colonel A. H. Van

Straubenzee,* one of the second group of cadets who came in early 1877, asserted that Ridout can "truly be regarded as the founder of our college drill and discipline."[28]

When General Selby Smyth inspected the college in October, he declared himself perfectly satisfied with the cadets' progress. "Each lad replied to my questions that he was very happy, contented, and comfortable, and certainly this was corroborated by the general appearance and demeanor [*sic*] of the whole." Selby Smyth showed his approval of the military side of the instruction by saying that the captain of cadets had performed his duties in a thoroughly satisfactory fashion.[29] The cadets indeed took their duties seriously, although at times with a certain levity. When Hewett instituted a 24-hour guard at the college gate (at weekends so as not to interfere with studies), one cadet challenged Mrs. Ridout's maid and received the reply, "It's me." The sentry answered, "Pass 'me.' All's well." When she returned a little later and said "It's me coming back again," he replied, "Pass 'me-coming-back-again.' All's well."[30]

Living conditions in the college were spartan. The Stone Frigate was inadequately heated by a furnace in the basement which fed hot air to the corridors but not to the rooms. A porch had to be added at the front door to keep out bitter winter winds that swept in from Lake Ontario.[31] Breakfast often consisted only of porridge. Mud and snow made the parade ground a quagmire and footscrapers at the doors were an essential piece of equipment.[32] Cadet life was thus by no means as luxurious as hostile press accounts alleged. A cadet did not have the personal servant that reporters imagined. Although college servants cleaned his boots, the floors, and the corridors, the cadet polished his own brass accoutrements and made his own bed. The first cadets were certainly neither "carpet knights" nor "Mackenzie's pets," as some newsmen christened them.[33]

The next break in the routine came on 20 and 21 December when the whole college went on Christmas leave;[34] but the cadets were soon back to face term examinations at the end of January. Those who were promoted started new courses in a new class in February. In June, at the end of the

---

*Colonel Arthur Hope Van Straubenzee (1861–1946), entered RMC from Trinity College School in April 1877, the first recruit from Kingston, and graduated in December 1880 as a company sergeant-major, standing second in his class; the first RMC ex-cadet to be commissioned in the Royal Engineers (in place of A. B. Perry who had had to withdraw), he served at RMC as instructor in mechanical engineering, practical geometry, and engineering drawing, 1886–93; afterwards he was an instructor at Chatham and also served in Ceylon, Britain, and Bermuda; during World War I he was commanding royal engineer, Salisbury Plain. He wrote several articles on the history of ex-cadets. Two brothers (Major B. W. S. Van Straubenzee and Major-General Sir Casimir C. Van Straubenzee) and his son (Brigadier A. B. Van Straubenzee) were ex-cadets. Sir Casimir also served on the staff 1898–1903).

first academic year, in high spirits at the prospect of release from restraint, all the cadets marched off the end of the St. Lawrence pier into deep water in full uniform. The next day, when leave was due to begin, Hewett called a full-dress parade. The miscreants feared that their leave would be cancelled or postponed; but, after they had been lectured severely about their "disgrace," they were merely reprimanded.[35] There was no need for further punishment; Hewett now had them well in hand. Young men who twelve months ago had been raw recruits were rapidly becoming disciplined soldiers.

Meanwhile certain important decisions had been made about the length of terms and about the entrance examinations. The college had opened in June 1876, because it was not until that date that staff and recruits could be collected and buildings made ready. The first eighteen cadets had arrived to begin an open-ended course. Nothing had yet been decided about the length of terms or about vacations. They must have soon begun to enquire when they would get leave and when their first term would finish.

The government's original intention had been to operate the college on a yearly basis, with new intakes once a year, and with promotion at the end of each yearly session. But 1 June, when the first course started at the end of the school year, was unsuitable for the commencement of a college term because school-leavers would get no holiday before reporting and because school final results would not yet be known to make selection possible. Therefore, in August 1876, Hewett recommended that there should in future be an annual summer vacation of eighty-two days, from 20 June to 10 September. The Adjutant-General agreed to this in principle. He disliked the West Point system whereby a cadet worked a twelve-month year and had only one three-month furlough during his whole course. Colonel Powell told the minister that although such seclusion might produce officers more thoroughly trained in their profession, it would curtail their personal knowledge of the country and also their understanding of men. He therefore supported Hewett's proposal for a vacation in July and August in accordance with university practice. He said that the actual dates could be adjusted according to experience. The minister's approval, which was given verbally, put into effect a timetable that was pregnant with significance.[36] Canadian professional officers were not to be a class or caste set apart from the rest of the community.

The regulations were then amended to bring in another class of recruits on 3 February 1877 for a new first term that would last until 22 June. A third entry would be admitted in turn on 10 September for a first term to run through to 2 February 1878. This introduction of six-monthly entries would fill the college more quickly and would be within the letter of the Act since, after 1 January 1877, a new annual batch could be admitted.

A full Military College course would consist of eight terms in four years. The first two years would include some voluntary subjects as well as those that were obligatory. The subjects in the third and fourth years would be largely voluntary. A student who failed to gain promotion three times, or twice in the same class, would be released.[37] A cadet would graduate at the end of four years if he had passed in one of the top three classes.[38]

It was possibly believed that many and frequent examinations would attract more applicants, but when the fourth entrance examination was held on 5 November 1876 to make up the second entering class the response was even poorer than on previous occasions. Twenty-four cadets could have been accepted, and at least fifteen were needed to make up a new class. Only seven candidates presented themselves for the examination, and three of these failed to qualify. The new class would thus start with only four. Therefore on 26 December 1876, Hewett wrote to the GOC to urge that steps be taken to increase the entry by arranging to accept candidates up to the end of February.

Accordingly, on 5 January, the Deputy Minister of Militia asked the GOC how the standard could be lowered for a supplemental examination, but for that examination only. He said it should be held in March. In Hewett's opinion the disappointing response had been due to poor publicity rather than to overly high standards. So, in a letter to the Adjutant-General on 6 January, he opposed any blanket reduction of the number of subjects in the entrance examination and said the passing mark should not be dropped below 40 per cent. He feared that any cut made officially now might never be restored. Conceding that at present, as there was no real competition, some candidates might be admitted even though they had marks as low as 35 per cent, he recommended that another examination be held in February and that it should be widely advertised. Two days later, however, he agreed that French, German, and freehand drawing should be dropped from new examinations which had been announced for March; and he agreed also that the passing mark should be 35 per cent. He also suggested that candidates might be admitted even though slightly over or under the regulation age.[39]

The four recruits successful in November reported early in February. After the examination in March seven more were accepted and were ordered to report on 2 April. They came in at various times up to 3 May. Number 26, who came in on 10 April, was only fourteen years and nine months old. The new "eighth" class, including two drops, numbered thirteen; the seventh class had sixteen out of the former eighteen. With these numbers it was possible for the college to go ahead,[40] though the second entry had lost much of its first term.

Despite these difficulties in obtaining enough qualified recruits, the commandant soon reported favourably on the academic progress of his Canadian charges. Although after the first mid-term examination in September 1876, he had found only "moderate, but not marked improvement," in January 1877 he was satisfied with the results. He noted that since the time of the entrance examinations there had been striking changes in the order of merit. He said that this was partly due to the inclusion in the curriculum of subjects that had not been required for entry, and partly to the emphasis placed in the course on mathematics, modern languages, military exercises, drill, and discipline. But he believed that it also showed that natural ability and powers of application had become effective when inadequate school preparation was left behind. Mathematics was the core of the new course. The professor of mathematics and artillery, Major Kensington, noted the continuation of some weaknesses, but by the second term he reported that commendable progress had been made in accuracy and in attention to instruction.[41]

As new classes were admitted at the end of each six-month period, Hewett introduced new subjects into the curriculum. In the first term the cadets had studied mathematics (which accounted for more than half of the total marks), geometrical drawing coupled with fortification, French, drills, and swimming; and some cadets took German as an extra voluntary subject. In subsequent years Hewett added compulsory study of military topography and surveying, theory and construction of artillery, fortification as a separate subject, military administration and law, military history essays, strategy and tactics, reconnaissance, descriptive geometry, painting and freehand drawing, geology (with alternation in chemistry or electricity), gymnastics, and equitation.[42]

To teach these additional courses new staff members were needed. And the difficulties experienced earlier in attracting staff from England were now compounded by the slowness with which the Canadian government authorized measures to recruit professors. In 1878 Hewett became so incensed that he wrote that unless new staff were promptly recruited the full educational programme could not be carried out and the cadets would become frustrated and would want to leave.[43] A year later he said that he could not proceed on leave to England while certain questions of importance for the early stages of the college's development were left unsettled; and he named the appointment of professors as one of his chief outstanding problems.[44]

The first professor of surveying had been Captain Hawkins, RA, who had helped to prepare the courses, had taught "diverse subjects," and had worked with Kensington with untiring zeal.[45] Hawkins' departure in 1877 to take another appointment was greatly regretted. His place was taken by Major J. R. Oliver, RA,* who came as senior professor. Another new appointment was Captain George Walker, RE,† the first professor of military engineering, who was much admired by the cadets and contributed greatly to the college's development.[46]

Hewett's ability and knowledge were important in the fashioning of the course. One of his first tasks in Kingston was the preparation of a report about the city's defences for the Adjutant-General of the Militia.[47] While this report was apparently intended for defence purposes, surveys of the area were useful for the instruction of budding engineers. Orders were therefore placed with the Ordnance Survey Office in Southampton, England, for copies of survey maps of the fortifications of the Kingston district. Eighty-seven sheets of these, including no less than fifty-seven different maps and plans, were obtained through the crown agents for the colonies. The cadets then made their own surveys of the college grounds: Cadet Irving's chain sketch drawn in 1877, which is still extant, provides valuable information about the layout of buildings in those early days.[48] In 1877 the study of fortification was separated from geometrical drawing, and sixty plates of "the French modern system, the same as Vauban's," were obtained along with twenty plates of conventional signs as used at the Staff College.[49] Thus from the beginning there was a special emphasis on engineering at the Kingston college.

Progress in other respects was slower. The number of applications

---

*Major-General John Ryder Oliver (1834–1909), of Irish Protestant stock, was educated at Caius College and Trinity Hall, Cambridge, where he won a mathematics scholarship; in 1855 he stood fifth among one hundred and fifty candidates for the Royal Artillery; he served in India during the Mutiny and was twice mentioned in despatches; like Ridout, he served on the Bhutan expedition, 1864–5, where he commanded the artillery of the left column and received another medal and clasp; in 1865 he passed the Staff College and also a special examination in mathematics; he later served at St. Helena, as brigade major of artillery at Aldershot, and in the Intelligence Department; appointed professor of surveying and military topography at RMC in 1877, he was named senior professor and in December was made a lieutenant-colonel in the Canadian militia; he succeeded Hewett as commandant of RMC in 1886.

†Major G. R. Walker, RE, educated at Trinity College, Dublin, and RMA, Woolwich, and prizeman at both places, was commissioned in the Royal Engineers in December 1865 and served in India from 1868 to 1872; he was assistant instructor at the School of Military Engineering, Chatham, 1874–7, and then went to RMC to become professor of fortification, descriptive geometry, and geometrical drawing; he left RMC in 1883. Major-General Sir Dudley Ridout, who was a cadet in Walker's day, has spoken of his "extraordinary influence" on the cadets: "All the R.E. instructors were really 'giants' " *R.M.C. Review,* XIII (June, 1927), 27.

received was low, especially from French-speaking Canadians.[50] When first regulations had been framed in October 1875, the examinations set in French, Latin, and German required "translation from the language" without specifying what language the translation was to be made into. English was obviously the one expected.[51] As there were apparently then no French-speaking candidates, this interpretation was not disputed. On 4 April 1876, when the military college appropriation was debated in the House of Commons, Hector-Louis Langevin, MP for Trois-Rivières and a former acting minister of militia, pointed out that this was invidious.[52] The examination regulations were, therefore, amended in an order issued by Colonel Walker Powell on 19 October 1876. Translation from Latin and German could be into and from either English or French according to the candidate's preference; but in the French examination, translation was still to be "from the language" (i.e. into English) and English grammar was compulsory for all candidates.[53] French was an alternative against German in the examinations held in December; but as a result of the need to lower standards, French and German were made optional subjects in the supplemental examinations conducted in February 1877.

In 1877, and again in 1878, as the number of French-speaking applicants was still very small, Langevin asked for a return showing the proportion of French-speaking cadets in the Military College.[54] On 4 March 1878 he told the house that French-speaking Canadians were unable to pass the entrance examinations because of the nature of the English requirement. He said that this explained why there was still only one French-Canadian cadet (No. 21, A. E. Doucet) although a total of forty candidates had now qualified. He added that Doucet had been educated in English schools. Langevin pointed out that, in an emergency, junior officers with a knowledge of French would be needed to lead French-Canadian troops, but that few English-speaking Canadians would be able to give orders in French. He therefore argued that, provided an applicant for RMC could make himself understood in English, a knowledge of French should be acceptable as an alternative to a knowledge of English.[55]

Hewett had, in fact, already proposed certain changes to make the college "more evidently open" to both French-speaking and English-speaking candidates in order to meet this kind of criticism. Though loath to agree that the high standard of English required of all French-speaking cadets should be relaxed, he was willing to make concessions on this point until such time as French was again made compulsory for all candidates in the entrance examination. But he advised against introduction of texts and required reading in French in the entrance examination as an alternative to English.[56] The Minister of Militia, Alfred Jones,* told the Commons that concessions were being made to enable French Canadians to enter the college, but he refused to consider any changes in the college course itself. For the present he would also not concede the re-introduction of compulsory French in the entrance examination. He said that the present problem was to get cadets into the college, not to drive them out.[57]

Another serious problem was the need for more accommodation. The original proposal for construction in 1875 had called for an educational block on the north side of the parade ground to be ready for use by 1877. A second barrack block on the west side of the square to match the Stone Frigate should follow. All three buildings would be connected by covered walks.[58] A contract for the north building (the present Mackenzie Building) to be built of "the best Kingston limestone" was signed by William Irving of Kingston and Prime Minister Alexander Mackenzie on 18 April 1877. A kitchen in the basement and a dining room right above it on the first floor were to be completed by 1 December; and the remainder of the building by 12 June 1878. The cost would be $45,475.[59] Work commenced in the summer of 1877, cut stone being ferried to Point Frederick by convict labour.[60] This building was ready for occupation by the following year and the administrative offices, classrooms, and dining facilities were moved into it. It was spacious, with high ceilings and wide corridors; and it was modern with bell-pulls and food elevators. It also had built-in gas conduits.[61] Unfortunately, however, the nearest gas supply was in Kingston across the Cataraqui River. A supply of gas was not laid on for several years and the whole college continued to be lit by 300 oil lamps which were a great fire hazard and needed cleaning daily.[62]

When this building was completed, Hewett pressed for the commencement of work on the proposed west wing; but here he had no success.[63] As a result, when numbers increased some cadets had to be housed on the top floor of the educational building. Sickness frequently reached epidemic proportions, probably because the water supply was defective,[64] and the lack of separate hospital accommodation exacerbated the accommodation problem. By the summer of 1878, the need for new buildings had become critical. Hewett said that unless facilities were provided the development of the college would be halted.[65]

The year 1878 was a critical one in the history of the college in several other respects. The entry in February had again been small. In June, lest

---

*Alfred Gilpin Jones (1824–1906), a Nova Scotia merchant, opposed Confederation, 1864–7; he was elected to represent Halifax in the Canadian House of Commons, 1867; minister of Militia in the Mackenzie government, 1878; lieutenant-governor of Nova Scotia, 1900–6.

cadets already in residence might decide to withdraw before completing their course and so aggravate the situation, Hewett proposed the imposition of a $100 fine on those who left before the end of the four years for which they had been signed. A few days later, on 1 July, Mrs. Denison requested permission to withdraw her son so that he could go to England to obtain a commission in the British army. Hewett had not had Denison in mind when he made his submission about the penalty: he was a promising cadet, his motive was entirely laudable, there was no surety that he could get a British commission if he stayed at Kingston, and his departure would be regretted. Weighing all these things, the Commandant told the Adjutant-General that although the government had a clear right to compel a cadet to remain for four years it might not always be wise to enforce it. Nevertheless, he recommended that Denison should pay the $100 penalty because without the maintenance of a stringent condition of this kind the college could not be maintained. His recommendation was approved on 10 July.[66]

The introduction of this fine for withdrawal reduced the danger of a serious leakage of cadets. The case Hewett had in mind when he proposed the penalty may have been that of Cadet Bridges, one of the recruits who had entered late in the second term, on 10 April 1877. Like Denison, Bridges was a good student, but when his family migrated to Australia leaving him in Kingston he became unsettled and began to fail his courses. Hewett therefore asked his father to pay the $100 fine and withdraw the boy. This ex-cadet, the first RMC dropout, became Major-General Sir William Throsby Bridges, chief of the Australian General Staff, founder and commandant of the Royal Military College, Duntroon, commander of the Australian Imperial Force in 1914, and the first Kingston ex-cadet to command a division in the field. He was mortally wounded at Gallipoli.[67]

The withdrawal problem was, however, a minor part of the year's difficulties. Prime Minister Mackenzie was privately considering plans for further military development in Canada that would create openings for the graduates of his military college,[68] but in 1878 he was defeated at the polls and Macdonald's Conservatives were returned to power. Hewett immediately asked for an interview with members of the new government, and the GOC submitted to it the correspondence about the rise and progress of the college.[69] However, not merely were Mackenzie's plans halted, but the very existence of the college was threatened. The new Minister of Militia, Louis F. R. Masson,* MP for Terrebonne, a French Canadian, shocked the Governor-General, the Marquis of Lorne, by saying that he

*Louis François Rodrigue Masson (1833–1903), minister of Militia, 1878–80; senator, 1882–4 and 1890–1903; lieutenant-governor of Quebec, 1884–7.

was reluctant to ask the Commons to provide the $70,000 a year needed for the college. Masson told Lorne that he thought it might be better to send twenty or thirty young Canadians to Sandhurst.

Lorne informed Hewett that he was not sure whether it was the classical nature of French Canadian education, or the lack of a Roman Catholic chaplain, that was at the bottom of French-Canadian dislike for the college, but he warned him that this dislike might lead to political difficulties. However, after reflection, he cleverly replied to Masson that he agreed with him. He told the Minister that he thought that the trouble with Kingston was that it tended to develop a "special Canadian, as against an Imperial, sentiment." This can hardly have been what Masson had believed, and it may have caused him to reconsider the question. The appointment of an abbé to the examining board also helped to allay French-Canadian grievances.[70] The college thus managed to survive the change of government. But its development had been impeded. Mackenzie's concept of RMC as part of a steadily expanding Canadian military establishment was apparently not held by his successor. Sir John A. Macdonald was inclined to proceed cautiously and in accord with political pressures rather than on a theoretical timetable.

By the end of 1878, however, the tide began to turn. The number of applicants for entry had at last begun to rise. They came from most parts of the dominion. Furthermore, the college had already gained some recognition in Canada and in England. General Selby Smyth, in his annual report for 1878, stressed that although he believed that the college had been established before the country was ripe for it, and although he felt that it had impeded the development of "more simple elementary establishments for instructing Regimental officers and non-commissioned officers," it was now a *fait accompli* and should not be allowed to slide back. He said that in time it would come to be appreciated "by people of different nationalities throughout the Dominion." He declared that, financial considerations aside, everybody was favourable to the college.[71] Certainly Macdonald could hardly suppress a college in his own riding.

Meanwhile Hewett had been introducing important features at RMC to enable it to achieve its objectives. Very soon after its opening a "reading room" had been organized as a club. At the first meeting, the date of which is not entered in the minute book, Captain Ridout took the chair and a committee was organized. A number of periodicals were ordered. From 28 January 1878, Hewett was chairman at Reading Room committee meetings on which staff and cadets were about equally represented. Both staff and cadets paid subscriptions and membership was voluntary. Prime Minister Mackenzie joined and gave a handsome contribution to put it on its feet. Although in some ways like a students' union or a cadet mess, the Reading Room was not restricted to cadets. (There appears to have been no officers' mess at the college; Hewett and his staff were probably given privileges at the Tête-de-Pont barracks mess.) In 1883 the head class servant and the mess butler were given NCO privileges in the Reading Room.[72] The Reading Room thus played an important role in early college life by helping to develop a strong corporate spirit on a sound intellectual basis. Cadet reading rooms remain an important part of RMC life, though now much changed and for cadets only.

Another important early institution has survived to the present with less radical change except that membership is not now voluntary as it was at the outset. A Recreation Club Fund was set up in 1876. In 1880 the word "fund" was dropped and about the same time a college boat club was organized as a subsidiary.[73] In April the Deputy Minister authorized repairs to a boat at an estimated cost of $8.00.[74] Cricket began even before the Recreation Club was organized: the *British Whig* reported on 14 July 1876 that the military cadets were practising that game.[75] Sports meets were held by the Recreation Club and trophies awarded. One of the first of which there is record was a challenge trophy won outright by Cadet Spelman, in 1879. He had won it before, which would put the start of track and field athletics back to at least 1878 when $50 was expended on athletics, perhaps for the purchase of the challenge bugle. In 1882 Sergeant Joly* won this prized athletic trophy given to replace the "Old Eighteen" bugle won by Spelman.[76] By this time college teams had already played away from Kingston, for it is recorded in 1882 that the Recreation Club contributed $10 to help Sergeant Twining pay part of his medical expenses incurred as a result of breaking his collar bone in a football match in Montreal.[77] The college sports colours, white and scarlet, appear to date from 1877.[78] Sports thus flourished at RMC from the beginning and the college quickly established a reputation.

The college had also quickly been recognized as a valuable addition to the life at Kingston. Hewett and his British army colleagues were men of aesthetic and intellectual interests as well as of social standing. They therefore helped to compensate for the loss which the city had suffered earlier through the withdrawal of the British garrison. Professor Ferguson rejoiced in their arrival, especially when he was invited to join the officers' mess at the school of gunnery. He told his wife at various times, "The officers are going to be a great acquisition to our little Society – and then they are all learned men & have been educated at Woolich [*sic*]"; "[the

---

*Major-General Alain Chartier Joly de Lotbinière, C.B., C.S.I., C.I.E. (1862–1944), graduated RMC, 1883; chief engineer with the Anzac Corps in Gallipoli and France.

cadets] are all nice gentlemenly men & I anticipate great pleasure & satisfaction in teaching them"; "Colonel and Mrs. Hewitt [*sic*] & the other officers & wives are a wonderful improvement to our society. ... The Hewitt's live in grand style but yet are very simple & nice": "the Grand Champagne Lunch at the Barracks given by Col. Straubenzie [*sic*] & Mrs. Hewitt's At-Home ... passed off splendidly."[79] It is clear that the establishment of RMC greatly enriched Kingston's rather thin provincial social life.

The college's status was also enhanced by the interest which the governors-general of that day, as of later times, took in RMC. In February 1877 the Earl of Dufferin presented medals to be awarded for combined moral, intellectual, and physical qualities: bronze at the end of the second year, silver at the end of the third year, and gold at graduation. No. 1, Corporal A. Wurtele was the first cadet to win the bronze medal.[80] Dufferin, who had already reported to England on the good condition of the new college, visited it officially on 6 September 1876 and wrote a personal letter to Hewett praising the staff and cadets and commenting on "the good tone which has already been established amongst them."[81] Dufferin's successor, the Marquis of Lorne, was also interested in RMC, and for the same reason as Dufferin, namely that he thought that it provided a valuable means of strengthening Canada and Canada's connection with Britain. Lorne renewed the presentation of governor-general's medals. When he went to Kingston in 1879 to lay a foundation stone at Queen's College, his wife, Her Royal Highness the Princess Louise, held a drawing room in the City Hall and RMC cadets commanded by Major Ridout and headed by the "A" Battery band formed the guard of honour. The next day the Governor-General visited the college to inspect the cadets and saw a review and sham fight. The Princess presented awards to prize-winning cadets. The Governor-General gave portraits of himself and of the Princess to the Reading Room and also a set of Sir Walter Scott to the library.[82] This was the first of many royal visits to RMC.

Another sign that the college was beginning to make its mark developed from a question which appeared in a Kingston newspaper. If the government could pay for the transportation of the Queen's Own Rifles from Toronto to Montreal to take part in a parade on the Queen's birthday, why should the RMC cadets not also be sent?[83] The next year the cadet body took part in a great parade in Montreal, was incorporated with the division of troops which passed in review, and took part with the militia in the manoeuvres that followed. The events were witnessed by thousands of spectators, very many of whom had come from the United States for the occasion.[84]

Guns for artillery training had been requested as early as 15 January

1877;[85] and four six-pounders with carriages, limbers, and side arms had been issued from Ordnance stores eighteen months later.[86] By 1880 cadets from Kingston had begun to carry off prizes for shifting heavy ordnance in competition with all the garrison batteries affiliated with the Dominion Artillery Association. In 1881, Company Sergeant-Majors A. K. Kirkpatrick and A. E. Hodgins* were selected to represent the association in a competition at Shoeburyness, England, and received silver cups from the British Artillery Association as a memento of this first visit of Canadian gentlemen cadets to Europe.[87]

Throughout the period 1876 to 1880 Hewett and Ridout worked amicably together and were eminently successful in building up the cadets' sense of their own dignity and in establishing the military prestige of the college. By militia order the cadet body was authorized to take the place of honour at the right of the line.[88] Ex-cadet F. Davis says that on the way back from church parades in St. George's Cathedral the cadets marched ahead of the gunners of the school in Tête-de-Pont barracks, an older unit. He relates that, not to be outdone, the gunners took an alternative route and tried to get to the Tête-de-Pont gate first in order to receive a salute from the college battalion as it passed. Naturally the cadets also doubled their step. The result was that both groups covered the distance at the double with the cadets winning by a short head.[89] Though this rivalry introduced an element of farce, it was a result of the official recognition of a leading status in Canada's armed forces which the college cherished until the closure in 1942.

Colonel Hewett, who was an artist of ability, personally designed a college crest, "a mailed arm bearing a maple leaf," symbolic of the relation of the cadets to their country. This appeared on the first graduation certificate and is still in use. He also selected as the college motto, the words "Truth, Duty, Valour," which he also used to urge upon his own son as a standard by which to live.[90] It was probably also Hewett who adopted from the Royal Military Academy the designation "gentlemen-cadets" which had been authorized for use at Woolwich by a royal warrant of 30 July 1744.[91] It has been said that it was first used in Kingston on a commandant's order dated 15 October 1877. It appeared in the roll of cadets in an entry dated January 1878.[92] Although not used in a second (and undated) edition of the 1876 *Standing Orders*, the phrase "gentlemen cadets" was used in place of "cadets" in all the new clauses in a

---

*Lieutenant-Colonel Arthur Edward Hodgins (1861–1939), graduated RMC, 1882; he was a civilian railway engineer and built military railways in the Transvaal and Orange River Free State during the Boer War; he was assistant director of light military railways in France during World War I.

revised version put out in 1883. The first college certificate awarded to
A. G. G. Wurtele in 1880 describes him as "gentleman cadet." The
designation thus gained official approval indirectly by customary usage.
As Hewett used "gentleman cadet" in his annual report for the first time
in 1878 and as he associated it with the addition of the word "Royal" to
the college name,[93] it was probably a demonstration of his conviction that
by that time the college he had organized had come to compare with those
he had known in England.

In his report for 1878, Selby Smyth had expressed the hope that, in the
near future, British army commissions would be offered to graduates of
the college and so create "another link in the chain that binds us all together." This he regarded as a preliminary step toward the establishment
of permanent force units in Canada, which might be interchangeable with
British battalions.[94] The first part of this aspiration had been under consideration for some time. To lead up to it Hewett had proposed that the
college should be renamed the Royal Military College of Canada, a title
like the name used by the War Office in his letters of appointment.[95] The
Canadian Privy Council approved this usage on 8 April 1878 and three
weeks later the GOC wrote to the War Office to ask that the title be used in
the next *Army List*, "it being greatly desired by the officers and cadets of
the College." The War Office promptly asked the Secretary of State for
the Colonies whether the governor-general-in-council had the power to
confer the title "Royal" without the Queen's sanction.[96]

Before this question was answered the Colonial Office received from
Canada a formal request that a commission in each branch of the "imperial military service" should be placed at the disposal of the Canadian
government to be offered annually as a reward to successful graduates of
the Royal Military College of Canada. At the same time Captain Montagu
Ommanney, now Crown agent for the colonies, received a private letter
from Hewett drawing attention to the new title of the college and saying
that it was he who had proposed the application for regular army commissions. Hewett asserted that the cadets of the first and second classes
at Kingston would be fully equal to Woolwich cadets and were fitted to
maintain the honour and social position of an officer. Asking for help in
persuading the War Office to offer British commissions, he declared that
rejection of the proposal "would be seriously felt and [would] be a blow
to the military and imperial feeling which is springing up" in Canada.
Shortly afterwards Hewett wrote to solicit the aid of the Governor-General
in an approach to the Duke of Cambridge. He said that the provision of
British commissions for Kingston cadets would diminish Canadian jealousy of imperial officers and would help to retain the imperial connection

through the continued acceptance of an "imperial" officer as commandant or, at least, of "imperial army" professors.*

The officials at the Colonial Office were well disposed to the plan because they felt that Canadians had shown conspicuous loyalty by applying in large numbers for commissions when war with Russia had seemed imminent in recent months, but they believed that many in the War Office would oppose it. Nevertheless, J. H[olland] minuted the request, "Yes, but it might be well to wait 'till we hear about the title 'Royal' which is used in these papers."[97] The undersecretary, Sir Robert Meade therefore informed the War Office that the Governor-General appeared "to have inadvertently omitted to obtain the Queen's sanction" in the first instance for the granting of the title "Royal," and stated that the Colonial Secretary was prepared to make the necessary submission to the Queen. Royal approval was granted in August 1878.[98]

On 28 June the Colonial Secretary forwarded to the War Office the application for commissions for graduates of "the Military College at Kingston."[99] The matter was then referred by the Commander-in-Chief to the governor of the Royal Military Academy, to the director general of military education, to the deputy adjutant generals of the Royal Artillery and of the Royal Engineers, and to certain other officers. These gentlemen were inclined to approve but requested full information about the entrance examination and courses. It was thought that, because of limited opportunity in Canada for certain types of experience, for instance to see the manufacture of ordnance, Canadian cadets should be required to take further training in England before being commissioned; but eventually it was decided that they should be commissioned on graduation and that, as officers, they should take any additional training they needed.[100] When the Canadian government requested more details of this training, it learned that Kingston graduates would in fact take the same artillery courses at Shoeburyness and the same engineering courses at Chatham as RMA graduates.[101]

The Duke of Cambridge then suggested that if no Canadian cadet wanted a cavalry commission (which would be likely because of the expense involved) two infantry commissions would be offered.[102] The Canadian government thereupon asked that if no applicant was qualified for the artillery and engineers, all four commissions might be given in the

---

*The British officers at RMC, and the British army commissions granted to RMC cadets, were usually called "imperial" in accordance with contemporary usage though strictly they should have been called "British." See Richard A. Preston, *Canada and "Imperial Defense"* (Durham and Toronto, 1967), p. 433 for a discussion of the use of the word "imperial."

infantry. This was conceded by the Duke.[103] The four commissions were available by the time the first class graduated in 1880.

Although Hewett had pressed for British army commissions, he was careful to insist that the commandant should have the right to refuse to recommend an applicant he thought unsuitable.[104] There is some evidence that he had doubts about the leadership qualities of some of the Old Eighteen. In 1879 he had found it necessary to reduce some cadet NCOs in rank, not for personal misconduct, but because they had not been effective. Reduction in rank proved to be no incentive to improvement because military feeling was not yet sufficiently strong in the college. Hewett therefore introduced a rule that in order to graduate a cadet must have become an NCO. He stated, "It is now understood that a cadet who, at the termination of his full four years, does not possess sufficient stability and firmness of character to control his own actions, or those of others ... is not fit for and cannot be permitted to attain the rank of a commissioned officer."[105] However, in 1880 he reported favourably on all the NCOs. Those cadets who had made the grade academically thus graduated in 1880. His plan therefore seems to have worked.[106] Nevertheless, when Battalion Sergeant-Major Irving failed out of the college in February 1880, no successor was appointed immediately. H. W. Keefer,* who eventually succeeded, was not made BSM until shortly before the passing-out ceremonies in June.[107] Hewett may have wished to avoid imposing onerous duties on a new man immediately before the final examinations. But it may be that he delayed because he was uncertain about the qualities of leadership of potential successors.

Four British commissions would not, however, go very far among the college's graduates. Hewett therefore drew up a proposal for a Canadian permanent force and submitted it to the Minister of Militia. Mackenzie had been thinking on these lines, but the Conservatives pigeonholed the proposal.[108] The need for jobs for RMC graduates was not a sufficient reason to reverse their opposition to a standing force. Instead the government issued a militia general order on 7 February 1880 which said that RMC graduates who did not receive British commissions would be commissioned in the militia and would remain on the militia list and be eligible for promotion provided they attended annual training with a militia unit as a supernumerary. Two years' absence would cause their removal from the list. It added: "So soon as there are a sufficient number of eligible graduates, appointments to the permanent Militia Corps will be made solely from this list; and after a sufficient length of service and rank has

---

*H. W. Keefer (1859–1887), a civil engineer, was killed by falling from the Vaudreuil Bridge. This family has sent cadets to RMC down to the present generation.

been obtained permanent Militia Offices will be filled therefrom."[109] This was as far as Macdonald would go to offer RMC graduates opportunities for appointment in government service. Efforts to secure an appointment in the Mounted Police for F. J. Dixon in 1879 and for W. M. Davis in 1880 had come to nought.[110] And the government was unwilling to consider the grant of preference for appointments in the civil service. RMC graduates must therefore be prepared adequately to compete with the graduates of the Canadian universities for these, and for other civilian positions.

Accordingly, for their final year 1879–80, the cadets of the first class who had survived thus far without repeating a term's work were offered courses in civil engineering. These courses were "voluntary" in so far as they were not necessary for graduation. The final year included civil surveying, the nature, production, and use of materials for construction, hydraulic engineering, the mechanics of materials, the design and execution of structures, architecture, and estimating. To undertake the extra teaching three civilian professors were appointed: R. Carr-Harris* for civil engineering, Forshaw Day† for drawing, and A. D. Duval‡ for French. Hewett had been instructed to select Canadian residents for these appointments. This eliminated some of the best qualified men from his short lists. Carr-Harris was in fact his fourth choice; and he was compelled to appoint Duval, who was actually a doctor of medicine rather than of languages, even though he thought him "not a person of very high standard of ability or experience."[111] Hitherto French had been taught by Ferguson, a learned jack-of-all-trades.

Duval's appointment was probably an effort to make RMC more acceptable to French Canadians. For, despite the signs that the college was becoming secure in other ways, the French Canadian problem continued. P. B. Casgrain, the historian, who was a member of parliament and whose son wanted to enter the college in 1879, told the Minister of Militia that the examination questions were harder for French candidates because they demanded a subtle knowledge of the English idiom and of English etymology.[112] Young Casgrain succeeded in passing and became No. 92,

*Robert Carr-Harris (1843-1923) railway construction engineer 1864-79; professor of civil engineering, RMC 1879-97; set up engineering courses at Queen's 1894; professor of general engineering, School of Mines, Kingston, 1898-1901. Eight sons and two nephews were RMC cadets.

†Forshaw Day, RCA (1832–1903), professor of drawing and painting at RMC, 1879–97. A number of his paintings are now in the college.

‡Arthur Duponth Duval, MD, professor of French, 1879–97. In 1883 Hewett recommended unsuccessfully that Duval be appointed the medical officer of the newly created "C" Battery in Victoria (Public Archives of Canada, MG 27, I, D 3, vol. 67, no. 3547, 16 Aug. 1883).

the third French-Canadian cadet. However, even though a French-Canadian professor had been appointed and there was a French Canadian on
the examining board, the number of French-Canadian applicants did not
increase significantly. In the first twenty-three years of operation there
were only twenty French Canadians among five hundred cadets; and in
the next fourteen years there were nineteen out of 500.[113] Nor does the
teaching of French appear to have been improved by the introduction of
a French-Canadian professor. Perry, one of the Old Eighteen, remembered
that Duval's teaching was confined to grammar and reading and that oral
French was entirely neglected.[114]

More immediately urgent was the problem of accommodation. On 26
August 1879, Hewett sent a long memorandum to the Adjutant-General
listing "works required to complete R.M.C. as designed ... to place it on
an equal footing with kindred institutions of Europe and America." He
divided the list into three orders of priority. All were needed by next year
but, if all could not be completed in that time, the first group, listed under
"A," should be completed in 1880. Otherwise, said Hewett, the college
"cannot possibly give the results which, in every other respect, it is
capable of doing." Group "B" should be completed in 1881 and "C" in
1882. List "A" contained the west barrack block; the commandant's
quarters; meat and ice stores and an enclosed backyard for the mess; a
kitchen, latrine, and fence for the outer gatehouse; one staff-sergeant's
quarters; an engine house for the water works; drill sheds for infantry and
artillery training and to include an engineering and modelling room, a
riding school, and a general store; and a chain rail around the north building. Class "B" listed a cadet hospital, two staff-sergeants' quarters, stables
for officers' quarters in the inner enclosure, a cadets' workshop, a racquets
court, the continuation of the water supply to the outer enclosure, and
ten servants' cottages because the old Navy cottages were too dilapidated
for permanent occupation. List "C" included the conversion of the north
end of the Stone Frigate into officers' quarters, a gymnasium to replace
the old blacksmith's shop, a library, museum, and chemical laboratory,
extensions to classrooms and the mess room in the north building, and
the introduction of gas in place of oil for lighting. These were formidable
demands.[115]

The report of the Board of Visitors for 1879 supported Hewett in these
requests. It noted that several cadet rooms that were too small for the
purpose housed two cadets and that five rooms in the north building that
were needed for other purposes were occupied as dormitories by fifteen
cadets. It argued that to keep up with technical development there was
need for scientific apparatus, models, laboratories, and a museum. It

noted the lack of horses for teaching equitation (an essential accomplishment of every staff officer of that day – the Old Eighteen hired horses privately for their riding lessons), and suggested that it could be met by adding horses to "A" Battery (to which the Commandant of that school objected), by the erection of a riding school, and by the appointment of a riding master. In his reports from 1879 onwards, Hewett repeated the request for increased barrack accommodation and for facilities and equipment for technical training and equitation. In 1880 he also stated that the practical course was incomplete because it did not include torpedo or submarine mining which was being adopted everywhere for the defence of ports.[116] On 3 February 1880 the Minister of Militia, Sir Alexander Campbell,* ordered that a copy of the requirements should be sent to the Minister of Public Works for consultation purposes with the proviso that he was not yet recommending any part of the programme.[117] It was several years before the government approved any of these requirements and it was twenty years before the major projects were undertaken. With Macdonald as prime minister the college's progress had noticeably slowed.

To make up for the lack of training in the new torpedo and underwater mining techniques, Hewett proposed that the graduating class should visit Halifax to witness demonstrations by the Royal Navy and the Royal Engineers. Hewett in his submission to the Canadian Department of Militia suggested that the visit could be coupled with visits to the fortifications at Halifax and the various engineering works and structures in Montreal, Matapedia, Quebec, and Acadia Mines (Londonderry), Nova Scotia. He also proposed to ask the parents of the cadets to pay part of the cost, to ask for reduced fares and free passage on the government's Intercolonial Railway, and to reduce the number from fifteen to the ten who had most distinguished themselves if fifteen was considered too many. When the Marquis of Lorne asked the home government to instruct the authorities in Halifax to stage the demonstrations he stressed the value of torpedoes for defence of the lakes, rivers, and seacoasts of Canada.[118]

Ten cadets went on the tour of instruction from 3 July to 20 July under the command at first of Major Walker, professor of military engineering, and, for the later part, of Colonel Hewett himself. The trip included a full inspection of the fleet and of the military installations. The party worked ten hours a day except on Sundays and each cadet made reports and sketches of his observations. Hewett was satisfied that the practical lessons learned were of great value to the cadets themselves and to Canada.[119] At the same time it was a gala outing, greatly appreciated as a finale to the

---

*Senator Sir Alexander Campbell (1822–1892), a law partner of John A. Macdonald and a close political associate who held many government offices.

course and as a pleasant change after the grind of examinations. One of the party, A. G. G. Wurtele, published an account to supplement the official reports and dedicated it "To the Commandant, Staff and Cadets to No. ∞ minus one of the Royal Military College of Canada." Wurtele's book tells of the inevitable larking that went on but is also a good account of and a fitting tribute to the professional value of the work that was done. He and his fellows were deeply appreciative of the opportunity that had been given them.[120]

Despite its undoubted success, the tour was in some ways an anticlimax, or at least an epilogue. The college careers of the Old Eighteen had ended on 2 July when, as the *British Whig* reported, the "West Point of Canada" staged "a brilliant closing." Prizes were distributed including the sword of honour to BSM Keefer. (A proposal to add a revolver to this prize had been turned down by the government.[121]) There were exercises in the gymnasium including sword and bayonet fighting, boxing, horse-vaulting, and displays on the parallel bars and rings. The cadet body marched past on the square in quick and double time with a "precision only equalled by 'B' Battery."* Deployed as skirmishers it demonstrated light infantry drill and then advanced in review order. Parading as artillery the cadets engaged in rapid charges and firing, and then dismounted the guns and dismembered and reassembled the carriages. Earth works which they had dug were on display; and when a mine was exploded on the shores of Navy Bay "the waters ... were not a little disturbed and then became black with debris." (This display and subsequent ones in later years did irreparable damage to the old hulks still lying in the bay from the War of 1812.) In the evening the commandant and staff of the college entertained the ladies and gentlemen of the city and garrison at a dance in the educational block where "a fine supper was spread." The press report of this forerunner of the June balls of the future declared that "every one was delighted."[122]

The Old Eighteen quickly became a living legend and its members were, quite naturally, regarded as the heroic founders of a great tradition. In his account of the instructional tour, Wurtele seems to suggest that while still in the college they were well aware of their own significance in the history of a great institution. He showed that as there were intakes twice a year, his class had seen seven new generations of cadets follow in their footsteps by July 1880. Bound together by a sense of being pioneers, they had rapidly developed a strong class spirit. Long before they graduated the first class was styled the Old Eighteen. Wurtele said that, as the

---

*"B" Battery had replaced "A" Battery in Kingston in June 1880.

college grew, discipline became more formal, but "the officers seemed disinclined to render our lives more burdensome and still granted to us, the seniors, the old privileges we had enjoyed in more primitive days when we alone formed their subjects." When the members of the top class were on their own they often enjoyed reminiscing about the first days of the college. Occasionally they would "growl" about the "cheek" of the last-joined recruits, but they never took the trouble to check it. "As the guilty ones had wisdom not [to] offend us personally, and no other term disapproved of what we passed over, they continued to live on unmolested."[123] Apparently systematic "recruiting," that is to say the disciplining of recruits by seniors, was not known in the era of the Old Eighteen, or at least it was not promoted by the senior class and is not legitimately a part of their tradition.

The Old Eighteen had made a contribution greater than they can possibly have realized. Canada was a land absorbed by the economic and political problems of a nation that was expanding peacefully from sea to sea; it had no aggressive intentions and it seemed remote from external danger. Except in brief periods of crisis few Canadians worried about the possibility of invasion or attack either from Europe or from the United States. Military preparations seemed more appropriate in countries not similarly blessed. If Canada were involved in a war, even with the United States, it would almost certainly be due to British policies in which Canada had had no say. Therefore if any Canadians thought that the future might make it necessary to defend their country or its interests by resort to arms, they took it for granted that Britain could and would stand by them and also that, if more were needed, improvisation would quickly bring an adequate Canadian military force into the field. No one envisaged the military needs of Canada's involvement in two world wars in the twentieth century. As a result of these things few Canadians took up part-time soldiering and most of these were more interested in the social side of militia activities than in professional training. Those who were more serious found themselves thwarted not only by lack of money and of arms but also by want of a satisfactory professional expertise. This lack the RMC graduates were being equipped to remedy.

Under the tactful and skilful direction of Colonel Hewett and his staff the Old Eighteen created a college with a professional military tradition, yet one that was also equipped to turn out graduates who could compete on favourable terms with the products of civilian universities, especially in engineering. The clue to their success was an unusual amalgam of academic subjects and military training. For four years a small number of young Canadians lived a regimented life of a kind unknown elsewhere in their country except, for a different purpose, in its monasteries. The principles upon which their training was built were derived mainly from the British army; but on the academic side their education, beginning from a less thorough school preparation, went much further than that given in any British cadet college. Lack of military employment for RMC graduates had been a guarantee against a decline in academic standards or in specialization in fields in which RMC graduates must compete for a living with men from Canadian universities. The maintenance of a sound military training depended on the continuance of British assistance, but it also grew out of the strength of the tradition that was established. As a result of the excellence of their training and education, the Old Eighteen, although only average young men who were not all gifted by nature with marked qualities of leadership, became the model of that valuable tradition.

The value of a college must be measured by the quality of its graduates and by the extent to which they fulfil its objectives. RMC had been established primarily to produce officers to strengthen Canada. Writing with reference to the overseas imperial naval and military service of the Old Eighteen, a later critic stated: "Some of the first batch of graduates from this college did not turn out at all creditably, for reasons of a personal and harmful nature and left the service. Fortunately this condition of things did not continue ... ."[124] This severe indictment of that first class of cadets which came to be revered for having established the great traditions of the college must be examined in the light of the facts.

Of the original eighteen, Denison left the college after two years. In 1880 he joined the South Staffordshire Regiment of the British army. Irving and Perley flunked out in February 1880; and Reed did not graduate in June.[125] Of the fourteen who graduated, six declined to accept commissions in the British army which therefore passed to others of lesser ability lower on the list. Those who accepted commissions were Company-Sergeant A. B. Perry, Royal Engineers (the top listed cadet who won the governor-general's medal), Sergeant C. Fairbank, Royal Artillery, Company Sergeant-Major H. Wise, and Sergeant H. Freer, Infantry. However, Perry broke his leg in a carriage accident on the way home to Napanee and after some hesitation decided to withdraw; and Fairbank resigned his commission in 1881. Freer served with distinction in Egypt in 1882, but Wise and Freer were both on half-pay in Canada soon afterwards: Wise was promoted captain in the Derbyshire Regiment in 1890 and became ADC to Lord Lansdowne, the viceroy of India, but resigned his commission because of ill health in 1897. Denison meanwhile rose to be a major in the South Staffordshires but in 1888 joined the Royal

Canadian Regiment.[126] The imperial service careers of those of the Old Eighteen who joined the British army were thus creditable but not spectacular.

Wise and Freer served as ADCs to General Middleton during the North-West Rebellion when their professional expertise must have been useful; and Denison served as ADC to the Earl of Aberdeen as governor-general, to Lord Roberts in South Africa, and to the Duke of Cornwall (later King George V) on a visit to Canada. He became an honorary brigadier-general in the Militia in 1916 and major-general in 1932. Dixon served in South Africa as historical recorder of the Royal Canadian Regiment and as a staff captain of railways and he remained in that country as a civil magistrate after the war. Rivers joined the Canadian Permanent Force in 1883 when the infantry schools were set up and, like Fairbank, served Canada both in South Africa and in the 1914-18 war. Perry commanded the Royal North-West (Canadian) Mounted Police as superintendent and on retirement in 1922, was appointed a major-general in the Canadian Militia.* W. M. Davis, city engineer of Berlin (Kitchener) and of Prince Rupert, B. C., and a lieutenant-colonel in the Militia, took the 54th Bn. of the CEF to Britain. The Old Eighteen thus gave greater military service directly to Canada than to Britain.

Thirteen of the Old Eighteen had careers that were primarily civilian; but five of these are among those listed above who served at one time or another in the armed forces of Canada or the empire. Three of the eight civilians worked most of their life in the United States. It is worthy of note that, in addition to a few senior service officers, this small class produced two presidents of engineering firms (Spelman and Fairbank), a superintendent of the Nevada School of Industry (F. Davis), a CPR divisional engineer and assistant chief engineer for the Transcontinental Railway Commission (MacPherson), and the director of the Dominion Testing Laboratory (Perley), as well as a senior civil servant in each of Ontario and New Brunswick, a district magistrate in South Africa, and two RMC professors. It seems, therefore, reasonable to say that the Old Eighteen proved the value of the academic education, and especially that of the engineering course set up in Kingston in 1876. They therefore fulfilled the secondary purpose for which the college was founded.

The credit for the successful launching of RMC in these formative years must go to Colonel Hewett. He was a man with a sense of dignity and authority, yet filled with human understanding. Proud of his aristocratic

---

*Major-General A. B. Perry, C.M.G., ADC (1860–1956), the most distinguished of the Old Eighteen (No. 13), lived the longest. He took the salute of the "new hundred" recruits at the re-opening of RMC in September 1948.

connections, he nevertheless made himself fully at home in Kingston's colonial society. His professional experience and scientific qualifications enabled him to build an engineering college on sound lines. His humanity gave it qualities that would provide the basis for a great tradition. His artistic interests ensured that cultural pursuits were not neglected. But most important of all, he had the strength of will, and the ability to steer RMC through difficult political waters and to overcome prevailing apathy about defence matters. He was a pragmatist, and was able to see not only what was needed but also what could be done in Canada. The successful graft of a first-class academic and technical college on a military foundation was his work.

4

THE

RIDOUT ROW

AND AFTER, 1880-1886

With the graduation of the Old Eighteen, the initial phase of RMC's growth had come to an end. It was now time to put the college on a normal operating basis at or near its full establishment. To bring this about the Board of Visitors in 1879 had recommended that the practice of accepting entries every six months should cease and that RMC classes should be put on a yearly basis.[1] Accordingly, as there was no longer a pressing need for recruits to fill up the college, the February entry was dropped. The class that had entered in the spring of 1877 graduated in 1881 after eight terms; but later classes that had entered in the second term were accelerated to graduate in only seven terms along with their comrades who had joined in the September before them. So, after June 1881, there were only four classes in the college instead of eight; and there was only one graduating class each year instead of two.[2] This was the arrangement proposed originally; and it was to persist henceforward except when the RMC course was reduced in length.

The 1879 board had also recommended that the upper age limit for entry to the college should be reduced by two years. As recruits were now thought plentiful a smaller reduction was accepted. The upper age limit was to be nineteen years and nine months at the time of entry.[3] As a consequence the cadet body began to be more homogeneous. The Board had further recommended that the admission quotas be by province rather than by military district,[4] but this third revision was not then adopted.

The RMC instructional staff was now considered complete at thirteen. It included seven British officers from the Royal Artillery and the Royal Engineers, five civilian professors who were Canadian, and the Captain of Cadets, Ridout, a Canadian but a member of the British army.[5] But Hewett was coming to the end of his assigned tour of duty in Canada, and other officers would soon be in a similar position. Therefore in May 1880 the Governor-General forwarded to the War Office a request that the commandant's services be made available for five years more. When Hewett applied for this extension, he claimed that before he came to RMC he had been given a personal undertaking by the adjutant-general of the Royal Engineers that his British regimental pay would be paid to him while he was at the college. He said that when the temporary arrangement granting him his regimental pay for the first two years ran out in 1877, he could not have afforded to take his family back to England had he wished to do so. He went on to say that, as it happened, he had felt unable at that time to leave the college at a crucial stage in its development. However, in that same year new regulations had been introduced in the army to prevent officers from receiving either regimental or reserve pay while serving in the colonies. Despite this discouraging development, the Governor-General had made strong representations on Hewett's behalf for special consideration for British pay on the grounds that he had had a difficult and important task to do, had done it well, and had spent his own money lavishly on hospitality to advertise the college. It was of no avail. A five-year extension was authorized but without either regimental or retired pay. As a consolation, the Colonial Office suggested that Hewett's name be put forward at the next opportunity for the colonial decoration, third class, that is the Cross of St. Michael and St. George.[6]

The British authorities were equally unwilling to make concessions for other members of the RMC staff. Captain Ridout was informed in 1880 that if the time came when he must retire from the army because he had not reached his "majority" by the age fixed by the regulations, he would be unable to draw his pension as long as he continued in Canadian employ.[7] Two years later Hewett failed to persuade the War Office to promise to extend the Canadian tours of duty of Kensington, Walker, and Major Oliver to the fourteen years that was sometimes permitted in the case of military professors at the British military academies.[8] The War Office's position could be defended on the grounds that it was preferable for an officer to return to his regiment if he wished to progress in his profession and also because it could be deemed advantageous to the college to have instructors whose knowledge of the army was up to date. Nevertheless, it seems that the War Office adhered slavishly to its regulations with scant regard for any special need to keep at RMC those British officers who had proved effective. It was apparently insufficiently impressed by arguments about the "imperial" value of the new Canadian college and about the need to foster it carefully.

The budget for RMC levelled out from 1880 onwards at around $58,000

ᴠᴏʟ. XIII.—No. 25.   MONTREAL, SATURDAY, JUNE 17, 1876.   { SINGLE COPIES, TEN CENTS. / $4 PER YEAR IN ADVANCE.

Lᴛ. Cᴏʟ. Eᴅᴡᴀʀᴅ Oꜱʙᴏʀɴᴇ Hᴇᴡɪᴛᴛ, R. E. Cᴏᴍᴍᴀɴᴅᴀɴᴛ.
From a Photograph by J. J. Abbott, Kingston.

Drill Square

C   B

Guns Parked.
CRICKET GROUND

FORT . FREDERICK

A. Future Educational and Mess Block.
B. Existing Block, now the whole College, but at the completion
of the new addition it will be Cadet Barrack only.
C. Cadet Barrack.
D. Covered passages for drill, &c., in wet weather.

Uɴɪғᴏʀᴍ ᴏғ Cᴀᴅᴇᴛꜱ.   Pʟᴀɴ ᴏғ Mɪʟɪᴛᴀʀʏ Cᴏʟʟᴇɢᴇ, ꜱʜᴇᴡɪɴɢ ɪɴᴛᴇɴᴅᴇᴅ ɪᴍᴘʀᴏᴠᴇᴍᴇɴᴛꜱ.

KINGSTON, ONT: OPENING OF THE CANADIAN MILITARY COLLEGE.

1 The opening of ʀᴍᴄ, from the *Illustrated News*, Montreal, 17 June 1876

1 Col. E. O. Hewett, C.M.G., first commandant 1875–86

2 Maj.-Gen. J. R. Oliver
commandant 1886–8

3 Col. R. N. R. Reade
commandant 1901–5

4 Col. G. T. Kitson
commandant 1896–1900

5 No 45, Col. E. T. Taylor
commandant 1905–9

6 Col. J. H. V. Crowe
commandant 1909–13

7 Maj.-Gen. D. R. Cameron
C.M.G., commandant 1888–96

2

3

4

5

7

6

1 No 624, Brig. W. H. P. Elkins
D.S.O., commandant 1930–5

2 Brig.-Gen. C. N. Perreau
C.M.G., commandant 1915–19

3 No 621, Brig. C. F. Constantine, D.S.O., commandant
1925–30

4 Brig. H. H. Matthews
C.M.G., D.S.O., commandant
1935–8

5 Col. L. R. Carleton, D.S.O.
commandant 1913–14

6 No 749, Brig. H. D. G. Crerar
D.S.O., commandant 1938–9

7 No 151, Lt-Gen. Sir A. C. Macdonell
K.C.B., C.M.G., D.S.O., LL.D., commandant 1919–25

1 No 816, Brig. K. Stuart, D.S.O., M.C., commandant 1939–40
2 No 1841, Brig. D. G. Cunningham, D.S.O., E.D., commandant 1944–5
3 Hon. No 2727, Maj.-Gen. H. F. H. Hertzberg, C.M.G., D.S.O., M.C., commandant 1940–4
4 No 2120, Brig. J. D. B. Smith, C.B.E., D.S.O., commandant 1945–6

5 6

5 No 1137, Brig. D. R. Agnew, C.B.E., D.S.O., commandant 1947–54
6 No 2184, Cmdre D. W. Piers, D.S.C., C.D., commandant 1957–60
7 Maj.-Gen. J. F. M. Whiteley, C.B., C.B.E., M.C., commandant 1947
8 No 2140, Air Cmdre D. A. R. Bradshaw, D.F.C., C.D., commandant 1954–7

7 8

1

2

3

1 No 2364, Air Cmdre L. J. Birchall
   O.B.E., D.F.C., C.D., commandant
   1963–7

2 No 2265, Brig. W. A. B. Anderson
   O.B.E., C.D., commandant 1960–2

3 No 2424, Brig. G. H. Spencer
   O.B.E., C.D., commandant 1962–3

4 No 2576, Cmdre W. P. Hayes
   C.D., commandant 1967–

4

per annum.[9] The progress of the college was, however, jeopardized because the Canadian government was somewhat unsympathetic and was inclined to economize wherever possible on its running costs. A second instructional tour for graduates was refused in 1881, presumably because of the expense.[10] Furthermore, in addition to the $100 fee for board and instruction, from 1883 on cadets were required to deposit $200 at the time of entry to cover articles issued to them and another $50 was paid in each succeeding year.[11] This may have been a necessary precaution against barrack and laboratory damage and for wear and tear of clothing. However, the extraordinary extent to which penny-wise governments and civil servants could go was shown when in 1885 several cadets who had not yet completed their course were released to take up British commissions offered by the War Office as a consequence of the Russian crisis, and their parents were required to pay the $100 fine normally imposed upon a cadet who had withdrawn voluntarily. One of the fathers who received such a bill was George Kirkpatrick, a Conservative MP, the leader of the party in the Kingston area, and a friend of Adolphe Caron,* the minister of Militia. Kirkpatrick protested to Caron but was unable to secure a relaxation of the regulations because other similar applications for relief had already been turned down. The government declared it would ask the War Office to collect the $100 from the pay of delinquents; and some years later, when the fact that others had not paid was raised in parliament, the government refused to return the money which it had collected in this way.[12]

Uncertainty about the college's future caused by apathy in London and Ottawa was increased by a number of basic difficulties at RMC that had not yet been overcome. The most important of these was the need for more accommodation and the need for assured employment for graduates. But before progress could be made on either matter an internal conflict arose which overshadowed all else. The introduction of a new company organization in 1880 had precipitated a quarrel that had been brewing for a long time between Colonel Hewett and Major Ridout. It raised fundamental issues in military education and it also threatened to destroy the college.

Ridout's pride had apparently been hurt by the slowness of his promotion in the army. Because it had taken sixteen years for him to be promoted to captain it was difficult for him to reach high rank, especially after new age and retirement rules were introduced. He was therefore sensitive

---

*Sir Joseph Philippe René Adolphe Caron (1843–1908), called to the bar, 1865, MP (Quebec county), 1873, minister of Militia, 1880–92, postmaster-general 1892–6, created K.C.M.G. for services in the 1885 rebellion.

about questions of relative rank. When he had helped to draft RMC *Standing Orders* in the fall of 1876, he pressed for a provision that members of the RMC staff should be ranked for military command from the date of their appointment in the college and not from the date of their commissions in the militia. When additions to the staff were sought in the spring of 1877 he urged "warmly but not improperly" that no one senior to him should be appointed. On that occasion he allegedly confided to a colleague, Captain Hawkins, that if Hewett appointed an officer senior to him he would use his powerful political friends in Canada to have the Commandant removed.[13] In 1877 Hewett had applied to have his instructional officers stepped up one local rank. The new senior professor, Oliver, was given the local rank of lieutenant-colonel in December. Ridout then petitioned to have his own local rank of major antedated to give him seniority over the rest of the military professors.[14] This does not seem to have been granted.

Trouble was precipitated by a reorganization of the college in 1880. A military college must educate as well as train; but in England separate staffs for these two very different functions had been condemned by the Dufferin Commission on Military Education, and the staff at Sandhurst had been amalgamated. Before he left home Hewett had become convinced that the two functions must not be kept apart. He also realized that in a college in a small country like Canada, separate instructional and disciplinary staffs would be too expensive. However, as the first class in 1876 was only eighteen strong, there was but one company and it was under the direct command of Ridout as captain of cadets. He accordingly reigned supreme in matters of discipline and basic military training. Thus at first education and training were under different officers and virtually separate. But at the end of 1877 Hewett announced that he intended to divide the cadet body into "divisions," and "to bring the instructional staff into more intimate relationship with the cadets."[15] This reorganization took place the following year. Nevertheless what he called the "keystone of the system," the appointment of the academic instructional officers to command the two divisions (or companies), could not immediately be put into effect because the proposed additional one dollar a day that each was to receive for performing those extra duties was not yet voted. It became available in 1879.[16] In the following year, circumstances having made modifications in the plan necessary, a four-company system was introduced. Each company was to be commanded by one of the academic instructors. The two dollars extra pay that had been voted was now divided four ways.[17] At the same time the academic instructional staff and also the cadet NCOs were given increased authority with greater powers of punishment.[18]

These changes seriously undermined Ridout's position and power. As the officer in command of the cadet company with quarters in the Stone Frigate he had for those first four years been closer to the cadets than any other officer, especially the Commandant who was in comparison a distant god. Hewett lived in town and his duties were not directly concerned with the cadets. They saw him most frequently on formal parades, when he was driving into the college in his barouche drawn by two fine bays, or at formal balls which he occasionally gave at his house. Ridout was not only with the cadets much of the time but he also had quarters in the Frigate. He was undoubtedly personally popular with them. They admired his soldierly appearance and his impressive performance on the square; they appreciated his affability off parade. He shared many aspects of their life.[19]

There has been considerable divergence of opinion about the exact nature of Ridout's influence over the cadets. Some have said that he was the only disciplinarian on the staff and that other officers knew so little about infantry drill and regimental procedure that when they were appointed to command companies they had to seek guidance from the cadets.[20] It was also frequently stated that Ridout, as a Canadian, was more able to deal with Canadian boys. This presumably meant that he seemed less distant, or less of a martinet, than the British officers, even though the latter were more concerned with academic matters than with discipline. Conversely, Hewett's friends, and possibly also the Commandant, believed that Ridout permitted the senior cadets too much licence, that he overlooked their loose habits, and that he was their "boon companion."[21] Indeed, Ridout seems to have treated the seniors as comrades rather than as pupils.

Although Hewett's plan to divide the cadet body and to appoint instructional officers to command companies was, as he claimed, based on principle, there can be little doubt that he also saw it as a means of breaking the special hold that Ridout had over the cadets.[22] The proposal which he made in 1879 to alter Ridout's appointment and title from captain of cadets to staff-adjutant[23] therefore came like a gratuitous affront to that proud officer who was already oversensitive about questions of rank and authority. Hewett claimed that as a staff-adjutant Ridout would be more useful to him and to the college and would in fact become his confidential assistant, but Ridout and his friends thought that a staff-adjutant would be "a mere office clerk" with a euphonious title.[24] Ridout also resented the fact that four academic instructional officers who were to take over the company duty that he had formerly done alone were to share the two dollars a day extra pay authorized for company commanders.[25] He smarted under a sense of grievance that was all the higher because, as technical officers, the professors were already better paid than he was.

It has been alleged that Ridout was ambitious to be commandant.[26] It has even been suggested that for five years he had pursued a deliberate policy aimed at ousting Hewett.[27] This may have been merely an addition to the current recriminations when matters came to a crisis, but Ridout's past jockeying for position gives some colour to the idea. Indeed, if he did not actually intrigue when at the college, he seems to have threatened to do so. It should be noticed that as soon as his Liberal friends came back to power in 1896, although he had long been retired from the army and had lived in England since 1881, he applied for the post of commandant.[28]

The personal antagonism between Ridout and Hewett was brought to a head by an anonymous letter in the Toronto *Mail* on 7 June 1880. Signed "Raglan,"* it originated from Kingston. The author of this letter said that the RMC staff had falsified the accounts to deceive the public; he complained about the cost of the college which he alleged was being operated in order to give British officers a job; he also mentioned the cost of the commandant's house which Hewett had never occupied; and he called RMC a "nest of snobbery."[29] Hewett was furious and wanted to take legal action against the newspaper; but before he could do so other letters followed.

On 27 June Ridout, suspected of being the author or the inspirer of this newspaper correspondence, wrote to seek the help of an old family friend, militia Colonel George T. Denison, the Toronto police magistrate. Claiming that his relations with Hewett were "never more cordial," Ridout asked Denison to use his influence to persuade the editor not to publish any more letters. He said that if they continued he would be dismissed.[30] On 3 July Hewett told the Adjutant-General that the letters must have been written by a friend of Ridout and that they were a consequence of the change in the structure of command which, he claimed, Ridout had at one time favoured but now disliked. He believed it possible that Ridout might not actually know who wrote the letters, but he was sure that he had talked about the college unwisely.[31] Then in December 1880, Hewett wrote an adverse report on the Captain of Cadets. Ridout promptly asked for a formal investigation of his conduct. However, Hewett insisted he

*The identity of "Raglan" has not been uncovered. It is tempting to think that it was a cadet disgruntled at having been left behind from the instructional tour (see above, p. 71).

had the right to evaluate his staff and he denied the request. At the same time Ridout refused to answer questions about the authorship of the "Raglan" letters. There the matter ended for a while with the two principals no longer on speaking terms. Although they worked in neighbouring rooms they communicated with each other by letter.[32]

This situation obviously could not continue for long. In February 1881 Hewett reported that Ridout and Kensington were close to the end of their five-year service in Canada and he asked that Kensington should be permitted to stay on. He did not request the continuation of Ridout's services.[33]

Three months later the room of Cadet Battalion-Sergeant-Major Campbell, a firm disciplinarian, was invaded; his furniture and clothes were thrown into the passage and saturated with water. Hewett immediately interviewed the cadets in small groups, but all denied responsibility. The Commandant then spoke to the whole cadet body in the presence of several officers and invited the cadets who had ragged the room to step forward. When no one did so, he said that he could no longer trust them because there were at least two liars among them. He added that 95 per cent were honourable.[34] A few days later Ridout told Professor Ferguson, Dr. Bayne,* and others that the Commandant had abused the cadets "as usual" and that he had insulted them by calling them a pack of liars. Ferguson promptly made it his business to report this statement to the Commandant who in turn requested the GOC of the militia to investigate the incident officially.

The matter was referred to the Board of Visitors. The Adjutant-General, Colonel Walker Powell, presided at a court of enquiry and officers and cadets were called as witnesses. It was clear from their evidence that the staff members who were present when the Commandant spoke to the cadets had not understood him to mean that he classified the whole cadet body as liars. The cadets, however, while agreeing that Hewett had said later in his talk that 95 per cent were honourable, and though each one knew that the offensive words did not apply to him personally, harboured resentment against Hewett. Each cadet believed that, although the words were used generally, others might think that he was involved. There was no doubt that Ridout had initiated his attack on the Commandant deliberately and that he had done so with some malice. The GOC,

---

*Herbert A. Bayne, M.A., PH.D., was appointed professor of experimental and natural sciences in 1879 to teach physics and chemistry; in 1884 he was called professor of physics, chemistry, and geology. He was a founding member and Fellow of the Royal Society of Canada (MG 26, A 1(a), vol. 82, no. 92). He died in 1886, allegedly of overwork.

General Luard,* therefore came to the conclusion that there were proper grounds for preferring against him a court-martial charge for conduct to the prejudice of good order and discipline. As it was obvious that Ridout could not longer serve comfortably under Hewett, and as he had already served beyond his pre-arranged term, Luard recommended that the War Office should be requested to withdraw him. This was approved by the Minister, Adolphe Caron.[35] Major Ridout was then given a three-month leave of absence before rejoining his regiment.[36]

When this decision became known, Ferguson was held responsible. All the cadets in his German classes, which were voluntary, therefore informed him that they had decided to drop the subject. Some of them advertised their German textbooks for sale and wrote insulting comments about him on the blackboard in his classroom. His picture was posted in the college with the caption "Judas – Reward $500 per annum,[37] a reference to an increase in Ferguson's salary that Hewett had just recommended. Hewett lectured the cadets about these actions; but he felt unable to take any disciplinary action against them because they had no general feeling of culpability and no realization that collective protest was a military offence. Nor could the leaders of the insubordination be identified.[38]

When the dismissal of Ridout was announced, news of all the related occurrences leaked to the press.[39] Cadets and ex-cadets wrote anonymous letters to newspapers. The Commandant was criticized and bitter attacks were made on the college. The RMC course was declared to be mainly preparation for an English commission which only wealthy men could afford. RMC's English officers were said to treat the Canadian cadets as if they were English private soldiers, to make nice sensible boys into insufferable snobs, and to turn out graduates who mostly went into business. One critic, a supporter of the militia, said "I fear some go over to brother Jonathan," and even added the preposterous notion that "in the case of a possible falling out with our cousins across the line we may find these young soldiers directing their genius against their alma mater."[40]

The Kingston *News* suggested that it would take a more impartial position by publishing, first Hewett's case as obtained from his friends, and then Ridout's reply in a later issue. But after Hewett's account had appeared Ridout threatened the paper with legal action because of what was said about him in the article; and he claimed that army regulations did not permit him to make an answering statement. Therefore the information

*Lieutenant-General Richard Amherst Luard, C.B. (1827–1891), fought in the Crimea and in China and also served in Ireland and Nova Scotia; he was GOC of the Canadian militia, 1880–4, but quarrelled with Caron and was withdrawn at the request of the Canadian government. His sons attended RMC.

published by the *News* remained one-sided.[41] Other papers said that Hewett was weak and jealous of Ridout. It was rumoured that the Commandant had been piqued because Prime Minister Mackenzie, on a visit, had called only upon the Captain of Cadets who had shown him around the college without taking him to the Commandant.[42] "One of the Old Eighteen" wrote to the *Globe* to say that no man was more fitted to be commandant than Ridout.[43] This correspondent was known to be Duncan MacPherson who, in consequence, lost a chance for an appointment to a proposed Halifax engineering company.[44] The *Globe* suggested that instruction should be separated from discipline and should be placed under a separate staff. It added that Hewett ought to be replaced by a better man.[45]

Meanwhile, Hewett realized that he had stirred up a hornet's nest. He circulated requests for testimonials about his work at RMC, and when these were received he had them printed. Former Prime Minister Alexander Mackenzie, who supplied a testimonial, complained afterwards that Hewett had not played fair with him because he had concealed the disharmony in the college. Mackenzie said that if he had known about this he would never have supplied the letter.[46]

When the cadets refused to continue with their German, Hewett became even more rattled. The copious notes that he sent in reply to Luard's letter of enquiry demonstrated that he had taken great care to handle the investigation of this matter properly in the presence of witnesses. His disjointed style suggests that he could not wait to draft a careful reply.[47] However, Ferguson, Kensington, and Walker all stated that, if called upon in court, they would testify that several times during 1880 and 1881 Ridout had stated that if he had to leave he would "drag the R.M. College with him." Ferguson also wrote to tell Hewett that, shortly before the court of enquiry, Ridout's lawyer had called him to his office, threatened that his client would make use of his important political friends, claimed that he "commanded" the columns of the *Mail* and of other Toronto papers including perhaps even the *Globe*, and promised that these would not spare Ferguson's name.[48] Ridout was rumoured to have begun legal proceedings against those who had maligned him, and Hewett feared lest he also might be sued.[49]

The question did not come to a court martial or, apparently, into the civil courts. Ridout went back to England and to promotion in the British army,* his expenses for the transportation of his family and his goods

*Ridout retired from the army with the rank of lieutenant-colonel on 10 August 1886. In May 1896 he was elected chairman of the Gillingham District Council, Kent, and became a justice of the peace. He was concerned about the welfare of

being paid by the Canadian government.[50] But the matter was carried into the Canadian House of Commons by government back-benchers. It was raised there in 1882 by C. W. Bunting, an obscure Conservative MP (Welland) who called for the correspondence relating to the removal of Major Ridout. Bunting was followed by another Conservative, F. W. Strange, MP for North York, who claimed to speak on behalf of members of the militia. He said that in 1875 many had thought a military scientific college was in advance of Canada's needs, and at present, he went on, "the college is receiving funds to which the active militia is entitled." He asked for statistics about the numbers who had graduated from the college and about their present availability to serve Canada. Dr. T. S. Sproule, MP for East Grey, and also a Conservative, called RMC a "useless luxury." Caron replied that he was sure that the information that had been requested, when it was produced, would dispel all doubts. He declared that since he had become minister some RMC graduates had been appointed to the college staff and also to the Mounted Police. Only one other voice was raised in defence of RMC; that of J. S. McCuaig of Prince Edward county, also on the government side of the house, who stated that the college had been a success and that he hoped that parliament would support it liberally.[51]

The formal motions for the returns, all in Bunting's name though he had not actually asked most of these questions, called for the correspondence about Ridout, for the changes in organization at RMC since its establishment, for the amount of Ferguson's salary, for the number of cadets he had taught and the number of lectures he had given between 1 November 1881 and 1 February 1882, for details of all the salaries and allowances paid to the RMC staff, for a list of graduates holding militia commissions and of the parades they had attended, and for a list of those cadets past and present who were born in the United States.[52]

When the answers were produced they revealed that the staff-adjutant's duties were now being performed temporarily by Lieutenant H. R. Sankey, RE,* an instructor teaching fortification, who was receiving a dollar a day

old soldiers and did a great deal to help them (*R.M.C. Club Proceedings*, 1894, p. 45). He died at Richmond, England, 25 September 1910. His son, Major-General Sir Dudley Ridout, K.B.E., C.B., C.M.G. and his grandson, Colonel J. H. H. Ridout, D.S.O., were RMC cadets. His wife, who was described by a colleague as "a nice little Englishwoman," had accompanied her husband on the Bhutan campaign in 1858; she died at the age of 88 at Neilsonville, PQ, on 14 January 1930.

*Captain Matthew Henry Phineas Riall Sankey, C.B., C.B.E.; commissioned RE, 1873; instructor in fortification, RMC, 1879–82; later director and consulting engineer to Marconi's Wireless Telegraph Co. and of many other companies; he wrote many books on engineering and was adviser to the Director of Fortifications and Works at the War Office, 1914–18; died 1925.

out of the two dollars that had been provided for officers in charge of companies. The four companies had been reduced to two and two other instructional officers were in command of them and were each receiving fifty cents a day. Ferguson's salary was still $1000 and he had done no teaching in the period stated. One hundred and thirty-two cadets had been admitted since 1876, seventy-five were still on strength, thirty-five had graduated, twenty-two had left without graduating. The greatest number at the college at any one time was ninety-two on 9 February 1882. (This number must have included the officers on the Long Course about which something will be said later.) Seven graduates were in the British army, one was in the Mounted Police, and two were instructors at RMC. The addresses of the remainder were not known and the means of calling upon them in emergency was merely the same as for the militia, namely by a general order in the *Canada Gazette*. The department had no information about the number of ex-cadets who trained with the militia; under existing regulations graduates were not required to be attached to militia units. Eight cadets had been born in the United States.[53]

Although this miscellaneous collection of information showed that RMC was not yet contributing much to the defence of Canada, it apparently satisfied the house. Several members made a tour of inspection of the college and were favourably impressed. When the RMC appropriation came before the house on 13 April, the Conservatives who had raised the hue and cry on 2 March were silent. From the opposition side, however, Mackenzie asked for a statement about the recent trouble in the college and about RMC's achievements. Caron then assured the house that all was in order. He said that he personally approved of the Mackenzie government's selection of Hewett as commandant. He was "the right person for the position." He also believed that those cadets who had gone into the British service would return to Canada and would bring back with them a widened experience. Liberal member G. W. Ross, a future minister of education in Ontario and later Mackenzie's biographer, stated that it would be a retrograde step if parliament closed the college; but he criticized its cost. He said that its staff was about the same size as that of University College, Toronto, which had five times its number of students. However, he added that he did not know any institution where a young man could get a better training than at RMC. He thought that the course should prepare the cadets for civil employment without their having to take further professional training.[54]

The Ridout row thus petered out. On the day of the appropriation debate Hewett reported from Kingston to the Adjutant-General as follows: "There has never been a period since the opening of the college at which the working of the Institution has been in so satisfactory a condition as it has been since the commencement of the current year. Everything is working most smoothly – Military offences are fewer and of slighter description without their existence being in any way overlooked or undetected – Studies and drills are proceeding systematically and satisfactorily and there is no friction in any department."[55] Though this must have been written to make a good case in connection with the debate in the house, it is probably an accurate appraisal of the situation.

The conflict between Hewett and Ridout was an unfortunate clash of personality of two strong men who had, each in his own way, made great contributions to the college which they had founded together. But it was more significant than a mere personal feud. It was even more than a dispute between the British and Canadian elements on the RMC staff which has sometimes been suggested to have been the cause of trouble; as a matter of fact the Canadian civilian professors and the British military professors were united against Ridout. It was also more than the result of an intrusion of the Canadian political party conflict into the administration of the college. The incident can only be properly understood as an outcome of the potential contradiction between the two different functions of a military college, namely education and training. Hewett, although an army officer, represented the academic side of the college; Ridout represented military training. Ridout's attempt to assert seniority over the academic professors and to retain sole control of training, if successful, would have given the college a certain bias. Parade-ground training would have tended to gain priority over educational and academic activities. If continued through the years this might have prevented the distinctive development of the Royal Military College of Canada and might have made it like other military colleges.

The Ridout incident also reveals the degree to which cadet spirit had grown. The cadets were unanimous. They stood fast together to conceal the identity of those among them who had invaded the BSM's room. They thought Ferguson's action (which he claimed was necessary for the good of the institution as a whole) a breach of their schoolboy version of the military code in which they were being trained by both Hewett and Ridout. They organized a successful boycott of Ferguson's classes which the Commandant could not break. Their cohesion in all these things was pregnant with possibilities for the magnificent camaraderie of the future RMC; but, since it was directed against the sentiments of the whole staff except Ridout, it carried with it the seeds of a dangerous brand of cadet independence of constituted authority.

Finally the conflict was important because it brought on, or out into the open, the dislike of some militia officers for RMC. When there was relatively little military interest in the country, rivalry between two military groups was bound to hurt both. This rivalry grew out of conflict over appointments. Mackenzie had intended that "the founding of the college should lay the foundation of a future military system"; and he had expected "that when the first batch left the college means would be found" to employ the graduates in the Canadian military service.[56] In the *Canada Gazette* of 7 February 1880, it had been announced that RMC graduates would receive commissions in the militia provided they performed certain military duties. It had said further that when they were (in Colonel Hewett's words) *"qualified by the necessary age, rank, and seniority* (but not till then)"* they would receive all the permanent commissions in the militia. Reporting this announcement, Hewett examined the possibilities for various types of military employment in Canada and the effect that the production of trained officers could have on the dissemination of military knowledge throughout the country. He concluded that "the full object of the college" would be attained "to even a greater extent than was anticipated." But in quoting the announcement about permanent commissions in the militia he used italics as above and his words in parentheses suggest that he may have had some doubts about when the proposal would be carried through.[57] The announcement seemed more designed to impose restrictions on the aspirations of RMC graduates than to offer them openings.

The reason was that the very few permanent commissions available in Canada were eagerly sought by militia officers; and they were also valuable patronage. At the same time the idea of a larger permanent force was disliked by the militia because it would be a competitor for financial support. A tirade in the Toronto *Mail* in June 1880, which said that Canadians did not want to be taxed to provide jobs for youths of aristocratic background, was believed to have been initiated by militia officers.[58]

The Marquis of Lorne therefore proposed that, as had been suggested in the parliamentary debate about the establishment of the college, RMC should offer training to the militia.[59] A short step was taken in June 1882, when militia engineers from Toronto and Montreal attended a week's training camp on Point Frederick under their own officers but with lecturers supplied by RMC. Two cadets were detailed as supernumerary officers.[60] Lieutenant Goodwin of the Montreal Engineers, Lieutenant Caleb C. Cole of the New Brunswick Artillery, and Major D. MacLeod Vince and all his officers of the Brighton Engineer Company of New Brunswick, applied to be allowed to take courses at RMC to qualify them for higher military appointments.[61] Depite the shortage of accommodation and the pressure on his staff, Hewett offered a six-month course.[62] From 1882 militia artillery officers attending the long and short courses at the Schools of Gunnery were given a "special course" of instruction in military survey-ing and engineering, strategy, tactics and reconnaissance, and military administration at RMC. Subsequently this became the RMC long course in which militia officers received instruction of a more advanced character than that which they received at the schools of gunnery.* Hewett made it clear, however, that the long course must not be regarded as equivalent to the RMC course because it was not based on an adequate educational preparation.[63] It will be seen later that this arrangement did not eliminate all militia jealousy. Moreover the problem of assuring employment for RMC graduates remained. The failure of Canadians to make greater pro-vision for defence in the following two decades was in part a result of this conflict of interest among the military.

One of the results of the Ridout affair, although not admitted to be related to it, was the resignation of Ferguson. He had been exonerated in a testimonial signed by Hewett and all the other members of the staff who said that the course he had taken was the only one which a gentleman of honour could have followed.[64] Furthermore, an application for a higher salary, which had been turned down in 1877 but had been re-submitted, had led to Hewett's recommendation that Ferguson should get that extra $500 that had aroused the ire of some cadets. The GOC noted on this recommendation that, although Ferguson had originally been appointed to teach German, English, and French, another professor had since taken over the French. Thus, the money spent on these subjects was exactly doubled. He nevertheless supported the increase. But the Canadian government turned it down.[65] English had been included as a separate course in the curriculum only in 1882,[66] perhaps as a device to keep Ferguson busy. However, Ferguson resigned in 1883 on the grounds that his work at Queen's College was now occupying more of his time. Hewett greatly regretted the loss of his first appointee in Canada; and he declared in another testimonial that Ferguson's professional experience had been very beneficial to RMC and to its standing in the country.[67]

A second staff problem was the replacing of Ridout. Applications began to arrive even before the vacancy was officially announced. Ex-cadet A. B. Perry, and also an officer in Cape Town named Captain Allen Cameron who had heard by February 1882 that Ridout had gone, sought the post.[68] Other applicants pressed their claims on political grounds. One applicant from "A" Battery, who claimed to be a Conservative, said that if British

---

*The long course of this period prepared militia officers for higher rank in the Active Militia and not, as in a later period, for Permanent Force commissions.

officers were really interested in their profession they would stay with the British army; and he added that as "B" Battery had just had a government appointment it was now "A" Battery's turn. Macdonald endorsed this letter "a strong case" and asked Caron to discuss it with him.[69] Another militia adjutant, also a Conservative, said that six MPs had recommended him for the job and that as the government had a financial surplus the Conservative government could now do anything it liked.[70]

However Hewett took Ridout's dismissal as an opportunity to confine the staff-adjutant to administration, to the care of stores, to finance, and to the command of the military and civilian substaff, leaving the instructional officers to take charge of all cadet work including infantry drill. He said that this was customary in continental armies and was now being introduced in England. He claimed that by reducing the pay of the staff-adjutant from $1600 to $1250, and by hiring two ex-cadets as company commanders and assistant instructors, a re-arrangement on these lines would cost no more than the old one. Forwarding this proposal for the consideration of the Minister, the GOC, General Luard, questioned whether a staff-adjutant of that kind would be an adjutant or only a quartermaster or paymaster.[71] When George Kirkpatrick of Kingston, the local Conservative party leader, wrote to tell Caron that the employment of ex-cadets would be popular and recommended Perry and J. B. Cochrane,*[72] the reorganization was promptly approved by the Privy Council; but with ex-cadets A. G. G. Wurtele† and Cochrane as the appointees.[73]

Kirkpatrick's intervention in the affairs of the college, although made in the form of a suggestion which, he said, could be ignored if not liked, was coincident with and typical of an increase of political interest in RMC as a means of patronage. Although the Conservative victory in 1878 had not led immediately to changes in staff or in contracts, or to the relaxation of the regulations in response to political pressures, it soon became clear that all these things were increasing. Hewett wrote to Caron in 1883 to say that he had been, and would continue to be, very careful not to receive fuel for the college except from the contractors authorized by the Militia Department.[74] Kirkpatrick told Caron that the Clerk of Works for the

---

*Lieutenant-Colonel J. B. Cochrane (1860–1946); RMC, 1876–80; assistant instructor in survey, military topography, chemistry, and physics at RMC, 1882–97; professor of physics and chemistry, 1897–1915; professor of survey, 1897–1904; Surveys Department, Department of Militia, 1914; director of survey, geographical section, General Staff, 1916–29; president of the RMC Club, 1899.

†No. 1, Alfred George Godfrey Wurtele (1857–99), assistant to William Ashe, D.L.S. in an investigation of the moving of boundary marks on the international border, 1881; assistant instructor in mathematics and geometrical drawing and lieutenant of cadets, RMC, 1882–97; member of the Medal Claims Board, Department of Militia, 1897–9.

construction of a drain at the college "should be one of our men, if competent" and that the engineer officers ought to be too busy with their teaching to do such work.[75] Kirkpatrick also recommended the Rev. K. L. Jones* to succeed Ferguson as professor of English by the statement that he was from "one of our oldest Conservative families" – and he got the job.[76] Parents asked that the regulations about age of entry and about residence requirements should be waived: "A very good friend of mine and a valuable man in politics is Mr. E. W. Rathbone [Rathbun]† of Deseronto [who] is desirous of getting his son into R.M.C. but the young fellow is 19, [and by the time of entry] a year beyond the limit of the regulations," wrote one applicant for special consideration.[77]

In cases of this kind Hewett usually advised the Minister that the regulations could be stretched provided there was room, provided the candidates were otherwise qualified, and provided no others who met the regulations had applied. Caron normally accepted this advice, although he would not always agree to waive the requirement for five years' residence in Canada.[78] But he did not stand as firmly on principle in regard to appointments. After Jones had received the professorship with political backing, another applicant appeared who claimed that Caron had promised him Ferguson's place and that he had consequently already resigned his former position.[79]

This increasing use of RMC for Conservative patronage led the Liberals to attack the college in 1883 and 1884 without the reservation they had shown in 1882 when the opposition had merely followed up a Conservative back-bench initiative. C. W. Weldon, a Liberal from Saint John, repeated the request for returns to show what proportion of RMC graduates were in British service and what proportion served Canada; and when Ross renewed his attack on the cost of the college he was joined by G. E. Casey, a militia officer, and by Edward Blake, one of the Liberal leaders. The Liberal position was that the original intention to use the college to provide trained personnel for government service had not been carried out. Caron replied that out of fifty-four graduates to date, eleven were in the public service of Canada, and eleven in the British forces. Twenty-three were in railway and engineering work. Only eight were in the United States; and two of the eight were employed building a branch line for a Canadian railroad. The Minister defended the high cost of the college by saying that the standards required for British commissions required the

*K. L. Jones, professor of English at RMC, 1882–97.

†Edward Wilkes Rathbun, born 1842, son of the founder of Deseronto, head of "The Rathbun Co.," and president of the Bay of Quinte Railway Co. He was described as "independent" in politics in 1898 and later sat in the Commons as a Liberal Independent.

use of specialists as teachers. He admitted that, because of lack of accommodation, the college was only able to take about seventy-five cadets instead of the hundred or more permitted by the Act. However, he said that when the college was brought up to its full establishment, the teaching staff need not be any bigger.[80]

But Caron was in fact not prepared to undertake the expensive building programme that was needed if the full number was to be admitted. As the opposition charged that the institution was costly and useless, their attacks helped to confirm this policy. Hewett's requests for new accommodation was therefore rejected. The Commandant then urged the examiners should not become unnecessarily severe because accommodation was limited and that all qualified candidates should be accepted. He declared that room could be made available by doubling up in bedrooms.[81] To alleviate the effect of overcrowding in classrooms which was said to give headaches to the staff and cadets, better ventilation was authorized.[82] Otherwise the only construction was a small observatory for use in connection with the teaching of surveying.[83] Hewett found Caron charming and friendly, personally solicitous about his welfare to the extent of sending him a bottle of cough medicine, always ready to defend him and the college against political attack, but noticeably hard to reach when demands for construction and expansion were being pressed.[84]

The problem of making beneficial use of the RMC graduates in Canada's interest was also difficult. Although the number of graduates was small, a large proportion were civilian engineers. Fewer of these had emigrated to the United States than experience with the first class had suggested might happen. RMC had, however, succeeded in an objective not envisaged at its founding, the production of officers for the British army. Although the achievements of the first RMC graduates who went into the British army had not been impressive, the prestige of the college had quickly been established by their successors who stood high in competitive examinations that matched them against graduates from British military colleges. Indeed, within a very short time the amount of initial training that was required of RMC ex-cadets after they went to England was reduced.[85] RMC was thus already making a small but highly satisfactory contribution to British military strength.

Up to 1882 little progress had been made towards the attainment of the college's primary purpose, the production of officers for employment in Canadian defence, mainly because Canada still had no permanent force. The need for the establishment of a permanent corps in Canada, and also for the provision of civilian public service posts for RMC graduates, was repeatedly urged by the GOC, by the Adjutant-General, and by the Commandant. RMC's contribution to Canadian defence was also low because few of its graduates entered the militia. It produced engineers who moved about a lot and were often employed in places remote from the more populated areas where the militia units were located. RMC graduates had therefore been put under no obligation to join a unit. Even so, while a few cadets may have attended the college to get an education without any intention of continuing in military service in either a full- or part-time capacity (as was sometimes alleged in the Commons), there is good reason to believe that many were anxious to keep up their militia connection even though their careers made the necessary regular training impossible.[86] The ex-cadets asked to be allowed to wear a distinctive uniform when parading with the militia.[87] It is worthy of note that Colonel Walker Powell, reporting on RMC in 1882 in the absence of the GOC, expressed the opinion that lack of a permanent force actually made RMC more useful, as it had a valuable influence upon the militia which had no other model.[88]

A year later the government at last prepared to set up infantry schools for militia training, the staffs of which constituted the first elements of a permanent force in the Canadian service apart from the artillerymen called out in 1870 to run the artillery schools. Many cadets and ex-cadets at once applied for positions on the staff or in the newly constituted "C" Battery.[89] When General Luard complained to the Governor-General that the staffs of the schools had been recruited on political, rather than military, grounds and that one of the officers selected had been convicted of drunkenness, the Prime Minister himself investigated the situation and replied that out of twenty-three officers, five were graduates of RMC, four were former British regulars, five were graduates of the artillery schools, and one had been appointed on political grounds. This was a grandson of Sir Étienne Taché, Macdonald's great French-Canadian colleague in pre-Confederation days, and he was the man about whom the accusations of insobriety had been made; Macdonald said that when he was a cadet this officer had once celebrated too well at a New Year's party.[90] Macdonald did not explain the other seven appointments or reveal whether they had been made for reasons of patronage. It is clear that patronage was necessary to maintain adequate political support for defence measures. As no RMC graduates were as yet more than three years out of college they could not be expected to have the senior appointments. Furthermore they had been trained primarily with a view to going into the engineers or the artillery. Nevertheless it could be held that RMC had been shortchanged in its share of the appointments to Canada's first infantry schools.

The continuance of parliamentary attacks on the college in 1883 and 1884 convinced many people that there was a plot on foot to do away with it. But it was difficult to organize the ex-cadets in defence of their *alma mater* because they were widely scattered and hard to locate. However, the growth of an RMC spirit had been shown by the request that ex-cadets should be entitled to wear a distinguishing uniform; and the ex-cadets living in the Toronto area decided to establish a club through which opinion could be mobilized.[91] An organizational meeting was held on 7 February 1884 at the offices of Messrs. Denison & Lowe, Barristers, 42 King Street East, Toronto. L. H. Irving, the first BSM, acted as chairman.[92] The minutes of this, and of later formal meetings, are preserved in Club's files. Irving and Denison then sent a circular letter to ex-cadets and received very encouraging replies. One such typical reply from the Punjab said that the idea was capital and that the writer would be glad to join the club.[93] A noteworthy feature was that among the organizers was a cadet who had left after two years and another who had failed out in the middle of the final year. The Royal Military College Club which they formed was thus not restricted to graduates. Its first annual meeting was held on 14 March 1885, and Irving was elected its first president.[94] The club's primary purpose was the promotion of the college's interests as a whole, rather than merely those of club members. Nevertheless, as one of the college's greatest impediments was the lack of provision for the employment of its graduates in the military service of Canada (as seemed to be shown by the recent appointments to the new militia schools), inevitably the club's most important task lay in that field.

However, during the following year that problem became less pressing. It had regularly been claimed that one purpose of the college was to produce graduates who could make a living in civil occupations but who would be available in emergency to train and officer armies for the defence of Canada and the empire; and emergencies on both levels occurred within twelve months of the formation of the ex-cadet club.

In 1884 General Garnet Wolseley had called for Canadian *voyageurs* to aid him in the navigation of the Nile to rescue General Gordon in Khartoum.[95] Although these were employed as civilians, Canadian militia officers helped to direct the service. A little later, due probably to an erroneous news report about Canadian intentions, New South Wales offered troops to aid Britain in the Sudan where General Gordon had been beset by the Mahdi. This offer was accepted but the War Office was clearly not enthusiastic about the idea of employing colonial detachments. It refused later colonial offers.[96] The troubles in the Sudan had not yet been settled when Russian troops destroyed an Afghan force at Penjdeh in Transcaspia on 30 March 1885. The War Office suddenly discovered that if a war with Russia followed, Britain would be very short of officers.

Therefore, on 15 April it informed the Colonial Secretary that during the current year, in addition to the four commissions ordinarily reserved for RMC, it was willing to offer twenty-six extra commissions to recent graduates, six in the artillery, ten in the engineers, and ten in either the infantry or the cavalry. It added that when the necessary conditional qualifications had been decided upon, it intended to offer commissions also to members of the various colonial local military forces including the Canadian militia.[97] Obviously the War Office had been able to offer commissions to RMC without hesitation and without qualification because experience had already given it confidence in the quality of the RMC product.

Meanwhile on 26 March a Métis force at Duck Lake in the Canadian North-West defeated a small force of Mounted Police and local inhabitants and sparked a rising that required the despatch of forces from Eastern Canada under General Sir Frederick Dobson Middleton.* On receipt of the news the Kingston cadets offered their services as a body; and this offer was forwarded to Ottawa. Their spirit was commended by the authorities but it was stated that the situation was not of such a nature that their college careers should be interrupted.[98] This was of course a sound decision. Examples of the use of cadets in war, the Virginia Military Institute cadets at the battle of New Market, the École polytechniciens in the siege of Paris, and the cadets of the Mexican Military Academy when American forces approached Mexico City (when the *cinco niños* became immortal by their self-sacrifice) had occurred when situations were desperate. Nevertheless, some thought there was a possibility that RMC itself might be attacked by rebel sympathizers from the United States. The cadets were therefore placed under the command of Professor Cochrane, who was appointed a captain in the militia for the purpose, and they did night picquet duty for three months of the term.[99] Hewett postponed a trip to England which he had planned, though only for a week, and he agreed to return immediately if cabled. But, while apparently concurring that there was some danger, he did not take it very seriously. He advised that a night-watchman would be more useful than sentries on Point Frederick.[100]

Much more important was the contribution that ex-cadets made to the expeditionary force. At the time of the outbreak of the rebellion eighty-eight had passed through the college. Of these twenty-four had gone into the British army. More offers of service came from the remainder than

---

*Lieutenant-General Sir Frederick Dobson Middleton (1825–98), GOC of the Canadian militia, 1884–1890, commanded the expedition to the North-West Territories; he had previously served in India during the Mutiny and in 1868 in Canada; in 1896 he became keeper of the Crown Jewels at the Tower of London.

could be used. Nevertheless about thirty ex-cadets served west of Winnipeg and seven were on garrison duty in the east, leaving only a few unaccounted for. Four RMC graduates had important appointments on the staff, two with Middleton, one with General Laurie,* and one with General Strange.†[101] The Kingston graduates were, as yet, all still young men and in junior ranks. Therefore they inevitably served in junior appointments. But the degree of their response had been remarkable.

The suppression of the rebellion was followed by recriminations when supporters of the militia attacked Middleton's caution and claimed that the victory had been won by the militia's dash rather than by his professional leadership. In the course of the ensuing controversy, a *Globe* editorial discussing Middleton's report asked what return "this expensive institution [RMC]" had made to Canada? C. O. Fairbank, one of the Old Eighteen, replied with facts and figures about the participation of ex-cadets. He said they had not been "lunching on raspberry jam" and that as time went on their value would obviously increase. Describing the RMC course itself, he said that it was tough, a case of the survival of the fittest, that drones were not wanted, and that RMC had proved that it deserved the best the country would give it.[102]

In 1883 RMC certificates of graduation, first or second class, were replaced by RMC diplomas of graduation with or without honours. This distinguished the RMC graduate more effectively from the militia holder of a drill certificate issued by one of the schools of artillery.[103] Several appraisals attest to the superior nature and the excellent quality of the RMC course. General Strange, former commandant at the artillery school, said that even though there was little or no competition for entry to RMC, the system of education there possessed solidity by contrast with the hustle and cram of the much shorter courses at Woolwich and Sandhurst.[104] Major-General Walker,‡ the son of an RMC professor, said some years later that the four-year course gave a much better preparation than the colleges "at home" and also gave a better grounding for life. A Kingston graduate, he said, had little to learn at the military engineering school at Chatham. He was already a trained civil engineer with an additional extra military training; all he lacked was experience.[105] Sir Charles Tupper, the Canadian high commissioner in England, relayed to the Minister of Militia a British reply to a request for information in connection with the

*Lieutenant-General John Wimburn Laurie, C.B. (1835–1912), served as Middleton's second in command in 1885.

†Major-General Thomas Bland Strange, RA (1831–1925), commanded the Alberta Field Force.

‡Major-General George Walker, C.B., C.M.G., D.S.O., RE (1869–1936), colonel-commandant, RE, 1935.

possible establishment of a military college in Australia: Sir Andrew Clarke, the inspector general of fortifications, had said that at Kingston a "most excellent and practical education in Civil Engineering is combined with a soldier's training." Clarke added that its graduates had no difficulty finding employment. Several had served under him. "I regard the Canadian Military College as one of the best of its class in the World. The training and results are in every way of a high order and the Americans themselves, I understand, say better than at West Point."[106]

With this kind of testimony to show that his work in Kingston was a success, Hewett felt able to leave it. He had been promoted steadily in the British army during his absence from it. He had become a lieutenant-colonel in 1879 and a colonel in 1881. In 1883 his CMG was promulgated. He had been considered for other appointments and in 1885 had been approached about taking command of the citizen forces in New Zealand. In that year his tour at RMC had been extended again to last until 1889, the full fourteen years possible in such appointments; and the Secretary of State for War said that this extension would in no way prejudice Hewett's future promotion or bring him compulsory retirement.[107] A year later, however, Hewett was offered the command of the Royal Engineers of the Western District in England at Plymouth. He resigned and left Canada in May 1886. His appointment as commandant officially ended on 15 July.

Hewett's later career further demonstrated the quality of the man who had set up the Royal Military College of Canada. In 1890 he was on a short list of British officers being considered for appointment as GOC of the Canadian militia.[108] In 1893 he was given the command of the Engineering School at Chatham; and in 1895 as a lieutenant-general he became the Governor of the Royal Military Academy at Woolwich. He died in office in 1897 as a result of a fractured leg incurred when playing tennis. Lieutenant-Colonel J. B. Cochrane, who served with all the commandants from Hewett to Carleton, considered Hewett "by far the most able and informed of them all".[109] Hewett's contribution to RMC had not been merely that he had founded the college and laid the foundations of its academic quality and its military traditions but also that he had skilfully enabled it to weather the storms that had burst around it in its early tender years. In 1886, after ten years of his care, RMC's future seemed assured.

5

MARKING TIME UNDER

OLIVER AND CAMERON

1886-1891

Hewett's resignation was a serious blow. He had qualities that made him a difficult man to replace. General Middleton announced officially that the success of the college to date was "largely attributable to the tact and ability he [Hewett] had brought to bear in the performance of his duties."[1] As George Kirkpatrick was to say when suggesting in 1890 that the first RMC commandant should be brought back to succeed Middleton as GOC, Hewett was "not a crank."[2]

Deputy Minister Eugene Panet* regretted Hewett's departure but claimed that the first commandant had had the foresight to prepare in Colonel Oliver "a worthy successor."[3] This seems to imply that Hewett had recommended his senior professor for the appointment. But circumstantial evidence suggests that he had not done so. To avoid the loss that he would suffer as a result of his sudden decision to leave, Hewett wanted the government to lease from him the house he had bought in 1879. To support this request he argued that if the college had suitable quarters to offer to a commandant, it would be able to attract "the best man."[4] As Oliver's lease on his house in Kingston still had some time to run,[5] Hewett apparently did not regard him as this "best man" and therefore, if he had earlier thought of Oliver as a successor, he had changed his mind.

Yet Oliver was indeed well qualified for the post. Although an artillery-man and not, like Hewett, a Royal Engineer, he was a distinguished

*Colonel Charles Eugene Panet (1829–98); senator 1874–5; deputy minister of Militia and Defence, 1875–98.

scholar. He had written textbooks on geology, geodesy, surveying, astronomy, and the theory of artillery projectiles. Moreover he had one important qualification that Hewett himself lacked, decorations earned on active service. Oliver was well known and had important connections in Canada. He had married Mary Hinds, the daughter of a Kingston banker, whose family was acquainted with John A. Macdonald.[6] He also knew the Minister of Militia at least well enough to correspond with him personally about a telescope that was borrowed for the new RMC observatory from the meteorological services in Toronto.[7] It is therefore not surprising that when the GOC, who had been acquainted with Oliver for a long time, recommended that he should be appointed commandant up to the end of his tour of duty at Kingston (the end of 1887 unless extended), the Minister promptly agreed.[8]

As Oliver believed that he would get no further employment and promotion in England, he wanted to extend his service in Canada until the time came for him to retire from the army. He thought this would be on 16 December 1889.[9] When he found that Caron needed to be reminded to publish the announcement of his appointment as commandant in the *Canada Gazette*,[10] Oliver sought some assurance of tenure. He then learned that his position was probably only temporary.[11] A man more in touch with current developments in the army was wanted. Caron regarded him as a stop-gap until the appointment could be filled more suitably. Oliver subsequently found that, as a result of changes in British regulations, he would retire from the army in 1888, a year earlier than expected. Faced with the prospect of the early termination of his employment at the college, he appealed directly to Macdonald to be allowed to stay on at least one additional year as commandant. He was supported by General Middleton and by Lieutenant-Colonel Frederick Denison,* a Conservative MP and militia officer, who argued that a commandant should be kept for five years. According to Denison, Oliver was the right man in the right place because he was good on theory and was also practical.[12]

But it was all in vain. Caron had made up his mind that Oliver must go.[13] In May 1888, he told the Prime Minister: "We must have in our college an officer who is in the Imperial Army, and Colonel Oliver has now left it."[14] Oliver took this decision with good grace. He recommended as his successor the commanding officer of the 17th Field Com-

---

*Lieutenant-Colonel Frederick Charles Denison (1846–96), second son of Colonel G. T. Denison II, a cornet in Denison's Horse, 1865, and later its commander; orderly officer to General Wolseley on the Red River Expedition, 1870; in command of the Canadian voyageurs in Egypt 1884–5; Conservative MP for West Toronto, 1887–96.

pany of Engineers at Aldershot, Lieutenant-Colonel Elliott Wood, C.B., R.E.,* who had seen much active service and had enjoyed rapid promotion.[15]

But a selection committee had been set up which advised that either Major George R. Walker, the professor of engineering at RMC, or Major Johnson William Savage, R.E., an instructor in field fortification at the School of Military Engineering at Chatham, would be better fitted for the post.[16] Caron accepted the committee's advice and formally recommended that the governor-general be asked to approach the Colonial Office to obtain the services of either one of these British officers as commandant.[17]

Meanwhile rumours that there was to be a new appointment at the college had spread rapidly. Major Hillyard Cameron,† the son of one of Macdonald's deceased Conservative colleagues in the party, wrote to him from India about the post: "Any appointment bringing in two or three hundred [pounds] a year would be acceptable." Macdonald sent this letter to Caron with the comment: "This is from the son of our old friend Hilyard [*sic*] Cameron. What answer shall I send?"[18] But another influence much stronger than that of Middleton or Denison, or even of the deceased Hillyard Cameron senior, was seeking to force Macdonald to bend Caron's will in a different direction. The Honourable Sir Charles Tupper was determined to find a place for his son-in-law, another Cameron.

Donald Roderick Cameron, a retired artillery officer, had, like Oliver, served in India. He had organized an Armstrong mountain battery of native troops for the Ambeyla campaign and had marched it from the extreme northwest of India to the northeast across difficult country in the most unhealthy season of the year to take part in the Bhutan campaign. On his journey, which took over three months, he did not lose a single day and suffered only one casualty. In the campaign, Cameron had independent command of a detached unit of artillery until he took over the battery when Oliver became sick. Cameron earned distinction as a dashing leader of native troops and was three times mentioned in despatches.

In 1869 Tupper arranged that Cameron should be appointed a member of the executive council which the Honourable William McDougall was to set up when he went to Fort Garry to administer the former Hudson's

*Major-General Sir Elliott Wood, K.C.B. (1844–1931); commissioned in the RE, 1864; served with distinction in Egypt and the Sudan 1882–5 where he was decorated and promoted in the field; engineer-in-chief, South Africa, 1899–1902.

†Major Hillyard Cameron was educated at Eton and Christchurch and served in the Bedfordshire Regiment in India. His father, John Hillyard Cameron (1817–76), had been Macdonald's rival for the Conservative party leadership in 1854 and continued to be a power in politics until his death.

Bay country for Canada. Cameron was to be the chief of the police and to command the militia. Against McDougall's orders, Cameron went out to meet some half-breeds and ordered them to remove a barricade. According to McDougall, he called it "that blawsted fence." The result was that the whole party was seized by the rebels and was hustled out of the territory. It is not surprising that McDougall thought him "an incorrigible madcap." When Cameron and his wife, Emma, were detained by the rebels, Tupper went personally to the west to rescue them from a "miserable sod cabin."[19] The whole affair showed that Cameron was not lacking in personal courage, though he was, perhaps, rather rash. (His personal bravery was confirmed in 1878 when he saved a boy who had capsized a canoe in the Rideau Canal at Ottawa. For this he received the bronze medal of the Royal Humane Society.)

Tupper then arranged for his son-in-law to lead the British-Canadian party on the International Boundary Commission set up to establish the location of the Canadian-American border between Lake of the Woods and the Rocky Mountains. The British government would have preferred an engineer rather than an artilleryman. Next, in 1883, Cameron became secretary to the Canadian delegation at an international conference in Paris on the protection of submarine cables. When Tupper went to London as high commissioner in 1884 he got the governor-general to ask the commander-in-chief to post Cameron from Sheerness to London so that his wife could be near her parents.[20] After declining an appointment to command the artillery in South Australia in 1885, Cameron went as Tupper's private secretary in 1887 when the Maritime politician was the Canadian commissioner at the fisheries conference in Washington.

While working on the boundary commission, Cameron had been called upon to estimate the cost of delineating the boundary disputed with the United States in the Alaska panhandle; and in his report in 1874 he had indicated the grounds upon which the best British case could be made there. He had also suggested that Britain should offer £100,000 for the Alaska panhandle territory. He thought this offer would be attractive to the Americans because they would then not need to spend £250,000 on marking the boundary and so would in effect get £350,000; but they had not been moved by this logic. Cameron's opinions about the location of the Alaskan boundary were expressed in a second report written in 1886 and were presented by Tupper in 1888 to the Colonial Office. These opinions were quoted in the tribunal hearings in 1903.[21] The coast doctrine, "an odd thing of gall and gossamer which Donald Cameron had woven in the cabalistic laboratory of his mind"[22] was the basis of vigorous but unsuccessful Canadian diplomacy to get a favourable delineation of the boundary. Cameron had thus had a series of important posts; but there can be no doubt that his connection with Tupper had been an advantage.

When Macdonald won the election of 1887 he promised Tupper that Cameron would succeed Middleton as GOC at the end of the latter's five-year appointment.[23] Tupper immediately tried to have Cameron replace Middleton earlier and to have the latter go to command RMC. Caron's reply was that he was not aware that Middleton was to retire; and he added, "I think also that, large as it is, Canada is getting too small for the Tupper family. Colonel Cameron would not be a propular [*sic*] appointment."[24] A year later Tupper saw a newspaper report that Governor-General Lansdowne was to ask for an extension of Middleton's term to 1892. He peremptorily told Macdonald, "kindly inform me whether either of those positions may be depended upon for Cameron and at what time as it is of great importance both to him and to me to have that information as early as is convenient to you."[25] A month later he cabled imperiously, "Please cable reply to mine 16 June. What can I depend upon? Very important I should know now."[26]

George Kirkpatrick, who appears to have been doubtful about the wisdom of retaining Oliver, wrote on 16 July from Kingston to inform Caron that he hoped there was no foundation for a rumour that was circulating that Cameron was to be appointed to command at RMC. He said, "I have strenuously denied it for the reason [for] which you allowed Oliver to go applies equally to Cameron. They are now both on the retired list. Moreover Cameron has never held any appointment or command or shown any qualification to justify his selection." He said that he knew that Caron had written to the Horse Guards to ask for a commandant; and he was sure that the Commander-in-Chief would not recommend Cameron. He had heard that Colonel Wood, a first-class man, was ready to accept. He concluded, "Do not let the Tupper interest force him [Cameron] on you."[27] However, on 1 August Tupper was able to write to thank Macdonald for "prompt action on the appointment" which he declared was of great importance to both Cameron and himself.[28] Macdonald had been unable to resist the importunity of the man who had brought Nova Scotia into Confederation.

The new commandant arrived in Canada shortly afterwards. A reporter quoted him as saying that the post at RMC had come unexpectedly just as he was on the point of taking a house in Germany to settle down.[29] The opposition press in Canada found this appointment useful. It vigorously condemned it and retailed the story of "Blawsted Fence" Cameron. The London *Advertiser* seized the opportunity to ask why a Canadian had not been considered.[30] In reply the *Ottawa Daily Citizen* argued that legal restriction of the RMC appointment to a "military officer" did not necessarily mean that it must be an engineer officer on the active list of the British army. It argued that Cameron's position as Tupper's son-in-law should not be a disqualification if he was in other ways qualified. It added that connection with a Canadian family by marriage should, indeed, tell in his favour.[31] Although the debate had by this time become a political issue, the opposition to Cameron had obviously come at first from within the Conservative party and had been based on doubts about his qualifications for the command.

Cameron was the same age as Oliver and, like him, became a major-general in retirement. He had some scientific attainments, though none to compare with those of his predecessor. He was believed by a newspaper-man to be a strict disciplinarian;[32] and his dashing career in his younger days would claim the respect of the cadets. But he had had no experience in military education and many of his recent appointments had not been military. An account of his work on the boundary commission in a recent book suggests that he was temperamental, touchy, proud, and moody.[33] Whether these charges are correct or not, it is clear that Cameron could not qualify as "the best man" Caron wanted and that his appointment was "political."

Only time would tell what effect this appointment would have on the development of the college which at that time still needed careful fostering. For, despite the respect in which Hewett had been held and the influence that he had come to wield, the first commandant had been unable to solve some of the chief difficulties under which RMC laboured. He had not persuaded the government to complete the building programme to enable the college to attain its projected enrolment; and he had been unable to secure the promise of enough military openings in Canada to serve the needs of its graduating classes. The appointments at this juncture, first of a temporary stop-gap, and then of a political nominee, were obviously unfortunate.

The crises of 1885 had seemed to justify the existence of the college but they had not actually lent much strength to the case for its further expansion. The prospect of war with Russia was not likely to move Canadians to produce more officers for the peacetime British army. It is true that there was some concern in Canada about the possible bombardment of ports, but Canadians generally believed that the Royal Navy and a few coastal guns would protect them. Moreover Middleton's success in the west had convinced many that the militia was efficient and was all that Canada needed. Therefore neither the Russian menace nor the rebellion in the west helped to increase public interest in the development of RMC.

For ten years after the militia schools were re-opened in 1883, nothing very effective was done to improve Canada's defences or military capability. A Canadian Defence Commission, created in 1885 as a result of pressure by the British Colonial Defence Committee, never got beyond the stage of collecting and calendaring all the important relevant documents. When Caron reported on its findings in 1888, he outlined what Canada had done for defence since 1867 by the establishment of the militia and of the military college; but he said that his immediate programme envisaged merely another commission of enquiry. The Governor-General succeeded in persuading the Macdonald government to agree instead to create a permanent defence committee on the lines of the British committee. However, this new organ (of which an RMC graduate with the Royal Engineers at Halifax, Lieutenant Lang,* was secretary) immediately withered through lack of proper terms of reference.[34] The basic reason for this inertia was that the Canadian government and people were engrossed with other activities and saw little reason to spend money on defence. In these circumstances the expansion of the military college was unlikely, whatever the quality of its commandants.

The most urgent problem at RMC was the shortage of barrack accommodation. In his last report (28 November 1885) Hewett had said that the commissioning of so many cadets into the British army had temporarily eased the pressure on space, but that if that relief had not come when it did, it would have been impossible to hold RMC entrance examinations in 1886. He had shown that the entry classes were increasing in size, and declared that if the proposed new barrack block were not commenced immediately, it would be necessary either to drop an annual examination from time to time or to reject an undue proportion of the candidates. He had also specified that the college needed a drill shed, quarters for two members of the senior staff and for two of the subordinate staff, a workshop, a bowling alley, and a rifle gallery; and he called for the replacement of the Stone Frigate's inadequate and dangerous hot-air heating apparatus by hot water or steam.[35]

A year later Oliver reported that a new heating system had now been installed in the Stone Frigate (but only in the corridors) and that an iron gate† had been placed at the outer entrance of the college. There had been complaints that the hospital in the basement of the educational block was,

---

*Lieutenant-Colonel John Irvine Lang-Hyde, C.M.G., O.B.E., F.R.G.S., formerly called Lang (1859–1940), was BSM in 1882–3 and won the sword of honour; commissioned in the RE, 1883, he was ADC to Lieutenant-General Sir Andrew Clarke, 1885–6, during which time he was employed to design defence works for Esquimalt; he later served in the Gold Coast and Nigeria; during World War I he was CRE, Newcastle-upon-Tyne.

†When the Memorial Arch was built this gate was removed to the other outer entrance to the east.

in addition to other deficiencies, full of overhead heating pipes. Oliver said that the government had approved the construction of a separate hospital building which would make the isolation of patients possible in the event of an epidemic. He repeated Hewett's plea for a new dormitory and in this he was supported by both the Deputy Minister and the GOC. The latter added that, even though the commissioning of cadets in the British army reduced the numerical strength of the college, intakes had led to doubling up in single rooms and to the use of the hospital accommodation as barracks.[36]

Plans for the proposed hospital were sent to the Department of Works in March 1887, and tenders were requested.[37] Some time later all the deposits were returned with the contracts not let, presumably because the bids were considered too high. George Kirkpatrick then told Caron that a dormitory was more urgently needed than an expensive hospital which would cost $25,000 merely to serve cadets with trifling ailments. Oliver confirmed this judgment.[38] Indeed by March 1889 seventy-five cadets were occupying accommodation that had been intended for fifty-nine; and the GOC said that if twenty-four recruits were admitted in the coming session some cadets would have to be billeted elsewhere. Deputy Minister Panet therefore got an architect to draw plans for a dormitory to house thirty-six cadets and an officer and his family; but he said it must not cost more than ten or twelve thousand dollars.[39]

Believing that the necessary dormitory was now assured, Cameron listed building priorities in his 1889 Report without again mentioning the need for barracks. He now put the hospital first. In second place he listed drill sheds, a modelling room, workshops, gun and artillery stores, a gymnasium, a bowling alley and a hockey "court." All these could be under one roof with a floor space of approximately 150 feet by 200. Thirdly he asked for a powder magazine.[40]

In 1890, $10,000 was included in the military college estimates for barrack accommodation;[41] but when plans for the proposed dormitory were sent to the college so that the site could be selected, Cameron declared them "to be quite incongruous with regard to style and material in connection with the existing premises, and also very defective in internal arrangements." The dormitory now being proposed was to be built of brick instead of limestone like the rest of the college buildings; and it had no plumbing. Cameron therefore refused to accept it. He called for a "general scheme embracing [all the requirements of the college as] a complete whole," and he stressed the urgent need for a separate hospital. As his refusal to accept an inferior dormitory led to protracted correspondence and inevitable delay, the appropriation automatically lapsed, but it was renewed from year to year and by 1892, $15,000 was included in the estimates for the dormitory. This amount was increased to $20,000 when a proviso that officers' quarters should be included had been added.[42] It was still probably not enough. By that time, however, serious developments of a different nature had made the construction of the dormitory in the near future unlikely.

Thus, despite the urgent need for more accommodation, no major construction was undertaken at the college under either Oliver or Cameron. Nothing new had been added at RMC since the observatory was built in 1885. A sand model for use in teaching tactics had been set up in a pre-college building;[43] but the weight of the sand soon caused damage to the floor and requests for a new model room were repeatedly turned down. Cameron therefore asked in 1890 for permission to build one with part of an appropriation for pontoons.[44] Almost the only additions in this period were a boardwalk (from the outer back gate to the inner gate) and a rough breakwater on the site of the old wharf. Electricity was considered but not introduced. However, some other changes were made: two tennis courts were constructed near the gymnasium; a building to lodge pontoons was erected; and a magazine was made or remade in old Fort Frederick which was later transferred to the care of the commandant of RMC for that particular purpose.[45] The major needs were not touched.

Two noteworthy exceptions to this story of procrastination and neglect must be examined. Within a few weeks of arriving in Kingston, Cameron had asked the government to buy a house in Kingston for his use as he had found that he could not lease one on a permanent basis. His brother-in-law, C. H. Tupper,* then put pressure on Caron who consulted Macdonald. The house Cameron had in mind was one on King Street that had belonged to the late Dr. Horsey.† It was said to have cost $25,000 when built and it was offered for sale at $15,000. Although a little nearer to the college than the houses in which Hewett and Oliver had resided, it was nevertheless some two miles away. Senator Michael Sullivan heard about the proposal and offered to buy the house and rent it to the government until a commandant's quarters was built on Point Frederick. This was some kind of political deal. Sullivan obviously wanted to get the house without having to compete for it in the open market; the advantage that was alleged to come to the government would be that it would not need to get parliamentary authority for a capital outlay and would not have to make a long-term commitment. Macdonald told Caron to go ahead.[46]

---

*Sir Charles Hibbert Tupper (1835–1927), at that time minister of Marine and Fisheries.
†This house, 157 King St. E., was later the residence of the area commander.

However, Sullivan must have been unwilling to pay the price fixed by an independent appraiser. The King Street House became government property.

When Caron was called upon to explain in the Commons how money had been obtained for the purchase of a commandant's house without specific appropriation, he said that the Minister of Justice had ruled that it would be proper to use unexpended portions of the RMC appropriation. On behalf of the Liberals, Sir Richard Cartwright strenuously objected to this "dangerous precedent."[47] The government had been noticeably less economical in this matter of a house for Tupper's son-in-law than it was in construction for cadet barracks. And a year later Caron spent a further $1,808.55 on alterations to the King Street house to meet Cameron's wishes because it was not in a completed condition when bought.[48]

A second instance in which Caron was prepared to undertake construction at the college was in the case of a favour he did for Dr. H. A. Bayne, the professor of chemistry at RMC. Bayne was a distinguished scientist who had organized a chemistry laboratory at the college and had recently taken on extra teaching because Oliver, having become commandant, was too busy. Bayne had also put the Department of Militia in his debt by undertaking the laborious testing of cartridges, powder, and silk cartridge bags that had been giving trouble.[49] When Major Kensington left his quarters in the grounds (the former commodore's house, now Hewett House, that had been rebuilt in 1875 as a commandant's residence) the building was divided into two parts. Offered quarters there, Bayne chose the part of the building that needed the least alteration to suit his needs; but he asked to have the drawing room enlarged to bring it out to the line of the main portion of the structure. Caron replied that, although he was anxious to avoid extra expense at the college, he would make an exception in this case because "as Professor of Chemistry you have given so much satisfaction that I am anxious to do what I can to make you comfortable."[50] Undoubtedly Bayne deserved whatever the Department of Militia could do for him; but the way in which Caron responded to his request, as also to the political pressure exerted on behalf of Cameron, contrasts strikingly with his lack of success in securing cabinet authority for major building projects of greater importance.

Staff problems proved to be almost as obstinate as the building programme. Oliver's work as commandant had prevented him from teaching the course in meteorology and astronomy in the observatory which had been built to provide opportunity for the cadets to use large instruments. Dr. Bayne, who had stood in for him, "took great pains" with it; but he died within a very short time. There were a great many civilian applications for Bayne's chair;[51] and J. A. Waddell* was appointed in 1886. Military appointments proved more difficult. About the same time as Bayne died, Major E. Raban† left to return to England. As professor of military engineering since 1883, Raban had shown himself to be a brilliant man and a fluent lecturer. He had gained public notice by blowing up an ice jam in the St. Lawrence River to open navigation a few days earlier than usual.[52] It proved much more difficult to replace him than to replace Bayne; and it was also hard to find officers when other military professors left in the following years. General Middleton, who went to England, was instructed to seek out suitable candidates.[53] But many who were approached refused to come to RMC.[54] Overseas service in areas where operations, and therefore promotions, were possible was more attractive.

At the same time the army regulations made it increasingly difficult to keep British officers who had proved effective staff members and who were willing to prolong their tours of duty. Major S. G. Fairtlough,‡ who had been a great success both as a teacher and a company commander, had personal reasons for wanting to stay in Canada. Deputy Minister Panet thought him one of the best officers that RMC had had and tried to keep him on. Fairtlough claimed that he was up with the latest artillery developments (for instance, that he knew as much about the guns of the new battleship, *Bellerephon*, as did those who handled them); and he asked to be employed at the college if he left the army. He said that he did not aspire to become commandant. But when he learned that if he were in Canadian employ he would lose his British army pension and that his wife would lose her right to a widow's pension, he decided instead to take a posting to India.[55]

When Major Edward Nash, RA, the professor of military history, administration, and law, left in 1889 it was some time before a replacement was found and Cameron had to teach artillery himself, a very unsatisfactory arrangement.[56] The War Office suggested that RMC should take an infantry officer but Caron insisted on an officer from the technical corps.[57]

*J. A. Waddell, B.A., PH.D., D.SC., professor of physics, chemistry, and geology, 1886–97.

†Brigadier-General Sir Edward Raban, K.C.B., K.B.E., RE (1850–1927), served against the Naga hill tribes, 1879–80; professor of military engineering, RMC, 1883–6; director of works at the Admiralty, 1895–1912, where he was employed on the construction of naval bases; a deputy director at the War Office in 1917.

‡Lieutenant-Colonel Samuel Gerrard Fairtlough, RA, instructor in mathematics and artillery, 1878–88; later served with distinction against Fodi-Silah, a slaver in Sierra Leone; died of fever there, 1894.

Eventually Major E. G. Edwards,* RA accepted the position. He proved to be quite satisfactory as a professor. However, he believed in the public ownership of property and of the means production and he decided to oppose John A. Macdonald in the Kingston riding. Edwards offered to drop the socialistic part of his platform if the Liberals would support him. When they decided to run their own man, there was a three-cornered fight. Macdonald at first told Caron to "take steps to quietly replace" Edwards who "need not know it now," but he soon changed his mind and said, "Don't act on this for the present." Edwards resigned from RMC; but in the election he polled only 29 votes against 1784 for Macdonald and 1301 for the Liberal.[58]

One possible solution for the staffing problem was to appoint graduates of RMC. Lieutenant A. H. Van Straubenzee, who had received the College's first commission in the Royal Engineers when Perry resigned it, had made a successful career in the British army. He was appointed instructor of military engineering at Kingston in 1886.[59] Ex-cadets Wurtele and Cochrane, who had taught at RMC as civilians (with militia commissions) for some years, were recommended by Caron for increases in salary if it could be done without raising the estimates.[60] Ex-cadets Percy Girouard† and Lieutenant J. I. Lang, RE, also applied for posts at the college. Girouard had not yet had enough experience; and the commandant thought Lang not fitted for the senior post for which he applied. Furthermore, when the Canadian Defence Committee became active, Lang's duties as secretary would take him away from the college too much. Professor Carr-Harris's consulting work for the Canadian Pacific Railway

---

*Major Eugene Eustace Gresley Edwards, RA, was professor of artillery and military law, 1 January 1890–2 August 1891. He apparently returned to England after he resigned and was on half pay from 11 April 1891 until 1915.

†Colonel Sir Edouard Percy Cranwill Girouard, K.C.M.G., D.S.O. (1867–1932), eldest son of Mr. Justice Girouard, graduated RMC, 1885; worked on construction on the CPR until he received one of the extra RE commissions offered in 1888; from Chatham he became traffic manager of the railways within the Royal Arsenal, Woolwich (1890–5) and published an article in the journal of the Royal United Service Institution (1891) which suggested the use of guns on railways for coastal defence; Kitchener chose him as director of railways in the Egyptian army and to build 588 miles of railway to support the Sudan campaign, 1896; president of the Egyptian state railways, 1898, director of military railways in South Africa, 1899–1902, and commissioner of railways in the Transvaal and Orange River Colony, 1902–4; in 1907 Winston Churchill appointed him high commissioner of the Protectorate of Northern Nigeria and in 1909 he became governor and commander-in-chief; his administration protected native rights against European speculators but in East Africa, 1909–12, where conditions were different, he facilitated white settlement; during the war he became director-general of munitions supply and afterwards was a director of Armstrong, Whitworth and Co. (Major G. G. M. Carr-Harris, "The Girouard Story," *R.M.C. Review* XLII (1961), 185–95; *ibid.*, XIII (Dec. 1932), 74.)

was not regarded as a parallel and was therefore not considered to be a precedent for permitting Lang to have outside interests. Neither Lang nor Girouard was appointed.[61] The policy of appointing graduates who had experience in the British army was, however, continued with marked success. Thus in 1895 the Royal Engineers sent two ex-cadets to staff the military engineering department. Captain Philip Geoffrey Twining,* RE, who had graduated in 1883, became professor of fortification, military engineering, drawing, and descriptive geometry and he had as his assistant, Lieutenant William Breck Lesslie,† who had graduated in 1888.[62]

Meanwhile Cameron had proposed a rearrangement of the college courses to concentrate each professor's teaching in the subjects closest to his special knowledge and to eliminate situations in which junior teachers were responsible to several different professors. Some changes were made but new appointments to complete the arrangement would have increased the budget and were therefore rejected by the Minister.[63] Cameron then suggested a more modest addition, a re-arrangement of the curriculum and staff most significant for the future. He proposed to use civilians to teach subjects previously taught by army officers until such time as officers could be obtained. Cameron argued that there was no reason why a teacher of subjects like astronomy and mechanics should not be a civilian. In 1890, Iva Martin‡ was appointed on a year-to-year basis to teach mathematics.[64] Instruction in professional military subjects was, of course, still given by officers.

A source of staff dissatisfaction was that, apart from the turnover of British army officers, there was little change in the staff and therefore little prospect of promotion. Furthermore, Caron's chief concern in all RMC staff problems was that nothing should increase his estimates. When the staff-adjutant, Major McGill§ applied for an increase in pay, Caron re-

---

*Major-General Sir Philip Geoffrey Twining, K.C.M.G., C.B., RE (1862–1920), graduated RMC, 1893; instructor and professor in military engineering, 1895–9; director of fortifications and works, War Office, 1918–20.

†Brigadier-General William Breck Lesslie, C.B., C.M.G. (1868–1942), BSM, 1887–8; commissioned RE; professor of military engineering, RMC 1895–9; Cdr 1st Australian Infantry Brigade.

‡Iva Everard Martin (1863–1951), professor of mathematics, mechanics, and astronomy, RMC, 1890–1920; director of studies, 1917–22; graduated first in his class in physics in the University of Toronto, 1886; university fellow and examiner, 1886–7; Auditor-General's Office, 1887–90; chairman of the Kingston Board of Education, governor of the General Hospital, director of the Canadian Club.

§Lieutenant-Colonel Sydenham Clitheroe McGill, second son of the Honourable Peter McGill (president of the Bank of Montreal and speaker of the Legislative Council of Canada), gazetted an ensign in the Royal Canadian Rifle Regiment, 1859; a captain when the regiment disbanded, 1870; he commanded the depot at Prince Arthurs' Landing during the Red River expedition; Cheshire Regiment, 1872–3; Canadian militia cavalry, 1876; staff-adjutant RMC, 1883–1900.

called that he had taken the position on the understanding that he would receive $1200 per annum and that there would be no prospect of an increase in salary. Later McGill was recommended for $1600 on the grounds that he was an efficient officer and next in seniority to Cameron; but probably his greatest asset and what got him the extra money was that he was supported by George Kirkpatrick, the local Conservative party boss.[65] The Reverend K. L. Jones and Dr. Duval, who taught English and French respectively, wanted an increase from $1000 to $2000 to bring them more into line with the other professors who received $2500.[66] Cameron claimed that with his revised establishment it would be possible to freeze salaries (which had been fixed by statute when the college was opened but had had to be exceeded)* and that new junior appointees should be made to understand at the time of their engagement that they could not hope for an increase in salary or for chairs that became vacant.[67]

By contrast with the difficulty in securing staff, applications for cadet-ships were at first plentiful. Oliver wrote three reports during the slightly more than two years that he was commandant and in the second two he said that interest in the college was growing and the quality of the recruits was improving.[68] From 1885 to 1888 twenty-four cadets were admitted each year.[69] But in 1889 and 1890 Cameron complained that (presumably to keep the numbers up) the examining board had admitted cadets who were deficient in mathematics, a fact which not only impeded their progress but also that of their classmates.[70] However, the number of applicants was now large enough to permit a stricter application of the regulations about age and residence in Canada though there were still occasional exceptions.[71] An Indian boy sponsored by the Indian Department was refused admittance because he was over the age limit;[72] and applicants who fell short of the required residence qualification were ruled inadmissible,[73] but General Middleton's son was admitted although his father had not yet been in Canada five years.[74] Middleton told the Duke of Cambridge that he sent his son to RMC because it was "one of the best considered institutions in the world and the cost wonderfully small."[75]

Caron's chief concern was to see that the college did not cost the government too much. In 1888 there had been a complaint in parliament that RMC gave a "free" education to gentlemen's sons. Kirkpatrick retorted that the most prominent cadets had been the sons of working farmers. But the Minister raised the fees for board and tuition from $100 to $200 per annum. With other charges it now cost $400 for the recruit year and $350 thereafter.[76] There was some grumbling, especially from

*Legislation was introduced in 1893 to amend the RMC Act to legalize salaries that had actually been paid since 1876 (House of Commons, *Debates*, I (1893), 3496).

those whose sons had already taken the examinations for entry. These recruits were therefore exempted for the first year.[77] In the long run the effect of higher fees was to restrict the number who tried the examinations; and decreased competition tended to lower the average quality of those who passed. This was a potential source of trouble.

The most serious problem arising from the growth of the number of applicants was that cadets from Ontario and from English-speaking Quebec proved to be better qualified. They therefore secured an increasing proportion of the places. As a result there were complaints from the Maritime provinces. The question was taken up by C. H. Tupper who was told by Caron that the examination was an open competition across Canada and not by province, and that entrance was strictly on academic merit. Adjutant-General Walker Powell then explained to Tupper how the process of selection worked.[78]

The weakness of recruits in mathematics suggests that there were deficiencies in the system of selection or in the quality of the applicants. There seems to have been some disagreement among the authorities as to what constituted the best system. Middleton had supported Cameron's request that higher qualifications in mathematics should be required, but Walker Powell claimed in 1890 that "the literary competitions for cadetships" were better than any other method of selection and he justified his statement by asserting that failures in promotion had been reduced to a minimum.[79]

To assess the soundness of these conflicting views about entrance requirements, it is necessary to investigate the standing of college cadets at this time. One of the effects of so many cadets going into the British army in 1885 had been that the top classes were seriously depleted. Competition fell away and the quality of cadets' work suffered.[80] In 1887 almost every professor reported adversely on the third class (those in their second year). They were described by various professors as "a very poor class," "not very bright *in toto*," and "indifferent at the top to very bad at the bottom"; and they only received praise ("doing very good work") in French and drawing.[81] It is possible that this decline in the quality of this particular class was in part caused by the poor example shown by the seniors who had remained behind. However, by the time this same supposedly poor class graduated in 1889 its results were very similar to those of classes in other years and Cameron praised it.[82] Although some had failed or had dropped a year behind, it seems that either the class had pulled itself together or that the standard had been lowered. The difficulties which the college experienced in the next few years suggest that the latter explanation may be the true one. In fact it was known in Canada that the War Office had already complained in the spring of 1889, before this class graduated, that the RMC graduates it had received from the class of 1888 were not up to previous standards.[83]

The probable explanation is that they had been selected from lower down the class list, but a change in the regulations from those of Hewett's day may also have helped to lower academic standards. In 1886 Oliver had introduced a modification to permit "excellence in one subject to counterbalance another" for promotion and graduation.[84] Although sound in intent, if this rule were administered too generously it could lead to lack of effort in difficult subjects. Cameron apparently believed that high marks proved the quality of the course and he did not realize that grades are merely symbols and can be manipulated. In his second report he noted that the number of honours cadets (those distinguished in seven subjects) was three times the average of preceding years and 66 per cent greater than in any year since the college opened;[85] and in 1892 he remarked on the continuation of the increase in honours graduates. But he noted that only one cadet, and then only by a few marks, had obtained distinction in mathematics.[86] The effect of Oliver's change in the rules and of the admission of cadets weak in mathematics had apparently had the inevitable consequence of lowering achievement in this important subject. The growth of the numbers of honours graduates was therefore not as healthy a sign as Cameron believed. It is perhaps a significant point that Cameron, who was small and slight in build (personal characteristics upon which hostile newspapermen delighted to comment), showed in each of his annual reports an extraordinary interest in the physical growth of individual cadets during their college career. He listed statistics of increases in height, weight, and chest measurements.[87] These were concrete gains that could not be denied. But the quality of the educational improvement was less easily established.

Cameron was oblivious to signs of deterioration in quality in the college, but he applied existing academic regulations firmly. When Cadets Burstall and Scarth failed their examinations in the second class in 1889, tremendous political pressure was brought to bear upon the commandant to secure their promotion. Burstall's failure (artillery) was admitted by his father, John Burstall, to be "through idleness [and] too much attention to amusements" and "to tennis and young ladies"; but the elder Burstall also complained that the college authorities had not warned the boy about his conduct until two weeks before the examination. He asked that his son be promoted or allowed to repeat. A Conservative in the Maritimes told Caron to "strain to the fullest every law or rule .... John Burstall is a true friend and has in the past used every effort in supporting our party"; and another wrote, "get General Cameron down and he will see some way out of the trouble. John Burstall worked their two coves as no one else did at our *two* elections." Burstall senior said, "tell Cameron if Harry takes after his father he will be a good hand at turning Grits into good Conservatives, a qualification which the son-in-law of so astute a politician as Sir Charles Tupper ought to appreciate highly." Cadet Harry Burstall claimed that John A. Macdonald himself had promised him that he would make an exception in his favour; and his mother, Fanny Bell Burstall, "an old Kingstonian," asking that no one should know she had written, pleaded with the Prime Minister to "put Harry back in College."

Cadet Scarth, who was the more serious failure, was the son of a Conservative MP, William B. Scarth, who was a personal friend of the Minister. Caron was very much distressed by the whole business.

But Cameron and Caron stood firm. Precedents were searched in the college records. Caron said there had been no exceptions to the regulations in his time as minister and that experience suggested that if Burstall and Scarth were promoted they would fail again and this would do them no good. At an earlier date two cadets had been permitted to write supplementary final examinations by the passage of a special order-in-council, but the cases of Burstall and Scarth were different in that they sought promotion. Cameron argued that to make exceptions in their cases would jeopardize the standards of the college. On 9 September 1889, Macdonald called a special cabinet meeting to discuss the two cases. Cameron and Caron were upheld but Burstall was offered a commission in "C" Battery in Victoria. Although he would have preferred the Mounted Police, he accepted it. It is noticeable that within a short time his father was writing again to ask another favour, namely that his son should be transferred to "A" Battery in Kingston.[88]

The letters on Burstall's behalf now in the Caron Papers not only show that the petitioners were astonishingly persistent in what they claimed was a righteous cause but also that their earnest pleas were mixed with a blatant assertion of claims based on political connection. However, it may be that Cameron had decided wrongly in one of these cases. For Burstall mended his ways and rose to be one of Canada's top soldiers in World War I.* Whether he would have learned his lesson if he had not been denied promotion at RMC, no one can say.

*This RMC failure was Lieutenant-General Sir Henry Burstall, K.C.B., K.C.M.G., C.M.G., C.B. (1870–1945) who served with the Yukon Force and in South Africa; he attended the Camberley Staff College and commanded the Royal Canadian Horse Artillery, 1907–11, the artillery in the Canadian Corps, 1914–16, and Second Division of the Canadian Expeditionary Force, 1916–18; quartermaster-General, 1919–20; inspector-general of the Canadian militia, 1920–8. He received the academic recognition that he had missed at RMC when Bishop's College gave him an honorary D.C.L.

William Hamilton Scarth, RMC (1887–9) became an inspector in the RNWMP, served in the South African War, and joined the South African Mounted Rifles.

Two years later Caron received a request of a similar nature from J. C. Patterson,* who was to become minister of Militia within a short time. This was for the promotion of another cadet who had failed and who claimed illness as an excuse. Caron again refused the request on the grounds that the failure was too serious.[89] Caron's stand against Conservative influence of this kind at RMC may have earned him enemies in the internecine struggles within his party which were to come when Macdonald died. Cameron also may have suffered as a result of antagonizing powerful people at a time when he was soon to need all the friends he could muster.

One source of potential support for RMC was the militia. As a result of their military interest, many of its members sent their sons to the college. However, the college competed with the militia for funds. The militia therefore needed careful fostering. In 1886 the college had inaugurated the long course for militia. The part held at RMC was of three months' duration. One of the first officers to take it was Major D. M. Vince of the Brighton Engineers who had asked for it five years before.[90] But in 1888 Oliver recommended the discontinuance of the volunteer engineer courses for NCOs and other ranks at RMC because they were a serious inconvenience and were a heavy load for the RMC staff. He said that if the militia engineer companies were supplied with tools they could undertake this training themselves. A year later Cameron similarly recommended discontinuing the short courses.[91] Any militia support for RMC which the long courses might have won was possibly offset by these recommendations to eliminate the short course. On the other hand it had now become regular practice for Royal Military College cadets to be attached to militia units during training camps, partly for the experience they could gain, but even more for the contribution they could make.[92] This would win friends for the college in some militia units.

Certain contemporary features of the college course and of college life also affected its popularity with cadets and potential applicants. The RMC equitation course which had begun only in 1881 came to a halt when the horses were taken away for the Northwest campaign. They were not immediately brought back when the troops returned. Oliver therefore arranged to hire horses locally.[93] The GOC proposed that a cavalry school be set up in Toronto with a detachment in Kingston to help train RMC cadets and militia officers on the long course,[94] but this was not done. In 1890 Cameron complained that the horses provided for riding were draught animals and were not suitable for the purpose. They balked at jumps. Riding was thus insufficiently and inadequately taught.[95]

*James Colebrooke Patterson, MP for North Essex; minister of Militia, 1892–5; lieutenant-governor of Manitoba, 1895–1900.

Sports, however, were increasing. In addition to cricket, football, and tennis, swimming was possible in early fall and late spring, and the college bought a thirty-foot sloop, *Yolande*, from Cadet Kirkpatrick when he graduated and left Kingston.[96] In winter the ice of the lake was a skating rink and playground. It has been claimed that ice hockey was invented in Canada by British army officers who had formerly played field hockey. Kingston, as one of the garrison towns, is a strong contender for the honour because Lake Ontario is a natural rink close to the heart of the city. The first formal game in Canada is said to have been played between Queen's College students and RMC cadets on the ice in the harbour in 1888.[97] A stick and cube-shaped puck from that game are now on display in the Queen's gymnasium. One year after that game the RMC commandant asked for the construction of a hockey "court."[98]

But of even greater importance for the future of the college was employment after graduation. Commissions in the British army remained the best military opportunities for RMC graduates; but so many were given in 1885, reaching down even into the second class, that when extra commissions in the Royal Artillery were offered by the War Office in 1886 only CSM Archibald Macdonell, a future RMC commandant, was willing to accept one.[99] Interest in imperial commissions had revived by 1888, especially in the Royal Engineers. Mrs. W. M. Lesslie, mother of the then BSM, noted that her son, W. B. Lesslie, would not get an RE commission because the second-in-command, Cadet Joly, had higher marks. She asked Caron to approach the War Office for extra commissions.[100] Perhaps in consequence there was again a list of extra British commissions, four in the Royal Engineers and two in the Royal Artillery, in addition to the usual four. The GOC said that this offer proved that the British government was satisfied with the RMC graduates it had commissioned earlier. He noted that there had been gratifying articles in the British press on the value of the college's contributions to the British army; and he proposed that cadets with a two-year military qualification certificate from RMC should be accepted for the British commissions that were now available for militia officers.[101] However, a belated announcement of more commissions in the Royal Engineers in that year "unsettled the cadets" because those who had earlier signified a willingness to accept one in the Royal Artillery would have preferred one in the Engineers where the pay was better. Oliver reported that out of thirteen graduates no fewer than ten wanted to enter the British army, two in the infantry, six in the engineers, and two in the artillery.[102] One graduate from a former class, who got an RE commission at this time through Caron's influence, was Percy Girouard.[103] He was to have the most distinguished career of all those many cadets who did well in the British army. In 1891 a commission in the Royal Army Service Corps was added but did not become an annual offering;[104] and in that year Major-General John Thacker, late of the Bombay Staff Corps, whose sons were at RMC, suggested that Kingston cadets ought to be put on a similar footing as Sandhurst cadets for appointments in the Indian Staff Corps.[105] Access to this corps was, however, not obtained for another five years when, following the practice in the other corps, one commission was offered annually to RMC.[106]

RMC's contribution to the British army was measured much more by its quality than by its numbers. In 1890 Lord Lorne spoke of the success of RMC graduates in the British army and said that a similar college was needed in Australia.[107] Several times during the 1880s Australian colonies had explored the possibility of duplicating the Canadian experiment. At the request of Queensland six copies of RMC regulations and of the instruction syllabus were sent to Brisbane.[108] In 1893 the Earl of Derby said that "for preparation for civil life and for military life," the education and training at the RMC now was "not excelled by any British or continental school."[109]

RMC graduates were now bringing honour to their *alma mater* by their courage and their ability. Thus, one of them, Huntley Brodie Mackay, who had been commissioned in the Royal Engineers, had served in Bechuanaland 1884–5, and as commanding royal engineer [CRE] in West Africa 1887–9, won the college's first DSO fighting tribes near Sierra Leone, and then became acting administrator of the British East Africa Company.* An ex-cadet, William Grant Stairs, also a Royal Engineer, was the first man chosen by Henry M. Stanley for an expedition to relieve Emin Pasha, who had been beleaguered in central Africa since the fall of Khartoum. Stanley invited him because he had been struck by the concise style and directness of Stairs' letter of application. On the expedition Stairs was wounded by a poisoned arrow and nearly died, but he carried on and shared with his comrades the most severe privations. A colleague, Dr. Mountjoy-Jephson, revealed something of Stairs' resourcefulness and fortitude when he recorded that, for their dinner on Christmas Day, Stairs proudly produced from the depths of his box a medicine bottle containing about a gill of whisky which he had secretly saved through all the starvation days. Henry S. Wellcome, the secretary of the testimonial banquet given Stanley on his return to the United States "after penetrating dismal forests and encountering ferocious savages," spoke of Stairs as a Canadian whom Stanley had praised for his skill in making geographical observations, for his generalship in command of small bodies of troops facing vastly superior forces, for his tact, and for his adroit

*Mackay died of fever in Mombassa in 1891.

strategems which won bloodless battles. New York newspaper correspondents wrote that this tall, fair, handsome, and unassuming young engineer officer blushed easily when praised and told his story in an entirely unaffected way. In Canada, Senator W. J. Macdonald asked Caron whether it would not be proper and possible to pass a parliamentary resolution expressing satisfaction for Stairs' manly conduct.[110] In 1892 Stairs was given the command of an expedition sent by King Leopold into Katanga; but he died soon afterwards at Chide on the Zambesi.

Another RMC graduate, William Henry Robinson, also served as CRE on the west coast of Africa (1889–92), and was killed when attempting to blow up the gate of a stockade at Tambi near Sierra Leone, the first ex-cadet to be killed in action. A fourth, Kenneth J. R. Campbell of the 6th Dragoon Guards, became deputy commissioner and vice-consul in the Oil Rivers District (Niger Coast Protectorate). For his part in an operation against the town of Brohemie,* he became the first ex-cadet to be "mentioned in despatches." These Canadian RMC cadets thus won fame for their contribution to the expansion of the British empire when (in Campbell's words) "Britain true to [her] instincts annexed the Oil Rivers, the largest and best share of that part of West Africa, but with a feeling that we should have had all and 'what do these foreigners mean by taking any at all,' "[111] words which show the strength of imperial sentiment prevailing in many quarters of Canada at that time.

Some cadets would have preferred military service in and for Canada,[112] but there were few openings for them. When an uncle of Cadet Carpenter applied for a permanent force commission for his nephew, the Minister told Macdonald: "We laid down as a policy, I think, the appointment of cadets as much as possible to our Permanent Corps. They are more efficient I need not say and if this rule were invariably followed it would, I think, give better results." However, Caron promised that he would not appoint cadets to the military staff without first informing Macdonald.[113]

When in 1891 Cameron enquired about the possibility of appointments for RMC graduates in either the Permanent Force or the Mounted Police, his application was supported by the new GOC, Major-General Herbert,† who was determined to reform the Canadian militia. Caron's reply, transmitted through the Deputy Minister, was that this was a matter which must

---

*Campbell afterwards became acting commissioner and consul general in the Protectorate. He won the Royal Humane Society's bronze medal for rescuing a native from a crocodile-infested river. He commanded the naval brigade in the relief of Peking during the Boxer rebellion and also served as a colonel in World War I.

†Ivor John Caradoc Herbert, later Baron Treowen, C.B., C.M.G. (1851–1933) was major-general and GOC of the Canadian militia, 1890–5; an officer in the Grenadier Guards, he had served in Egypt in 1882 and as military attaché at St. Petersburg.

be settled by the whole government.[114] In 1893, when Caron had left the department and the Permanent Force was being organized, John Burnham, Conservative MP for Whitby, enquired about a commission in the Permanent Force for his son who was in his graduating year at RMC. He said that even if the son was eligible for a British commission he did not want him to have one. After a delay of four and half months the request was put to the cabinet and was then "filed for reference in case of need."[115] Caron's explanation in 1891 for the failure to give preference to RMC graduates for militia staff commissions was that it would be unfair to militia officers who had borne the brunt of hard times which some graduates had not had to face.[116] The obvious conclusion that can be drawn is that the government, which was reluctant to increase the size of the Permanent Force, was unwilling to earmark for RMC the few permanent commissions that it had at its disposal lest it thereby arouse opposition in the militia.

Faced with this problem, the commandants and even the British commander of the militia sought to find outlets for RMC graduates in civil occupations. In 1887 General Middleton said that the government should provide employment for RMC graduates. "The want of such employment sends men out of the Dominion." But he thought this was not all loss. Sooner or later they would return "with increased and valuable experience" which would be an asset to Canada.[117] All that could be expected, however, was that the government would consider RMC applicants favourably for public service positions. To have given the graduates from the college automatic employment would have aroused political opposition. The chief difficulty was, of course, that employment by the government was dispensed as patronage by the party in power.

In these circumstances it was imperative to stress subjects in the college that would help to prepare graduates for private civilian occupations. It was therefore necessary to gain recognition for the RMC course and to make arrangements for further specialized education where necessary. Alexander Morris,* the chairman of the Board of Queen's College and a member of the Ontario legislature, talked to Principal G. M. Grant and Colonel Oliver in 1887 about arrangements for the recognition of the military college course as a step towards degrees in arts and engineering in the universities. He said that such recognition in arts would permit an RMC graduate in Ontario to be called to the bar in three years instead of five. Recognition in engineering would enable RMC graduates to obtain the status of civil engineers. He added that Canadian university degrees were

*Alexander Morris (1826–89), lieutenant-governor of Manitoba and the North-West Territories, 1872–7 and MLA, Ontario, 1878–86; a member of Queen's College Board of Trustees, 1880–5 and its chairman, 1883–5.

recognized by the British universities. Morris' proposal was unofficial and he did not suggest how much credit should be given by the universities for the RMC course. A pencilled comment on a sheet attached to this letter in the Caron Papers asked whether the universities could do this and yet be consistent with their charters.[118]

RMC's quest for recognition of its status and function in the civilian educational and professional world meant that greater emphasis would be placed on its contribution to the civil life and development of Canada and also on the academic elements in its curriculum. At the same time the quality of its military training and of its education in military technology had to be maintained because of its small, but significant, contribution to imperial defence through graduates who went into the British army and because of the potential, but as yet only slightly exploited, professional influence that it exerted over the Canadian militia and therefore on the defence of Canada. The college was now well integrated into the social and political life of the Kingston community. The gentlemen cadets, being at an impressionable age, helped to make that connection more permanent by the extent to which they married into Kingston families. Through the publicity given to the exploits of some of its graduates in distant Africa, but also through the acrimony developed in public criticism and debate in the press and in parliament, RMC was becoming known nationally and even throughout the British empire. But the college continued to operate at little more than half of its proposed strength. Within two or three years of Cameron's arrival as commandant it had become obvious that the check to RMC development dating from Macdonald's return to power in 1878 was likely to be prolonged. As in all defence matters in Canada, the root of the problem was apathy growing out of a sense of security. A secondary cause was that the college had become increasingly involved in politics. The serious effects of this apathy and of this political involvement were soon to be revealed.

6

POLITICS

"RECRUITING"

AND DECLINE, 1891-1896

Six months after the *Ottawa Citizen* criticized the appointment of Cameron in 1886, the *Toronto Daily Mail* carried an article signed "Not a graduate but a friend" which declared that the Militia Department was giving military appointments to supporters of the government and that Canada was not making use of RMC graduates but was allowing them to go elsewhere, including the United States. In support of claims for the good quality of the college cadets, the writer of his letter quoted Major-General John W. Laurie, second-in-command of the Northwest expedition and a Conservative MP, and Lieutenant-General Sir Frederick Middleton, the GOC. Another anonymous letter in the *Militia Gazette* signed "Paterfamilias" developed the same theme but with greater bitterness. Then on 1 December, 1888 the *Woodstock Sentinel Review* argued that "unless some responsible proportion of these graduates can be retained in the service of Canada, the College ought to be abolished. ... What is wanted, however, is not the abolition of the Military College but a radical reform of the motives and methods by which the Department of Militia is at present managed."[1]

One of the leaders in what soon appeared to be an organized political campaign was L. Homfray Irving, a member of the Old Eighteen and a founding member of the RMC Club, who allegedly admitted that because the government as a whole was too strong, its opponents had planned to sow discord among its supporters by personal attacks on Caron.[2] But the Minister was not without his defenders. Colonel George T. Denison, claiming that he was under no obligation to the Militia Department, told Caron that he was determined to defend him against the "Liberals' Treason and Yankee plotting." He accused the "Grits" of attempting to stir up racial controversy and he declared that every man who went on the Northwest expedition was indebted to the Minister because, as he said, "you looked after us." He went on: "Since then you have withstood the General's attempt to increase the Permanent Force of drones at the expense of the Militia and the Country."[3] This statement suggests the way in which opinion in the country about military questions was aligned with party strife. On the whole the Conservatives supported the militia. The Liberals accordingly tended to be for RMC and even for the idea of a professional force. But these lines were not very clearly drawn. Many Conservative leaders sent their sons to RMC; and there were many Liberals in the militia. And the Liberals, of course, were prepared to attack the Conservatives' administration of the college for the sake of political gain.

Controversy flared up in 1889 when it was alleged that recommendations for imperial commissions were being given on political grounds.[4] A large number of Canadian newspapers joined in the debate; and the English periodicals, the *Army and Navy Gazette* and the *Broad Arrow*, described this as a "little war" in Canada.[5] In the course of this newspaper war the *Canadian Military Gazette* attributed an attack on the Militia Department, which was signed "Canadian," to Major-General Oliver. When this allegation was brought to his attention, the former RMC commandant, now in retirement in England, wrote to Caron to deny all knowledge of the authorship of that letter or of any other correspondence to the press.[6] Caron, courtly as ever, replied promptly that he had never for one moment believed that Oliver had written the "Canadian" letter and was well aware that he would not have countenanced such anonymous publications.[7] The Minister must have known that it was the opposition in Canada that was behind these criticisms of the way in which the college was developing.

When the militia estimates came up in April 1889, Sir Richard Cartwright associated this press attack on Caron with his action in appointing Cameron commandant. Cartwright and Alfred Jones, a former Liberal minister of militia, vigorously criticized the selection of a retired artillery officer, instead of an active-list engineer, to command RMC. After reciting all the objections to the appointment, Cartwright said that it was idle for Caron to deny that the commandant had been chosen on political grounds. He said that in his view the only way to keep politics out of the college was to ask the British government to send an officer "of their own selection." Caron claimed that he could not remember whether the proposal to appoint Cameron had been initiated by the Canadian government or by the War Office; and he categorically denied that any other officer had been recommended. Cartwright, who probably knew that this was false, sceptically expressed a hope that Cameron would discharge his duties in a satisfactory manner.[8] When the final vote on the item was taken, a formal Liberal amendment condemning the purchase of the comman- dant's house as inexpedient and as a misappropriation of public funds was defeated by the Conservative majority on division.[9]

The opposition next sought to have the operation of the college offi- cially investigated. In the following session Dr. J. M. Platt, Liberal mem- ber for Prince Edward county and a militia officer, asked when the RMC Board of Visitors had last met. He was told by the Minister that it was in 1881.[10] Implying that there had been favouritism at RMC in the distri- bution of the British army commissions, Platt then requested the publica- tion of the college's examination results. Macdonald construed this as an attack on his government, rather than on the college, as indeed it was.[11]

Three months later Platt drew attention to Cameron's proposed re- organization of RMC. He said that it would reduce the number of "respon- sible professorships which must be held by military men from five to two"; and he asked whether the government intended to carry out these "extra- ordinary changes." When Caron replied that the government had not yet had time to consider the Commandant's Report, Frederick C. Denison asked whether the government intended to appoint a board of visitors. The Minister's reply was a masterpiece of diversion. Without admitting that the board had not met in recent years, he said: "There is a Board of Visitors which has been in existence almost since the College was started." Challenged again later on the subject, he declared that, as the college was under the GOC who inspected it regularly, the board had not been found necessary.[12]

However, before these questions had been asked in the house, General Middleton had urged Caron to assemble the board and to include on it two members of the House of Commons.[13] Later that year the board visited RMC for the first time in a decade. It consisted of four militia staff officers, the Adjutant-General, Colonel Walker Powell, Colonel Gzowski, Colonel Theodore Juchereau Duchesnay,* and Colonel W. D. Otter,† along with a local Conservative member of parliament, Kirkpatrick. Its

---

*Lieutenant-Colonel Theodore Juchereau Duchesnay, a member of a French- Canadian military family, became a lieutenant in the 100th Prince of Wales' Royal Canadians in 1858 and transferred to the 25th King's Own Borderers in 1860. After service in England and Gibraltar he became brigade major in the Canadian militia at Rivière du Loup in 1862 and CO of Military District No. 7 in 1876.

†General Sir William Dillon Otter, K.C.B., C.M.G., C.V.O. (1843–1929) joined the Canadian militia in 1861 and served during the Fenian raids; he became commandant of the School of Infantry in December 1883 and commanded the centre column during the campaign in the Northwest, 1885; chief of the Canadian General Staff, 1908–10 and inspector-general, 1910–12; director of internment operations during World War I.

report[14] was a whitewash. It declared that the college was "a useful and necessary institution that is providing such an education as is now needed, and that the graduates emitted from year to year will carry with them and retain for future use, all the military knowledge it is possible to provide under the existing circumstances." The board took note that there had been criticism of the inclusion of military subjects in the RMC curriculum. Opponents had suggested that these were more appropriate in countries where there were large standing armies. The board's view was that "for many reasons the amalgamation of subjects was and is a necessity. ... It is no impediment to an officer if he possess the power of applying in time of need the fund of useful knowledge he may acquire in civil life after he graduates." The visitors said that the college was, as its name implied, a military one, but that it also had a civil object. "It could never have fulfilled the purpose for which the existing education is required if it had been a Civil College having also a Military side."

RMC policy was in fact to maintain the principle of teaching civil subjects in a predominantly military college, to seek recognition for the civil education that was given, and to prepare RMC graduates for civilian, as well as military, careers. Oliver had therefore opened negotiations with the professional societies and the universities in 1888.[15] A stumbling block in the case of the Ontario Law Society was that the RMC course lacked Latin. Oliver proposed that, as Latin had been required for entry to the college, a smattering could be given to polish it up. He suggested that the professor of English might teach it.[16] However, in 1891, without Latin being introduced, the Ontario Law Society laid down terms on which RMC graduates would be admitted to the bar. They were placed on a par with university graduates. Passing the obligatory and voluntary entrance examination and the college's first-year examination exempted cadets from matriculation; graduation reduced the period of study required of them from four to three years.[17] The Medical Council of Ontario similarly relieved RMC graduates of the need to take its matriculation examination.

In 1887 the Ontario legislature had included RMC graduates, along with those of the Toronto School of Practical Science and of McGill College, among those for whom apprenticeship for a land surveyor's certificate would be shortened by one year.[18] In 1892 Professors Carr-Harris and Mayne* called the attention of the GOC to a bill in the Ontario legislature to amend conditions for the certification of land surveyors in the

---

*Major Charles Blair Mayne, RE, professor of surveying, military topography, and reconnaissance, 1886-93; he was described by General Cameron as a "man whose versatility and ever active unselfish zeal" won many friends outside the college; assistant director of fortifications and works at the War Office, 1905-7.

province. The federal Minister of Militia, Mackenzie Bowell, wrote to the provincial legislature and received in return a letter from the president of the Ontario Land Surveyors' Association defining its position on the question. The gist of this argument was that theoretical training was not enough.[19] However, the Ontario government continued to place RMC graduates on the same level as the graduate engineers of the Ontario School of Practical Science, exempting them from matriculation, and requiring of them only one year's apprenticeship in place of three. In 1894 the province of Quebec followed the dominion and Ontario in recognizing the RMC course for the purposes of certification for land survey work.[20] The Canadian government was able to utilize this part of the RMC training in 1894 when the GOC ordered a survey of parts of eastern Canada along the border with the United States. He obtained the services of the RMC professor of engineering, Captain A. H. Lee,* and a party of graduating cadets to do the work. Although the survey was not contoured and was not of great accuracy, it was much more than an exercise; and it helped to train RMC cadets for careers as surveyors.

By this time the number of RMC graduates practising civil engineering was already impressive. In answer to a question in the House of Commons in 1891, it was noted that fifty-one graduates of the college as of that date had been listed as employed in that profession in Canada; and six more had been commissioned in the Permanent Force and were "liable to perform Military Engineering [at] any time."[21] In 1893 the staffs of the militia schools were organized as a regiment of infantry and a regiment of cavalry to constitute the first permanent units in Canada. On 29 March 1894 William Mulock,† Liberal MP for North York, asked how many students had joined RMC since 1876, how many had graduated, how many were in the public service of Canada, and how many were in the service of the imperial government. He also asked further questions about the cost of the college, its present size, about the commandant, about his salary, and what had been spent on his house.[22] When answering most of these

---

*Arthur Hamilton Lee, Lord Lee of Fareham, P.C., G.C.B., G.C.S.I., G.B.E. (1867–1947); as a lieutenant in the Royal Artillery, he was professor of military history, surveying, military topography, reconnaissance and tactics at RMC, 1893–6 and was a local captain in the militia; a very personable and able young man, he was a popular lecturer on military subjects; he organized the military survey of the Canadian border, 1894–6; he retired from the army in 1900, was a military correspondent in Cuba, and a member of parliament; first lord of the Admiralty, 1921–2 and British representative at the Washington Conference, 1921–2. (T. L. Brock, "Lord Lee of Fareham: Professor of Strategy and Tactics, R.M.C., 1893–98," *R.M.C. Review*, XLIII (1962), 159–65.)

†William Mulock, QC, vice-chancellor of the University of Toronto, 1881 and Liberal MP for North York, 1882; he became postmaster-general in 1896.

questions on 10 April, the Minister of Militia said his department did not have records to show how the graduates were being used. Within less than a month Captain Ernest F. Wurtele,* the secretary of the Royal Military College Club of Canada was able to furnish the department with the required information. Since the opening of the college, 379 recruits had been accepted of whom 363 actually joined and 195 graduated. Twelve cadets and ex-cadets had died and the careers of sixty-two were not known. Sixty-five had not yet left the college. Of the remainder, both graduates and non-graduates, eighty-four had joined the British army or colonial forces and police, ten had joined the Canadian Permanent Force, ten the North-West Mounted Police, nineteen the various public services of the dominion and provinces, and four the RMC staff. Seventy-two others were in engineering, mines, railways, and architecture. Twelve were in business or financial houses, four were in law (three of them as students), four were farmers, there was one in each of the church and medicine, and one was a university student.[23]

Of the ex-cadets thus listed for every one who was in either the Canadian Permanent Force or the public service of Canada, there were two in the imperial service and two more employed privately on various kinds of engineering projects in Canada. If the aim expressed at its founding, to contribute in a secondary way to the development of Canada, had been intended to include private employment as civil engineers, RMC was making a significant contribution in that respect and also an equal contribution to the British army. But it was not being fully used by the dominion government for defence purposes. However, the number of those who had gone into business, law, and other such professions was only about half of the small number employed by Canada. The small size of this business group suggests that there was no serious departure from the college's proper function, especially as these ex-cadets were all available in emergency.

On 23 May 1894 Captain Wurtele requested the Department of Militia to secure the recognition of the RMC diploma by what he called the Institution of Civil Engineers of Canada on an equal footing with those of other educational establishments. This was referred to the Commandant who was instructed to prepare a statement about the curriculum which Wurtele had said would be required.[24] The Canadian Society of Civil Engineers had been set up in 1887; but according to the British North America Act

*Lieutenant-Colonel Ernest Frederick Wurtele, v.d. (1860–1936), graduated RMC, 1882; engineer, accountant, and militia officer; retired 1917 when in command of the 19th Infantry Brigade; honorary secretary-treasurer of the RMC Club, 1892–1913, and editor of its *Proceedings*; associate editor *R.M.C. Review* for ex-cadet news, 1926–36; first honorary member of the RMC Club.

the registration of engineers is primarily a provincial concern. Recognition by the dominion body had therefore only a limited value. Furthermore the provinces and the provincial universities might be affected by RMC's intrusion into this sphere. Wurtele's request therefore provided a weapon with which the Liberals could attack the government.

Mulock, as vice-chancellor of the University of Toronto, took exception to the development of non-military education in RMC on the grounds that it was a contravention of Parliament's purpose in founding the military college in 1874 which he declared was "to provide properly qualified persons to take charge of the professional corps, not to educate persons in a general way for the ordinary affairs of life." In the debate on the RMC vote on 29 June he protested that education of the latter kind was within the exclusive jurisdiction of the various provinces. He complained of the high cost of the college and he noted that appointments in the Permanent Force were not kept for its graduates but were given to unqualified individuals for political reasons. He said that in 1878 it had been promised that RMC graduates would get preference in the Permanent Force, but this had never been fulfilled. It would be better, he thought, to send young men destined for the British army to the old established military colleges in England rather than that the object for which RMC had been founded should be perverted.

In reply the Minister, J. C. Patterson, argued that when Mackenzie founded the college he had intended to give the cadets an education that would make them useful in civil life and at the same time provide a reserve of military professional experience in case of emergency. He claimed that his department did give preference to RMC cadets for the Permanent Force and also that it employed them without respect to political connections; but he noted that if RMC were given the monopoly of all permanent commissions this would actually not amount to more than two a year. He said sarcastically that he was sure that his opponents did not want him to make a substantial increase in the Permanent Force merely to find military occupation for the graduates of the college. He claimed that the *per capita* cost of the professors at RMC was no higher than the cost of professors at the University of Toronto but that the former worked harder since they had a ten months' session and were tutoring cadets from early morning until ten o'clock at night.[25]

By this time the college had become involved in patronage in other ways than its failure to get militia commissions. Political influence, favours, even bribes, were barely concealed. A letter in the Caron Papers from Gooderham Ltd. which says that a case of whiskey was on the way to the Minister[26] without mentioning a bill suggests the extent to which such practices were taken for granted. RMC jobs automatically went to

Conservatives and the government kept a "preferred list" of firms from which supplies must be bought.[27]

Party leaders in Ottawa tried to maintain that RMC patronage was not a local matter.[28] But Kingston was Macdonald's riding. Although he lost his seat there in 1878 to a Liberal Reformer, Alexander Gunn,* the Prime Minister retained a very lively interest in the administration of its patronage and sometimes personally intervened.[29] It was therefore not easy to distinguish national from local interests and pulls. Sir John himself rarely said "No" to a friend, or if he did he said it so obliquely that he managed to convey the idea that he had said "Yes"; and all competing cliques argued their case on what they alleged to be Sir John's interests or Sir John's wishes.[30] At times there was even doubt about who was on which side politically. G. A. Kirkpatrick, the local party leader, protested that one firm which regularly supplied RMC had consistently opposed Macdonald at all elections.[31] Conversely, Caron sometimes thought that Liberals were getting RMC business. He told Oliver on one occasion: "I do not wish to bring any political pressure to bear but think that with your usual tact you can quietly tell [Major] McGill [the Staff Adjutant] that he is not to go out of his way to help Grits who certainly never would have appointed him to the position which he occupies."[32] A Kingston correspondent declared that Major William King, the local superintendent of stores in Kingston, was a Liberal and "should be stopped giving his friends patronage that don't belong to them."[33] When elections came near, demands for patronage, and friction between Conservative cliques, increased.[34] Macdonald won back Kingston from Gunn in 1887, but only by seventeen votes out of a total count of over 2700.

Inevitably conflicts and abuses multiplied. Firms on the preferred list systematically overcharged;[35] Conservative newspapers assumed that they could copy advertisements from other papers and simply send a bill to the government; Kingston newspapers thought that if advertisements were placed in other cities, Kingston should not be left out;[36] and local party hacks thought they should be employed even though, as in one case, it could be said that "he does not work every day, nor ever when bad weather occurs and ... physically he is not able to do a proper day's work ... ."[37] Cameron, being a political appointment himself, was in no position to take a firm stand even if he had wanted to do so, which is doubtful. Caron's efforts to decide between competing cliques within the party, and to prevent the most flagrant of abuses,[38] probably resulted only in the loss of friends in the difficult days ahead when he was himself charged with corruption. The net result was that RMC was increasingly besmirched with political mire.

*Alexander Gunn, a mason and contractor, Liberal MP for Kingston, 1878–87.

The situation was more serious when the politicians reached out to influence the control of teaching appointments with which, in the very early days, they had not interfered to any great extent. Just before the crucial election of 1891, George Kirkpatrick received a short list of eight applicants for the professorship of English being vacated by the Reverend Mr. Jones. He picked out two, the Reverend Clarendon Worrell,* whose brother J. A. Worrell was a prominent Conservative, and Mr. Robert Marshall, the editor of the Conservative Kingston *Daily News.* Caron liked the look of Worrell and he got the job.[39] He proved to be satisfactory; but the method by which he was appointed could, of course, lead to future trouble.

The most important result of political involvement at RMC was the strengthening of the opposition to the Commandant. The War Office held that as Cameron was a retired officer he was out of touch with modern developments; and British officers in Canada distrusted him because of his political connections. Day-to-day administration of the college had hitherto come under the adjutant-general, presently a militia officer who had formerly been in parliament. Major policy decisions had been handled by the deputy minister who also had political associations, but professional British soldiers believed that civilian control in Canada inevitably meant political interference in military matters. Therefore General Herbert, who came as GOC in 1890, decided to take the direction of the college over from the Adjutant-General and, by concerning himself more with its affairs than had any of his predecessors, to lessen the Deputy Minister's supervision. The GOC was able to do this because he was ex-officio president of the college. In 1894 Herbert protested against an order that the Commandant should address all his letters to the Adjutant-General to be dealt with by the GOC "as each case may require." He saw this as a means of emphasizing the Deputy Minister's authority, and argued that as the college was a military institution it should not be under the control of a civilian.[40] However, by the end of that year the Commandant was again communicating directly with the Deputy Minister.[41] Herbert's assumption of control over RMC on the grounds that it was a military institution had thus been effectively rejected, either because it weakened the Canadian government's hold over the college, or, as the British soldiers no doubt thought, because Cameron and the politicians disliked it. The attempt to lift the college above politics had thus failed.

*The Right Reverend Clarendon Lamb Worrell (1854–1934) held various curacies and rectories in Ontario; principal of Brockville Collegiate Institute, 1882–4; professor of English literature at RMC, 1891–1904; rector of St. Marks' Barriefield, 1891–1903. Appointed bishop of Nova Scotia in 1904, archbishop in 1915, he was primate of all Canada, 1930.

This failure had the unfortunate effect of making some influential military men doubt its value.

Meanwhile events inside the college had attracted unfavourable public attention. It has been seen that in the days of the Old Eighteen there was apparently no system of "recruiting," a term used at RMC to mean the systematic and organized disciplining of first-year cadets by their seniors. R. W. Leonard,* stating in 1893 that "fagging and hazing and such child-like practices" were unknown when he was a cadet, described his own initiation in 1879. Five days after he joined, a senior imitated the sergeant-major's voice and ordered him to parade with the rest of the recruit class. The recruits were marched into the coal cellar and left there in total darkness. Then they were brought one at a time before a "court" consisting of "titled dignitaries of European and African armies" appropriately garbed. The trial was humorous and punishments, if any, were slight.[42]

What had been harmless fun tended in the course of time to grow into something quite different. The cadet victory in the Ridout-Ferguson incident in 1881 had helped to foster a growing sense of power and independence in the senior classes. By 1888 a considerable amount of hazing had developed. General Middleton's letter to Caron on this subject must be quoted at length:

I propose going to Kingston to inspect the battery and school there, and I intend speaking to the gentlemen cadets there. You remember the talk about "hazing" some time ago, and that I desired Oliver to stop it at all hazards. This he has been working at ever since and he had naturally taken the side of the junior cadets, which has caused dissatisfaction among the seniors, who also think themselves aggrieved by the alterations in the regulations last year which prevented them from having almost uninhibited leave to go to town, etc. All this culminated the other day in a row between the seniors & juniors which was at once stopped. Since that all their leave has been stopped. Now I want you to authorize me to say that if this hazing is carried on in the slightest degree that the sergt-majors & sergeants & corporals shall all be sent away without respect to former character or anything else. This would stop it and if they did their duty "hazing" would soon be a thing of the past.[43]

The date of this letter, May, suggests that by 1888 "recruiting" at RMC lasted throughout the academic year and not, as at RMC in Leonard's day and in other educational institutions today, just for the first few days or

*Lieutenant-Colonel Reuben Wells Leonard (1860–1930) graduated RMC, 1883; served as transport officer in the Northwest rebellion before becoming a CPR engineer. In 1911 Robert Borden made him chairman of the National Transcontinental Railway Concern, the forerunner of the Canadian National Railways. His interest in Coniagas Mines and Cobalt, Ontario, made him wealthy. He established the Leonard Foundation in 1916, a scholarship scheme for white Protestants. Leonard presented Chatham House in London to the Royal Institute of International Affairs.

weeks of a college career. As some RMC cadets came from English public schools, and as all undoubtedly knew about the hazing of freshmen in North American fraternities, it may be assumed that RMC recruiting stemmed from an amalgamation of the English fagging system and American hazing, reinforced by the military authority conferred upon senior cadets as part of their training for leadership. Whatever merit could be ascribed to one or all of these customs, recruiting could obviously easily get out of hand when higher authority was weak or when individual seniors had a sadistic streak. Something of this kind had apparently happened by 1888.

Caron's reply has not been found. If Middleton spoke to the cadets in the way in which he proposed, it is likely that the practice waned for a time. However, four short paragraphs in Cameron's report of 1890 suggest that two years later all was still not well in the cadet body and that the practice had persisted. He wrote:

The general conduct of the Cadets has been satisfactory.

I regret extremely that a few individuals have deprived me of the great pleasure and pride I experienced last year in speaking of the frank manliness and honourable ambition of all.

I have every confidence that the upright example and powerful influence of their comrades will enable the erring ones to happily forget the time when they *would have perverted the bestowal of distinctions* due only to attainments and to a sense of honour which were not theirs.

Were I to permit my words of general approbation to be understood, for a moment, as applicable to those exceptional individuals, I should fail in giving due weight to the expression of my opinion of the cadets as a body, of their honourable principles, and of their manly pride in and care for the reputation of their College.[44]

The words "would have perverted the bestowal of distinctions" suggest that senior cadets had either usurped privileges or had been guilty of hazing. That it may have been hazing is suggested by the fact that soon after this time the college required that all entering cadets sign a declaration: "We sincerely promise to abstain – during our connection with the Royal Military College – from using physical coercion to [*sic*] any cadet and to discourage others from doing so, unless required in the discharge of duty. We further promise not to combine in any way to enforce our views on any fellow cadet." The first extant statement of this kind dates from September 1892.[45] It may be taken for granted that offences had made such a signed undertaking necessary.

Early in the session 1894–5 what Cameron called in his Report a "serious breach of discipline, but not of a savage brutal kind" came to his attention.[46] The recruits had been "caned" with T-squares by cadets of the third class (second year) on 25 September and 1 October. One recruit named Plummer had evaded the second caning by some means and run away from the college. When Cameron informed Plummer senior that his son would be charged with desertion, the Commandant learned of the caning incident. It had taken place in Cadet Denison's room. In the orderly room on 10 December, when charges of desertion were preferred against Plummer, the prisoner and the Commandant separately asked Cadets of the second and third classes to answer two written questions: whether they had used physical violence against recruits, and whether they knew of it. All replied in the negative except Cadet Carr-Harris, the son of the professor of civil engineering, who stated that he did not care to answer the second question. Cameron must have suspected these denials. On further investigation a third-class cadet named G. L. Bennet, who had answered both questions in the negative, was definitely incriminated. The rest of his class then asked to be permitted to confess that they were all involved. They were warned that such a confession must be voluntary and that they must not expect any leniency. They admitted guilt on those terms and the whole class was sentenced to twenty-eight days confinement to barracks on charges which included making false statements.

Meanwhile the conduct of the second class was also being investigated. It was discovered that four cadets who had on three occasions denied that they were aware of the hazing had in fact been present when it occurred. These cadets asked that, in the written confessions which they were to sign, the words "flogging" and "T-squaring" should be amended to read "caning." On 16 October they were rusticated until January and were ordered to catch the next train out of Kingston.

One of the four was D'Arcy Weatherbe,* the son of Justice Robert L. Weatherbe of the Nova Scotia Supreme Court. In an exchange of letters with the Commandant, the judge complained that the punishment hurt him as much as his son because the boy was being deprived of an education that the father could not obtain for him in Nova Scotia. He then said that he would not say that his son was innocent but proceeded to question Cameron's handling of the case. Cadet Weatherbe had apparently not been present the first time that the recruits were beaten. On the second occasion

---

*Lieutenant-Colonel D'Arcy Weatherbe (1874–1960), RMC, 1892–6; after a brief service in the British army he devoted his life to travel and exploration: "Probably the most noted traveler of the century. ... Few men have had so varied and colourful a career" (*R.M.C. Review*, XLII [1961], 174). He had adventures with Chinese brigands, escaped from Russia with confidential documents (1917) and returned there with Kolchak, kept open communications between Iraq and Iran in World War II, and was in Kenya during the Mau Mau rebellion.

Plummer had escaped a chastisement which, it could be argued, was not correctly described as a "flogging." The judge said that the beating was actually done with a "short cane or rattan about the size of my rather large penholder (two feet or less)." He therefore maintained that his son had not made false statements in the orderly room because Plummer was not chastised then and because there was no "flogging" in a strict sense of the word. The only possible charge against him, said the judge, was a violation of the promise made on entering the college not to acquiesce in "physical coercion." But, Judge Weatherbe argued, as there was no resistance by the recruits there had been no "coercion"; and as no reference had been made to this original undertaking at the time of the trial, this question was immaterial to the charges made against his son. Justice Weatherbe claimed that there might therefore in fact be no evidence worthy of the name of evidence to substantiate charges of "flat falsehood" against "20 of some of the flower of the young gentlemen of Canada." Weatherbe also protested that his son had been sent away so hastily that he had had to borrow his train fare, had been without money for a hotel or cab en route and in Halifax, and had arrived home without books with which to study.

In reply Cameron defended his disciplinary actions, but stated that criticism of his administration of his command should be referred to the government, not to him. To this the judge replied with vague threats that he might ask for the Commandant's dismissal. About the same time, as he was obviously out of his depth in this legal exchange, the Commandant referred the papers to his Minister and was instructed to answer no more letters from the judge. Towards the end of November, when Mrs. Weatherbe was at King's College, Windsor, seeking an alternative education for her son, the four rusticated cadets were recalled to Kingston for reinstatement. Judge Weatherbe hailed this as a victory.

This was, however, by no means the end of the matter. One of the third-class cadets who had served his twenty-eight days' confinement to barracks was F. H. Courtney,* whose father was the bishop of Nova Scotia. The Bishop learned of his son's conviction of falsehood "from a citizen here" in Halifax. Some time later, after the second-class cadets were reinstated, using arguments strikingly similar to those advanced earlier by the elder Weatherbe, the Lord Bishop wrote to Cameron to request the removal of "the stigma" of "this degrading charge of falsehood" from his son. He said that he had heard that the second-class cadets who had been rusti-

*Lieutenant-Colonel Frederick Harold Courtney, D.S.O. late RA (1875–1937); commissioned in the RGA, 1897; served in India, Arabia, Gibraltar, Malta, and Egypt and throughout World War I.

cated were being reinstated and he argued that the charge against the other class should now be expunged. Professing a dislike for "what is popularly known on this continent as 'hazing' ..., unmanly, brutal, ungentlemanly, and unChristian conduct," he nevertheless maintained that no one would object to "the exercise of reasonable discipline by seniors upon uppish, conceited and pig-headed juniors." He argued that the only offence his son had committed was that of "standing by his whole class." In reply Cameron shrewdly informed the Bishop that action of that latter kind was in fact "very closely allied to what in military life would be called 'mutinous insubordination.' " Moreover he could not condone falsehood.[47]

By this time the newspapers had got hold of the story. RMC cadets were being branded as "cads, snobs, cowards, ruffians, bullies, thugs, tyrants, beasts, and brutes." The cadets resented these charges so much that they voluntarily signed a unanimous declaration "to correct the false impressions which have arisen from the commission by some of our members of irregularities [which have been] characterized, we think very unfairly, as brutal and therefore repugnant to the feelings of the country." But they weakened their case by proceeding to "express regret that such irregularities have occurred." Their declaration went on: "While we plead that our conduct has had the sanction of very generally prevailing usage, we pledge ourselves for the future to do our utmost to prevent its recurrence." In forwarding this revealing statement at the cadets' request to the Minister, Cameron stated that he had investigated three anonymous allegations that had been made in the press and had found one of them to be utterly baseless. In the case of the other two, "where the knowledge to confirm or deny was certainly available ... confirmation and denial were alike refused. One of these cases – that of alleged burning the body of a cadet over a gas jet was inconsistent with the fact that there was no gas jet at the college where the diabolical act could have been perpetrated."[48] It seems obvious from the language of these various statements that there had actually been abuses.

The weakness of the college's administration in allowing the growth of questionable practices that could easily become intolerable was brought to the attention of the House of Commons when the RMC estimates were next considered. On 3 July 1895 Frederick C. Denison, MP, the father of the cadet in whose room the recruiting had taken place, moved that the appropriation for the college be reduced by the amount of the Commandant's salary, $3,163.22. Denison, who was a Conservative, stated that he had always "cordially supported [this item] with the object of having a first-class military college in Canada to educate our young men in the higher branches of the military art," but if the college was not properly managed it was a waste of public money. He referred to the Plummer case, to boys having been compelled to purchase raffle tickets even if unable to afford them, and to the fact that the cadets needed to purchase extra food. He said that it was well known that all these things went on. If the Commandant was unaware of them, as Cameron claimed he was, it was time the college was commanded by an officer who would attend to his duties more carefully. Discussion in the house then widened to the whole question of the value of the college as presently constituted.[49]

The reasons for the general attack on the college which now followed lie much deeper than the cases of hazing to which Denison had referred. However, the Minister's reply to the specific complaint about hazing and a statement during the debate in the House on the subject may be mentioned first, since they presented the standard arguments on both sides of this difficult question. The Minister of Militia, A. R. Dickey,* a Tupper supporter in the schisms that rent the Conservative party in the following year and therefore probably very ready to defend Tupper's son-in-law as far as he could, put forward the official college views of the matter. He claimed that "if a young man who is being educated for a soldier cannot stand the hazing that well-bred Canadian youths will put him through, he had better find out sooner rather than later that he has missed his avocation." In reply Lieutenant-Colonel Sam Hughes, Conservative MP for North Victoria and a future minister of Militia,† declared that things had changed since the Minister went to the University of Toronto and that some of the hazing conducted in universities at the present time would be a discredit to "any University even in Timbuctoo." He said that the Minister's remarks would be taken up everywhere and that college authorities would have more trouble than ever in "keeping the boys in line."[50]

Richard Walkem, QC,‡ speaking to the RMC Club later that year on the subject of the effect of the RMC training on the character and social relations of the cadets, emphasized that the punishment recently meted out to offenders amply proved that both fagging and hazing were absolutely forbidden at RMC.[51] But there can have been little real determination to eliminate a practice which, as the Minister's statement shows, was regarded by many in authority as a valuable element in the training given in the college. Anyone who could not "take it" was automatically classed as a weakling. Few apparently considered the possibility that one who had the courage to refuse might in fact be a potential Napoleon. Nor did they

*Minister of Militia and Defence, 1895–6.
†Minister of Militia and Defence, 1911–16.
‡Richard T. Walkem, QC, born 1840, Kingston lawyer, lecturer on equity at Queen's College, writer on legal matters and local history.

consider the effect on the character and future conduct of these students who administered arbitrary punishment irresponsibly by methods no longer countenanced in the British army or the Canadian militia. In these circumstances it could hardly be expected that the cadets themselves would stop to consider what effect their actions might have on public opinion and therefore on the future of their college.

The hazing incident did not cause the parliamentary attack on the college in 1895; it merely triggered a renewal of complaints that were of long-standing. What made these complaints much more effective in 1895 was the difference in the political scene from that of five years earlier when Macdonald still dominated the administration and when Caron could side-step all challenging issues. In 1891 the Old Chieftain had been laid to rest in an impressive ceremony in Kingston with cadets of RMC in full number one dress uniform standing at the four corners of his bier in Kingston's magnificent crepe-draped city hall. One of these cadets recalled long afterwards: "I can see him now, a very small man with tiny feet in patent leather boots and a big nose. He was dressed in his Privy Council uniform with his dress sword beside him." The recruits marched with arms reversed all the way up Princess Street to the Cataraqui cemetery.[52] The Staff-Adjutant, Major McGill, who organized the parade, probably did not realize that this marked the peak of RMC's prestige and stability for years to come. He could not have anticipated the disintegration of the Conservative régime that would follow Macdonald's death. The collapse of the party was hastened by the early retirement of Macdonald's successor, Sir John Abbott, through sickness, and by the sudden death in Windsor Castle of the next prime minister, Sir John Thompson, who was the Conservative party's real strength after Macdonald was gone. Sir Mackenzie Bowell, the fourth head of government in as many years, was unable to hold the party together.

One source of Bowell's difficulties was that a series of political financial scandals had corroded party harmony. In the course of the cabinet shuffles, Caron had been moved to become postmaster-general in 1892. The Department of Militia had been given in quick succession to Mackenzie Bowell, to J. C. Patterson, and to A. R. Dickey. General Ivor Herbert, who had been appointed GOC of the militia by Macdonald on 20 November 1890, was a vigorous able soldier with good connections in England. He was a protégé of Lord Wolseley, who was attempting at that time to reform the British army. Herbert, skilfully taking advantage of the weakness of the ministers and of their desire to do something to compensate for long neglect, introduced long-overdue reforms and the reorganization of Canada's tiny Permanent Force. He called for improvement in the training of officers; but he did not immediately ask the government to carry out the old promise that when RMC graduates had enough seniority they would get preference for its few commissions. Herbert's postponement of this step until 1895 naturally revived the old RMC sense of grievance. At the same time it left the college open to the criticism that it was not doing all that it should to produce officers for the defence of Canada.[53]

The prospect of a British commission was still the most attractive feature of the college for many applicants. But the British commissions were few in number and Canadians were usually without inherited incomes that British officers needed and so could not afford to serve in the cavalry and infantry, or even in the artillery. In some years, therefore, the commissions in these corps were not accepted. Hence rivalry for the single Royal Engineers commission was fierce. There were charges of favouritism and of political interference with the recommendations forwarded to the War Office. Furthermore the majority of the cadets who had no hope of gaining a British commission had little incentive to study. As a result of these things and of the increase of fees in 1889, RMC had become a school where the sons of relatively wealthy men were educated for civil careers. This opportunity for civil careers after graduation was what kept the college alive. But as the exemptions from matriculation and the shortening of the courses for further professional education were given on passing grades at RMC without regard to quality or place on the class list, there was in fact little to stimulate competition and effort within the college. Meanwhile, the emphasis put on civil careers led to public criticism that this was not the purpose for which the college was set up.

Not unnaturally in these circumstances RMC's recently won prestige began to decline as rapidly as it had grown. Two or three years later than the time we are considering, a new commandant, Colonel Kitson was to declare that the War Office had "not thought much of some of the cadets who had been sent home lately recommended for commissions."[54] He made it quite clear that the reputation which RMC had gained earlier as a result of its graduates' performances in the British army had been tarnished under his predecessor. To some extent this decline in quality was caused by the wholesale commissioning done from 1885 to 1888 which had reached far down the list of the graduating class and had even taken cadets from the second year. Inevitably the quality and preparation of some of those who went to the British army was lower than in earlier years when only one commission was available for each arm of the service. That many good cadets preferred careers in Canada also contributed to this apparent deterioration. Furthermore, as graduating classes became smaller, there were fewer from whom to choose. But the principal reason for decline was the lack of real academic competition and stimulus within the college which became obvious in times of large-scale commissioning to the British army during international crises. An important contributory cause was the inadequacy of some of the staff and especially of the commandant.

A recent historian of the demarcation of the Canada-United States boundary has said that "Cameron's mismanagement almost brought about the demise of that once proud and hopeful institution [RMC]."[55] This judgment neglects to take into account the root of the college's difficulties, that for political reasons, or from lack of need for defence, the government had not made provision for the proper use of the college's graduates. Nevertheless it is substantially correct. General Cameron was a failure as a commandant. He was too old for the job, out of touch with the modern army, without experience in military education, and temperamentally unsuitable. On the boundary commission he had "rubbed everybody the wrong way." His irritability and stubbornness had made co-operation and negotiations with the Americans difficult; one of his subordinates had described his cutting of the meat ration when food was plentiful as "the act of a madman." His obituary described him as one "who ruled the common actions of his life ... with almost military method and order."[56] Kirkpatrick, seeing him perform at RMC, warned Caron that he would not do as GOC. "You will find General Cameron too fussy and too obstinate."[57] In 1890 Cameron complained that his works officer was receiving orders that bypassed him, and that he must have full control of all militia officers taking instruction at RMC; when he did not get his way, he sent in his resignation. Caron disdained to accept it.[58] He knew only too well that Cameron was a political appointment and that to accept the resignation was impossible. His bland ignoring of the gesture was indicative of his opinion of Cameron's behaviour and temperament.

Cameron's annual reports, which are garrulous and amorphous when compared with the precise reports of both his predecessors and his immediate successors, showed nothing of a decline in the college's standards.[59] In fact he reported each year that the quality of the top cadets was continuing to improve and that their marks were establishing new records. The lowest marks were at about the same level as those of earlier classes, but the average quality of the classes as a whole was actually declining and this was not offset by the spectacular results recorded at the top. Later investigation was to suggest that the marks of many of the poor ones were inflated.[60] Cameron's reports also carefully played down the decline in the number of graduates. In the years 1888 to 1894 the number in the recruit class had fallen from twenty-four to fourteen and in 1895 the number of graduates was only eight. But Cameron reported that for the first time in the history of the college every graduate got an honours diploma.[61] Laurier's statement at the Colonial Conference of 1897 – "I can say I think that the Military College has been a great success until five years ago but I am sorry to say that the man we have at the head of the College allowed it to go down a little"[62] – seems entirely justified.

Denison, although a supporter of the government, had begun an attack upon the administration of the college in order to secure Cameron's removal since the ordinary rules of retirement did not seem to apply. Cameron was alleged to have claimed that his appointment was for life. It was inevitable that the Liberal opposition should follow up with an attack on the government's administration of the college. George E. Casey, a militia officer and an advocate of civil service reform who represented Elgin West, produced figures which purported to show that it had cost $4,533 apiece (and even as much as $8000 in the last year) to educate two hundred cadets of whom only eleven had entered the Canadian Permanent Force. He said there were "two professors to each cadet, almost," and that $1000 was spent on servants for each graduate. A. Amyot, the lone Independent Nationalist in the House, interjected that this expensive "emigration school" ought to be abolished. William Mulock again declared that it was against both the spirit and the letter of the British North America Act for the dominion government to set up a college for general education.[63]

Denison's motion was defeated. The college estimates were approved. But the government convened the Board of Visitors to report on the college in the fall of 1895; and, as a result of the insistence of the RMC Club, the 1895 Board of Visitors included an ex-cadet, Duncan MacPherson, one of the Old Eighteen, now a divisional engineer on the Canadian Pacific Railway. The board's report, signed by MacPherson and the three militia staff officers, argued that to get full value from the instructional staff the number of cadets should be increased. But it declared that this could not be done unless the long overdue west barrack block was erected without unnecessary delay. It also declared that the drill at the college was out of date and that (according to evidence brought before the board at a time when the Commandant had been asked to withdraw from its deliberations), "there is slackness in discipline." It therefore recommended that the college should be brought more under the supervision of the GOC. It said that the instruction in French should be modernized and also that the civil engineering in the college should be more progressive. Finally, after suggesting that RMC graduates should be given preference in the Permanent Force, it approved the combination of military and civil instruction. But it concluded that the commandant ought to be changed every five or seven years, ought to be on the active list of the British army, and ought to be of no higher rank than a lieutenant-colonel.[64]

The fifth member of the Board of Visitors, Sandford Fleming, a distinguished engineer and financier, and the chancellor of Queen's College, disagreed with the tenor of these findings. He had withdrawn at an early stage from its deliberations. In a minority report which he sent direct to the Minister, Fleming was willing to agree that RMC had proved to be a useful institution and that its establishment had been of national importance. But he said he thought that it should now be radically changed because things had altered since it was founded. He admitted that a good civil education should be the groundwork of a military, as of all other professional educations; but, following the argument of Mulock of the University of Toronto, he said that constitutionally a civil education was not one of the functions of the "general [i.e. the federal] government." He said that it had cost $5,510 for each of the thirteen and three-fifths graduates produced annually since 1880 and that of this the federal government had paid $3700. The share of the cadets' parents was more than the remaining balance of $1,450 because there were other expenses. He said that the universities could now do this job more cheaply. The Royal Military College at Kingston should therefore become a military college and be nothing else. So constituted, the course of instruction need not exceed two years. He said that, to fill it up, liberal inducement including guaranteed appointments should be offered to a sufficient number of well-educated young men imbued with military and patriotic zeal.[65] Fleming thus elaborated Mulock's argument that a military college producing civilian engineers was unconstitutional.

In addition to these reports for publication, the Board of Visitors also prepared an extra confidential report in which it declared that the Commandant did not take the degree of interest in his work that he ought. It found that this was the reason for the prevailing lack of confidence in the college. The board said that there was a feeling among staff and cadets that there could be no improvement until there was a change of commandant. Secondly, this supplementary report alleged that three professors were unsatisfactory. Wurtele was said to be not up to his work and was unsuited to it; Duval, it was considered, had become careless and did not secure the results he should; and the engineering instruction of Professor Carr-Harris was declared to be neither modern nor progressive and should be improved. On the other hand the board commended Captain Cochrane for his zeal, energy, and ability and recommended that he be made a professor and given an increase in pay and promotion in rank.[66]

As soon as he received the board's reports, A. R. Dickey sent Major-General W. J. Gascoigne,* the new GOC, to Kingston to inspect RMC. Gascoigne was not a man of great perspicacity. He reported that there appeared to be a thoroughly contented spirit among all the cadets. Perhaps this contentment was induced by his extraordinary request that, in consideration of this being his first visit to the college, the cadets should get a week's extra holiday at Christmas, a request that even royalty never made. But he also submitted a supplementary confidential report in which he agreed that the Commandant was too old for his job. However Gascoigne's only aim in Canada was to please the government. He suggested that the RMC appointment should be thrown open to an exceptionally smart, energetic officer of the Canadian militia for a short term of office renewable at the option of the government. Obviously this recommendation would have rendered the appointment more liable to use as political patronage; and it could not have provided the necessary modern military expertise. Gascoigne had a flair for misunderstanding the nature of any problem. When approving the work of the military professors, he suggested that the employment at RMC of more Canadians now in the British service would help to counter the prevailing notion that the granting of four British commissions to RMC cadets meant a permanent draining away of Canada's few trained military men. But this had never been a significant criticism and was not a real issue. Gascoigne criticized only one civilian professor, Duval, who, he said, was unable to hold the cadets' attention or to impart instruction. Apparently Duval was so poor a teacher that even Gascoigne could see it. The GOC urged that RMC graduates should get preference for Permanent Force commissions because he thought, without any apparent evidence, that if this were not done the British government might withdraw its liberal offer of regular army commissions for which there was fierce competition at home.

Dickey appears to have asked Cameron to report on his teaching staff at RMC. The Commandant did so two days after Gascoigne's visit. From some of the phraseology of this report it seems likely that Cameron already knew something of the criticisms that the board was going to make including even those in its confidential report. The visitors, of course, may merely have adopted some of his own complaints about his staff.

Cameron told the Minister that Captain Twining and Lieutenant Lesslie, two ex-cadets recently appointed to the department of military engineering, were too new for him to assess; and he understood that there had been no question about the performance of Lieutenant-Colonel McGill,

*Major-General Sir William Julius Gascoigne (1844–1926), entered the army, 1863; served in Egypt and the Sudan 1882–1885; GOC Canadian militia, 1895–8; K.C.M.G. 1901.

1 Professor I. E. Martin, M.A., director of studies 1917–22
2 No 600, Lt-Col. E. J. C. Schmidlin, M.C., S.M.E., senior professor 1926–33
3 Col. H. J. Dawson, C.M.G., D.S.O., M.A., director of studies 1922–6
4 Professor F. H. Day, B.A., M.SC., senior professor 1933–4

1

2

3

4

1 Professor L. N. Richardson, M.A., M.SC., senior professor 1934–41

2 No 759, Professor H. H. Lawson, B.SC., senior professor 1941–2

3 Dean J.R. Dacey, M.B.E., B.Sc., PH.D., F.C.I.C., principal and director of studies 1967-78.

4 No 1557, Col. W. R. Sawyer, O.B.E., E.D., B.SC., M.SC., PH.D., LL.D., D.SC.MIL., F.C.I.C., vice-commandant and director of studies 1948–67

5 The "Old Eighteen." *standing l to r* S/M Mortimer (staff), No 11, J. Spelman, No 9, C. A. DesBrisay, No 17, H. W. Keefer, No 4, W. M. Davis, No 15, F. J. Dixon, No 14, J. B. Cochrane, Capt. Ridout, No 2, H. C. Freer; *seated l to r* No 6, S. J. A. Denison, No 1, A. G. G. Wurtele, No 5, T. L. Reed, No 13, A. B. Perry, No 7, L. H. Irving, No 12, C. O. Fairbank, No 18, D. MacPherson, No 3, H. E. Wise, No 16, V. B. Rivers; *front* No 8, F. Davis, No 16, G. E. Perley

1

3

2

WINNERS OF THE VICTORIA CROSS AND
GEORGE CROSS

1 No 1866, Lt-Col. C. C. I. Merritt
V.C., E.D. (Dieppe raid, 19 Aug. 1942)

2 No 943, Air Marshal W. A. Bishop
V.C., C.B., D.S.O., M.C., D.F.C., LL.D.
(10 Aug. 1917)

3 No 1815, Air Cmdre A. D. Ross
G.C., C.B.E., C.D. (30 June 1944)

4 Memorial Arch at the main entrance of RMC, erected in 1923 by the RMC Club of Canada. Designed by John M. Lyle, the arch is constructed of buff Indiana limestone on a base of granite from Quebec

1 Cadet uniforms   1923–42

2 Funeral procession of Sir John A. Macdonald, Kingston, June 1891, with the battalion of gentlemen cadets as a guard of honour

1

1 TRH Princess Elizabeth and the Duke of Edinburgh with the Commandant,
Brig. D. R. Agnew, during the royal visit to RMC, 12 Oct. 1951

of Captains English, Lee, Moren, and Cochrane, and of Professors Day and Worrell. He said that Dr. Waddell, the professor of physics, had higher scientific qualifications than were required at the college and was a good teacher, although he had little sympathy with indifferent students; but Cameron declared that he would not risk a change in this department unless it was certain that someone better could be found. However, he did repeat a recommendation which he claimed he had made earlier, that Captain Wurtele should be replaced as instructor of mathematics because he was lacking in the power of lucid explanation and had a discouraging manner with students.

Cameron's chief complaint was about Dr. Duval. After the board's visit, Cameron had notified Duval in writing that his pupils had been thought poor in spoken French and that he seemed to concentrate too much on "isolated verbal inflexions." Duval had replied that the cadets would not apply themselves to the subject and that they pretended that French was a difficult language for all English-speaking people except those of superior intellect; the cadets had told him that many English people who had lived for years among French people had not learned to speak French. Duval defended his methods. He protested that he had taught many other subjects including music, Latin, physics, chemistry, mathematics, and astronomy, as well as French for thirty years. He had found that it is always better to go slowly and secure solid foundations "if we intend to erect a solid building." He said that his teaching of French was as successful as that of other subjects at RMC and particularly as that of mathematics in which RMC cadets were, according to him, very much behind French students. He ended by blaming the government for not promoting competition by giving RMC graduates a monopoly of government posts.

Passing Duval's reply to the Minister, Cameron denied the charges about RMC's alleged poor standards in mathematics. Cadets began the study of calculus by the end of their second year. He said the college was not intended to produce professors of mathematics. Therefore some parts of the subject, like the theory of numbers, were not taught. He then referred to comments that had been made outside the college to the effect that the instruction in civil engineering was neither modern nor progressive. Not being acquainted with the subject himself he had asked Professor Carr-Harris to comment on these criticisms and had been impressed by his replies. The Commandant said it would be impossible to find a more conscientious and inspiring teacher than Carr-Harris who had shown him that he used up-to-date textbooks and had listed his practical experience in engineering projects undertaken from 1864 to 1889.[67]

In March 1896 General Cameron protested that he had only now seen the Board of Visitors' Report. By this time his father-in-law, Sir Charles Tupper, had become prime minister; he therefore felt more secure and became extravagant in his demands and assertions. He wrote a detailed rebuttal of the charges made against his administration. He argued that as the Minister and GOC were changed frequently it was imperative in order to ensure continuity that there should be no time limit to the commandant's tenure of office. Denying that the college's drill was antiquated, he quoted a Sandhurst Board of Visitors in support of his position that high efficiency in mechanical military drill, obtained at the cost of lessening other more essential mental acquirements, would be a mistaken approach to the work that the college should do.[68]

General Cameron dealt separately and at even greater length with Sandford Fleming's report. In contradiction to what Fleming had suggested, "men thoroughly educated in military principles," he upheld rather, "thoroughly educated military men." He claimed that the RMC course, though not exactly identical with a university pass B.A., was equivalent to one. He asserted, with some cause, that Fleming's proposal to have men who had been previously educated in civilian institutions take a two-year professional course at RMC would not work. Canadian schools did not prepare students as adequately for a military college as English schools where there were often special army classes; and Canadian university graduates would not enter RMC. He pointed out that up to July 1893 no single graduate of a Canadian university had taken advantage of the existing privilege of direct commissioning in the British army. He said that because RMC graduates did not usually go on to further training in the army as did the graduates of the British military colleges, the RMC education and training should be superior to that in the British colleges. He declared that Canadian universities did not give courses to suit the requirements of the military student in Canada; for instance, engineering students in the universities did not learn French. Cameron then produced statistics to show that although it cost the University of Toronto endowment $2,180.56 to produce one B.A. graduate it cost the Canadian government only $1,271.39 to produce each graduate of the Royal Military College.[69]

Meanwhile in the House of Commons the government had resisted all efforts by the opposition to discover whether the reforms recommended by the visitors would be carried out. Finally in April, having been unable to get a satisfactory answer, Mulock used the parliamentary device of moving the adjournment of the house so as to precipitate a debate about the condition of the militia and especially about RMC and its use for general educational purposes. In the course of the debate there were references to the existence of the board's confidential reports, but their content was not disclosed. In face of bitter attack, those who supported the college as it stood argued that as Canada, unlike Britain, did not have a military caste a general education was necessary at RMC to attract applicants. Because the general subjects given there contributed to a military purpose, they were declared to be within the meaning of the constitution.[70]

At the closing exercises in June, Cameron delivered his usual annual address. As was his custom he added this address as a supplement to his year-end report. In it, after announcing the grant of an Indian staff corps commission to RMC cadets, he noted that the hostile campaign against the college, which had raged in the press and parliament since the beginning of the session, had reported in the *Canadian Military Gazette* and had broadcast throughout the country, and even to the British press, the idea that the college lacked discipline, that its drill was antiquated, that its cadets were drunkards,* and that its staff were "unworthy of belief." Cameron had obtained formal denials of the charges of drunkenness signed by every cadet and staff member.[71] He declared that in 1893 Lieutenant-General Sir Andrew Clarke, the Inspector General of Her Majesty's Fortifications, had said that RMC graduates were better than those from Woolwich. But he admitted that this statement had been qualified. General Clarke had added: "It is true we get only one or two from there so perhaps they are the best the College can produce." Cameron claimed, however, that a year later a royal commission on army entrance examinations in Britain had also said that RMC cadets were better informed than those of Woolwich.[72]

Cameron then went on to repeat his familiar boast that there had been more high marks in recent years in the college than at any time in its history. To refute the charges about drill he sarcastically noted that in the *Toronto Mail and Empire*, which had led the attack on RMC, a picture showing a parade of gentlemen cadets of the Royal Military College was headed, "Steady as a Rock: Head of [Toronto's] Queen's Own Rifles passing Saluting Point."[73]

However, Tupper's government fell on 8 July 1896 and Cameron's protection was thereby removed. The new Liberal Minister of Militia, Dr. F. W. Borden,† after considering all the reports about the college,

---

*An ex-cadet of that era has stated that there was much drinking in his time but very little drunkenness. The cadets got liquor from a speakeasy in Barriefield run by a man named Tom Burns. As this cadet, when a recruit, was the only one with a bicycle he was frequently sent by seniors for supplies. Once he was spotted by an officer also on a bicycle who pursued him to the Frigate. The recruit hid the bottle and suspended the bicycle out of the window to avoid detection. Brock, Reminiscences of No. 338 Alfred La Rocque.

†Sir Frederick William Borden (1847–1917), minister of Militia and Defence, 1896–1911, a medical doctor, MP (King's county, NS) 1874–82, 1887–1911; K.C.M.G., 1902; LL.D. (New Brunswick), 1911.

including the confidential ones which he had found in the files, at once instructed General Gascoigne to ask for the RMC Commandant's resignation. This resignation was submitted on the day on which the request was received.

In September, Borden tabled the confidential reports in the House of Commons as justification of his action. Cameron objected to their publication in this way on the grounds that they damaged his personal reputation. He said that he had not been given an opportunity to reply to them and he tried to disparage them by saying that the previous government had not thought fit to act upon them. He also declared that he had not in fact seen them before they were tabled. Borden replied that he could not explain the actions of his predecessors in office, and he added coldly: "Had I supposed it possible that the late Government had not furnished you with a copy of the document, I should certainly have done so." He concluded, "I trust that you will not consider any continuance of this correspondence necessary."[74] So was written the finale to an unfortunate period of RMC's history. Cameron went; and the Staff-Adjutant, Major McGill, became acting commandant until the new government's policy could be announced and put into effect.

In the early 1890s, RMC's reputation had thus plummeted. A fundamental reason for this was the lack of a large enough permanent force in Canada to absorb the output of the college. This had made the college turn more to its second purpose, the production of civil engineers. If this were the college's sole reason for existence, it could be argued that its existence was unconstitutional or unnecessary. The use of RMC for political patronage when it had no clearly established value to the country opened the door wide to criticism. As the exemptions given for civilian professions did not depend upon competition, academic standards declined. On top of all this an outbreak of hazing, the result of cadet independence and of staff weakness, fostered public hostility. The result was a series of heavy attacks in the Commons. The college came close to extinction.

Yet in several respects RMC maintained certain of its earlier more valuable characteristics and prestige. Its graduates were still attracting attention by their exploits throughout the empire, if one can judge accurately from a series of articles printed for publicity purposes in the *Canadian Magazine* and the *Proceedings* of the RMC Club.[75] The purpose of these articles at a time when RMC was under serious criticism was to demonstrate that Canada needed a military college and that RMC fulfilled that need. The introduction in the former periodical pointed to the plight of China, at that time being overwhelmed by Japan because of Mandarin scorn for the military profession and general neglect of higher military education. China at least had an excuse that Canada lacked, an army two million strong. The editor of the *Canadian Magazine* argued that, whatever the cost, "formal, full, and effective recognition of the vital national interests involved in the purposes for which the Royal Military College had been established should not be longer withheld."[76]

The articles by writers from militia headquarters, the RMC staff, the ex-cadet club, and the cadet battalion described the contemporary condition of the college in favourable terms and explained its value to Canada. RMC was said to be unique in that it differed from the universities in its military training, and from all other military colleges in that it prepared cadets for civilian, as well as military, life. It was the only place in Canada where anything more than the mere rudiments of military training could be obtained. It developed character, honour, and social poise. The cadets lived under a system of control unknown to their civilian friends. However, one professor, the Reverend Clarendon L. Worrell, warned that parents should not regard the college as a reformatory and protested that many recruits arrived with inadequate academic preparation. But he declared that RMC cadets worked under ideal conditions and acquired a thorough knowledge of the military art. He had less to say about academic achievement; but he noted that there was now a library of about three thousand volumes which was, however, inadequately housed.[77] CSM G. R. Frith admitted that the cadets spent their spare time in the evenings playing whist and singing to the music of banjos and mandolins and that the energy they spent preparing for the June ball, "*the* dance par excellence," exceeded that spent on the more sober part of their education.[78]

These articles effectively support the conclusion that academic standards had fallen off at RMC. "In the matter of study no man need overexert himself," wrote two NCOs but hastily added that most cadets got through a considerable amount of work, especially in military and engineering subjects with a practical application.[79] Despite the small size of its establishment, RMC was still successful in some sporting and similar contests. In 1895 the cadets had done poorly in hockey and football, but in 1892 they had lost by only one point in a two-game series with Queen's at football. In track athletics they could hold their own with other Canadian colleges and universities. The boat club, which had declined a few years before, had been revived and was as good as in its best days.[80] Without doubt, the man chiefly responsible for this sporting success was Sergeant-Major J. Morgans,* instructor in gymnastics, fencing, boxing, and infantry

---

*Sergeant-Major J. Morgans, Scots Fusilier Guards, had won British army medals for "marching order races" and "single-handed tug-o'-war" before coming to Canada. In Kingston he had a private gymnasium and taught calisthenics to the city's young ladies, at the Ladies' College, and at Queen's College. After leaving RMC he toured with a wild-west show and then became instructor to the Royal Grenadiers at Toronto.

drill from 1878 to 1897. Morgans excelled at sculling and rifle-shooting. In 1888 he was hailed as the fencing champion of North America with foils, swords, and bayonets. He held this title against all-comers from Canada and the United States until 1895. The following year Morgans took a bayonet-fighting team from RMC to Toronto and, to everybody's surprise, defeated a team selected from all the militia units in the area.[81] This triumph, and the favourable publicity which it attracted, was some compensation for the unfavourable press that RMC had had in the past few years. It may have helped to reinforce the idea that there was much good in the college and that it could be resuscitated.

7

KITSON'S

REFORMS

1896-1901

Lord Lansdowne, the secretary of state for war, was concerned about what was happening at the college in Kingston, not so much because of the threat to RMC's potential contribution to the general defence of the empire, but for the more immediate reason that Britain offered five commissions annually to the college's graduates. RMC's graduates were alleged to have fallen off so badly in quality the military authorities in England were considering cutting down the number that they would take.[1] Hence Lansdowne kept a watchful eye on the situation and relayed the information he collected to the Colonial Office. At the time of the Liberal victory in July 1896, he learned from John M. Courtney, the Canadian deputy minister of finance, that most of the Liberals and many Conservatives were opposed to RMC and were prepared to shut it down.[2]

The criticism most frequently heard was that because RMC graduates did not get preference for the Canadian Permanent Force and for the Canadian civil service most of them went into civilian occupations. Allegedly many also left the country and the empire altogether. From a different angle came the charge that they contributed little or nothing to the militia. However, in addition to a gross exaggeration of the numbers who moved to the United States, these criticisms were based on the fallacy that Permanent Force commissions could save RMC. In fact, the total number of commissions available in Canada would not have been enough to keep the college going even if all were reserved for its graduates. Furthermore, Canadian commissions were not as glamorous an inducement to young Canadians to enter RMC as were British commissions. Although many members of both political parties were prepared, twenty years after the event, to praise Mackenzie's wisdom in setting up a college to provide a substructure for Canada's military future, no one in political life had the temerity to suggest an expansion of the Permanent Force in order to make openings for the college's graduates. Therefore the future of RMC continued to depend on the retention of the British offer of commissions along with a curriculum that would not only satisfy the War Office's requirements but would also prepare cadets for possible civilian careers.

It was indeed very clear that the amalgam of military and civil elements at Kingston had been the basis of the college's early success and must for the foreseeable future be the means of keeping it alive. A British officer, Major-General E. Harding Steward, RE, Inspector General of Warlike Stores for New Zealand, had told the Minister of Defence in Victoria, Australia, in 1889:

In Canada ... a military training *pur et simple* would not attract a sufficient number of students, the "leisure class" in the colony being very small indeed. It was therefore decided to graft an efficient course of instruction in civil engineering and practical mining on a military course and to trust to the drill and military discipline at the college and the surroundings to model and stimulate the growth of the military instincts of the students. ... Such a course cannot fail to have a lasting effect on the students, for submission to discipline becomes in time natural to them, their minds being moulded at a period of life when they are most receptive and attentive. ... 'the Canadian military students are known, when called on to serve, to make admirable officers, full of self-reliance and resource, and to be at the same time excellent business men, whose training in civil engineering and practical mining while at college, must make them valuable members of the community, particularly in the newly opened provinces.'[3]

But RMC's unique combination of military training with general and technical education was in jeopardy when the Liberals took over the government in 1896; and if the double-headed curriculum were abandoned, the college would collapse.

Changes advocated by those critics who were hostile to the college but were not yet committed to its abolition were ominous for its future. Many politicians and news editors, and also some militia officers, thought that the command of the college should go to a Canadian; and General Gascoigne had gone even further when he suggested that it should be an officer from the militia. A development of that kind would have reduced the confidence of the War Office in RMC and would have cost it its imperial commissions, for as yet no Canadian militia officer had enough of the right kind of military experience to do the job properly. At the same time the opposition in some circles to RMC's emphasis on non-military education threatened to take away those subjects that served to attract recruits who had little hope for one of the few British commissions available but who could obtain at the college, as a secondary reward, an education to fit them for a civilian career. Their presence was necessary to keep classes up to a reasonable and economical size as well as to produce experienced military graduates who could be relied on in an emergency to turn from their civilian careers to the defence of their country. Either a militia commandant, or the institution of a purely military course would have been almost the same as a summary closing of the college.

The question of the command was the more immediate problem. In addition to ambitious militia officers, there were some Canadians retired from the British army and some British retired officers who had served in Canada, or had relatives there, who thought that the change of government gave them a chance for a new career as commandant of RMC. One of these was Major-General T. A. Strange,[4] the former commander of the Canadian artillery and an applicant for the post of commandant twenty years earlier when Hewett was appointed. A second was Major-General J. Van Straubenzee, RA, an imperial officer who had retired in 1895.[5] As was noted in an earlier chapter, a third was the former RMC staff-adjutant, Lieutenant-Colonel J. Bramley Ridout.[6] None of these possessed the qualifications demanded by all those who had the interests of the college at heart, namely that a commandant must be on the active list, but they all had influence in high places. If their friends could have emulated Sir Charles Tupper, RMC would have received a second Cameron and that would have been fatal.

The new Minister of Militia was Frederick W. Borden, a medical doctor from Nova Scotia who had had a long interest in the militia in which he had served at the time of the Fenian raids. Although there has been much criticism of him because of the intensity of his political interest, and although he did not impress British statesmen favourably,[7] it must be remembered to his credit that during his long period of office from 1896 to 1911, the Canadian militia was thoroughly reorganized. The *Broad Arrow* said of Borden that "no Minister of Militia has done so much towards making the Canadian forces so thoroughly efficient and ready for the field as he."[8]

A good commandant was urgently needed. Courtney had put all the blame for RMC's decline on Cameron who had, he alleged, "run the institution into the ground." He said that what was needed was "a man of great patience and tact – and of good temper and firm in decision – capable of undoing quietly and steadily all Cameron's mistakes." He told Lansdowne that, "for local reasons," Sir Richard Cartwright, the minister of finance and a power in the cabinet, wanted to see the college maintained and prosper; and he implored the help of the War Secretary in ensuring the selection of a good man when the time came.[9]

The Royal Military College Club at its twelfth annual meeting held in Kingston on 29 February 1896 had been very much concerned about the unsatisfactory state of the college and especially that the 1895 Board of Visitors' Report had not been acted upon. In July, as soon as the results of the election were known and Borden was sworn in as Minister, E. F. Wurtele, the club's secretary, sent him a copy of the printed minutes of the February meeting and also a copy of an extract from the *Broad Arrow* of 7 March 1896 where it had been recommended that Cameron should be replaced by a younger man on the active list.[10]

However, as Courtney reassured Lansdowne, the new Canadian cabinet was not being swayed on this subject by political considerations. It intended to appoint a British officer. Courtney urged that an engineer or artilleryman should be sought out.[11] He proved to be a good prophet. The Canadian cabinet acted with unusual alacrity, perhaps to forestall the pressures that would build up with time. Only eleven days after Cameron's resignation, the Governor-General cabled the Colonial Office to ask the War Office to select an RMC commandant from the active list; and a few weeks later that Canadian government stressed the need for haste.[12]

The question was urgent because the situation in Kingston was getting worse. One indicator of the college's condition was the number of recruits that it could attract. From the time of Cameron's appointment the number entering RMC had fallen steadily from twenty-four in 1887 to eleven in 1891. In 1892, when the press attack on Cameron had diminished, it had climbed back to twenty-five, only three short of the average that could be taken in any one year if the college operated at full establishment. But from 1893 to 1895 the entry class had again fallen – from seventeen to thirteen. Although General Cameron and others attributed the unwillingness of Canadian boys to enter RMC to the lack of military appointments for its graduates, these statistics show that the interest of recruits, or of their parents, was in fact related to the state of public opinion. The Plummer incident in 1894 had renewed parental doubts and suspicions and had again discouraged applicants.

In the summer of 1896, fourteen qualified, but after attacks in parliament had mounted again, five recruits who were accepted did not report in September. This was the largest number to fail to accept an appointment since the college had opened in 1876.[13] The entry class was therefore down to nine, about the same as the number that had graduated that year. Cameron's dismissal, which had come after the entrance examinations were held, had thus obviously not restored confidence. For the first time since 1876 a supplementary entrance examination was planned, but no candidates appeared when it was held in November. There had been inadequate advertising,[14] but that was not the whole explanation. The college was still in bad odour with the public. The parade state, now only forty-five, had reached its lowest level since 1878.[15] With recruit classes thus falling steadily in numbers it was obvious that RMC would soon fade out of existence unless drastic measures were taken.

The War Office's choice of a commandant to put RMC back on its feet was made by 6 November. He was Major Gerald Kitson of the King's Royal Rifle Corps,[16] that is to say an infantryman and not, as had been urged, a member of one of the technical corps. Kitson was one of the disciples of the new Commander-in-Chief, Field Marshal Lord Wolseley, and had a lot of staff experience and a good active service record. Aged forty as compared with his predecessor's sixty-two years, he would bring vigour and new ideas.* The situation was too desperate for remonstrations because a technical officer had not been recommended. Kitson's personal characteristics might compensate for the deficiency, and he was accepted with little delay.

Kitson came immediately to Canada and F. W. Borden told him that drastic steps were needed. He undoubtedly also stressed the need for economy. The new commandant carefully obtained a promise from the Minister that he would be given time to look the situation over and make his own proposals before radical changes in the RMC staff were made.[17] He may have been alerted to the need for such a promise of freedom from political interferences by an incident that occurred as soon as he landed in Halifax; there he was accosted by a most persistent office-seeker, Charles deW. MacDonald, M.A. of MacDonald and Jones, Halifax solicitors, thereby showing that the rehabilitation of the RMC was now in danger of being as much troubled by Liberal patronage as it had formerly been afflicted under the Conservatives. MacDonald, the adjutant of the 63rd Halifax Rifles, had been encouraged by Gascoigne's proposal that RMC

---

*Major-General Sir Gerald Kitson (1856–1950) had been commissioned in the First Regiment of Foot but almost immediately transferred to the King's Royal Rifles; he was ADC to the brigadier-general, Aldershot, 1884–5 and to the GOC of the Western District, 1885–6; a district staff officer in Bengal, 1890, he was deputy assistant adjutant-general at Meerut, 1890–2 and assistant adjutant-general at Umballa, 1892–4; for service in the Manipur campaign in 1891, he was mentioned in despatches and won a medal with clasp; he had attended the Staff College at Camberley in 1885–6 and was promoted lieutenant-colonel in 1896 on taking up the Canadian appointment; after his service at RMC he became military attaché at Washington and then commandant at Sandhurst, 1902–7; he held various commands in India and was quartermaster-general, 1909–12 after which he commanded a division; he retired from the army in 1918.

professors should be selected from the militia. He therefore sought Duval's place as professor of French. He brushed aside suggestions that the appointment ought to go to another French Canadian. In a series of most belligerent letters during the second half of 1896 he said Duval's unfitness was "universally known," denounced the "partyisms" that had made possible the appointment of Cameron whom he described as a "consummate cad," and belittled the knowledge of German of the former RMC professor, Mr. Ferguson. He suggested that there were other means of appeasing the Liberal friends of Duval, Wurtele, and "Old Carr-Harris ... if they have any."[18]

There are no other patronage letters as brazen as MacDonald's among the extant correspondence about appointments to RMC in 1896. His letters are, however, enough to demonstrate the nature of the pressures put on Borden and the cabinet by Liberal supporters hungry for spoils after eighteen years in the political wilderness. Borden's patience with a man he obviously had no intention of satisfying shows how deeply the system was ingrained. It may also show that, although the Liberal government was prepared to follow the usual custom and displace its political opponents from some parts of the government service, RMC was one institution that it would treat with greater deference. Yet Kitson must have seen MacDonald and his like as threats.

When he arrived in Kingston the new commandant quickly assessed what constituted the chief problem at RMC. In a letter to Borden, he reported that some of the professors were so ineffective as teachers that the cadets laughed at them; yet he asked for more time. Remedial action should wait until after the results of the June examinations were known when he would submit recommendations for reform. He assured the Minister that already he could see a way to economize, for although a hospital was needed, he felt that as much space was wasted, it could be fitted elsewhere than in its present location in the basement,[19] and so he could avoid building a new hospital block.

But Borden was apparently anxious not to wait until June before deciding on a policy for the college. He gave Kitson verbal instructions to present a scheme by which the course at RMC could be reduced from four years to three.[20] It is not clear from the extant evidence whether this idea of a reduced course stemmed from the Minister or from the Commandant.* Kitson replied on 1 February that to maintain the efficiency of the college a reorganized curriculum should drop studies that could be described as luxurious and should be restricted to those subjects that were

*Borden told the Commons later that he had not liked the idea but that Kitson convinced him, House of Commons, *Debates*, 1898, III, 7022–94.

essential, firstly for cadets entering the Canadian civil service and Permanent Force, and secondly for those commissioned in the British army. Freehand drawing should be dropped. Military engineering should cover only what was necessary for entry to the imperial service. Strategy should be omitted. Physics, chemistry, geology, and mineralogy should be reduced to the proportions required for a modern civil engineer and made as far as possible into options. French should be confined to the first two years only and English to the first year. Mathematics, civil engineering, and civil surveying, being especially important, should keep the same number of hours as already assigned. The reduction to three years could be made by combining the present first and second years. In fairness to the current first-year class Kitson suggested that the British government should be asked to give ten commissions in 1899 instead of five.

Kitson told Borden that if this scheme were approved it would be possible to make certain reductions in the size of the staff. The services of the professors of freehand drawing, physics, and French, and also of an assistant instructor in mathematics, could be dispensed with. He said that as the English course would be reduced, there would not be enough work for a professor of English. Unless it was considered essential that a French professor should teach French, he preferred that Mr. Worrell, the professor of English, who was thoroughly acquainted with the French language, should teach that language rather than Mr. Duval, the present professor. He also proposed that one of the two instructors of military engineering should take over the elementary instruction in English and receive $250 extra salary for it. With certain other adjustments he hoped to save $6000 a year on teaching staff salaries and $1300 a year on the wages of the subordinate staff.

Kitson urged that these economies would make possible a reduction of fees. He thought this necessary for the welfare of the college above all else. Principal G. M. Grant of Queen's, who had been most helpful to him,[21] had told him that university fees in Canada were about $200 a year as against RMC's $350. Kitson also proposed the abolition of the fine of $100 for withdrawal; and he said that the entrance examinations should be set and marked by the RMC staff rather than by the outside board of examiners, thus effecting a further saving.[22]

To influence Kitson to act more quickly about the staff, Borden sent him evidence of certain malpractices at RMC. Kitson had known that some RMC professors had been in the habit of telling the cadets the questions they were going to set in examinations; and he had heard that they had even "gone so far as to mark blank papers." But Borden's evidence (the exact nature of it is not now known but it probably consisted of information collected from ex-cadets) completely shook his confidence in his teaching staff. He had already come to the conclusion that the cadets were potentially sound.[23] He therefore now formally forwarded to Ottawa his proposals for a radical reorganization of the college and the dismissal of Professors Forshaw Day, Waddell, Duval, and Wurtele.

Sir Richard Cartwright was acting minister of militia because Borden had been injured in a train accident. Cartwright, it will be remembered, was especially anxious to ensure RMC's welfare. He thought that the reduction to three years which Kitson proposed might need an amendment to the RMC Act.[24] However, he quickly steered the whole scheme through the cabinet. Everything was approved in April except the proposal that Dr. Worrell should teach the French courses. Kitson deplored the rejection of this recommendation but understood the political necessity that inspired it. Duval was, nevertheless, one of the professors who was to be dismissed as part of the process of reorganization. Israel Tarte, the French-Canadian Liberal leader, took Kitson to task about this. He suggested that the Englishman was displaying racial bias, but Kitson defended his action and believed that he convinced Tarte of its validity. Dr. Duval was expected to be able to bring political pressure to bear in attempt to get the cabinet's decision reversed. But Kitson declared that "without entering into those charges which have been brought against him by ex-cadets," a glance at his past examination papers would easily prove to any sane man that Duval was incompetent.

Kitson had left the decision about Carr-Harris for further consideration.[25] But a month later, he agreed with Borden's proposal that for the good of the college he also should be replaced. The Board of Visitors' Report had shown that he was popular because he was easy-going, but the cadets had no confidence in him. His untidy personal habits had lost him their respect. He appeared in class looking as though he had slept in his clothes. He never gave punishments and his classes were disorderly. The cadets played tricks on him, for instance by knocking his transit off plumb. Carr-Harris had worked hard since Kitson's arrival. Kitson confessed that he was not himself an expert in civil engineering and, therefore, was not a reliable judge of the professor's fitness; but he thought he seemed out of date. He therefore recommended that like the others, Carr-Harris should be dismissed by an order-in-council so that the action could not afterwards be called in question.[26]

Kitson said he did not expect immediate improvements to follow these alterations. He would not despair if the entry in 1897 was again small. The cadets had given an excellent gymnastic display which was greatly appreciated; and Kitson took a cricket team to play games in Toronto for the sake of the publicity. He told Borden that if there was not a marked increase in applicants in June 1898, little more could be done to improve the popularity of the college and he would be inclined to recommend that it should be closed. Meanwhile things were going well.[27]

Borden had already begun to tackle the root problem, employment prospects for RMC graduates. He told the Adjutant-General that he would only ask for three commissions in the Permanent Force annually from 1897 to 1900, but he wanted five thereafter. He would also ask the provincial governments to match these.[28] He wrote to his colleagues in other departments and also to ministers in the provinces to ask that civil service jobs be reserved for cadets. He aimed at getting five places in the federal civil service for RMC graduates as well as the five in the provinces in engineering, surveying, and the educational branches.[29] He does not seem to have obtained many definite promises but no doubt the publicity obtained by appeals had some importance for the future. Borden also undertook to advertise the college more widely through the press. It is noticeable that these advertisements stressed that the RMC course led to civilian employment and did not take into account the possibility that the reductions in civilian subjects about to be made might affect the amount of credit granted to RMC graduates for entry to various professions.

Rumours of the impending drastic changes at the Royal Military College led Sam Hughes, a militia officer and now opposition defence critic, to ask questions in the House of Commons in April. What had General Gascoigne meant when he had said last August that changes would be made in the general administration of the college? And what were the "great and many advantageous changes" at which Kitson had hinted at an RMC Club dinner on 27 February? Cartwright replied that no changes had been carried out and that Kitson's report was still being considered.[30] But a month later a prominent militia officer, Lieutenant-Colonel Richard Tyrwhitt, Conservative MP for Simcoe South, asked for a return to show the changes to be made at RMC, details of the staff, the number of classes to be in attendance at any one time, the proportion of time to be spent in various activities, the amount of the deposit, and the number of applications that had been received before the reorganization was decided upon.[31] When replies were slow in coming, Sir Charles Tupper pressed for them. In June news that members of the teaching and subordinate staffs had been dismissed brought more questions from Tupper about the propriety of the government's action. He was told that the dismissals were either on grounds of incompetence or of redundancy and that the government reserved the right to take any action it thought desirable in the interests of the college, compensation being made to individuals affected thereby. He was also told that the individuals dismissed had all received adverse reports under the previous government. They had, in fact, also received much consideration and more notice than had General Cameron.[32]

Opportunity for a thorough discussion of the college came when the RMC vote was discussed in the house. As Tupper had planned to leave for England on private business, the Acting Minister considerately brought the RMC item to the committee on supply a day or so early so that Sir Charles could be heard. Cartwright disclosed that many on both sides of the house had come to the conclusion that the decline in the college was so serious that it ought to be closed down. Nevertheless the government had thought that RMC's past contribution to Canada and its importance in Canadian relations with Britain had shown that it would be a pity to destroy an institution that had fostered overseas a good impression of the military qualities of Canadian youth. The government had therefore instructed Colonel Kitson to reorganize the college in an effort to make it effective.

In reply, Tupper claimed that the Conservatives, when in power, had maintained RMC in accordance with Mackenzie's objectives, namely as a military college which secondarily educated for civilian life. He protested that the college was in a sound condition when the Liberals took it over. He claimed that Cameron's distinction as a scientist was proved by his recent selection by the Royal Geographical Society to represent it at a meeting in Halifax. He made another equally absurd statement, that General Gascoigne had sought to dismiss Cameron because the cadets' hair was too long and the commandant himself was untidy in his dress. To do this, Tupper said, the GOC had sought to take over control from the minister so that he could dismiss a commandant who was senior to him in rank. Tupper then made slighting references to Kitson's youth.[33] It was a ridiculous speech, Tupper at his worst, making debating points without facts.

When the debate was resumed three days later, Sir Charles Tupper had left for England. G. E. Foster, the opposition leader in the Commons, then suggested that the Acting Minister should postpone what he had to say about RMC until the following session when Tupper could answer them; but Cartwright would not allow Tupper's fantastic charges to remain unanswered so long. He said that ex-cadets in the imperial forces as well as General Gascoigne had criticized Cameron's administration of the college. The GOC had simply acted on instructions, and not through personal animosity, when he reported confidentially to the previous government. He stated that whatever Cameron's scientific qualifications were, he had clearly been unsuitable for the RMC command and that Kitson had qualities that Cameron lacked. It would take time to see whether the changes were effective, but one indication was that applications had already jumped from "scarcely more than eight or ten" to "something like forty." Possibly going beyond the facts, he stated: "I believe some more have been refused on the ground that there are more applying than we have vacancies for." He showed that competition for entry and a raising of the standard of matriculation was essential when the course was being reduced from four years to three.

Now that the question could be debated without being distorted by Tupper's presence and family involvement, opposition to the changes at RMC was very weak. It was limited to assertions that a reduction to three years would make it more difficult for the college to carry out its declared mission. One Conservative, Dr. T. S. Sproule, was unable to understand that increased competition for entry to the college would automatically increase the quality of the work done there. He wanted to abolish RMC on grounds of expense and to rely on the military schools to produce officers. There was also some concern about the treatment of the discharged members of the staff, particularly of Captain Wurtele whose career from his RMC cadet days was outlined in the house. But retired and active militia officers on the Conservative side including the former ministers of militia were emphatically of the opinion that Mackenzie's concept of a military college had been what Canada needed. Colonel Tisdale,* Minister of Militia under Tupper, said he wanted the college to be "second to none in the world." Caron went even further: "There was a time, I remember, when Canada did not stand in the proud position which she occupies to-day in Great Britain. Our present position is due to the fact that our Royal Military College cadets were able to take their places side by side with the men who had been trained in the [British] military service. It was also due to the fact that ... [Militia] teams which were sent to England showed not only that loyalty existed but that Great Britain in her Canadian subjects found men who were prepared to take their share in fighting her battles and who were able to fight these battles side by side with the best men that England could send to the front." (It will be recalled that some RMC cadets had been members of winning Canadian militia teams in Britain.) There was thus no real opposition to the retention of the military college, or to the idea that it should seek to give both military training and general or civilian education; but there was doubt about whether it could be effective after drastic curriculum reductions had been made.[34]

Although Kitson's desire to await the results of the June examinations had been over-ruled, he cautiously decided to make those examinations a

*David Tisdale (1835–1911), QC, minister of Militia, May-July, 1896.

test of, or justification for, action against those members of the staff who had already been warned that they might be dismissed. Obtaining outlines of the RMC course, he caused examinations to be set and marked by McGill professors. He then compared the results with those obtained in the same courses the previous Christmas. Dean Bovey of McGill, who supplied the external examiners, told him that the comparison showed that several of the RMC professors were practically useless. "The French examination in particular was an awful fiasco." The standard in freehand drawing was "miserably low" and suggested that Forshaw Day's teaching had been wasted time. The civil engineering results also revealed that instruction in that subject had been abominable and the cadets were "lamentably ignorant of many branches of the subject."[35]

To justify the dismissal of staff, Kitson announced details of these examination results in a special report in June. In the Christmas test marked by Carr-Harris, whose fate was not yet decided, the high had been 95 per cent, the low 58 per cent and the average 70 per cent. In an examination of the same students marked by Professor Cecil B. Smith of McGill in June the comparable figures were 69 per cent, 28 per cent and below 50 per cent respectively.[36] Similar contrasts were to be found in the other subjects. Bovey assured Kitson that the examinations had been set on the syllabus and that, as the results seemed harsh, his professors had actually marked the papers leniently.[37] But the external examination was, of course, a different examination paper set at a different time of the year, and was therefore not an absolute contrast. Furthermore, despite their alleged leniency, it is possible that the McGill professors, one of whom was soon to be a candidate for an RMC appointment, marked more severely than they would have done for their own students. Uncertainty about the future must also have unsettled both staff and students at RMC. Nevertheless, the differences were so marked that past criticisms of RMC's academic standards seemed justified.

Carr-Harris had given term marks of 100 per cent to eight top cadets and 50 per cent to the poor students who made up the remainder of his class. When he was asked to re-adjust these grades to more realistic figures in order to support the Commandant's refusal to recommend those at the bottom of the list for imperial commissions, he replied that his conscience would not let him do such a thing. Kitson therefore now lost all confidence in him and was quite ready to dismiss him along with the others.[38] The professors who were to lose their jobs at RMC were treated generously. Claims for special consideration were heard. For instance, Day's service in the Royal Navy was counted towards his pension. Gratuities were calculated on the basis of one-tenth of a year's pay for each year of service with a proportionate allowance for broken periods; and with an extra eighteen months' gratuity in lieu of longer notice of dismissal.[39] Wurtele was found other employment in the service of the government.

With regard to the cadets, Kitson decided that it was no use retraining in the junior class the worst failures who in the past would have been allowed to go on from year to year. He therefore asked their fathers to withdraw them. Others were given summer reading and were promised a supplementary test in the fall.[40]

Because the purge at RMC in 1897 coincided with the change in government it has been portrayed as a political turnover. This is a very distorted interpretation. The original critical report on the college, and even the charges against the individual staff members who were dismissed, had been made while the Conservatives were in office. It would be gross miscasting to portray Gerald Kitson merely as a Liberal political tool. He had reported on the proposed staff changes to the GOC before he discussed them with Borden. It is true that, like Hewett, he was always aware of the need to tread carefully in the political arena, but his reforms and the dismissals they involved have every appearance of being his own idea of what was needed and not something done merely to please the Minister. Kitson should rather be seen as a determined and dedicated military reformer bent on removing abuses and restoring the efficiency of the college.

Kitson's own personal contribution was on the military side, where immediate improvement came relatively easily. He added rapid and gymnastic marching between breakfast and classes, compulsory revolver and rifle practice, marks for outdoor drills and gymnastic exercises, and nearly a week's camp with "A" Battery of the Royal Canadian Artillery. He also reintroduced the practice of attaching some cadets to summer militia training camps.[41] By June he was ready to show off the quality of RMC drill which he declared was now in conformity with the latest drill manual published in 1896. The Montreal Diamond Jubilee Celebration Committee asked him to bring cadets to take part in a review and Kitson saw this as an opportunity to gain more publicity for the college. The Montreal committee put up $175 and Kitson asked the cadets themselves to furnish $2.00 each, which they would be able to do as they would have to give up their annual ball which cost them $5.00 a head. He asked the government, "as in Lord Lorne's day," to put up money for transportation and he suggested $100.[42] In 1899 he took a cadet gymnastic team to the Toronto Military Tournament where it gave a "fine performance" that "completely brought down the house & was easily the feature of the whole entertainment."[43]

But Kitson was anxious above everything else to restore RMC's prestige in Whitehall. He suggested that the last two cadets on the graduation list, because they were "idle," "weak," "rough," and "uncouth," should not be recommended for a commission if refusals higher up the list gave them possible reversions. He declared that the current stiffening of the British army promotion exams would make it hard for these two to progress.[44] Borden assured Kitson that if any unpleasantness arose from this decision, with which he personally agreed, he would support him heartily.[45]

Perhaps because of expected political implications, there was delay in the announcement of the recommendations for commissions. By early August parents were becoming impatient.[46] Soon there were rumours of political interference. In September, a member of the provincial legislature complained that he had heard there had been favouritism and that a cadet with glasses who could not recognize a fellow cadet across the room had been given a commission because his father was important.[47] The most persistent complainant, however, was a Halifax medical doctor whose letterhead proclaimed that he did not believe in internal medicines. His son had been left $1000 a year by a relative provided he graduated at RMC and received a commission. The boy would lose this legacy if Kitson's decision to refuse a recommendation was not reversed. Kitson could see no reason for changing his mind. He said that he was personally responsible for ensuring that the cadets that he recommended were in every way fitted for the imperial service. He was sure the cabinet and Minister would not want him to recommend cadets he thought would bring discredit on Canada and the military college. He said that the boy would succeed elsewhere but would be unhappy in the army.[48]

The boy's father decided to take this matter up at the highest level. He believed that Tupper would ask questions when parliament met; he circulated printed copies of testimonials to prove, among other things, that his son neither smoked nor drank. Kitson replied with affidavits, including one from Captain Lee, which made allegations about cheating, and another one that mentioned Carr-Harris's practice of never giving less than 50 per cent term marks as proof that the boy was not as good as his marks suggested. In January the complainant accused Kitson of having tried to get cadets to break, rather than sign, the pledge of abstinence. There is a reply to this in the form of an unsigned draft of a letter which Kitson seems to have intended to send to the father. It is dated 26 February 1898 and says that no criticism has ever been made of the son's character "except by you. ... you told me he had learned to drink at R.M.C."[49] It is a pity that this "retort complete" was not sent to the irate but misguided parent. However, the commission was apparently not granted.

Kitson's reforms on the academic side were impeded by the 1896 reduction in the length of the course to three years. But he aimed to preserve and foster the scientific and technical elements. The standard required in the entrance examination was considerably raised so that the time taken up in teaching elementary subjects could be cut down. To raise the standard of French in the college, French was made obligatory in the entrance examination and Latin, which was not taught at the college, was put on the optional list.

But the most important need for the future of the college was that the staff members appointed to fill vacancies left by some of the dismissed professors should help to repair its academic standing. The crucial appointment was in civil engineering. To succeed Carr-Harris, E. F. Wurtele, the secretary of the RMC Club, recommended three ex-cadets who had followed that profession since graduation, Duncan MacPherson and W. M. Davis of the Old Eighteen, and Lieutenant R. W. Leonard who had graduated in 1883.[50] Kitson, however, had been impressed by Cecil B. Smith* of McGill who had conducted the external examinations in civil engineering. He enquired about Smith's availability through Dean Bovey. Although the appointment at RMC was considered by some to be no promotion for him, Smith was prepared to accept.[51] Bruce Carruthers, the president of the Kingston Liberal Club, who supported Davis because he was a practical man, said that Smith was "much too theoretical."[52] Meanwhile John V. Ellis, MP for Saint John, had sent Cartwright an eighteen-page testimonial in favour of Professor Stephen Dixon of the University of New Brunswick.[53] But the Minister was already committed to Professor W. R. Butler,† of King's College, Windsor, Nova Scotia, who was associated with him in engineering work and in business deals connected with the erection of dikes to reclaim land in King's County, Nova Scotia. Kitson told Borden that he preferred Smith. He wanted to have the letters about him laid before the cabinet, but he said that if the Minister insisted on Butler he was prepared to give way.[54] Borden's reply caused Kitson "anxiety and worry." The Minister insisted, so Kitson apologized and professed that he was grateful because Borden had been "exceedingly kind in letting me have my own way about the college" in so many other respects. He would do everything in his power to make Butler's appointment a success.[55]

Later Kitson reported that Butler was "getting on capitally ... "; the class seemed to like him and was working more energetically. Butler, who

---

*Cecil Brunswick Smith, B.SC., M.ENG., railway engineer, member Ontario Hydro-Electric Power Commission, 1906–7.

†W. R. Butler, M.E., A.M.I.C.E., professor of engineering, King's College, Windsor; professor of civil engineering, RMC, 1897–1917.

found he preferred the fall in Ontario to that in the Maritimes, was optimistic about what could be accomplished at RMC. He found the library small but he personally bought books; and he asked if he could get them into Canada free of customs duties. He also asked Borden whether he could take on consulting work and he told him that Kitson seemed to like the idea.[56] As time went on Butler came to like RMC "more than at first." He was particularly pleased that Kitson was no longer disappointed that Smith had not been selected and he declared that no one could have given him more consideration than the Commandant.[57] It is noteworthy that Butler continued to be associated with Borden in land reclamation in Kingsport, Nova Scotia. His appointment was no doubt a piece of personal patronage on the Minister's part but the new professor of civil engineering seems to have turned out very well.

The vacancy in French was also filled politically. Israel Tarte recommended a French army officer, Captain J. D. Chartrand,* who seemed to Kitson to be "as good a man as we are likely to get at the $1000 salary." He had been dismissed from the army because his leave of absence was not renewed on account of debts that he could not pay.[58] That there was nothing else known against him seems to have counted for more than more positive qualifications which were not mentioned.

Although patronage thus continued to flourish, the revival of the college was quickly apparent. When Kitson arrived there were forty-five cadets. Thirteen of these graduated in June, one was withdrawn for health reasons, four failed, and two others "withdrew after the examinations." This left the college with only twenty-five returning cadets for September. However the new class was thirty-one and one other returned from sick leave. The total for 1897–8 therefore stood at fifty-seven.[59] Kitson reported to Borden that only one room in the college was big enough to take all the cadets at the same time.[60] This remarkable reversal of the trend in recruiting continued in the following years. In 1898 the strength at RMC jumped to seventy-four; in 1899 it was eighty-seven; and in 1900, despite the commissioning of twenty-one cadets for war service without graduating, the number was seventy-six.[61] By 1898 Kitson was able to suggest dispensing with newspaper advertising which, he said, did not appear to have much effect on recruitment.[62]

In 1898 outside examiners were again sought. Professor Butler asked Borden to ensure that Cecil Smith of McGill should not be employed to mark civil engineering. Having been thwarted about the appointment, he could hardly be expected to be free from bias.[63] Kitson was able to report

---

*Captain J. D Chartrand, professor of French, 1897–1905, formerly an officer of the Chasseurs d'Afrique (information from Colonel L. F. Grant).

that in all subjects examiners were selected who had nothing to do with the instruction of the cadets in the subjects they were being examined in and that the results were fair. There were only eight graduates. From all years in the college three cadets had been commissioned, one had failed, and three had been withdrawn.[64] In the following year, 1899, after two cadets had withdrawn through sickness and one had been dismissed for misconduct, there were four failures and fourteen graduates. It was now said to be difficult to obtain outside examiners and the examinations were once more marked by the professors who gave the courses. To reassure the Minister that abuses would not recur, Kitson personally checked samples of the marking.

Apparently, rigorous academic standards had been restored. Kitson expected the increase in the number of applicants to bring better quality. He reported that thus far all who had qualified for entry to RMC had been accepted; but he remarked that, as the increase continued, the ceiling imposed by accommodation and establishment would soon be reached and entry would then become sharply competitive. A side result of the obviously greater academic pressure on cadets was an increase in the practice of cramming for examinations. However some who had no hope of passing, or who were congenitally idle, were still to be found in the college. Kitson asked that he be given power of summary dismissal in such cases.[65]

An interesting sidelight on the reform of RMC and the restoration of sound academic standards appeared in a controversy about the passage of a bill in Quebec to prevent unqualified engineers from practising in the province. Duncan MacPherson, one of the Old Eighteen, and other ex-cadets were among the leaders in working for this change. They were bitterly opposed by Professor R. Carr-Harris, now at Queen's. Carr-Harris saw the bill as a move by established engineers to impose severe restrictions on new graduates. He hoped to win the support of the RMC Club. He told its members that RMC graduates now had to go to McGill for a year to qualify as practising engineers because the RMC course had been reduced in length. He said that this had "depressed" the college.[66] This shows that Kitson's reforms, although they had improved the quality of the instruction, had made it harder to qualify as a professional engineer. This was a consequence that Kitson, interested chiefly in obtaining better qualified officers for the British army, had apparently overlooked. Nevertheless, Carr-Harris got no support for his campaign against the bill, either in the RMC Club or in RMC itself.

The decline in numbers at the college during Cameron's day had removed the pressing need for more barracks. On his arrival Kitson had been warned against expensive projects, but his first annual report, in which he pointed out the greater stress that was being placed on drill, stated that a new infantry and artillery drill shed was needed for use in winter.[67] He made the same request a year later; and in 1899 he was able to report that both it and the hospital had been put into the estimates for 1899–1900. In that year he also reported that numbers were once again producing overcrowding but that he could manage for the immediate future by making better use of space and by creating six new rooms.[68] However, if the number of cadets continued to rise, the "wing" that had been planned many years earlier would be urgently required. Kitson could forget the warning against expense because he was now confident of the success of his reform and revival of the college. He declared that increase in numbers would mean the need for more staff but that the cost would be offset by the greater revenue from fees. Although he balked at carrying out a father's request to stop his boy from smoking,[69] Kitson moved to improve conditions at the college by curbing what Borden called delicately, "the matter of the liquids," that is to say cadet drinking.[70] He imposed a "pledge" on recruits on arrival. Whatever one may think of this device there can be no doubt that there was a vastly different atmosphere on Point Frederick soon after his arrival.

On the military side, summer service with the militia camp had been made an obligatory part of training. First-year cadets served without pay, but those in the second and third years were paid as second lieutenants. The numbers who were eligible to go to camp became so large that Kitson proposed in 1899 that attendance should be made a privilege or prize and that he should be given the authority to select those who would go.[71] In addition, each year a party of RMC cadets continued the survey of the country that had been begun by Captain Lee in 1894. London, Prince Edward county, the frontier at Detroit and along the St. Clair River, Toronto, and Niagara were covered. Maps made by these survey parties were to prove useful in connection with militia exercises which became more common as the century drew to a close.[72]

The improvement of RMC's prestige was by no means due only to the change of commandant and the change of government. Largely as a result of the Venezuelan crisis at the end of 1895, Canadians were now more conscious of the need for defence. At the Colonial Conference in 1897 when Laurier had pointed to the decline of the college in recent years, he had continued: "We hope that with new management it will be restored to its former standard, which was very good, I believe."[73] Cartwright told Borden that Canada was entering a new era and suggested that the time was ripe for a thorough reform of the military.[74] Laurier brought out as

GOC of the militia, Major-General E. T. H. Hutton,* another of Wolseley's protégés. Kitson had been a brother officer of Hutton in the 60th Rifles and addressed him as "My Dear old Curly." He greeted the prospect of his appointment as GOC with expressions of delight.[75] As soon as he learned in May that it was a possibility, he ordered extra drill for "the unfortunate cadets" (his own words) to prepare them for Hutton's visit to RMC even though he could hardly come that term.[76] As Hutton did not arrive in Canada until August and did not visit the college until October, extra drill imposed in May suggests that Kitson was a little premature. He apparently gave little heed to the possibility that it might be at the expense of the academic programme, which shows that his interest was in military training rather than in education.

Hutton had had earlier experience of colonial militias in Australia and was a confirmed believer in their value as additions to the military strength of the empire. He talked of the development of a "national" army in Canada based on the militia, using the word "national" to mean pertaining to Canada and not, as it was still sometimes used in the colonies, to apply to the British nation including the colonies. The new GOC realized that the most serious deficiency in Canada was trained senior staff officers. He therefore turned to RMC to produce them.

As soon as Hutton arrived, Kitson took up the question of the long course, which he had revived in 1897, but for which militia officers could rarely spare time from business. In 1897, through the GOC's influence, a "capital class" of thirteen or fourteen had been collected and Kitson offered to give the course in the autumn as well as in the spring; but in the following year there were only six or seven, and these were "boys who were being crammed for the examinations for the Imperial Service who don't interest one very much." Kitson therefore asked Hutton to look into the question, at the same time warning him that militia officers were in most cases so ignorant "that we have to start them with 'vulgar fractions.' "[77]

It was too late to set up a class for the fall term of 1898; but Hutton promised that he would see that there was a good class in the following spring, and he said that he also wanted to discuss with Kitson the training of Canadian officers for staff duties. At Hutton's request, Kitson worked out a programme for a staff course modelled to a great extent on the course at the British Staff College at Camberley except that surveying and

---

*Lieutenant-General Sir Edward Thomas Henry Hutton, K.C.B. K.C.M.G., D.L., K.R.R.C., commandant in New South Wales, 1893–6; GOC Canadian militia, 1898–1900; an advocate of mounted infantry, commanded mounted troops other than cavalry in South Africa; GOC Australia, 1901–4, 21st Division 1914–15.

higher reconnaissance were not considered necessary at Kingston. The theoretical part of the course covered the movement of troops, military history, and the framing of orders. The practical portion was to be carried out by "staff rides."[78] Hutton then obtained the approval of the Deputy Minister by showing that an efficient staff could be produced for the militia at no more cost than the travelling expenses and lodging allowance of the officers who took the course.[79] At the opening of this course in Kingston in 1899, Hutton told its fourteen members that this was the first step in the reorganization of the Canadian militia, that it was being watched with the greatest interest by the authorities at home, and that "nothing could be more important, more absolutely vital to the forces of the Dominion than the creation of a General Staff if in any way they are to be looked upon as an Army." Twelve officers completed the course which was very successful.[80]

Meanwhile Laurier had also agreed to the establishment of a defence commission to report on Canada's military preparedness. Composed of British officers and two Canadian ministers, the Leach commission toured Canada and reported on the state of the militia. Its report included a description and assessment of RMC. The commissioners stated their opinion that Kitson was doing valuable work not only in the professional training of cadets for subsequent employment in civil life but also in raising their moral standard and tone. The report said that only a small percentage entered the college in hope of an imperial commission. Service in the Permanent Corps or the North-West Mounted Police offered little inducement because, though the pay was better than in the imperial service, promotion was slower and there was no pension. Of one hundred and fifty-nine qualified RMC graduates, there were only ten in the Permanent Force and twenty in the Active Militia. (Two Permanent Force commissions offered to RMC in 1898 had not been taken up.[81]) The commissioners found it difficult to understand why so few served in the militia and they noted that although one hundred and twenty were on the list of reserve officers, and available in the event of war, they received no training in time of peace. They alleged that "a large proportion have left the country," which was only true if those who took imperial commissions were included. The commission found that the reduction of the course from four years to three, although strongly criticized at the time, had been "beneficial," but it did not specify what the benefits were. It recommended that all Permanent Force commissions and all Mounted Police commissions should be reserved for RMC graduates and that they should also have preference for appointments on the Inter-Colonial Railway, the Department of Marine and Fisheries, and government public works generally. It also recommended that application should be made to the imperial government for appointments in the India Public Works Department, the Indian police, the Indian Forest Department, and administrative and police services in the crown colonies.[82]

Hutton had worked closely with the commission and, though the Leach report was never published, incorporated some of its findings in his own annual reports. He was able also to carry out some of its recommendations, notably those in regard to RMC. In 1899 he announced that the Permanent Force and Instructional Corps were in future to be largely officered by RMC graduates. All Royal Canadian Artillery commissions and half of the infantry and cavalry commissions were to be reserved for RMC.[83] Two Army Service Corps commissions were also now allocated annually to RMC, making the total of imperial commissions available seven instead of five.[84]

Hutton wanted to ensure that Kitson, whom he regarded as his second-in-command in Canada, would be senior to the members of the staff courses at RMC.[85] He therefore had him made a full colonel. He had to obtain authority from the War Office because the Canadian Militia Act did not make provision for promotion beyond the rank of lieutenant-colonel. This promotion was also a tribute to Kitson for his success in the rehabilitation of RMC.

RMC's revival renewed interest in it in Australia. Applicants were sought for the Queensland Artillery in which prospects were said to be good because the Australian colonies were on the verge of federation.[86] Furthermore, ex-cadets continued to make their mark in the imperial army and to bring glory and honour to their alma mater. Captain H. C. Smith of the Royal Dublin Fusiliers was mentioned in dispatches by Kitchener after the Battle of Khartoum and later received the Order of the Medjidie (Fourth Class). Lieutenant Girouard was appointed president of the Egyptian Railway Administration at a salary of £2000 a year. In Canada, Major Robert Cartwright* became assistant adjutant-general at militia headquarters and Captain C. C. Van Straubenzee was appointed professor of artillery, administration, and law at RMC.[87] Lieutenant Heneker† gained distinction in another way. He had been commissioned in the

---

*Lieutenant-Colonel Robert Cartwright, eldest son of Sir Richard Cartwright, was at RMC 1878–81, where he won many academic prizes; he was a railway engineer in Manitoba, served in the 1885 campaign, and in South Africa where he was four times mentioned in dispatches; AAG for Musketry, Ottawa, 1901, and Musketry Officer No. 11 MD, Victoria during World War I.

†General Sir William Charles Gifford Heneker, K.C.B., K.C.M.G., D.S.O., A.D.Q. (1867–1939), graduated RMC, 1888; commissioned in the Connaught Rangers; GOC., 8 Division, France, 1916–18; divisional commander, Army of Occupation; GOC-in-chief, Southern Command, India, 1928–32.

100th Prince of Wales's Own Royal Canadians. The regimental history makes the somewhat boastful assertion that Heneker was one of Canada's star hockey players "recognized as the best shot at goal in the whole Dominion."[88] At the college itself Sergeant-Major F. Fraser surpassed all previous prizewinners by obtaining every possible decoration during his college course.[89]

So marked was the progress of the college that even the ranks of Tuscany could scarce forebear to cheer. Sir Charles Tupper's private secretary, A. E. Blount, obtained for his employer a list of the RMC graduates who had distinguished themselves either in the imperial service or in any other line since their graduation.[90] Tupper visited RMC and then spoke in the house in praise of Mackenzie, Hewett, and Girouard. Significantly he made no reference to Cameron. He approved the reduction in fees, but he expressed doubt about the wisdom of the reduction of the length of the course. Then when Borden praised Kitson, Tupper called out, "Hear, Hear." Not to be outdone, Borden replied by pointing out that four out of five of the military professors at RMC were graduates of the college. After first praising Kitson, he lauded ex-cadets Girouard, Van Straubenzee, Twining, Stairs, Robinson, Campbell,* Dobell,† McKay [*sic*],‡ Ridout,§ Carey, and Joly de Lotbinière. He showed that out of a total of two hundred and sixty-eight [*sic*] graduates up to and including 1898, eighty-eight had gone to the British Army, twenty-one to the Canadian Permanent Force and the Mounted Police, and twenty to the various civil services in Canada. Fifty-five were engineers on railways or elsewhere and thirty-five were in commerce and business. Only twelve civil engineers had gone to the United States, that is to say no more than 5 per cent of the total had left the British empire. When Finance Minister Cartwright stated that "we do not go far enough to recognize R.M.C. in the

---

*Captain Kenneth Jeffery Rawken Campbell, D.S.O., RMC 1879–81; joined the Gloucester Regiment as a private, served in operations in the Niger Coast protectorate, 1884; commissioned 6th Dragoon Guards; acting commissioner and consul general, Oil River protectorate, 1891–5; Peking expedition, 1900; served in both navy and army in World War I.

†Lieutenant-General Sir Charles MacPherson Dobell, K.C.B., C.M.G., D.S.O., F.R.G.S. (1869–1954), graduated RMC, 1890; Royal Welsh Fusiliers; commanded the allied force which captured the Cameroons, August 1914; an army commander in the Middle East, 1916; divisional commander, Third Afghan War, 1919.

‡Captain Hunley Brodie Mackay, graduated first in his class in 1881 and was commissioned in the RE; acting administrator for the British East African Company; he was awarded the D.S.O. in 1889.

§Major-General Sir Dudley Howard Ridout, K.B.E., C.B., C.M.G., RE (1866–1941), son of Major J. B. Ridout, captain of cadets at RMC; graduated RMC, 1885; intelligence officer in South Africa and GOC Singapore during World War I; died 1941.

Civil Service," Sproule, the MP who had long ago taken up a role as RMC's chief critic, retorted that the graduates of other Canadian universities should get equal chances for employment by the government.[91] However, as if to hammer home the extent of the renaissance by improvement in sport, towards the close of the year RMC won its first Dominion Intermediate Inter-collegiate Rugby (football) Championship.[92]

The war in South Africa came before Kitson had completed his work at the college. In June 1899, he watched the graduation of the combined classes who had entered in 1895 and 1896, that is before he arrived. There were only fourteen, the others having fallen by the wayside. Kitson described the fourteen as "an exceptionally fine lot of men" and recommended nine of them for imperial commissions. The strength of the college in September was eighty-seven and he looked forward keenly and confidently to the graduation of the first class that he had admitted himself. This would occur in June 1900. When the Special Force for South Africa was organized in October, no fewer than eight of the twelve officers who had taken his first staff course were selected for it. Kitson reported that there was little doubt that the staff course had been of value to all concerned.[93] It placed the coping stone on the success of his command at RMC.

Before very long, however, the war began to have unfortunate direct repercussions on the college. Because of the organization of the Special Force Kitson was ordered on 16 October to return to their respective depots six officers of the Royal Canadian Regiment who were then taking the militia long course. Its number was thus reduced to eight.[94] Despite Kitson's doubts, Hutton insisted that the second staff course should take place as planned in the following spring and should last the full four months. He told Kitson that the new course should study the Red River campaign, the beginnings of the Franco-Prussian War, and the embarkation and disembarkation of troops. He also contemplated a more advanced course for selected colonels who gave promise of becoming useful brigadiers. This commanders' course would run concurrently with the fourth month of the staff course. The latter should therefore be confined to tactics and to the drafting of orders, leaving strategy and staff administration for the more senior course. The onset of war had shown that a course of this kind was much needed. Hutton was also determined that "the excellent system which you [Kitson] have assisted me in starting" for the purpose of building a Canadian general staff should not be interrupted.[95]

Things were, however, not going as well as they seemed. The question of Canadian participation in the war had been very controversial and had rent the country. The Governor-General and the imperial officers in

Canada, as also many militia officers and Canadian imperialists, had done all they could to arouse public feeling and to force the Laurier government to act. Hutton had been suspected, perhaps wrongly, of having been privy to the release of information about British proposals that had compelled the Canadian government to agree reluctantly to the formation of an expeditionary force, despite considerable opposition among its own supporters. Both Hutton and Kitson were hand in glove with the imperialists. Kitson urged Dr. George Parkin, the headmaster of Upper Canada and the ablest of the group, to stir up popular feeling by mass demonstrations in order to "brace up our political people" in support of the war.[96]

Kitson discussed this question with Parkin when he was in Toronto buying horses for the First Battalion of the Canadian Mounted Rifles which had been ordered to South Africa in December. Hutton had succeeded in thwarting Borden's original intention of assigning the purchase of the horses by contract to a Liberal member of parliament. Under his direction Kitson and his officers chose the horses and are said to have given satisfaction to the battalion's officers who showed their appreciation (and incidentally embarrassed the recipient) by presenting the RMC commandant with an engraved silver cup. The Minister, however, was concerned lest the prices paid in a seller's market, higher than those paid to the Mounted Police for similar horses, would be criticized. It is possible also that he believed that it might be alleged that the patronage had passed to the Conservative opposition. He therefore appointed an independent agent to check the purchases. This individual was, however, no other than the horse dealer who had been denied the original contract. Kitson was insulted, and Hutton declared his intention of putting "the matter very clearly and pointedly to the Minister" to show how a British officer felt about such delicate matters.[97] The outcome was that the incident became a pretext for Hutton's dismissal. He left the country in February for England and soon got a command in South Africa.

An immediate consequence of this was the collapse of the second staff course at RMC after it had run only seventeen days. Lieutenant-Colonel H. H. Burney, an imperial officer on the RMC staff, and some of the officers forming the course, had been ordered to South Africa and others were needed at their military duties. The course was therefore cancelled.[98] Meanwhile the impact of the war was beginning to be felt also on the cadet college which must have already suffered somewhat when members of the military staff, including the commandant, were employed on special duties connected with the organization of the forces for South Africa.

The college was soon affected in another way. Colonel Hubert Foster,* the quarter-master general who had organized the first contingent in October because Hutton was absent in British Columbia, had later had an interview with the Commander-in-Chief, Lord Wolseley, in England about what was needed further. Wolseley asked whether Kitson could "furnish good boys for commissions." Foster replied, "certainly." Wolseley then revealed that the War Office was at the end of its resources for officers and was giving active service commissions to untrained British militia officers. He asked for twenty or thirty RMC cadets fit for regular army commissions. He warned Foster that it was desirable that they should have private incomes as "a boy's position with only his pay [was] rather cruel." This condition always produced difficulty as far as Canadian applicants were concerned. Wolseley told his visitor to pass this message on to Governor-General Lord Minto† and to let him know at once how many could be recommended.[99]

Before he left Canada, Hutton persuaded Minto to inform Wolseley in a private cypher cable that Kitson was able to furnish the required officers.[100] Soon afterwards Major McGill, the staff-adjutant at RMC, received a wire from Borden asking for detailed information about cadets of two years standing and more. Kitson immediately jumped to the conclusion that, unless this request was in connection with Lord Strathcona's regiment of horse which was then being formed, the Minister had received an official offer of imperial commissions for RMC cadets and must be keeping it from him. He therefore sent Minto's private secretary a copy of regulations which he had had drawn up and which stated that the seven annual commissions now given to RMC graduates for the imperial army would only be offered to the top fourteen members of the class unless the commandant made special exceptions when all the commissions were not taken up. He insisted that he and his officers must have control of the offer of commissions to cadets. Even an offer of commissions in Strathcona's Horse "plays the mischief with the discipline of the college, when commissions are offered to the cadets at the bottom of the class."[101]

Instructions to select candidates for extra imperial commissions were in

*Colonel Hubert J. Foster (1855-1919); RE, 1875; after service in Halifax, he became QMG of the Canadian militia, 1898; Intelligence Department War Office; attaché in Washington; Challis Director of Military Science, University of Sydney and lecturer on staff duties.

†John Elliot Gilbert, Earl of Minto, G.C.M.G., K.G. (1845–1914), Scots Guards, served in Afghanistan (1879) and Egypt (1882); as Viscount Melgund he was military secretary to the Marquis of Lorne, governor-general of Canada, 1883–6, and chief of staff to Middleton on the Northwest campaign, 1885; governor-general of Canada, 1898–1904; viceroy of India, 1905–10.

fact already on the way to the college, but Kitson soon found that there was difficulty in getting "decent cadets" to accept them. "Unfortunately our present senior class are a very poor lot, & apparently their parents are afraid of their boys being shot in South Africa." He hoped to be able to get "5 good fellows"; he said that if cadets of one-and-a-half years' standing were acceptable he could supply any number.[102] There was considerable delay before these recommendations went to London and before the actual offer of specific commissions was made. As a result the cadets and their parents became very anxious and kept "bullying" Kitson to get an answer.

Perhaps as a result, and to show what could be done further, Kitson communicated directly with General Grove at the War Office about a request for more regular officers from RMC and he received a reply that two commissions would be offered in the Royal Engineers, four in the artillery, five in the Army Service Corps, and two or three in the infantry, a revision of what had already been sent officially through the regular channels. Despite his experience with the senior class, Kitson believed that he could get "a good lot of youngsters."[103]

He was, however, suspicious of the Minister's intentions with regard to the imperial commissions in the regular army that were to be offered to the militia and which had formerly been distributed by the GOC who had now been dismissed. He also wanted to keep the RMC commissions distinct from the militia commissions even though the former were now to be offered to the junior classes and not merely to RMC graduates as in peace years. He told Minto that all the best young men of the militia were in South Africa and many there would give anything for a permanent imperial commission. He believed that unless the selection of applicants was made by three imperial officers "the British Army [would] be shot with all the useless ruffians, the lame, halt & blind that were piled into Strathcona's Horse."[104]

Kitson soon began to suspect also that political patronage might affect the college's share of the imperial commissions. The recommendations that he had forwarded to the Chief Staff Officer were returned and he was told that the government of Canada had not yet accepted the offer. Furthermore, he was severely reprimanded for having corresponded directly with the War Office on the subject. He defended himself by saying that his letter was a private one; but he at the same time declared that he had a right to correspond officially directly with the War Office on the subject because the War Office was always writing directly to him. He told Minto: "This Minister of Militia is really a terrible fellow, and will ruin his Gov[t] if he doesn't take care."[105] However, when Minto took a strong stand, the matter was settled by an arrangement whereby the imperial officers in Canada would recommend applicants for imperial commissions to the Minister who would then have the right of disapproval but not of nomination. The possibility that the imperial commissions could be used for "political corruption" by being given, as Kitson put it, to "a collection of politicians' friends' sons," was thus avoided.[106]

This conflict about who should select cadets for the imperial commissions may have had a disturbing affect on cadet demand for them. In March, four cadets from the second class at RMC were commissioned in each of the artillery and the Army Service Corps, and in May, four more from the same class took artillery commissions. Of three more commissioned in June in the Royal Engineers, only two were in the first class and on the list of graduates. The graduating class also provided one officer for the Canadian forces in South Africa. Eight other cadets who were commissioned later in the year were all from later classes.[107] As Kitson had begun to fear, some of the first class that he had seen right through the college seemed to have turned their backs on military service. The war had brought a restlessness that had apparently also affected the final examination results: five of the graduates were required to write a supplementary examination before receiving their piece of parchment. The *British Whig* reported that the *esprit* of the senior class in the college had been strangely affected. "They seemed to have imbibed an aversion to conditions in the imperial army." It alleged that they were "nearly all going to courses in engineering and mining in Montreal and Toronto."[108]

The *Whig* sent its reporter to find out about conditions at RMC. Although he claimed that his sources of information were cadets who had passed and who were therefore not suffering from a case of "sore head," the reporter's findings have all the earmarks of the prejudiced whining that low morale produces. Cadets alleged favouritism in the allocation of prizes, favouritism in the grant of the privilege of supplementary examinations, bias in grading, and also that they had been used as guinea pigs for a lecture to be delivered later elsewhere by a professor who gave only one lecture in the term. They claimed that professors called cadets by abusive names; and that in order to get a cadet into trouble had tried to tempt him with liquor to make him violate the pledge he had taken on entering the college. As supreme evidence of the attitude of the class, the reporter noted that the traditional RMC practice at closing exercises of carrying the professors around the groups and transporting them to their rooms, had been restricted to two only, and that a "decree" had gone out among the cadets that no others were to be so "honoured." It had been mutually agreed that any cadets who did not conform to the wishes of the majority of the class in this respect would be thrown into the lake.[109]

Kitson complained that he and his management of the college were being attacked in the local press because some cadets had grumbled and had made groundless accusations. He said that after three and a half years he was "pretty sick of this school" where he had done all the good he was likely to be able to do. He had found it an "ungrateful task." In one sentence in a letter to Minto, in which he asked advice about applying to succeed Captain Lee as military attaché in Washington, he put his finger on one cause of trouble. He wrote: "It shows their bitter spirit of animosity, they [the Canadian press] never seem to lose a chance of having a slap at one of us [imperial officers]."[110] The problem, as Laurier had said when he reported on Hutton's dismissal to the House of Commons, was that the imperial officers in Canada found themselves unable to serve two masters when controversial issues arose, like participation in the war. What he meant was that they therefore resorted to political propaganda and to questionable channels of communication and they objected more vigorously than ever to the patronage that infected Canadian political life. Laurier claimed that the GOC had failed to understand his position as an officer "in the employment of and subject in all respects to the government of Canada, ... the adviser but not ... entitled to control the Department of Militia."[111] Kitson had warned Hutton before he accepted the post as GOC that he must be willing to accept this subordinate position,[112] but in the midst of war fever neither man was able to maintain such a tame role.

The graduating class was undoubtedly affected by the political controversies that raged around them and probably also by the fact that the official and unofficial activities of the college staff connected with the war had reduced the time the military professors devoted to class work. Hence, whereas Hutton had told the RMC Club in 1898 that he had found that the anxiety and ambition of the cadets was to serve her Majesty "anywhere but in Canada,"[113] in 1900 half of the first class to go right through the rehabilitated college under Kitson went to civil occupations despite the war in South Africa. It is not surprising that the Commandant was thoroughly dejected and that he felt that all his work had been in vain.

The spirit of institutions is, however, greater and more lasting than that of individuals or small groups. Although the graduating class in 1900 did not show the same temper as the cadet body in 1885, when the whole college volunteered for service in the Northwest, that class was in fact well represented in the war in South Africa. It had entered thirty-one strong in 1897. Fifteen of its members served in South Africa, some with British commissions either obtained through the government or privately. Others served in the ranks. Fourteen who graduated in 1900 did not go to South Africa but three of these were commissioned in the Permanent Force a few years later and five served during World War I. Only six are known not to have served either in war or as career officers. Two others cannot be accounted for. The morale of the class in its graduating year was thus a passing phase.

In addition to the graduating class, cadets from junior classes and ex-cadets from pre-reform days also volunteered. At the outset of the war the RMC Club wired to the Minister: "Graduates R.M.C. offering for South Africa, if required will be pleased to forward names." Borden answered immediately: "Shall be glad to receive names of graduates volunteering." One hundred and thirteen ex-cadets served in South Africa, some of them among the one hundred and sixty officers who served in the Special Force, and at least as many more with the British army and forces from other colonies. Five were killed and several were wounded. The number of RMC decorations received was high in proportion to the size of the college's representation: one K.C.M.G., two C.M.G. s, seven D.S.O. s, twenty-two mentioned in dispatches by Kitchener, five by Sir Redvers Buller, and two by Sir Charles Warren.[114]

Some RMC graduates were especially useful on railway administration. Lieutenant-Colonel Girouard was director of railways with Captain Joly de Lotbinière as his deputy director of the Bloemfontein line and Captain H. C. Nanton* in the same capacity on the Kimberley line. Lieutenant-Colonel H. S. Greenwood commanded the Central South African Railway Volunteer Corps and was in charge at Johannesburg. "The little English clerk at the station speaks their names with a respect almost amounting to the reverence he bestows on the titles of the lords and baronets who are leading the warlike yeomanry to the front," wrote Lieutenant E. W. B. Morrison,† and he added that another young Canadian engineer, Captain MacInnes,‡ the son of Senator MacInnes of Hamilton, was credited by the local press as being chiefly responsible for saving the station from the Boers.[115]

---

*Brigadier-General Herbert Colborne Nanton, C.B., C.I.E., late RE (1863–1935); RMC 1879–83; Northwest campaign, 1885; served in India and South Africa.

†Major-General Sir Edward Whipple Bancroft Morrison, K.C.M.G., C.B., D.S.O. (1867–1925), journalist, served in South Africa, GOC Canadian Artillery, 1916–19, later master-general of ordnance and adjutant-general.

‡Brigadier-General D. S. MacInnes, Royal Engineers, graduated RMC, 1891, served against the Ashanti and in the Balloon Section in South Africa. He played a big part in the formation of the Royal Air Force.

RMC had thus justified its existence when war involved the empire. But the Canadian Permanent Force was still not large enough to absorb more than a tiny proportion of the college's output. It was because of this that the college's curriculum had had to be shaped to meet the needs of civilian professions. In a time of great confusion, of political controversy, of perplexity, and of recrimination about the war in South Africa, a few of the young graduates had thought more about getting started on their immediate careers than of their duty to fight in distant lands. But larger numbers of their classmates and others not yet within sight of a graduation certificate and a professional career, as also more mature ex-cadets whose RMC spirit was still strong, had stepped in to fill the breach and had added further laurels to RMC's already impressive tradition of service. In an appreciative article to the London *Times* on the occasion of Kitson's resignation, Dr. Parkin, its Canadian correspondent, said that RMC was doing "exceedingly good work, not only for the Dominion, but for the Empire."[116]

8

THE EVE OF

WAR

1901-1914

Canada's involvement in the South African War had followed closely upon strained relations betwen Britain and the United States over Venezuela and also upon a disagreement over the Alaskan boundary. All these events drew attention to the lack of adequate military preparation in the dominion and to the need for a thorough reform of the Canadian Permanent and Non-Permanent Active Militia. Preliminary measures had been taken by Generals Herbert and Hutton before the war. The GOC from 1902 to 1904, Lord Dundonald,* organized the departmental corps needed to create the balanced force that Hutton had recommended; but, like Hutton before him, he was dismissed because he failed to accept subordination to the civil power in Canada in matters which he believed purely military. However, the minister of Militia and Defence who was responsible for his dismissal, Frederick Borden, was equally anxious to overhaul the Canadian militia; and his Conservative successor as minister from 1911 to 1916, Sam Hughes, was also a zealous advocate of the doctrine of military preparedness. Although there was still much opposition to military expenditures, budgets were a little more generous. So, in the dozen years before Canada was plunged into a far greater conflict, the dominion began to build up an effective part-time military force organized for operations, and an efficient permanent component to train it.

This renovation of the Canadian militia was matched by expansion and growth of the reformed RMC. There the first problem was to find a suitable successor to Kitson. While one was sought, Major Casimir Van Straubenzee, the senior military professor, carried on as acting commandant.

---

*Lieutenant-General Douglas M. B. H. Cochrane, Earl of Dundonald, K.C.B., K.C.V.O. (1852–1935), Life Guards, served in Egypt, commanded cavalry and mounted troops in South Africa, GOC Canadian militia, 1902–4.

The first ex-cadet to command the college, his appointment was an indication of the degree to which the college's graduates had now progressed. One strong influence affecting the RMC appointment was that Laurier's government wanted to find a good place for Colonel Otter, whose service commanding Canadian troops in South Africa had been highly praised in the Canadian press and had won him a great reputation with the public. The command of RMC seemed a possibility for him.[1] But the Colonial Office feared that if Otter were appointed he would become a permanency in the position. He would lose touch with military developments and the college would relapse into that degenerate condition experienced under General Cameron. It was also suggested that if the War Office lost confidence in the officer who commanded RMC the granting of British commissions might be re-considered. Although this withdrawal was soon realized to be unlikely, the maintenance of a supply of Canadian officers for the British army was a valid reason by itself for Britain to seek to ensure the college's efficiency.[2]

Lord Minto, the governor-general, was anxious to foster the imperial connection by keeping British officers in posts like that at RMC. Therefore, although he agreed that Otter was a good soldier, he pointed out that Otter lacked the educational and staff training needed to head the college.[3] To enable Canada to reward the officers who had done well in South Africa, Minto suggested that Britain should hand over Halifax and Esquimalt to be governed by the dominion. The Colonial Office refused even to consider this transfer of the bases, but an anonymous official commented that, as the War Office had not always been careful to send the best men to the garrisons in Canada, there was no reason why a distinguished Canadian officer should not be appointed to their staffs.[4] Meanwhile the War Office which, according to the Colonial Office, had come to regard the appointment at RMC as a "regular piece of [its] military patronage,"[5] recommended Major Raymond N. R. Reade of the Shropshire Light Infantry*[6] for the post without waiting for a request to come from Canada.

Annoyed at being forestalled and committed, Borden immediately protested that Canada should have been consulted before a British officer was recommended. He said that he knew nothing about Reade, and he asked to be informed of his qualifications.[7] Borden declared he would accept

*Major-General Raymond Northland Revell Reade, c.b., c.m.g. (1861–1943), a grandson of the second Earl of Ranfurly, served in Afghanistan and West Africa and had staff appointments in Egypt and Aldershot; DAAG (intelligence) South African war; after commanding RMC (1901–5), he served in Malta, Scotland, and the Straits Settlements; poor health prevented service in World War I; British representative on the Inter-Allied Military Mission to Greece, 1918 (CO 42/866, p. 24).

Reade as commandant of RMC if another place could be found for Otter; he suggested that Otter replace Colonel Hubert Foster as QMG of the militia. But to make that appointment possible, it would be necessary to find a place for Foster. Borden asked whether the QMG, who wanted RMC, could go to Kingston instead of Reade. As Foster was regarded as too poor a disciplinarian for a cadet college, the War Office was compelled to promise to find a place for him at home. Borden then accepted Reade as commandant.[8]

Reade's qualities and qualifications served him well in this appointment. Though neither an engineer nor an artilleryman, as would have been preferred, he had stood in fourth place in his staff college examination, had held important staff and administrative appointments, and had seen much fighting in South Africa. His comments on RMC examination results show an academic interest and outlook. He said in 1901 that low marks could be explained by the fact that the best cadets had gone to South Africa but he criticized standards in French, physics, and chemistry. When the war could no longer account for poor results in 1904, he again criticized the examination results, this time in surveying and physics. What is noteworthy is that on both of these occasions his criticisms were accompanied by sound and constructive proposals for improvement: smaller classes for French, the introduction of entrance tests in physics and chemistry, and separate instructors for physics and surveying. Reade also showed concern to build up the RMC library. He recalled the government-owned technical books held on charge by the professors and put them on the library inventory. He also extended RMC library privileges to the Permanent Force officers in the Kingston area.[9] A significant development under Reade was the completion of long-awaited construction, a twenty-five bed hospital adjacent to the educational block, an electric power plant, and a large gymnasium to the south of the Stone Frigate. He also secured separate quarters for the staff-adjutant and his family (in what was later called Panet House after its first occupant), and he built an extension at the rear of the Stone Frigate for bathroom facilities. Both of these additions increased RMC's dormitory accommodation.[10] The college was beginning to grow.

But the foremost difficulty to be overcome was the problem of integrating the college with the militia, Canada's chief military potential. Although Borden had told the Commons in 1901 that all recipients of Permanent Force commissions must now be either RMC graduates, college matriculants, or militia officers who had passed the long course, and that only the RMC graduates were eligible for the artillery, he noted that for three years no graduate had taken a Canadian artillery commission.[11] One reason for this was, of course, that those cadets who wanted a military career had gone to South Africa.

Major-General O'Grady Haly,* the elderly British officer appointed GOC after Hutton was dismissed, attempted an explanation. He said in 1901 that in the time they spent at RMC the "*students* [he may have used the word deliberately] do not imbibe any soldierly ambition or acquire a taste for Military employment." Consequently he was unwilling to do much to develop the college, as is obvious in his attitude to equitation at RMC. The war had greatly magnified the importance of horses, yet riding instruction at RMC was still extremely weak. O'Grady Haly said that, as the college did not produce many officers for the Permanent Force and the Active Militia, it would be wasteful to improve its riding facilities, and he therefore recommended that those cadets who took Permanent Force commissions should be sent to Toronto to take a riding course with the Dragoons.[12] Later, in testimony before the British Royal Commission investigating the conduct of the South African War, he said that the Kingston college produced officers for Britain rather than Canada.[13] But while in Canada he had done little to help those cadets who wanted British commissions to acquire the necessary skill on horseback. He had, in effect, been prepared to let the RMC die as a military institution in failing to teach a skill that was still important at that time.

The Canadian government paid little attention to this old man and his poorly thought-out ideas, but O'Grady Haly had provided RMC's foes with heavy ammunition. They were only too willing to use it. In the House of Commons in 1902, Dr. T. S. Sproule, RMC's most persistent critic, erroneously ascribed the GOC's criticism to the Commandant; he declared that it showed that RMC had entirely failed to achieve its objectives. Borden easily refuted this attack on the military spirit of RMC cadets and on the college's military value by simply announcing the number of RMC cadets in the British army, the number who had fought in South Africa, and the number of RMC trained engineers who had come forward from their civilian occupations to join the Special Force.[14] However, Reade informed Governor-General Grey,† who passed it on to the Colonial Secretary, that it was in fact true that many cadets preferred civilian employment, for

*Major-General Richard Hebden O'Grady Haly (1841–1911), 84th Regiment, ADC to adjutant-general and GOC Canadian militia, 1870–9; after staff college in 1881, he served in Egypt (1882) and the WO Intelligence Department (1882-4); GOC, 1900-2.

†Albert Henry George Grey, Earl Grey (1851–1917), son of a private secretary of Prince Albert and Queen Victoria; a liberal MP; governor-general of Canada, 1904–11, and one of the most popular to hold that post.

instance on the extension of the Grand Trunk Railway, because a career as a British officer required private means which few possessed.[15] Service in Canada, although better paid than service in the junior ranks in the British army, lacked certain of the latter's advantages – the prospect of adventure, interesting appointments, and pensions. Reade pointed out that all West Point graduates entered the army, but he noted that their education at the academy had been "practically free." He therefore proposed that fees should be reimbursed to those RMC graduates who entered the Canadian Permanent Active Militia, and that RMC graduates should be required to serve for three years in the Active Militia.[16]

With regard to permanent commissions, Lord Dundonald bluntly stated at the college's closing exercises in 1902 that the employment of RMC graduates was beyond the limits of his competence.[17] He thus publicly, and in front of the audience that was most immediately interested, issued a direct challenge to the politicians under whom he served, revealing that the responsibility for solving this difficult employment problem lay with the government. A year later he suggested that a $500 bonus should be given to an RMC graduate on appointment to a Permanent Force commission and that time at RMC should count toward the new militia pensions. But the part of his report which included these proposals was suppressed when he quarreled with the Minister.[18] Because of his bluntness and lack of tact, Dundonald had no immediate success in these projects, as in most of the other things for which he campaigned. But many others were pressing for similar objectives. In particular the RMC Club was anxious to bring about changes at the college; and the quality of the club's membership was beginning to make it influential and prestigious.

These years before World War I saw many ex-cadets rise in fame and position throughout the empire; and their achievements did not pass unnoticed in Canada. In 1900 Girouard was knighted. In the same year Captain J. I. Lang became British commissioner in Lagos. Lieutenant-Colonel S. J. A. Denison was ADC to the Duke of York when he visited Canada in 1901. Captain A. Joly de Lotbinière was in charge of the construction of an electric power plant in Mysore, India, which was claimed to be the largest in the empire if not in the world. At home Perry became commissioner of the Royal North-West Mounted Police; and other graduates began to reach places close to the tight oligarchy that dominated the higher ranks of the Permanent and Non-Permanent Active Militia. Major G. M. Kirkpatrick,* RE, an officer in the British army, was

*General Sir George Macaulay Kirkpatrick, K.C.B., K.C.S.I., late RE (1866–1950), son of Sir G. A. Kirkpatrick, *qv*, RMC, 1882–5, DAAG (intelligence) South Africa; chief intelligence officer, Orange River Colony, 1901–2; DAQMG, Halifax, 1902–4;

appointed deputy assistant quartermaster-general at headquarters in 1902; Captain H. A. Panet,* staff-adjutant at RMC in 1900, later went to the headquarters staff; Lieutenant-Colonel G. A. S. Hamilton† was appointed commanding officer of the 3rd Regiment, the Victoria Rifles of Canada, and was one of the youngest such officers in the militia. Furthermore two ex-cadets attracted attention by patenting newsworthy inventions. Captain MacPherson produced a safety switch and frog for use on railways and Major F. M. Gaudet‡ a target for miniature ranges.[19] The three years at the turn of the century thus saw RMC graduates make solid achievements in a number of directions. There can be little doubt that this gave the representations of the ex-cadet club greater weight.

The nineteenth annual meeting of the RMC Club in Toronto on 25 April 1903 passed three resolutions addressed to the minister of Militia. These requested that an ex-cadet be regularly included on the Board of Visitors, that the four-year course be restored, and that the pledge of abstinence from alcohol which was imposed on cadets be abolished. Dr. Borden replied that he would always be willing to receive suggestions from the club about the composition of the board but that he could not promise to do more than consider favourably the proposal about club representation; he said that experience with the three-year course did not thus far justify abandoning it, but he would keep an open mind on the subject; and he promised to refer the question about the pledge to the next Board of Visitors.[20] A little later he spoke of the biggest problem that the club and college faced, the employment of RMC graduates; in a speech on 8 October he said that they ought to be more widely employed by the government and added that the new Intelligence Branch would take two or three of them.§ This statement was published in the club's *Proceedings.*[21]

Borden was more concerned at this time with a much bigger problem than RMC, the Canadian militia. He was determined to improve the militia

DAQMG, War Office, 1904; GSO1 in India under Kitchener, 1906; inspector-general, Australia, 1910–14; CGS India, 1916–20; GOC British troops in China, 1920; GOC-in-C India, 1923–7.

*Major-General Henri Alexandre Panet, C.B., C.M.G., D.S.O. (1869–1951), graduated RMC, 1891; served in the South African war; staff adjutant RMC, 1901–5; AAG militia headquarters, 1905–7; DAG, 1907–9; commanded RCHA Brigade and 2nd Division Artillery, France, 1916; adjutant general, Canadian militia, 1923.

†Lieutenant-Colonel George Arthur Sicotte Hamilton (1871–1948), RMC, 1888–90, 14th Regiment Canadian militia, 1890; lieutenant-colonel 1900; crossed with First Contingent, CEF, 1914, but returned to Canada; worked in the Ministry of Munitions during the war.

‡Colonel Frederick Mondelet Gaudet, C.M.G., died 1947; RMC, 1883–7; superintendent Dominion Arsenal, 1896–1913; CO 22nd Battalion, CEF; managing director National Filling Factory (munitions) in England.

§These officers were later affiliated with the Royal Canadian Engineers.

but at the same time to assert the Canadian government's authority over it. The Minister was henceforward to be advised by a militia council of soldiers and civil servants modelled on the new British Army Council; and the militia lost its British general officer commanding and was placed under the Militia Council. In future, the chief of the general staff (who had in effect replaced the GOC) need not be a British regular officer. These reorganizations brought about by the Militia Act of 1904 inevitably affected the college. The minister became its president in place of the GOC; but day-to-day direction remained, as before, with the adjutant-general who, in the eyes of the GOC and often in actuality, had in the past been unduly susceptible to political influence. However, as the commandant henceforward reported to the secretary of the Militia Council instead of, as earlier, to the GOC, civil supremacy was more firmly established. The intermittent dispute about the control and direction of the college was eased. At the same time military efficiency was increased.

A development that affected RMC more immediately was the expansion of the Permanent Force to provide garrisons for Halifax and Esquimalt when those bases were taken over from Great Britain in 1904–5. According to Earl Grey, twenty-three cadets had joined the Permanent Force on 1 July 1904,[22] but this figure must have included some who came from earlier classes. In that same year the Commandant reported that because of the superior attraction of civil engineering opportunities, RMC graduates continued to be reluctant to join the Permanent Force. He therefore recommended that a fixed number of commissions in it should be offered to the graduating class annually as "King's cadetships" to promote the idea that the best men in the class ought to take up military service in Canada.[23]

The militia reforms and the expansion of the service brought a welcome change in the government's attitude. Borden offered a Permanent Force commission to every cadet who graduated in 1905,[24] and Grey told the Colonial Secretary that there would be twenty-nine appointments* and

*In view of this great improvement in RMC's position, Grey had "the strongest feeling of annoyed vexation" at reports from England that Dundonald, who had retired on half pay in England and was therefore beyond the control of His Majesty's Government, had made a "most improper and indecent speech" that included "disparaging remarks about the attitude of R.M.C. cadets to the military authorities." Grey told Laurier, who had pressed him to publish the figures and all the correspondence about the commissioning of RMC cadets, that Borden's "energy and ability" as shown in his efforts to increase the militia's efficiency deserved commendation; but he could find no report of the speech in the British press and began to doubt whether it had ever been made. It seems likely that someone who felt that Dundonald had been badly treated had spread outdated information about the college (Douglas Library, Laurier Papers, microfilm, series B, reel 184, p. 20318, 11 July 1905).

that twenty-seven more had applied.[25] Actually only twelve of the graduating class of that year went into the Permanent Force; nevertheless, as the number who went to the British and Indian armies dropped to three,[26] it appeared that a new trend had begun. Captain R. M. Collins, the Australian secretary of defence, who visited the college in October, ascribed this change to the introduction of pensions and to better prospects of promotion in the militia.[27] In the following year, 1906, however, when six graduates took British commissions, only two joined the Canadian Permanent Force.[28] The tide had not yet turned. But in one other respect there was a significant permanent difference. Borden told the House of Commons that the number of applicants for RMC was now so large that "it is really becoming a matter of competition to get into the college."[29]

Borden was, however, as yet unwilling to take the next obvious step, the introduction of a requirement that all RMC graduates who did not take a regular commission in either the British army or the Canadian Permanent Force Active Militia must serve for a stated time in the Non-Permanent Active Militia. In 1908, when this matter was being discussed by the Board of Visitors, the Commandant, Colonel Taylor,* indicated the difficulty involved: compulsory militia service would cause problems because RMC graduates did not always live near militia units; however, he obtained support for his proposal that RMC graduates should be posted to any unit they chose rather than be placed merely on the reserve of officers.[30] He did not specify other factors, that militia commissions were still valuable patronage, or that senior militia officers did not relish the appointment of better trained junior officers, but no doubt these arguments had influenced government policy.

The Minister accepted the fact that "there are always some [graduates] who do not care to adopt the profession of arms." He tried to make room in government service for some of these by persuading his cabinet colleagues to agree to offer places to the RMC graduates of 1906. Although several departments replied that they had no suitable technical appointments, Laurier thought there might be one or two places in the RNWMP, and Public Works offered one place, as did the patent branch of the Department of Agriculture. But the Chief Engineer in Railways and Canals, who had the most attractive appointments at his disposal, does not appear to have answered. In 1907 three members of the senior class, expressing a preference for the Railways Department, sought civil service employment, but when graduation day came the government had not yet acted on their applications. Even the Militia Department itself, which had advertised that it would give three clerkships to RMC graduates, had

*Colonel Edward Thornton Taylor (1850–1921), commandant, RMC, 1905–9; retired 1916 but commanded labour corps in France (1917).

not yet done so. Another suggestion, that an approach should be made to the provinces to take RMC graduates, appears also to have come to nothing.[31]

The employment problem thus continued to plague the college. It left RMC open to the charge that it was merely performing functions that should more properly be carried out by the universities. For the Conservatives, G. E. Foster questioned whether a military college that trained young men only for the civil business of the country was worth keeping and suggested that officers could be given their preliminary general education in the universities. Laurier replied that military technical education could not be separated from other branches of knowledge which were indispensable to a young soldier; and Borden insisted that although the time might come when the universities would be used to train officers, it was not yet here.[32]

Meanwhile the RMC Club was developing a great *esprit*. In 1903 it had commissioned Mr. Alfred Hewett* of Toronto to write a college history. In 1906 the club's annual dinner was held at the college and a homecoming reunion had the effect of further stimulating loyalty; the practice began of calling the roll by having each member rise in his place in his turn and announce his college number and name in order of seniority. The following year for the first time the Old Eighteen Loving Cup was circulated around the table.[33] The toast to "absent comrades," meaning those who had fallen in action or who had died, was beginning to recall larger numbers. Five ex-cadets had died of wounds or were killed in action in South Africa: Lieutenant C. C. Wood, Loyal North Lancashire Regiment, Captain C. A. Hensley, Royal Dublin Fusiliers, Lieutenant Osborne, Captain T. W. Chalmers, Canadian Mounted Rifles, and Captain J. H. Laurie, Royal Lancaster Regiment. The annual publication of the club's *Proceedings*, which had commenced in 1891, provided a means of keeping ex-cadets in touch, and gave publicity to ex-cadet opinion.

The prestige of the college had risen, and for some years the British War Office had received favourable reports about it. Governor-General Lord Grey, a frequent visitor to RMC, referred to it regularly in his despatches. In 1905 he attended its boxing championships where he saw some "baddish" knockouts; but he reported to the Colonial Secretary that the next day all the victims were on parade. Grey said that the BSM, E. J. C. Schmidlin,† had eight boils on his legs but that "he [Schmidlin] told the

---

*Efforts to identify this man as a relation of the first commandant have failed.

†Major-General Edward James Schmidlin, M.C. (1884–1951), BSM, 1904–5; Governor-General's medal; senior professor RMC, 1926; director of Engineering Services, Ottawa, 1933–40; QMG, Canadian army, 1940; head Mechanical Engineering Department, Queen's University, 1942–6.

doctor that he would rather die than miss the gym display and parade, ... [and he] went through several most difficult gymnastic exercises, some of which must have been most painful, without a single flinch. After this performance the Doctor renewed the plasters and discharged a lot of matter ... but the young hero was at the head of his men on parade ... the next morning and as smart and alert as possible. ... A college where this spirit exists is a valuable national asset. [This] handsome, modest, British-looking boy of German descent ... ought to go far."[34] Grey took Schmidlin with him to West Point, the first RMC cadet to visit the academy in uniform, and the BSM wrote a report on the visit which was sent to the War Office because it threw "new light on West Point."[35]

From 1906, the Board of Visitors persistently advocated that RMC graduates be properly used in the service of Canada. The board was becoming an increasingly important body. In the colleges' early years a fiction had been maintained that the board was, as the law seemed to require, a permanent body, but it had been called into session only very irregularly. After the upheaval of 1895, which had been precipitated by the publication of a Board of Visitors' report, this board seems to have met annually, although its report was not printed. In 1902 Sam Hughes asked in the Commons whether a Board of Visitors' report would be published. Borden replied that publication was not usual, but that if the house so desired, the report could be tabled and it would then be published.[36] This does not seem to have been carried out, however.* After the establishment of the Militia Council, the board was called regularly, and from 1907 its report was published annually. Its proceedings were now fuller and much more important. The chiefs of the General Staff, unlike their predecessors the general officers commanding, restricted their reports on RMC to a statement of the numbers admitted to the college. The commandant's report was also now much briefer, giving more details about strength, staff, graduates, and prizes. The Board of Visitors' report covered all major developments, the curriculum, progress in building programmes, and the state of discipline.

Frequently the board was obviously expressing the ideas of the commandant. Colonel Taylor, Reade's successor, made much use of the Board of Visitors to present his ideas to the government and to the public. However, as the board at various time included senior soldiers, prominent educators, and members of parliament, it was more than the commandant's

*A Board of Visitors with seven members was appointed on 12 May 1902. In 1903 a board of three members, all of whom had been on the 1902 board, was set up (DM 14266, 30 May 1902). The next report that has been located is for 1906 (DND, HQ C417). From 1907 the board's reports were included in the *Sessional Papers* of the following year.

mouthpiece or sounding board. From 1910 there was always an ex-cadet member. These developments were so noticeable that when General Sir John French inspected the militia in 1910 he said "the outside direction of the college is largely in the hands of the Board of Visitors, which reports to the Militia Council." He added that the board did not always include the CGS who, he considered, ought always to be a member.[37] The truth was that senior officers from headquarters had often failed to attend when appointed to the board. French is generally an unreliable witness about RMC but his report shows that the Board of Visitors, even if it did not have the directing role which he had imagined, had become a body of great influence.

The nature of that influence needs further elucidation. As Borden appointed Sam Hughes, the opposition's chief defence critic, to be a member of the board in 1902 and, even to be its chairman in 1910, it is obvious that the Minister was not afraid of the board's investigations. On the contrary, he found them a useful means of putting pressure on parliament. Throughout this period the Commons continued to be reluctant to vote money for defence. Every RMC vote was scrutinized carefully and every proposal for construction led to questions either about the operation of the college or the need for its existence. It was not the militia colonels who now blocked RMC's development; a rapid expansion of militia training facilities had removed the root cause of their jealousy. Opposition to RMC now came principally from MPs who were against all defence spending, especially to support British imperial policy.

Some French-Canadian members of parliament were prominent among those who invariably sought opportunities to criticize the college. Although the college was becoming better known in English-speaking Canada, it had not succeeded in drawing large numbers of French-speaking boys. In the period from 1900 to 1914 only nineteen French Canadians appear among five hundred cadets enrolled, an average of little more than one a year.[38] A few French-Canadian families, noticeably those in which the military tradition went back to the ancien régime, sent their young men to RMC. But the language and cultural barriers remained formidable obstacles. Although those French-Canadian cadets who came to RMC usually fitted in well and succeeded according to their respective abilities, they often found it harder to adjust to the rigorous discipline imposed by the college authorities and by the seniors. They submitted to it less readily than the English-speaking boys, many of whom had come from private boarding schools where the discipline was not dissimilar. French-Canadian recruits sometimes felt that they were being victimized because of their race; seniors who had charge of them found them both different and difficult. One such ex-cadet of a slightly earlier period recalled that as a recruit he felt picked upon by an English officer and by his seniors and that he was rescued from this victimization by the staff-adjutant and by a fellow French Canadian; that individual he revered as a "great patriot."[39]

The college authorities and the Militia Council were anxious to resolve this difficult problem. They attributed this poor French-Canadian response to lack of awareness of the college in Quebec. The Adjutant-General therefore proposed that to arouse French-Canadian interest the cadets should parade in Ottawa; Colonel Reade retorted that an appearance at the horse show in Montreal would have more effect. But probably in neither city would the audience for such displays have been predominantly French. Yet the Adjutant-General stubbornly persisted with his idea, perhaps with the hope of pleasing members of parliament.[40] In 1908, RMC cadets took part in the tercentenary parade on the Plains of Abraham in Quebec City in commemoration of Champlain's landing; and the RMC Club of Canada donated $500 towards the preservation of the battlefield as an historical monument.[41] If this was intended as a gesture towards Anglo-French harmony it was poorly conceived and was hardly likely to win the hearts of French-speaking Canadians. The ceremonies in Quebec, despite their emphasis on the conquest, may have temporarily assuaged French-Canadian nostalgia for the past; but in the long run they served only to increase French-Canadian national spirit.

Another problem related to the ethnic question was the quality of French instruction in the college. J. D. Chartrand, the professor of French, was very popular with the cadets and sought the support of Laurier in his efforts to increase the amount of French that was taught.[42] His successor, J. M. Lanos,* started Le Cercle du College Militaire Royal de l'Alliance Française to foster interest in the language. The Cercle's founding membership in 1906 embraced 50 per cent of the cadet body; that this was not mere temporary initial enthusiasm was shown two years later when that proportion had risen to 80 per cent.[43] Clearly a real effort was being made to strengthen French teaching at RMC. But Lanos, like Chartrand, was a native of France and not a French Canadian. The realities of Canada's ethnic problem were obviously not well understood at that time.

French-speaking Canadians were often opposed to the introduction of British officers for staffing the college. On the other hand, the RMC Club's attitude on this question probably coincided with views expressed in the *Natal Witness* of 3 April 1903 which were reprinted in the club's *Proceedings*. An anonymous soldier who was advocating a military college for

*J. M. Lanos, professor of French, RMC, 1905–18.

South Africa wrote: "Many people send sons to Kingston to have them under the eye of British officers – if these were withdrawn the commissions would be withdrawn and the college would fall to the ground. It stands to reason that if Commissions in the Imperial Service are granted by the War Office they will insist on the grantees being trained under the eye of a man they can trust."[44] Dr. Borden told the Commons that Canadians would be used to instruct at RMC if they were qualified. Some members protested that the only national qualification should be that RMC instructors must be British subjects, and any professional officer, whether British or Australian, would do equally well; however all members appeared to believe that a Canadian should be preferred.[45]

Many of the British staff officers at the college were in fact Canadians serving in the British army. They had probably been selected partly because they were willing to accept a tour of duty at home and partly because they would be welcomed as compatriots. In 1905 the RMC Club urged that the commandant and staff should be the very best officers available.[46] In that year Reade was succeeded by Colonel E. Thornton Taylor,[47] a McGill graduate who had attended RMC where he had won the sword of honour in 1882 and was battalion sergeant-major. He was the first RMC cadet to attend the staff college course at Camberley (1895). After joining the 2nd Battalion of the Cheshire Regiment, Taylor had served both with his regiment and on the staff in India and Burma, frequently in instructional positions. An energetic man with great physical endurance, he was fond of climbing and of shooting tigers. He possessed an "almost boyish enthusiasm." Although more at ease with a gun than with a pen,[48] he seemed a good choice when Canada asked for a Kingston graduate to command RMC.

No doubt the personal relations between British officers and Canadians on the college staff were usually excellent. But from time to time there were rumours of difficulty. Under a Canadian commandant one might expect these problems to diminish. However, in 1906 the Toronto *News* carried a report that the independent attitude of the British officers at RMC had led to a showdown. It said that these officers had been compelled to recognize their subordination to the Canadian militia commander in the district. Borden countered the report by saying that in fact Taylor, the new Canadian commandant of RMC, had only asked to be commissioned in the militia and that the Militia Council had decided to revive the practice of giving militia commissions to all the British officers employed at the college.[49] Two years later rumours reached the Militia Council that relations between the British officers and the Canadians at the college were strained because the former habitually spoke in slighting terms of the Active Militia.⁵⁰ It was also reported that one ex-cadet who was said to have stood at the head of his class had resigned from the Permanent Force as a protest against the advancement of a British officer who was brought out to Esquimalt.⁵¹ Obviously there was much national rivalry between the Canadians and the British officers in the Canadian forces. Taylor's appointment does not seem to have solved this problem at RMC.

Yet Taylor tried hard to conciliate various interests. The sons of ex-cadets were now reaching the college entrance age. Through the Board of Visitors he pressed for a reduction of the residence requirements for the sons of Canadian officers serving with the British army; Taylor also proposed a reduction of RMC fees for the sons of militia officers. The board approved the first suggestion and it was introduced within a couple of years; but the government turned down any reduction of fees. The board itself rejected another of Taylor's suggestions that would have pleased not only the college staff but also those Canadians who sent their sons to RMC as a preparation for civilian professions. This was a return to the four-year course. The board stated that RMC already included the most useful of the non-military subjects of a university course; but it thought too much time was spent on mathematics and too little on military subjects to prepare the cadets for the responsibilities of command. It agreed that a four-year course would be one way of solving this weakness, but it felt that an extension in the length of the course might lead to competition with the universities with which, as RMC was not equipped for practical work, the college could not "hope to compete." The board was also afraid that the Canadian Society of Civil Engineers would be unwilling to recognize an RMC diploma as equal to a university degree in engineering.⁵² Obviously the reduction to a three-year course had not only made the maintenance of a high standard of military preparation more difficult, it had also caused the college to fall back from the position that it had attained in the 1880s in civil engineering *vis-a-vis* the civilian universities. Those few RMC graduates who had gone on to do engineering in a university before the South African War had been permitted to graduate in one more year; from about 1905, when many more went on to degree courses, they were required to do two more years. Later enquiries found that all the staff and forty out of fifty-nine parents who were approached on the subject were in favour of the four-year course.⁵³ But the government shied away from the expense.

In its annual reports the Board of Visitors continued to praise Taylor. But he had been less than successful in dealing with some disciplinary problems. The principle of fostering responsibility by leaving the exercise of authority to the senior cadets invariably had a possible weakness, and if not carefully supervised, it could bring trouble. "Recruiting" could be defended on the grounds that it was an initiation into the new and more mature society of the cadet body, that it taught obedience to youngsters who had often been indulged, and that it created pressures and tensions which helped the recruit to face the trials and tribulations of an alien and often hostile world. However, recruiting was always liable to get out of hand. When trouble occurred it was not easy to decide whether a weak recruit had been unable to accept reasonable pressures or whether seniors with sadistic temperaments had gone beyond reason. No one seems to have considered the possible danger to the often immature seniors, that this exercise of arbitrary authority might foster undesirable qualities and not a true sense of responsibility among them. Whenever there was trouble, the invariable reaction of the authorities was to issue denials, partly because of their belief that in principle recruiting was worthwhile.

In 1906 Colonel Taylor investigated a report that had appeared in the *Ottawa Citizen*, alleging that the illness of a cadet had been caused by hazing. The Commandant reported to the Adjutant-General that he "was justified in denying absolutely that there was any truth" in the story. Soon afterwards, however, Taylor had to admit that he had been wrong. He stated that though there had been no hazing when he was a cadet, the practice was now widespread. He declared flatly that there was no real discipline in the college and no regard for the truth. As the senior class had no real regard for discipline, he had taken special measures to deal with the situation and had withdrawn disciplinary powers given to the seniors twenty-five years ago. He had placed the juniors in a separate class under two NCOs of the second class.

One of the military staff, Major Mosely, interceded with the Commandant on the seniors' behalf. He said that they had understood that "T-squaring" (beating a cadet on the seat with a T-square) which had been the cause of the injury to Cadet J. A. P. Marshall was permissible. However, discipline improved after the power to award punishment drills was taken from the seniors. Taylor began to take a more lenient view of the matter. But he concluded a report to the Adjutant-General which gave all this information by saying that he would stamp out "objectionable" practices although it would take some time to restore the prestige of the college to its former high level.[54]

In his official annual report later the same year, Taylor stated that conduct and discipline at the college were only "fair" and "poor" respectively. But he went on: "I am most confident that I shall be able to report a great improvement in both, in the autumn, and I trust that the gentlemen-cadets are beginning to realise the true meaning of the word 'discipline.' "[55]

The Board of Visitors henceforward made a special point of asking the seniors and the recruits whether there was any hazing in the college; they always received answers in the negative and came to the conclusion that it had been stamped out. When a member told the board on one occasion that he had heard rumours of ill feeling between senior and junior classes, all the cadets who were interrogated, seniors and recruits alike, flatly denied it.[56]

Nevertheless a recruit of this period who returned to the college later as staff-adjutant has stated that in the 1910-11 period recruits were "licked" with rifle slings if they were thought to "need it." Once the entire recruit class got the strap. Referring to other practices that developed later, this ex-cadet said that although at table recruits were required to throw bread to seniors on demand, they were allowed to relax while eating and to have all they wanted. He said that they did not get up as early as did the postwar recruits and there was no cadet-imposed "bending" (punishment drill).[57]

A "B" Company order book kept by a recruit in 1909 confirms that the visitors were never told the truth about hazing. Amid a few rather brief entries that show the names of recruits detailed for particular duties and of those who were officially punished by the seniors, it gives information about recruiting and a long account of initiation. Some cadet practices were amusing, though rather unsophisticated in modern eyes. The first entry in the order book records that Cadet Vivian Bishop* was "Spider Orderly" for the week beginning 27 September, and his duty was to catch the spiders with which the Frigate, like all Point Frederick, abounded. Another entry concerns legitimate punishment; even in sub-zero weather cadets had to leave their windows fully open at night, and Cadet Dansereau was awarded one "drill" for having his window closed. Another punishment, described as "5 blows," was meted out to a French Canadian, Cadet Le Blanc,† for "gross impertinence." Recruit E. K. Stewart‡ (sometimes spelled Stuart by the diarist) was at various times spider orderly, orderly to draw the seniors' baths, and window orderly to close their windows before they got out of bed.

But the most important entry in the order book is a seven-and-a-half page account of the initiation of recruits. This had no place in a book of

*Colonel Clarence Vivian Bishop, M.C. (1890–1945), graduated RMC, 1913; commissioned RCHA; with Canadian Corps, CEF, during World War I; CO "E" battery, RCHA, Winnipeg; CO Esquimault Fort, 1940; CO Fixed Defences, Atlantic Command Headquarters, Halifax, 1944.

†Captain M. J. R. Beaudry Le Blanc (1893–1959), graduated RMC, 1913; Royal Canadian Dragoons in World War I; RCMP; in World War II.

‡Eric Kennedy Stewart, RMC, 1909–12.

official orders, and the recruit who thus preserved his personal diary deserves our gratitude for information not usually recorded. After lights out on Tuesday, 22 September the recruits were awakened and summoned to the guardroom where they were told that the next day would be the most important one of their college careers. They were ordered to speak to no one all day and to report to the Fort Frederick martello tower clad in "canvas," that is fatigue dress, at 7:15 PM. They were also asked whether they could swim. This led them to speculate that they were to be thrown into the lake or put down the well. On Wednesday, whenever seniors were not around, most of the recruits broke the silence rule; a few did so even when they were under observation, speculating, of course, on the ordeal that lay ahead of them. Late in the afternoon when they took their canvas clothes to be secreted in the tower, some of them seized the opportunity to reconnoitre the well. As they found that it was half full of boards and held very little water, the lake seemed a more likely destination. After it became dark, the recruits went to the Fort and changed their clothes. The seniors then appeared wearing their greatcoats and with hoods and masks over their heads to conceal their features. Disguising their voices they called the roll. "Soon the fun began." Individual recruits were detailed to do "stunts" such as "scrambling like eggs" – that is rolling on the ground from one end of the recruit line to the other which made the performer reel like a drunken man when he stood up. Others were set to kiss and hug everybody in quick succession, to enact love scenes, and to repeat "sweet sayings" over and over again like a phonograph. Recruits who laughed at their fellows' antics were promptly "straightened up" by a few sharp blows.

While these "stunts" were being performed, the tunnel sally-port through the Fort's embankment was being prepared. Then, one by one, the recruits were taken to the "darkest depths" where they were grabbed by unseen hands, hurled roughly against the wall, and dazzled by a blinding light. Those who kept their eyes closed were made to open them by "gentle persuasion." While kissing what was alleged to be a Bible (actually a literature book), each recruit was compelled to take an oath to serve the king faithfully and to respect the college seniors "above all." Punishment was then inflicted on them ("mine was fifteen blows," said this recorder) on the grounds that they had broken the silence rule during the day. Each recruit bent over and was struck on the seat with a thick hickory rod. After the punishment the recruit was told to walk slowly down the tunnel "still stooped over." Men on either side wielded sticks as though beating carpets. If a recruit moved too fast, he was called back to run the gauntlet again. The anonymous writer concludes: "After coming out of the tunnel we were left to ourselves for a minute or so. Our backs and legs were covered with welts and bruises from the beating. Some had lumps like eggs on their legs to remind them of the tunnel." Subsequently the recruits were again set to doing "stunts." Some were ordered to march and were not given an "about turn" until up to their waists in the lake. After a check of the roll to see that none had escaped, they were ordered to return to the Frigate without being seen. They were commanded to race over the parapet and were told that the last up would get something to "quicken his movements." "The race was a great scramble and the last up never went back that I know of."

This account shows that initiation at RMC resembled fraternity initiation in American and Canadian colleges as it was practised until recently. The recruit who described it thought it "not bad, although some of the seniors were a bit too handy with their sticks. When it comes to getting a blow on the leg which leaves a bruise about four inches in diameter and which swells up as big as an orange the affair goes beyond a joke." Part of the proceedings the recruits thought very unfair, as when cadets of the second class were present, not merely as spectators, but using sticks as much as they pleased. That was said to be "no fun."[58]

Fraternity initiation in the United States could be quite as rough as this. What was different at RMC was, firstly, that the rites were supported by the military authority which the seniors exercised and, secondly, that such disciplinary practices were not always restricted to one night or one week of initiation. Any infraction of rules by a recruit during his first year, or any failure to show due respect for seniors, could merit summary punishment in the form of a sharp blow with a swagger stick. Billy Bishop's son stated that when his father, the famous air ace, was a recruit in 1911, each first-year man was soundly trounced every Saturday night on the theory that seniors, however vigilant, must have overlooked some recruit crimes during the week.[59] Bishop was "profoundly depressed by the indignities" of his first year at the college, which included being compelled to eat a live spider. However, his service as a recruit had a humorous side. He was detailed as the "recruit" of a senior who had the same surname but was not related to him, Vivian Bishop. A recruit normally made his senior's bed, kept his room tidy, and took care of his comfort. Because of the similarity of name, Billy had an extra duty; he had to call his senior "daddy" and kiss him goodnight on the forehead each evening.[60] Humour of this kind was common among the cadets; sometimes initiated by recruits as a "spoof" against a senior, it gives evidence of a light-hearted strain running through the senior-recruit relationship which often softened the asperity.

An ex-cadet who was a recruit in 1902 has testified that the account in the order book shows that recruiting had become more severe by 1909 than in his day. He said that when he was a recruit the pressure eased off after initiation, although a certain amount of fagging continued. Cadet NCOs could award official punishment drills and sometimes awarded extra drill unofficially. This informant said that the problem with recruiting was that it operated unevenly. Some seniors were much harsher than others. Certain juniors got off lightly because they were already acquainted with seniors at their private schools.[61] Recruiting was an important, perhaps an essential, part of the RMC system. But it needed to be firmly controlled. Developments in Taylor's time showed how easily it could get out of hand, and there were always critics ready to pounce on abuses in order to attack the college as a whole. Taylor was fortunate in this instance that the question did not become public.

However, one other matter involving cadet discipline, raised in the House of Commons, led to some notoriety for the college. Petty pilfering, often common and even accepted in communal societies of young men, had become endemic at RMC where cigarettes and cake were apparently regarded as fair prey. When losses of more valuable articles of personal property and of money became serious, Taylor authorized the use of marked money as bait. When the bait disappeared, he ordered a court of enquiry. After he had received the report of the court, Taylor preferred three charges against a cadet who was apparently widely suspected by his fellows. This boy's father came to Kingston and rejected a proposal that the matter be referred to the civil police. The boy elected to be tried by the commandant instead of by court-martial. Two charges of a more serious nature were dismissed; but Taylor convicted the accused of stealing a silver cigarette case although that incident had occurred several months earlier, the boy had returned the cigarette case (without its contents) immediately he was asked about it, and the owner of the case had stated that he did not believe that the accused intended to keep the case.

The boy's father was a Conservative member of parliament. Colonel Sam Hughes brought the matter before the house and dramatically protested against what he called "sweat box" interrogations of witnesses at RMC when an accused was not present to hear what was said about him; he also complained that the Commandant had acted in this case as both accuser and judge. The case had in fact been handled in reasonable conformity with the normal military processes of courts of enquiry as Hughes, who was a militia officer, must have known; and a charge of theft could have been laid in a civil court on the basis of the evidence presented. Hughes was on sounder ground however when he argued that the case should have been dealt with in a military court as "improper possession," a military offence that includes the possession of a comrade's property when there is no evidence of intention to deprive the owner permanently. Hughes and the accused's father loudly proclaimed that the incident showed that Taylor was unfit to be commandant of RMC.[62] It certainly appears that Taylor had acted hastily and injudiciously, much as he had done earlier when reporting about the hazing.

Taylor was not without defenders. In addition to the general testimonials presented by the Boards of Visitors, some parents of cadets and some prominent citizens wrote to Laurier to say that Taylor had had a good influence on the college. Maurice Hutton, the principal of University College, Toronto, who had a son at RMC, deprecated Hughes' parliamentary attack. He said that he was sure that Hughes did not speak for other parents. Laurier replied that he felt that Dr. Borden's reply had been in good taste and that he was sorry that he could not say as much for some of the other speeches.[63] The Bishop of Ontario, W. L. Mills, also wrote to support Taylor because he had introduced good reforms at the college which, the bishop said, had previously been notorious for card-playing and drinking. He believed that Hughes was motivated by political purposes and he asked whether a statement of Taylor's case could be made in the House.[64] Laurier replied that that was a matter on which Taylor himself must decide.[65] However, it was apparently decided that the matter should be let drop and no statement was made. But the Conservatives did not forget; they hounded Taylor until he had gone back to England. Dr. Borden then admitted in the Commons that "we have had more successful commandants"; and he pointedly remarked that the new appointee (Colonel Crowe) had first-class qualifications.[66] The first ex-cadet commandant had not been an unqualified success; perhaps it was more difficult for a Canadian appointment to be non-partisan.

Colonel Taylor had probably not been personally responsible for yet another error of judgment that had bought heavy fire upon the college during his time. This was in connection with the construction programme. A new gymnasium had been brought into use by the time he arrived. Its basement had been planned with the idea that it should hold a swimming pool and a shooting range.[67] The pool was, however, dropped, a wise decision because the basement was very much too small for both purposes. The next project approved by the government was a stable to cost $18,000. Then, to replace the old naval cottages near the observatory which had long been condemned, a preliminary $10,000 was appropriated to build new servants' quarters.[68] There were to be two terraces of these, each with eight small four-roomed cottage houses with basement kitchen facilities. The original estimate for the sixteen four-roomed cottages (later known as Ridout Row or Hogan's Alley) was $96,000. By 1909 the total cost had mounted to $107,152,[69] at over $8,000 for each house. This high cost merited the attacks of opposition members who said that, even though the occupants were to be NCOs rather than servants, they must surely be the most expensively housed people of their station of life in all Canada. The opposition's suspicion of political jobbery seems confirmed. Its criticism of inefficiency in government planning and spending was supported by the fact that, although parliament had provided for building a stable, it could not be used for some years because quarters for the grooms had not yet been provided. The fault lay not in the commandant, or even in individual members of the government, but in the whole governmental fiscal process which was incapable of eliminating graft or insuring efficiency. Unfortunately the resultant publicity was also detrimental to the college.

Public criticism of RMC in 1907 and 1908 did not affect its growth and development. Despite the lack of guaranteed employment for cadets, the revival of the college begun under Kitson continued steadily under his successors. By 1909 RMC's strength topped the hundred mark. There were now cadets from every province and every territory, even the Yukon. Only the numbers from Quebec were disappointing because of continued lack of French-Canadian interest.[70]

When Colonel Taylor completed his tour of duty in 1909 the Militia Council decided not to continue the experiment of using a Canadian commandant from the British army. This decision was not a result of dissatisfaction with the retiring incumbent but was made because the imperial (defence) conference earlier that year had agreed to co-ordinate the military forces of the empire under the guidance of an "Imperial General Staff," some members of which would be in the dominions. Borden took care that the British officers of the Imperial General Staff did not become a Canadian section of the Imperial General Staff like those in Australia and New Zealand. He scattered the British staff officers across the dominion. He at first also opposed the proposal that two should be posted to RMC,[71] either because he thought that they would be wasted there or because he thought they might form a nucleus of British officers that would be too independent or powerful. However, he eventually yielded on this point and two came to Kingston. The main work of these two senior British staff officers at RMC was with pre-staff college courses for Permanent Force officers. They only occasionally gave lectures to the cadets.[72] But they added an important element of professional expertise to the college.

At a time when military professionalism was growing in Canada, and when some Canadians were beginning to anticipate that before very long

Canada might find herself plunged into war, it seemed necessary to get the very best possible commandant for RMC. Because the two British staff officers were posted to RMC, it became increasingly important that the commandant should have had superior professional experience. The Militia Council's willingness to maintain the practice of appointing a British officer as commandant, even if he were not a Canadian, derived from this need. Henceforward the commandant must have passed the Staff College and have been a successful first grade staff officer.[73] To obtain a man with these qualifications it was necessary to raise the salary which had remained as in 1875.[74] The new rate was said to be $200 less than he received in his previous appointment, but Major J. H. V. Crowe, RFA,* accepted the appointment.[75] Crowe had been ADC to the governor of the Punjab, had attended Staff College, and had served on the intelligence staff in South Africa. In 1904 he had become chief instructor at the Royal Military Academy, Woolwich; and four years later had received command of the 28th Brigade, Royal Field Artillery (RFA). He was the first technical officer since Cameron to command the Royal Military College of Canada. The appointment of an artilleryman with his qualifications suggests that RMC was at last considered an important asset in British and Canadian defence planning – and properly so.

Growing fear of Germany was now bringing big changes. Military development was hastened throughout the empire and there were obvious implications for the college. Even before it had been fully realized that Germany was determined on a menacing course of action, RMC cadets had been required to attend at least one militia camp in order to graduate.[76] Then in 1910 the Department of Militia ruled that every cadet who did not enter either the British army or the Canadian Permanent Force on graduation must become attached to the Militia within two years of leaving the college and must attend two militia camps. This was indeed a revolutionary step in the college's development. The Commandant was thus able to report in that year that for the first time every RMC graduate was taking a commission.[77] RMC graduates were attached to militia units as supernumeraries; to get a lieutenancy there had to be a vacancy and there were therefore still complaints that ex-cadets were not properly used.[78] However, this regulation was a step in the right direction.

Colonel Crowe's reports on the college's activities were much more informative than those of his predecessor. But the interest and activity of

*After he left RMC, Crowe became GSO 1 at army headquarters in India. During World War I he commanded the artillery in East Africa under General Smuts and published an account of the campaign, *General Smuts' Campaign in East Africa in 1918*. He wrote several military handbooks and contributed to various periodicals and to the *Encyclopaedia Britannica*. He retired as a brigadier-general and died in 1922.

the Board of Visitors increased also and its thinking became spacious. With Hughes as chairman in 1910 it noted that it understood that the government intended to construct a covered drillshed to double as a skating rink; and it discussed a proposal to provide a rifle range on the west side of the peninsula to replace the one on the east side that had had to be abandoned some years earlier because of danger to the citizens of Kingston. Cadets would have fired across Navy Bay at "heads" bobbing up out of the water when wires were pulled on shore. On a more prosaic level the board wished to remedy a situation in which forty-eight out of one hundred and five cadets shared rooms and in which the corridors in the dormitory had to be used for storage. It talked about plans for the next hundred years and for an increase of 200 per cent in numbers, that is to say for an establishment of three hundred cadets. The board noted that a proposal to put another story on the top of the Frigate (which, if carried through, would have entirely destroyed the fine lines of that structure) would "scarcely suffice" to meet the need for accommodations.[79] After the board had adjourned, the Master-General of the Ordnance, who was one of its members that year, proceeded to investigate what would be entailed by expansion on the scale that had been envisaged.[80]

Close upon the heels of the 1910 report of the Board of Visitors came that of General Sir John French, the successful cavalry commander in South Africa and the future commander-in-chief of the British Expeditionary Force on the western front. In the course of his inspection of the Canadian militia in 1910, RMC and the Canadian artillery were all that met his unqualified approval. Of the college, French wrote: "I have heard much of the Royal Military College at Kingston, and from what I have observed I feel sure that the celebrity which the institution has earned throughout the Empire on account of the good work it has achieved is fully justified." He favoured the continuation of its combined civil and military curriculum because it gave "to a large proportion of its [Canada's] brain power the advantage of military training and education"; but he thought that RMC graduates ought to be compelled to serve in the militia for at least ten years. He said the college had a good library but no reading room; and he criticized the lack of dormitory accommodation, the doubling up of cadets in study-bedrooms, and the lack of a covered riding school and of a covered rink. He also urged that the course should include an historical study of a campaign.[81]

Major-General P. H. N. Lake,* inspector general of the militia, a British officer who had served for a long time in Canada, and who pos-

---

*Lieutenant-General Sir Percy Henry Noel Lake, K.C.B., K.C.M.G., C.B. (d.1940), QMG Canadian militia, 1893-8; CGS, 1904-8; inspector-general, 1908-10; CGS India, 1912-15; commanded Mesopotamian Force, 1916.

sessed the complete confidence of the Canadian government, commented on French's proposals in an official paper that was published by the Department of Militia. He said that some of French's recommendations had already been carried out, others would be adopted, and the remainder depended upon the money being made available for building purposes.[82] The Militia Council was inclined to the belief that the time might come when RMC, like Sandhurst and West Point, would be restricted to candidates for regular commissions, but it was not yet prepared to accept the need for planning for such a large scale of expansion as the board recommended and for such a long period ahead. It therefore ruled that construction should be limited to present needs. Within these narrower limits, the government began to investigate the means by which the college could be enlarged to carry out General French's recommendations. For the present, projects for expansion were to be limited to accommodating two hundred cadets but designed to permit future growth.[83]

The most important building that was commenced immediately was a new dormitory across the square from the Stone Frigate. This was in effect the additional dormitory originally planned as long ago as 1875. It was now to be set much further back than the one proposed at that earlier time when only a very small parade square would have been created. The board's recommendation for a uniform style of architecture for the college was adopted. The new dormitory was not built of brick as proposed in the 1880s but was limestone like the educational block. Two squash courts which Montreal friends of the college had presented in 1909[84] were placed on the shore of Navy Bay to the south of the new group of buildings that had been completed there, the gymnasium, Panet House, and the water-pumping plant. In 1910 the Board of Visitors recommended that the often proposed rink that would double as a drillshed should be built immediately, but it was not erected. A sea wall was built in Navy Bay, and the water front there, which had been an eyesore for years, was tidied up. The old naval cottages, which dated from 1822, were demolished.[85] One member of parliament even campaigned for several years to get the Department of Militia and Defence to accept responsibility for putting a new roof on the Fort Frederick martello tower because the old one had been blown off in a storm.[86] In 1907 Colonel Taylor was asked to oversee repairs to the tower; but a year later he protested that the cost should not come out of the RMC appropriation for 1908–9.[87] The roof was replaced in this period.

RMC's revival and growth after the South African War had been marked by noteworthy achievements in sports and in allied forms of extracurricular activities. Dundonald, who had been concerned about the effect of the use of electric cars and long hours of office work on the physique of the men in the city militia units, had reported that at RMC physical training and gymnastic exercises brought a surprising development in the measurements of the gentlemen cadets' chests.[88] As the average complement of the college during most of the following decade was below a hundred, and as it had only a three-year course, RMC's success in competition against much larger institutions was quite remarkable. RMC won the intermediate intercollegiate championship in hockey in 1904, 1905, and 1906; in football in 1909, 1910, and 1911; and in tennis in 1909 and 1910. In 1912 it took a place vacated by Ottawa University in the senior intercollegiate competition.[89] Cadets, and ex-cadets also, excelled at cricket, and in gymnastics the cadets were superb. General Sir John French stated in his report that he had never seen a finer gymnastic display than that put on for him by the cadets.[90] In joint athletics (track and field) meets with Queen's College which were held annually, it was not unusual for cadets to win every event for which they were eligible. The RMC boxing tournament was so vigorous that one report stated that ladies present turned away their heads from the sight of so much blood.[91] RMC's prowess in sports became so well established that rumours that the Minister had ordered the abolition of boxing inspired a sarcastic newspaper cartoon that portrayed the cadets drinking pink tea.[92] Finally, in an activity even more appropriate to their military profession, the Canadian cadets did well in competition with their brothers-in-arms in England. In 1901 an annual shoot against Sandhurst with rifles and revolvers was inaugurated by using the mails. The Canadian college won the rifle competition in the first year and repeated that victory frequently thereafter; but its first win with the smaller weapons did not come until 1913.

During this same period some of the college's unique traditions were developed or consolidated. These were a subconscious part of the morale-building process so necessary in an institution of this kind. The recruits' obstacle race over a gruelling course set up by their immediate predecessors was already well established as an annual event. So also was "Copper Sunday," an annual church parade to St. George's Cathedral which was said to date from 1882 or even earlier. It was so named because the gentlemen cadets took up a collection of copper coins. It seems that it was not unusual for the collection plate to be dropped on the floor to create a disturbance. Perhaps for this reason no collection was taken on two copper Sundays during the period: the cadets gave flowers for the altar instead.[93] Another college tradition, an annual minstrel show with burnt cork faces and female impersonators, which dated from about 1880,[94] was "revived in 1905." However, in 1904 there had been a spontaneous rag on 17 March when some cadets dressed themselves up in tablecloths and colours appropriate for St. Patrick's Day and paraded around the college. The minstrel show on 14 February in the next year included the distribution of a cake "as large as a clothes basket." In 1906, in addition to the minstrel show in February, the recruits entertained their seniors by a stage show on 17 March and were rewarded with a cake.[95] Thus the traditional annual RMC "cake walk" on St. Patrick's Day when recruits performed before seniors and staff, which was to outlast the minstrel show as an annual event, was derived from a combination of two quite different sources. It would be interesting to be able to identify the Irishman who initiated it.

The old gymnasium had been a poor place for social functions. It was small, it doubled as a gunshed, and its floor was old and uneven. For some years at the turn of the century the June ball was held in a classroom. The new gymnasium provided a much better setting for stageshows and also for the ball, the great social event of the year not only for cadets but also for guests from Kingston and elsewhere. At stage presentations and at balls the decorations became elaborate.[96] For the June ball in 1911 the outer door was guarded by mounted dragoons. A stuffed effigy of an infantryman was placed over the entrance to the ballroom. In that year an ex-cadet presented the college with a proscenium arch for the stage in the gymnasium.[97] In 1910 the ball had to be cancelled because of the death of Edward VII; but the cadets discovered one advantage that could be squeezed out of bilingualism: the Alliance Française held a dance instead of the ball. At that dance the traditional blanket-tossing of the graduating senior cadet officers was duly carried out after the last waltz.[98] In 1913 the June ball had again to be cancelled because of the accidental drowning of two cadets.[99]

The college had now come to be greatly admired by those who knew it. When Grey left Canada in 1911 and was unable to pay a final visit to RMC, he wrote a eulogy to the Commandant which is worth quoting but should be read with the realization that he was undoubtedly unaware of the hazing that was practised: "I do not think there is any institution in the whole of Canada in which I am more interested than I am in your college. I regard R.M.C. as one of the formative influences for good on the national character. You turn out men who hit hard but hit fair, above the belt everytime, men who would rather lose a game playing fairly, than win an advantage by dishonourable means. It is because the influence that radiates from your college is of a clean-handed high-souled generous manliness that I regret so much that I am unable to say goodbye to you on the 21st. I would wish that your yearly output, which I believe to be of such admirable quality, were double the quantity. ..."[100]

In these years between the South African and Great Wars other dominions were seeking to build their own military potential through colleges like RMC. They found they had to choose between two "systems," that of Sandhurst and of West Point by which only regular army officers were trained (in the former for the infantry and cavalry, and in the latter for all arms), and that of Kingston, by which officers were trained for the reserve as well as for all arms of a regular force. Many people believed that the Kingston all-inclusive civil military system was preferable for British dominions with their relatively small requirements. There were several proposals that it should be copied. Hutton proposed it in 1902 for Australia.[101] Officers from all three British dominions in the southern hemisphere visited Kingston to look it over in 1909–10.

One of these visitors was Colonel W. Throsby Bridges, the RMC ex-cadet who had become chief of the general staff in Australia and who was the Australian representative on the Imperial General Staff in London. Bridges reported to the Australian Minister of Defence that on his way home to establish an Australian military college, he had "inspected" RMC, Kingston.[102] What he meant by "inspection," whether a formal parade or a personal investigation of the Kingston system, is not clear. His diary shows that he did not spend much time at the college during his visit.[103] Like many students, he probably believed quite erroneously that he already knew all there was to know about his *alma mater*. Some of his compatriots were inclined to protest that the Kingston system would do nothing for "citizen forces," the Australian equivalent of the Canadian militia.[104] Bridges' criticism was of a very different nature, that it did not do enough for the Permanent Force. With the international scene growing darker, it seemed to him wasteful to train officers without getting full use of their services after graduation. Duntroon therefore copied the West Point system, a four-year course training for all arms.[105] South Africa, on the other hand, seems to have favoured the Kingston system; but like New Zealand it did not set up a military college at this time.[106]

In the four years before the war with Germany, RMC graduated one hundred and twenty-three gentlemen cadets, just three short of the number of officers who were commissioned in the Canadian Permanent Force during those same years. But of this total, only twenty-three actually joined the Permanent Force. Nineteen others joined British units. A glance at Table I which gives detailed figures for each year shows that RMC could have supplied Canada's Permanent Force with all the officers it commissioned during those crucial prewar years. This raises the question why, when the regulations were altered in 1910, all RMC graduates were not required to take Canadian Permanent Force commissions instead of Mili-

TABLE I

RMC COMMISSIONS AND PF COMMISSIONS[107]

	1911	1912	1913	1914	Total
RMC graduates	32	27	36	28	123
RMC imperial commissions	7	4	6	2	19
RMC Canadian PF commissions	6	9	6	2	23
Total Canadian PF commissions	28	40	34	25	127

tia commissions. Of course so basic a change could have been introduced to apply only to cadets recruited after the revised regulations were announced. It would, therefore, not have affected the output before 1914.

The failure to make this revolutionary change is easier to understand when it is remembered that the smaller requirement that RMC graduates should do militia service had been unpalatable and slow to come. Resistance to further change came from several sides. Militia officers did not want to lose the chance of Permanent Force commissions, politicians did not want to relinquish patronage, and parents did not want their sons to take on an obligation for a lifetime career in return for the benefits of a disciplined education. Moreover, filling the complement of Permanent Force commissions would have meant the elimination of the British commissions which were regarded by many people as Canada's contribution to imperial defence and as a valuable tie with Britain. The British commissions were popular with applicants for the college and brought in many recruits who did not in the end win one. Another and perhaps greater obstacle was that RMC served the purposes of those Canadians who were prepared to accept a responsibility to train for defence but who did not think it necessary to serve until there was an emergency. Professional military service seemed out of line with Canada's interests and Canada's needs. It was thought that in peacetime military service should not prevent young men from following civilian careers. This attitude is the more understandable when it is remembered that, even after war was declared in 1914, the policy of "business as usual" held sway in Britain and the empire for some time. This attitude was demonstrated at RMC when in 1907 the introduction of compulsory militia camps led the Commandant to propose that cadets should be sent to camp in August before term started. He was overruled from headquarters on the grounds that this would interfere with the normal holiday period; parents would not like to have to bring their sons back from summer cottages before the usual time.[108] Thus, although cadets had to meet the new regulation which required that they train with the militia before they could graduate, the holiday routine of the social class from which most of them came must not be disturbed.

This evidence, more than any other, shows the place that RMC held in the pattern of Canada's social life. Its fees were still sufficiently high to restrict entrance on the whole to professional classes and business people of at least moderate means to whom a disciplined education with training for responsibility and leadership especially appealed. This was the class that also sent its children to civilian colleges, but there were probably fewer sons of the Canadian manse in RMC than in the universities. The records show that there was a high proportion from the upper middle classes. Out of about four hundred cadets of the 1876–1900 period whose fathers' occupations are known, nineteen were the sons of gentlemen, forty-one were the sons of army and navy officers, one hundred and sixty-eight were the sons of professional men, one hundred and nine were the sons of business men, and twenty-seven were the sons of bankers and other financial men. Only fourteen gave their father's occupation as farmer. Eighteen were the sons of leading men in political life.[109] There can be little doubt that the college served a relatively small but very influential part of the community.

A proposal in 1911 for a change in the curriculum shows that the need to prepare for two different kinds of career, civil and military, was becoming stronger rather than weaker despite the darkening shadow of war. To meet the needs of a growing number of cadets who did not wish to take either civil or military engineering, and perhaps because of increasing numbers and higher technical standards, the curriculum was re-examined. As a return to the four-year course was considered out of the question, Colonel Crowe suggested that alternative courses should be offered in the third year. To enable those who planned to take up a civilian career to go further in their civilian engineering, the course in military engineering should be altered and much of it omitted. This would enable those who did not take the civil engineering course to do more military work and also more languages. The Board of Visitors also advocated in 1912 that more time should be given to English and that political history should be introduced.[110]

The details of these changes were not spelled out and that they were not implemented before the war led to drastic cuts and a different emphasis. However, what is known of them suggests certain things. The three-year course was apparently an inadequate preparation for both a civil and a military career. The solution that was proposed was, in effect, the introduction of an alternative course to the engineering one, which would include more humane and social studies. This was intended to serve the needs of both reserve and regular army officers. As the proposed introduction of non-technical studies was to be coupled with more advanced military training, it seems that it was accepted already that there was a need to improve the general, in addition to the technical, education of potential army officers. This was an interesting anticipation of the direction in which RMC was to move a generation later.

By August 1912 the strength of the college had risen to one hundred and twenty-four and there were one hundred and twenty candidates for admission of whom only about forty could be accepted. Obviously so high a degree of selectivity meant a great increase in the quality of the cadet body. It showed that the college was now widely regarded as a success. RMC's most obvious value was connected with the growth of the technical services of the army where Canadian expertise and willingness to pioneer new methods sometimes meant that the embryo Canadian forces anticipated developments in the British army. Thus Bruce Carruthers, an RMC graduate who had gone to the British army as a Hussar lieutenant and who had served later as a sergeant in South Africa with the Royal Canadian Regiment, campaigned to have Canada set up a separate signal corps. This was done by a special general order of 24 October 1903. Carruthers became inspector of signalling. As a result Canada had a separate signal corps before World War I and was the only part of the British empire with one. From 1905 signalling was taught at RMC by Captain C. Russell Brown, RE, and the college began to produce officers trained adequately for the new Canadian Signalling Corps.[111]

RMC's connection with the Royal North-West Mounted Police similarly showed the value of the Canadian military college. Between 1882 to 1891 eight RMC graduates had been appointed to the force with the rank of inspector. By 1899 four of these had become superintendents. Four served in the South African War and three eventually transferred permanently to the Permanent Force. A. B. Perry became the commissioner of the RNWMP in 1900 and Z. T. Wood the assistant commissioner in 1902. As the force was relatively small, the number of graduates needed from RMC was small. But RMC thus served as a useful training college for this world-famous force which, until the western provinces were organized in 1905, was partly military in nature. Although the Canadian Permanent Force took more graduates after 1904, the link between RMC and the RNWMP remained important for many years to come.[112]

RMC's contribution to the armed strength of Canada and the empire was based on quality rather than quantity. It produced only a small number of the officers required for either the regular or the part-time forces of

Canada. In both cases it produced a leaven rather than the mass of the dough. Perhaps its greatest contribution was that at an impressionable age a number of selected young Canadians lived a life entirely subject to strict military discipline. They thus gained a degree of military experience that would make them invaluable when great armies had to be fashioned hastily from a population unused to military methods and manners. In those armies RMC ex-cadets had an obvious advantage in the competition for promotion and appointments and in the contribution they could make.

Quite apart from its direct contribution to Canadian and empire defence and militia service, RMC provided certain other services for defence purposes. The college was the location of a gymnastic course for militia NCOs and also of the long courses for militia officers. In 1912 the latter became the required qualifying course for candidates for the expanding Permanent Force. In 1913 the RMC Commandant, commenting on this innovation, pointed out that the RMC military qualification certificate given to cadets who had passed the military content of the RMC course satisfactorily but had not gained a diploma did not qualify its holder for a permanent commission although the RMC course was considerably longer than the period of training given on the long course.[113] The long course was under the supervision of the commandant of RMC, but the young officers who took it were apparently not lodged in the college.*

The most valuable service provided by RMC for the Permanent Force was the preparatory staff course. The number who took it was very small but their quality was excellent. The Board of Visitors noted in 1911 that the two Canadian officers who had taken this course topped the list of overseas candidates at Camberley. But it proved to be very difficult to get the required two qualified British staff officers who, along with the

---

*One of them was the future Brigadier-General A. C. Critchley who helped set up Imperial Airways and to introduce dog-track racing in England. An R.A.F. Air Commodore in World War II, he later went blind. Critchley has told of some of the scrapes he got into while taking the long course and he gives a brief glimpse of rivalry between the gentlemen cadets of the college and the junior militia officers on the long course. Critchley wanted to take the Commandant's daughter to the theatre but her father disapproved. However, he bought a ticket for a theatre seat next to those occupied by the Taylor family, waited in the lobby until they arrived, and then walked down the isle with them as if he were with their party. Later, when he was called to take a part in a play at short notice, he seized the opportunity to embrace the daughter frequently before her father's eyes. Mrs. Taylor told him that he was bound to pass the long course at the first attempt. The Colonel would not have him back to repeat it at any price. [Brig. A. C. Critchley] *Critch: The Memoirs of Brigadier General A. C. Critchley* (London, 1961), pp.27-30.

commandant, directed the course. In 1912 five GSO 3 s refused the posting because, although the pay was the same as in England, living in Canada was more expensive.[114]

The increasing acceptance of RMC by Canada in the prewar years was demonstrated by the noticeable success of Colonel Crowe in contrast with the difficulties experienced by several of his predecessors. Crowe was a small man; in his plumed hat he resembled the bird whose name he bore. The cadets liked him because he was able to unbend. A keen actor, he delighted them on one occasion by appearing on the stage wearing red underwear.[115] Unlike so many of his predecessors, Colonel Crowe steered clear of all political troubles as long as he was in Canada. Undoubtedly this was not merely due to his personal qualities but also to the recognition that Canada faced dangerous times. RMC was accepted warmly before 1914 because it was realized that it served a valuable national purpose and also the cause of the empire.

9

TESTED IN

WAR

1914-1919

When the war began in August 1914, Canada's military strength was negligible by European standards. The Permanent Active Militia consisted of about 3000 men organized for instructional purposes rather than for operations, and the Non-Permanent Active Militia had an enrolment of just over 70,000 but was not militarily effective as it stood. In 1910, with Dr. Borden's approval, Brigadier-General W. D. Otter, Chief of the General Staff, had chaired a mobilization committee to prepare plans to put the six divisions of the militia on a war footing and to make good their deficiencies in an emergency; and the following year Colonel W. G. Gwatkin,* who was borrowed from the War Office, had drawn up mobilization plans to provide a force for home defence and a smaller expeditionary force for service abroad. However, in a burst of super-patriotic feeling because Britain was in danger, Sam Hughes, the minister of militia, ignored previous planning, bypassed intermediary commands, and sent nightletter telegrams direct to militia units calling for volunteers for a Canadian expeditionary force. His "call to arms," although soon modified,[1] symbolized what was in many respects true, that Canada's famed Canadian Corps in the war of 1914–18 was an improvisation.

Certain factors, the arbitrary divorce of the CEF from the militia organization, the great size of the force that was ultimately engaged, and the very different nature of this war from anything that had been anticipated, have tended to minimize the value of Canada's prewar military preparations to the war effort. One element of the CEF in particular, the officer corps, did not lend itself easily to improvisation or innovation after war had been

---

*Major-General Sir Willoughby Garnons Gwatkin, K.C.M.G., C.B. (1859–1925), late of the Manchester Regiment, was chief of the General Staff of the Canadian militia, 1913–20.

declared. A recent study by an RMC graduate and regular army officer states: "It was the Militia Officer that permitted the creation of the 1st Canadian Division and ... held the C.E.F. together in its early formative days in action. It was around the Militia Officer that the Canadian Corps was built... ."[2] By the end of the war militia-trained officers held most of the command and staff appointments in the corps (except that the two key positions, brigadier-general, General Staff and deputy adjutant and quartermaster-general were, significantly, still held by officers of the British army).[3] Only in the infantry was it found possible for a Canadian officer who had no pre-war experience to rise to the command of a unit,[4] but the availability of Canadian militia officers was particularly important for the two technical corps, the artillery and the engineers. Despite its limitations, this prewar militia training made possible a force that was almost exclusively Canadian. Without those officers, Canadian troops would have had to be drafted to the British army as auxiliaries.

Militia officers could serve this important function in World War I partly because it was a kind of war the military had not foreseen and which did not necessarily require all the techniques that a professional officer had acquired. But what was even more important was that the officers who had trained with the militia before the war included many men of outstanding calibre from many walks of life. Though their military training could not compare with that of a regular officer, their intrinsic ability was often much superior.[5] The Canadian divisions and the corps became *élite* formations in the allied armies, not merely because they contained, as Liddell Hart has said, "matchless attacking troops,"[6] but also because of the personal quality of many of the Canadian militia officers who rose to command and staff them after the first-class British regulars who had ably guided their development in the early days of the war were replaced.

RMC's part must be evaluated in the light of these circumstances. The three-year course at the college, although not equal to a regular officer's peacetime experience, came closer to professional military training and experience than did the part-time training of the militia officer. Its graduates were therefore in some ways better prepared in the fundamentals of military life and the military ethic than were Canadian militia officers. But RMC was too small to produce more than a tiny fraction of the officers required by Canada during the war. However, those ex-cadets who had either militia or permanent force experience, and especially the latter, had an advantage in their favour that could not be gainsaid. RMC's value to the war effort must therefore be assessed qualitatively rather than quantitatively. Before a full appraisal can be made it is necessary to examine the policy pursued at the college during the war and also the extent of the contribution made by its graduates – by those who had passed through earlier classes as well as by those who were commissioned directly to war service.

Canada's involvement in war affected the college at once, for RMC had always relied heavily on British officers for its teaching staff. In August 1914 four of these men were in England on leave; they rejoined their regiments, and did not return to Canada. One of the British staff officers at the college to give staff training was called in to help with the instruction of the cadets; but he too was summoned to England in November. The following month the Commandant, Colonel L. R. Carleton,* was also recalled for war duties. Thereupon the Staff Adjutant, Major Perreau,† was appointed acting commandant in addition to his previous duties. With only two members of the military staff left, he was hard pressed to carry on with the military part of the curriculum which was now more important than before.[7]

The cadets chafed at the idea of the college being maintained on a peacetime footing when Canada was at war. Eighty-nine candidates had written the entrance examinations in the spring of 1914, fifty-six had qualified, and fifty-four reported to RMC soon after war was declared. These new recruits brought the total strength of the college up to one hundred and twenty-eight.[8] As soon as the college opened, many of the cadets, even some of the recruits, asked to be commissioned immediately in the hope of joining the CEF. All assumed that, as they had in effect "taken the King's shilling," they were destined to serve in the war and they hoped to see action before this "short war" came to an end.[9] With all the cadets pressing or hoping for commissions and with some of the essential military staff already gone, the future of the college was uncertain.

The wisest policy to adopt was not at first clear. It could be argued that a small college that educated as well as trained would not be able to meet the need for officers for swollen wartime forces, however much its course might be shortened. Junior officers, according to this reasoning, could be produced in much more adequate numbers in military schools or in officer-training units. Moreover those young men who wanted a postwar military career would obviously be anxious not to miss an opportunity for active service. As the war was prolonged it would become increasingly

---

*Brigadier-General Lancelot Richard Carleton, D.S.O., p.s.c. (1861–1937), Essex Regiment; served in South Africa, 1900–2; instructor at the Royal Military College, Sandhurst, 1907.

†Brigadier-General Charles Noel Perreau, C.M.G. (1874–1952), Royal Dublin Fusiliers, had been severely wounded in South African war; he was staff-adjutant at RMC, 1911–14; acting commandant, 1915–16; commandant, 1916–19, with the rank of temporary brigadier-general from December 1918.

difficult to justify a college that prepared cadets to be professional soldiers if they were kept back from the front while wartime officers were commissioned from the ranks or direct from civilian life in a much shorter time. Also to be considered, however, was that after the war Canada and the empire would need regular forces and it was important that their officers should be well educated and well trained, however much experience they might have gained in actual fighting.

The policy that evolved came as a result of *ad hoc* decisions. When the college re-opened in September, following precedents in previous crises, the War Office offered twenty extra commissions in the British army to RMC cadets. Some of these were given to members of the class that had graduated in the previous spring, but others were offered to members of the senior class entering their third year at the college. The principle was adopted that the minimum qualifying period at RMC before recommendation for a commission in either the British or the Canadian forces during the war should be one year.[10] Some cadets who had already been at the college for a year were disappointed when the War Office commissions were handed out. These were organized into an army class with the prospect that by Christmas they might get a commission in one of the services;[11] this class dropped civil engineering in order to concentrate entirely on military subjects. The RMC wartime course was not, however, entirely a military training course. The remainder of the cadets of the second year, including all those who would not have reached the age of eighteen (the War Office's minimum age for commissioning) continued on the peacetime curriculum but with greater intensity. Faster progress was possible because intercollegiate sports were cut and out-of-town games dropped.[12]

When the army class was commissioned at Christmas 1914, or soon after, twenty-eight new recruits were admitted, some from among those candidates who had failed to qualify for a place the previous September, and others from among matriculants at Canadian universities. In 1915 commissions were again offered at Christmas to those who were eighteen. But it had been found that the recruits admitted after Christmas in 1914 had been severely handicapped by their late entry, and the Commandant therefore advised that the experiment not be repeated.[13] However, to utilize the facilities as much as possible, and to meet the wishes of young Canadians who when still under the regulation age wanted to prepare themselves for a commission, twenty candidates were again admitted in January but restricted this time to matriculants or others who passed a special examination.[14] This pattern was to persist throughout the war. In effect there was, at the maximum, a two-year course with an accelerated peacetime curriculum and intakes twice a year; those cadets who were old enough to be commissioned could go into an army class for concentrated military training.

Commissions were offered as they became available and cadets were given their choice according to their place on the class list. The War Office continued from time to time to accept RMC cadets for commissions in the British army, the first preference of many Kingston cadets not merely because it was likely to promise a better career after the war but also because its officers went overseas much more quickly than those in the Canadian army. As the war went on, there was a persistent demand for officers to make up for heavy losses at the front; therefore the requirement of at least one year's service at RMC before a recommendation for a commission was not always maintained.[15] Thus, RMC's war policy was to take Canadian boys who were not yet old enough for a commission and give them as much peacetime education and training as possible until they became of age for immediate commissioning and active service.

At Christmas in 1914, twenty-nine cadets had been commissioned in the British army, twenty-nine in the Canadian Permanent Force, and twenty-five went to overseas contingents. Adding these to the graduates of the previous class who had gone before, one hundred and thirty RMC cadets had been commissioned during the year. Some who were too impatient to wait for commissions enlisted in the ranks, and 95 per cent of these were almost immediately promoted to officer rank. Later in the war a number enlisted in the Royal Flying Corps or its successor, the Royal Air Force. RMC cadets thus sought commissions eagerly throughout the war. In report after report the Commandant drew attention to the proud record of cadet determination to serve the empire and Canada in battle.

Meanwhile, staff problems at the college had continued to be difficult. The Canadian government was convinced that without Perreau it would have to close RMC.[16] Therefore Perreau was persuaded to suppress his natural desire to rejoin his regiment and to stay on as commandant although the decision left him vulnerable to hostile criticism. He was given promotion in local rank and in December 1918, in recognition of his services at RMC, was made a temporary brigadier-general; the Governor-General then asked the War Office to raise him from his substantive rank of major in the British army.[17] Perreau undoubtedly served Canada well during the war but it was at the cost of damaging his career. After he returned to England he commanded a battalion of his regiment, but his only subsequent appointment was as a commander of the 116th Infantry Brigade of the Territorial army, 1923–7. There were too many other men of equal seniority who had operational service.

Following most of the British regulars at the beginning of the war, many of the college's civilian staff also left for service. Mr. O. T. Macklem,* an instructor in civil engineering, joined the cyclist section of the Second Overseas Contingent in the first year of the war;[18] and Major H. J. Dawson,† an assistant instructor in mathematics, followed soon afterwards to command the 59th Battalion.[19] Other losses through sickness and age meant that the RMC instructional staff that remained was much overworked, especially when the midyear recruits needed extra coaching in mathematics and French. Then the Professor of French, M. Lanos, a French citizen, was recalled to his native land for military service despite Canadian protests that he was unfit and was performing valuable war service in Canada. He was soon invalided and returned to Kingston, but he died shortly afterwards, allegedly as the result of the extra strain imposed upon his constitution. The Canadian government asked the French government to make provision for Lanos' widow and children who had been left in strained circumstances in Kingston. To fill his place, it also asked France to find a young, married French officer who had had teaching experience and who was incapacitated by war service. But the officer recommended by France became seriously ill before leaving home, and his replacement, M. Vattier,‡ did not arrive until after the war was over.[20]

*Professor Oliver Tiffany Macklem, B.SC. (1883–1959), graduated RMC (1905) and McGill (1908); instructor in civil engineering, RMC, 1908; commissioned in the cyclist corps, CEF, became staff captain, 4th Canadian Infantry Brigade and was attached to the APM staff, Canadian Corps, Paris; associate professor of civil engineering at RMC, 1920; became professor and head of the department, 1933; retired, 1938.

†Colonel Herbert John Dawson, C.M.G., D.S.O. (bar) (1876–1926), B.A., 1898, M.A. 1899 with the gold medal (University of Toronto) for the highest honours in mathematics; fellow at University College; postgraduate student at Harvard until impeded by ill-health; became an associate of the Institute of Actuaries; assistant instructor in mathematics at RMC from 1901; commissioned in the PWOR and later commanded the regiment; associate professor of mathematics, 1915 and organized the 59th Battalion for overseas service; commanded the 46th Battalion in France, 1916 and won the D.S.O. at the Somme; awarded the Belgian Croix de Guerre, 1918 and the C.M.G., 1919; he was four times mentioned in despatches; after the war he commanded the 7th Infantry Brigade and was offered the position of GSO2, Military Division 3 but instead returned to RMC as professor of mathematics; became director of studies in 1922.

‡M. Georges Vattier, L. ès L., professor of French at RMC, 1918–25, had studied in Caen and Paris. When he came to Kingston he was unable to speak English. He held strong views on the differences between European French men and French Canadians which he expressed in his *Essai sur la mentalité canadienne-française*. He loved Canadian outdoor life but returned to France in 1925 and was later proviseur du lycée française in Salonika, Greece. Persecuted for his pro-British sentiment by the Vichy government, and watched by the Gestapo, his village was the first one to be liberated by parachute troops in the Normandy invasion on 6 June 1944.

RMC solved its wartime staff problem by the use of officers and civilians who were unfit for active service. On 1 August 1916 Captain H. C. Wotherspoon* was appointed staff-adjutant and an ex-cadet, Captain H. H. Lawson,† came to teach engineering. Two officers from the British army and Mr. W. R. P. Bridger,‡ who had been teaching mathematics at Trinity College School, Port Hope, were appointed in 1916 and 1917.[21] In May 1918 Major A. D. Fisken,§ M.C., an RMC graduate who had been overseas three years and wounded as many times, was brought in to teach tactics and trench warfare.[22] In view of the current need to foster the military content of the course so as to make it of practical value to cadets who would soon be in action, the latter appointment had a special value. Further practical experience was also gained when the burning of the parliament buildings in Ottawa (alleged to be arson) revived fears of another Fenian invasion from the United States, and special cadet guards were mounted at the college and nightly patrolled the ice of Lake Ontario.[23]

Despite pressures caused by the war, the college's emphasis on the academic element in its course not merely remained strong but actually increased. A year before the war began, Sam Hughes, a former schoolmaster, stated publicly that he intended to reform the academic programme at RMC. It was rumoured at that time that he proposed to make Professor Iva Martin of the mathematics department a "director of studies" to take charge of the syllabus.[24] Nothing came of this immediately, but in 1914 the Board of Visitors, who were also concerned about the

*Major H. C. Wotherspoon, 46th Durham, staff-adjutant at RMC, 1916–19.

†Major Horace H. Lawson, B.SC., E.I.C., O.L.S., RMC, 1907–10, was engaged in survey work in various parts of Canada, 1910–14; a lieutenant in the CFA with the CEF, he was invalided home, 1916 and appointed instructor in the Royal School of Artillery before moving to RMC as instructor and company commander; became associate professor of engineering, 1917, professor, 1938 and senior professor, 1941; in 1942 he was loaned to the Survey Wing, A-1 CATC Petawawa.

‡Professor William Reginald Pritchett Bridger, M.A. (1884–1962), graduated from Cambridge University, 1906 and taught in Newbury Grammar School and Trinity College School, Port Hope, before succeeding Professor A. Laird as head of the department of English at RMC, 1917. With Professor T. F. Gelley he founded the *R.M.C. Review* in 1920 and from 1922 edited and published in the *Review* the proceedings of the RMC Club. In 1930 he was made head of the department of modern languages and history. When the college closed in 1942 he was appointed librarian, officer in charge of records, and archivist. When the college reopened in 1948 he resumed the headship of the department of English, retiring in 1949 in which year the RMC Club honoured him by election as an honorary life member with the number H2828.

§Major Arthur Douglas Fisken graduated RMC, 1910; went to France with the 20th Canadian Battalion; instructor at RMC, 1918 and later a civil engineer in Toronto; president of the Vancouver branch of the RMC Club in the 1920s and a member of the National Council and vice-president in the 1940s.

college's academic standards, recommended that their number ought to include an "educationist," preferably from Queen's University so that he could keep in constant touch with the commandant. In the same report the board agreed with the Commandant that the qualifying standard for entry was too low and should be raised from 33 per cent to 50 per cent in the obligatory subjects.[25] A year later, it recommended that the civil engineering, survey, and military engineering departments should be combined under the professor of civil engineering; and also that the senior professor of "the scientific department" ought to act as the commandant's educational advisor.[26] Then on 10 May 1916 Professor Martin was appointed director of studies. In the following year changes were made in the entrance examinations; general knowledge, drawing, chemistry, "and drill" were eliminated and Latin was made compulsory. The board and Colonel Perreau decided that the over-all percentage required for entry should be raised to 60 per cent, the matriculation level in the Canadian universities; and the board also discussed a proposal to recommend the re-adoption of the four-year course. Although it was considered inadvisable to make a decision on this latter point during wartime,[27] it was remarkable that the other changes to strengthen the academic side of the course had been made while a war was in progress. War had, in fact, given new urgency to the work done at RMC; military training was stepped up, and a cadet of that day has declared that the cadets applied themselves with a greater intensity to all their studies.

The reason given for the appointment of a director of studies was that, as commandants changed frequently, and as each was inclined to stress training for his own corps, it was impossible to maintain a reasonable continuity in the curriculum.[28] Carleton and Perreau were not technical officers. They were therefore less qualified than some of their predecessors to head an institution in which an increasing emphasis was being placed on scientific studies. Under them the RMC course presumably began to lay heavier stress on military drill and infantry tactics. The appointment of a director of studies capped other developments which stressed the desire to maintain the academic quality of the college. Although the transfer of military engineering to the control of the professor of civilian engineering might be explained as a wartime expedient, the discussions about a possible return to the four-year course suggest that RMC's academic status after the war was being considered. Thus while the college was used to produce junior officers for immediate active service, the superior academic qualities that had been its hallmark in the past were reinforced.

As no new recruits came to RMC in January 1918, the graduation of the army class the previous December cleared the way for the arrival of ten officers, thirty-two cadets, and twenty-nine ratings from the Royal Canadian Naval College which had been rendered homeless by the Halifax explosion on 6 December 1917. A temporary wooden building was erected south of the new Fort Frederick dormitory for use as a naval college gymnasium and a "quarter-deck" for "divisions" and "evening quarters." Other college accommodation was shared with the sailors. Because the navy was the senior service in the British tradition, the Naval College claimed, and was allowed, precedence on parade. But RMC cadets were a year or two older on the average than the naval cadets and the college had long enjoyed a traditional privilege of taking "the right of the line" when parading with other troops. The naval claim was therefore found irksome; inevitably, as when there had been rivalry with the Artillery School in previous years, the party in the rear on church parade from St. George's Cathedral took another route to Point Frederick and moved at the double.[29] Despite this spirited competition the association of the two colleges was a friendly one and was an example of determination to co-operate fully for the sake of victory.

While the war was in progress it brought to Canadians generally a much greater understanding of the need for military preparation in time of peace. On 25 March 1915, Dr. J. W. Edwards,* the Liberal-Conservative member for Frontenac County, when speaking on the budget debate in the House of Commons, paid glowing tribute to RMC and to the contribution that it was making to the war effort; he read into the record the names of those cadets, including members of the graduating class of 1914, who had taken commissions at the outbreak of the war and at the end of the year.[30] The war in fact developed a new attitude in those who were responsible for the college. Despite the pressure of wartime needs, it loosed pursestrings that had hitherto slowed construction. Soon after the completion of the front portion of the new dormitory (then called Fort Frederick like the martello tower, but now named Fort LaSalle), the board repeated the recommendation made before the war that an extension should be added to the educational building; it also urged the addition of two wings to the Fort Frederick dormitory.[31] On 3 September 1917, the House of Commons voted $150,000 to enlarge the education block and $100,000 to complete the dormitory.[32] The college grounds were improved by the planting of many ornamental trees,[33] classrooms and dormitories were refurnished, and a chlorination and filtration plant was installed.[34] As the war drew to its close, the Board of Visitors pressed

*Dr. John Wesley Edwards, B.A., M.D. (1865–1929), a graduate of Queen's, was clerk of Frontenac County, 1899–1907 and MP for Frontenac 1908–29; minister of Immigration and Colonization, 1921.

Prime Minister Sir Robert Borden to provide yet more accommodation "as a War measure."[35]

The reputation which RMC gained in war and which produced this more sympathetic attitude among legislators did not depend on the college's immediate value for the training of junior officers, but rather upon the contribution made by the ex-cadet body as a whole. The number of former cadets who volunteered in the emergency was a tribute to the college's founders who had planned with this in mind. When this number is added to the number of cadets commissioned immediately before and during the war, the figures are impressive.

By August 1917, the last date on which a cadet could have entered the college in time to get a wartime commission, 1,378 recruits had been accepted since RMC opened in 1876. But thirty-seven of these had not joined and twenty-two more had stayed in Kingston less than six months. Among a number of others who were withdrawn at their own or their parents' request were undoubtedly some more who had also found a military life uncongenial; these ought, perhaps, to be subtracted from the total of trained or partially trained cadets available for active service in 1914–18, but as the number of such cadets cannot be estimated, they must remain in the tally. Since 1876 seventeen cadets had been discharged from the college as medically unfit; and ninety-six cadets and ex-cadets had died. The total number of former cadets who were unavailable for all these various reasons was about two hundred. The number who could have served was therefore 1,178.

Wartime statements that 914 cadets served in either the British or the Canadian forces were later revised by W. R. P. Bridger who claimed that a more correct figure would be 982; but it may be that his estimate included those ex-cadets who were "frozen" in essential civilian war work.[36] Nothing is known about the postwar careers of three-quarters of the ex-cadets for whom no war service can be shown; and it may be assumed that some of these had been incapacitated or had died and that others had served without the fact being realized at the college. If the calculation of the proportion of RMC cadets who served in the war is based only on those about whom information was available to Professor Bridger, the proportion of college cadets who could have served and did so was 95 per cent. But practically all those cadets who graduated after the war began went automatically into the services. If these are not included in the calculation it can be said that about 80 per cent of those who went through RMC in peacetime and were available are known to have actually served. Probably some of the remaining 20 per cent served and others were unfit. These various calculations therefore give substantial support for a statement made by one who signed himself "Ex-cadet" in the *Canadian Defence*

Quarterly: "So far as is known every [RMC] cadet who could possibly have served did so."[37]

Even more impressive conclusions can be drawn from the record of ex-cadets in the war. As at least 390 of the 982 RMC ex-cadets and cadets who served in the war were with the British, the Indian, or some other empire force, there were fewer than six hundred in the Canadian Permanent Force in Canada and in the CEF, that is to say little more than 2 per cent of the latter's total officer component. What is remarkable is that when the First Canadian Division went overseas, 22 per cent of its commanders and staff officers were RMC ex-cadets; moreover, at the armistice, the percentage of RMC ex-cadets among the officers of the whole CEF was 23 per cent. By that time, although Corps Commander Sir Arthur Currie was a former militia officer, two of his four divisional commanders, Major-Generals Sir Archibald C. Macdonell and Sir Harry Burstall, were from RMC, as was the GOC of the short-lived Fifth Division, Major-General Garnet B. Hughes.* Two of Currie's seven artillery commanders, Brigadier-Generals H. C. Thacker and Henri A. Panet, and three of his six engineer commanders, Major-General W. B. Lindsay, Lieutenant-Colonel S. H. Osler,† and Lieutenant-Colonel J. Houliston,‡ were also ex-cadets. Nine out of fifty-five brigade majors in the CEF[38] and Major-General Percy E. Thacker,§ adjutant-general of the Canadian Overseas Forces, were all RMC graduates.

Remarkable too was the record of those ex-cadets who were in the British and other empire forces. There they had greater opportunity but also greater competition. During the war these British army regular officers from RMC gained a prominence out of all proportion to their numbers. Before the war ended the college could boast two lieutenant-generals (G. M. Kirkpatrick and C. M. Dobell), nine major-generals, and seventeen brigadier-generals in the British army. Major-General W. T. Bridges, who commanded the Australian Imperial Force until his death at Gallipoli,

---

*Major-General Garnet B. Hughes, son of the minister of Militia, commanded the 1st Canadian Brigade in France, 1915–17 and the Fifth Canadian Division organized in England in February 1917 but disbanded February 1918.

†Colonel Stratton Harry Osler, C.M.G., D.S.O. (1882–1931), graduated RMC, 1903; commissioned RCE, 1904; CO 5th Field Company, RCE, 1915 in France, CRE, 2 Div., CO2 Brigadier, CE; assistant director of engineers, militia headquarters, Ottawa, after the war.

‡Colonel John Houliston (1868–1937), graduated RMC, 1890; CRE Canadian Corps Troops, 1918.

§Major-General Percival Edward Thacker, C.B., C.M.G., p.s.c. (1873–1945), RMC, 1890–4; commissioned Permanent Force, 1895; served with the Yukon Field Force, 1898–1900 and in South Africa, 1901–2; Camberley Staff College, 1907–8; assistant adjutant-general, Ottawa, 1909–10; director of military training, 1911; lieutenant-colonel, Lord Strathcona's Horse, 1912; imperial General Staff at the War Office, 1912–14; adjutant-general, Canadian Overseas Forces, 1917–19.

had begun his military career in Kingston. Colonel G. N. Johnston* was director of ordnance and commander of permanent artillery in the New Zealand Defence Force. And many other ex-cadets had ranks and appointments not greatly inferior to these. RMC had proved its worth when Canada was at war.

A like tale is told by the statistics of the number of decorations won by RMC ex-cadets. Captain W. A. Bishop,† was awarded the V.C.; he had been commissioned in the Canadian Mounted Rifles in 1914 but had transferred to the RFC in France in 1915. When training as a pilot, Bishop was at first rejected on the grounds that he was too heavy-handed on the controls, but through assiduous practice he became the best aerial marksman on the station and so was allowed to qualify for his wings. He proved to be a determined and aggressive fighter with only one aim in life, to down enemy aircraft. Credited with the destruction of seventy-two German planes, he was the allies' leading war ace. Colonel Eddie Rickenbacker, the outstanding American pilot, testified: "Billy Bishop was a man absolutely without fear. I think he's the only man I have ever met who was incapable of fear." Bishop had that courage which Napoleon said was rarest, "the courage of the early morning."[39] Between April and August 1917, he won the M.C., the D.S.O., and the V.C.; in August 1917 he got a bar to the D.S.O., and in July 1918 the D.F.C. The citation for the latter stated that he had destroyed twenty-five enemy planes in twelve days, five of them on his last day of service at the front; it concluded, "his value as a moral factor in the R.A.F. cannot be overestimated."

Three other ex-cadets were recommended for the highest decoration for valour in the British empire: Captain E. D. Carr-Harris, RE, who was killed in action in November 1914; Major F. Travers Lewis, 54th Battalion, CEF, killed in action in March 1917; and Acting-Major G. A. Trorey, RFA, reported missing 21 March 1918. The number of other war decorations received by RMC cadets was as follows: K.C.B., 5; C.B., 17; K.C.S.I., 1; C.M.G., 51; C.B.E., 1; O.B.E., 10; D.S.O., 118; D.S.O. and bar, 6; D.S.O. and two bars, 2; M.C., 125; M.C. and bar, 12; D.F.C., 4; foreign decorations, 62; mentioned in dispatches, once 128, twice 57, three times

*Brigadier-General George Napier Johnston, C.B., C.M.G., D.S.O. (1867–1947), graduated RMC, 1888; commissioned RA; served in India, New Zealand, Canada, United Kingdom and Egypt; organized the New Zealand Divisional Artillery, 1914 and commanded the artillery of the Australia-New Zealand Division at Gallipoli and the New Zealand Artillery in France; CRA, 52 Lowland Division, 1920–4.

†Air Marshal William Avery Bishop, V.C., C.B., D.S.O., D.F.C., E.D., LL.D. (1894–1956), RMC, 1911–14; Canadian Mounted Rifles, 1914; transferred RFC, 1915, the leading British war ace of World War I; private business, 1919–36; appointed Canada's first air marshal, 1936; director of recruiting for the RCAF during World War II, helped with the Commonwealth Air Training Plan.

27, four times 6, five times 6, six times 3, and seven times 2 (the highest number given in the war). One hundred and forty-seven former cadets had been killed in action, more than 10 per cent of those who served.[40] This record was a remarkable one for a relatively small college located in a country with little military tradition and one which in peacetime had been geared to educate its cadets for civil life as well as to train them for a military career.

Wartime decorations are of two kinds. Some reward personal deeds of heroism; others mark successful service of a more general kind. These latter are often given in considerable numbers in routine fashion to the holders of particular appointments or to a proportion of the personnel involved in particular operations or wartime activities. Acts of bravery performed by junior officers bring credit on a college from which the recipient came and which helped to develop his character, but they should probably be attributed as much to the individual's own characteristics as to his early training. Distinguished service, on the other hand, although often marked by awards given to officers holding certain appointments, relates more specifically to previous preparation. It is noteworthy that RMC ex-cadets received many awards of both kinds, for instance one Victoria Cross and over a hundred Military Crosses and Distinguished Flying Crosses on the one hand and a similar number of c.m.g.s and d.s.o.s on the other. Clearly RMC men featured both in action and in important work of a more technical nature and in command and staff duties. Younger men like Bishop served in close combat. More senior officers who had graduated earlier used their training and experience in more remote, as well as in very close, support. That so many awards of both kinds were gained is evidence that RMC was producing junior officers for immediate service who were also men capable of success in the higher ranks.

The RMC ex-cadets who served in important positions in World War I had come through several different channels. Many had been commissioned in the British army, mainly as technical officers. RMC's strength in this field had been well established before the war, as can be seen, for example, in the service of Brigadier-General D. S. MacInnes, a graduate of 1891, who first served in the Royal Engineers in Africa. He then became DAQMG at Halifax, and subsequently DAAG Canadian militia because of his knowledge of both the British and Canadian forces. In 1910 he was made secretary of a subcommittee of the Committee of Imperial Defence which recommended the formation of the Royal Flying Corps; MacInnes also had much to do with the reorganization of the British Army Signal Service. After being wounded during the early months of the campaign in France, MacInnes returned to the War Office and in 1916–17 was director of aeronautical equipment; he was responsible for eliminating much confusion that had grown up in procurement for the Royal Flying Corps and he helped to increase aircraft production greatly. Despite the effects of his war wound and the general deterioration of his health as a result of the retreat from Mons in 1914, he worked untiringly and was one of the founders of the future Royal Air Force. Anxious to return to the front, MacInnes was made Commanding Royal Engineer, 42 Division, and was later inspector of mines at army headquarters. He was killed on active service in 1918.[41]

Ex-cadets who reached high rank in the Canadian forces had either risen in the Permanent Force or had come from civilian life and the militia. It was symbolic of RMC's contribution to the ultimate victory that the two divisions which represented the CEF in the ceremonial march across the Rhine bridge at Cologne (13 December 1918) were headed by RMC men, Lieutenant-General A. C. Macdonell and Lieutenant-General Sir Harry Burstall. Even more spectacular was the work of the chief engineer of the Canadian Corps, Brigadier-General W. B. Lindsay, who had also been a prewar Permanent Force officer. Lindsay obtained the appointment as chief engineer of the CEF when General J. Armstrong, another RMC graduate, was injured in a railway accident. The new Commanding Royal Engineer was short, fat, and seemingly lethargic, but his appearance concealed an extraordinary energy. General McNaughton, whose counter-battery work depended on Lindsay's roads behind the front, said that he was "stout but professionally alert." Lindsay built the roads and the tunnels needed for the Vimy assault; he also built the first Canadian-style plank road in France to counter the appalling condition of the ground and had to set up a makeshift sawmill to cut the planks.[42] He was said to have taken part in every major engagement in France and was mentioned in dispatches six times. As they had in South Africa, RMC graduates excelled in railway construction and control.

The Royal Military College of Canada had never at any time been considered as a means of producing officers for forces of the size that Canada fielded during the 1914–18 war. Its prewar purpose had never been more than the provision of officers for Canada's peacetime militia, permanent and non-permanent, the training of civilians who could be relied on to come forward for an emergency of a much smaller scale than that faced in 1914, and the preliminary military education of a few Canadians who wanted a permanent career in the British army. Yet in the very different circumstances that pertained in the war with Germany, the RMC trained man stood up well by comparison with officers obtained through other channels. In the technical corps of the British army RMC graduates were clearly above the general average, probably because they were already a highly selected group. In the CEF the relatively smaller number of RMC graduates, especially those who had served between graduation and the war in the Permanent Force, rose to important positions.

European reserve corps were usually officered by men who had had inadequate training for war, and the armies of all the combatant powers included a very high proportion of officers who were not regular officers and who had had little or no previous military experience. A wartime study of these weaknesses in the German army concluded that "only in connection with the officers' corps of the active army and under its guidance were the officers of the reserve able to render such valuable service to the Fatherland. ... They [the reserve officers] became professional soldiers ... they acquired a training which they had lacked in peacetime when their adoption of the profession of arms had been only an incidental experience."[43] The CEF had to depend on regular officers from the British army for this kind of aid and example. However, the fact that Canada had long had a military college with a three-year course also helped. The German writer above concluded that in the education of an officer, "intellectual development in all the departments which directly or indirectly concerned the soldierly profession is of great importance in relation to ... military duties, but first and foremost in importance is the training of character, the cultivation of a distinguished mode of thought."[44] Character here is used to mean more than moral strength and a good reputation, although these are an important part of it. What RMC had been able to instil during three formative years of a young man's life was the spirit of service, of obedience, of persistence, of loyalty, and of single-minded devotion to a military purpose, all of which were necessary to the exercise of military leadership. By his education at the college, in a concentrated period of "living according to rule," the ex-cadet was better prepared in these qualities than was most of his comrades, even than those who had had a long period of part-time service in the militia. In the muck and mire of the trenches, and in staff duties that called for resolution amid seeming chaos and horror, RMC training had stood the test.

It has sometimes been said that Canada came of age on Easter Sunday at Vimy Ridge. Certainly Canada's great military contribution in the war as a whole, fully integrated with that of the empire yet noticeably distinct in its Canadian character, marked the beginning of Canadian nationhood. It is equally true that RMC's contribution to the Canadian achievement fully justified the college's existence. Alexander Mackenzie's prescience was vindicated on the fields of France and Flanders.

10

RESTORED IN

PEACE

1919-1930

When the war ended the Militia Council decided to put RMC back on a peacetime footing. This meant that cadets still in the college who had taken the entrance examination in 1917 and 1918 in the expectation of an early wartime commission would stay the full three years. The council also decided to restore the four-year course[1] and to make preparations to increase the college establishment to three hundred cadets. Major-General Sir Archibald Cameron Macdonell, who was selected as commandant to carry out these tasks, declared that the restoration of RMC was a result of its "present high standing ... in the Dominion [which was] due largely to those who fell in Flander's fields and to the magnificent response of the graduates during the war, and the high positions filled by Graduates."[2] But the prevailing sentiment in Canada for the next decade and a half was against all military institutions which seemed to many people to be just a step towards a repetition of the horrors of 1914–18. Excessive trust was placed in the achievement of peace through the League of Nations. In these circumstances, the college suffered through neglect and was exposed to attack; yet its existence helped to keep alive a military spirit that would come into its own when war again threatened.

Macdonell had been chosen to put the college back on its feet after the wartime dislocation because he was one of Canada's greatest fighting soldiers. Fiercely proud of the military reputation of his Highland and Loyalist ancestors, Macdonell had worked hard as a cadet at RMC, but only on subjects that had a military connotation.[3] He had stood fourth in his class and had won a diploma with honours in 1886. He had also been prominent in sports, representing Ontario in rugby football against Quebec and excelling at cricket, a game which he still played vigorously when he was commandant and which he hoped to re-establish "firmly" at the college. Offered a British commission on graduation from RMC, Macdonell had been forced to resign it almost immediately when his father failed in business. He had then been commissioned in the new Mounted Infantry unit in Manitoba and from there had transferred to the Royal North-West Mounted Police in which he served twenty years. When Currie became corps commander in France, Macdonell took over the 1st Division, and after the armistice he led the men with the "Old Red Patch" into Germany. He had been mentioned in despatches seven times. The troops called him "Fighting Mac," but as he was a man of colour and personality and with the eccentricities that frequently go with greatness in leadership, he was also sometimes called "Batty Mac." At RMC this eccentricity showed itself when he regularly barked "You're fired!" at those who irritated him, for instance by mis-spelling his name, only to apologize and retract a little later.

Macdonell's loyalties and emotions were simple and unaffected. When the men of his 1st Division sailed from Southampton to be demobilized, he watched them with streaming eyes. Whenever he spoke of the Mounted Police, the 1st Division, or the King, he always solemnly clicked his heels together and stood for a moment at attention.[4] At the end of the war he had been looking forward to enjoying his retirement. An appointment at RMC would bring him little more income than the pension which he would have to forego, and would introduce into his life yet another possessive loyalty that would become hard to relinquish. Nevertheless the call of duty triumphed and "Fighting Mac" and his war horse Casey came to Kingston.[5]

To Macdonell RMC was the nub of the defence forces of his beloved Canada. He therefore conceived great plans for developing its physical plant, its staff, and its curriculum to enable it to perform its proper role adequately.[6] His reputation, his wide contacts, and his personal qualities helped him to achieve a few of these goals. He built up the college's public image. The long list of distinguished visitors in the years when he was commandant was evidence of the interest taken in RMC by those who had served in the last war; foremost among those who came was Edward, Prince of Wales, who had met Macdonell in France; General Sir Arthur Currie, Macdonell's chief as Commander of the Canadian Corps and now chairman of the new RMC Advisory Board (which had replaced the Board of Visitors), came many times; other military visitors included Lord Byng of Vimy, Admiral Sims of the United States Navy, Major-General Sir Philip Twining, an ex-cadet, Commissioner A. B. Perry, one of the Old Eighteen, Lieutenant-Generals Sir R. E. W. Turner and Sir H. E. Burstall, Major-Generals J. H. MacBrien, Sir E. W. B. Morrison, E. C. Ashton, the Honourable J. E. B. Seely, and Brigadier-General W. A. Griesbach.*[7] All these were Macdonell's comrades in arms. Another came for Copper Sunday, Lieutenant-Colonel the Reverend F. G. Scott, who had been chaplain of the 1st Division, Macdonell's friend and a fellow "Highlander."[8] Sir Archibald Macdonell lavished on the college the affection and care of a great heart and he commanded respect and admiration. He brought RMC international and national fame by his presence.

Macdonell did much to strengthen RMC's position in the Kingston community. He invited businessmen and civic leaders to lecture at the college. He helped to revive the Kingston Historical Society after the war and was its president from 1920 to 1926 including the year 1922 in which Kingston celebrated the 250th anniversary of its first settlement. He supervised the erection of tablets on various historic sites in the city and vicinity. He was interested in the society's project to open the Murney martello tower as an historical museum in 1925 and was largely responsible for its renovation.[9] In 1925 the society passed a resolution hoping that Macdonell would "long continue" as its President.[10] Most important of all he cemented the college's relations with Queen's University. Principal Grant had lectured at RMC when Macdonell was a cadet and had been impressed when he met him.[11] The association then begun was long lasting and when Macdonell was commandant he assiduously fostered friendly relations with Queen's University. Sports contests were resumed after the wartime break in a most amicable spirit. In 1922 Queen's gave Macdonell an honorary LL.D degree in recognition of his leadership of the 1st Division and of his work at RMC. Macdonell reported that this honour strengthened the already cordial relations between the two institutions and that it was much appreciated by all ranks at RMC.[12]

Macdonell's first step at the college was to bring back the old scarlet uniform which had been practically abandoned during the war in favour of khaki. But because of the expense, the red mess jackets which cadets had worn for formal dinners since 1897 were not included in this revival. Restoring the uniform could not by itself, however, restore and develop the college. There had been one hundred and two candidates in 1919 but only thirty-one obtained the required 60 per cent qualifying mark over all

*Lieutenant-General Sir R. E. W. Turner (1871–1961), GOC, 2nd Division, 1915–16; CGS Canadian Overseas Forces, UK, 1916–19. Major-General J. H. MacBrien (1878–1938), CGS, Canadian Overseas Forces, 1919–20; CGS Canadian militia, 1920–3. Major-General Sir E. W. B. Morrison (1867–1925), GOC, artillery, 1916–19, adjutant-general 1922–3. Major-General Ernest Charles Ashton, C.M.G., M.D., C.M. (1873–1956), adjutant-general, 1918–20; QMG, 1920. General the Right Honourable J. E. B. Seely, C.B., C.M.G., D.S.O. (1868–1947), secretary of state for war, GOC Canadian Cavalry Brigade, 1914–18, later Baron Mottistone. Major-General the Honourable William Antrobus Griesbach, C.B., C.M.G., D.S.O., K.C. (1878–1945), GOC 1st Infantry Brigade, 1917–19; MP, 1917; senator, 1921.

subjects. Twenty candidates who had made only 50 per cent were therefore admitted. The number who were successful in the entrance examinations in 1919 was so low that the Militia Council's desire to build the college up to a strength of three hundred seemed to be threatened.

Macdonell investigated the matter carefully and came to the conclusion that, as it stood, the RMC entrance examination was not in line with the provincial examination which governed entrance to the universities and that it was not within the reach of the majority of Canadian schools. He therefore reduced the number of subjects required but restored the standard of 60 per cent overall and 50 per cent in each subject. At the same time the upper limit of the entrance age was lowered from twenty-one on the first of January preceding the entrance examination to nineteen on the date of admission to the college.* These changes were timed to coincide with the restoration of the four-year course in place of the prewar three-year course about which Macdonell had said: "[It] was obviously a failure – all were agreed on that point." Macdonell's reason for this belief was that the reduction to three years had caused military training to decline;[13] the academic professors agreed with him because their work could not go far enough.

The executive committee of the Royal Military College Club passed resolutions approving this proposed extension of the course from three to four years which it, of course, had long advocated; but it questioned the lowering of the age of admission and what it considered a parallel lowering of entrance standards. It protested that the extra year should not be added to the beginning of the course, where it would usurp the functions of the preparatory schools, but should come at the end so that those cadets who did not accept a regular commission on graduation could become professional engineers immediately or could qualify for a year's reduction in the time required to obtain a degree at a university.

Macdonell's reply to their protest shows that his primary concern was with RMC as a source of officers. He informed the Militia Council that the three-year course had originally been adopted by dropping the first year. He said that, with the slight increase that had been made in the work covered by the entrance examinations, a cadet without any previous training and grounding in his military work had been expected to enter what had earlier been known as the "hard 2nd year." While he was a recruit, with "all that that means and stands for," the cadet had been expected to make up one year's military subjects, training, and discipline. The result

*The upper age limit of twenty-one years had prevailed for some years, possibly dating back to 1897 when the RMC course was shortened to three years. Apparently at this time provincial quotas for entry were introduced, but I have found no record of the new regulation.

was that cadets often got off to a bad start, there were many complete failures, and an appalling wastage. Many who graduated lacked the polish that the old four-year course had imparted. Macdonell said that the new entrance examination, which was in line with university matriculation, would put the college within the reach of every Canadian boy who applied himself to his studies at a high school as well as of those who attended the "Public Boarding Schools" (he meant the private residential schools). As a result there would be greater competition for places, the door would be open to the sons of all taxpayers, and there would be a degree of choice that would ensure the entry of cadets with brains who, with RMC's increased facilities, would go far. Macdonell's revised entrance regulations were approved by the Board of Visitors who recommended that the standard for entry should be that of the junior matriculation in the various provinces.[14] The adoption of this policy in 1922 automatically cancelled the holding of the special RMC entrance examinations.[15]

The second major problem that Macdonell had to cope with was a building programme. When he arrived the west wing of the proposed new educational building for which money had been appropriated by parliament in 1919 was already well on the way to completion. The foundation stone had been laid on 16 June 1919 by the Governor-General, the Duke of Devonshire, who had come to RMC to attend a service of thanksgiving for the safe return of those ex-cadets who had taken part in the war. The occasion was long remembered, partly because the day was very hot and the Duke spoke at some length with the cadets standing at attention; as a result several had fainted.[16] The building was almost ready for occupation within a year; it provided classrooms for tutorial groups on the West Point model, a large assembly hall, offices for the staff, a chemistry and physics laboratory, a machinery hall, and a modern science hall. One of the classrooms in the old administrative building was now transformed into an extra messroom and there were also messrooms for the senior and subordinate staff in that building.[17] In 1920, at the suggestion of ex-cadet Lieutenant-Colonel F. A. Wanklyn, M.C.,* and through the generosity of Sir Herbert S. Holt,† the father of three ex-cadets, two hangars were provided free of cost from imperial war surplus stores in Canada and erected as a covered rink. The Canadian National Railways "free-freighted" the sheds from Deseronto to Kingston. In 1922 the parade ground was enlarged by paving it to the front of the Fort Frederick dormitory.

But the chief barrier to the growth of the college was a lack of dormi-

---

*Lieutenant-Colonel Frederic A. Wanklyn, M.C., graduated RMC, 1909.
†Sir Herbert Samuel Holt, civil engineer, president of the Royal Bank of Canada from 1908.

tory accommodation. Recruits could only be admitted as graduates left. Fifty-six were due to go in 1921, thirty-nine in 1922, and fifteen in 1923; the number that could come in would therefore decline. Macdonell said that all the fifty or sixty candidates who successfully qualified annually for "Canada's National Institution" ought to have an opportunity to enter upon its course of instruction. Therefore more accommodation ought to be provided within the next few years by adding the two wings proposed for the Fort Frederick dormitory; when the wings were completed, a mess-room for three hundred cadets would be needed and also a gymnasium. After that the second wing of the new educational building (which would replace Mackenzie's old administrative building) and a second new dormitory should be considered.[18]

In the years immediately after the war, several members of the House of Commons spoke in favour of proposals for construction at RMC. Thus, Mr. Mackenzie King, the leader of the opposition in 1920, said he would not oppose the money to complete the college's educational building: "I entertain the highest opinion of the work being done at that institution. ... The services performed by the college extend far beyond the immediate work it does in connection with the Militia, although in that connection also it has been very useful."[19] A year later the Honourable Charles Murphy, another Liberal, gave as his reasons for supporting the college that it was a Liberal foundation, that it had turned out most of the engineers under whom the great public works in Canada had been constructed, and that Sir Archibald Macdonell, "than whom there is no more accomplished soldier or thorough gentleman on the face of the earth today," was its commandant.[20] But by 1922 the House of Commons had begun to set its face once more against military expenditure including that for RMC. Macdonell saw the north wing of the dormitory almost ready for occupation before he left, but the east wing of the educational building to replace the Mackenzie building was never undertaken. As a result the new "Tudor Gothic" wing remained attached to the old administration building which was frankly Victorian in style. The rest of the building programme had to wait until the eve of World War II and some of it was not completed until after that conflict.

Thus, although Macdonell did not in fact succeed in doing very much in the way of construction, his tour of duty saw great improvement to the grounds, though possibly the chief credit for this should go to Captain F. Vokes, RCE,* who had begun landscaping during the war and who

*Major Frederick A. Vokes, RCE; a retired sergeant-major in the Royal Engineers, he came to RMC from Dublin as foreman in charge of works, 1910; quartermaster and Honorary Lieutenant, supervising RCE district officer, and assistant instructor, 1915; captain, 1920; major, 1925; retired 1935 but recalled as works officer, October 1939 to July 1943.

continued to work at it afterwards.[21] Macdonell was the first to suggest that there should be a drive around Point Frederick outside the fort so that visitors could get the full flavour of the college's magnificent location. Nevertheless, all that he actually achieved in this area was the erection of a hundred and ten foot flagstaff on the centre battery from which a union jack was visible for several miles.[22] It was said that his aim was to show passing American vessels that the Point was "British" soil!

One aspect of his planning was more fruitful. His historical sense was shocked by the fact that nothing at RMC distinguished it from any other military college in the empire. He therefore sought to stress the significance of the college's historical location, of its immediate past, and of Canada's history. He called for copies of pictures of Wolfe and Brock, and also of the college's founder, Alexander Mackenzie. As he was a great admirer of the fighting qualities of the French-Canadian soldier, he also hung portraits of Montcalm and of Salaberry in the college. Furthermore, Macdonell gave Great War names to all the roads and areas of RMC.

More important still was his plan to make the assembly hall in the new educational wing a Valhalla commemorating the achievements of the Canadian Corps. Named in honour of the Corps commander, Sir Arthur Currie, this hall was decorated with the likenesses of the CEF's leaders and with the badge, battle-patch, number, and name of every Canadian unit serving on the Western Front on 11 November 1918. Major Stuart Forbes painted the insignia as a free gift to the college. Macdonell said that "no greater incentive or inspiration could be given to the Gentlemen Cadets of the Royal Military College of Canada than the sight of the emblems worn by the Canadian Corps."[23]

As its war memorial, the Royal Military College Club of Canada offered to present a memorial arch to stand at the entrance to the college. Macdonell thought this arch should not be erected at the college entrance but should stand a little way down the drive, perhaps near the old observatory, so that a visitor would see it at its most advantageous point before he made the slight curve that brought him within sight of the college buildings.[24] However, the granite and Indiana limestone arch, built at a cost of about $75,000, was actually placed yet nearer to the highway and to the new LaSalle Causeway where it could be seen by those who passed on one of Canada's most important highways. Two large bronze tablets on the inner side of the arch bear the names of the ex-cadets who gave their lives for their country in World War I.

Macdonell made the staircase in the administration building into a memorial stairway decorated with the photographs of all those ex-cadets who had died on military service.[25] He converted the basement and first floor of the Fort Frederick martello tower into a museum to portray the history of the dockyard and the college; and in the adjacent lunette was placed a general staff display sand tray depicting a sector of the Western Front.[26] In 1920 he authorized Professors W. R. P. Bridger and T. F. Gelley* to publish a bi-annual *R.M.C. Review* which was to fulfil the functions of the former *Proceedings* of the RMC Club by giving news about ex-cadets and also of a college yearbook to take the place of the single volumes that had been occasionally produced in the past. Edited from 1920 to 1950 by Bridger who had thoroughly identified himself with RMC and with its spirit, the *Review* also published articles of military interest and stories about the history of RMC and its graduates. T. F. Gelley, who had come to RMC from Khaki University to teach English and history, was the *Review*'s business manager and sports editor until 1940.

Macdonell's only experience in the educational field had been in instruction given in the Mounted Police.[27] In his annual reports he paid high tribute to the aid he received from his director of studies, Iva Martin, who had had thirty years of teaching experience. Macdonell said of him, "time has sharpened rather than dulled the edge of his keenness on producing sound academic teaching ... ."[28] Martin was a good teacher and he wanted to ensure a high standard in the college. When the new postwar staff was recruited he called them to listen to a lecture in which he demonstrated the way that gentlemen cadets should be taught. Then he had each member of the staff give individual tuition to cadets; he also planned inspection visits to classrooms. He used professors to fill gaps in other departments, especially when the small classrooms of the new educational building permitted division into sections based on ability so that the weaker cadets, whom Macdonell called the "duds," could be given more time.[29] Martin believed this "co-operative system" would give better results than one that employed teachers as specialists. He said he thought it less detrimental to the "embryonic mentality of the cadets."[30] But his reports to the commandant are so vague and so general that one is led to have doubts about his influence on the staff; furthermore his emphasis on teaching method, laudable though it no doubt was in intention, suggests a school rather than a university approach. There is therefore little wonder that the Minister of

*Lieutenant-Colonel Thomas Fraser Gelley, M.A., a graduate of Manitoba, served in the 28th Battalion in France and Germany in World War I; instructor in English and history, RMC, 1919; co-founder, business manager, and sports editor, *R.M.C. Review*, 1914–42; coach of college hockey team for many years; directing staff, senior officers, and company commanders' courses, RMC, 1941; GSO1 to organize Canadian civil affairs staff course, 1943; CMHQ, London, 1944; registrar and librarian, Khaki University, 1945; librarian, NDC, at RMC, 1946, registrar RMC, 1948; secretary-treasurer, RMC Club, 1958.

Militia and Defence, Hugh Guthrie,* when describing RMC in the House of Commons, used the rather damning praise that its standard of entry was "considerably higher" than that of Ontario high schools.[31]

It was probably Macdonell, rather than Martin, who sought to equate RMC with the universities in order to establish the college's academic reputation and to get credit for graduates who went on to further study.[32] Nevertheless, Macdonell was convinced that "by its very inception" RMC could never become a degree-conferring university,[33] which appears to mean that he thought that its military objective and the military content of its course was an insurmountable obstacle.

Yet, he did much to bring the college into line with the universities. He proposed, but did not get, a board of governors. Instead, the Board of Visitors, which made an annual inspection, became in 1922 the Advisory Board, which was intended to act more continuously.[34] In 1922, after some years of delay, Macdonell was instrumental in obtaining an RMC calendar in which the curriculum would be given stability and publicity.[35] He set up an academic board of the heads of departments chaired by the director of studies to look over the written examinations of all failures and to explain to the commandant why a cadet should not go on with his course.[36] He secured representation of the college at the conference of Canadian universities.[37] And he succeeded in getting the long-sought pension for civil members of the staff to put them on a par with their military colleagues and with the faculties of the universities.[38] He may have sought some of these changes to strengthen his own position by the introduction of sound procedure, but they gave the college a system of academic control more like that of a university and somewhat less subject to arbitrary action and change.

When the RMC Club raised the question whether the additional year should have been added to the beginning, rather than to the end, of the course, Macdonell argued that it would be impossible to obtain from the universities a blanket promise in advance that RMC cadets would be admitted to the final year of their course in engineering. He said that it was necessary to wait until the system was in operation so that the quality of its graduates could be proved. He then directed Professor L. F. Grant,† an instructor in the department of engineering and an ex-cadet, to investigate the possibility of accreditation for the RMC engineering course with

*Hugh Guthrie, PC, K.C., MP, minister of Militia and Defence, 1920–1.
†Lieutenant-Colonel Leroy F. Grant, born 1884, graduated RMC, 1906; commissioned in the Royal Canadian Artillery; taught civil engineering at RMC and president of the RMC boat club; responsible for beginning intercollegiate competition in sailing in Canada in 1937; after his retirement from RMC, he lectured at Queen's University and was secretary of the Engineering Institute of Canada and an alderman of the City of Kingston.

the Engineering Institute of Canada. Grant quoted one passage from the report of the seventh conference of Canadian universities where a speaker had alleged that RMC graduates were often preferred to university graduates for appointment in geographical survey and also a second from a Canadian magazine which had reported that the railroads "wanted men from high schools and colleges and from schools like the Royal Military College, men who want a chance." He concluded that "graduation from this Institution can be and should be sufficient in itself to assure success to graduates of good standing." But he said that the course should be thoroughly overhauled to make sure that it was fully equal to the first three years of engineering in any Canadian university. The RMC graduate would then have a clear choice between going on for one further year of study at a university or of taking up his professional career immediately in civil engineering.[39]

In 1921 the military and civil engineering departments had been amalgamated under Colonel E. J. C. Schmidlin, the professor of civil engineering and an ex-cadet of the college. A draft copy of the proposed RMC calendar was sent to the War Office to ascertain British views on the qualifications that would be required by candidates for RE commissions. The reply that was received was that a course in mechanical engineering would be preferable. Macdonell was prepared to introduce this change but the Director of Engineering Services of the Canadian militia vetoed the proposal on the grounds that in the Canadian service the work mainly done by the RCE was in the civil field.[40] The Chief of the General Staff emphasized that the four-year course had been reintroduced at RMC not only to benefit those cadets who wished to proceed to a university, but also because the experience of the last war had shown the desirability of improving the general educational qualifications of Canadian officers in every possible way. Specialization at RMC should therefore be limited to the fourth year, the standard and scope of which ought to prepare cadets for admission to the fourth year at McGill University. An exception could be made for those cadets wishing to study chemistry who could begin their specialization in the third year.[41]

Macdonell had suggested that the universities should be asked to accept into their fourth year those RMC graduates who had made 75 per cent. Others who made over 50 per cent would be able to enter the third year.[42] This proposal was approved by the Advisory Board and was accepted by the universities. Toronto and Queen's accepted RMC graduates with high standing in their fourth year of civil engineering and in their third year of mechanical, electrical, chemical, mining, or metallurgical engineering. McGill required one or two conditions in connection with economics and highway engineering.[43] Accordingly, the achievement of a passing standard in four years at RMC was not accepted as the equivalent of three years in a university. However, competition to obtain a mark that would cut out one year of work at a university must have stimulated the application of the brighter students.

Macdonell's primary interest was in the military parts of the college training. One of his first steps on arrival had been to ensure that the administration of the cadet wing would be carried on in the fashion of the best battalions in the service. The college was re-organized more like an infantry battalion, with the battalion sergeant-major as commander, with two company sergeant-majors as company commanders, and with two company sergeant-majors as platoon commanders; the rank of quartermaster-sergeant was introduced and the remainder of the NCOs were attached to sections. Control and discipline and the issue of stores were carried out in the same manner as in the army. Each company and each platoon had a senior staff commander; there was a cadet daily orderly officer as in a regiment.[44] In 1923–4 the BSM and CSM were renamed the senior and junior under officers respectively to make them equivalent within the battalion to commissioned officers. Macdonell's aim was to see that during four years at the college each cadet, in addition to taking the full military engineering programme, became familiar with the work of the cavalry, artillery, and infantry. For meal parades cadets were trained to form up as either a regiment of cavalry, a battery of artillery, or a battalion of infantry. Macdonell instituted a cavalry week, an artillery week, and a "trek" during which the battalion bivouacked and manœuvred in infantry operations.[45] He also taught the tactics of trench raids to impart lessons learned in the last war. He obtained bridging equipment from surplus war stores and the cadets bridged Navy Bay. By 1935 this was the only equipment of that kind in use in Canada.[46]

The Director of Studies, Iva Martin, felt that as a result of Macdonell's interest in military training the academic part of the curriculum was being crowded out. But he did not make this complaint public until he was on the point of retiring under the new pensions act. In a final report Martin stated that for thirty-two years RMC had been deficient in its educational aims and objectives. He argued that as commandants had been solely responsible for policy there had been lack of continuity because of the short period of their tenure of the office; for this reason he said that he had recommended to the government that a director of studies should be appointed. This step had been ineffective, however, because the director's authority was subject to the approval of a commandant whose educational experience was necessarily inadequate. He noted that since the government did not apparently intend to complete the eastern wing of the educational building, the drafting room which was to have been in that wing would not become available. He complained bitterly that General Macdonell had refused to allow the use of Currie Hall in its stead. In his opinion the director of studies, who should be a civilian, ought to have the right to appeal over the head of the commandant to the Minister in the Militia Council. He alleged that the cadets were at present too frequently distracted from their studies by unexpected privileges of a social nature; and he concluded by saying that if the building programme were not carried out and the college was not increased to a strength of three hundred, the staff which had been recruited since the war would be underemployed.[47]

Commenting on these statements in a report to the Department of National Defence, Macdonell protested that military officers were not necessarily inferior to civilians as teachers. He said that he had allocated the "old" naval gymnasium (which had been built in 1918 for the naval college) for use as a temporary drafting room. Martin's proposal of a dual system of control was impracticable, he claimed, and added, possibly with little foundation, that for years Professor Martin had attacked football, hockey, and social leave. Brigadier A. G. L. McNaughton, deputy chief of the General Staff and the director of military training and staff duties, described Martin's report as "the vindictive effort of a conceited individual who is piqued at not being assessed by his associates at his own valuation,"[48] which may be not far from the truth. There is evidence in General Macdonell's diary that Martin had caused trouble by behaviour not connected with his work in the college,[49] and the Director of Studies may have borne a grievance because he was prematurely retired on pension. Nevertheless, Martin performed a useful service by drawing attention to the fact that the effort to introduce higher academic standards at RMC conflicted with the Commandant's natural concern for military training and had been hampered because Macdonell's authority had hitherto been virtually unchecked. Martin was also probably right in his inference that it was difficult, if not impossible, for some military officers to understand the problem of maintaining academic standards.

After Martin's retirement, Lieutenant-Colonel H. J. Dawson, the professor of mathematics, succeeded to his office. When Dawson died in 1926 his place was taken by Lieutenant-Colonel E. J. C. Schmidlin, the professor of engineering who, although he performed the same duties as Martin, was not given the title of director of studies but reverted to the former description, senior professor. This implied that Martin's claims for the academic side of the college had been rejected.

Another perennial problem of cadet officer training came to a head during Macdonell's commandantship as a result of the desertion of a recruit named Arnold who went over the ice to the United States during the night of 5 February 1924. He left behind a letter addressed to his section commander, Corporal J. E. Ganong, in which he said: "I am not – before God – quitting. Certainly things can be no worse in the future than what I have stood in the immediate past and I have no complaints – it was a square deal, though I will say I was trying." Arnold intimated that there were private reasons for his action that were definitely not of a dishonourable nature, and he said that he would always keep the ideals of the college in mind.[50] It was, however, assumed that Arnold's action had been precipitated, if not caused, by a recent caning. His flight precipitated an inquiry into the operation of a basic principle at RMC, that the senior cadets were responsible for enforcing discipline, and into RMC recruiting practices. Before examining those practices the story of the Arnold case must be told.

On the Saturday previous to his departure Arnold had failed to attend a hockey game when ordered to do so, and when challenged on the subject, he lied and asserted that he had been present. As this was the third time the boy had been caught in prevarication, the BSM (later senior under officer), E. W. Crowe,* decided to deal with the offences formally in his orderly room. He awarded Arnold twenty strokes with a swagger stick, eight of which were to be at the discretion of his company commander, and two weeks extra parades.[51] From evidence submitted later it seems that Arnold's leave was also stopped "until further notice." When the corporal punishment was inflicted, the bamboo cane split. But as the punishment did not seem to the administering cadet officer to be very effective, he applied the optional strokes with another cane.[52]

In a lecture given to the cadet officers on their appointment at the beginning of the academic year the staff-adjutant, Major E. H. deL. Greenwood,† a former RE officer and ex-cadet, had told them: "corporal punishment by cadets is not permissible." However, he immediately added: "At the same time it is thought that certain offences can be dealt with in nor [sic] other way and, as a very exceptional case, should it seem necessary to the BSM that a cadet should receive corporal punishment from other cadets, a proper Court-Martial should be convened with a CSM as Presi-

---

*Captain Ernest W. Crowe, born 1902, F.A.S., F.A.I.A., BSM and governor-general's silver medal, 1924; actuary; captain, McGill COTC, 1941–6; had much to do with the restoration of RMC in 1948.

†Major E. H. deL. Greenwood, born 1892, BSM, graduated RMC, 1913; commissioned RE; lost a leg early in the campaign in France in 1914 but served again at the front and then at the War Office; RMC staff-adjutant, 1914–24.

1

2

3

CADET ATHLETIC ACTIVITIES
IN THE 1960s

1 Cross country racing

2 Football

3 Basketball

MORE CADET ATHLETIC
ACTIVITIES IN THE 1960s

1 Gymnastics
2 Hockey
3 Boxing

1

2

3

4

5

6

CADET ACTIVITIES
IN EARLIER DAYS

4 Equestrian drill
5 Pontooning
6 Camping

1

CADET ACTIVITIES IN EARLIER DAYS

1 Canoe gunwale race
2 Artillery training

2

3 Recruits at drill, 1889
4 Bayonet drill

3

4

1 RMC *c* 1885 – with a cricket game in progress

2–5 Scenes from various annual
recruit obstacle races

2

3

4

5

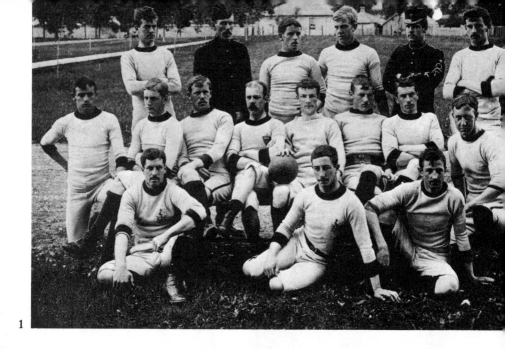

1 RMC soccer team, 1892

2 The first RMC hockey team, 1888. Winners of the first organized hockey game in official Canadian records

dent. ... Punishment of this nature, however, should not be given unless for continued offences after other punishments have failed."[53] The BSM assumed that this gave him authority to award corporal puishment; but he was technically in error when, while depending on Greenwood's authority given in this lecture, he heard the case himself instead of delegating it to a subordinate. The punishments he awarded to Arnold exceeded the three days' defaulters' drill permitted him by the college regulations.[54] However, although the regulations had not been officially changed, Major H. T. Cock,* the OC of "A" Company, had on his own initiative substituted for his company a scale of corrections in the form of extra parades in place of defaulters' drill to make the punishments fit the crimes;[55] and BSM Crowe apparently followed that precedent.

Arnold went to an uncle in New York who told him what Crowe was reported to have said about the offence that he had committed. Presumably this information had been passed on by another uncle in Kingston who had conducted a search for him when he disappeared and was feared lost on the ice. While refusing to give details, Cadet Arnold hinted at what were described as "the indecencies, indignities, and punishment to which he had been subjected"; and he threatened to shoot Crowe. He said that he was not learning at RMC because he had had no time to study, and he said that he could acquire all the bad habits exemplified in his seniors without going to the college.[56] Arnold's father admitted that the boy had been wrong to leave the college, but he claimed that in the circumstances he had no other option; it would have been hard for a recruit to substantiate charges against the seniors. Major Arnold asked for a full investigation of the incident and declared that he believed it would reveal an unsatisfactory state of affairs in the college.[57] Macdonell, who was a personal friend of Major Arnold, agreed to have the matter investigated and asked Arnold to see that his son was present to give evidence on oath.[58]

Major Arnold had already told the press in his hometown, Regina, that his son had been forced to leave RMC as a result of repeated and most severe hazing. Reporters from Toronto therefore began to ask the college for information; General Macdonell gave them an account of the affair and believed that he convinced them that a mountain had been made out of a molehill.[59] However, the Attorney-General of Ontario, W. F. Nickle, a Kingstonian, referring to the startling stories of irregularities that had appeared in the press, informed the Commandant that "all groups or individuals, whether within barracks, university or college, are under the

*Major Harry Tredennick Cock, M.C., K.O.Y.L.I., transferred to RCR; instructor in tactics, RMC, 1923–5.

Law," and that if they took the enforcement of the law into their own hands "apprehension and trial must necessarily follow." He said that, as he was anxious not to do an injustice to any cadet, he wanted a full report from the Commandant.[60]

The Adjutant-General, Major-General Panet, then ordered an official inquiry and sent two officers from headquarters in Ottawa, Colonel Sutherland-Brown and Lieutenant-Colonel B. W. Browne, to participate. He instructed Macdonell to detail Colonel T. V. Anderson,* who was a staff officer at the college, as chairman. The instructions first given to the Court of Inquiry were that it should investigate the circumstances connected with "Arnold's sudden departure from the college" and also "all charges made or inferred against the good name of the College or any of its students or staff."[61] However, the second and wider inquiry was not included in the statement of purpose announced at the opening of the proceedings,[62] perhaps because it might have prejudiced the line of investigation of the specific problem of Arnold's departure. Major Arnold claimed that this wider inquiry had been omitted because of a desire to "whitewash rather than to probe." As a result he said he would not ask his son to give evidence but the boy would do so before any court at which the public were represented, where provision was made for the skilled examination of witnesses, and where the inquiry would cover the whole ground.[63] Major Arnold seemed to be hinting that he would take the case into the civil courts.

The inquiry proceeded without Arnold and with Colonel W. P. Gibsone, director of organization and personal services, National Defence Headquarters, as chairman in place of Colonel Anderson. It interrogated all the principals including the Commandant and the Staff-Adjutant, and also a number of recruits selected at random. All the witnesses were asked questions concerning the allegations made about the administration at RMC as well as about Arnold's case.

In a paragraph which appears to have been added as an afterthought to its findings, the court reported that it found it "difficult to believe that any serious charge against the Administration, rules, customs, and conduct of the College could be sustained." If there had been any isolated abuse it would be "due to the characteristics of the individuals concerned and not to wrong methods in the administration of the College." It said that it was impressed that Crowe was a "young gentleman who has no idea

*Colonel Thomas Victor Anderson, D.S.O. (1881–1968), graduated RMC, 1900; CSM, 1900; 14th PWOR; instructor in civil engineering, RMC, 1902–6; RCE, 1905; wounded 1917 and became commandant Canadian Engineers Training Centre, England; GSO, RMC, 1921; DMT 1925; inspector-general central Canada, 1946.

of brutality or vindictiveness." It found that all the younger cadets were enthusiastic about the college and that they respected their seniors. It also came to the conclusion that Arnold had not left because he had been caned.

By specifically rejecting the idea that he had left because he was caned, the court implied that there was another reason. But it had simply listed and denied the charges that had been made in the press without proceeding to investigate them thoroughly. These charges were that corporal punishment by senior cadets was rife at RMC, that recruits had to do menial work for seniors, that as a result they had insufficient time to study, that a case had come to light where a recruit had written an essay for a senior which he should have done himself, and that there were irregularities at the college which were not known to the senior staff.[64]

The court's only attempt to explain Arnold's departure was a general reference to evidence given by Crowe, by the Staff-Adjutant, and by the Medical Officer. What Crowe had said was that there was "really no such thing" as recruiting, but he had also stated that recruits were required to do some services for the seniors. His explanation was that without this the government would have to provide the seniors with servants in order to enable them to carry out their duties; and he claimed that there was no interference with studies. Major Greenwood had testified that corporal punishment had always been given at the college but that it was now much less "promiscuous" than in his time as a cadet. He said that a cadet orderly room was not required to report to him when it inflicted punishments. (This was in fact a departure from one of the basic principles of judicial systems, both civil and military, that punishments should be duly reported to higher authority.) The Staff-Adjutant had added that discipline was entirely under the control of the cadets "with as much observation from the Superior Staff as is thought necessary," and that this was to teach them responsibility, to build up their characters, to improve their judgment, and to teach them to take command. He said that in the past there had been a few cases of recruits running away at the beginning of the year but that this was the first time one had left after he had been at the college several months. He thought this was because cadets were being taken in at a younger age than before the war. The Medical Officer, Lieutenant-Colonel R. J. G. Gardiner,* had testified that during his first term Arnold had been in the hospital for several weeks with appendicitis and had later suffered first a sprained leg and then a very badly sprained knee. While in

*Lieutenant-Colonel Robert J. G. Gardiner, M.D., C.M., F.R.C.S.(C), F.A.C.S., RO (CAMC), medical officer at RMC (1920–33), professor of medical jurisprudence and assistant professor of surgery at Queen's University.

the hospital the boy had complained of being nervous and unstrung; but the Medical Officer had concluded that he was merely homesick. The court had thus offered no explanation for Arnold's desertion except homesickness.

The conclusion that could be drawn from this investigation was that Arnold had personal weaknesses that had made him incapable of accepting a reasonable amount of discipline and training; and the evidence of many witnesses appeared to substantiate this. It was said that Arnold had seemed to have no "chums," he had been moody and withdrawn, he had been appointed the senior cadet in the recruit class for the first half of the term but had become "slack" when the position was taken away from him; though he had no difficulty with his studies other recruits had not asked him for help as they did of other members of the class. Evidence was also given that when he was the class senior Arnold had inflicted corporal punishment on some of his classmates; after he was demoted he had been similarly punished by the new class senior. Finally, as time went on, his classwork had fallen off.

Macdonell's statement to the press had been on these lines. Major Arnold wrote to point out that the General had made certain erroneous statements in this press interview; Macdonell had said that young Arnold had received only twelve strokes with the swagger stick, while in fact he had received twenty; he had omitted to mention the "indefinite" restriction of leave; he had said that the boy had not told the seniors that he had relatives in Kingston to whom he might have turned for encouragement, whereas in fact he had publicly invited his classmates to visit them; and when confinement to barracks prevented him from keeping appointments to visit his relatives, seniors had phoned to say he could not come because he was "on duty"; Macdonell had said that a swagger stick was incapable of inflicting pain and that the punishment was more mental than physical, an extraordinary statement which Major Arnold did not even bother to contradict; and finally, he had stated that Arnold had "lost" his seniority, which seemed to imply that he had been demoted for incompetence, whereas it was merely a normal rotation of command.

The father noted that the main charge against Arnold was that he had lied. He countercharged by saying:

the recruits had been instructed by the seniors to lie on any and every occasion when a senior might otherwise be implicated and to lie to any and everyone save and except to the seniors themselves. If questioned a recruit is always to say that he is doing whatever it may be for the B.S.M. who is the only senior authorized to impose tasks, or that he is doing a message for a Company

Sergeant-Major who is entitled to a runner. If checked for being improperly dressed he is to say that he has already been checked by a senior to emphasize the senior's efficiency. If questioned by a civilian [he has] to give no information "but to shoot a strong line." If questioned by the staff, as to falling asleep in class, or if inflicted such punishment as necessitated medical attendance [he has] to give a plausible excuse.

He said that a year earlier when the Medical Officer brought a case of injury caused by recruiting to the attention of the Commandant, the boy stated that he had fallen down stairs. Arnold claimed that his son had said nothing on these matters until the Commandant had made false statements to the press. He suggested that General Macdonell had been misinformed by those whom he had trusted.[65]

At the same time Major Arnold sent Macdonell a copy of the letter which young Arnold had written when he arrived in New York. This letter said:

In leaving the College I took what was perhaps the most important step in my life but I know you will believe me when I tell you that it was not done in impulse or because I am a "quitter." I stayed as long as I did because I wanted to be quite sure that I was doing the right thing.

The College itself is all that you told me and all I thought. The staff are white and the course is just as good as the syllabus. The discipline is only what a fellow would expect and just what he needs and the physical training simply wonderful. As you know I have done pretty well in my classes, but honestly, Dad, it was because I was pretty well up when I came. There is simply no chance to get an education here. The whole atmosphere is against it and a recruit is simply not allowed to study and I really feel that I can spend four years much more profitably, so far as education is concerned, than by completing my course here. By going when I did, I can still get my senior matric this June, and so not lose any time and that means saving a whole year at University.

This sounds pretty bald Dad, but you have always trusted me and I know you will now till I get a chance to talk to you and explain.

The next day Major Arnold wrote again to tell Macdonell that he had more information to give to the press; he said that he would do everything in his power to clean up the "rotten condition" of the college. But he offered to wait until the following Saturday if the Commandant would promise to investigate the general situation personally and satisfy himself about the state of affairs concerning the recruits.[66]

Macdonell was taken aback by the evidence that his own statement to the press had been so full of errors; and he was apparently impressed by the tone of young Arnold's letter to his father. He therefore agreed to investigate.[67] Twenty-four hours later he wrote to the Chief of the General Staff, General MacBrien, the following revealing letter:

I think that I should lose no time in letting you know that as far as I have got with my investigation, the Report made by Major Arnold, though overstated in some instances, seems fairly correct, as far as we, Perry,* Greenwood and myself can judge. The whole 1st Class is mixed up in it. The spirit of R.M.C. has always been that the 1st Class took care of discipline amongst the Cadets themselves, and we all had firm faith in them, but this proves that drastic changes will be necessary; we have been living in a "Fools' Paradise." Major Arnold wishes to return home and wants a statement from me clearing his son. It must be admitted his son had good reason for wanting to leave and he considered running away the lesser of two evils, the alternative being to come to me. Could you authorize me to issue a statement to Major Arnold on these lines as we do not now feel that blame attaches to his son[?] The question of the treatment and punishment of the 1st Class [i.e. fourth year] calls for careful reflection, certain cases such as wearing plain clothes [the only reference to this offence in the documents] etc., could be dealt with, but the whole thing is serious and the whole class involved and I think that you and the Militia Council will have to deal with it. They are young fellows just entering life and I am most anxious the future shall not be ruined ... .[68]

Macdonell then wrote to Major Arnold on the lines which he had suggested. He completely exonerated Cadet Arnold by saying that he was quite justified in running away.[69] He received from Major Arnold a reply with the comment: "It is the letter of a soldier and a gentleman: written with the courage of one and the courtesy of the other."[70]

Macdonell now set up a new court of inquiry chaired by Colonel T. V. Anderson. This uncovered evidence of misuse of privilege and breach of regulations by the seniors. There had been gambling at mah jong and also drinking that had been encouraged by ex-cadets who had brought liquor into the college.[71] With regard to recruiting, General Macdonell said in his evidence to the court that in November 1921 he had decided to abolish the use of juniors as fags by seniors because, although the senior could be a "big brother," the "other side," which had not existed in his day as a cadet, was not so pleasant. It was "un-Canadian and undesirable" but had become a tradition which no mere order could "smash." The classes of '22 and '23 had been educated to put his wishes in force. He said that the class of '24 was considered a splendid class and had lived under the new system for three years. He claimed that it was now definitely established that, "Instigated and bolstered by Ex-Cadets [they had] deliberately decided to reintroduce "recruiting" and illegal punishments. Evasion and deception became necessary to keep it from the staff, and one thing led to another. One Under Officer stated to me: 'We considered we could make a much greater success of the College by re-introducing "recruiting" in all its

*Lieutenant-Colonel K. M. Perry, D.S.O., RCR, son of No. 13, Major-General A. B. Perry; graduate of McGill; professor of tactics and battalion commander, RMC, 1920–4.

phases. We considered loyalty and duty as sticking by and protecting one's own class and complying with the many and urgent requests from the Class of '21.' ... When it came to the point of following your orders, Sir, or carrying out our pledges to Ex-cadets, we decided to do the latter."

Macdonell said that "espionage" [by which he really meant careful supervision] could have checked this situation but that it was diametrically opposed to the trust that he had put in the seniors. He repeated that the class of '24 had reintroduced "recruiting" after a lapse of two years and had added previously unknown punishments. He had to admit, however, that the "recruits were very smart under their secrecy system this year."[72]

The Commandant decided to punish the senior cadets and to take other steps to prevent a recurrence of the unfortunate affair. The senior class had already been restricted from going on leave for ten days. Charges that the seniors had used recruits to do research for their essays, and even to write them, were referred to Lieutenant-Colonel Dawson for investigation. They were dealt with on 19 March and several cadet NCOs and seniors who were either reprimanded or punished were presumably convicted on these offences. The Senior Under Officer was reduced to the ranks on a charge of raffling a government T-square which had come to light during the investigation. All the remaining under officers, the company sergeant-majors, and the company quartermaster-sergeants, were reduced to the rank of sergeant. The NCOs were reduced a step in rank. The cadet NCOs lost their privileges and their powers of punishment and members of the senior staff were detailed to sleep in the dormitories. Specific instructions about recruit duties were issued.[73] The senior NCO was now V. C. Hamilton, the cadet officer who had administered Arnold's punishment; but he was personally very popular and therefore able to make a success of a very difficult appointment.

Arnold had kept open the possibility of his return to the college until the matter was concluded; but as he had lost most of his first year he decided not to come back. His father claimed that it had been admitted that the trouble had been caused by the college and that as a result of it he had lost the fees which had already been paid; he therefore argued that he should not be required to pay whatever charges were still outstanding.[74] He does not appear to have paid them.

The Arnold case is important, not because it was particularly outrageous, but rather because Major Arnold had persisted in his demand for an investigation of the abuse of a fundamental principle of officer-cadet training – the allocation of responsibility. It shows how easily this training method could get out of hand. General Macdonell came out of the incident fairly well. It has been alleged that the whole business occurred simply because a weak cadet stirred up press hostility. But the documents reveal that although Macdonell was induced to investigate personally only by Major Arnold's threat of more revelations to the press, his investigation quickly convinced him that there had been serious abuses. However, it is possible that he was in error about the extent to which he had succeeded in eradicating recruiting in the previous two years and therefore that the seniors of '24 were actually punished for carrying on a tradition that had been handed on to them.

What seems to have happened is that during the war recruiting had continued but had necessarily been imperfect since the seniors were themselves invariably barely out of their recruit year and did not know much about the traditions of the college. Thus, one of the wartime seniors ordered a recruit to clean his boots, a task which, under the RMC tradition, was never required of a recruit because it was considered "menial."[75] After the war, the continuance of the class of '21 through three years with the same BSM raised it to a position of power which probably engrained the worst of the wartime accretions. Furthermore, anxious to re-introduce the old traditions on proper lines, and undoubtedly instructed by ex-cadets inevitably prone to exaggeration, seniors of that period had overdone it. In September 1921 General MacBrien told Macdonell that the father of a cadet had complained that ragging had become too severe. One cadet was alleged to have been treated by the medical officer for bruises received in beatings. This father had complained that in some cases recruits had to get up at 4:30 AM to clean boots and kit, that they could not eat until the seniors had finished, and that they were often ordered away from the table before they had finished. On 30 September 1921, Walter B. Kingsmill,* an ex-cadet and a member of the Board of Visitors, had written to tell Macdonell that he had heard criticism of the moral life of the college, of drinking at the June ball, and of recruiting. He thought recruiting necessary but that periodically it went beyond the bounds of reason; he had been told by the father of an ex-cadet that at present it was so severe that work was impossible.[76]

Macdonell had checked this situation in November 1921 and believed that he had put things right. But the practices apparently continued to flourish. The seniors had become convinced that the staff knew what was going on, which was in many cases true; but the awe in which the great

---

*Lieutenant-Colonel Walter Bernard Kingsmill, D.S.O. (1876–1950), graduated RMC, 1898; Osgoode Hall, 1901; Canadian infantry, World War I and deputy judge advocate general; president, RMC Club, 1920–1; won the Old Eighteen Bugle three times and presented a replacement.

war hero Macdonell was held by the staff was such that no one cared to disabuse him about the "fool's paradise" in which his trusting nature had placed him. Furthermore, there was all too little supervision by the staff over what happened in the dormitories where recruits were frequently herded into boiler rooms and subjected to loudly shouted orders and abuse by relays of seniors until they fell from sheer exhaustion.[77] The corporal punishment at RMC, although alien to modern ideas and even to the Canadian army of that day, was not unlike what still went on in private schools. This aspect of the Arnold affair was therefore perhaps less serious than the fact that the seniors' attempts to stiffen the recruits by what they regarded as RMC's traditional disciplinary methods were a potential threat to the quality of the academic work at the college. Furthermore, when cadets concealed what was going on they were led to break the code of honour which they professed.

Recruiting at RMC was not abolished after the Arnold incident, though caning with a swagger stick had ended in dramatic fashion. As the Advisory Board had reported, recruiting was customary in all military colleges where seniors are normally given authority in order to train them for command. The development of contact with West Point, which began in 1923, may have increased the severity of RMC's system.[78] The systematic disciplining of recruits not only taught them to respond quickly to commands but also the important lesson that command is an impersonal relationship. At RMC recruits were expected to be prepared for certain "emergencies" which became traditional; for instance, every recruit must be able to give a senior a light for his cigarette on demand, and it had therefore become customary for recruits to carry three bundles of ten matches in his field service cap.

Sir Archibald Macdonell was well aware that this system of discipline put heavy pressure on the recruits. The seniors had been given the upper floors of the Fort Frederick martello tower for use as a common room but they had subsequently abused the privilege by rolling cannon balls down the stairs. Macdonell then took the place from the seniors and allocated it to the recruits as a haven where they could take refuge.[79] This incident should have taught him that the seniors needed supervision. One result of the system was that in their common misery, recruit classes found cohesion and a great loyalty. Most recruits found their first year acceptable because they looked forward to the day when they would carry on the tradition and could use recruiting to bring their own juniors up to RMC standards; they believed that it was recruiting that made RMC superior and would also make them superior men.[80] One ex-cadet, who recorded his recruit year impressions immediately after graduation (by which time they must have mellowed and changed somewhat), believed that the rigid discipline of this period was the basis of the success of the RMC graduates of this era not only in the services but also in the professional and industrial life of Canada.[81] Yet the system was directly contrary to the milder discipline which the RMC graduate would be called on to administer when he joined a unit; and some ex-cadets must have found it difficult to change from the one to the other. The example of tolerant discipline shown by the college military staff, which one critic has suggested was a corrective for the wrong ideas which RMC seniors developed,[82] cannot have been very effective because the college was quite unlike any normal unit of the permanent force or the militia.

The Arnold case brought RMC a great deal of adverse publicity in the press; and reference was made to the affair when the college appropriation was debated in the Commons. The Minister, Edward M. Macdonald of Pictou, read into Hansard the report of a subcommittee of the Advisory Board which had investigated the subject. It had come to the conclusion that the irregularities had been a breach of standing orders and that recruiting, which it said the seniors had "mistakenly" believed would improve the smartness and discipline of the junior cadets, had endangered the health of some of the juniors and had forced upon them menial and objectionable duties. There had been no personal viciousness but the loyalty they gave to each other had led to deceptions which were a breach of the high standard of honour instilled into and maintained by the cadets in other respects. The committee found that Macdonell's faith in the honour of the cadets was so strong that he had placed too much reliance upon the senior cadet officers. It said that steps to remedy these evils had already been taken. The only additional suggestion it could make was that special care ought to be taken to ensure that study hours were not interfered with.

Agnes MacPhail, member for Grey South and a militant pacificist, then produced figures which purported to show that RMC cadets were receiving an education that cost the government $1750 a year but that they paid less than $400 a year. She said the main object of the college was to produce a class of snobs whose chief duty was to carry the swagger stick with which the state provided them. She then moved that the RMC vote be reduced by $100,000. Her motion precipitated a debate which was largely favourable to the college. Reference was made to its contribution both in war and peace, and many of its distinguished graduates were mentioned by name: Colonel Bishop, the Carr-Harris family, Lieutenant-Colonel Cassells who was a barrister in Toronto, Sir Percy Girouard, Captain William Harty of the Canadian Locomotive Company in Kingston who had received two war decorations, Lieutenant-Colonel Kingsmill, who had also been called to the Bar, Kirkpatrick, Lackie (Leckie), Lieutenant-Colonel Bartlett McLennan who was killed in action in France, and General Nanton, another graduate who had made Canada famous. It was argued that "if there is one agency for democratizing our Canadian Army it is the Royal Military College" which, so it was said, had helped to destroy the feeling that the officer class in Canada was a special class. Since most cadets came from the wealthy middle class or from professional backgrounds, the latter protest was not entirely convincing, but it is true that Canada did not have a large and powerful military élite. Miss Mac-Phail's resolution, which had been based on emotion rather than reason, was negatived without a division.[83] It did not find much support.

On the eve of the graduation of the class of '24, its seniors were restored to the ranks they had held before the Arnold case broke. This was a popular decision. To the delight of the staff and all the cadets they reappeared in their old places on the graduation parade. But the college's image had been somewhat tarnished in the public eye and its former prestige could not be easily restored.

General Macdonell stayed on as commandant for a full academic session after the incident, long enough to overcome its disturbing impact on the college itself and to avoid any inference that he was dismissed. In his last report which he issued in 1925 he noted that with the complete absence of recruiting the fourth class (first year) had done better academically than ever before. On the other hand the senior cadets in the first class had "not done themselves full justice." They had developed a "captious attitude of mind" and had complained that the loss of the services of recruits for cleaning their kit had left them with too little time for study. The Director of Studies also noted that the second class (which had not been allowed to have recruit labour) had similarly fallen off. Both classes had complained about extra parades on Wednesdays and Saturdays. Macdonell thought that the first class should be granted more privileges by making some of their equitation and physical training courses optional.

However, along with the alleged decline of effort in studies there went what Macdonell paradoxically called a "revulsion" in favour of the service. In that same year, 1925, thirteen cadets were recommended for commissions as compared with the four or five that had been the maximum in previous years. Seven of these went to the Canadian Permanent Force. This was a creditable development which offsets some of the hostile criticism.

Macdonell therefore seemed justified when he pleaded for more time for the college to develop stability. He said that the process of restoring RMC after the war had led to many changes which had been "terrifically upsetting" at a time when order was being brought out of chaos. He felt that a sound system had now been established and that it ought to be given a fair trial.[84] He thus left to his successor Colonel C. F. Constantine,* an officer whom he had personally selected to become a member of the RMC staff, the task of consolidating his work.

The increasing value of the college as a source of Permanent Force officers helped to silence its critics. Constantine was informed in November 1925 that the Department of Militia intended to expand the college facilities over the next ten years so that it could not only handle three hundred cadets, but also a five-month staff college preparatory course of ten officers of the Permanent Force and the RCAF, the long course for ten militia officers and Permanent Force NCO candidates for Permanent Force commissions, a seven-month physical training course for officers and fifteen other ranks, equitation courses, and "such other special courses for the military education of officers of the Royal Canadian Navy, the Active Militia (P.F.) and the Royal Canadian Air Force as may be required." The policy of attaching cadets who were candidates for the Permanent Force and the RCAF to those forces for summer training was to be continued and was to be applied also to the RCN. Part of this special summer training and accommodation for the officers on course should be provided at the college.[85]

Two years later the number of cadets had climbed to 201, and could not go higher unless new accommodation was provided. Constantine therefore reviewed the various plans that had been made since 1910 when an establishment of three hundred had first been proposed as the eventual goal. He referred to Macdonell's building programme and pointed out that one wing of the dormitory, the eastern half of the educational block, the mess and recreation building, and another new dormitory to the south of it had not yet been built. He said that the dining and kitchen facilities, the classrooms, and the library had all reached their capacity and that these were the limiting factor preventing further expansion. Until the proposed cadet mess and recreation block was provided, no further increase

*Major-General C. F. Constantine, C.B., D.S.O. (1883–1953), was the son of a superintendent of the RNWMP; graduated RMC, 1905; an outstanding athlete and CSM; in England he played rugger for Blackheath and Harlequins, two of the leading British teams; commissioned in the RCA; brigade major of the 1st Division Artillery at the beginning of the war; after serving on the staff he commanded 5th (Canadian) FA Brigade; became professor of artillery at RMC, 1919; he did the Camberley course and returned as professor of artillery, 1921–3; became OC of the RCHA and commandant of the Royal School of Artillery; commandant RMC, 1925–30; GOC, MD7, 1930; DOC of MD6 during World War II; retired, 1944.

in numbers was possible. The plans for the mess and recreation building had been deposited with the Board of Works but the money had not yet been appropriated; he could not find that the rest of the programme had ever been approved.[86] Constantine said that when the new dormitory was built, the Stone Frigate could be utilized for the Permanent Force and Non-Permanent Force courses, some of which were already being undertaken at RMC.

All that occurred immediately, however, was the building and equipping of a new mechanical engineering shop which Constantine had recommended in 1926, thus releasing the space under Currie Hall for use as the much needed drafting room.[87] Since the other accommodation required was not constructed, the college strength levelled off at two hundred. The problem of accommodation was referred to a select committee on building which met in September 1928 and in the spring of 1929,[88] but without immediate result.

As in the years before the war, the bulk of the college's graduates went into civil life; but graduates were now required to serve in the Non-Permanent Active Militia unless there was no unit near enough to their homes to make this possible. As a militia commission in some units was a socially desirable prize and difficult to obtain, this regulation acted as an inducement to encourage applications for entry to the college. The high proportion of graduates that did not take up a military career continued to require that the academic content of the course be adequate to secure continued recognition by the universities and the professional societies. Some new accreditations were obtained. In 1926 the Institute of Chartered Accountants of Ontario decided to give RMC graduates an exemption of one year in its five-year course; the following year Quebec agreed to admit RMC graduates into law courses on the same terms as graduates of the universities; and the Nova Scotia Law Society exempted RMC graduates from its preliminary examinations in the course of the 1927–8 session. This left only Prince Edward Island and New Brunswick making no concessions.[89]

Concern for the academic standing of the course led to two other important developments. Constantine reported that several of the civilian members of the staff were taking measures to improve their academic qualifications;[90] and in 1927 the Advisory Board suggested that an approach should be made to the universities to ask them to give a special bachelor of military science degree to those RMC graduates who completed their studies in the universities. It added that if that could not be arranged, RMC might give the degree itself. But this proposal was coldly received by the two men who most mattered. The Deputy Minister thought neither of these proposals practical. The Chief of the General Staff commented that the universities did not like special degrees, did not have the chairs of military studies necessary to make the B.M.SC. degree possible, and that the course at RMC did not go deep enough to give degree status in military subjects; this, he believed was more appropriate at the staff college level where the letters p.s.c. (passed staff college) could already be earned.[91]

Thus, within ten years of the end of the war, RMC had been restored and expanded on lines that largely followed the nineteenth-century pattern, with a four-year course that both produced civilian engineers and candidates for other professions and gave a basic military training for all arms. Although at times cadets had asked for the introduction of specialization on either the military or the civilian side according to their particular interest, the course that had been developed since the war was, in accordance with a general staff memorandum of 20 August 1923, a general one in which all cadets took the same subjects with a heavy emphasis on mathematics.[92] It was designed to meet the needs of the services and to give a sound basic education. Specialization was eliminated, with one exception; about 1924 (the records do not show the exact date) specialization in chemical engineering had been introduced in the third year to meet university requirements. Some ex-cadets wanted to broaden the course by the addition of more humanities and cultural subjects, but Colonel E. J. C. Schmidlin believed in a general rather than a specialized education for engineers.[93] In 1929 the Advisory Board agreed that the intensive study in chemistry should be ended in order to permit more chemistry to be taught generally. This was tried on an experimental basis in 1930 and by 1932 the dual course had gone and there was a "unified syllabus."[94] Engineering drawing and descriptive geometry were moved into the first year to allow more time in the later years for English, economics, advanced chemistry, mineralogy, and engineering geology.[95] Colonel McNaughton, the chief of the General Staff, told Sir Robert Borden that he was prepared to cut the strictly military side of the course in order to include constitutional history.[96]

The curriculum that had emerged after the war was thus general with a bias on the civil engineering side. It retained a strong military content common to all arms, and was noticeably similar to the West Point course. Indeed, the new educational building had been planned with small tutorial classrooms on the West Point pattern. Unlike the shorter courses at Sandhurst and Woolwich, the four-year RMC course was designed for cadets whose preparatory education was not as complete as was the case in England and for whom the RMC course went as far in military education as they required. The aim at Kingston, therefore, was to give as complete a general military education as possible, with the scientific basis that an officer had now come to need, and with a literary and cultural element to provide the essentials of a liberal education.[97]

During the nineteen-twenties the idea of using the summer months for military training became firmly entrenched, a distinct change from the period after the Boer War when it had apparently been customary for many of the cadets to spend their vacations with their families at summer cottages. The RCAF appears to have been the first after the war to propose using the summer for training; in 1922 it had offered flying training to RMC cadets but the offer had been virtually ignored. Cadets at that time were said to believe that they got enough "playing soldier [at RMC] without spending the summer at it."[98] A year later Professor Dawson attempted to find summer employment for cadets in the civil service but the invariable reply was that the RMC's two-month vacation was too short when compared with that of university students. However, by 1923 the practice of attachment to militia training camps that had begun shortly before 1914 was in full operation and individual cadets were attached to school cadet corps camps to act as adjutants.[99] A year later, eight cadets signed up for the summer courses with the RCAF; training was intensive from early morning to late at night, and during working hours the RMC cadets wore flight-sergeant's uniforms to save their "blues." It was believed that most of the eight would get their coveted "wings" in three summers.[100] In 1925, "in order to improve the military knowledge of cadets and to awaken their interest in the various arms of the military service with a view to their applying on graduation for commissions" it was decided that a number from the first and second classes (the third and fourth years) would be attached to the RCE, the RCA, the RCCS, and the RCAF with the status of second lieutenants.[101]

The war had served to strengthen the traditions which had been developed by RMC in the old days. In addition to the Currie Memorial Hall, the Memorial Arch, and the Memorial Stairway, a large flag of memory had been made; it consisted of a union jack on a background adorned with 1100 green maple leaves each bearing the name of an RMC cadet who had served in the war; in the centre, red maple leaves perpetuated the memory of those who had made the supreme sacrifice. This flag was presented by RMC to St. George's Cathedral for safekeeping. Until it began to disintegrate in 1934 it hung in the north gallery which RMC cadets occupied on church parade.[102] In 1921 the college obtained a warrant to validate its coat of arms which had been used without that authority since Colonel Hewett's time.[103] At General Macdonell's suggestion the college became the repository of the officers' mess plate of the 1st Battalion of the

Prince of Wales's Leinster Regiment, formerly the 100th Prince of Wales's Own Royal Canadian Regiment of Foot, which had originally been raised in Canada but which had now been disbanded. Finally, in addition to the recruiting that has already been mentioned, other old customs were carefully brought back. The cake walk had been resumed by 1921 and the minstrel show was also revived in 1922 and flourished strongly for a time, no doubt inspired by the fact that it was similar in nature to the entertainment popular with the troops on the western front. In 1923 it was sponsored by the Kingston Rotary in the Grand Opera House in aid of Dr. Barnardo's boys' home. In 1927 it got a new title, The Pill Box Review, and the cadets carried out the time-honoured custom of entertaining the patients at Rockwood.[104] But this seems to have been about the last year in which this form of entertainment took place. Perhaps it was hard for amateur performers to compete with the new talking pictures which arrived in Kingston in 1929. However, the recruits continued to attempt to do so annually in their cake walk which lampooned the staff and seniors.

One measure of the renewed vigour of RMC in the 'twenties was its success on the sportsfield. The great interest taken in sport is shown by the fact that the commandants' reports from 1923–4 to 1926–7 begin with a long account of the fortunes of RMC's teams immediately after a report on discipline and before the educational and training programmes were discussed. By 1930 the college had won the intermediate intercollegiate title in rugby football for the fifth time in nine years, and the dominion title for the fifth time in college history. In the decade it had also won titles in senior intercollegiate athletics (track and field), intermediate intercollegiate hockey, senior intercollegiate harriers, and intermediate track. Despite the growth of the college since the early part of the century, it was now even more overshadowed in size by its rival universities; these triumphs, therefore, with teams coached by members of the military and teaching staff, were quite remarkable and were in large measure due to the superior physical condition of the cadets.

Of even greater historic interest was the inauguration of the annual hockey game with West Point which developed after General Macdonell, Professor Iva Martin, and Major Greenwood visited West Point to study its curriculum. General McArthur, then superintendent of the academy, agreed to arrange a hockey game which the RMC cadets won 3–0 in February 1923. RMC senior cadets then voted money from the furnishings account for a trophy for annual competition; but as the Superintendent could not promise a return game the trophy was presented to the academy as a souvenir of the first game. However, in 1924 West Point cadets came to play in Kingston, the first time they had been allowed to leave the

United States in their historic uniforms. RMC won again and in fact continued to beat West Point regularly until the beginning of World War II. These annual international contests, in which a special "no penalties" rule operated, attracted some public attention and served usefully to foster good relations between members of the forces in the two countries.

One other international contest should be mentioned. In 1921 the Lafferty Cup for athletics and swimming was given for competition between the cadet colleges of the British empire. Presented in memory of General F. D. Lafferty* who had served in both Sandhurst and Kingston, it was operated by an exchange of times and performance by mail. Against the larger Sandhurst, and against Duntroon in Australia where the climate is more congenial for athletics, Kingston rarely shone.

But the real test of the value of an educational institution is not success on the sportsfield; it is rather the progress of its graduates. In the 'twenties between one-quarter and one-half of each RMC class went into regular military service in Canada or Britain. There was a steady flow of RMC cadets into the Canadian technical corps, the signals and the engineers. British RE commissions were not quite as eagerly sought after as before the war, because other opportunities had increased, and although the influence of dedicated British officers remained important at the college, there were fewer of them.[105] Those RMC cadets who went to the British army continued to do well. Lieutenant-General Sir William Heneker, one of RMC's most distinguished officers in the British army, showed that although the Kingston cadet left college to enter the army two years later than the product of Sandhurst, his longer training quickly enabled him to leave his British brother officers behind. He said, "it is remarkable how many of these Kingston cadets do choose" to do so. General Heneker attributed the success of RMC graduates in the British army to greater initiative, to their drive and confidence, to their superiority in field sketching, map reading, and reconnaissance, and to their better grasp of tactical problems.[106]

The success of the graduates of these years is proved by the number who rose to high rank in the Canadian and British armies. Out of two hundred and nineteen in the graduating classes between 1924 and 1930, that is in the first operating years of the four-year course, two RMC graduates became lieutenant-generals, eight became major-generals or of equivalent rank in other services, and nineteen became brigadiers or the equivalent. There was also one superintendent in the Mounted Police.

*Brigadier-General Frank Delamere Lafferty (1877–1920), RMC, 1892–6; RNWMP, 1896–9; RCA, 1899; South Africa; staff-adjutant RMC, 1905–6; gunnery instructor, Quebec Citadel, 1913; superintendent, Dominion Arsenals, 1917.

Among those who made a career in civil life, five became presidents of major national corporations and one of these also became a senator. Another cadet of this vintage, Walter Gordon, became a cabinet minister. Nor are these the exceptions that prove the rule. The solid success of most of the others is harder to tabulate but considerable. RMC in the 1920s thus made a contribution to the national life of Canada that was out of all proportion to its small size.

RMC's contribution during these years stemmed from the military prestige that Canada won in World War I and was established by Macdonell's qualities of leadership. Probably Macdonell was personally responsible for developments that strengthened the academic standing of the college, but the priority which he gave to its military purpose, and his emphasis on training for the tactics of the recent war, placed limitations on possible progress on the academic side. However, recruiting, and public hostility on account of it, paradoxically fostered the growth of a tremendous spirit and morale within the college which found full expression in remarkable successes on the sports fields. RMC consciously aimed at the development of character and the gentlemen cadets were convinced that the college gave them something that could not be found in any other educational institution in Canada. Although he was not as colorful as Macdonell, because of his sterling qualities of leadership, his interest in sport, and his co-operation with Schmidlin Constantine maintained this supremacy until the end of the decade.

11

CURRICULUM

REVISION

AND MORE RECRUITING 1930-1939

RMC had been firmly re-established in the decade after World War I but the prewar Canadian sense of remoteness from European quarrels, which had served to slow the college's earlier progress, had given way to a widely held determination to stay out of a repetition of the Great War "blood-bath" at almost any cost. This new isolationism had an effect similar to that of the earlier remoteness but was more positive in nature. Many Canadians regarded military preparations of any sort as dangerous steps towards involvement in an overseas war. For this reason, and because it could be argued that pressing social and welfare needs should have priority, especially after the onset of the great depression in 1929, public money was allocated for defence only grudgingly. RMC, because it was one of the more permanent forms of military organization in the country and therefore one of the most secure against pacifist and isolationist attacks, was for a long time bitterly opposed by extremists. The general public and the majority of parliamentarians were either vaguely hostile or apathetic. Only a few, who were liable to be denounced as warmongers, gave consistent support to the college. Not until Canada began reluctantly to rearm in 1936 did the tide turn and the college at last became some-what more appreciated. In these circumstances RMC's survival was due to the fact that the governments of the period, although influenced by popular emotions, were aware that it was worth maintaining even when it could not be fully developed.

In 1928 the RMC Act had been amended to remove certain statutory controls, long since ignored, on the size of the cadet body and on the cost of the professorial staff. While some Conservatives expressed concern in this debate lest parliamentary authority were being weakened, members of both major parties spoke enthusiastically about the value of the college.

The only serious note of dissent in parliament in this period came from Miss Agnes MacPhail in 1931 when she objected to RMC not only on pacifist grounds but, as in 1924, because it allegedly taught snobbishness and also provided a cheap education for the sons of the rich.[1] The passage of the amending act, and the elimination a year later of the chemistry option, seemed to suggest that the general course without options that had emerged in the decade after World War I had proved itself and would now have some degree of permanence. RMC's curriculum had become more like that at West Point than at any time before or since. But during the 'thirties every side of college life was subjected to re-evaluation and criticism and, by the time war came again, considerable progress had been made with a thorough overhaul designed to make RMC serve its ultimate objectives more effectively and to keep it abreast of contemporary developments in education. Nevertheless, the expected numerical growth had not taken place.

In 1927 the cadet body numbered two hundred at the commencement of the academic year, and this was to be its level for the next decade. Even though a few cadets each year withdrew at their own or their parents' request, there was serious overcrowding of the existing facilities. Nevertheless, not merely did successive governments make no effort to carry out the forecast made both before and after the war, that the RMC establishment would be raised to three hundred cadets, they were also very slow to provide the necessary dormitories and other accommodation promised as long ago as 1919 to house the present numbers.[2] In 1931 the Advisory Board declared that accommodation provided fifty-five years before for ninety cadets was now serving two hundred, that the kitchen was unsanitary and had been condemned by the medical authorities, that the rooms now used for dining were needed for classrooms, and that the *esprit* of the college required a hall where all cadets could dine at the same time. It said that since RMC was Canada's "only national education institution" its facilities should be "consistent with our national dignity"; instead they were poorer than those of private and provincial educational institutions. The board added that now when building costs were low because of the current economic blight, the government should take the opportunity to anticipate future needs.[3]

In the year this recommendation was made, a disastrous fire in the administration building made necessary the rebuilding of part of that structure. This reconstruction had one benefit. Much of the small library (except for many of the science books in professors' offices) had been destroyed or damaged, and when repairs were effected the building was slightly enlarged so that the library could have more space.[4] However, this forced rebuilding served to explain or excuse failure to undertake any new construction. The sole exception was a physics laboratory, provided because the one which was to have been put in the abandoned project for an east wing of the new educational building was now not forthcoming; a makeshift one-storey structure made with cement blocks, it was placed between the new mechanical engineering laboratory and the administrative building and, like the mechanical engineering building, was built by men from an unemployment relief camp. It looked more like a factory or warehouse than a college building. Neither of these additions did anything whatever for Canada's "national dignity," and the government's penny-pinching led to protests that future construction at RMC should conform to a uniform architectural style. Finally, in 1933, before construction on a more satisfactory scale could begin, another fire destroyed the boathouse; once again emergency rebuilding was necessary and other things were delayed.[5]

However, during the depression the college did not suffer as much from emergency economies as did other branches of national defence and the universities. Furthermore, in 1933 foundations for projected mess and recreation buildings were also dug by men from the relief camp for the unemployed. This camp had been set up under the command of the RMC Commandant on Barriefield lower common as a measure to fight the depression.[6] The new building, now known as Yeo Hall, was begun in 1935 and was ready for use a year later. The mentality of the depression years had at last been partly sloughed off. The structure was of limestone and in an architectural style similar to that of the west wing of the educational building and the Fort Frederick dormitory (today called Fort LaSalle). It included a large dining hall, kitchens, and a gymnasium. By August 1937 the south wing of Fort Frederick had been added and it was joined to the new mess building by an arch and upper passage. It provided forty-two extra cadet rooms and there were also three small suites for single officers.[7] This new accommodation relieved the heavy pressure on space in the college, but it did not provide for expansion. To meet this need for growth, in 1935 the men from the relief camp began to excavate foundations to the south of the mess building for a third dormitory which, it was suggested, should include an indoor swimming pool.[8] But when the relief camp was closed in 1936, digging stopped. Despite the rearmament programme which began halfheartedly in 1936, money to build the new dormitory at RMC had not been appropriated when the war began in 1939, and new accommodation at RMC had barely caught up with the expansion of the college that had occurred immediately after World War I.

The first significant change at RMC in the 'thirties came in the sports programme. Constantine's most notable contribution to the college had been to foster RMC's remarkable successes in intercollegiate competition which had already been well established under Macdonell. However, in the eyes of his successor, Brigadier W. H. P. Elkins,* the cadets had begun to assume that sports were "paramount during the games season." He said that this "seriously affected the application of the majority ... to their studies." Elkins was a classmate and friend of Constantine and, like him, an artilleryman with a good war record. But he believed that Constantine's great interest in sports had had harmful results, so he introduced a rule in 1931–2 which barred cadets with academic averages below 40 per cent from the hockey and football teams. He was able to report an immediate improvement in the quality of classwork and also that the college had enjoyed another successful year in intercollegiate competition.[9]

Elkins' next step was to divide the cadet battalion into six companies instead of two.[10] A compelling reason for this change was that it made possible much greater cadet participation in intramural sports. There were thirty intercompany hockey games in 1933–4 as compared with only one the previous winter; and a minimum of seventy-two cadets took part in them as compared with eighteen. Intramural football was similarly stepped up. In 1932–3 the college's success in intercollegiate sports fell away somewhat.[11] The following year the Commandant reported that the college teams were "again unsuccessful" but he added that enthusiasm nevertheless remained high. Happily a year later, RMC won the intercollegiate intermediate rugby championship once more and had a successful basketball season.[12] Not only had Elkins fostered a new and more realistic attitude to games, but it seems that it had not seriously affected RMC's ability to win.

The influence of Lieutenant-Colonel E. J. C. Schmidlin may have been a powerful factor in this re-assessment of the place of sport in the college curriculum. A classmate of both Constantine and Elkins, Schmidlin had been their BSM, had won the governor-general's medal, the crown and crossed flags for signalling, the crossed rifles for marksmanship, and the crossed swords for gymnastics. A man of powerful intellect, of great powers of persuasion, and of eminence as an engineer, he was on good terms also with both of his former subordinate cadet officers, Constantine and Elkins. The downgrading of the office of director of studies to senior professor, which had coincided with his appointment, had not in any way reduced the impact of his strong personality. It seems reasonable to assume

---

*Major-General W. H. P. Elkins, D.S.O. (1883–1964), graduated RMC, 1905; commissioned RCA; attached RHA India, 1908–10; France 1915–19; OC, RCA and staff officer artillery duties, Ottawa.

that it was he who advised Constantine in 1927 and 1928 to re-arrange the commandant's annual report to give a less prominent place to sport. Under Constantine the paragraphs recording RMC's triumphs on the sportsfield had been placed in the second paragraph after the report on discipline, and they were now moved to the end. It was probably also Schmidlin who had persuaded Elkins to introduce the academic eligibility rule for participation in games.

The problem of revising the RMC curriculum to achieve the objectives of the college more effectively proved to be much more complicated than this re-assessment of the place of sport. Broadly speaking, RMC's aims were to produce officers and engineers, and to give a general and cultural education to meet the needs of both these groups and of other cadets who wished to take up civilian occupations other than engineering. In addition, all were given a certain basic military interest and training. At this time the universities were raising their standards of entry and were introducing greater specialization, especially in engineering faculties. RMC's four-year general course in civil engineering with its heavy emphasis on mathematics, the only course available since 1929, was all that Colonel Schmidlin believed the RMC Act would permit; and it made possible the general cultural education for engineers in which he firmly believed. But many others now thought that it was out of keeping with developments elsewhere. During the decade before war came in 1939, the authorities in the college and in Ottawa sought to change the course to reconcile various conflicting desires and interests. This objective stimulated much discussion about the college's purpose and its curriculum, and also about the length of its course and the qualifications required for acceptance.

Some universities now required senior matriculation for entry. Consideration of RMC's entrance qualifications was precipitated by the keenness of the 1932 competition to enter, which was, perhaps, a consequence of the depression. As more than half of the recruits had qualifications higher than the required junior matriculation, many repeated at RMC work that they had already done at school, and some became bored. Recruits who entered with junior matriculation were those with very high standing, and some who came in with senior matriculation suffered by comparison with classmates who on paper were less well qualified. The failure rate at the end of the first year among students who had entered with advanced qualifications was therefore disproportionately high. Nevertheless the General Staff proposed that all candidates should henceforward be selected a year in advance of their actual entry on the basis of the applicant's junior matriculation plus additional evidence that he had pursued further study in mathematics, English, French, physics, and chemistry at the senior matriculation level. Colonel Schmidlin informed the Advisory Board that if this change were introduced, the RMC course could then be re-arranged by dropping some elementary science work to make room for more advanced work in the sciences in the fourth year and also for further studies in imperial geography, military history, and economics. It was expected that the resultant increase in the standard attained at RMC would be reflected in the credits granted by the universities to RMC graduates.[13]

Some members of the Advisory Board in 1932 thought that it would be preferable to require the senior matriculation certificate itself as a condition for entry; but others had already pointed out that courses at that level were not available in the schools in some provinces. In an attempt to compensate for the differences between the educational standards of the provinces it was suggested that provincial interview boards should be set up and that there should be an order of merit for each province. The new regulations for entrance, based on junior matriculation plus further work where it was available, were then approved by the board in 1933. They were put into operation the following year, but without the proposed provincial interview boards.[14]

Meanwhile, civil engineering had lost some of its earlier glamour as a profession, partly because the great days of western expansion had ended. By 1930 the slump seriously reduced constructional work and industrial growth. Graduate engineers therefore found it hard to get employment. As Canada was becoming developed industrially and now had great urban and metropolitan centres, there were more opportunities in other professions in the cities. Many parents therefore wanted their sons to prepare for law or accounting, or to go into business. Some of these thought that RMC's four-year course with its heavy mathematical bias was too long for their purpose. Accordingly in 1935 and 1936 a number of ex-cadets brought to the RMC Club proposals that the college courses should be shortened to three, or even to two, years.[15]

Some ex-cadets, mainly from Ontario, complained that the prevailing system of provincial entrance quotas meant that lower standards were possible from some provinces than from others.[16] The quota system, which had operated since 1922, had been administered on the basis that if enough qualified candidates did not come forward from a province to fill its quota, the resultant vacancies were filled on a nation-wide roster of merit. This meant that the quota for Ontario and that for English-speaking Quebec (which was kept distinct from that for French Canadians in the province) were the only ones that were consistently overfilled. Occasionally one of the Maritime provinces, and more frequently towards the end of the 'thirties one or more of the western provinces, produced enough qualified candidates; but for most of the period Ontario provided half of the cadet body and the lowest entrants from Ontario and English-speaking Quebec were often better prepared than some who had come from other provinces at the bottom of the original quota list.

In contrast to the ex-cadets mentioned above, members of parliament and Maritime members of the Advisory Board repeatedly asked why their provinces were not more fairly represented at RMC. Disproportionate representation also had serious implications from a national point of view, especially when it included a marked underrepresentation of French Canadians. In 1937 French Canadians from Quebec held only fourteen of the forty-two vacancies in the college which were available to them on a *pro rata* basis,[17] and French Canadians outside Quebec were given no special consideration. One source of difficulty was that only a few French-Canadian schools, such as Mont St. Louis and Académie Commerciale, provided the scientific preparation necessary for entry to RMC. As there was now no special entrance examination, open competition on a nation-wide basis, which some critics proposed, would have been very difficult to administer, and the old style special examination was unsatisfactory because private residential schools had special classes to prepare for RMC and could resort to cramming which ordinary high schools could not do.[18] The sons of wealthy families would thus be favoured. Open national competition for entry would have made the disproportionate representation of the provinces even worse. But a more rigid application of the provincial quota system would have introduced unqualified candidates and would have excluded some recruits better able to take the RMC course. In face of this dilemma efforts to revise the provincial quota system in 1937 proved fruitless.[19]

In 1936 Colonel Schmidlin, who had left RMC and was now quarter-master-general, addressed the RMC Club executive at considerable length about standards for entry to the college and the length of the course. Declaring that RMC's chief purpose was to produce officers and engineers, he said now that engineering was becoming more advanced and specialized at the universities, it was imperative that an RMC graduate should progress as fast as possible at the college in order to cut down the time needed to obtain a degree at a university.[20] Brigadier H. H. Matthews,* who had

---

*Major-General Harold Halford Matthews, C.M.G., D.S.O. (1877–1940), British Columbia Horse at Valcartier camp in 1914; CO 8th Canadian Infantry Battalion; gassed at Ypres and Mt. Sorel; CO Canadian Training Area, Hastings; GSO2 to Lieutenant-General Sir Archibald Macdonnell, 1st Division, April 1921; became assistant director of military intelligence; director of military operations and intelligence; CO No. 13 military district at Calgary. Commandant RMC 1935–38; adjutant-general 1939–40.

recently succeeded as commandant, then told Schmidlin: "You have demolished the theory of the three-year course fully and completely."[21] Nevertheless, although the club decided to take no official stand on the issue, its executive brought the proposals for shortening the course to the attention of the Advisory Board which set up a subcommittee to examine them.[22]

The result of this investigation was very unsatisfactory. Only fifty-two ex-cadets answered a letter asking for their opinions. This was said to be partly because those in the regular forces felt constrained from taking a stand on such a matter. The largest group of those who answered, eighteen in number, favoured maintaining the four-year course, thirteen wanted a three-year course, and smaller numbers suggested various other policies including further study of the matter. The subcommittee therefore decided to recommend that the question should be referred to a larger committee which should include "educationists" as members and should take advice from experts. However, as the problem was closely related to proposals for the re-introduction of specialization at RMC which had now come up for reconsideration, the Advisory Board decided to defer further discussion about reducing the length of the course until a decision had been reached on specialization.[23]

The new commandant in 1935, Brigadier Matthews, was a prewar militia officer who had had a good war record and a successful career in the Permanent Force after the armistice. He was much more intellectual than either of his two immediate predecessors, neither of whom could make an extempore speech, for example. As has been seen, Constantine was primarily interested in sport. Elkins, who had a sounder understanding of the relative importance of sport, was excessively concerned with decorum; he had ordered the staff to wear morning dress when the Advisory Board visited and to attend monthly bridge nights in dinner jackets. Constantine and Elkins had both had long associations with the college and Kingston. Matthews was not an ex-cadet and his connections in Canada were mainly with the West. Some thought that as an outsider he could not possibly understand the college's problems, but he was a man of wide experience and a fresh eye may have been an advantage. He was aided during his term of office by the urgency of the international situation which began to bring home to Canadians the need for military preparation and the value of an institution like RMC. By 1938, when he was appointed adjutant-general, Matthews had endeared himself to everybody at RMC by his quiet courtesy and consideration. More important than this, he had made great changes at the college, both in the curriculum and other aspects of college life. Finally, the physical expansion of RMC, for which his predecessors should receive some credit, came during his period of office.

Matthews' most important contribution was the re-introduction of a specialized curriculum at RMC. Realization that the course needed revising stemmed partly from complaints that the needs of the armed services were not being met. In England the courses at Sandhurst and Woolwich had undergone drastic revision in recent years. At Sandhurst new subjects had been introduced to broaden a cadet's education and to teach him to think for himself, and new military ones had also been added.[24] At the same time graduates of Woolwich proceeding to Chatham for further training as Royal Engineers were now often sent on to Cambridge University to take a degree. RMC graduates in the Royal Engineers were required to follow the same path. In 1932 it was found that some of these ex-cadets were experiencing difficulty with mathematics at Cambridge, allegedly because they had taken mathematics early in their course in Kingston and by the time they arrived at Cambridge the subject had become rusty. In other respects they were ahead of their English comrades in scientific preparation,[25] because of courses introduced by Schmidlin.

Nevertheless, by 1937 the RMC course not only failed to cover all the military work done at Sandhurst and Woolwich but also no longer gave an adequate preparation for entrance to engineering in the Canadian universities. Although RMC graduates with high standing could still get into the fourth year in civil engineering at a university, changes in the applied science faculties at McGill and Toronto, coupled with the elimination of the chemistry option at RMC in 1932, meant that the RMC graduate was admitted only to second year in chemical engineering. Queen's still admitted them to the third year but made it clear that this was a special concession and that it was unhappy about making it.[26]

It was this inadequacy, rather than the lack of purely military courses that precipitated a change in policy. On 29 March 1937 Dr. W. R. Sawyer,* an ex-cadet who had been appointed to teach chemistry at RMC wrote to Dr. J. L. McKee,† the professor of physics and chemistry, to recommend a solution to the problem of university entry by the re-introduction of specialization.[27] His proposal was supported by the Senior

*Colonel William Reginald Sawyer, O.B.E., E.D., M.SC., PH.D., LL.D., D.SC. Mil., F.C.I.C. (1901–1967), graduated RMC, 1924; Queen's University, 1924–7 and McGill University, 1927–31; Harvard Chemical Laboratories, 1931–5; department of physics and chemistry, RMC, 1935–9; GSO1, chemical warfare, northwest Europe; director of Weapons Development, Ottawa, 1945–8; vice-commandant and director of studies, RMC, 1948–67.

†James Lyttle McKee, M.SC., PH.D., instructor in chemistry, RMC, 1921; professor, 1934–42.

Professor and approved by the Commandant. Matthews then persuaded National Defence Headquarters to set up a committee chaired by Adjutant-General Constantine to consider whether the introduction of specialization should be considered by the RMC Advisory Board. After considering various opinions about university attitudes and cadet needs, and after hearing from Dean A. L. Clarke of the Faculty of Applied Science at Queen's, the chairman of the committee concluded that a good case had been made.[28]

General A. G. L. McNaughton, president of the National Research Council, advised Brigadier Matthews that discussion of the case for specialization at RMC should not be argued on the basis of personal claims of individual cadets to get access to a higher level in the universities, but rather on general military necessity. He declared that under modern conditions a thorough and more particularized scientific training was necessary for the fighting services. He suggested that it would pay military units to accept a subaltern from RMC with a lower standard of training in strictly military subjects if this was because additional time had been given at the College to broadening the cadet's general education especially in the scientific subjects. He was anxious, he said, that there should be no over-emphasis at RMC on drill and purely mechanical exercises, for instance, in manual skill in handling machine guns: "These sort of subjects can be better learned on the barrack square ... after joining [a unit]."[29] Thus McNaughton made it perfectly clear that the introduction of more specialized work in the sciences at RMC and the preparation of cadets to take a B.SC. degree had a military as well as a civilian purpose; and he showed that it could be instituted by a reduction in the amount of drill and other mechanical training processes which military instruction involved.

One other proposal for solving the academic problem at RMC was that the college should give the degree itself. This idea was put forward in the House of Commons by Dr. James J. McCann, the Conservative member for Renfrew South. However, the leader of his party, R. B. Bennett, argued that an RMC degree was impossible because the college operated under section 91 of the BNA ACT. If the college became a purely civil institution, under section 93 it could not receive federal support.[30] To prevent this kind of reasoning from blocking his curriculum proposals, Matthews carefully explained, as McNaughton had done, that the introduction of specialization was necessary primarily to meet military requirements: "The idea, first and last, is that RMC is a military training school."[31]

That these were not empty words is demonstrated by the measures Matthews had already taken to strengthen the military side of the curriculum. When he came to Kingston he had noticed that "in a College whose only justification for existence lies in its being a Military College, the military academic subjects have been and, to some extent, are still considered by the Cadets as being of secondary importance." He believed that the root of the trouble was that the GSO 1, who was the senior military officer on the staff under the commandant, had his hands full with the staff college preparatory course, the militia staff course (theoretical and practical), and the senior militia staff course (theoretical and practical). Matthews therefore introduced a chief instructor of military subjects to co-ordinate the various branches of cadet military training.[32] It is not clear who was appointed to the post, but Lieutenant-Colonel K. R. Stuart, the GSO 1 at that time, was more concerned with cadet activities than his predecessors had been. Matthews gave the military courses better classroom facilities, and he said that when the new optional courses were introduced it would be necessary to emphasize the military elements in a graduate's training by listing on his diploma the military courses that he had taken.[33] An ex-cadet who revisited the college about this time has recorded his impression that the effectiveness of the practical military training, which seems to have at first declined since those immediate postwar years when Macdonell had stressed infantry training for the kind of war in which he had just fought, has been greatly improved.[34]

Earlier in 1937, in a circular letter to parents to explain the optional courses that were to be introduced, Matthews had said that with specialization in the fourth year, the class would be divided into three groups: those preparing for, firstly, the Permanent Force non-technical corps, secondly, the civilian non-engineering professions, and thirdly, the Permanent Force or civilian engineering. The syllabus would be designed to suit the different needs of each group.[35] Thus, by 1939 the RMC course was reorganized so that the first three years became a basic science course with some English, French, history, political and economic science, and imperial and international affairs; in addition, in the first three years the cadets took courses in military history and military engineering, infantry training, weapon training, and equitation. In their fourth year they could choose between options in civil engineering, mechanical engineering, electrical engineering, chemical engineering and chemistry, and mining and metallurgical engineering, or they could follow a general course with more advanced work in the non-scientific subjects listed above.[36]

Two years after specialization was first proposed, Matthews was able to report that arrangements had been made with the universities to supplement the practice by which RMC graduates were admitted to the fourth year in civil engineering. Toronto had agreed to accept "specially recommended" graduates into fourth-year chemical, electrical, and mechanical engineering; McGill would accept them into fourth-year chemical engineering; and Queen's would accept RCM graduates commissioned into the Permanent Force in its fourth-year electrical and mechanical courses. Other cadets who were "recommended" could enter third-year university courses in these fields. The commandant reported in the summer of 1939, that ten members of the 1938 graduating class, which was the first class with specialization, had gone on to university. (Actually twelve went, all or almost all, into the fourth year.) Matthews also noted that one of them had entered "the difficult course in aeronautical engineering in Toronto."[37] No doubt these new arrangements were agreed to by the universities because many of those RMC graduates who had been recommended in the past had stood very high in their university classes.[38]

Matthews believed that the course at RMC, as amended, should not be thought perfect but should be subject to regular revision to meet changing needs. He called for the introduction of more imperial and international history, and he argued that the next step should be to require all who entered to have senior matriculation.[39] He boasted that a cadet entering RMC with junior matriculation could now earn an engineering degree in five years, that is to say in the same time as a student who took senior matriculation at school and four years in a university. He added that in addition the cadet would get a military and cultural education. There were indeed a few bright junior matriculants who did the engineering degree through RMC and a university in this way. However, it must be remembered that the trend was towards entry to RMC with senior matriculation, and also that graduates could not go on to the universities in the fourth year in three out of four fields of engineering unless "specially recommended" or into the university in the third year unless "recommended." It was the abler students who went on, and they usually did exceptionally well.

The practice of attaching RMC cadets to militia training camps which had been introduced before the war and revived by Macdonell had, as a result of the depression, declined in the early 'thirties. All camp vacancies may first have been offered to the graduating classes, but in 1934 the *R.M.C. Review* noted that in the previous summer the second class had, apparently for the first time in recent years, been offered temporary militia commissions to attend summer training with the Royal Canadian Horse Artillery which was usually open only to graduates. Five of the third-year cadets accepted.[41] In the spring of 1934, the whole college went to Petawawa for training under canvas. This was a revival of the kind of practical training which Macdonell had carried out on "the trek." The cadet who reported the training at Petawawa stated that this was the first time that many of these particular cadets had slept in a tent.[42] Their summer training thus gave them a small experience of a kind of practical soldiering that seems to have declined in the years midway between the two wars. By 1939 it had again become regular practice to attach RMC cadets to military training schools during the summer months.[43]

About the time that summer training with the militia dropped off, the Royal Canadian Navy introduced a scheme for training RMC cadets for commissions. Started as an experiment with nine volunteers in 1930, seven of whom qualified as RCNVR special service sublieutenants, this course continued at Halifax throughout the 'thirties. The result was that some RMC cadets like G. C. D. W. Piers* left RMC at the end of their second year to take commissions in the RCN as career officers.[44]

But the most important part of the RMC cadet's military training was the four years that he spent under strict military discipline in the college, a community organized on military lines. At Kingston, as at all other military academies, discipline was primarily administered by the senior cadets. Recruiting continued to be an important part of the total disciplinary and military training picture. It had changed considerably in nature over the years. Before 1914, initiation, after which recruiting had eased, had flourished; but that had been replaced, at least in theory, by the recruit's obstacle race which had deliberately channelled the punitive physical elements in the initiation process into an organized public activity. As a result of the Arnold case, corporal punishment had been officially forbidden. The net result of these two changes was that recruiting had become a year-long suppression of the recruits that was psychological rather than physical and was in some respects more onerous than before. One unfriendly critic wrote that the "ram-rod enforced" recruiting of the pre-1914 era, which he claimed had been "public knowledge," had been replaced by a secret "star-chamber" system in which a recruit could be "crucified."[45] If the exaggerations of his language are disregarded, this anonymous critic can be seen to have put his finger on the chief characteristics of recruiting at RMC as it developed between the wars.

Recruiting was designed to foster the habit of instantaneous response to orders on the premise that no man could give orders until he had learned how to take them. Therefore, from the day he entered the college until midnight during the June ball (except for a few specified periods of welcome respite), the recruit was badgered by seniors with orders and questions deliberately designed to trip him in order to provide justification for punishment. Among other things, the recruit had to know details of the

*Vice-Admiral Desmond William Piers, D.S.C., C.D., ADC, RCN (born 1913), RMC, 1930–2; midshipman, RCN; escort group commander, Atlantic convoys, World War II; director of Naval Plans and Operations, 1950; senior naval officer afloat (Atlantic), 1952; commandant RMC, 1957–60; assistant chief Naval Plans, 1960; chairman, Canadian Joint Staff, Washington, 1962.

college history,* he had to be able to name all the college buildings, and give the names and college numbers of his seniors and of the ex-cadet members of the staff. The earlier practice whereby all recruits had to respond to any seniors' call had been reintroduced and each recruit was detailed to a senior to clean his kit (though not his boots), make his bed, and run his errands. Recruits also had certain orderly duties to perform and had to do emergency fatigues, including clearing snow from the rink. Recruiting often included what was called "flat physical training" or "bending," the punitive drilling of recruits in dormitories. These tasks, duties, and pitfalls were an addition to the normal military hazards, dirty buttons or boots, and uniform that had not been adequately "whisked" to meet the exacting standards of an inspecting officer or of a senior cadet who made no concession even though scarlet and navy showed every tiny cotton thread and speck of dust. The most extreme form of this process of disciplining the first-year class was the so-called "shit-meeting" in which the recruits were herded into a room to be harangued, drilled, and bullied, often with the accompaniment of a lot of shouting and abuse.[46]

The recruits had the Fort Frederick martello tower area as a sanctuary, where recruiting was not permitted. They were also occasionally given a period of respite known as "lids off," especially after intercollegiate games. John Windsor, who entered as a recruit in 1939, tells that the evening "lids off" given after the recruits' annual obstacle was not of much use to them.[47] The obstacle race entailed climbing high walls plastered with grease, wading or swimming through pools of evil-smelling water, and climbing obstacles with the aid of rope ladders or by co-operative effort. After the race the recruits were invariably so tired and dirty that it took them what was left of the evening to clean up before they fell asleep. In some years, however, some of them were able to enjoy the tea dance that followed the race.

For many recruits life at RMC was miserable. No doubt some, who were lazy or careless, did benefit from this training, but certain boys for one reason or another became the permanent targets for attack. Each year several were unable to accept the rigorous disciplining and left the college. A few ran away. The majority, however, quickly took a curious pride in being able to outdo their classmates by accepting without showing visible resentment punishment that was so often undeserved. Many endured recruiting as a necessary ordeal not too different from what went on in residential schools. Some detested the system. But recruiting undoubtedly

*Some of the "facts" were incorrect. For instance some classes learned that the Stone Frigate was built in 1789. In 1923 the Kingston Historical Society had put up a plaque giving this date. The Frigate was actually built in 1819.

brought cohesion to the recruit class and a feeling of accomplishment, perhaps even of strange exaltation such as men find on a yet greater scale amidst the crudities of war. Recruiting was a period of initiation into a select group that prided itself on its superiority. It was a powerful factor in building the RMC spirit. (Modern sociologists describe this kind of initiation as a rite that marks entrance into a restricted social or professional group with its own pride and privileges.) Recruiting was thus partially responsible for the homogeneous group that RMC cadets and ex-cadets became in Canada and in the armed services.

People who did not themselves experience recruiting tended to be critical of it. Some who suffered under it now extol its virtues. Among ex-cadets there are differences of opinion about the system as it operated in the middle 'thirties. Some senior classes took steps to reduce the lengths to which recruiting went because they thought that it had exceeded reasonable limits. However, the fact that a veil was very deliberately drawn over the practice at the time (a veil that still exists in many minds today since some ex-cadets believe that recruiting ought not to be discussed by outsiders) makes the separation of fact from fiction and the elimination of wild exaggeration extremely difficult. It is hard to get at the truth and to make a rational appraisal. All that the historian can do is show both sides of the question and accept the fact that contradictory opinions are still irreconcilable.

Windsor says in his autobiography that the reasons for recruiting were not evident to him at the time but that it did more than make him and his classmates alert and physically fit. "It taught us to keep cool under pressure. ... More than that it developed in us a very real loyalty to our classmates so that punishment, even unjust punishment, would be accepted in silence sooner than say anything that would bring trouble on the class or its members. Like Benjamin Franklin ... we felt we had to hang together or hang separately."[48]

As has been said before, no doubt one of the most important effects of the disciplinary system at RMC was the development of a code of loyalty to the class. It was born in the common misery of the first year, sustained by the disciplines of the second and third years, and crowned by the responsibilities born in the senior year. It should be added that between seniors and their recruits a curious mutual respect and even affection often developed. On the other hand some recruits carried into later life an undying hatred of bullies who had tormented them at RMC.

Windsor also said that the "only consolation [for recruits] was that in three years, if we stood the pace, we too would rise to the Olympian heights and become cadet N.C.O. s with recruits of our own to train."[49] Most cadets came to be convinced that the RMC system was the best method of "making boys into men," which was the accepted cliché to explain recruiting. Generally, the seniors were anxious to see that this long-standing tradition of the college, as they regarded it, this essence of all that made the college great, should be maintained despite criticism from hostile politicians, fond mammas, timid politicians, and Ottawa bureaucrats. They also rejected any interference by the staff.

It was ceaselessly drummed into recruits by seniors that disloyalty to the college, untruthfulness, and deceit were the most heinous offences or, in cadet vernacular, "slimy." Many ex-cadets are convinced that the character training thus instilled served them in good stead in later life. Some claim that it gave an RMC ex-cadet the ability to endure adversity, for instance in Japanese prison camps. (This latter cannot be regarded as fully proved, of course, since the qualities enabling men to withstand an oppression that was, after all, infinitely worse than anything adminis-tered at RMC, may well have been inborn rather than acquired in cadet life.) It is certainly true that during the 'twenties and 'thirties the RMC system of training produced a very large number of able men whose sterling qualities responded magnificently to the test when war came. Whether those who refused to accept the discipline and left the college were misfits who would, as one ex-cadet has suggested, have been unable to succeed in any walk of life or were, conversely, boys with highly strung temperaments who could under different treatment have been made into good officers, is a question that can not easily be answered. Nor is it pos-sible to agree with absolute confidence that it was the recruiting system at RMC that produced some of the great Canadian military leaders of World War II, though it may possibly have been a partial cause.

Recruiting was part of the training of seniors as well as of recruits. It gave the seniors experience of command. Clearly such training had great potential value. However, it gave them more powers than they were likely to possess for many years in their careers and authority that was subject to less check from above than in the services. Furthermore, inevitably some seniors used as an excuse for bullying the pretext that they were doing the recruits good. The distinction was hard to draw and the only sanction against abuse was the disapproval of fellow class members. This was usually relatively ineffective. More serious still, the code of honour and truthfulness positively asserted by the seniors for the maintenance of relations within the cadet body did not extend to relations between the cadets and the staff. Recruits were regularly warned not only that they must not complain about their treatment but also that they must deceive the staff if questioned about it. The seniors believed that the administration of this form of discipline was their own business and nobody else's, they ignored orders to abandon objectionable practices, they prevaricated by denying the existence of abuse, and they compelled the recruits to equivocate also. Oddly enough some of the latter appear to have done so with enthusiastic conviction. The net result was what would be called today "cadet power."

Inevitably there were complaints that RMC recruits were being mistreated. In November 1932 an anonymous letter to the staff-adjutant claimed that the writer had the support of three ex-cadets in his efforts to eliminate the excesses of recruiting. He had encountered cadets on vacation in Toronto who had said that it took the form of "tortures" in the basement of the new building. The writer threatened to complain to the Minister of National Defence, to Miss MacPhail, and to his member of parliament.[50]

Accordingly the Staff-Adjutant, Major "Hans" Logan, who it should be noted was not an ex-cadet, instructed that flat physical training (PT) was to be ended, but that correctional arms drill could continue. The only result appears to have been that flat PT without rifles was replaced by flat PT with rifles because a senior could always explain that away as "correctional drill." A year later Senator Griesbach was told during a formal investigation of hazing at the University of Alberta that the worst hazing in Canada was at RMC. Griesbach was urged to ask questions about it in the house. Ottawa was undoubtedly sensitive to criticism about the reputation of its military college. It was widely believed that another Arnold incident might lead to RMC being closed down, or at least to the abolition of the "class system" at the college and therefore to the cessation of the traditional enforcement of discipline by senior cadets. Accordingly, instead of raising the matter publicly, Griesbach wrote personally to the commandant to ask for information.

It happened that just at this time BSM Peter Riordon had decided on his own initiative, but with the support of his classmates, to reintroduce weekly "bending" in order to smarten the recruit class. Perhaps as a result of Griesbach's enquiry, and because a flat servant reported blood on the floor of the recruits' recreation room (it had come from a bloody nose), the duty officer kept watch and found BSM Riordon "bending" the recruits in their sanctuary, the Fort Frederick martello tower.

General Elkins reported to Ottawa that Riordon had been caught "conducting physical training exercises ... in the dormitory" contrary to orders.[51] Almost all the members of the whole senior class, who were convinced that the recruits could not be properly trained unless they were punished physically, declared that if the BSM were disciplined and demoted they would take collective action, would refuse to take over his appointment, and would even consider resignation from the college. They were convinced that the Commandant, under pressure from Ottawa, was ruining the college. However, when Elkins summarily reduced Riordon to corporal, the seniors' protest fizzled out.[52]

The seniors' reaction to one of their own class being disciplined for a blatant breach of the regulations and for what they knew was a deliberate attempt to oppose official college policy suggests that despite the recruiting process which they had themselves undergone, they still had much to learn about obedience and discipline. This opinion is reinforced by evidence of the extent to which they themselves broke regulations when it suited their purpose and flouted authority even in the presence of the recruits they were training. The fact that they disagreed with regulations, took a chance on being found out and punished, and accepted punishment philosophically if caught, does not deny this general conclusion. The seniors, despite the authority they wielded, were immature. It was impossible for them to understand, as their elders saw at the time and as many of them were to appreciate later, that it was not merely wrong but also harmful to force on the recruits a code which seniors broke if they wished. But it is also true that the harsh cadet code at RMC had certain advantages. It gave the seniors a degree of self-confidence that would serve them well in later life. It gave them a smartness of appearance which they never lost. And it taught them that the command relationship in the armed forces should be an impersonal one.

A most damaging aspect of recruiting was that it fell so heavily on the first-year cadets that those who lacked strong determination to study wasted their year academically, with serious consequences for those recruits who were at the bottom of the class. Yet, even with the pressures of recruiting, wastage rates in the first year were not as high as in the universities, probably partly because RMC's restricted establishment eliminated the weaker applicants. In *Fight the Good Fight* T. L. Brock* wrote: "The academic classes ... are a blissful haze of sitting at ease against the backs of seats ... dozing, or even literally falling asleep, happily away from the ever-demanding Seniors."[53] His account of the permanent state of physical exhaustion of the recruits and of the extent to which their thoughts were concentrated on evading trouble suggests that the first year must have been a loss academically. Recruiting cannot have failed to lower the general academic level of the recruit class through loss of time and

*Thomas Leith Brock, B.A., B.A.SC., M.SC., F.C.I.C., RMC, 1930–4; Aluminum Company of Canada; author of many articles related to the history of the college; member of the RMC Museum Committee; RMC Club historian.

emphasis on different values; Macdonell had found that when recruiting was abolished the class results of the first year immediately improved. A wasted first year must inevitably have affected the quality of the college as a whole. Conversely, the good results achieved by the better students who went on to the universities suggests that the RMC recruiting system did not hamper those with ability. However, this potential threat to the academic standards of the college was especially prejudicial at a time when RMC was seeking to improve its accreditation for those who went on to the universities. It is therefore not surprising that when Brigadier Matthews was seeking to introduce more advanced studies and specialization to improve the accreditation rating of the RMC diploma in the universities, he took simultaneous steps to curb recruiting.

Matthews had begun to attack abuses in the practice of recruiting within a few months of his arrival at the college. In a talk to the new BSM and the CSMs in the presence of the GSO 1, the staff-adjutant, and both company commanders, he pointed out that as commandant he was responsible to the minister of national defence; the staff and cadets were similarly responsible to him for all that they did. He said that abuses had grown up which would have been avoided if this channel of responsibility had been properly observed. Notes for his lecture reveal his thoughts. He believed it was necessary to ensure that "zeal for the cause does not prevail over our common sense and better judgment." He declared that delegated authority, vested only as a privilege, had come to be considered a right. However, as RMC was a public institution supported in the main by the taxpayers, disgruntled parents had a legitimate right to carry their complaints direct to the government. Therefore over-zealous recruiting could defeat "the whole object for which we ... work and drags the good name of the College in the mud."

Matthews appealed to the cadet officers to co-operate with him to see that practices were not allowed that might interfere with a cadet's health or studies or morale, that might savour of persecution, vindictiveness, or reprisals for what had been done the seniors when they were themselves recruits, or of the visitation of the sins of older brothers on younger ones now attending the college. (In one case, however, an elder brother ex-cadet requested seniors to treat his recruit brother roughly because he had been "spoiled" at home). He suggested that they should see that orders were not issued in an overbearing manner or with abusive language, that "stupid practices" like addressing seniors in high-pitched staccato voices and knocking on doors until knuckles were skinned, were abandoned, and that flat PT and all other forms of interference with recruits during study period were abolished. He said that recruits, who by long tradition had

had to "double" across the square, must not be compelled to run along the sidewalks around the square.[54]

The cadets regarded Matthews as a pleasant person who need not be taken too seriously. He seemed to them to lack dynamism and vigour. As a result he made only limited progress by appealing for their co-operation. Therefore in 1936 or 1937 he tried a new tack. This time, so that there could be no misunderstanding through the process of relaying his wishes, he addressed the whole senior class. He told them that the college was steeped in traditions, some good and some bad. In addition "questionable practices" had crept in during and since the war which had led to adverse criticism from outside, some of it fair, some of it based on exaggerated gossip. He said that where there was smoke there was fire and that the time had now come to make some changes. After repeating his concept of his own responsibility and of the responsibility of cadet NCOs to him, he listed changes that were to occur. No "restrictions" were to be enforced on recruits at table in the mess. "Torpedoing" or "submarines" (the practice of creeping under the table and throwing a tumbler of water in the lap of an unsuspecting victim), compulsory tucking of napkins at the neck, and sitting at attention and on the edge of the chair [undesirable practices imported from West Point] were to cease. There was to be no shouting in the dining room; "checking" was to be done quietly, food and plates were not to be thrown about, and there was to be no sending of unnecessary messages or compulsory telling of jokes. "In short, behaviour was to be consistent with proper table manners as would be required in your own home." The enforcement of these changes was to be the responsibility of the NCO in charge of the table or company. Matthews also repeated what he had told the cadet officers a year earlier, that unofficial punishments, flat PT, shouting and abusive language, and exaggerated styles of responding to questions and of walking were to be abandoned. The "drops" (cadets who had to repeat their first year), were not to be "recruited" under any circumstances.

Matthews was aware that changes of this order could not be made in a day. It would require moral courage on the part of seniors to resist the "siren calls" of their predecessors. He said that he had spoken thus so that he would not be forced to "break someone on the wheel for wilful defiance of constituted authority." Matthews was well aware that because he was not an ex-cadet his task was the more difficult, but he suggested that as all the officers on the staff except the Commandant and one other had gone through the college, the seniors should go to staff ex-cadets for advice. But this second attack on the abuse of recruiting, although it probably had a sobering effect on some seniors, was little more successful than the first.

Many were still convinced that the hallowed tradition of recruiting was the basis of RMC's excellence. The fundamental principle in the whole college system was, indeed, that the seniors carried real responsibility. Undue day-to-day supervision seemed a denial of that principle. Matthews was prepared neither to introduce continuous supervision nor to take ruthless measures for the discovery and punishment of individual offenders in order to achieve his end. He believed that the final eradication of abuses could only come about if the cadets undertook it themselves. This was in conformity with the principle upon which the system was based.

By tradition, inspecting officers only visited the dormitories during the day when the cadets were in class. It is said that recruiting was at a minimum in that part of the Fort Frederick dormitory that was close to the officers' bachelor quarters and was greatest in the Stone Frigate where no officers were lodged. When Major Logan, the staff-adjutant, walked from his office to his house across the parade square in front of the Frigate, the seniors called for quiet and a halt in recruiting until he was safely out of earshot. Faculty members of that day admit that the noise that often emanated from the dormitories left no doubt about what was going on inside, but they did nothing about it. All that would have been necessary was for officers or members of the faculty to visit the dormitories at frequent intervals without previous warning. The civilian members of the staff thought this was not their business, and some of the ex-cadet officers on the faculty did not interfere because they believed in the principles behind recruiting and thought that staff intervention to weed out abuses would destroy its value. Obviously there was a complete breakdown in communications between the members of the staff and the responsible authority, the commandant, a breakdown as serious as that between staff and seniors. The military system of that day raised a commanding officer so far above his staff that he was never fully informed what was in their minds. And they were so anxious to carry out his supposed wishes as indicated by his nod or glance that they often failed to carry out his real intentions.

Some ex-cadets on the staff were determined to tackle this problem. Lieutenant-Colonel Kenneth Stuart who came to RMC as GSO 1 in 1933 sensed on his arrival that things had greatly changed since he graduated in 1911. He noted that although the cadets saluted him punctiliously, all his friendly greetings were politely ignored. When he questioned a cadet about this, he was answered politely but in an unintelligible manner. The cadet did not look at him straight in the face but stared directly to his front. When Stuart tackled the BSM on the subject he discovered that as soon as it was clear that that young man realized he was being questioned about the relations between the seniors and the recruit class he took refuge behind "a wooden face." Efforts to penetrate this barrier proved futile. From Brigadier Elkins and two other ex-cadets on the staff at the time, Majors Agnew and Brownfield, Stuart learned that under the cloak of college tradition a code of behaviour had evolved which, in his opinion, had no relation to the true traditions of RMC, and had no real value in the training of officers.

Stuart was an able and articulate officer who had not allowed his military training and career to eradicate his capacity to think for himself. Although an ex-cadet, he was able to look at college practices with detachment. Furthermore Stuart was not the man to miss the chance of expressing his opinions or of taking vigorous action. Although busy with the militia staff courses, he concerned himself with the code and discipline of the cadet body. He prepared and apparently delivered a lecture to the senior class in or about 1937 in which he went thoroughly into the origin and practice of recruiting. He said that after the war a new tradition had been developed by imaginative members of the "recruit-senior" class of 1918. It was based on information from unrepresentative ex-cadets and influenced by the advice of senior cadets of the Naval College when it was located at RMC. Stuart also thought that the beginning of the West Point hockey series had brought in certain West Point customs that had the flavour of that academy's Prussion originator. He believed that by 1925 a hybrid system had been firmly consolidated which, he said, still persisted.

Stuart said that the most noticeable feature of this system was the lack of contact between the staff and the senior class who firmly believed not only that the commandant and staff were necessary evils that they had to tolerate but also that the senior class was responsible for the maintenance of discipline at the college and for the conditioning of recruits to make them a credit to RMC. The seniors, he said, failed to see that the abuse of their privilege of administering discipline was potentially prejudicial to the future of the college as well as to the military career of the commandant. He said that the system had given birth to a situation whereby principles of ethics had no place in relations between the staff and the cadets. "Putting it over" on the staff had become laudable, and this included cribbing in examinations. He pointed out that the prevalence of lying to the staff was a strange parody of the first two words of the college motto, "Truth" and "Duty." Stuart believed, perhaps unjustly, that the only criterion at which the seniors aimed was smartness on parade and some degree of mental alertness. He was on sounder ground when he said that the whole basis of the system was punishment. He argued that "true discipline is purely a condition of the mind and should be based not on fear of punishment but on confidence, respect and loyalty to one's self, to one's comrades and to one's superiors." He declared that petty bullying which was inherent in the cadet code might attain superficial results in the way of smartness but that it would never produce true discipline: it was the negation of modern army practice. "It is out of date and should never be tolerated in this modern age." Stuart believed that physical smartness helps towards success but was not the chief means of achieving it. "The successful man is one plentifully endowed with moral and mental attitudes."

After outlining in his lecture the nature of the responsibility of the cadets to the commandant, Stuart said that at RMC the cadet's loyalty to the class and his comrades did not include loyalty to the commandant and the staff. In the previous two years he had been informed by senior members of the class that flat PT in all its forms was non-existent, but he had subsequently discovered that this was not the case. "In the same period two senior NCOs of the Senior Class had been caught 'flat-footed' lying to the Staff [but] the seriousness of the offence did not seem to worry [them]." Recruits had run away as a result of "mental torture" and "any recruit that runs away may be compared to a dagger directed at the very heart of the College." Incidents had been the subject of parental letters to the Commandant, to NDHQ, and to members of parliament. These had threatened the existence of the college but had been hushed up by ex-cadet influence in Ottawa. One BSM and one CSM by their lack of judgment in applying the code had created situations in which some parents had proposed to withdraw their recruit sons and had only been prevented from doing so by the commandant's tactful persuasion. Stuart said that he realized that the system could not be changed in a day. The two previous senior classes had "recognised in word their prior responsibility to the Commandant" but in practice had found it more difficult to carry out than they had imagined. Changes were slowly being introduced to remedy the situation and the Commandant had no intention of easing up on them. Stuart called for a new "staff-cadet code" and the end of the cadet code which, he said, "since the war has been the cause of so much acrimony and discord and, at times, has threatened the very existence of the College."[55]

By 1938 Matthews and Stuart, aided by Majors Brownfield* and Agnew, apparently believed that they had succeeded in reducing the severity of recruiting. Yet John Windsor talks in his autobiography as if many of the practices that were supposed to have been eliminated, for

*Major-General Harold Oswald Neville Brownfield (1895–1958), graduated RMC, 1914; RCA France and Belgium, 1915–18; associate professor of tactics, RMC, 1934–7; BRA 1st Canadian army, 1945.

instance torpedoing, were still in full swing in his day.[56] While he may
have been exaggerating occasional incidents or may even have been merely
repeating old tales, what he said must have had some basis of truth, for
General Crerar* claimed later that in 1938–9 he persuaded the seniors to
abandon some of the "excesses" and "stupidities."[57] The abolition of all
abuses would obviously be a slow business. The root of the difficulty was
that no one at RMC wanted to destroy the principle whereby the seniors
carried responsibility for discipline because it had obvious value for training. How could the seniors be brought to exercise responsibility wisely
without the exercise of supervision that would in fact destroy much of the
value of the system? At RMC the tendency for oppression of recruits to
grow rather than diminish, which had been inadequately checked by the
staff in the past, was difficult to reverse without striking at principles that
were not in themselves bad. It is impossible to say whether the evil elements in recruiting would have been eradicated if the war had not come in
1939.

In the interwar period the college had been steadily turning out graduates trained for careers as officers. A useful indicator of the college's
value to Canada in this period is the number of Permanent Force commissions taken by ex-cadets. In 1938 Ian Mackenzie, the minister of
National Defence, reported to the House of Commons that the total number of RMC ex-cadets who had taken fulltime commissions in Canada
since the college opened was two hundred and forty-one, and the number
in the British and Indian forces was two hundred and thirty-four. He said
that this represented 19.8 per cent and 19.0 per cent respectively of the
graduate body, that is to say 38.8 per cent all told. But as many cadets
had not graduated and some had taken commissions without graduating,
this figure is an inflated one. However, the figures which he had given
earlier for the number commissioned each year from 1926 to 1937 from
the graduating class totalled one hundred and twenty-four, that is to say
almost 35 per cent of all the graduates of those years.[58] Nevertheless, the
Chief of the Air Staff, Air Vice-Marshal G. M. Croil,† whose service was
hungry for good potential officers, declared that the number who took
permanent commissions was too small in recent years. He suggested that
every graduate of RMC ought to be required to take a commission if one
were offered to him.[59]

*General Henry Duncan Graham Crerar, PC, C.H., C.B., CD, ADC, D.SC. Mil., LL.D.,
D.C.L.; graduated RMC, 1909; commissioned Canadian militia; served in France,
1915–18; professor of tactics, RMC, 1928–30; commandant 1938–9; GOC, First Canadian Army, 1944–5.
†Air-Marshal George Mitchell Croil, C.B.E., A.F.C., chief of the Air Staff, RCAF,
1939–44.

The records at RMC show that some cadets were commissioned in the regular forces either before graduation (for instance those commissioned in the executive branch of the RCN who were required to leave RMC after two years) or some time after graduation and that these were not always included in the general figures given in the commandant's report and to parliament. From 1928 to 1939 there were three hundred and ninety-six cadets who graduated from RMC out of seven hundred and thirty-nine who had entered. Of these one hundred and fifty-three were commissioned in the Canadian services and fifty in the British. So in the eleven years before World War II 27½ per cent of those who entered the college became career officers, and this was equivalent to 50 per cent of the number who graduated.

It is noteworthy that whereas the number who went to the British forces during the period remained fairly constant, there was a considerable increase in Canadian commissions during the 'thirties. Only in 1927 and 1937 did British commissions outnumber Canadian commissions. Also, the college produced some officers for the air force, and to a smaller extent for the navy, as well as for the army. Of the fifty British commissions, thirty-six were in the army and fourteen in the RAF. The breakdown for the Canadian commissions is one hundred and eighteen army, twenty-seven RCAF, and eight RCN. RMC was thus on the way to becoming a tri-service college before World War II. Graduates who did not take a regular commission went into the militia where their contribution was of a different, but not necessarily unimportant, order of magnitude; their role came to be more truly appreciated with advent of war in 1939.

It has been noted that RMC produced officers for the air force and navy as well as for the army. The RCAF's interest in RMC as a source of officers, shown by the offer of summer training courses back in 1922, led to the appointment in 1931 of Squadron-Leader C. M. McEwen, M.C., D.F.C., RCAF,* a World War I "ace" who had scored twenty-two "kills," as an Air Staff Officer at RMC to represent the air service on the instructional side. From about 1932 all cadets were given instruction in the history and organization of the air force and special classes were given in air tactics.[60] However, RMC regulations prohibited cadets from flying during term except on duty. In 1936 G. C. D. M. Holman,† who had a commercial pilot's licence, sought permission to fly with the Kingston Flying Club at weekends in order to maintain his skill. Although Adjutant-General

*Squadron-Leader C. M. McEwen, M.C., D.F.C., RCAF, served in France and Italy in World War I.

†Air Commodore (now Brigadier-General) Donald Morison Holman, C.D., RCAF; graduated RMC, 1938; chief of Logistics Division, Air Material Command headquarters, 1963; Directing Staff, NDC.

Constantine feared that flying would interfere with studies, the CGS, Major-General E. C. Ashton, gave his approval because there was a great shortage of service pilots. On this occasion the Chief of the Air Staff had declared that private flying was of little value for service training, but eighteen months later the RCAF offered "familiarisation flights" to RMC cadets and proposed that arrangements should be made to attach them to RCAF units for summer training. In 1939, twenty-five places for flying training with the RCAF were offered on similar lines to the training courses already available in the RCN, the artillery, the engineers, and the signals.[61] The increase of RCAF training and the possibility of Canadian participation in the Commonwealth Air Training Scheme led to proposals in May 1939 that the RCAF staff officer should be withdrawn from RMC. This was opposed by the Commandant and the Chief of the Air Staff on the grounds that, although the RMC course could not be amended to include as much air force training as was needed for an RCAF commission, an air force officer's presence had a valuable influence in stimulating the interest of RMC graduates in the RCAF. Air Vice-Marshal Croil minuted a report on the question: "To my mind we must endeavour to make it [the college] take the place in our service that Cranwell takes in the RAF."[62]

Although training for the naval services was much less developed at RMC, those cadets who planned to apply for naval commissions after two years at the college were said to be able to get their "training in sail" in a whaler lent by the RCN in 1936 and in dinghies presented to the college by the RMC Club; but these activities were never seriously regarded as equivalent to the training provided in *H.M.C.S. Venture* or in the RCN.[63]

Before RMC's contribution during the second war is examined, some aspects of the college's place in peacetime Canada and in its Kingston setting should be noted. Immediately after the first war the college still drew predominantly upon the residential and other preparatory schools for its cadets. Thus, in 1919, when thirty-nine came from that source, only eight came from ordinary high schools. By 1935 that situation was well on the way to being reversed, the numbers being fifty-nine from high schools as against nineteen from the "prep" schools. Despite this trend, and even though it was always possible to show that a few cadets came from lower middle class or even working-class backgrounds, the families that sent their sons to RMC were still largely in an upper social and economic bracket. Many, of course, had military connections, and for retired officers it provided the kind of education in which they believed at a cost they could afford. It is noticeable also that some family names had begun to appear frequently on the rolls: Osler, Carr-Harris, Van Straubenzee, Wotherspoon, Wurtele, Keefer, Kingsmill, Wood, and Anderson. By 1935 cadets had begun to arrive whose fathers and grandfathers had attended the college. RMC provided a tertiary education for these families that was the nearest thing to the upper class schools and colleges of the old world that could be found in Canada. It carried with it a connotation of social superiority that the Canadian universities did not as a rule possess.

For Kingston this had important implications. Since the middle of the nineteenth century Kingston had been left behind by cities that had grown commercially. With the development of road transport in the 1920s it also began to lose its importance as the main warehouse centre between Toronto and Montreal. Queen's University and RMC were therefore of very great economic and social value to the city. RMC's social pre-eminence helped to preserve some of the nineteenth-century social attitudes and customs that were gone or going elsewhere. As so many Kingston girls married cadets, Kingston became the place to which officers often retired. The city therefore retained something of the flavour of an old garrison town. Visitors were always impressed by this and by the sight of RMC cadets marching rigidly in the streets, never loitering, crossing roads at right angles and at corners, and behaving favourably as compared with the alleged slackness of contemporary youth. The smartness of RMC cadets gave Kingston streets, which were already different by virtue of their "eighteenth century vistas," a distinctive flavour unknown anywhere else in Canada.

It is not surprising that the people of Kingston, especially its civic and social leaders, were very sympathetic to the college and its aims. Thus, on the day the Arnold case broke in the *British Whig*, that newspaper ran an editorial about the prevalence of lying among young people and suggested that corporal punishment was sometimes the only way to check it; although this was not related directly to the incident at the college the inference was obvious and libellous.[64] A member of parliament for Frontenac said that he had lived near the college all his life and had never heard of any trouble between the cadets and the citizens.[65] The college and the cadets were undoubtedly popular, though it was a popularity not unmixed with envy. There was a love-hate attitude, especially on the part of those who did not share RMC's social hospitality.

This was even marked in the attitude of junior members of Queen's University. The senior members of the university showed a real appreciation of the value of the college and were willing to admit recommended graduates to degree courses; and some of the Queen's faculty, for instance, Principal Taylor, sent their sons to be educated at RMC. But the undergraduates at Queen's found the uniformed cadets were serious rivals in athletics and also for the hearts of the limited supply of young ladies in the city. There is a story (probably apocryphal) that after one hard-fought football game between the two institutions when the undergraduates had advanced menacingly on the small cadet cheering section, Sir Archibald Macdonell himself, a great friend and admirer of Queen's, gave permission for the cadets to wear their belts (which made formidable weapons) at the next encounter. Conversely, a member of parliament told the Commons in 1937 that when at Queen's he and his fellow students had regarded it as their duty to check cadet snobbery, and they had succeeded. (He was, however, a wholehearted supporter of the military college.)[66] RMC and Queen's always lived in close but uneasy harmony and with the friction between local rivals that was inevitable when college loyalties became strong and tempers high, especially in fiercely contested sporting events. Yet in times of crisis and difficulty they stood together. When fire burned part of the RMC education wing in 1931, Queen's students went to help RMC cadets and the fire department, and the University immediately offered the use of its dining rooms and of classrooms for the RMC final examinations, an offer that was gratefully accepted. There had grown up between the two institutions a relationship that was unusual and perhaps even unique.

By the eve of World War II RMC had thus become apparently yet more firmly established in the social life and military organization of Canada and of Kingston. It had undergone a thorough internal reform and revision and was on the point of emerging as a very different institution while maintaining all that was best of the old traditions. Many of its graduates had entered either the regular forces of Britain or of Canada and a slightly larger number were in the militia where they maintained their military interest and were prepared for a future emergency. It should be noted, however, that the majority of those who were to serve in the coming conflict had been trained under the unrevised curriculum and subjected to the unreformed system of recruiting. Whether they could have been better, or would have been less effective, had the system been changed earlier is an unanswerable question. It is perhaps worthy of note in this connection that the principle of entry on the basis of an academic qualification was already firmly established. Brigadier Crerar told a college benefactor and mother of a deceased ex-cadet who asked for favourable consideration of a cadet applicant: "I should emphasize, however, that academic standing is of primary importance in the grading of candidates from each Province, and should he not gain a place on that basis there is little or nothing to be done on his behalf".[67] Entry to RMC was not to be obtained by "pull."

12

THE SECOND

WORLD WAR

1939-1945

In August 1914 Canadians had found their country involved almost overnight in a war which few of them had foreseen and the nature of which no one had anticipated. It was very different in 1939. Almost everybody was convinced that with the new weapons available another war would be even more devastating than the previous one, and the danger signals had been hoisted in Europe for several years. In 1938, by carrying the world to the very brink of catastrophe, Munich had dramatized the widespread fear of war without showing how to prevent it. A year later, throughout August, traditionally the month when Europe went to war because the granaries were full, "incidents" on Germany's eastern border kept the world's nerves on edge. The tension was unbearable and could not last indefinitely. When war came it seemed to some people almost a relief.

In 1914 war had come upon RMC during the summer vacation. By the time the college had re-assembled in September, the CEF had been ordered to concentrate at Valcartier and, though their full implication had not yet been realized, Canada's intentions had been made clear. In 1939 the German invasion of Poland on 1 September, and the British declaration of war two days later, came when cadets were assembling in Kingston from all parts of Canada to start the new session. The cadet NCOs and the recruits reported on 28 August. The remaining seniors followed a few days later. Some heard the news of the beginning of war in Europe when they were on the train.[1] All found an atmosphere of tension and uncertainty at the college which, like the country as a whole, abounded with rumours. Each cadet speculated what the future would bring for him personally. Would the college continue as usual? Would it be altered? Would cadets be commissioned at once? Would they go straight to war? No one had the answers.

Canada was not yet at war. In accordance with his long-announced policy, Mackenzie King delayed Canada's declaration until 10 September when parliament could share in the decision. However, Permanent Force leave had been cancelled on 24 August and on the following day volunteers from the militia had been called out to mount guard on vulnerable points. On 1 September the Permanent Force was put on active service, but those who were on the RMC staff were instructed to return to their duties after reporting to their units. The cabinet also ordered the organization of a Canadian Active Service Force (CASF) of two divisions which had been planned for some years.[2]

On the same day the Canadian Prime Minister asked Mr. Chamberlain what Canada could do. The Secretary of State for the Dominions replied that the provision of naval vessels and facilities and of air force personnel would have most immediate value and that the present British policy was to avoid a rush of volunteers for the army. But the United Kingdom high commission in Ottawa indicated that Britain hoped that Canada would eventually send an expeditionary force overseas, though at present only a small Canadian token force and some technical units and personnel were required. On 16 September the Canadian cabinet decided that one division should be sent to Britain.[3]

No definite wartime policy had been decided in advance for RMC. A 1937 mobilization plan had suggested that one means of bringing the Permanent Force up to strength would be to use RMC ex-cadets and the cadets of the two top classes in the college.[4] In 1938, at the height of the Munich crisis, Brigadier H. D. G. Crerar, who had just taken command of RMC, had recommended that the role of the college in war should be set down in advance. There was no reason, he said, for breaking the tradition of both war and peace that RMC provided officers for the Canadian services. Therefore, after the two top classes had been commissioned in accordance with the mobilization plan, the rest of the college should be put on a wartime footing and the military content of college courses increased. At the outbreak or later the college should be reorganized into three wings, one for each service, and each cadet should choose the one he preferred. New entrants should be accepted for a one-year course at age seventeen with junior matriculation to take a course which would bring them up to the level of senior matriculation. The army and air force wings should have one hundred cadets each and the navy wing thirty. Crerar stated that, as 90 per cent of the officers of the forces in time of war would be obtained from short courses in "royal" (the old name for the militia schools) or air force schools, RMC should not duplicate their work. Since entry to these officer-producing units would be at age eighteen, RMC graduates could go on to finish their precommission training in those schools. He suggested that, after release from war service, RMC graduates with senior matriculation would be able to take a course in applied science at a university.[5] Although the Department of National Defence sought information about Britain's plans for Sandhurst and Woolwich,[6] it did not follow Crerar's advice to lay down a manpower policy for RMC before war began.

However, after the Canadian declaration of war, Major-General T. V. Anderson, the chief of the General Staff, called a meeting on 21 September in his office in Ottawa to draw up a policy for the college. Among those who attended were the previous, present, and next commandants, Major-General Matthews, Brigadier Crerar, and Colonel Stuart, respectively. This meeting accepted plans for the commissioning of the two top classes and agreed to recommend that the first and second years should continue until May or June 1940, when their members would also be offered commissions. Thereafter "special war courses only" would be conducted in the college. The details of these would be laid down later.[7] According to this plan RMC would close as a cadet college in 1940 and all officers would come from officer corps training units (OCTUS).

Six days after this meeting, Crerar telephoned Ottawa to ask what he could tell the cadets. He had heard that a policy had been approved by the Minister. He wanted to announce it because the young men were getting "very restless."[8] Having received the information and permission which he requested, the Commandant informed all parents by letter on 29 September that the college was to be changed over to a purely military college and that cadets who did not wish to take a commission should leave immediately. In a moving address to the whole college, he revealed that the first class would graduate at Thanksgiving, that is within three weeks time, and be commissioned. The second class would follow at Christmas. He added that the two lowest classes would be struck off strength in May or June 1940 when RMC would become an officers' training establishment for special war courses of one year's duration. He also announced that he was himself leaving to take up a war appointment.[9]

The announcement that the two lowest classes would be commissioned by 1940 was greeted by some ex-cadets with considerable surprise because they understood that there was a surplus of officers in the CASF. In Toronto Captains Nicol Kingsmill* and C. H. Walker† had organized a "refresher" course for RMC ex-cadets to bring them up to date with military

---

*Lieutenant-Colonel Nicol Kingsmill, graduated RMC, 1929; a Toronto lawyer; served overseas in World War II; secretary-treasurer of the RMC Club and president, 1951–2.

†Colonel Charles Harold Walker (1900–1965), graduated RMC, 1920; Osgoode Hall; called to the bar, 1924; staff-adjutant, RMC, 1939–42; headquarters staff England and Italy, 1942–5.

developments.[10] Some cadets and ex-cadets who were keen to get commissions had been disappointed that their services had not yet been accepted. The executive of the RMC Club therefore sought a clarification of the announced policy from the Commandant. Colonel Stuart, now director of Military Operations and Intelligence, who was present as an elected member of the club when it met the Commandant to express concern about future policy at RMC, reported to the CGS that, although Crerar stressed that there were plenty of commissions available for RMC cadets and ex-cadets in the navy and in the air force, some members of the club persisted in regarding the college as primarily a military college producing officers for the army. Stuart also suggested that the club should be asked to prepare a list of ex-cadets who wanted to offer their services.[11]

The executive then obtained an interview with the Minister of National Defence, the Honourable Norman Rogers,* and informed him that it would be a pity to have two classes of cadets graduate in June 1940 only to be added to waiting lists already filled with more mature officers. They suggested that if it was likely that more officers would be needed by that time it would be wise to bring about forty recruits from the ranks of the CASF into RMC at Christmas so that they could be ready to be commissioned by December 1940. If this were not done no new officers would be produced at RMC *until* June 1941.[12] Their proposal for overlapping courses of officer-cadets would have given continuity to the traditions of the college and would have retained it as a source of officers during the war. What is not clear, however, is whether the ex-cadets realized at this time that the official announcement might mean that RMC would be exclusively used for purposes other than a cadet college.

In fact the future of the college was not yet settled. A discussion between General McNaughton and Mr. Rogers on 4 October 1939, the day when the RMC Club's executive first met to discuss RMC, suggests that the Minister was not as convinced as his chief military advisers that a vast extension of the land forces was inevitable and would require so very many officers that they would have to be trained elsewhere than at RMC.[13] Nevertheless Rogers told the delegation from the RMC Club that he could not rescind an order which had been issued only after he had given the matter his full consideration. However, he promised that if the situation should have changed by next May he would reconsider the policy.[14]

The RMC Club executive realized that it could not oppose a policy which was based on factors about which it was at present ignorant. Hence, its

---

*Norman McLeod Rogers (1894–1940), professor of political science, Queen's University, 1929–35; minister of Labour, 1935; minister of National Defence, 1939–40.

members felt that they must postpone further protest against plans which seemed to them to be likely to turn RMC into an officer training establishment "without the cultural background to be obtained through the Universities, or the intangible but character building processes which have been the backbone of the Royal Military College throughout its history."[15] They had registered their opinion and must now accept patriotically what the country's leaders decided.

No gentleman cadet in the college had withdrawn in response to the Commandant's circular letter of 29 September. On 14 October, in an atmosphere even more highly charged with emotion than that of a peacetime graduation parade, forty-three cadets of the first class marched off to the tune of "Auld Lang Syne."[16] They were going to war. But the historians of the Canadian Corps of Engineers record sardonically that those who went to that regiment found on reporting to Halifax that they had to go straight to the Nova Scotia Technical College to take more courses.[17] With the graduation of the third-year cadets in December, a "sombre and businesslike" affair when snow covered the parade square, the prewar mobilization arrangements for RMC had been duly carried out.[18] It still remained to be seen whether the further arrangements made at the meeting of 21 September in the CGS's office would be put into effect and whether RMC would close as a cadet college for the duration of hostilities.

Brigadier Kenneth Stuart* had succeeded General Crerar as the commandant of RMC on 15 October 1939. The war in Europe did not at first lead to heavy fighting and was being prosecuted by the Chamberlain government in Britain with a noticeable lack of vigour. In view of the nature of this "phony" war, the CGS recommended to the Minister in November that a decision on the nature of the war courses to be held at RMC should be deferred until the spring. The Minister approved.[19] Meanwhile Stuart had made several changes at the college to suit the needs of a shortened course and to meet the exigencies of war. He reorganized into four companies the two classes left in the college after the graduation of their seniors. "There were now no recruits and naturally no recruiting," wrote the editor of the *R.M.C. Review,*[20] a change which no one seems to have deplored. Stuart also suggested that to make up for the loss of Permanent Force members of the staff, the civilian members should be called out as members of the Non-Permanent Active Militia (NPAM);[21]

*Lieutenant-General Kenneth Stuart, C.B., D.S.O., M.C. (1891–1945), graduated RMC, 1911; commissioned RCE, 1911; GSO1 RMC, 1934–7; professor of tactics, RMC, 1937–8; director Military Operations and Intelligence, 1938–9; deputy chief of the General Staff, 1940–1; vice-chief of the General Staff, 1941; chief of the General Staff, 1941–3; chief of staff Canadian military headquarters, London, 1944.

as officers they could give military instruction and also help with similar instruction outside the college. Stuart apparently also acted on the assumption that without definite orders about the future of the college, he should plan in expectation that the class that had entered in 1939 would have a full two years' course. But, in the 1 February issue of *Maclean's Magazine* in 1940 it was stated that the government intended to use RMC for courses for officers of the active force and that in June of that year the college would cease to be a cadet college. Stuart immediately called the attention of the secretary of the Department of National Defence to the potentially harmful effect of this statement which sounded like an official announcement. He said that the "so-called fourth class" (those who had entered in 1939) would not graduate until June 1941; moreover, it was not yet decided that RMC would be used to train officers rather than gentlemen cadets or that it would be restricted to the army. Finally he stated that since November, when it had been agreed to postpone a decision about plans for RMC, misunderstandings had arisen; as the current political situation had altered considerably, he thought that a policy should now be announced. He suggested that the Advisory Board, which by law should meet annually, ought to be summoned to advise the Minister on the subject. In his view a press release should state that recruits would be accepted on the same basis as before the war but the length of the course they would take should not be stipulated.[22]

On 29 February the CGS reminded the Minister through the Adjutant-General that the decision made in November to postpone an announcement of a war policy for RMC had been taken because it was necessary to wait to see whether there would be heavy fighting and casualties in the spring.[23] However, in March, before this would be certain, Mr. Rogers visited RMC on his own initiative and discussed the matter with the Commandant. He agreed with Stuart's concept of future policy for the college and also, subject to the approval of the CGS, that it should be announced in a press release. Stuart's draft for this proposed release stated that in war the college would have the same aims as in peace, the production of a portion of the broadly educated young men required for commissions in the armed forces. It would also have the same conditions of entry. But the course would be reduced to two years with a longer academic session and would include as much military training as in the former four-year course. The cadets would be divided into two groups according to their scholastic standing, the higher group to cover work equivalent to two years of engineering at the universities and the lower group to do work equivalent to senior matriculation and first-year university. All cadets would be obliged to join the services on graduation.[24]

General T. V. Anderson, chief of the General Staff, was opposed. An advisory board was not expedient in time of war, he said, and he wished to prevent a precipitate announcement of policy. On 3 March he wrote to inform the Minister that Stuart had been present at the meeting in November when it had been laid down that special war courses only would be held at RMC, and he pointed out that it was still too early to know whether the expected spring offensive would occur. If one came and continued through the summer, "we would have to contemplate a very different picture to that now before us in respect to requirements of reinforcements" and might regret a commitment to a two-year course at RMC "as we would be open to the criticism that we had allowed the educational factor to out-weigh the officer-producing one." He suggested that the press release should therefore be held in abeyance for two months.[25]

The Minister at first agreed that no announcement should be made until he had had a chance to talk to Anderson, his chief military adviser. Nevertheless, on 3 April he instructed the CGS verbally to draft a press release in conjunction with Stuart. Anderson described this release as a "change in policy." There were to be two-year cadet courses at RMC with a longer academic year and a higher military content. All graduates would take commissions. This notice was sent for publication in the newspapers on 5 April.[26]

In May, Lieutenant-Colonel C. R. S. Stein,* the staff-adjutant, announced to the college on behalf of the Commandant that, as the government had recently decided that an applicant for a Canadian commission must be at least twenty years old, the present third class would not be offered commissions until June 1941. Ex-cadets everywhere heard about this revised policy with delight.[27] A new intake of recruits, one hundred strong, the largest recruit class since World War I, arrived in Kingston in August 1940. One noticeable change was that they were issued khaki battledress and officers' barathea instead of the traditional blues and scarlet. They were organized in classes according to their academic standing rather than their year of entry and were required on graduation to take commission in the RCN, the RCNVR, the CASF, or the NPAM, or to join the British Commonwealth Air Training Scheme. The whole policy was, however, specifically stated to be subject to change without notice in accordance with the progress of the war.

Brigadier Stuart in co-operation with the Senior Professor, L. N. Richardson,† then proceeded to introduce curriculum changes which he

---

*Major-General Charles Ramsay Stirling Stein, RCE (born 1897); war certificate RMC, 1915; staff-adjutant, 1936–40; brigadier, General Staff, army headquarters; COC 5th Canadian Armoured Division, 1943.

†Lorne N. Richardson (1886–1958) came to Kingston with the Royal Naval College of Canada and remained at RMC as professor of mathematics, 1922; director of studies, RMC, 1934–41; adviser on education, RCN, 1941; Carleton College, 1946.

had envisaged when he was chief instructor at the college. According to the editor of the *Review*, these changes resulted in an improvement of the results obtained by RMC graduates. Stuart's brief nine-month tour of duty was thus very effective in bettering the standard of the academic side despite the increase of military training.[28]

Major-General H. F. H. Hertzberg succeeded Brigadier Stuart as commandant on 5 July 1940. The grandson of a colonel in the Norwegian army, Hertzberg was a graduate of the University of Toronto, and had worked as a civil engineer before World War I. He had been a prewar militia officer, had first become commanding royal engineer of the 1st Canadian Division, and had then commanded the 3rd Bridgade. After the war he had remained in the Permanent Force and had served as GSO 1 at RMC from 1925 to 1929. In 1938 he had been promoted major-general and appointed quartermaster-general. The appointment to the college of so senior a soldier with a rank of major-general was due to increased responsibilities that the commandant of RMC had now assumed.

Diversification had begun at RMC sometime before Hertzberg arrived. The RCN had requested facilities for an officers' course as early as 27 September 1939 but had been told that space would not be available for it until after the second graduation in December.[29] Commencing on 8 January 1940 successive eight-week courses, each with thirty-three RCNVR officer-students, had been held in the Stone Frigate which was appropriately re-commissioned HMCS *Stone Frigate* as a tribute to its historic past. The depleted college staff assisted with teaching in the naval courses and received help in return. Both groups of instructors also gave lessons in artillery, signals, and ordnance training centres in Kingston and to the Queen's University Canadian officer training corps (COTC).

After Hertzberg took command, three senior officers' courses of two weeks' duration each were held at RMC during July and August while the cadets were away. These had a total enrolment of one hundred and sixty-six officers. During the year 1940 there were also five company commanders' refresher courses of various lengths with one hundred and ninety-three officers attending, and a four-week intelligence course with forty-one in attendance.[30] RMC was thus extensively used for senior courses while still a cadet college.

In July 1940 General Crerar had been brought back from Canadian military headquarters in London, where he was senior Canadian combatant officer, to become the chief of the General Staff in Ottawa. In the ensuing months, spurred by the crisis presented by the fall of France and the aerial siege of Britain (which took the place of the spring offensive that Anderson had been expecting), Crerar proceeded to plan a Canadian army of five or six divisions. Its officers were trained in the corps schools and a Canadian officer cadet training unit was established in England in August 1940.[31] The army also needed facilities for training staff officers. In November, on behalf of the CGS, Brigadier Stuart, now vice chief of Staff, sent to the corps commander in Britain, General McNaughton, a cipher message which shows that the new Minister of National Defence, Colonel J. L. Ralston* had authorized the implementation of a plan to use RMC for courses for senior officers.

Stuart said in this message that he had at first interpreted the Minister's authority to mean merely that no more regular classes would be admitted. He had now learned from Colonel E. L. M. Burns,† who had returned to Canada from Canadian military headquarters in London, that the Corps Commander thought the cadet college ought to be closed down altogether in June 1941. However, Stuart told McNaughton that the Director of Military Training had informed him that accommodation for one hundred and fifty officers would be all that the staff course would need, and he recommended that the present junior class of cadets should complete its second year. It could be billeted in the Stone Frigate and thus leave the whole of Fort Frederick for officer accommodation. Stuart added incidentally that J. H. V. Young,‡ the deputy master-general of the ordnance, had told him that the RMC Club would accept with good grace the ruling that no further recruit classes would be entered.[32] Accordingly, on 21 December Major-General B. W. Browne, the adjutant-general, outlined a new policy for RMC on the lines of Stuart's suggestions. The present classes would each complete their two-year course in June 1941 and June 1942 respectively, and there would be no new entry classes until the cessation of hostilities. RMC would be used to accommodate a senior officers' course, a company commanders' course, and possibly a junior staff course.[33]

At an RMC Club dinner at the end of March, General Crerar announced the plan to have no more entry classes and to use RMC for the education of existing officers rather than for the training of new officers. Two weeks later he wrote a personal letter to the president of the club to explain this

---

*Colonel James Layton Ralston, PC, K.C., C.M.G., D.S.O., LL.D., D.C.L. (1888–1948); minister of National Defence, 1926–30, 1940–4. He succeeded to the post the second time when Rogers was killed.

†Lieutenant-General Edson Louis Millard Burns, D.S.O., O.B.E., M.C., LL.D. (born 1897); war certificate RMC, 1915; instructor, 1924–6; GOC 1st Canadian Corps, 1944; deputy minister Veterans' Affairs, 1950–4; commander UN Emergency Force (Middle East), 1956–9; adviser to the Canadian government on disarmament, 1960.

‡Major-General James Vernon Young, C.B., O.B.E. (1891–1961), graduated RMC, 1911 and went to MIT; 3rd Artillery Brigade, World War I; a leading industrialist; master-general of Ordnance, 1942.

decision. Canada would need three thousand new officers within the next year. Recent government decisions to introduce compulsory military training and to commission all army officers from the ranks must inevitably affect the function of the college in time of war. The army could not afford to wait for two years for a very limited number of "particularly efficient young officers" when experience had shown that it was possible to train young men to an adequate standard for war needs in a much shorter time. He said that two different systems of commissioning officers to perform the same kind of duties could not be maintained side by side. Reason dictated that the role of the college must be changed if it was to perform its full national obligation. He concluded: "I believe that this temporary 'changeover' in function is in the interests of the State and, indeed, of the College itself. When a nation and an Empire are fighting for their lives, sentiment and traditional conception cannot be the deciding factors. Also I am convinced that after this war is over, and the time comes for the re-constitution of the Battalion of Gentleman-Cadets, that those who have passed through R.M.C. in pre-war years, and who will then be charged with the responsibility of the successful re-establishment of the College, will not fail in the task that will be theirs."[34]

There were no further protests from the RMC Club. Its members were well aware that the war situation was critical. They were uneasy about the possible effect of a break in continuity, but they had not yet begun to worry about the possibility of a permanent closure. Crerar's reference to the re-opening of the college had dampened their powder. They had not realized the significance of the fact that at this very time when the army was thinking only of its immediate problems of officer training, the other services were planning with an eye on the long-term future.

The graduation in June 1941 left only one class at RMC. The war was noticeably changing the college in other respects also. During the summer of 1941, in place of training camp, RMC cadets were taken on a tour of the growing military installations in Canada before going to summer training. When they returned to Kingston in August they found themselves rapidly outnumbered by officers under instruction at RMC. At the beginning of the war the RMC riding establishment had been converted into a motor vehicle training school. Scarlet and blue had been entirely replaced by khaki. Only the "RMC" on their shoulders, their lack of rank badges, and their pillboxes in summer and fur headdress in winter distinguished cadets from the officer students in the college. Hitherto the only woman on the RMC staff had been a nursing sister, but now four stenographers were taken on strength. During the summer months drumhead services were held on the football field in place of indoor services in Currie Hall. In

1941, in addition to officers' courses of the kind conducted the previous year, there were Canadian junior war staff courses, field security courses, and radio technicians' courses attended by fifty airmen and run by the RMC staff under Major C. C. Cook. Finally the chemistry department undertook research in chemical warfare.[35] The RMC cadets were quartered in HMCS *Stone Frigate* and the student officers in Fort Frederick.

Physically the appearance of the point was also changing, partly as a result of the war but more through the completion of wartime projects and from other accidental causes and the passage of time. The dominion and provincial governments had completed the road around Point Frederick to give tourists and visitors an opportunity to see the magnificence of RMC's location. The Holt rink near the guardroom had collapsed from sheer age and was replaced by an open air rink in the same place. A breakwater had been completed to the south of the boathouse. Finally, now that the horses had gone, the wire fences that disfigured the point were removed. Thus once again the grounds of RMC, now plentifully covered with shade trees and no longer as bare as they were when the college opened in 1876, were beautified in the course of a war.[36]

The traditional West Point hockey game was among the war casualties, for when Canada went to war, the competition had to be suspended since the United States was neutral. After Pearl Harbor it was possible for the series to be resumed, but the only wartime game was played at West Point in 1942. There was now only one class in the college. The result, West Point's second victory in the series, seems in retrospect a symbolic harbinger of the end of an era in RMC's history.

Nearly four months later the final day to close the college arrived. After the Governor-General, the Earl of Athlone, had inspected the battalion, the cadets moved off the square in slow march following their colours. The RMC Club had marked this great solemn occasion by timing its annual meeting at the college to coincide with the final closing exercises. The ex-cadets paraded to the memorial arch for a service of remembrance for those of their colleagues who had fought their last fight. After motor cycle, physical training, and gymnastic displays by the cadets, the scene was transferred to St. George's Cathedral. General Hertzberg marched at the head of the battalion across the LaSalle causeway to the cathedral, which was crowded with college relatives, friends, and local citizens. They were attending a ceremony of great significance in the life of Kingston and of Canada. On arriving, the commandant knocked three times with the hilt of his sword and asked permission of the churchwarden, Professor W. R. P. Bridger, to lay up the RMC colours in the cathedral. When the ceremony had been duly completed and the congregation had been addressed by the Lord Bishop of Ontario, the cadet battalion marched back to the college. There it gave three cheers for His Majesty the King and was dismissed. The June ball that evening, despite the war, was gay and colourful. It was the last event in a long and crowded day.[37] RMC still existed in name, but it was now merely a place where various military courses were given. It had ceased to be a cadet college.

It is instructive to compare the military college policy promulgated by Canada in World War II with that which was adopted in the earlier conflict and with the policies devised in both wars in Britain and the United States. It will be remembered that in the first war RMC had remained a cadet college and had given courses shortened to as little as one year which continued to include some of the earlier general educational content. In 1914–18 and 1939–45 Sandhurst became a wartime officer training unit producing officers in six-months' courses instead of the usual eighteen or twenty-four and it was supplemented by other similar OCTUs. In the first war Woolwich similarly graduated those classes in residence prematurely and introduced a six months' course, but by 1916 the "Shop" began to lengthen its course again until it reached twelve months. In 1939 RMA Woolwich had been subject to severe criticism because its location had become unsuitable and because its course having been reduced to eighteen months between the wars could not meet either the military or the technical requirements. When war came it closed down summarily never to re-open. In both the wars West Point reduced its four-year courses by early graduations but maintained much of their general educational value. In the war a three-year course policy, matching that in civilian colleges, was deliberately introduced. The final comparison is perhaps the most significant. The RCN in 1942 opened a cadet college with a view to producing officers after the war. Despite all the rationalizations for what happened to RMC in this same year, it is difficult to avoid the conclusion that the decision to close the college was induced by a state bordering on panic, that it was short-sighted, that it may have been furthered by senior officers in the Permanent Force who had come from the militia and who were jealous of RMC rivals for appointments, and that it clearly gave rise to the possibility that the various groups who opposed RMC would be able to join together to see that it did not re-open after the war.

The departure of the cadets left the facilities on Point Frederick fully available for use for staff training. Until his retirement in 1944 at the age of sixty, General Hertzberg, who was admitted to the RMC Club as an honorary member with the number H2727, remained commandant. The name "Royal Military College" was retained. Hertzberg and his successors, Brigadier D. G. Cunningham,* Brigadier J. D. B. Smith,† and British Major-General J. F. M. Whiteley,‡ were appointed "Commandants of the Royal Military College of Canada" but this was now the command of a training establishment. The junior war staff course was enlarged and, because it was equivalent to the intermediate staff course at Camberley, was redesignated the Canadian war staff course. In 1943 the senior officers' course and the company commanders' course were fused into a field officers' course which in December 1943 made way for a Canadian civil affairs staff course organized and directed by Lieutenant-Colonel T. F. Gelley of the RMC staff. Along with these various staff officers' courses RMC was used for various intelligence courses for officers and other ranks and for courses for field security personnel. In 1943 five Canadian Women's Army Corps (CWAC) officers took the junior wing of the Canadian war staff course.[38] By 1944 the training of officers at RMC had largely relieved the serious staff problem of the Canadian army.

Important as these courses at Kingston undoubtedly were, they could have been carried on elsewhere, though perhaps not as conveniently. What could not have been provided by a substitute was the service RMC contributed through its ex-cadets. RMC's real role in the war must therefore be measured in terms of the achievements of its own sons rather than of the courses that used its buildings in wartime.

The number of available ex-cadets was very much greater than in 1914–18. The 1937 mobilization plan had noted that one means by which militia units could fill out their complement of officers in the event of war was by appointing RMC ex-cadets. Recruiting officers were therefore forbidden to enlist them in the ranks lest their services be misused.[39] As soon as the war began ex-cadets clamoured for military appointments. The CASF and the NPAM could not absorb them fast enough to suit every one. By the end of 1940 there were well over nine hundred in the services, nine had been killed in action or had died on active service, one was reported

*Brigadier Douglas Gordon Cunningham, D.S.O. (born 1908); graduated RMC, 1929; law practice in Kingston; adjutant of the PWOR; brigade-major of a Canadian infantry brigade which took part in the Dieppe raid, 1942, and GSO1 1st Canadian Corps, 1943; brigadier, 9th Canadian Infantry Brigade, 1944; commandant RMC, 1944.

†Major-General James Desmond Blaise Smith, C.B.E., D.S.O., C.D., C.ST.J., ADC (born 1911); graduated RMC, 1933; GOC 4th and 5th armoured brigades and 1st infantry brigade during World War II; commandant RMC, 1945–6; later Military Secretary Cabinet Defence Committee; Canadian military representative SHAPE, 1951–4; commandant NDC, 1954–8; adjutant-general 1958–62.

‡General Sir John Francis Martin Whiteley, G.B.E., K.C.B., M.C. (born 1896), late RE (a British officer exchanged from the Imperial Defence College to set up a joint services staff college, later called the National Defence College, in Canada); commandant RMC, 1947.

missing, and one was a prisoner of war. A year later the number had risen to eleven hundred, with twenty-one killed, two missing, and two captured. By the time the war ended, one thousand three hundred and fifty-eight ex-cadets had served in the forces and another sixty-nine had been engaged in special war work, making a total of one thousand four hundred and twenty-seven, or over 80 per cent of those eligible.[40]

This number is more than half as large again as that of the RMC ex-cadets who served in World War I, but fortunately the number of deaths was rather less, 114 in 1939–45 as against 147 in 1914–18. In the first war Canada's total fatal casualties had been 9.65 per cent of the total men enlisted and officer casualties were 12.9 per cent; in the second war the comparable figures were 3.86 per cent and 8.3 per cent of a much larger total enlistment. For RMC ex-cadets the percentages of the total engaged who lost their lives in the first and second wars were 15 per cent and 8.3 per cent respectively.[41]

About 71 per cent of the RMC ex-cadets who served in the war were in the Canadian army. Of these more than 30 per cent were in technical corps: the Royal Canadian Engineers, the Royal Canadian Electrical and Mechanical Engineers, and the Royal Canadian Corps of Signals. It is important to notice that RMC had thus produced specialists for the needs of the new mechanical warfare though their number was much too small to satisfy more than a fraction of its voracious demands. A little more than 30 per cent of RMC ex-cadets in the army were in the armoured units and the infantry. Ten per cent of the ex-cadets in the army were on the General Staff. The 20 per cent of the ex-cadets who were not in the army were in other services: 12 per cent in the RCAF, 5 per cent in the RCN and RCNVR, 8 per cent in the British and Indian armies, and 1½ per cent in the RAF. There were a few individuals in the Royal Navy, the Australian army, the United States forces, the RCMP, and other allied services.[42] A number of other ex-cadets were "frozen" to their jobs in important war work in industry and science in Canada.

A big difference between the Canadian military efforts in the two wars was that in World War II Canada no longer had need to borrow British staff officers and commanders. The destroyer on which General H. D. G. Crerar and his staff crossed the English Channel during the Overlord operation in 1944 was commanded by an ex-cadet and future commandant, Lieutenant-Commander D. W. Piers, RCN, who noted that history was being made. He wrote that this was "the first time a Canadian Army Commander had proceeded to the invasion of enemy territory in a Canadian warship." *Algonquin* flew the Canadian army standard at the starboard yardarm, and General Crerar read the lesson in the service on the upper deck and addressed the ship's company.[43] Colonel Stacey has shown that it was the NPAM which to no small extent had produced the leaders who had built and led the army that was put in the field. At the end of hostilities, three out of the five fighting divisions were commanded by men who had begun the war as captains or majors in the militia. This is clear evidence of the value of the part-time citizen soldier. But it does not depreciate the complementary value of the very much smaller Permanent Force. Regular soldiers made distinct and invaluable contributions to the shaping of the prewar militia and also to the forces that served in war. Moreover, as Stacey said, the Permanent Force played a part out of all proportion to its size, four hundred and fifty-five officers all told when the war began: "A man who had devoted his life to the study of military affairs should be a more useful soldier than an amateur; and it was fortunate that the country had a few professionals available in the crisis."[44]

Elsewhere Colonel Stacey has commented on the advantages that accrued to Canada from maintaining a military college in peacetime. Small in relation to the wartime army, it had nevertheless been a valuable source of qualified and well-educated leaders and technical officers both for the regular army and the militia.[45] Had its output during peace gone exclusively to the regular force, as is customary in most other countries, RMC's contribution would have come to the militia only secondhand. It was therefore undoubtedly an advantage when the emergency came the RMC graduates had been commissioned in both the regular and the part-time forces. RMC graduates had been an important influence in the militia before the war, and many of the militia officers who rose to the top on active service were from the college.

In addition to this general contribution, RMC ex-cadets were directly and personally involved. General Crerar led the Canadian army to victory in Europe in 1945. At the close of hostilities one of his two corps commanders, Lieutenant-General G. G. Simonds,* and two of his five divisional commanders, Major-Generals H. W. Foster† and C. Vokes,‡ were RMC graduates and prewar regular soldiers. Generals Simonds and E. L. M. Burns had organized the first junior war staff course in Britain. Major-General Burns also commanded a division under General Alexander with distinction.

The four officers who held the appointment of chief of the General Staff

*Lieutenant-General Granville Simonds, C.B., C.B.E., D.S.O. (born 1903), graduated RMC, 1925; RCA; associate professor of artillery and instructor in tactics, RMC, 1938; GOC 2nd Canadian Corps, 1944–5; CGS, 1951–5.

†Major-General Harry Wickwire Foster, C.B.E., D.S.O. (1904–1962), MQ certificate RMC, 1922; McGill University; a Permanent Force officer; GOC 1st Canadian Infantry Division, 1944–5; GOC, 13th Brigade Group in the Kiska operation.

‡Major-General Christopher Vokes, C.B., C.B.E., D.S.O. (born 1904), graduated RMC, 1924; GOC 1st Canadian Infantry Division, 1943–4 and 4th Canadian Armoured Division, 1944–5.

in Ottawa during the war were all ex-cadets: Major-General T. V. Anderson, and Lieutenant-Generals H. D. G. Crerar, K. Stuart, and J. C. Murchie.* Out of seventy principal appointments at National Defence Headquarters and in the Canadian Army Overseas, thirty-one were held by ex-cadets (this tally of course includes men who moved from one office to another and who are therefore counted several times). At the end of the war there were in the Canadian army and air force, one full general, four lieutenant-generals, nineteen major-generals, fifty-eight brigadiers, one air marshal, and eight air commodores who had all begun their military careers in the college. Although this list included several who retired before the end of the war, it is an impressive testimony to RMC's value to Canada.

Moreover, although the proportion of Kingston graduates who served in the British army was much smaller than in the previous war, there were in the British and Indian forces two lieutenant-generals, two major-generals, seventeen brigadiers, one air commodore, and one naval captain. One hundred and sixty-two cadets reached the rank of colonel or above in the Canadian forces and thirty-seven in the British forces. Four hundred and thirty-three were decorated (including seventy by foreign governments) and two hundred and eleven were mentioned in despatches.[46]

Statistics of this kind are dry ways of measuring achievement and accomplishment and perhaps some of these awards and appointments followed upon the seniority and service of career officers. They nevertheless show the size of the contribution made by a small college whose total annual strength had never exceeded two hundred, that is, an average of fifty in each year.

Conditions of active service naturally revealed the excellence of RMC's scientific and engineering bent. For instance, Colonel C. J. Bermingham,† RCE, startled the British by his use of Canadian construction "bull-dozing" methods.[47] Demolitions were carried out in many areas by ex-cadets including some in far flung parts of the earth, notably in Malaya by Major H. C. DeBlois,‡ RE.[48] Brigadier D. H. Storms§ helped to develop pre-fabricated bituminous surfacing for runways that could be laid quickly for mobile tactical airfields.[49] Colonel W. R. Sawyer of the Canadian army's

*Lieutenant-General John Carl Murchie, C.B., C.B.E., C.D., D.SC. Mil. (1895–(1966), MQ certificate RMC, 1915; RCA, France, 1915–17; vice-chief of the General Staff, 1942–4; chief of the General Staff, 1944–5.

†Colonel Cornelius John Bermingham (born 1900); left RMC, 1921 to become a civil engineer and port construction contractor; commander, Army Group Engineers during the war.

‡Major Howard Crawford DeBlois (1913–1948), graduated RMC, 1934 and Cambridge University; RE.

§Brigadier Douglas Huick Storms (born 1893); graduated RMC, 1913; became chief engineer (works) RCE during World War II.

chemical warfare unit, and a future RMC director of studies, provided smoke to cover the crossing of the Rhine and elsewhere Brigadier Sir Godfrey Rhodes, an engineer who had gone from RMC to the British army, was director of transport in Teheran.[50]

Lieutenant-General G. G. Simonds, commanding the 1st Canadian Division in Normandy, by ingenious use of new tactics, blew a corridor through German defence lines at the Falaise gap. He operated tanks at night by firing Bofors tracer shells down the line of advance. He also used "artificial moonlight" from searchlights to improve visibility and green marker shells to identify boundaries. Although the attack did not go completely as Simonds had planned, his tactics were, in the words of the official historian, "fully justified by the event."[51]

All the stories of heroism and excellence in the performance of duty by ex-cadets cannot be included but some must be told even at the risk of seeming discriminatory. The first great test of Canada's newly expanded armed forces did not come until the Dieppe raid on 19 August 1942. General Hertzberg, writing to General Crerar, who had broadcast a statement about the closing of the college, commented that the record of RMC ex-cadets at Dieppe was "beyond words." The Victoria Cross, Canada's first in the war, was won by Lieutenant-Colonel C. C. I. Merritt, an RMC graduate, a barrister, and a peacetime militia officer in the Seaforth Highlanders of Vancouver, whose wife had seen him off to war with the admonition: "Don't try to win any medals, Cec. Just come home."[52] Merritt commanded the South Saskatchewans who landed on the beach at Pourville. He gallantly led many attacks in the face of galling fire. When the enterprise failed, he held off enemy attacks until the main body of troops on his beach were evacuated. His rearguard force fought until its ammunition was exhausted and it was compelled to surrender.[53] Victoria Crosses are awarded for individual acts of heroism of such a rarity that they are often thought not to provide very convincing evidence of the excellence of the background from which the hero came. However, Merritt's achievement was supported by other facts about Dieppe that were the basis of Hertzberg's boast. Of the twelve DSOs awarded for service in the Dieppe raid or staff work in its preparation, no fewer than five went to former gentlemen cadets.*[54]

Reference may also be made to heroism of a somewhat different kind, that of Lieutenant Joseph-Maurice Rousseau, CIC, who was killed when

---

*Of the many RMC officers at Dieppe, none was more colourful than Major Dollard Ménard who after graduating had elected to serve for two years with a Sikh regiment on the northwest frontier because it was more likely to be exciting. He returned to serve with his own countrymen when war came. Ménard literally talked his way back; he obtained transportation as a "sailor" on several naval vessels en route to Canada (Robertson, *The Shame and the Glory: Dieppe*, p. 7).

on secret operations in enemy-occupied Alsace.[55] Mention should be made of Air Commodore A. D. Ross* who lost an arm when he rescued the pilot and air gunner of a burning bomber in which the bombs were exploding as he worked. Ross was awarded the George Cross.[56] However, perhaps the most historic contribution was that of Squadron-Leader L. J. Birchall,† a future commandant. Sir Winston Churchill once said that the news that the Japanese had broken into the Indian Ocean marked for him the most dangerous moment in the war. Birchall spotted the Japanese fleet approaching Ceylon and was able to send a warning back to his base before he was shot down and imprisoned. In prison camps Birchall was a thorn in the flesh of the Japanese guards, and at the risk of his life kept a secret record of their activities for use after the war.[57] Another RMC ex-cadet, Group-Captain John Francis Griffiths, RAF, had been the first airman to sight the German fleet in Heligoland Bight on 13 December 1939 and was the first Canadian to be decorated in this war after shooting down several enemy airplanes.[58] Lieutenant-Commander D. R. B. Cosh, RCNVR, a naval airman who had been at RMC, attacked *Tirpitz* in a Norwegian fjord.[59] Also at sea, Lieutenant-Commodore W. P. Chipman, RCN(R) was the executive officer on *Wild Goose* on what was described by the First Lord of the Admiralty as "the most outstanding cruise undertaken in this war by an escort group."[60] Finally, Lieutenant-Commodore H. R. H. Kirkpatrick, RCNVR commanded a Canadian motorboat flotilla attacking enemy shipping in the English Channel.[61]

A variety of other services were rendered by various other ex-cadets such as Captain I. E. MacPherson of the Indian army who commanded Gurkhas,[62] and by Lieutenant-General Sir G. N. Cory, an RMC graduate who had joined the British army and was inspector-general of foreign troops in Britain.[63] The traditional tie between RMC and the British army had many other beneficial results and none more remarkable than the saving of the Canadian brigade's guns at Brest in 1940. The garrison commandant at Brest during the evacuation happened to be Colonel W. B. Mackie who graduated from RMC in 1910 to join the British army and knew some of the officers of the 1st Canadian Brigade personally. He therefore proved willing to intercede with higher authority to obtain permission for the Canadians to load their guns on the ships despite overcautious peremptory orders that all *matériel* must be destroyed. As a result the twenty-four guns, and also twelve Bofors, seven predictors,

*Air Commodore Arthur Dwight Ross, G.C., O.B.E. (born 1907); RCAF; graduated RMC, 1928.
†Air Commodore Leonard Joseph Birchall, O.B.E., D.F.C., C.D., ADC (born 1915); graduated RMC, 1937; commandant, RMC, 1963-7.

RMC BUILDINGS   1 Mackenzie Building

2 Stone Frigate and Old Gymnasium

3 Fort Frederick Martello Tower

1

2

3

1 Yeo Hall

2 Currie Building

3 Senior Staff Mess

4 The senior staff, on the occasion of the visit of the Governor-General, the Earl of Bessborough, May 1932

4

1

1 Cadets celebrate Canada's centennial
   The cadet wing marching past the Governor-General, the Rt. Hon.
   Roland Michener, C.C., C.D., on Parliament Hill, 26 May 1967

2 Graduation parade

3 Graduates march off with the colours

2

3

GRADUATION ACTIVITIES

1 Conferal of diplomas
2 Cadet wing on parade
3 Graduation parade, 1967
4 June ball

1

2

3

4

5

5 Ex-cadet memorial service, 1946

6 Parade of ex-cadets

6

1

2

1 The gallery

2 The foyer

3

3 Mr. J. W. Spurr, chief librarian,
with Dr. W. K. Lamb, dominion
archivist and national librarian,
Ottawa, and the Rt. Hon. Vincent
Massey (centre), in whose
honour the building was named.

4 RMC Massey Library

4

three Bren carriers, and various other vehicles which the gunners added on their own initiative, were taken back to England to strengthen defences that had been seriously weakened by the defeat in France.[64]

RMC cadets also served in many important capacities connected with the direction and prosecution of the war, the security of Britain and Canada, and the administration of conquered territory. Thus Lieutenant-Colonel H. A. Davis, RE, went as a member of the military mission that accompanied Sir Stafford Cripps to Moscow in 1941;[65] Lieutenant-Colonel C. M. Drury,* RCA, was military attaché in Washington before going as CRA in the 4th Canadian Armoured Division with the 2nd Corps in Europe;[66] and Major P. W. Cook, RCA was chairman of the Canadian Joint Intelligence Committee in Washington.[67] Lieutenant-Colonel R. Theo DuMoulin was president of allied military courts in occupied Germany.[68] Captain E. H. C. Leather, CIC, an ex-cadet who had served in the RCA, and who later became a British MP and received a knighthood, wrote a manual for the Home Guard called *Combat without Weapons*.[69] At home in Canada Lieutenant-Colonel T. A. H. Taylor commanded the Pacific Coast Militia Rangers organized to watch for Japanese raids in the vast mountain fastnesses of British Columbia.[70] Finally, but not least, Colin Gibson† became the first RMC ex-cadet to be a cabinet minister when he was appointed minister of national revenue in 1940. In 1945 he became minister of national defence for air.[71]

A meaningful assessment of RMC's full value in the war is hard to make. The college was not involved as a unit and indeed ceased to exist as a cadet college. Its former members were scattered throughout the services and across the world, and the sum of their achievements is hard to reconstruct. Statistics of ex-cadet service, casualties, and decorations, and accounts of individual valour and achievement, impressive though these are, do not tell the whole story. However, it is clear that had Canada not had a productive cadet college before the war the task of welding the nation's manhood into an efficient war machine would have been more difficult than it actually proved. As in World War I, RMC supplemented the work of the militia, giving a degree of professionalism and knowledge of military procedures, and particularly of the military ethic, in a way that a part-time

*Brigadier Charles Mills Drury, PC, D.S.O., C.B.E., QC, MP (born 1903), graduated RMC, 1929; practised law in Montreal; GOC (temporary major-general) 4th Canadian Armoured Division, 1945; deputy minister of National Defence, 1949; minister of Industry and minister of Defence Production, 1955.

†Colonel Colin William George Gibson, PC, M.C., V.D., LL.D. (born 1891); graduated RMC, 1911; Royal Fusiliers, 1914; practised law from 1919; lieutenant-colonel Royal Hamilton Light Infantry; MP 1940; minister of National Revenue, 1940; minister of Defence for Air, 1945; secretary of State, 1946; minister for Mines and Resources, 1949.

militia could not do to the same extent. As the number of RMC graduates was much larger than in 1914, the college's contribution was proportionately greater, perhaps not in relation to that of the militia which had also grown, but in so far as it was now less necessary for Canada to borrow from the British army. The militia, the Canadian Permanent Force, and RMC were all like a leaven working in a mass of dough to produce the efficient fighting Canadian forces on the victorious allied side in the war. If Canada had had no RMC, Canadian initiative probably would have won through and Canada would have made a useful contribution. But the existence of RMC made the task less difficult. The cost of the college during peacetime had been a small premium which, if it did not give the country full insurance against the needs of war, provided valuable assistance when the emergency came.

13

THE STRUGGLE TO

RE-OPEN

1942-1948

When RMC's closure as a cadet college was announced in 1941, ex-cadets everywhere were uneasy about the imminent break in the great tradition which they had shared; but before the battalion had laid its colours on the altar in St. George's Cathedral, they had begun to worry about something much more serious, that the college might drop completely out of the public mind. Allan Mitchell, the current president of the RMC Club, feared that cessation of the enrolment of new cadets would mean that parents and the public generally would soon "forget that the place ever existed." He therefore thought that the RMC Club should publicize the college in the newspapers. He suggested that the club should ask its branches to pool resources which could not be used actively during the war for any other purpose. With these the executive could finance articles about ex-cadets and their activities to be placed in newspapers in Toronto, Montreal, Winnipeg, and Vancouver. He proposed to use stories which Professor W. R. P. Bridger, the editor of the *R.M.C. Review*, was collecting from ex-cadets all over the world.[1]

Mitchell's scheme was not put into operation. However, when the college closed, the RMC Club showed its appreciation of the work that Bridger was doing by urging that he should continue it,[2] and as he stayed on at RMC as librarian and archivist, he was able to keep the *Review* going. Ex-cadets wrote to tell him about their own exploits or about those of other ex-cadets whom they had met in the course of their duties. These were published in whole or in part as appropriate. Though the *Review* did not have a wide circulation beyond club members, it served a very useful purpose by helping to maintain their interest in their *alma mater* and by keeping the RMC spirit alive. "Bill" Bridger, as he was known to all, thus made an important contribution to the eventual re-opening of the college.

In November 1943, when he thought that the end of the war was drawing measurably closer, Mitchell again raised the question of the future of RMC. In a letter to Lieutenant-General Stuart, now chief of the General Staff, he noted that the navy, "having whistled for wind in the doldrums for twenty years, understands the importance of a favourable breeze." He declared that the RCN had "feathered its nest" with permanent buildings from coast to coast and also with a permanent college for officers (HMCS *Royal Roads*). He asserted that this naval college would still be operating when "C.C.F. anti-militarism" and "high-finance sound money economy" impinged upon what was left of "the efforts of today's gallant fighting men." Mitchell told General Stuart that the army slept: "There is a break in the great tradition of R.M.C. ... A once great living organism – a great bond of unity for Canadians from Halifax to Vancouver – fades in the memory."[3]

Stuart had gone to London to take command of the Canadian army overseas as chief of staff; but before this letter was sent on to him it was read by Major-General J. C. Murchie, the vice chief of the General Staff, who was also an ex-cadet. Murchie told Mitchell he had not yet received a reaction from General Stuart but that "the person who is slated to be the new C.G.S., is not likely to look with favour on the re-opening of the College." Who was meant is not clear for, after the post had been left vacant for some months amidst suggestions that it should be downgraded to adjutant-general, Murchie was himself appointed. Meanwhile Mitchell had once more proposed that the club should publicize the college and had suggested the possibility of getting a "ghost writer" for this purpose.[4] The name of Grattan O'Leary was mentioned in this connection.[5] But General Murchie was "not enthusiastic" about publicity and the proposal was dropped.[6]

Nevertheless, in March 1944 after members of the RMC Club had gathered in Ottawa and had discussed the possibility of getting RMC re-opened, their new president, W. H. O'Reilly, made a direct approach to the Minister of National Defence to ask for an assurance that there were plans for that eventuality. Mr. O'Reilly's letter stated the case formally and well. It read as follows:

The re-opening of the Royal Military College of Canada is a burning question with all Ex-Cadets, if I am to judge from the representations that have been made to me from all Canada, from those serving in the field and from the three score attending a recent meeting of the Ex-Cadets in Ottawa.

You are fully aware of the proved value of the Royal Military College to Canada.

You know the proud record of Ex-Cadets in every theatre of war since the coming-of-age of the Royal Military College. You know that there are now over 1300 Ex-Cadets serving in the present conflict.

You know that the Royal Military College is one of our great democratic institutions, which is vitalized by the cadets who come from every walk of life and from every Province of Canada.

You know the place Ex-Cadets have taken in the civilian life of our country, and you know of their anxiety to serve Canada in the most effective manner possible in war and in peace.

You know the training given to the youth of Canada by the Royal Military College in the past has been of inestimable value to the country.

We know we would be doing Canada a disservice if we did not now urge upon you the importance of re-opening the Royal Military College to cadets at the earliest possible moment.

Canada must have an army post-war. The army must have junior officers. These officers must be highly trained. While at the cessation of hostilities you may have plenty of junior officers, you must remember that the pre-war training of the Royal Military College covered a four-year period. Hence no new highly trained junior officers could be available for the army under a minimum of three years.

Canada will need, and need badly in the undoubtedly trying post-war years, youth trained in the traditions and ideals of the Royal Military College, not only in the Army but in civilian life.

We believe that trained Canadian youth will be our greatest asset, and regret that the necessity of war brought about the closing of the Royal Military College to cadets.

All this indicates the necessity of re-opening the Royal Military College to cadets without delay.

We hope, sir, you are in a position to advise us that plans are now being laid to re-open the College to cadets prior to the cessation of hostilities.

The Royal Military College Club of Canada, representing all Ex-Cadets, offers its services to you at any time you wish to call upon it for advice and experience.[7]

Canada had not yet begun to think about the postwar training of army officers, but in Britain a committee had been set up by the Army Council in January 1944 to study the problem of educating officers to meet the scientific and technical requirements that the present war had proved were now all important. It was headed by Dr. H. L. Guy,* a noted scientist and engineer. The Guy Committee reported in June in favour of a new "Imperial Military College" to produce cadets for the British and Indian armies. This college, if it had been accepted, would have been a combination of Woolwich, Sandhurst, and the Royal Military College of Science. The Guy Committee had considered an alternative plan of producing officers through the universities but had rejected it.[8]

When a copy of the Guy report reached Canada in February 1945, Major-General J. V. Young, the master-general of the ordnance (an ex-cadet), urged that a similar study should be made of Canadian needs. The

*Sir Henry Lewis Guy, C.B.E., F.R.S., D.SC., M.I.MECH.E., F.AM.SOC.M.E. (1887–1956); secretary of the (British) Institution of Mechanical Engineers, 1942–51.

Minister of National Defence, now General McNaughton, was in favour. But nothing could be done in detail until the government had decided what the establishments of the postwar army and the reserve army would be, and a policy had been drafted for Canada's postwar defence organization.[9]

In June the service chiefs presented proposals for a peacetime navy of 20,000 officers and men, an air force of 30,000, and an army of 55,000 to be raised by universal service, the whole to cost an estimated $290 million. The cabinet defence committee decided that firm estimates of the peacetime force were not yet possible but announced in the house in September that for immediate planning purposes figures of about half these strengths would be used. As this reduction fell most heavily on the army, the need for the introduction of universal military training was eliminated.[10] Despite this reduction, the war with Hitler had inspired revolutionary changes in the Canadian attitude to defence questions. As after 1918, the main instrument for preserving world peace was to be an international agency. But it was now generally agreed that the new agency, the United Nations Organization, must be adequately backed by the armed strength of member states and must not attempt to rely as heavily on moral pressure as the League had done. As a result of Canada's war experience, and because the Americans had sloughed off their traditional isolationism, the smaller country was ready and willing to maintain forces at least four times as large as in 1939 and to face the possibility that they might have to be used. Prime Minister Mackenzie King, whose personal predilection to avoid international implications or entangling ties had been largely responsible for Canada's prewar military ineffectiveness had been swept along by the tide of events. Canada's withdrawal of her occupation forces from occupied Germany in mid-1946 because she did not have the same status as other occupying powers was the last gasp of an old spirit. From 1947, when the cold war hardened, Canada began to face the realities of a dangerous world with a new determination to accept responsibilities and to maintain the force to meet them either through the UN or in co-operation with like-minded allies.

Greatly expanded forces would require more officers. When the war ended in both Europe and Asia, the re-opening of RMC was immediately raised in the House of Commons in September 1945. Lieutenant-General Charles Foulkes who had commanded the 1st Canadian Corps in Europe was now chief of the General Staff. He advised the new minister, Douglas C. Abbott,* to reply that RMC was currently being used for the training of

*The Honourable Douglas Charles Abbott, PC, (CAN), B.C.L., LL.D. (born 1899); minister of National Defence for Naval Services and minister of National Defence (army), 1954–6.

officers in staff duties, but that the army intended to resume the training of cadets in 1946 under conditions that were now under consideration.[11] It is noticeable that there was no assurance here that RMC would be re-opened as a cadet college. Nevertheless in October, General Foulkes told the chiefs of staff of the other two services that the re-establishment of RMC as a means of training cadets for their first appointments in the army was being considered. He recommended that a tri-service system of training should be considered.[12]

On 8 November Foulkes appointed a committee of eight army officers to consider arrangements for the provision of officers for the active force.[13] Its chairman was Brigadier L. M. Chesley,* an ex-cadet who had served in World War I, had returned to the army from a business career in 1939, and was now deputy chief of the General Staff. The Chesley committee also included three other ex-cadets: Brigadier G. P. Morrison,† Brigadier J. P. E. Bernatchez,‡ and Lieutenant-Colonel G. J. H. Watts-ford,§ as secretary. The navy and air force agreed to send representatives to sit with this committee and take part in its deliberations, though without any commitment to accept its recommendations. One of these, Wing-Commander F. R. Sharpe,‖ was an ex-cadet. Another was a former member of the RMC faculty, Dr. Percy Lowe,# at that time director of naval education. Some of the ex-cadet members of the committee had served in the militia before the war and others had gone directly into the Permanent Force. The committee and its associated members also included officers who had entered the Permanent Force through the universities or who had come from the British army and militia officers who

---

*Brigadier Leonard McEwan Chesley, O.B.E., E.D. (born 1898); war certificate RMC, 1917; RGA World War I; in business in Montreal, 1919–39; Directorate of Staff Duties, World War II; deputy CGS and director of Staff Duties, 1946–8.

†Brigadier George Power Morrison, C.B.E. (born 1895); war certificate RMC, 1915; RCA; CEF Siberia; Defence Research Board, Canadian Joint Staff, London, 1951–5.

‡Major-General J. Paul Emile Bernatchez, C.B.E., D.S.O., C.D., LL.D. (born 1911); graduated RMC, 1934; OC 3rd Royal 22nd Regiment; vice-CGS 1961–4; Colonel Royal 22nd, 1964.

§Brigadier George James Harrison Wattsford (born 1911); graduated RMC, 1933; Lord Strathcona's Horse.

‖Air Marshal Frederick Sharpe (born 1915); graduated RMC, 1933; RCAF; vice-chief of the Defence Staff from 1967 (as lieutenant-general).

#Commander Percy Lowe, M.A., PH.D. (1900–1959), governor-general's medal at Trinity College, Toronto; demonstrator in physics, University of Toronto. 1920–1; instructor in mathematics, RMC, 1921; instructor in signals, Queen's University COTC, 1939–42; instructor-lieutenant commander, RCN College, Royal Roads, 1942; director of Naval Education, Naval Service HQ, 1944; professor and head of mathematics department, RMC, 1948; chairman of the division of science, 1959; elected member of the Kingston Board of Education, 1956.

had graduated in a university and had followed a civilian career. It could thus claim that it had a "considerable variety of military and civil education and background."

The Chesley Committee was instructed to make recommendations about the provision of officers for the postwar active force, about the educational requirements of candidates, and about the way they should be trained. It was also "to consider and recommend the basis upon which the Royal Military College will be used in the post-war period." The chairman told the committee that it had been announced that RMC would re-open in September 1946. He added that it was necessary to ensure an adequate supply of French-speaking officers and that there should be arrangements for promotion from the ranks.

The committee met eight times, considered several different "plans," and listened to the opinions of fourteen different witnesses. Three plans were strongly favoured. Plan A proposed to eliminate RMC as a source of officers and to use the site for a two-year course for the military training of university graduates. Plan B proposed to enlarge RMC so that it could provide the total annual requirements of the active force, to make it free, and to impose on all its graduates (who would have received a course leading to a degree at a university) an obligation to serve in the active force. Plan C proposed to enlarge RMC to produce from 50 to 70 per cent of the officers needed by the army and to have a parallel officer training scheme in the universities to prepare the balance.

Most of the witnesses who appeared before the committee appear to have favoured the third, or mixed, plan, but there was some difference of opinion about whether officers trained at RMC should go on to take their degree at a university. Almost all agreed on the advantages of a cadet college training and were aware that it might be difficult to get the best quality graduates from the universities. However, Brigadier G. Walsh,* an ex-cadet who spoke for the Royal Canadian Engineers, emphasized that his corps needed a degree given by a recognized university. Conversely, Lieutenant-Colonel W. R. Sawyer, also an ex-cadet and a former member of the RMC faculty, suggested that RMC should itself "advance" to degree-granting status; he said that it should now be possible for the civil service to pay enough to attract the necessary staff.[14]

Meanwhile, after the first two sessions of the committee, General Foulkes had given further instructions to Brigadier Chesley. He said it

*Lieutenant-General Geoffrey G. Walsh, C.B.E., D.S.O., C.D., B.ENG. (born 1909); graduated RMC, 1930; Nova Scotia Technical College and McGill University; chief engineer First Canadian Army, 1944; CGS, 1961–4; vice-chief Canadian Defence Staff, 1964.

was not necessary to call the Army Commander, General Crerar, as a witness because he was overseas. The Chief of the General Staff suggested that Crerar's opinion could be ascertained by a single member of the committee. General Crerar, who had closed the college in 1942, might have been committed by his statements at that time to favour re-opening it, but as he was not called, his views on the question were not made known. The Chief of the General Staff made four other lengthy comments about the academic standards required of officers which leaned towards the adoption of a university plan: he said that if a mixed scheme were adopted, university graduates should be compensated in some way because the scales were "loaded against them"; he wanted to know what obligations would be imposed on RMC cadets if they were given a degree at the college; he deplored suggestions that the committee should discuss the production of reserve officers; and he said that the committee should make sure that its recommendations were feasible and practical, especially in regard to the capital cost of re-equipping the college and building the necessary new accommodation.[15]

The Chesley Committee began its report with an estimate of how many officers would be required. The total officer establishment had been settled at 2605 officers of all corps. Using prewar wastage rates the committee calculated that this meant an annual intake of 182 officers, but for planning purposes it decided to work on a basis of 150 per annum. It then proceeded to explore the cost of re-opening the college, the difficulties which would face the re-establishment of civil instruction there, and the advantages and disadvantages of a university as against a military college for the education of career officers. While it thought that there was much to be said for continuing RMC as a federal institution, throughout its discussions the committee was obviously concerned lest there might be opposition to re-opening it to train reserve officers. It could see the broadening effect of drawing officers from several sources but it argued that a common source would "obviate unfortunate suspicion that special advantages accrued to graduates from any particular source." The report stated that it was necessary that all technical officers should have a university degree and that it was desirable that all other officers should have one. It concluded that the ideal method of producing officers for the active force would be to give a complete military education in RMC with a university type course and degree to cadets who should be educated at public expense and should engage to serve after graduation. This would require a pre-RMC course for French-speaking cadets to make them fluent in English. But it calculated that the cost of such a plan, based on an establishment of six hundred cadets, would be $1,711,591 per annum and that the capital costs might run up to as much as $10 million. The cost of the pre-RMC course for French-speakers would be additional to this. Therefore the committee recommended a plan to produce all officers through the universities and to give them their military training at RMC after they had been provisionally commissioned. It stressed that RMC would have a "continuing function," as a postgraduate military training establishment for commissioned officers.[16]

On 15 February the Chairman of the committee was instructed by the Vice-Chief of the General Staff to co-operate with the deputy chief and director of military training to prepare a memorandum on officer training for him to submit to the minister. This memorandum was to propose "three phases" or parallel roads to a commission: from the universities through RMC; from high school through the universities and RMC including credits for Canadian Officer Training Centres [COTC] qualifications; and, for other ranks, by scholarships to the universities and RMC. Brigadier Chesley was specifically instructed that the memorandum which was to be drafted was not to include a four-year complete RMC plan.[17]

General Foulkes' plan for the provision of officers for the Canadian army was submitted to Defence Minister Abbott on 28 February, 1946. The Chief of the General Staff said that in order to get the highest possible competence in economic, political, and technical subjects, as well as in purely military matters, and in order to maintain homogeneity in the officer corps, regular army officers should almost all be educated in the universities. He had therefore asked Dr. James S. Thompson, the president of the University of Saskatchewan, and president of the National Conference of Canadian Universities, to show how the universities could give academic credits for certain subjects that had a military application. He suggested that by subsidizing the universities to give tuition in these subjects the officer establishment of the present University Officer Training Corps could be considerably reduced. He stated that the university portion of the new plan would cost only $900,000 as against the $917,300 that the COTC's now cost the country. He also anticipated that the new plan would attract a better type of student than the COTC.

The Chief of the General Staff proposed that officer-cadets should be paid as second lieutenants for training in three summer vacations. He said that the total cost of producing an officer by the new plan would be $9,995.25. This would include a six-month postgraduate military course at the Royal Military College. His calculation was based on the premise that there would be two thousand officer cadets in the four-year scheme in the universities from which one hundred and fifty officers (that is almost one-third of each annual class) would accept commissions in the army annually. General Foulkes proposed that up to 20 per cent of the required one hundred and fifty officers should be selected from the ranks and should go through the university scheme with the rest. These would receive tuition fees and their service pay throughout the academic year in addition to their pay during summer training. This "other ranks training plan" would cost $41,850, a sum which had been included in his calculation of the total cost of producing an officer. However, if the "other ranks" plan were subsidized by the canteen fund, the cost of producing an officer could be reduced to $9,649.64. Finally, Foulkes said that under the prewar system it had cost $31,291 to produce an officer at RMC and a further $2,580 to finance him to a university degree, a total cost of $33,871. He therefore claimed that his new university plan would produce the same result with a net saving of $24,221.36 per officer.[18]

Such drastic economy in the cost of officer training was bound to attract the interest of politicians faced with enormous problems of postwar reconstruction. Furthermore, the war had brought a general realization that the modern officer must have a better scientific preparation than had been traditional in earlier days, and a genuine case could be made for suggesting that this academic preparation could best be obtained in the well-established science and engineering faculties of the universities. There was also a widespread feeling that an officer should be more closely identified with the community as a whole and should not be part of an exclusive caste. Finally it was believed that every effort should be made to ensure that officers were selected and trained by a democratic process. The university plan with the "other ranks" scheme which had been built into it seemed to meet all these conditions.

However, there were hidden reasons for the decision not to restore RMC as an officer-producing unit. These stemmed from old antagonisms. In the 1920s and 1930s rivalry between the militia on the one hand and the Permanent Force on the other had been strengthened by the growth and greater efficiency of both elements. RMC had become more closely associated with the Permanent Force because of the increasing number of its graduates who had become career officers in Canada. The militia's attitude to the regular soldier, one of respect intermingled with envy and frustration, therefore tended to carry over to embrace the ex-cadet. During the war a new Canadian army had been built up largely with officers drawn from the militia but also with many more who came directly from civilian life in all parts of Canada. Most of these new officers had had little or no previous contact with each other. The much smaller number of RMC ex-cadets, whether former regular officers or not, had old associations and connections that set them apart. This served to strengthen their distinctiveness within the army. They became very conscious of their tradition and of their earlier military training and preparation for war.

A letter to Professor Bridger from an ex-cadet with the 5th Armoured Division reveals the strength of this not unnatural sentiment and of its ramifications. He wrote:

Here at the "Big Maroon Machine" we consider ourselves very much an R.M.C. Division. General Hoffmeister is not an ex-cadet, but all four brigadiers are: C.R.A. – Brig. J. S. Ross (2116), Brig. Cumberland (1769), Brig. Johnston (1855) and Brig. Lind (2016). Then there's Chips Drury (2382) as A & Q.; Jack Christian (2211) as C.R.E.; Harris Widdifield (2066) as O.C. Sigs.; John Sinclair (2482) as B.M.R.A.; Pete Hertzberg (2685) on the G. Staff, and myself as A.D.O.S. Up until a short while ago, too, the C.R.C.A.S.C. was "Sparky" J. L. Sparling (1760) and his brother Brig. H. A. (1878) was C.R.A. "Kits" Jordan (1858) has the G.G.H.G. while Bob Smallian (2362) and Bob Cameron (2563) had Field Squadrons R.C.E. until a few weeks ago.

From the Ordnance point of view, my cousin "J.A.W." (2703) holds forth as D.D.O.S. at Army H.Q.; Tony Townesend (2004) is A.D.O.S. Cdn. Sec. G.H.Q. 1 Echelon here and Fred Slater (2483) is A.D.O.S. at 1 Div. where he recently relieved "Joe" Lake (2398). ... Elliot Durnford (1526) is A.D.O.S. Army Trps.

While in Brussels a few weeks ago I was very surprised to run into Henri Emond [a member of the R.M.C. French department]. ... Luckily both Jack Christian and Chips appeared shortly and of course joined us. It is truly amazing the circumstances under which ex-cadets always seem to turn up. ... [signed] Bob Bennett, No. 2435.[19]

This letter tells something about the extent of an RMC oldboy network within the army overseas. Ex-cadets appeared to others to be an exclusive inner caste or clique and many brother officers felt that this was used to their advantage. Inevitably this special inner group aroused a jealous reaction. Beneath the acknowledged camaraderie of war there was a latent rivalry between those who had been at RMC and those who had not. At the same time the success of former militia officers who rose to high command strengthened the venerable myth that derived from a false interpretation of the War of 1812 that a reserve force officered by citizen soldiers had been historically the most appropriate means of providing for Canada's defence. Hence, although the desirability of a larger permanent force for the future was now generally accepted, the belief that a large reserve was needed persisted and had been strengthened by the experience of two great wars. The idea of obtaining the officers for the Permanent Force from the universities instead of from RMC was in some ways an extension of this old militia myth. Paradoxically the fact that RMC had also in the past been closely associated with the militia, to which slightly more than half of its graduates had gone, served to help to strengthen the case against it in a day when a permanent force was realized to be essential. It is also probable that some of the public hostility aroused by stories of abuses in "recruiting" lingered on. General Foulkes, who had come into the Permanent Force from the University of Western Ontario, had shown where his feeling lay in these old antagonisms when he told the Chesley committee that, within the army, the scales were loaded against a university-trained officer in a mixed plan.[20]

The Chief of the General Staff's recommendation to the Minister to eliminate RMC as a cadet college had been anticipated by efforts to secure its restoration. In December 1945, before the recommendation was made and perhaps before it was suspected, the Vancouver branch of the RMC Club held a reception for General Crerar. It invited government leaders, educationists, and prominent local citizens. In a later *R.M.C. Review* it claimed that this reception had "started the agitation for more publicity for the College."[21] Then, soon after the Chesley committee reported, and about six weeks before the Chief of the General Staff made his recommendation to the Minister, news of what was contemplated leaked out by the "grape vine." David W. MacKeen, the president of the RMC Club for that year, called a meeting of the executive in Kingston on 18 and 19 January which selected a deputation consisting of Brigadier D. G. Cunningham, until recently commandant at RMC and now back at his law practice in Kingston, Hugh Mackenzie,* and MacKeen himself, to interview the Minister. Their enquiries confirmed that the rumour about the proposal to eliminate RMC was substantially true.[22]

On 23 February an editorial in the Kingston *Whig-Standard* took note of a speech by Mr. Abbott in Toronto and of rumours that were circulating that RMC would not re-open. The newspaper argued that the record showed that in every past war RMC graduates had provided a substantial proportion of the officer material of high quality. It claimed that while most of Canada's officer strength during the last war had been provided by the militia and the wartime officer training centres, RMC graduates had had much to do with the success of those establishments. The *Whig-Standard* believed that Canada needed a fully trained officer cadre of professional soldier calibre in order to make wartime expansion possible and that this could best be supplied by RMC supplemented by the university COTCs. The paper admitted it had a local vested interest in RMC but it declared that it would have supported a military college for Canada wherever it happened to be situated.[23] On 19 March a new Kingston branch of the RMC Club was organized and immediately decided to circulate this

---

*Hugh Alexander Mackenzie, O.B.E., F.C.A. (1901–1963); graduated RMC, 1921 as BSM and governor-general's medallist; quarter-back Toronto Argonauts in the Grey Cup, 1921; an accountant, became general manager and vice-president of Labatt's Breweries, Ltd.; assistant to the chairman of the Wartime Prices and Trade Board; president, RMC Club, 1960.

editorial to other branches and to urge that all ex-cadets should write to their members of parliament.[24]

The action of the Kingston branch sparked the creation of special sub-committees in other branches. On 29 March Colonel S. H. Dobell,* the comptroller and executive assistant to the principal at McGill, who was chairman of the Montreal subcommittee, approached the Minister personally and was given information which suggested to him that the figures which the Chief of the General Staff used were open to question. Colonel Dobell secured a promise that no announcement would be made about the future of RMC until the ex-cadet club had had time to make further enquiries and further representations. A special committee of the club executive formed from the six branches closest to Ottawa was authorized to take whatever steps it considered necessary. Its members were Major-General Young, Brigadier Cunningham, Colonel Dobell, Lieutenant-Colonel Nicol Kingsmill, Hugh Mackenzie, Lieutenant-Colonel J. Douglas Watt,** and Captain E. W. Crowe. Colonel Dobell was appointed chairman and Colonel Watt secretary.

The special committee made plans for a wide publicity campaign to be launched at short notice if one became necessary, but at the same time Captain Crowe obtained information in Kingston to enable the committee to draw up its own estimate of the cost of re-opening the college. This work confirmed Colonel Dobell's earlier impression that the figures about the cost of officer training which General Foulkes had given the Minister were very wide of the mark. When he saw Mr. Abbott again and told him the committee's estimate, the Minister, without necessarily accepting the revised figures, was sufficiently impressed to agree to hold up his announcement about the university training plan until the RMC Club's special committee had had an opportunity to meet him and his advisers in Ottawa. He also accepted the committee's proposal that, to save time, it should first talk with the Chief of the General Staff.

The RMC Club committee met in Ottawa on 2 April and decided to urge the re-opening of the college. Convinced that if the facts were considered by responsible, impartial, and public-spirited citizens, its case would be accepted, the committee proposed to suggest that educationists and other civilians should be consulted. To obtain the necessary information on which to make a case, it planned to ask for help from National Defence

*Colonel Sidney Hope Dobell, D.S.O., LL.D., C.A. (born 1900); war certificate RMC, 1918; RFA; CFA France; McGill COTC; CO 6th Field Regiment, RCA, 1942; comptroller, McGill University, 1947; President, RMC Club, 1947.

†Lieutenant-Colonel James Douglas Watt, O.B.E., K.C., E.D. (1903–1951); graduated RMC, 1925; a lawyer; CO 6th Light Anti-Aircraft Regiment, World War II; prosecutor in war crimes trials; president, RMC Club, 1950–1.

Headquarters. The next day the club's committee met with General Foulkes, the Vice Chief, and his two deputies. The discussions lasted all day. Ultimately the Chief of the General Staff agreed to join with the RMC Club special committee in recommending to the Minister the appointment of a committee that would include non-military specialists. The chairman of the committee, appointed by the Minister, was Brigadier Sherwood Lett,* a lawyer who had served overseas in both wars. The other members were Brigadier S. F. Clarke,† representing NDHQ, with Colonel D. Ménard as his alternate; Dr. W. A. Mackintosh, head of the economics department (and future principal) of Queen's, presently special adviser to the deputy minister of Finance, representing the minister of Finance; Dr. James S. Thompson and Abbé Arthur Maheux, archivist of Laval University, for the National Conference of Canadian Universities, with Dr. Sidney Smith as alternate; Dr. O. M. Solandt, the director general of defence research; and Lieutenant-Colonel W. F. Hadley, the chairman of the Conference of Defence Associations. The RMC Club's representative was Lieutenant-Colonel J. Douglas Watt, K.C., who, against his expressed wish, was retained by the club on a professional basis so that he could give the fullest possible time to the committee's business.

At the time of its interview with the Chief of the General Staff, the RMC Club's committee had been given copies of the Chesley report and of the Chief's recommendations to the Minister. A quick examination convinced its members that the figures in them were quite inaccurate. However, as the Lett Committee was to meet on 20 May, Colonel Dobell's committee decided that it would not have time to present a full brief at the outset. It therefore circulated to the members of the Lett Committee a preliminary statement of its views and when the committee met on 20 and 21 May, Colonel Watt pressed that it should not act hastily but should meet a month later to hear prepared statements and witnesses. After "considerable argument" the Lett Committee agreed to this procedure. The RMC Club's special committee thus gained time to prepare a brief to present at the postponed session.[25]

The club had been promised the fullest possible co-operation at National Defence Headquarters for the collection of the figures and information necessary for the presentation of its case. However, the special committee found that many of the officers it approached, apparently because they were aware that they held opinions that differed from those

---

*Brigadier Sherwood Lett, C.B.E., D.S.O., E.D., LL.D. (1895–1964); deputy CGS, 1947–8.

†Major-General Samuel Findlay Clarke, C.B.E. (1909–1968); deputy CGS, 1945–7; CGS, 1958–61; general manager, Independent Coal and Coke Co.

of their Chief, were reluctant to discuss the principles involved or to provide information about costs.[26] Furthermore the time which had been allowed for the preparation of the brief was realized to be too short. Therefore Colonel Dobell and his committee decided not to attempt to prepare a complete plan for re-opening RMC which might be easily refuted on the grounds that it was misinformed, but rather to concentrate on an examination and criticism of the proposals that had already been made. They also decided that it would be poor policy to give an impression of "indulging in mere destructive criticism of the military authorities." They determined that their brief should be couched in moderate and restrained language.[27]

The brief presented to the Lett Committee on behalf of the club was over forty pages long. It included two appendices and a table of costs. Despite the voluntary self-restraint of the committee members, it was quite outspoken. It stated that the report of the Chesley Committee, which it pointedly called "the Military Committee," contained "so many errors of fact, of inference, and of omission, that we cannot believe that its authors were free to bring in a factual objective recommendation. ... On the contrary, we are forced to the conclusion that they were required by higher authority to work backwards from a pre-decided recommendation, which they then had to endeavour to substantiate and justify."[28] It said that the Chesley Committee's report contained so many inaccuracies that the RMC Committee had come to the conclusion that those who prepared it had never expected that it would be subject to investigation. The recommendation made by the Chief of the General Staff to the Minister was declared to be equally inaccurate and the RMC Club critics warned that it ought to be "taken with the very greatest reserve."[29]

The club's brief argued that the university plan would not work. It said that the plan could not be applied uniformly to all universities because of differences between them. It would therefore be politically unsound. The brief stated that in the recommendation made by the Chief of the General Staff the annual cost of the university plan had been understated by one and one-half million dollars because he had failed to include the costs of summer training, summer pay, transportation, the pay of the military training staff at the universities, and the cost of the administration of the programme at headquarters. The brief declared that Canadian military history showed the value of reserve forces but that the atmosphere in the universities had often been antagonistic to the armed forces; therefore they might not produce enough career officers. Also university students often took summer employment to complement their winter term work and many would be loath to go to the three summer camps required in the new scheme. As the university plan would not require a commitment to service before graduation, there was no evidence that the required number of officers would be forthcoming. The brief noted that the Chesley Committee had expressly said that the scheme might not be successful.

It went on to say that 44 per cent of RMC's graduates in prewar years had become regular officers and the remainder had helped to train the reserve forces. RMC would also provide a permanent officer-training system that would resist waves of pacifism and could survive economic depression. By contrast the university scheme was a paper scheme that could be destroyed overnight by those in power. Colonel Dobell's committee then challenged the military committee or the Chief of the General Staff to prove that graduates from RMC had obtained special advantages in the service. It said that to suggest that promotion had been on any other basis than ability and training was to indict the army's High Command. It claimed that the reason why RMC ex-cadets did well in the service was because the RMC cadet had had a better training at an early stage in his career. Finally, it stated that the university plan was the most expensive scheme of the three that had been proposed. An RMC confined like West Point to cadets with a precommitment to the service would be the least expensive method of producing officers. However, for political reasons, and to minimize or postpone capital costs, it recommended a combined plan using both RMC and the universities.[30]

The Lett Committee sat again on 25, 26, and 27 June 1946 to consider the club's brief and other briefs and evidence. Principal Wallace of Queen's University, who was called as a witness, professed doubts about the willingness of universities to grant academic credit for military subjects in the manner postulated in the university plan. He stated that "the Royal Military College was an institution which had proved its worth, and that, therefore, we must have very good reason before it is removed." At a later session, Brigadier Clarke said that, as the Lett committee had agreed with the Chesley Committee that the degree standard was necessary for all officers, "it was now only a matter of confidence as to whether or not we could get sufficient annually from universities or whether it would be necessary, in addition, to re-open RMC to ensure the required intake." However, the committee as a whole, with good reason, was impressed by Brigadier Cunningham's reminder that the university scheme was "experimental." It came to the conclusion that although it believed that a mixed plan would be more expensive than reliance only on the universities, it would recommend the re-opening of RMC along with the university scheme.[31]

Shortly after reading the Lett Committee's report the Minister told the members of the RMC Club's special committee that he would make his decision and implement it as soon as he could obtain all the information necessary for a recommendation to the cabinet. Colonel Dobell believed that Mr. Abbott made up his mind on the subject early in the fall, but for some months, owing to pressure of other cabinet business, he was unable to make a public pronouncement. When he was pressed on the subject, he authorized the RMC Club to announce at its annual dinner on 21 November the good news that the cadet college would be re-opened in September 1947.

Soon afterwards there were rumours of a cabinet shuffle, but Mr. Abbott reassured Colonel Dobell that if he did leave the defence post his successor would re-open the college. However, the changes that ensued involved much more than a mere change of minister. The government had decided to move towards close integration of the three defence ministries and the armed forces. Brooke Claxton,* who succeeded Douglas Abbott, was made responsible for all three services, and not just for two services (Abbott had held separate portfolios for defence and navy. Colonel the Honourable Colin W. G. Gibson, an ex-cadet, was minister of national defence for air until 1945–6.) Furthermore the government had decided that the defence estimates were to be greatly reduced. The annual intake of one hundred and fifty army officers, on which all planning had been based, was thus clearly now too high. On the other hand, there was public pressure for the closer integration of the services because it was believed that the past war had demonstrated the need for more preparation for combined operations than had been customary before 1939. Although these ideas seemed visionary to many military men who were used to three separate services, serious study had to be given to their implications for officer education and training. Therefore the Dobell Committee, although it kept in touch with Mr. Claxton, did not press him to issue the public pronouncement about re-opening which had been promised.[32]

Allan Mitchell, the former president of the club who had begun to press for arrangements to re-open back in 1942 when the college closed, was on first-name terms with the new minister. As a result in April 1947, he was able to secure from him the following statement of the government's intentions: "We aim to extend Royal Roads so as to cover Air Cadets in September 1947 and probably will extend its scope so as to cover Army as well in 1948. While this is indefinite yet, it is our present intention to re-open RMC in September 1948 as a college to prepare officer personnel on the same footing as Royal Roads, with senior matriculation as entrance

*Brooke Claxton, PC (Can), DCM, QC, LL.D. (1898–1960); minister of National Defence, 1946–54.

and probably a three-year course equivalent to two years at the university, though the details are not yet worked out. Of course this plan may have to be changed, but it is my hope that it will be possible to carry it out."[33]

HMCS *Royal Roads*, which Mr. Claxton proposed should become a tri-service cadet college, had been set up by the navy during the war. Unlike the army, the RCN had had almost no regular and reserve officers at the beginning of the war to be the nucleus of the vastly expanded service that war required. The Royal Naval College of Canada had been established at Halifax in 1911 and had been housed briefly at RMC after the explosion in 1917. It had then moved on to Vancouver Island but had been closed for economy reasons within five years. Senior officers were aware that the problem of producing officers was acute, and were determined to prevent prewar conditions from recurring. Therefore they planned not only for immediate war needs but also for postwar requirements.

On 28 August 1940 the Director of Naval Personnel, Captain H. T. W. Grant, brought Professor L. N. Richardson, the senior professor at RMC who had served throughout the life of the former Royal Naval College of Canada, to meet the Minister of Defence for the Navy, Angus L. Macdonald,* in order to discuss plans for training naval officers. The Minister was told that a permanent naval college could train officers for the merchant marine as well as for the navy. He was therefore willing to consider something of longer duration than the short wartime courses that were then being used to produce officers. He also accepted as logical the idea that Canada should not send its naval cadets for their preliminary training to England but should produce its own officers following the pattern of the Royal Navy. The three men were agreed that the educational standard at RMC was good but they all felt that for naval cadets a naval atmosphere was important. They thought that the reasons why the former naval college had been costly were that the number of cadets it trained was small. The larger numbers now expected in the new college would reduce the cost. There was thus a general agreement that a new naval college should be established in Canada.[34]

Following this meeting, Captain L. W. Murray, RCN† and Professor Richardson visited Annapolis. They found that the US Naval Academy system was not suitable for Canada because the numbers there were much larger and because American policy was to complete cadet training before sea service. They believed that the superintendent of the academy actually

*Angus Lewis Macdonald, PC (Can), K.C., B.A., LL.B., S.J.D., LL.D. (1890–1954); minister of Defence for Naval Services, 1940–5.

†Rear-Admiral Leonard Warren Murray, C.B., C.B.E., RCN (born 1896), deputy chief of the Naval Staff; later commander-in-chief Canadian North-West Atlantic Command.

preferred the British system of bringing junior officers back from sea for a "post-graduate course." Professor Richardson added that the course at Annapolis also differed from the British system because it lacked specialization. Therefore Captain Murray proposed that, after preliminary college training in Canada in a college which should be re-established in British Columbia because its weather was milder in winter, RCN cadets should serve at sea and then should take the Royal Navy's acting sub-lieutenant course at Greenwich. He thought that until the war ended the Canadian course should be two years. Thereafter it should be three years.[35]

On 19 March 1941, Captain Grant, noting that $150,000 had been put in the naval estimates for the purpose, asked the Director of the Canadian Naval Service to call a meeting to decide what steps were to be taken to open the naval college by autumn.[36] Two weeks later he summarized the arguments for and against a college. If Canadian youngsters wanted to become naval officers now, they had to go to Dartmouth in England. The new plan would keep them out of the war zone, and would also give a longer academic education than the English college. The navy staff officers had recommended a two-year course, with entry age from fifteen to seventeen, but Grant opposed the use of HMCS *Royal Roads* for this purpose because it was now employed for wartime courses.[37]

HMCS *Royal Roads* near Esquimault on Vancouver Island had been commissioned on 13 December 1940 to meet the need for officers for the corvettes which Canada operated in large numbers on Atlantic anti-submarine duties. The name was taken from a body of water which was an anchorage well known to mariners in the age of sail because it was a sheltered place where ships could ride out storms in safety. The RCN had acquired a stately mansion overlooking the Royal Roads called Hatley Park; it had formerly been the residence of the Honourable James Dunsmuir, a premier and lieutenant-governor of British Columbia.[38] With a substantial house, magnificent grounds, and good safe sailing for small boats in all seasons close at hand, HMCS *Royal Roads* was an admirable place for training naval officers.

Despite Captain Grant's caveat, the war committee of the cabinet approved the establishment of a permanent Royal Canadian Naval College at HMCS *Royal Roads*. On 10 December the Treasury Board recommended that it should open in the fall of 1942, that the total number of cadets accommodated should be one hundred, that the course should be one, two, or three years according to conditions prevailing at the time, and that the cadets should be under naval discipline. Captain J. M. Grant, RCN,* was

*Captain John Moreau Grant, RCN, commanding officer *H.M.C.S. Royal Roads*, 1940–4.

named commandant. Professors Lorne A. Brown* and Clarence C. Cook,† former members of the RMC faculty, went as lieutenant-commanders to head the departments of mathematics and physics respectively. Lieutenant-Commander W. M. Ogle,‡ who had been an instructor in modern languages and history at RMC (1931–2), was director of studies.

It had originally been proposed that entry to the naval college should be at junior matriculation level with senior matriculation in mathematics, physics or chemistry, or English,[39] but when the college was formed it was decided to use a special entrance examination at approximately junior matriculation level and to interview all candidates. Royal Roads trained cadets for the executive branch, the engineer branch, and the accountant branch of the RCN and the course was to be for two years in both war and peace.[40] The navy would offer regular commissions to as many college graduates as it required and the remainder would be under an obligation to join either the RCN reserve or the RCNVR.[41] Thus the RCN, as RMC ex-cadets noted wryly, planned carefully for postwar officer production at the very time when the army closed its military college in circumstances that seemed to suggest that the closure might be permanent.

The prewar RCAF, like the RCN, had no large pool of officers from which to expand its forces for war purposes. The British Commonwealth Air Training Plan had solved its immediate problem, but when the war came to an end it, too, was anxious to find a means of training officers for the larger peacetime air force that it confidently expected Canada would maintain. When Air Marshal Robert Leckie,§ the chief of the Air Staff, found that the Chief of the Naval Staff, Admiral G. C. Jones,‖ believed that the future of Royal Roads was in doubt, the two men discussed the possibility of joining forces to attempt to keep the RCN college in existence for use by both services.

Leckie argued that the requirements of the two services were not dissimilar. He said that both required a large proportion of their regular service officers to have an educational standing approximately of the level

*Lorne Alexander Brown, M.A. (born 1893); associate professor of mathematics RMC, 1921–42; instructor commander, Royal Roads, 1942–8, director of studies, Royal Roads, 1948–54.

†Clarence Cecil Cook, M.SC. (born 1894); instructor in physics, RMC, 1924–42; instructor-commander, Royal Roads, 1942–8; director of studies, Royal Roads, 1954–61.

‡Lieutenant-Commander William M. Ogle, M.A., instructor-commander, Royal Roads, 1941; director of studies, 1945.

§Air Marshal Robert Leckie, C.B., D.S.O. (born 1899); a graduate of the Curtiss flying school; destroyed two zeppelins during World War I; transferred from RAF to RCAF as director of Training, 1940; CAS 1944.

‖Admiral George Clarence Jones, C.B.; chief of the Naval Staff, 1944–6.

of senior matriculation in Ontario and to enter about the age of eighteen or nineteen. He said that basic training in the two services did not differ radically, especially as many naval cadets were now entering the fleet air arm. He said that the RCAF had in mind a college which, "while not perhaps equivalent of a university education in all subjects," would give specialized service education in selected subjects.[42]

The proposal for joint use of Royal Roads was approved in principle by the Minister of Defence for Naval Affairs early in 1946 and, in order to permit an announcement to be made to parliament in the fall, officers of both services were set to work out details. The chief difficulty was that the air force wanted the entry level to the college to be senior matriculation while the navy contended that its special examination, which was at a lower level, had proved very satisfactory.[43] The Deputy Chief of the Naval Service had argued that to wait until boys had obtained their senior matriculation would mean that the college would lose students to the universities.[44] Nevertheless, the RCAF stuck to its guns. It believed that the naval college had been inadequately advertised and that the number of applicants from which it had selected its cadets was "hopelessly inadequate" for RCAF purposes.[45] It therefore wanted to eliminate the special entrance examination so that the college could draw more widely on the school population, and it refused to be moved by naval arguments that the provincial standards differed and that without a special examination the selection of cadets would be open to political pressures.[46]

The Naval Commandant of Royal Roads favoured the use of the senior matriculation examination.[47] Dr. Percy Lowe, the director of naval education, who strongly preferred special examinations to the use of the provincial matriculation results because the former would cut down wastage, pointed out that advancing scientific standards might eventually mean that naval officers must be educated to the level of two years after senior matriculation or three years after junior.[48] The RCAF also learned that although graduation from the Royal Roads two-year course was considered equivalent only to one year at university, a good percentage of the RCN cadets had already obtained their senior matriculation before coming to the college.[49] Furthermore it noted that the Canadian army was considering a three-year course at RMC equal to three years at a university and a degree for its officers, that the United States army and navy both had four-year courses, that the RCN had a programme of activities at the universities during the scholastic years, and that the RAF was said to be contemplating making Cranwell a three-year course with a degree standard.

By all these standards Royal Roads was academically inferior. A brief on RCAF policy training (stated to be a "trend of thought" not in line with "present plans") dated 15 November 1946 suggested that, if the air force college was established at Royal Roads, it should have a four-year course equal to a university course; otherwise, the plan should be dropped and the RCAF should turn to the universities for its officers. However, this "trend of thought" had come too late and was marked by W. A. Curtis,* Air Member of the Air Staff, "the die is now cast."[50] The RCAF had adopted an entrance examination in English and mathematics at the senior matriculation level and the navy had to accept this because the only alternative that the RCAF would consider was the full senior matriculation standard.[51] On 21 January 1947, the Minister for National Defence, Mr. Claxton, recommended to the cabinet, the re-establishment of the RCN college at Royal Roads so that in the interests of economy it could also train officers for the RCAF. It would be supervised by a board of governors which would include senior officers of both interested services. It would be known as HMCS *Royal Roads* (the RCN-RCAF College).[52]

Mr. Claxton had agreed to the establishment of the RCN-RCAF College as a first step towards carrying out the government's desire to foster inter-service co-operation by giving the officers of all the three services, "as far as is humanly possible ... much the same general education ... the same environmental influences during part at least of their training ... and [the opportunity to] get to know each other and know about the work of the other Services."[53] He next set up an interservice committee to advise how this aim could best be put into effect on a permanent basis. This committee was instructed to work towards a joint system of officer training to come into effect by September 1948. The members of the committee, although representing the different services, were expected to look at the problem not so much from the point of view of their own service as "with [a] regard to the defence needs of Canada as a whole." They were to investigate the educational requirements of each service, the qualifications for entrance to Royal Roads and RMC, the length of the course or courses, the proportion of practical training to be included in the curriculum, policy in regard to fees, scholarships, payment for cadets entered from the ranks, the rank that should be granted in each service on graduation, and the need for further professional or academic education after graduation. The committee was also instructed to co-ordinate its recommendations with existing schemes for training officers in the universities and from the ranks.

*Air Marshal Wilfred Austin Curtis, C.B., C.B.E., D.S.C., E.D., LL.D. (born 1893); World War I fighter-pilot, RNAS; deputy commander-in-chief RCAF HQ overseas, 1941–4; CAS, 1947–53.

Mr. Claxton asked a retired senior air force officer, Air Vice-Marshal E. W. Stedman,* to take the chair. He told Stedman that if the committee became deadlocked because of differences of opinions between the services on any important matter, this should at once be reported to him so that he could discuss the point at issue with either the chairman or with the committee. Claxton also gave the chairman his own views. He believed that modern war required staff officers, training officers, and senior executive officers with educational standards that would enable them to deal not only with extraordinary weapons systems but also with scientific and other technical personnel; that the officers of the three services should have attained equal educational levels; and that officers who came from the universities or the ranks should be on the same footing as those from cadet colleges.[54]

The members of the Stedman Committee were Commodore G. R. Miles and Commander Percy Lowe from the RCN, Brigadier S. F. Clarke and Colonel W. R. Sawyer from the army, and Air Commodore D. M. Smith and Group-Captain R. C. Ripley from the RCAF. After five meetings, although the committee had reached a general agreement that technical officers on all three services should have a university degree or higher qualification, it could not agree on the qualifications for non-technical officers. The army was adamant that all officers must reach the degree standard. The navy and air force, anxious to get their young executive and air crew officers to sea and in the air as soon as possible, were satisfied with the present system of two years at Royal Roads with, in the case of naval officers, a subsequent postsea course at Greenwich. Stedman duly reported this disagreement to the Minister and was instructed to produce two alternative plans supported by "as near unanimity as possible," one for the education of all officers in all three services to a degree standard either at commissioning or later, and a second on the assumption that something short of the degree requirement would suffice in the case of non-technical officers.[55]

Accordingly the Stedman Committee submitted on interim report on 26 June which stated that the degree standard could be reached in the navy by a year at university after completion of training to lieutenant rank, in the army by four years at RMC, and in the air force by four years at RMC which would involve some loss of air crew training. If a standard set at one year short of the degree were adopted, the navy would be satisfied with the present arrangement; but a three-year course at RMC would not meet the army's minimum requirements, and the RCAF would still find that cadet

*Air Vice-Marshal Ernest Walter Stedman, C.B., O.B.E. (born 1898), director-general of air research, RCAF, 1941–6.

training cut seriously into flying training. The interim report therefore recommended that RMC should be re-opened on a four-year, three-service basis in September 1948 but that Royal Roads should continue for the present to take two-year cadets for the RCAF and the RCN (and not for the army) until further study had been made of educational requirements.[56]

General Foulkes saw at once what the result would be. He declared that it was "utter stupidity" to imagine that a naval or air force cadet would take a four-year course at RMC if he could get a commission in two years through Royal Roads. He said he was prepared to accept a three-year course at RMC, if that was all that was possible, provided the system was uniform for all services, and even though this would mean that technical officers would have to go on to a university for two more years. But he declared that the other two services were thinking only of their immediate requirement for junior officers and not enough about future requirements for senior officers capable of controlling combined operations for whom a much higher standard of academic education was needed. He declared that he also felt that the naval belief that officers must go to England to be trained was a serious indictment of the efficiency of Canada's "armed forces" and out of line with the probability that future co-operation would be more with the United States than with the United Kingdom. In his opinion it was bad policy to bring officers back to academic work after they had been four or five years away from it when it might have become hard for them to pick up the threads again.[57] Since the naval course at Greenwich conferred no academic standing, the Chief of the General Staff had shrewdly put his finger on a weakness in the RCN case. The plain fact was that the navy was unwilling to admit the need for improving the formal academic preparation of its officers because it placed major emphasis on sea service.

The RCAF, however, had different grounds for its stand. It was less bound by tradition than the navy. It was also ambitious to produce officers sufficiently highly qualified to command the combined operations expected in the future. Being already equipped with a system of short service commissions to provide many of the junior officers it needed for operations, its defence of the two-year course had been out of line with its real interest and may have been motivated more by the desire to adhere to the recent agreement made with the RCN to share Royal Roads than by a real appreciation of its own service needs. Stedman suggested to the RCAF members of his committee that their main consideration should be to plan for the man who would still be in the service twenty years from the present time.[58]

Meanwhile a subcommittee of the Stedman Committee had made recommendations about the opening of RMC in 1948 in conjunction with Royal

Roads. These were studied by another interservice committee chaired by Air Vice-Marshal W. A. Curtis, who had been appointed to consider the executive action that was now necessary. Subject to revision of the findings of the Stedman Committee in its final report, the Curtis Committee recommended to the Minister as follows: entrance should be by senior matriculation; there should be two qualifying examinations in English or French and mathematics; 50 per cent of the entrants should be selected in order of merit on provincial quotas determined by population and the remainder in open competition; the basis for selection should be on the results of the qualifying examination and matriculation examinations, a personal interview, and a medical examination; both colleges should require the payment of fees and should prepare for regular or reserve service at the option of the cadet except in the case of those selected from the ranks; the academic year should coincide with that of the universities thus leaving the summer for service training; the four-year curriculum proposed by the army should be accepted; technical officers in all services should attend for four years and should be sent for a further year to university at public expense to obtain the degree required; army officers in non-technical branches should attend for four years; army officers and technical officers for the RCAF and for the RCN who started at Royal Roads (other than those selected for training by the RN at Keyham) should transfer to RMC to complete the four-year cadet course; every effort should be made to obtain an academic staff of the highest calibre because the success of RMC would depend upon it; and Royal Roads should continue on its present plan for the intake of 1948.[59]

This Curtis plan was substantially that followed in September 1948 but with two important revisions. Royal Roads was brought into line at the outset and was not allowed to continue temporarily on its old basis after RMC was re-opened, and by October 1947 the RCAF had reversed its stand on the length of the course and had decided that all applicants for its long service commissions must take the four-year course.[60] This change came after the RCAF had circularized the universities and discovered that Royal Roads graduates could get no "blanket credit" on transfer to the universities, but only senior matriculation plus individual subjects in the first year for cadets with high standing. The higher academic level that had come with the creation of the RCN-RCAF College would therefore necessitate a campaign for a reappraisal of the college's status.[61] RMC's former reputation and revised course would more easily obtain the credit status that the air force wanted. The airmen had also realized that their scheme of direct entrance for short service commissions could satisfy most of their needs for junior officers. The Chief of the Air Staff's (CAS) conference therefore decided that, as there would be four long summer vacations for flying training including that after graduation at RMC, air crew could qualify from the Canadian services colleges. The air force henceforward adopted the army's proposals for the four-year course.[62]

The Stedman Committee was able to sum up all these developments in its report to the Minister on 20 November 1947 when it recommended that the Canadian services colleges' courses should be equivalent, year for year, with university courses in combined arts and engineering. It suggested that RMC should have a four-year course which could start at either college for cadets of all services except for certain naval cadets. Naval cadets, except those in the electrical and ordnance branches, would be entered only at Royal Roads. RMC should be ready to take Royal Roads graduates into its third year by 1950.[63]

The Stedman Committee had noted that there was no possibility of Canada having a third military college. The question of rotation of command and of other appointments between the services thus became important. As the RCN insisted that Royal Roads must remain HMCS *Royal Roads* (a claim which was eliminated in 1949 when the Minister ruled that the college was not a ship), the CAS on 9 February 1948 decided to withdraw his consent to the appointment of the next commandant from the navy. He demanded that rotation be put into immediate operation. He also insisted that the director of military studies and the senior administrative officer should be rotated; but he agreed that the director of academic studies must be the best man available and could therefore be a civilian. When this was discussed by the CAS conference, it was agreed that as the director of studies at the colleges might be a civilian, he should not be vice-commandant and second-in-command.[64]

The RMC director of studies' position was strengthened by the nature of the faculty that was to be recruited. As the postwar plan for officers required a university standard of education, it was necessary that the faculty should be equivalent to that of a university. But there was an acute shortage of qualified professors in the country, and it was thus especially important that the salaries offered should be competitive. A submission to the cabinet requesting a suitable salary scale noted that the present scale was twenty years old, that the nature of the course had changed, and that the number of students would be doubled. The new course was a four-year university course with options in arts, commerce, and engineering. The arts course, which included some science and engineering, would reach a degree standard. The engineering course would be equal to the first four years of a five-year engineering course. It was also intended eventually to give graduate courses at RMC. The submission noted: "The pre-war Royal

Military College was operated more like a high school than a university."
The reference here was not to the quality of the staff or of the instruction
that it imparted but to lack of specialization in teaching, to insufficient
incentive (apart from sporadic efforts) to research, and to an administration that was more centralized and autocratic than that of a university.
However, it should be noted that many Canadian universities in the 1920s
and 1930s suffered from one or more of these faults and that only a few
of them had succeeded in eradicating all of them before World War II.
To attract staff to replace that which had been scattered in 1942 and to
bring it up to the required number, it was necessary to establish the college
as a first class seat of learning, "equal in all respects to our leading universities." This meant that there must be facilities for the staff to do
research.[65]

The academic excellence of RMC was safeguarded by a system of organization devised by Brigadier Agnew and recommended by Brigadier
Megill, the army member of the Stedman Committee, which was opposed
by both the other services. The director of studies was to be vice-commandant and the command of the cadet battalion was to be exercised by
the commandant personally and not by another officer appointed specifically for this purpose. But this system was to be set up only at RMC
because it alone gave a four-year course. The director of studies was to
co-ordinate the military and academic training at RMC and the aim was to
ensure that there were not two competing staffs but just "one staff." The
director of studies was to represent RMC at the National Conference of
Canadian Universities, in which RMC held membership from prewar days,
and it was understood that the conference would accept him as the equivalent of a vice-principal. RMC routine orders were to be issued by the staff-
adjutant.[66] But the Chief of the General Staff could see no reason for
sending a lieutenant-colonel to command the cadet battalion at RMC when
the course was only 15 per cent military in content, when the battalion was
only one hundred strong, and when there would be three company commanders, one from each service, with the rank of major or its equivalent.[67]
(These officers also doubled as service staff officers and as associate professors of military studies.) The result was that the status of the director
of studies at Kingston was automatically enhanced. It is clear that this
structure (which was modified a few years later in so far as the command
of the cadet wing was concerned) was established in order to give the
fullest possible influence in the college to the first postwar director of
studies, Colonel Sawyer, who had been closely involved in the planning of
the curriculum and whose academic status and military rank permitted him
to perform the dual role.

The permanence of the director of studies, as compared with the transitory tenure of commandants, increased his importance and also helped to strengthen the academic side of the college. This was furthered by the introduction of a new staff member, the registrar, to keep academic records formerly maintained by the staff-adjutant and to administer the academic programme. The college thus became more like a university in its organization and the transfer of credits was facilitated. The first registrar was a former RMC professor, Lieutenant-Colonel T. F. Gelley.

Several lesser problems were also settled. Royal Roads changed its title from the RCN-RCAF College to the Canadian Services College, Royal Roads, on 29 July 1948; but the Curtis subcommittee had recommended that the Royal Military College of Canada should retain its historic name because the word "military" did not pertain solely to the army.[68] The question of a uniform for the cadets provoked some discussion. The navy wanted to introduce the service uniform as soon as possible, but the air force was willing to adopt a "neutral" uniform.[69] Some individuals, whose opinion was solicited, produced unusual suggestions. Thus General Simonds, the former GOC of the 2nd Canadian Corps, who was now at the Imperial Defence College in London, proposed a mixture of the uniforms of the three services.[70] The uniform that was adopted was the old RMC blue undress jacket, a blue battledress, and a blue field service cap. This was to be used at both colleges. Finally it was decided that the word "battalion" should give way to the word "wing" to describe the cadet body and "battalion-sergeant major" to "cadet wing commander" to identify its senior cadet officers. Subunits and ranks would be renamed with "neutral" titles to recognize the college's tri-service composition. A picturesque naval touch was added by the use of the boatswain's pipe in place of the bugle to call cadets to parade.

Finally, the accommodation necessary for the restored cadet college was provided by transferring the Canadian Army Staff College and the new National Defence College to the old RCHA depot at Tête-de-Pont barracks which had been renamed Fort Frontenac in the 1930s in recognition of an historic French past. General Whiteley became commandant at Fort Frontenac and the two senior colleges began to move, somewhat reluctantly, to less spacious quarters. In 1947 Brigadier D. R. Agnew, the first commandant of the restored RMC, arrived in Kingston with instructions to prepare for the re-opening in September of the following year.

14

THE CANADIAN SERVICES
COLLEGES
1948-1962

Brigadier D. R. Agnew was well suited for his task. Even before his cadet days he had learned from relatives and friends about RMC's traditions. Because of World War I his course was truncated and he went straight from the college to the front. As a result he was ever afterwards conscious of the advantages of the full peacetime course that he had missed. Experience on the staff in the 'thirties gave him insight into the development of the college since the war and also an appreciation of its potential. He was aware that the break with the past, which threatened ancient traditions, could be used to eliminate what was undesirable and to introduce necessary innovations. Finally, he knew that he had to do over again what Hewett had done successfully in 1875, namely lay the foundations for great future development.

One hundred recruits reported to RMC on 8 September 1948. Struck by the parallel with 1876 and the Old Eighteen, Agnew called them "The New Hundred." By the time of the official opening ceremonies on 20 September, although they had not yet been fitted out with uniforms but wore blazers and flannels, Regimental Sergeant-Major C. C. Coggins, a prewar member of the RMC staff, had them ready to present a creditable parade. The Minister of National Defence told them: "War is not inevitable, but neither is peace certain, and until it is, no self-respecting country, particularly one with the record as well as the resources of Canada, can afford to ignore her defences."[1] He added that he hoped that when the products of the Canadian Services Colleges became admirals, generals, and air marshals the result of their tri-service cadet training would mean that they would be at least on speaking terms with each other. As they marched past to the tune of the college song, "Precision"* Major-General

*There have been several college songs. *Precision*, composed by Madame Chabot,

A. Bowen Perry, No. 13 at RMC and the last surviving member of the Old Eighteen, took the salute, an interesting link on this auspicious occasion with the beginnings of what the Minister several times called "the old College."

The new college was in some ways rather different from the old one. It was intended that by September 1951 RMC would be twice as large as it had been before the war and would have an establishment of four hundred. This meant that it would need the dormitory that had been planned for a generation. Secondly, it was also now formally tri-service instead of just a military college from which some cadets incidentally went into the air force and the navy. Thirdly, only 22 per cent of the recruits in the first year of the Canadian Services Colleges came from private schools as compared with 83 per cent of those at RMC in the first year after World War I. One reason for this difference was the growth and improvement of the staff and the equipment in Canadian high schools, especially in the larger cities. High school graduates were now able to compete effectively with those from private schools at the new senior matriculation entrance standard. Also, a relative decline in the affluence of many of the middle-class families who had sent their sons to RMC meant that graduates of private schools turned increasingly to university scholarships or to occupations more profitable than soldiering. Finally, the war had shaken the rigidity of the social structure of the nation and had awakened wider interest in the possibility of a career as a service officer.

Another important change was that, as a result of the break with the past, recruiting could be more effectively controlled at the outset. The Minister, whose brother-in-law was a former BSM* and who had therefore heard about the recruiting practices in the old RMC, gave categorical instructions that abuses were not to be tolerated. Brigadier Agnew, when a member of the prewar staff, had striven to check recruiting. He now insisted that the New Hundred should voluntarily subject themselves to certain aspects of the traditional recruit's character-developing discipline, like "running the square"; but he was equally determined to prevent brutality and humiliation when the new classes came in. He delayed granting the prewar authority to seniors until the fourth year and he rotated appointments for the first three years. The Staff-Adjutant, Major Geoffrey

---

wife of Professor Charles Chabot of the department of modern languages, with lyrics by Professor T. F. Gelley, was published in 1941 in the *R.M.C. Review* and was adopted as a "regimental marching tune." (W. R. P. Bridger, "Notes on R.M.C. Songs and Waltzes," *R.M.C. Review*, XXIV [1943], 84–6.)

*Mr. Claxton's brother-in-law was BSM Donald Savage, graduated RMC, 1916; killed in action the same year.

Brooks,* also an ex-cadet, was similarly keen to reintroduce the manly and honourable traditions of the past but to check the growth of such unsavoury practices as had harmed the welfare of cadets, interfered with the progress of first-year studies, and at times threatened the very existence of the college. In the first three years of the new régime recruiting was dropped and anything so designated was disavowed. But the inevitable tendency of such practices to grow, coupled with the fact that recruiting had some useful purposes, soon restored elements of the old customs, although at first in a limited and less objectionable fashion.

The most significant development was on the academic side. The curriculum was planned and developed by Colonel Sawyer who had worked on it for the Stedman Committee before he became director of studies. As a result of his background as a scientist and his experiences as a soldier during the war, Sawyer was fully convinced of the need for greater attention to scientific studies. Both he and Agnew believed that the preparation of a service officer involved two distinct but overlapping processes, military training and a general and professional education. They were aware that training and education often conflicted. The curriculum in other military academies and colleges often attempted to combine, with more or less success, military training and the professional education of an engineer or a scientist. All military colleges also gave some place in the curriculum to humanities and social sciences, often because these were regarded as important tools, for instance English as a means of effective communication. But arts subjects almost invariably suffered more severely than mathematics and the sciences in the clash between training and education and all too often became exposure courses in which it was almost impossible to fail and in which, as a result, cadet effort was minimal. Colonel Sawyer's solution for this dilemma was, for a scientist, novel. Agnew and he planned not merely to strengthen the teaching of the sciences but also to give English, French, history, and economics a more prominent place in the college. The narrowing effect of military training and of a scientific education would thus be offset by more serious study of humanities and social sciences. The result was a considerable growth of the arts departments at RMC and of measures to recruit staff members from the universities.

As Sawyer was an ex-cadet and a soldier, he agreed with the Comman-

*Colonel Edward Geoffrey Brooks, D.S.O., O.B.E. (1918–1964), graduated RMC, 1939; brigade major, HQ, 3rd Canadian Infantry Division; GSO2, director weapons and development, 1946; staff-adjutant, RMC, 1948–49; CO 2, RCHA, Korea; directing staff, Canadian Army Staff College, 1955–6; director Artillery, director of Army Combat Development.

dant about the need to retain the traditions, the discipline, the spit-and-polish smartness of the old RMC which had been largely responsible for building character and producing leaders. But they believed that these aspects of training could flourish along with the more highly developed curriculum which he intended to introduce. Intelligent boys need far less time than ordinary recruits in the ranks to learn the technique of putting on a smart parade. This principle, which General McNaughton had enunciated before the war, was to be the principle on which the new RMC was to be built.

The first two years of Colonel Sawyer's course were to be the same for all cadets: military studies, English, French, history, mathematics, physics, chemistry, engineering drawing, and descriptive geometry. In his third year the cadet could choose between a general arts course or engineering. If he chose the former he selected five arts courses with a major and minor subject in addition to military studies. Engineers specialized in the civil, mechanical, electrical, or chemical branches. About 20 per cent of the four-year engineering course consisted of humanities and social studies, and the general course cadet could do as much as 80 per cent of his work in these subjects.[2]

Thus, unlike most military colleges, RMC had very much greater flexibility and opportunity for specialization and in this respect was akin to a university. Where it differed from most civilian engineering schools and arts faculties was not in the amount of military work, which was minimal, but in that it gave a broader basic education. With four academic sessions of instruction in four years, the RMC course was much longer than at the Royal Military Academy, Sandhurst (which had combined RMA Woolwich and RMC Sandhurst), where in the years immediately after the war a course consisted of three terms amounting to eighteen months altogether. Furthermore the new Canadian RMC course had less military content than RMA. British officers received their scientific and engineering training later at Cambridge University or at the Royal Military College of Science.

Canada's RMC also differed from its American opposite numbers. Although the course was of similar length, four years, and although the apportionment between military training and education was much the same at West Point and Annapolis, the American academies followed the principle of giving to all cadets or midshipmen what was considered the ideal programme of subjects for training a service officer. There was thus a set pattern which permitted alternatives only in one or two subjects (more advanced languages or a different history course). The academies were thus, in the American tradition for undergraduate colleges, general rather than specialized, but unlike American civilian colleges they went to the opposite extreme from the free elective system. Differences in scholastic ability were recognized by placing students in small classes divided according to competence, thus permitting each student to progress according to his capacity; but this practice had the effect of tailoring the passing standard to the students' ability instead of assuming a level of achievement which all must attain. Weekly tests and assignments fostered regular study rather than long-term understanding.*

RMC was quite different. It was assumed that different individuals and different branches of the service required different kinds of basic education and that the rigorous training of the mind in almost any academic sphere could be of value to the future officer. RMC's new course was based on a principle inherited from Britain that specialization would permit a more advanced and therefore a more useful education for either regular officers or for those cadets who elected to follow a civilian career and serve in the reserve forces. Naturally instruction at RMC in every subject introduced material that had a military application or connotation. But this was incidental rather than fundamental.

Perhaps the clearest evidence of the broadening of the interests of RMC cadets despite this more specialized curriculum was the multiplication of extracurricular activities. Debating, international relations clubs, dramatics, a cadet periodical called *The Marker*, a revived Alliance Française, and greater cadet participation in the production of the *R.M.C. Review* were among many departures that showed the vigour of cadet intellectual life. The only obvious difference from a university campus in this respect was the absence of junior branches of political parties.

The most obvious visible change on the academic side was the development of laboratories and the library. The basement kitchen became a library stack, and laboratories made use of prewar facilities with some extension of accommodation, for instance a chemical engineering laboratory was set up in a disused cellar. There was a generous supply of equipment to replace and greatly increase what had been loaned to the Naval College in 1942. The library started in 1948 with a valuable small collection of 17,000 volumes that had been collected by Professor Bridger during his long career. His successor, John W. Spurr,† who came to Kingston in 1949, quickly built up a basic teaching and reference library to serve the needs of the new curriculum and at the same time set out to work to achieve what had been Bridger's ambition, that RMC should

---

*The American service academies introduced many course options in the early 1960s with the new US Air Force Academy leading the way.

†John W. Spurr, B.A., B.ED., chief librarian, RMC from 1949.

eventually possess the finest military collection in Canada.[3] With the more generous and academically oriented policy of the postwar period this aim was realized within a decade. To house the collection, the Chief Librarian planned, and in 1960 obtained, a new library building (which also included for the immediate future offices for the humanities and social sciences). RMC's new library was named the Massey Library in honour of the Governor-General of Canada, the Rt. Hon. Vincent Massey, who showed great interest in the college where he had given a brilliant lecture on the need for a humanistic education for officers.*

Colonel Sawyer found that the recruitment of the faculty that he needed to ensure university level instruction was not easy. As soon as the war ended, university student populations skyrocketed, as discharged servicemen used their veterans' rights in university courses. University salaries, which had been comparatively low, had begun to rise in order to compete with industry and with American universities; civil service salaries rose more slowly and it was therefore not easy to find men of the required calibre. When the college opened in September only one new civilian appointment had been made. The first year was mainly taught by members of the prewar staff and officers borrowed from the services. But with an improved salary scale the establishment slowly filled up. One attraction was the real encouragement given to research. With the aid of grants from the Defence Research Board, the National Research Council, and, later, the Canada Council, excellent work was done in many spheres including low temperature physics, military history, chemistry, and electronics. Colonel Sawyer repeatedly emphasized his belief that research and teaching went hand in hand and were the joint bases of excellence in the academic world.

In the course of four years, an RMC cadet now covered more of the humanities, social sciences, mathematics, and natural sciences than a student who started from the same senior matriculation level in a three-year general B.A., or "pass arts," course in a university. A cadet who took the engineering option was one year short of a degree which could be completed at McGill, Toronto, Queen's, and other Canadian universities. At the same time he also had a course in military studies each year which was arranged on a tri-service basis and was intended to lay the foundations for his professional military interest, for the formation of the military ethic, and for the absorption of basic military knowledge. During the academic year he lived a life organized on military lines. In the summer he was attached to the service of his choice. Whereas before the war the

---

*Vincent Massey, "Education and the Officer," *R.M.C. Review*, XXXIV (1953), 146–51.

RMC cadet's summer military training had lasted only about six weeks and had been hampered by limited equipment and facilities, he now got twelve or more weeks in first-class service schools, in flying training, or at sea in each of the three summer vacations before RMC graduation (and for engineers in a fourth summer) when he began to learn his profession.[4]

The academic development in the new RMC must not be thought to be a complete break with the past. The course instituted in 1948 was possible only because it was a development of what had been planned in 1936. Colonel Sawyer, who had worked on the revision in 1936, was the architect of the postwar curriculum. Its full fruition was achieved because RMC had never been a normal military college. The Kingston college had always had two aims, military excellence for those cadets who wanted a military career, and high academic standards for those who were going to the universities or direct into civilian professional life. The need to secure and promote accreditation in the civilian educational world had meant that RMC's academic standards had been less subject to the corrosive influences that are present in all professional schools, and especially in military academies, where the exigencies of professional technical needs may hamper insistence on intellectual quality and effort. The new academic excellence was in line with the old RMC tradition but went far beyond it in achievement.

In other respects many of the old RMC traditions were deliberately restored. The new uniform had been derived directly from the old, and the RMC winter fur cap, the pill-box, and the scarlet tunic were soon reintroduced. Many other old customs were brought back. The recruits' obstacle race and the harriers race were run again. Copper Sunday was re-established, the Cake Walk was deliberately revived, though admittedly with varying degrees of success, and the June ball came back, at first in May because the academic year was shorter. In 1962 Brigadier W. A. B. Anderson* opened the re-established RMC Museum in Fort Frederick to display the collection of arms presented to the college by Walter Douglas† and to illustrate the college's own history and service. The West Point hockey series was also resumed, but no longer with a straight run of victories, for hockey had become more popular in the United States. There

*Lieutenant-General William Alexander Beaumont Anderson, o.b.e., c.d., b.a. (born 1915), graduated RMC, 1936; RCHA; Staff College Camberley, 1941; personal assistant to General Crerar, 1942; GSO 1, 1944–5; DMI, Ottawa, 1946–9; Commandant 1st Canadian Infantry Brigade, Germany, 1954–5; vice adjutant-general 1959–60; Commandant RMC, 1960–1; adjutant-general 1962–5; chief of Mobile Command, 1966.

†Walter Douglas (1870–1946), MQ certificate, RMC, 1890; Columbia School Mines, NY; mining engineer; chairman of the Board Southern Pacific Co., Mexico. The arms collection was from the estate of General Porfirio Diaz, president of Mexico.

was also an expanded sports programme with much more opportunity for intercollegiate games as well as for spirited intramural competition. If RMC's teams did not always fare as well as their predecessors in the 'twenties and 'thirties, they nevertheless maintained a good record for a small college. However, coaching in the universities was now producing a better state of physical fitness and competence among rivals, and RMC no longer enjoyed a special advantage in that respect. Still, the 1968 college competes in twenty-two intercollegiate sports as compared with only ten before the war.

Finally, the new college once more saw the pageantry of yet another Royal visit in 1951 when Princess Elizabeth and the Duke of Edinburgh came to Kingston and reviewed the cadets on parade. The new college showed on that day that it could match the old in the external trappings of the military panoply, and larger numbers provided a more impressive spectacle. The cadets on parade maintained the same standard of excellence as of old. Although some ex-cadets complained that an equal degree of snap and precision was not seen on Kingston streets as in their own day, this was often merely a matter of individual opinion, and there is no doubt that RMC cadets were still very impressive when contrasted with the appearance of many modern youths. Certainly the young ladies obviously thought so and, strangely enough, such were the mores of the new age, competition for "dates" did not seem to have as adverse an effect on relations with male students at Queen's as it apparently had had in former days. Times had changed and manners with them. In this, as in other respects, RMC was adjusting to new ways of thought and a new age. RMC's social contacts with Kingston citizens were more numerous and less formal and the college became even more popular in the city. Staff and students took part in more social and cultural events. And Kingston was appreciative of the fact that the re-opening in 1948 had restored a lost glamour to the city.

The tri-service experiment inevitably created problems, stresses, and strains in the maintenance of the sound traditions of old. The first batch of Royal Roads cadets who arrived at Kingston in 1950 to form the new third year (at that time the senior class in RMC) were not yet well enough known to be given rank and appointments. When commands were rotated a few weeks later many of them assumed responsibility, with the result that most of the cadet officers were cadets from the western college. Former RMC cadets then complained that a new and more rigid discipline was being introduced. They claimed that traditional RMC discipline was different from that of Royal Roads because it was based on the recipient of an order understanding its purpose.[5] In future years there were other problems: the third-year class was always the largest in the college but had little responsibility; some who came from Royal Roads (and later Collège Militaire Royal de St Jean) and had already tasted command and privilege found it hard to drop back; and there were inevitable problems of divided loyalty. Perhaps this problem of loyalty was the most important difficulty in the tri-service system. In most military academies, the college and a single service (and even a football team) are inextricably identified as a single entity in the cadet's mind. At the new RMC there were loyalties to three services, to three colleges, and to two linguistic backgrounds, in addition to a programme in which academic interests enjoyed a vigorous life within a sometimes uncongenial military atmosphere. Brigadier W. A. B. Anderson, who served only part of a normal tour as commandant* because he went on to a higher position at Ottawa, stressed to the staff the fact that, despite differing functions, they had a single objective, the production of superior service officers. There must therefore be only one staff, fully united in sentiment and ideals.

But some of the tensions produced by these conflicts of loyalty went much deeper, and also much higher, than the difficulties of adjustment experienced by cadets transferring from one college to another in the middle of their academic career or than problems of civil-military relations within the college. Command and staff appointments were divided between the three services. Rotation had to be adjusted to preserve a balance. As there were at first only two colleges, rotation of command would mean that at any given time one service would not have a command in one of the Canadian Services Colleges. It was expected that rotation between the services would commence at Royal Roads in 1949 where a sailor had had command ever since the college was opened up to RCAF cadets in 1947. Early in the year the Chief of the Naval Staff stated that as summer naval professional training was about to begin at Royal Roads it would be most desirable to extend the term of the present commandant, Captain H. S. Rayner, RCN.† But the RCAF had already selected an officer to succeed to the command of the college, and the navy admitted that it would have been satisfied with rotation if there had been three colleges so that each service could have one command.[6] When the RCAF sent a team of officers to look over Royal Roads on the assumption that a change of command would mean that the RCAF would also administer the college, the navy was incensed. Furthermore, Captain Rayner protested that if he

*On General Anderson's appointment as adjutant-general, his unexpired term was filled by Brigadier George Hylton Spencer, O.B.E., C.D., A.D.C., B.SC. (born 1916), graduated RMC, 1938; CO 1st Field Squadron, RCE, 1942; Camberley Staff College, 1944; Canadian Planning Staff, SHAPE; Imperial Defence College, 1957; commandant, RMC, 1962–3.

†Vice-Admiral Herbert Sharples Rayner, D.S.C., C.D., RCN (born 1911); commandant, Royal Roads, 1948–9; chief of Naval Staff, 1960–4.

were relieved of a post which he had held only one year instead of for the normal navy tour of two years, it would look as though he had been "fired."

Ultimately at a meeting of the chiefs of staff and the Deputy Minister on 16 June it was decided that Royal Roads would continue to be administered by the RCN regardless of the service from which its commandant came. At the same time there were suggestions (which were not immediately carried out) that the tour of naval commandants for the service colleges might be extended to three years instead of two, that the post of commanding officer of the cadet wing and of vice-commandant at Royal Roads should be abolished, and that the director of studies should be a civilian.[7]

Group-Captain J. B. Millward,* an officer with prewar experience in teaching who succeeded Captain Rayner at Royal Roads, recommended that the teaching staff should be civilian, that naval personnel on the faculty who only had the B.A. degree should be replaced by better qualified civilians, and that senior faculty appointments should be made at Royal Roads like those at RMC. He noted that there was a large failure rate in the junior term at the western college and suggested that the academic work load was too heavy by comparison with the universities.[8] However, he had aparently not realized that failure rates in first year at university were equally great. Nor had he taken into consideration the fact that Royal Roads had proportionately fewer applicants than RMC and therefore did not get as highly qualified students. RMC failure rates in the first year were also high and to some extent this was because the problem of adjustment for the students, difficult in a civilian university, was even more difficult in a military college. But the temptation to lower academic standards and to reduce the curriculum in order to increase output, which would inevitably have depreciated quality, was firmly resisted.

In other respects rotation of command went smoothly except that the RCN found in 1951 that it had no suitable senior officer to spare and nominated the current commandant, Brigadier D. R. Agnew, to fill its vacancy at RMC. He was succeeded in 1954 by the first air force officer to command the college, Air Commodore D. A. R. Bradshaw† after which the RCN selected in 1957 Commodore D. W. Piers, whose appointment to Point Frederick brought a reminder that a broad pennant had flown there over a century ago when the place was a royal dockyard and naval base.

*Air Commodore James Bert Millward, DFC (born 1911); commandant Royal Roads, 1949–52; air attaché Washington, 1955; directing staff NDC, 1957; director ROTP, 1960.

†Air Vice-Marshal Douglas Alexander Ransome Bradshaw, DFC, C.D., RCAF (born 1912), graduated RMC, 1934; OC 420 (B) Squadron RCAF, 1941–4; commandant RMC, 1954–7; commodore RCAF Air Division in Europe, 1963.

Cadets destined for the RCN "graduated" from the Canadian Services Colleges after two years and proceeded either to sea service or to the RN Engineering College at Keyham. However, in 1949, as a result of disciplinary difficulties in the navy, a commission of enquiry chaired by Vice-Admiral E. R. Mainguy reported that one source of difficulty was that RCN officers trained in Britain were not properly prepared to deal with Canadian ratings. The report recommended the lengthening of the Royal Roads course.[9] In 1950 Mr. Claxton told the CGS that he wanted all naval cadets to take the full four-year course at the Canadian Services Colleges.[10] Nevertheless, there were still "midshipman graduates" from RMC in 1955 and 1956.

This move towards a full four-year degree standard course for all Canadian service officers did not carry through immediately because the trend in that direction was halted by a growing demand for officers resulting from Canada's increasing military commitments. Anticipation of the nature of war in the nuclear and missile age, the NATO treaty of 1949, and the invasion of South Korea in 1950, brought changes in policy. They led to increases in the size of the armed forces, to the creation of a standing army plus the maintenance of a small permanent nucleus with a large reserve, and to a demand for officers greater than could be satisfied by existing methods. It had also become clear that plans for training officers in the universities had not produced the hoped-for numbers. Clearly the decision to re-open RMC instead of rely on officers from the universities had been vindicated. However, some officers, including General Guy Simonds, who succeeded as chief of the General Staff when General Foulkes became chairman of the Chiefs of Staff Committee in 1951, thought that the solution of the officer problem was to make the Canadian Services Colleges course a two-year one and to reduce the standard of entry to junior matriculation. The RCAF insisted that the four-year course on senior matriculation must be retained for all its long service officers. To meet the increased demand for junior officers the army set up a short service officer school at Camp Borden and the navy re-established the wartime HMCS *Venture* at Esquimalt. The Minister then submitted to the Cabinet Defence Committee for consideration proposals to introduce a two-year course to produce line officers through the Canadian Services Colleges and the universities, to continue the four-year course at RMC for technical officers, and to use degree courses at the universities to produce officers in technical fields which could not be taught at the services colleges.[11] These proposals were eventually transformed into a completely new plan for the production of officers.

By this time the critical shortage of junior officers had been eased by the emergency measures taken by the services. In 1952 the Minister of National Defence outlined to the executive of the National Conference of Canadian Universities in Quebec a regular officers training plan (ROTP) by which students would be provided with a full four-year university education and paid a substantial living allowance in return for a commitment to serve for three years with a permanent force commission. This offer was first made to cadets already in the services colleges and in the COTC's and other services' contingents in the universities. Soon afterwards it was extended to high school students who had reached the senior matriculation level. It must be remembered that fees, with a system of scholarships for academic ability, had been retained throughout the history of the old RMC, of Royal Roads, of the RCN-RCAF College, and of the Canadian Services Colleges up to this time; and it had been possible for any graduate to take a reserve instead of a regular commission. In 1954 the Chiefs of Staff decided that the ROTP would become practically the only path through the services colleges.[12]

The ROTP was designed to attract applications from among the large number of high school graduates who were unable to attend a university for financial reasons. The Canadian Services Colleges therefore became, more than ever before, a cross-section of the youth of the nation drawing from all classes from coast to coast, including "new Canadians" and boys from various ethnic origins. This made RMC more national in composition than any Canadian university. The introduction of ROTP had the incidental effect of largely excluding some of the sons of professional men, of ex-cadets, and of serving officers who had not yet made up their minds to become career officers. However, past experience showed that many former reserve cadets, including some who had high academic standing, took regular commissions at the end of their course. These had now been lost in favour of many at the bottom of the list of entrants who dropped out after a year or so because they could not gain academic promotion. Thus, although the total number of regular commissions from the service colleges increased slightly after the introduction of the exclusive ROTP plan, it was not as productive as the mixed reserve and ROTP scheme (which had operated for two years, 1952 and 1953). Furthermore, whereas fee-paying students who applied voluntarily for a commission looked forward to a lifetime career, many of the ROTP cadets accepted the obligation to serve for three years merely to get a cheap education and these looked forward to an early release from service. Dr. Percy Lowe, a vigorous critic of the ROTP policy, argued in an article in the *R.M.C. Review*, that there was a decline in quality after the mixed plan was dropped.[13] In 1961, when these trends became clear in Ottawa, it was arranged that up to 15 per cent of each annual entry could be selected from applicants who did not wish to assume the obligation to serve for three years in one of the regular services.

However, experience demonstrated that Canadian Services Colleges ROTP graduates were much more likely to make a career in the permanent forces than university ROTP graduates. Throughout the period with which we are concerned the ROTP graduate, whether from university or a service college, was required to serve for three years after graduation. Statistics given to the Canadian Services Colleges Advisory Board in 1967 showed that in the fourth year after graduation 64.5 per cent of services colleges graduates were still in service as compared with 45.1 per cent of university ROTP graduates. After nine years the retention rate was even more favourable from the services colleges, 58.8 per cent for the colleges as against 33.9 per cent for the universities. These figures prove conclusively that the RMC Club's efforts to re-open the college after the war had been fully justified.

About the same time that the ROTP was introduced another equally important development occurred. One limitation on the number of young Canadians who could qualify for the Canadian Services Colleges was that some provinces had no equivalent of the Ontario grade thirteen and senior matriculation, and entries from those provinces therefore came to RMC and Royal Roads at a disadvantage. Furthermore, the French-Canadian education system in Quebec did not provide the same kind of scientific preparation as those of the English-speaking provinces. Whereas the population of Canada in 1952 was 27.5 per cent French-speaking, the percentages of French-speaking officers in the three services were 2 per cent in the navy, 12 per cent in the army, and 4 per cent in the air force. The comparable figures for enlisted men were 11, 20, and 16 per cent respectively.[14] There had only been two French-Canadian students in the RCN-RCAF College and only about 10 per cent among the New Hundred at RMC. Clearly this situation needed remedying for reasons of national interest.

The army therefore explored the possibility of establishing a preparatory school in Quebec which would bring students up to the level of the grade thirteen in Ontario and feed them into the service colleges system. The army barracks at St. Jean, thirty miles south of Montreal, had been inspected with this in mind in March 1952.[15] The Minister's memorandum of 26 May 1952 to the Cabinet Defence Committee with various proposals for expanding officer training included the information that all the universities approached, except Laval, accepted the idea of giving a two-year course for potential officers. Laval which had turned it down said that

French-Canadian families would not be interested in such a course without a degree and it could not be grafted on to the system of classical colleges. Laval itself was not interested in conducting a preparatory course for the services colleges. Therefore the Minister proposed that such a course should be conducted under service auspices. He added that if it was justifiable to do so, two more years like those at Royal Roads should be added. Such a college would attract Quebec students and would be on a sound academic basis.[16] The matter was thought so urgent that plans to put it into effect were rushed. In June, Mr. Claxton gave instructions that the proposal to open that college in the fall "should stand" and pointed out that at the close of the war the Khaki University had been opened in the United Kingdom on as little notice and had been successful. Two names were discussed for the new college, Royal De Salaberry College and Royal d'Iberville College. The staff, including the director of studies, were to have had experience of senior high school or junior university teaching. The college was to be administered by the RCAF.[17] Nine days later, announcing his plans to the Commons, the Minister said that the new college at St Jean was "primarily designed to meet the special circumstances of French-speaking candidates but will be open to students from all over Canada."[18]

St Jean, which was chosen as the site of the new venture, had a long military history. The first fort there had been built by the French in 1666 and rebuilt in 1748. It was situated on the invasion route of the Richelieu River and Lake Champlain. In 1760 after advancing British troops captured Ile aux Noix, the fort at St Jean was evacuated and burned. Re-established after the war, it was captured in 1775 by American insurgents but was quickly recovered and henceforward was strongly held by Governor Guy Carleton who added two redoubts and a palisade. When besieged by General Richard Montgomery it was held by six hundred and fifty men of the 7th foot and one hundred French-Canadian volunteers under the command of Major Charles Preston of the 26th foot. The fort held out for seven weeks but was surrendered with the honours of war on 2 November after its garrison had suffered forty-three casualties. The fall of St Jean led to the evacuation of Montreal. St Jean was also important during the war of 1812 and in the rebellion of 1837 and continued to be garrisoned by the British. Later it became a station of the Canadian Permanent Force and in 1939 was the depot of "A" Squadron of the Royal Canadian Dragoons. Since 1945 it had been a Canadian Army Training School.[19]

Instead of De Salaberry College, which at first seemed likely to be chosen, it was decided that the new Quebec college would be called Le Collège Militaire de St Jean, and on 18 July 1952 the Governor-General was requested to seek the Queen's permission to use the title "Royal." Hence the third Canadian Services College became Le Collège Militaire Royal de St Jean or simply CMR. Claxton's proposal to use junior university and senior high school teachers was inadequate for the three-year course that was planned. A faculty with more advanced qualifications was therefore sought. Instruction was to be given in both French and English and special efforts were made to promote bilingualism. Colonel Marc L. Lahaie* was appointed commandant.

The haste with which CMR was established, and the need for special qualifications for its faculty, inevitably brought teething troubles. These included a considerable wastage at the end of the college's second year (which was the equivalent of RMC's first year) even though a large number had already dropped out a year earlier. Consideration was therefore given to direct entry from CMR into the services, but it was soon concluded that three years' training was not sufficient preparation for an officer. A proposal to send CMR cadets to a university for two more years to take a degree was thought impractical because the universities would not give year for year credit to the services colleges which had courses in military studies, military training, compulsory sports, and also wide and varied standards of entrance. The degree thus obtained in five years of study would therefore only be a pass B.A. To add a third and fourth year at CMR was seen to be more expensive than sending CMR graduates to finish their course at Kingston where the staff and facilities already existed. Accordingly, in 1955 CMR cadets joined with those from RMC and Royal Roads in the third year as had originally been planned.[20]

The supreme test of a military college is the success of its graduates in war. The first products of the Canadian Services Colleges did not have long to wait. By the time the class that had entered in 1948 had graduated, Canada was involved in the Korean War. The army therefore decided to send all its RMC graduates immediately to active service in Korea. There were some who believed that the stronger academic programme must inevitably have weakened the old military spirit and efficiency. But the success of the graduates who went directly to Korea quickly disabused them. Lieutenants D. G. Loomis, RCA, H. C. Pitts, PPCLI, A. M. King, RCR, and C. D. Carter, RCE, were awarded the Military Cross. Graduates of the old college were also decorated: Lieutenant-Colonel H. W. Sterne with the D.S.O., Major E. C. Schmidlin with the Military Cross, Lieutenant-

*Brigadier Marc Louis Lahaie, D.S.O., C.D. (born 1913); McGill University, 1932–5, Université de Montréal, 1940–1; DMT, Ottawa, 1949–51; commandant CMR, 1952–7; military attaché, Paris, 1959–63.

Colonels E. A. C. Amy and E. G. Brooks with the o.b.e., and Majors L. E. Leach and J. S. Orton with the m.b.e.[21]

Partly as a recognition of valuable service in Korea, but also because the demand for the immediate service of junior officers had begun to decline, the army decided in 1953 to send all its Canadian Services Colleges graduates to university to complete a degree course. The Chief of the General Staff, General Simonds, was keen on the broadening effect of attendance at university. Cadets who had taken a general course and who had already covered at rmc more subjects than were necessary for a pass degree were also sent to university at public expense, many of them to take a pass degree. This programme was very costly as officers sent to the universities received full pay and allowances as well as tuition fees. Some rmc graduates who repeated the same work neglected their studies and failed. By introducing this plan, the army made inevitable a reconsideration of the decision not to grant degrees at rmc.

In 1954 Air Commodore Bradshaw sent to the Chief Secretary of the Department of National Defence a proposal that degree-granting powers should be obtained for rmc. He noted that industry now invariably required that applicants for higher administrative and technical employment possess an academic degree. Cadets entering the armed forces wanted to obtain their degrees before their service career so that they would not have to embark upon an academic course when they retired and needed other employment. The granting of an rmc degree would thus remove one disadvantage suffered by the rmc-rotp cadet when he competed with the university output. The Commandant also noted that the rmc general course already equalled a university degree in arts and that the further recruitment of staff for rmc was hampered by the stigma that rmc was not a degree-granting institution. rmc courses were now shaped to meet the requirements of the universities but if rmc gave its own degree they could be shaped to meet the needs of the services. Eliminating the practice of sending rmc graduates to complete a degree at the universities could mean a substantial economy of about half a million dollars a year. However, the Commandant concluded by saying that the award of degrees in engineering was not contemplated in the near future.[22]

Under the British North America Act the authority for degree-granting power in Canada rests with the provincial governments. It was possible that a degree for military personnel might be constitutional under that section of the Act which gives the federal government power to organize the defence of the country. Nevertheless, when it was decided that rmc would become a degree-granting institution, an application for a bill to give the college the necessary powers was submitted to the province of Ontario. While this procedure was being discussed it was decided in Ottawa that the college would grant degrees in engineering as well as in arts and science. To do this it was necessary to reorganize the course to introduce specialization earlier, but the RMC policy of giving engineers more courses in the humanities and social sciences than they would get at a university was to be maintained. A second change was the introduction of a three-week spring term in each annual session between the final examinations and the passing-out parade and June ball. By this device, which necessitated a slight shortening of the summer military training period, the number of engineering courses was increased and was made comparable with that in the universities. After the Act was passed it took three years to produce engineering graduates of degree standard. However, an additional course in the arts departments in the third and fourth years had already been added for a few selected students of high academic calibre and this made specialized honours degrees in arts subjects on the Canadian pattern, as well as general course degrees, possible immediately. The first RMC degrees in arts and science were given in 1959 and the first degrees in engineering in 1962.

Military academies in the United States had given academic degrees for some years before World War II. RMC's degree plan was different in that it provided for a variety of specializations that would be valuable not only in civilian life but also in military service and would reduce the need for special service courses after graduation. The average student went further both in military training and in academic study under the mixed RMC plan than in systems where the two sides of a military preparation were more carefully separated. Moreover, Korea suggested that nothing of the old RMC military spirit had been lost. The Canadian Services Colleges were somewhat different from the old RMC that ex-cadets had sought to re-establish after the war; but most greeted the new system and its innovations with great enthusiasm. After World War II Canada's RMC quickly gained unique academic distinction and attracted world wide attention. It won new laurels to add to a record that was already written large on the pages of the military history of Canada and of the commonwealth.

Peacekeeping services in which Canada played an important role gave added weight to the argument that modern armed services required highly educated officers such as were produced in Kingston. As part of the new Canadian Services Colleges it embarked on a new career of service to Canada in roles in which scientific scholarly soldiers were needed. A senior ex-cadet from the old college had, in fact, already shown the way. General E. L. M. Burns, who had commanded a division in Italy and been deputy minister in the Department of Veterans' Affairs after the war, had become the first commander of the United Nations Emergency Force in Egypt. Later he was appointed the Prime Minister's special representative at disarmament talks in Geneva and the government's adviser on disarmament. Burns' career showed that the prewar RMC had served to develop the qualities needed for such important international and diplomatic duties. It was believed that the new Canadian Services Colleges were even better equipped to prepare officers not only for war but also for work of a very different kind. The Canadian soldier in the Congo and Cyprus was as much a diplomat as a fighting man.

As part of the new Canadian Services Colleges, the Royal Military College of Canada has thus embarked on a new career of service to country in an age when scientific and scholarly soldiers are needed as never before. The Canadian governments, civil servants, and senior officers who reestablished and transformed the college and who fostered this unique national institution deserve the nation's gratitude. The Royal Military College of Canada and its sister colleges are places of which Canada and Canadians can well be proud.

REFERENCES

CHAPTER 1, PAGES 3 - 19

1 "Visit of the Hon. Alexander Mackenzie, then Premier of Canada, to Fort Henry and Fort Frederick," from notes made by Colonel de La Cherois Thomas Irwin, C.M.G., *Royal Military College of Canada Review: Log of H.M.S. Stone Frigate (R.M.C. Review)*, IV (Nov. 1923), 27. Colonel Irwin placed this incident in 1875. A letter of Mackenzie's shows that it occurred in 1874, Public Record Office of Northern Ireland (PRONI), Dufferin Papers, D1071H/H4/4, pp. 23–4, Mackenzie to Dufferin, 14 June 1874.

2 Sidney Forman, "Why the United States Military Academy was Established in 1802," *Military Affairs*, XXIX (1965), 16.

3 The Hon. J. W. Fortescue, *A History of the British Army* (13 vols., London, 1930), XIII, 559. For an account of the low state of both general and professional education of many British officers in 1870 see Major-General Sir Alexander Bruce Tulloch, *Recollections of Forty Years' Service* (Edinburgh, 1903), pp. 167–70.

4 Sir John Smyth, *Sandhurst* (London, 1961), p. 98.

5 The quotations and information in this and the following paragraphs are from: Public Archives of Canada (PAC), RG 8, C 33, pp. 80–3, A. G. Douglas to Major-General (Wiltshire) Wilson, 30 Aug. 1816; pp. 84–7, "A Plan for the Establishment of a College in Canada"; pp. 88–9, Douglas to Sir J. C. Sherbrooke, Quebec, 24 Oct. 1816; pp. 92–3, Douglas to Colonel Addison, 14 Nov. 1816.

6 Public Record Office (PRO), CO 42/381, Memorial to the Admiralty by Officers on Half-Pay, Township of March, 20 May 1826; Bathurst to Maitland, 30 Oct. 1826; Maitland to Bathurst, 18 April 1827.

7 Canada, House of Commons, *Sessional Papers*, I (1867–68), no. 35, *Report of the State of the Militia for 1867*, appendix no. 7, p. 105. (Hereafter *Militia Reports*, which appear in *Sessional Papers* for the following year, are cited by the year to which they refer.)

8 RG 8, C 816; "Proposed Regulations for School of Instruction, which have received the approval of the Lieutenant General Commanding," *Militia Report, 1871*, p. 91.

9 *Militia Report, 1867*, p. 7; *Militia Report, 1868*, p. 19.

10 C. P. Stacey, *Canada and the British Army, 1846–1871: A Study in the Practice of Responsible Government* (revised ed.; Toronto, 1963), p. 262.

11 RG 7, G 21, vol. 168, no. 259A I (1869–70), Lindsay to Governor-General, 27 May 1870.

12 *Militia Report, 1870*, pp. 32–6.

13 "The examination [for a commission] was very simple and was passed almost as a matter of course, for it would have been unforgivable breach of etiquette for officers of one regiment to plough a candidate sent up by another," Field Marshal Sir William Robertson, *From Private to Field Marshal* (Boston, 1921), pp.32-3.

14 Francis J. Dixon, "Military Education in Canada," in J. Castell Hopkins, ed., *Canada: An Encyclopaedia of the Country* (6 vols., Toronto, 1898), IV, 444.

15 *Militia Report, 1871,* pp. 55–6.

16 *Militia Report, 1872,* p. xxvi. In his report for 1870 Ross had proposed a staff college for Canada, but without effect (p. 36).

17 Royal Archives, Windsor (RAW), Cambridge Papers, Williams to Cambridge, 25 April 1862.

18 *History of the American War* (3 vols.; London, 1865–6).

19 C. W. de Kiewiet and F. H. Underhill, eds., *Dufferin-Carnarvon Correspondence, 1874–1878* (Toronto, 1955), pp. 141–2.

20 Lieutenant-Colonel H. C. Fletcher, *Memorandum on the Militia System of Canada* ([Ottawa], 1873), pp. 5, 8–12.

21 Dufferin Papers, D107H/H2/4, p. 16, Kimberley to Dufferin, 3 July 1873.

22 A copy of Fletcher's *Memorandum* is in the Macdonald Papers (PAC, MG 26, A 1(a), vol. 100, 39616–35).

23 CO 43/699, Lisgar 156, Lisgar to Colonial Office, 24 Aug. 1871; *ibid.,* War Office to Colonial Office, 25 Sept. 1871.

24 Dale C. Thomson, *Alexander Mackenzie: Clear Grit* (Toronto, 1960), p. 115, quoting Commons, Debates, 2 May 1870; Richard A. Preston, *Canada and "Imperial Defense": A Study of the British Commonwealth's Defense Organization, 1867–1919* (Durham, N.C., 1967), pp. 71–2.

25 PAC, Militia Department, Deputy Minister's Papers (DM), Registers 9053, Privy Council to Deputy Minister, 29 Dec. 1873; Dufferin Papers D1071H/H3/1, pp. 8–10, Dufferin to Mackenzie, 31 Dec. 1873.

26 William Buckingham and Geo. W. Ross, *The Hon. Alexander Mackenzie: His Life and Times* (Toronto, 1892), p. 379.

27 Cambridge Papers, Cambridge to Dufferin, 22 Jan. 1874.

28 Dufferin Papers, D1071H/H3/1, pp. 8–10, Dufferin to Mackenzie, 31 Dec. 1873.

29 Great Britain (GB), *Parliamentary Papers,* 1868–69, XXII, 1–59, *First Report of the Royal Commission appointed to enquire into the Present State of Military Education, and into the training of Candidates for Commissions in the Army; ibid.,* 1870, XXIV, 215–507 and XXV, 223–832, *Two Reports of the Royal Commission on the State of Military Education and on the teaching of Candidates for Commissions in the Army, Evidence, Appendices and Index,* 4 parts, 1869–70.

30 Sir Alfred Lyall, *The Life of the Marquis of Dufferin and Ava* (2 vols., London, 1905), I, 145–9; Harold George Nicolson, *Helen's Tower* (New York, 1938), p. 136.

31 *Parliamentary Papers,* 1870, XXIV, 504. He said he knew nothing about cavalry and so could not express an opinion about how its officers should be trained.

32 Dufferin Papers, D1071H/H1/3, pp. 182–6, Dufferin to Carnarvon, 30 April 1874.

33 PAC, Militia & Defence, D.M. Papers (henceforward cited as DM) Register 9099, Powell [to Deputy Minister], 17 Dec. 1873.

34 *Militia Report, 1873*, pp. xiii-xiv. Cf. Washington's argument to congress in favour of a military academy in the United States: "A thorough examination of the subject will evince that the art of war is at once comprehensive and complicated; that it demands much previous study; and that the possession of it in its most improved and perfect state, is always of great moment to the security of a nation" (Jared Sparks, *The Writings of George Washington* ... [12 vols., New York, 1847–48], XII, 72).

35 George T. Denison, *Soldiering in Canada* (Toronto, 1900), p. 188.

36 T. B. Strange, *Artillery Retrospect of the Last Great War, 1870: with its Lessons for Canadians* (Quebec, 1874), pp. iv, v; Captain Richard J. Wickstead, *The Canadian Militia* (Ottawa, 1875), pp. 94–5.

37 *Parliamentary Papers*, 1870, XXV, 635–7, Colonel P. MacDougall, *Account of the System of Education at the United States Military Academy at West Point*. A précis is in *Militia Report, 1873*, appendix no. 9, pp. 221–3.

38 RG 9, II A 1, vol. 604, Commission on the Defence of Canada, v, Colonel Fletcher, "Report on West Point," 365, 369, 375, 435, 477, 481, 499.

39 Dufferin Papers, D1071H/H1/3, pp. 148–54, Dufferin to Carnarvon, 24 April 1874.

40 *Ibid.*, D1071H/H3/1, pp. 120–4, Dufferin to Mackenzie, 7 May 1874.

41 Cambridge Papers, Dufferin to Cambridge, 29 May 1874; Dufferin to Carnarvon, 2 April 1875; de Kiewiet and Underhill, eds., *Dufferin-Carnarvon Correspondence*, pp. 141–2; CO 42/735, Dufferin 83, Dufferin to Fletcher, 26 March 1875.

42 Dufferin Papers, D1071H/H2/5, p. 107, Carnarvon to Dufferin, 10 Aug. 1875.

43 *Ibid.*, D1071H/H4/2, pp. 155–6, Mackenzie to Dufferin, 5 Aug. 1878.

CHAPTER 2, PAGES 20 - 47

1 27 Vict., c. 36, *Acts of Parliament of the Dominion of Canada* (Ottawa, 1876).

2 Canada, Library of Parliament film, *Parliamentary Debates, 1873–74* (debates reported by the newspapers, Ottawa *Times*, Toronto *Gobe*, Toronto *Mail*), p. 100.

3 *Militia Report, 1870*, p. 36.

4 *Debates, 1873–1874*, p. 100.

5 DM 02603, Major General 306, 21 Feb. 1876.

6 *Militia Report, 1873*, p. xiii.

7 A. J. Kerry and W. A. McDill, *The History of the Corps of Royal Canadian Engineers* (2 vols., Ottawa, 1962), I, 23–31, 40, 52–3; *Militia Report, 1875*, p. xviii; *Ibid., 1871*, pp. 90–1; *Ibid., 1872*, p. xxviii; *Ibid., 1873*, p. 41.

8 *Militia Report, 1874*, pp. ix, x.

9 Cambridge Papers, Dufferin to Cambridge, 30 April 1874.

10 *Debates, 1873–1874*, p. 100.

11 *Ibid.*, pp. 100–3.

12 *Ibid.*, p. 100; 27 Vict., c. 36.

13 *Debates, 1873–1874*, p. 100.

14 *Ibid.*

15 A. M. Carr-Saunders and P. A. Wilson, *The Professions* (Oxford, 1933), pp. 157–8.

16 Sir Richard John Cartwright, *Reminiscences* (Toronto, 1912), pp. 135–7.

17 DM 9657, "Petition of the Inhabitants of Kingston, 20 [sic] May, 1874."

18 *Ibid.*, Sullivan to Cartwright, 19 May 1874.

19 Dufferin Papers, D1071H/H4/4, pp. 23–4, Mackenzie to Dufferin, 14 June 1874.

20 DM 06966, Montagu to Mackenzie, 23 July 1874.

21 *Ibid.*, 28 July 1874.

22 *Ibid.*, Walker Powell to Mackenzie, 28 July 1874.

23 T. Stewart Webster, "John A. Macdonald and Kingston" (unpublished MA thesis, Queen's University, 1944), pp. 121, 123, 127.

24 DM 0766. An application for appointment, 24 Nov. 1874, mentions Kingston as the location of the college.

25 Richard A. Preston and Leopold Lamontagne, eds., *Royal Fort Frontenac* (Toronto, 1958), pp. 17–82.

26 Richard A. Preston, ed., *Kingston Before the War of 1812* (Toronto, 1959), pp. xxxvii–xlvii, lxxviii–lxxxix.

27 C. P. Stacey, "Commodore Chauncey's Attack on Kingston Harbour, November 10, 1812," *Canadian Historical Review*, XXXII (June, 1951), 126–38.

28 J. M. Hitsman, "Kingston and the War of 1812," *Historic Kingston*, no. 15 (Jan., 1967), 50–60.

29 C. Winton-Clark[Dr. R. C. Anderson], "A Ship Builder's War," *Mariner's Mirror*, XXIX (1943), 139–48.

30 *Kingston Gazette*, 21 Dec. 1816; T. L. Brock, "H.M. Dockyard, Kingston, under Commissioner Robert Barrie, 1819–1834," *Historic Kingston*, no. 16 (Jan. 1968), pp. 3–22.

31 *Kingston Gazette*, 14 Dec. 1816.

32 Richard A. Preston, "The Fate of Kingston's Warships," *Ontario History*, XLIV (1952), 87–96.

33 Richard A. Preston, "Broad Pennants on Point Frederick," *Ontario History*, L (1958), 81–90.

34 Cambridge Papers, Colonel James Conolly to General Williams, 23 June 1861; PAC, A-308, Newcastle Papers (film), p. 146, Head to Newcastle, 25 June 1861.

35 RG, 7, G 1, vol. 180, Canada no. 282, Lugard to Colonial Undersecretary, 15 Oct. 1870; RG 7, G 9, vol. 53 [Charles Tupper] to [Lugard], 6 Dec. 1870; [Canada], Order-in-Council, PC 331, approved 6 Dec. 1870.

36 Dufferin Papers, D1071H/H1/3, p. 214, Dufferin to Carnarvon, 9 June 1874.

37 *Ibid.*, D1071H/H2/5.1, pp. 19–20, Carnarvon to Dufferin, 9 July 1874.

38 Brigadier O. F. G. Hogg, "The Royal Military Academy in the 18th Century," *Journal of the Royal Artillery*, LXXXI (1954), 1–16; F. G. Guggisberg, "*The Shop*": *The Story of the Royal Military Academy* (London, 1900),

p. 2, dates RMA from a royal warrant of 30 April 1741.

39 Dufferin Papers, D1071H/H2/5.5, pp. 35–40, extract from a letter from Sir Lintorn Simmons, 25 Aug. 1874.

40 PRO, Carnarvon Papers, 30/6/27, p. 129, Dufferin to Carnarvon, 2 Oct. 1874; 30/6/14, pp. 23–4, Carnarvon to Cambridge, 20 Oct. 1874; 30/6/14, pp. 25–7, 33–4, Cambridge to Carnarvon, 28, 31 Oct. 1874; CO 42/729, Dufferin 427, 1 Oct. 1874.

41 Carnarvon Papers, 30/6/27, p. 187, Dufferin to Carnarvon, 12 Nov. 1874.

42 DM Registers 9665, 9666, 9733, 9758, 9759, 9899, 9911, 0112, 0767, 01325.

43 *Ibid.*, Registers 0766, 0801.

44 CO 42/729, Dufferin 427, Minute by Carnarvon, 17 Oct. 1874, 1 Oct. 1874.

45 Cambridge Papers, J. C. Vivian to Colonial Undersecretary [copy] 2 Dec. 1874.

46 *Army and Navy Gazette*, 12 Dec. 1874.

47 Cambridge Papers, Carnarvon to Cambridge, 10 Dec. 1874.

48 Carnarvon Papers, 30/6/14, pp. 49–50, 55, Cambridge to Carnarvon, 11 Dec. 1874.

49 *Ibid.*, pp. 53–4, Carnarvon to Cambridge, 14 Dec. 1874.

50 Dufferin Papers, D1071H/H2/5.13, pp. 53–4, Carnarvon to Dufferin, 10 Dec. 1874.

51 *Ibid.*, D1071H/H2/5.3, p. 34, Carnarvon to Dufferin, 26 May 1874.

52 Carnarvon Papers, 30/6/14, pp. 78–80, 81–2, 90–1, Cambridge to Carnarvon, 27 Feb., 19 March 1875; pp. 82–3, Carnarvon to Cambridge, 1 March 1875.

53 Dufferin Papers, D1071H/H2/5.17, pp. 69–70, Carnarvon to Dufferin, 11 March 1875.

54 Carnarvon Papers, 30/6/14, pp. 94–6, Carnarvon to Cambridge, 17 March 1875.

55 Macdonald Papers, vol. 318, 32–7, "Qualifications of Colonel Hewett for appointment of Commandant Royal Military College"; *Canadian Illustrated News*, XIII (17 June 1876), 391; W. R. P. B[ridger], "The First Commandant," *R.M.C. Review*, VII (June 1926), 31; W. R. P. B[ridger], "Lieutenant-General E. O. Hewett, C.M.G.," *R.M.C. Review*, XIX (Dec. 1938), 27–8; Richard A. Preston, "A Letter from a British Military Observer of the American Civil War," *Military Affairs*, XVI (1952), 49–60; Richard A. Preston, "Military Lessons of the American Civil War: The Influence of Observers from the British Army in Canada on Training in the British Army," *Army Quarterly*, LXV (1953), 229–37.

56 CO 537/106, Dufferin telegram, 31 March 1875.

57 CO 42/738, War Office to Colonial Office, 13 April 1875.

58 CO 537/106, Dufferin telegram, 19 April 1875.

59 CO 42/736, Dufferin, confidential, 20 April 1875.

60 CO 42/738, War Office to Colonial Office, 23 July 1875.

61 *Ibid.*, p. 517, M. F. O.[mmanney], Minute to Meade, 18 July [1875].

62 Dufferin Papers, D1071H/H5/10.1, p. 38, Chesney to Dufferin, 6 Aug. 1875.

63 Carnarvon Papers, 30/6/14, pp. 141–2, Carnarvon to Cambridge, 6 Aug. 1875.

64 *Ibid.*, pp. 144–7, Cambridge to Carnarvon, 7 Aug. 1875 (2 letters).

65 Queen's University, Douglas Library, Mackenzie Papers, pp. 928–9, Hewett to Mackenzie, 21 July 1875; pp. 945–6, Mackenzie to Hewett, 9 Aug. 1875.

66 co 42/737, Dufferin 154, 15 Nov. 1875.

67 co 42/736, Vail to Dufferin's secretary, 19 April 1875, in Dufferin, confidential, 20 April 1875.

68 *Canada Gazette*, IX (12 Nov. 1875), 612–3.

69 co 42/737, Dufferin 146, 8 Nov. 1875.

70 *Canada Gazette*, IX (24 Dec. 1875), 816–7.

71 DM 02257, (RG 9, II A 1, vol. 109) [Canada] Order-in-Council, Regulations, RMC; RG 9, II A 1, vol. 117, PC 1247, 17 Dec. 1875.

72 Canada, House of Commons, *Debates*, 1875 (19, 25, 26 Feb.), pp. 253, 329, 393.

73 DM 02242, 25 Oct. 1875.

74 DM 02446, 28 Dec. 1875.

75 *Ibid.*

76 RMC, Massey Library, Ferguson Papers, George Ferguson to his wife, 28 Oct., 29 Nov., 1, 6, 8, 13, 22 Dec. 1874, 7 Nov., 19 Dec. 1875.

77 Dufferin Papers, D1071H/H2/2.1, p. 61, Carnarvon to Dufferin, 20 Jan. 1876.

78 Ferguson Papers, George Ferguson to his wife, 7 Feb., 13 March 1876.

79 co 42/745, War Office to Colonial Office, 30 May 1876.

80 RMC *Standing Orders*, 1876–1883, p. 108, approved by GOC, 5 Dec. 1876.

81 DM 9516, Powell, deputy adjutant-general, militia, 25 April 1874, approved 2 June 1874.

82 M. & D. Registers AG2513, Deputy Minister of Militia to Adjutant-General, 7 Dec. 1874.

83 DM 01069, Lieutenant-Colonel Wily, Director of Stores, 29 Jan. 1875.

84 Ferguson Papers, George Ferguson to his wife, 29 Nov., 13 Dec. 1874; House of Commons, *Debates*, 21 March 1876, p. 757. (*Mackenzie called the Stone Frigate* "the stone fort, a large building 170 feet long and 4 chains high," a description which adequately identifies it.)

85 Major H. Logan, "Chapter One of a History of RMC.," Canada, Department of National Defence, Armed Forces Historical Section, Library.

86 DM 02217, Commandant RMC to Deputy Minister, 14 [15?] Oct.

87 House of Commons, *Debates*, (21 March 1876), p. 757.

88 Ferguson Papers, George Ferguson to his wife, 7 Nov. 1875.

89 DM 02243, Hewett to Adjutant-General Militia, 23 Oct. 1875; Adjutant-General to Hewett, 1 Nov. 1875.

90 DM 02293, Hewett to government architects, 9 Nov. 1875, Colonel Walker Powell, Memo, 15 Nov. 1875.

91 *Ibid.*; DM 02657, Adjutant-General to Deputy Minister, 13 March 1876.

92 DM 02494, 13 Jan. 1876.

93 DM 02805, 02831.

94 DM 02275.

95 DM 02345.

96 DM 02769, 02908.

97 DM 02272.

98 DM 02590, 02650.

99 DM 02591, 02625, 02694, 02695, 02697, 02756, 02863.

100 DM 02828.

101 DM 02688.

102 DM 02435, Major General, 22 Dec. 1875, "Uniform of Cadets," folder only; "R.M.C. Dress Regulations, 1876 Pattern of Uniform" and "The Origin of the Uniform worn by the Gentlemen-Cadets," *R.M.C. Review*, VII (June 1926), 66–8.

103 *British Whig*, 1, 2, 6 June 1876; *Daily News*, 1, 2, 5, June 1876.

CHAPTER 3, PAGES 48 - 76

1 *Militia Report, 1875*, p. xiv.

2. *British Whig*, 10 Jan. 1876, quoting the *Almonte Gazette*; ibid., 13 March 1876.

3 DM 02725, Major General 566, 12 April 1876.

4 *British Whig*, 21 March 1876.

5 *Ibid.*, 22 May 1876.

6 *Ibid.*, 1 June 1876.

7 *Mail*, 5 May 1876.

8 *Militia Report, 1876*, appendix (A) to Half Yearly Report, Military College, p. 211; *Militia Report, 1877*, p. xv; *ibid., 1879*, p. 61.

9 G. Walker, "The Royal Military College of Canada," *R.M.C. Review*, VIII (June 1927), 24.

10 *Commandant's Report, 1876*, p. 211.

11 *Globe*, 16 Nov. 1881.

12 Brigadier-General S. A. Denison, *Memoirs* (Toronto, 1927), p. 20.

13 Major-General A. B. Perry, "RMC's First Four Years, 1876–1880" (ms, Massey Library), p. 2.

14 *Ibid.*, p. 3.

15 Denison, *Memoirs*, p. 21.

16 Perry, "RMC's First Four Years," p. 4.

17 *Commandant's Report, 1876*, p. 207; Walker, "Royal Military College of Canada," p. 26; DM 02818, 20 May 1876; DM 03033, 13 Aug. 1876.

18 *Daily News*, 1 June 1876; Perry, "RMC's First Four Years," p. 5; Canada, House of Commons, *Sessional Papers*, XIII, no. 5 (1880), no. 8, appendix 11, "Royal Military College, Board of Visitors' Report, 1879," p. 326.

19 *Militia Report, 1876*, p. 199.

20 Perry, "RMC's First Four Years," p. 5–7.

21 One of the Old Eighteen [No. 8, Frederick Davis], "Reminiscences of the Royal Military College," *R.M.C. Review*, XIX (June 1938), 19.

22 DM 03001, 28 July 1876, an empty docket endorsed "approved."

23 *Commandant's Report, 1876*, p. 208.

24 Perry, "RMC's First Four Years," p. 8.

25 Davis, "Reminiscences of the Royal Military College," p. 20.

26 Perry, "RMC's First Four Years," p. 8.

27 RMC *Standing Orders* [5 Dec. 1876], I, 4, 8, 9, 23, and III, 1; DM 02667, 12 March 1876.

28 Colonel A. H. Van Straubenzee, "The Military Founders of RMC," *R.M.C. Review*, XXIII (Dec. 1942), 47–8; Massey Library, Dixon Scrapbook, p. 53.

29 *Militia Report, 1876*, p. xi.

30 Denison, *Memoirs*, pp. 23–4.

31 DM 03323, 4 Jan. 1877.

32 DM 03104, 19 Sept. 1876.

33 Duncan MacPherson, "Foreword," *R.M.C. Review*, VII (June 1926), 10.

34 Massey Library, Major H. M. Logan, RCR, "Notes for the History of RMC," p. 51.

35 Perry, "RMC's First Four Years," p. 11.

36 DM 03004, 22 Aug. 1876.

37 Massey Library photostat, H. B. Mackay to "Drewie," 24 Sept. 1879.

38 *Board of Visitors' Report, 1879*, p. 330.

39 DM 03333, 5 Jan. 1877.

40 Logan, "Notes," p. 93; *Commandant's Report, 1877*, pp. 255–7.

41 *Commandant's Report, 1877*, p. 208.

42 *Board of Visitors' Report, 1879*, pp. 337–40.

43 DM 04588, 3 June 1878.

44 DM 05784, 16 July 1879.

45 *Militia Report, 1877*, p. xii; *Commandant's Report, 1877*, pp. 255–6.

46 Note by Major-General Sir Dudley Ridout, in *R.M.C. Review*, VIII (June 1927), 27.

47 "Report on the defences of Kingston," RG 9, II A 1, vol. 601, 337–413, 30 April 1875.

48 *R.M.C. Review*, XIII (Dec. 1932), 44.

49 DM 04622, 10 June 1878.

50 *Commandant's Report, 1879*, p. 342.

51 RG 2, Series 1, vol. 115, PC Order-in-Council 1078, 26 Oct. 1875.

52 House of Commons, *Debates*, I (4 April 1876), 1044.

53 DM 03333, 5 Jan. 1877.

54 House of Commons, *Debates*, III (12 Feb. 1877), 30; *ibid.*, IV (4 March 1878), 735.

55 *Ibid.*, IV (4 March 1878), 737; Canada, House of Commons, *Sessional Papers* (1877), no. 34, "Return of Candidates for the Military College ... distinguishing those of French Origin from the Others...." [not printed]: DM 03572, 20 April 1877; *Canada Gazette*, 13 Oct. 1877.

56 DM 04243, Hewett to Selby Smyth, 27 Feb. 1878.

57 House of Commons, *Debates*, IV (4 March 1878), 737.

58 *Canadian Illustrated News*, XIII (17 June 1876), 390.

59 Massey Library, "Articles of Agreement between William Irving and Her Majesty Queen Victoria, 18 April 1877.

60 Perry, "RMC's First Four Years," pp. 9–10.

61 DM 04234, 26 Jan. 1878; 06249, 24 Jan. 1880.

62 *Board of Visitors' Report, 1879*, p. 325; RG 9, A 2, vol. 6, 3665, 16 Oct. 1883.

63 *Commandant's Report, 1878*, p. 438; *1879*, p. 347; *1880*, p. 267.

64 *Board of Visitors' Report, 1879*, p. 331.

65 *Commandant's Report, 1878*, p. 438.

66 Logan, "Notes," p. 81 *verso*.

67 DM 05653, 6 June 1879; RG 9, II A 2, vol. 4, 2637, 7 June 1879; Massey Library, Bridges Letters; Major Warren Perry, "The Military Life of Major General Sir William Throsby Bridges," *Journal of the Royal Military College of Australia*, XXXIX (Dec. 1961), 69–79.

68 PAC, Dufferin Papers, microfilm, reel A 411, Mackenzie to Dufferin, 5 Aug. 1878.

69 DM 05006, 5 Nov. 1878.

70 W. S. MacNutt, *Days of Lorne: Impressions of a Governor-General* (Fredericton, 1955), p. 180; Cambridge Papers, Lorne to Cambridge, 6 June 1879.

71 *Militia Report, 1878*, p. xxix.

72 Massey Library, R.M.C. Reading Room Minute Book; Logan, "Notes," p. 57 *verso*.

73 Logan, "Notes," p. 57.

74 DM 03563, 19 April 1877.

75 *British Whig*, 14 July 1876.

76 Logan, "Notes," p. 57. The Old Eighteen Bugle could be retained when won twice, *R.M.C. Review*, VII (June 1926), 61.

77 Logan, "Notes," p. 57 *verso*.

78 Massey Library, Logan, "Revised Notes," p. 46.

79 Massey Library, Ferguson microfilm, George Ferguson to Elizabeth Ferguson, various dates, 1876; *ibid.*, "Sunday," 1876.

80 *Commandant's Report, 1877*, pp. 251, 254.

81 Logan, "Notes," pp. 28, *verso*–29; Marchioness of Dufferin, *My Canadian Journal, 1872–1878* (London, 1891), p. 368; Dufferin Papers, microfilm reel A 411, Dufferin to Mackenzie, 7 June 1877.

82 *Militia Report, 1879*, p. 21; Thomas Faughnan, *Stirring Incidents in the Life of a British Soldier: An Autobiography* (Toronto, 1879), pp. 331–4.

83 *Daily News*, 10 May 1878.

84 *Commandant's Report, 1879*, p. 345; DM 05605, 17 May 1879.

85 DM 03351, 15 Jan. 1877.

86 DM 04635, 17 June 1878.

87 *R.M.C. Review*, VIII (June 1927), 46; *Commandant's Report, 1881*, p. 255.

88 Directorate of History, Canadian Armed Forces HQ (D. Hist.), Militia General Orders, 29 Feb. 1884, referring to Regulations and Orders, 1883. If the story told by G. C. Davis is correct, this precedence had been established before 1880.

89 Davis, "Reminiscences of the Royal Military College," pp. 20–1.

90 *Daily News*, 12 Feb. 1878; Duncan Macpherson, "The Royal Military College of Canada, with Sidelights on its Early History," *R.M.C. Review*, VII (June 1926), 10; Logan, "Notes," p. 65.

91 *R.M.C. Review*, VII (June 1926), 65.

92 Logan, "Revised Notes," p. 50; C. C. Darling, "Gentlemen Cadets," ms in Massey Library.

93 *Commandant's Report, 1878*, p. 438.

94 *Militia Report, 1878*, p. xxix.

95 CO 42/738, pp. 491, 518, War Office to Colonial Office, 13 April, 23 July 1875. The War Office letters called it the "Royal Canadian Military College."

96 CO 42/775, pp. 673–5; RG 9, II A 2, vol. 4, 2000, 6 April 1878.

97 CO 42/753, Dufferin, 138; Cambridge Papers, Hewett to Lorne, 7 June 1879.

98 CO 42/755, p. 676; WO 32/817/058/5300, Colonial Office to War Office, 3 Aug. 1878.

99 CO 42/753, pp. 452–4.

100 WO 32/813/058/690, 1879.

101 CO 42/759, pp. 309–11.

102 WO 32/813/058/690, 1879.

103 DM 04517, 5 Nov. 1878.

104 Cambridge Papers, Hewett to Lorne, 7 June 1878.

105 *Commandant's Report, 1879*, p. 344.

106 *Ibid., 1880*, p. 273.

107 *Ibid.*, p. 285.

108 DM 06327, 24 Feb. 1880.

109 *Canada Gazette*, XIII (7 Feb. 1880), 1071.

110 DM 05417, 26 March 1879; 06617, 21 June 1880.

111 DM 04588, 3 June 1878.

112 DM 06181, 17 Dec. 1879.

113 Research by T. L. Brock.

114 Perry, "RMC's First Four Years," pp. 10–11.

115 DM 06196, 8 Jan. 1880.

116 *Board of Visitors' Report, 1879*, pp. 326–33, 335–6; *Commandant's Report, 1879*, pp. 346–7; *ibid., 1880*, p. 267; *ibid., 1881*, p. 256; *R.M.C. Review*, VII (June 1926), 36–43; DM 06594, 11 June 1880.

117 DM 06196, 8 Jan. 1880.

118 CO 42/760, Lorne, Secret, 10 March 1880.

119 Addendum to *Commandant's Report, 1880*, pp. 274–5.

120 A. G. G. Wurtele, *The Non-Professional Notes of the Cadets' Tour of Instruction ...* (Quebec, 1881).

121 DM 06514, 7 May 1880.

122 *British Whig*, 2 July 1880.

123 Wurtele, *Non-Professional Notes*, pp. 12–3.

124 J. Hampden Burnham, *Canadians in the Imperial Navy and Military Service Abroad* (Toronto, 1891), p. 228.

125 DM 06283, 6 Feb. 1880; *Commandant's Report, 1880*, p. 264.

126 *R.M.C. Review*, VII (June 1926), 12–24, 36–43.

CHAPTER 4, PAGES 77 - 98

1 DM 08453, 6 March, 1882; *Board of Visitors' Report, 1879*, p. 336.

2 *Commandant's Report, 1880*, pp. 264–5.

3 *Board of Visitors' Report, 1879*, p. 336.

4 *Ibid.*, p. 336.

5 *Militia Report, 1879*, p. xvii.

6 CO 42/761, pp. 226–38; CO 42/770, pp. 238–42.

7 CO 42/761, pp. 578–82; CO 42/765, pp. 528–31.

8 CO 42/773, pp. 596–600; CO 42/774, pp. 380–7; CO 42/776, pp. 434–7.

9 Victoria State Library, Australia, "Statement of Expenditures for Militia and Defence of the Dominion of Canada, 1867–1900."

10 DM 07423, 20 April 1881. The docket is empty and the reason for the decision is not given fully on the cover.

11 RG 9, II A 2, vol. 7, 3995.

12 PAC, Caron Papers, vol. 12, 155; vol. 88, no. 7050; House of Commons, *Debates*, XXIV (1887), 1268.

13 DM 08457, 4 March 1882, p. 62.

14 DM 03555, 7 April 1877.

15 *Commandant's Report, 1877*, p. 256.

16 *Ibid., 1878*, p. 439; *Board of Visitors' Report, 1879*, p. 332; Logan, "Notes," p. 80 *verso*, Powell to Hewett, 6 Feb. 1880.

17 *Commandant's Report, 1880*, p. 263.

18 DM 6372, 17 March 1880.

19 Davis, "Reminiscences of the Royal Military College," p. 21.

20 Dixon Scrapbook, clippings, "Veritas, Kingston," from *Mail*, 7 Nov. 1881, "One of the Old Eighteen," from *Globe*, 16 Nov. 1881.

21 *Ibid.*, pp. 50–2; *Globe*, 5, 9, 15, 16 Nov. 1881; *Daily News*, 7 Nov. 1881.

22 Logan, "Notes," p. 96 *verso*; *Daily News*, 21 June 1878.

23 *Board of Visitors' Report, 1879*, p. 311.

24 *Globe*, 15 Nov. 1881.

25 Panet to Hewett, 6 Feb. 1880, quoted in Logan, "Notes," p. 70 *verso*.

26 Logan, "Notes," p. 44.

27 *Daily News*, 7 Nov. 1881.

28 DM A 15056, 27 July 1896.

29 *Mail*, 7 June 1880.

30 Logan, "Notes," p. 45 *verso*.

31 *Ibid.*, pp. 45 *verso*, 46.

32 *Ibid.*, p. 45.

33 DM 07262, 23 Feb. 1881.

34 *Daily News*, 7 Nov. 1881.

35 DM 08457, 4 March 1882, pp. 47–67.

36 *Globe*, 8 Nov. 1881.

37 Dixon Scrapbook, p. 50, clipping from Toronto *Mail*.

38 DM 08457, 4 March 1882, pp. 79–82; *Globe*, 8 Nov. 1881.

39 *Globe*, 5 Nov. 1881.

40 Dixon Scrapbook, clipping from *Mail*, 4 Nov. 1881, by Cincinnatus, Woodstock.

41 *Daily News*, 7 Nov. 1881; *Globe*, 9 Nov. 1881.

42 Perry, "RMC's First Four Years," p. 11.

43 *Globe*, 16 Nov. 1881.

44 DM 08144; DM 08155.

45 *Globe*, 17 Nov. 1881.

46 House of Commons, *Debates*, XII (13 April 1882), 863.

47 DM 08457, 4 March 1882, pp. 79–81.

48 DM 08208, 22 Dec. 1881.

49 DM 07119, 5 Jan. 1882.

50 DM 08013, 24 Oct. 1881.

51 House of Commons, *Debates*, XII (2 March 1882), 190–1.

52 *Ibid.*

53 DM 08449, DM 08450, DM 08451, DM 08452, DM 08453, DM 08454.

54 House of Commons, *Debates*, XII (13 April 1882), 863–4.

55 DM 08585, 14 April 1882.

56 Dufferin Papers, microfilm reel A 411, Mackenzie to Dufferin, 5 Aug. 1878.

57 *Commandant's Report, 1880*, pp. 270–3.

58 Dixon Scrapbook, clipping from *Daily Mail*, June 1880.

59 MacNutt, *Days of Lorne*, p. 181.

60 *Commandant's Report, 1880*, p. 272.

61 DM 07121, "Report on Attendance of Militia Officers at RMC for Courses of Instruction," 9–11 Oct. 1880.

62 *Ibid.*

63 *Commandant's Report, 1882*, p. 190; *ibid., 1883*, p. 221; *Militia Report, 1883*, appendix 5, Report of the Regiment of Artillery, p. 195; PAC, CEF section, Cummin's transcripts.

64 Ferguson microfilm, Commandant and staff to Ferguson and Bayne, 14 Oct. 1881.

65 DM 07570, 7 June 1881.

66 *Commandant's Report, 1882*, p. 189.

67 Ferguson Papers, Hewett to Ferguson, 3 Oct. 1883.

68 DM 08101, 7 Nov. 1881; DM 08554, 27 Feb. 1882.

69 Macdonald Papers, vol. 200, 84386, John G. Holmes to Macdonald, 5 Nov. 1881.

70 *Ibid.*, vol. 200, 84410, Lewis to Macdonald, 2 Dec. 1881.

71 DM 08044, Hewett to GOC, 1 Nov. 1881.

72 *Ibid.*, Kirkpatrick to Caron, 4 Nov. 1881.

73 RG 9, II A 2, vol. 6, 15 Dec. 1881.

74 Caron Papers, vol. 64, no. 3111.

75 *Ibid.*, vol. 65, no. 3515.

76 *Ibid.*, vol. 64, no. 3114; vol. 70, no. 4017.

77 *Ibid.*, vol. 91, no. 7711.

78 *Ibid.*, vol. 77, no. 4962; vol. 79, no. 5295, 5950; vol. 84, no. 6121. General Luard's sons were admitted although their father had not been five years in Canada (RG II A 2, vol. 6, no. 3853, 24 March 1883).

79 Caron Papers, vol. 74, no. 4508.

80 House of Commons, *Debates*, XIV (1883), 858–60; XVI (1884), 1163.

81 Caron Papers, vol. 73, no. 4357, Hewett to Caron, 4 July 1884.

82 *Commandant's Report, 1883*, p. 222. This may have been the occasion when large ventilators were added to the roof of the Stone Frigate.

83 DM A 186, 6 Oct. 1883.

84 Caron Papers, vol. 78, no. 5086, Hewett to Caron, 28 Dec. 1884; *Ibid.*, vol. 80, no. 5380, Hewett to Caron, 22 Feb. 1885.

85 *R.M.C. Review,* IX (Dec. 1928), 83.

86 Macdonald Papers, vol. 100, Walker Powell to Macdonald, 11 May 1882; DM 97324, 16 March 1881.

87 DM 09838, 28 July 1883; MG 27, I D 3, vol. 64, 3058, 9 Aug. 1883.

88 Walker Powell, *Report on Royal Military College, 1882* in Canada, House of Commons, *Sessional Papers,* XVI (1883), no. 6, p. 179.

89 DM 06415; DM 09421, 28 March 1883.

90 Macdonald Papers, vol. 82, Lorne to Macdonald, 21 June 1883; Macdonald to Lorne, 10 July 1883. Cambridge Papers, Lorne to Cambridge, 6 Aug. 1883.

91 S. A. Denison, *Memoirs,* p. 26.

92 *R.M.C. Review,* VII (June 1926), 44.

93 Massey Library, E. Taylor to L. H. Irving and S. A. Denison, 23 June 1884.

94 *R.M.C. Review,* VII (June 1926), 44.

95 C. P. Stacey, *The Nile Voyageurs, 1884–1885* (Toronto, 1959), *passim.*

96 Preston, *Canada and "Imperial Defense,"* pp. 162–3.

97 CO 42/783, 69–75.

98 *Canada in the Great World War,* V (Toronto, 1920), 360.

99 A. G. G. Wurtele, "Notes and Reminiscences," *R.M.C. Review,* VIII (June 1927), 82; *ibid.,* VII (June 1926), 23.

100 Caron Papers, vol. 79, no. 5334, Hewett to Caron, 14 July 1885.

101 *Canada in the Great World War,* V, 360; Caron Papers, vol. 87, no. 6650, Metcalfe to Caron, 5 July 1885; House of Commons, *Debates,* IV (1885), 2913.

102 Caron Papers, vol. 92, no. 9238. (See also *Globe* of 29 March 1886, and two weeks earlier.)

103 *Canada in the Geat World War,* V, 357. (See RMC Register also.)

104 T. B. Strange, *Gunner Jingo's Jubilee* (London, 1893), p. 378.

105 G. Walker, "The Royal Military College of Canada," *R.M.C. Review,* VIII (June 1927), 26.

106 Caron Papers, vol. 114, no. 11915, Sir Charles Tupper to Sir Adolphe Caron, 23 Jan. 1886.

107 DM *despatches,* I, 67, 9 April 1885.

108 Cambridge Papers, Stanley to Cambridge, 5 Aug. 1890.

109 *R.M.C. Review,* XXIV (1943), 109.

CHAPTER 5, PAGES 99 - 121

1 Canada, House of Commons, *Sessional Papers,* XX (1887), no. 8 [S.P.] 9, "Report of the General Officer Commanding the Militia, 1886," p. xvii. (Hereafter *GOCs' Reports,* which appear in *Sessional Papers* for the following year, are cited by the year to which they refer.)

2 Caron Papers, vol. 145, no. 14128.

3 Canada, House of Commons, *Sessional Papers,* XX (1887), no. 8 [S.P.] 9, "Report of the Deputy Minister of Militia," 1886, p. ix. (Hereafter *Deputy Ministers' Reports,* which appear in *Sessional Papers* for the following year, are cited by the year to which they refer.)

4 DM A 3565, 7 April 1886.

5 Caron Papers, vol. 93, no. 9382, Oliver to Caron, 16 May 1887.

6 *Ibid.*, vol. 14, no. 11930, Denison to Macdonald, 18 Jan. 1888.

7 DM A 186, 6 Oct 1883; Caron Papers, vol. 78, no. 5110.

8 DM A 4030, 10 Aug. 1886.

9 Caron Papers, vol. 93, Oliver to Caron, 2 April 1887.

10 DM A 4030, 10 Aug. 1886.

11 Caron Papers, vol. 20, p. 184.

12 *Ibid.*, vol. 114, no. 11930; DM A 6652, 2 May 1887.

13 Caron Papers, vol. 24, p. 290.

14 *Ibid.*, vol. 24, p.154.

15 *Ibid.*, vol. 122, no. 12451.

16 DM A 8276, 2 June 1888.

17 DM Reports, vol. 10, no. 6406, 2 June 1888.

18 Caron Papers, vol. 123, no. 12504.

19 *Ottawa Daily Citizen*, 16 July 1888; G. F. G. Stanley, *The Birth of Western Canada* (London, 1936), pp. 65, 75; H. George Classen, *Thrust and Counterthrust: the Genesis of the Canadian-United States Boundary* (Don Mills, 1965), pp. 125–7.

20 Cambridge Papers, Lansdowne to Cambridge, 27 May 1884.

21 *Dominion Illustrated*, III (30 Nov. 1889), 342; CO 807, vols. 49 and 53; US Senate, Documents, 58th Congress, 2nd Session, 1903–4, Alaskan Boundary Tribunal, XVI, 345–6; XVII, 108, 160–1; XX, 545; R. Craig Brown, *Canada's National Policy: a Study in Canadian-American Relations* (Princeton, 1964), pp. 289–91.

22 Classen, *Thrust and Counterthrust*, p. 351.

23 Macdonald Papers, vol. 284, no. 130468, Tupper to Macdonald, 15 June 1888.

24 Caron Papers, vol. 108, no. 11401, Macdonald to Caron, 10 Aug. 1887, Tupper to Macdonald, 27 July 1887; Macdonald Papers, vol. 201, no. 84978, Caron to Macdonald, 15 Aug. 1887.

25 Macdonald Papers, vol. 284, no. 130471, Macdonald to Caron, 15 June 1888.

26 *Ibid.*, vol. 284, no. 130478, Tupper to Macdonald, 16 July 1888, cable.

27 Caron Papers, vol. 123, no. 12527, Kirkpatrick to Caron, 16 July 1888.

28 Macdonald Papers, vol. 284, no. 130485, Tupper to Macdonald, 1 Aug. 1888.

29 E. F. Wurtele, "Notes of Some 40 to 50 Years Ago," *R.M.C. Review*, IX (Dec. 1928), 82.

30 Quoted in the *Ottawa Free Press*, 14 July 1888.

31 *Ottawa Daily Citizen*, 16 July 1888.

32 *Ibid.*; *Dominion Illustrated*, III (30 Nov. 1889).

33 Classen, *Thrust and Counterthrust*, pp. 125–34, 145–7. See also John E. Parsons, *West on the 49th Parallel: Red River to the Rockies, 1872–1876* (New York, 1963), pp. 96, 116, 154.

34 Preston, *Canada and "Imperial Defense,"* pp. 180–81.

35 *Commandant's Report, 1885*, p. 197.

36 *Deputy Minister's Report, 1886*, pp. ix–x; *GOC's Report, 1886*, p. xvii; *Commandant's Report, 1886*, p. 191.

37 DM A 4051, 16 Aug. 1886.

38 Caron Papers, vol. 112, nos. 11709, 11771.

39 *Ibid.*, vol. 132, no. 13025.

40 *Commandant's Report, 1889*, p. 204. On 17 Nov. 1888, the GOC asked for a "Stickey" court for RMC cadets, DM, A 8496; unfortunately this docket is empty and the details are wanting. The following quotations are from this same source.

41 Caron Papers, vol. 145, no. 14118, Kirkpatrick to Caron, 19 July 1890.

42 DM A 10246, 9 Aug. 1890.

43 *Commandant's Report, 1886*, p. 191.

44 DM A 9859, 13 March 1890.

45 *Commandant's Report, 1887*, p. 211; *Militia Report, 1891*, Report of the Architect, Engineer Branch, p. 155; DM A 10512, A 10587, A 11829; DM Register [A] 14334, 3 Dec. 1895.

46 Caron Papers, vol. 127, no. 12809; DM A 8638, 13 Jan. 1889.

47 Canada, House of Commons, *Debates*, I (1889), 34; II (1889), 1534.

48 Caron Papers, vol. 145, no. 14118; DM A 13305, p. 2.

49 Caron Papers, vol. 97, no. 9845; *Commandant's Report, 1886*, p. 190.

50 Caron Papers, vol. 78, no. 5135; vol. 10, p. 397.

51 DM, A 6051, A 6063, A 6192, A 6195, A 6196, A 6197, A 6198, A 6199, A 6227.

52 *Commandant's Report, 1884*, p. 207.

53 Caron Papers, vol. 107, no. 11252.

54 CO 42/804, War Office to Colonial Office, 13 August 1890; *ibid.*, 28 August 1890.

55 Caron Papers, vol. 111, no. 11634.

56 CO 42/800, Stanley 90; CO 24/801, WO 23 Sept. 1889; *GOC's Report, 1889*, p. 1.

57 DM A 8631, 7 Jan. 1889.

58 Caron Papers, vol. 148, no. 14315.

59 *GOC's Report, 1886*, p. xvii; *Commandant's Report, 1886*, p. 190.

60 Caron Papers, vol. 11, p. 178.

61 DM A 6194, 3 Oct. 1886; DM A 9086, 4 June 1889.

62 Kerry and McDill, *The History of the Corps of Royal Canadian Engineers*, I, 41.

63 *Commandant's Report, 1889*, pp. 202–3; DM A 9130.

64 *Commandant's Report, 1889*, p. 202; *GOC's Report, 1889*, p. 1; DM A 14536; *Commandant's Report, 1891*, p. 110.

65 Caron Papers, vol. 22, p. 453; DM A 9082.

66 DM A 8478, 9 Nov. 1888.

67 *Commandant's Report, 1889*, p. 202.

68 *Ibid.*, *1887*, p. 211; *1888*, p. 214.

69 Caron Papers, vol. 25, pp. 309–10.

70 *Commandant's Report, 1889*, p. 201; *1890*, p. 153; DM A 9660, 19 Dec. 1889.

71 Caron Papers, vol. 97, no. 10090.

72 DM A 6300, 17 Dec. 1886.

73 Caron Papers, vol. 22, pp. 366–7.

74 *Ibid.*, vol. 118, no. 12227.

75 Cambridge Papers, Middleton to Cambridge, 30 Jan. 1888.

76 DM Reports to Council, vol. 10, no. 6405, 1 June 1888; House of Commons, *Debates, 1889*, II, 1361.

77 Caron Papers, vol. 132, nos. 13145, 13191; vol. 133, no. 13188; DM A 8217; DM Reports to Council, vol. 11, nos. 6978, 6991.

78 Caron Papers, vol. 25, pp. 309–10; vol. 125, no. 12616.

79 *Adjutant-General's Report, 1890*, p. 2.

80 *Commandant's Report, 1886*, p. 187.

81 *Ibid., 1887*, pp. 206–10.

82 *Ibid., 1889*, appendix A, pp. 207–08.

83 RG 9, II A 6, vol. 2, 681, Laurier ms, 58519 (copies of imperial despatches), War Office to Colonial Office, 11 April 1889.

84 *Commandant's Report, 1886*, p. 187.

85 *Ibid., 1890*, p. 152.

86 *Ibid., 1891*, p. 109.

87 *Ibid., 1889*, p. 205.

88 Caron Papers, vol. 137, no. 13506; vol. 30, pp. 36, 87, 332, 485.

89 *Ibid.*, vol. 156, no. 15054.

90 *Commandant's Report, 1886*, p. 190.

91 *Ibid., 1888*, p. 216; *1889*, p. 206.

92 *Militia Report, 1890*, report of the inspector of engineers, p. 150.

93 *Commandant's Report, 1886*, p. 189.

94 *GOC's Report, 1886*, p. xviii; *ibid., 1888*, p. xviii.

95 *Commandant's Report, 1890*, p. 153.

96 DM A 2289, 27 Aug. 1885; Massey Library, G. M. Kirkpatrick, "Diary," p. 16.

97 Illustration, *R.M.C. Review*, VI (May 1923), 76.

98 *Commandant's Report, 1889*, p. 204.

99 *Ibid., 1886*, pp. 186–7.

100 Caron Papers, vol. 113, no. 11876.

101 *GOC's Report, 1888*, p. xvii.

102 Caron Papers, vol. 122, no. 12452.

103 *Ibid.*, vol. 124, no. 12539.

104 *Commandant's Report, 1891*, p. 109; DM A 17520; House of Commons, *Debates*, II (1894), 4310–11.

105 DM A 11456, 10 Nov. 1891.

106 DM A 14710, 16 March 1896.

107 Bridger, "The Second Decade," *R.M.C. Review*, XXIII (Dec. 1942), 53–5.

108 DM A 10346, 19 Sept. 1890.

109 *Commandant's Report, 1893*, p. 143.

110 Henry M. Stanley, *In Darkest Africa ...* (London, 1897), p. 15; A. Mountjoy-Jephson, *Emin Pasha and the Rebellion at the Equator* (New York, 1890), p. 356; Caron Papers, vol. 142, no. 1380.

111 Lt. Kenneth J. R. Campbell, "The Capture of Brohemie, Niger Coast Protectorate, West Africa," RMC Club, *Proceedings*, 11th meeting, 1895, pp. 58–67.

112 For example, Cadet J. M. Clapp, DM A 6752, 1 June 1887.

113 Macdonald Papers, vol. 201, no. 85039.

114 DM A 11016, 18 June 1891.
115 DM A 12750; DM Report, vol. 15, no. 9689.
116 PAC, Cummins' Transcripts.
117 *GOC Report, 1887*, p. xvii.
118 Caron Papers, vol. 105, no. 11089.

CHAPTER 6, PAGES 122 - 48

1 Quoted from Bridger, "The Second Decade."
2 Caron Papers, vol. 26, p. 380, 10 Dec. 1888; vol. 128, no. 12836, 22 Dec. 1888.
3 *Ibid.*, vol. 129, no. 12876.
4 Bridger, "The Second Decade," p. 53.
5 Caron Papers, vol. 8, *passim.*
6 *Ibid.*, vol. 136, no. 13449, 25 June 1889.
7 *Ibid.*, vol. 29, p. 397, July 1889.
8 House of Commons, *Debates*, 1889, II, 1357–61.
9 *Ibid.*, 1705–6.
10 *Ibid.*, 1890, I, 245.
11 *Ibid.*, 1925, 1064; Caron Papers, vol. 133, no. 13188.
12 House of Commons, *Debates*, 1890, II, 3622, 4026.
13 Caron Papers, vol. 133, no. 13205, 24 Jan. 1890.
14 *Board of Visitors' Report, 1890*, p. 171.
15 Bridger, "The Second Decade," p. 53.
16 *Commandant's Report, 1888*, p. 215.
17 *Ibid., 1894*, p. 35; RMC Club, *Proceedings*, 29 Feb. 1896, p. 25.
18 Stats. Ont., 55 Vic. 34, 18(1).
19 DM A 11784, 30 March 1892.
20 RMC Club, *Proceedings*, 1895, p. 26; *Commandant's Report, 1894*, p. 35; Kerry and McDill, *History of the Corps of Royal Canadian Engineers*, I, 62.
21 DM A 11206, 12 Aug. 1891.
22 House of Commons, *Debates*, 1894, I, 386.
23 DM A 13305, 30 March 1894.
24 RG 9, II A 2 (Reports to Council), vol. 15, 10631, 26 June 1894.
25 House of Commons, *Debates*, 1894, II, 5098–113.
26 Caron Papers, vol. 65, no. 3251, 29 Oct. 1883.
27 *Ibid.*, vol. 130, no. 12993, 26 Dec. 1888.
28 *Ibid.*, vol. 24, p. 131, 7 May 1888.
29 For example, Macdonald's endorsement, "Private. My dear Caron. Be as strict as you please for the future but wind up satisfactorily with these people. J.A.McD," *Ibid.*, vol. 130, no. 12993, 26 Dec. 1888; Macdonald Papers, vol. 201, no. 81570, 24 March 1891.
30 For example, Caron Papers, vol. 21, p. 285, 28 Sept. 1887.
31 *Ibid.*, vol. 104, no. 10889, 3 June 1887.
32 *Ibid.*, vol. 21, p. 285, 28 Sept. 1887.
33 *Ibid.*, vol. 157, no. 15200, 28 Aug. 1891.
34 For example, *ibid.*, vol. 142, no. 13872, 1890, etc.
35 *Ibid.*, vol. 24, p. 131, 7 May 1888.

36 *Ibid.*, vol. 159, no. 15332.
37 *Ibid.*, vol. 23, p. 336, 26 March 1888.
38 For example, DM A 8625, 29 Dec. 1888.
39 Caron Papers, vol. 148, no. 14322, March 1891.
40 DM A 13317½, 9 April 1894.
41 DM A 13649, 10 Nov. 1894.
42 *Canadian Magazine*, IV (1894–5), 432.
43 Caron Papers, vol. 117, no. 12120, 4 May 1888.
44 *Commandant's Report, 1890*, p. 158, appendix A, 26 June 1890. The italics are mine.
45 DM A 13696, 30 Sept. 1896.
46 *Commandant's Report, 1895*, p. 43.
47 DM A 13696, 30 Sept. 1896, Cameron to Deputy Minister, 29 Sept. 1896, forwarding his correspondence with Judge Weatherbe and Bishop Courtney in 1894.
48 DM A 13696, 30 Sept. 1896.
49 House of Commons, *Debates*, 1895, II, 3781.
50 *Ibid.*, 3799, 3810.
51 RMC Club, *Proceedings*, 1895, p. 91.
52 *Weekly British Whig*, 11 June 1891; Brock ms, "Some recollections of No. 308, Col. H. D. L. Gordon."
53 *GOC's Report, 1894*, p. v.
54 PAC, F. W. Borden Papers, no. 3111, 1 July 189[7].
55 Classen, *Thrust and Counterthrust*, pp. 126, 147, 310.
56 Parsons, *West on the 49th Parallel*, pp. 36, 116, 154.
57 Caron Papers, vol. 145, no. 141128, 12 July 1890.
58 *Ibid.*, vol. 145, no. 14145, 12 Sept. 1890; DM A 10119, 21 June 1890; DM A 10605, 29 Nov., 12 Jan. 1890.
59 *Commandant's Report, 1892*, p. 17; *ibid., 1893*, p. 142; *ibid., 1894*, p. 34; *ibid., 1895*, p. 43.
60 F. W. Borden Papers, no. 3111, 1 July 189[7].
61 House of Commons, *Debates*, 1895, II, 3782–3; *Commandant's Report, 1895*, p. 43.
62 CO Misc. 111, *Report of Colonial Conference, 1897*, appendix A, p. 74.
63 House of Commons, *Debates*, 1895, II, 3790–7.
64 [Canada], *Reports in reference to the Royal Military College for the year 1895* (Ottawa, 1896), "Board of Visitors Report, 1895," pp. 1–8. (A copy of this volume is in the RMC library.)
65 *Ibid.*, pp. 9–11.
66 *Ibid.*, Canada, House of Commons, *Sessional Papers*, 1896, 2nd Session Supplementary Return 15, printed for distribution only.
67 DM A 14333, 29 Nov., 3 Dec. 1895.
68 *Reports in reference to the Royal Military College, 1895*, Canada, House of Commons, *Sessional Papers*, Supplementary Returns, 1896, pp. 12–17.
69 *Ibid.*, pp. 18–22.
70 House of Commons, *Debates*, 1896, II, 6679–767.
71 DM A 14779, 10 April 1896.
72 *Commandant's Report, 1896*, p. 28.
73 *Ibid.*, pp. 29–30.

74 *Reports in reference to the Royal Military College, 1895,* Canada, House of Commons, *Sessional Papers,* Supplementary Returns, 1896, 15a, 15b.

75 [Frederic W. Falls], "The Royal Military College of Canada," *Canadian Magazine,* IV (1894–5), 261–8, 377–88, 428–32.

76 *Ibid.,* p. 377.

77 *Ibid.,* pp. 386–8.

78 *Ibid.,* pp. 438–9.

79 *Ibid.,* p. 440.

80 *Ibid.,* p. 442.

81 RMC Club, *Proceedings,* 1907, pp. 142–8.

CHAPTER 7, PAGES 149 - 78

1 House of Commons, *Debates,* 1897, II, 4802 (R. Cartwright, 21 June 1897); F. W. Borden Papers, no. 3111, 1 July 189[7].

2 CO 42/845, WO to CO, 19 July 1896.

3 Victoria, Parliamentary Papers, 57/1889.

4 F. W. Borden Papers, no. 394, 5 Sept. 1896.

5 *Ibid.,* no. 406, 7 Sept. 1896.

6 DM A 15056, 27 July 1896.

7 Kenneth Young, *Arthur James Balfour* (London, 1963), pp. 224–5.

8 Quoted in Morgan, *Canadian Men and Women of the Time* (Toronto, 1912), p. 121.

9 CO 42/845, pp. 111–12, WO to CO, 19 July 1896.

10 F. W. Borden Papers, no. 81, 20 July 1896.

11 CO 42/845, pp. 111–12, WO to CO, 19 July 1896.

12 PRO, Index 15388, CO 42/845, Aberdeen telegram 26 Aug. 1896; Aberdeen 249, 27 Aug. 1896; Aberdeen telegram 8 Oct. 1896 [Destroyed], CO 42/845, p. 132, WO to CO, 13 Oct. 1896.

13 Logan "Notes," p. 273.

14 F. W. Borden Papers, no. 733, 27 Oct. 1896; *ibid.,* no. 763, 2 Nov. 1896.

15 Logan, "Notes," p. 273.

16 CO 42/845, WO to CO, 6 Nov. 1896.

17 F. W. Borden Papers, no. 1361, Kitson to Borden, 20 Jan. 1897.

18 *Ibid.,* nos. 25, 54, 55, 110, 152, 333, 428, 500, 667, 929, 1121, 1300, July 1896 to Jan. 1897.

19 *Ibid.,* no. 1361, 20 Jan. 1897.

20 DM A 15586, 1 Feb. 1897. Kitson's first official proposals of the reorganization are not in the Deputy Minister's file. The following details are from the Borden Papers, no. 1426, 1 Feb. 1897.

21 F. W. Borden Papers, no. 1670, 27 March 1897.

22 *Ibid.,* no. 1426, 1 Feb. 1897.

23 *Ibid.,* no. 1670, 27 March 1897.

24 *Ibid.,* no. 1693, 31 March 1897.

25 *Ibid.,* no. 1847, 25 April 1897.

26 *Ibid.,* no. 2094, 23 May 1897; Brock ms., "Family and R.M.C. Recollections of No. 338 Alfred La Rocque."

27 F. W. Borden Papers, no. 1847, 25 April 1897.

28 Logan "Notes," pp. 282, 282*v*, 283.

29 F. W. Borden, Outletters, III, 23–4, 18 Jan. 1897.

30 House of Commons, *Debates*, 1897, I, 791.

31 *Ibid.*, 2447.

32 *Ibid.*, II, 3540–4108.

33 *Ibid.*, 4480–502.

34 *Ibid.*, 4893–903.

35 F. W. Borden Papers, nos. 2135, 2162, 2269; DM 04588.

36 *Commandant's Report, 1897*, pp. 36–7.

37 F. W. Borden Papers, no. 3114.

38 *Ibid.*, Kitson to Borden, 18 Nov. 1897.

39 *Ibid.*, no. 2270, 9 June 1897.

40 *Commandant's Report, 1897*, p. 35.

41 *Ibid.*, pp. 36–7.

42 F. W. Borden Papers, no. 2135, 29 May 1897; no. 2171, 7 June 1897.

43 PAC, Hutton Papers, p. 343, 17 May 1899.

44 F. W. Borden Papers, no. 3111, 1 July 189[7].

45 *Ibid.*, Kitson to Borden, 27 Oct. 1897, enclosing FWB to Kitson, 12 July 1897.

46 *Ibid.*, no. 3423, 6 Aug. 1897.

47 *Ibid.*, MPP [unsigned] Ottawa, 12 Sept. 1897.

48 *Ibid.*, Kitson, 27 Sept. 1897; *ibid.*, Kitson to Borden, 18 Nov. 1897.

49 *Ibid.*, L. G. Power to Borden, 28 Oct. 1897; Kitson to Borden, 18 Nov. 1897; J. G. Bennett, MD, to Borden, 30 Dec. 1897; J. G. Bennett to Borden, 6 Jan. 1898; anonymous draft 28 Feb. 1898.

50 *Ibid.*, no. 3258, 19 July 1897.

51 *Ibid.*, no. 3114, 2 July 1897; no. 3440, 9 Aug. 1897.

52 *Ibid.*, no. 3437, 8 Aug. 1897.

53 *Ibid.*, no. 3053, nd.

54 *Ibid.*, no. 3141, Butler to Borden, 7 July 1897; no. 3490, Kitson to Borden, 13 Aug. 1897; Walter Lawson to Butler, 18 Dec. 1897; Butler to Borden, 13 Nov. 1897.

55 *Ibid.*, Kitson to Borden, 22 Aug. 1897.

56 *Ibid.*, W. R. Butler to Borden, 13 Nov. 1897.

57 *Ibid.*, Butler to Borden, 4 Dec. 1897; Lawson to Butler, 18 Dec. 1897.

58 *Ibid.*, no. 3490, 13 Aug. 1897; no. 3505, 14 Aug. 1897.

59 *Commandant's Report, 1897*, p. 35.

60 F. W. Borden Papers, Kitson to Borden, 22 Aug. 1897.

61 *Commandant's Report, 1898*, p. 43; *1899*, p. 33; *1900*, p. 55.

62 Logan "Notes," pp. 281–2*v*. Kitson complained to the Adjutant-General in July 1898 that the only result that newspaper advertising achieved was a heavy charge against the college appropriation.

63 F. W. Borden Papers, Butler to Borden, 5 Dec. 1897.

64 *Commandant's Report, 1898*, p. 43.

65 *Ibid., 1899*, p. 35.

66 RMC Club, *Proceedings*, 1900, pp. 109–18.

67 *Commandant's Report, 1897*, p. 36.

68 *Ibid., 1899*, pp. 34, 36.

69 F. W. Borden Papers, no. 1361, 20 Jan. 1897.

70 F. W. Borden, Outletters, III, 28–9, 18 Jan. 1897.

71 *Commandant's Report, 1899*, p. 35.

72 *Ibid., 1897*, p. 35; *1898*, p. 43; *1899*, p. 34, etc.

73 CO Misc. 111, *Report of Colonial Conference, 1897*, appendix A, p. 74.

74 F. W. Borden Papers, no. 1612.

75 Hutton Papers, p. 341, 17 May 1898.

76 *Ibid.*, p. 344, 17 May 1898.

77 *Ibid.*, p. 346, 20 Aug. 1898.

78 *Ibid.*, p. 350, 1 Nov. 1898; pp. 735–9, no. 1204, 25 Aug. 1898.

79 DM A 17169, 4 Nov. 1898.

80 Hutton Papers, pp. 735–9, 1 Feb. 1899.

81 *Commandant's Report, 1898*, p. 44.

82 PAC, Leach Commission Report, 1898, pp. 63–4.

83 *GOC's Report, 1899*, p. 27.

84 PAC, Minto Papers, pp. 103–4.

85 Hutton Papers, p. 66, 1 Sept. 1899; *GOC's Report, 1899*, p. 27.

86 *Ibid.*, pp. 1493–4, 17 Aug. 1899.

87 Bridger, "The Third Decade," *R.M.C. Review*, XXIV (June 1943), 33.

88 Lieutenant-Colonel F. E. Whitton, *The History of the Prince of Wales's Leinster Regiment (Royal Canadians)* (2 vols. Aldershot, 1926), I, 376–7.

89 Bridger, "The Third Decade," p. 33.

90 DM A 17485, 21 April 1899.

91 House of Commons, *Debates*, 1899, III, 7022–4.

92 Bridger, "The Third Decade," p. 35.

93 *Commandant's Report, 1899*, pp. 33, 35.

94 *Ibid.*, p. 34; Militia Order, 1899, no. 212.

95 Hutton Papers, pp. 1559–60, 11 Nov. 1899.

96 *Ibid.*, pp. 507–9, Christmas Day 1899.

97 *Ibid.*, pp. 1644–6, 11 Jan. 1900.

98 *Commandant's Report, 1900*, p. 55; Canada, House of Commons, *Sessional Papers*, 1900, no. 49, p. 101.

99 Hutton Papers, pp. 615–16, 27 Dec. [1899].

100 Minto Papers, vol. 17, p. 26, 7 Jan. 1900.

101 *Ibid.*, vol. 21, pp. 100–2, 27 Jan. 1900.

102 *Ibid.*, pp. 105–6, 30 Jan. 1900.

103 *Ibid.*, p. 124, cable, Grove, military secretary, WO, to Kitson, 20 March 1900.

104 *Ibid.*, pp. 119–23, 22 March 1900.

105 *Ibid.*, pp. 128–30, 7 April 1900.

106 *Ibid.*, pp. 125–7, 3 April 1900, pp. 133–4, 14 April 1900, pp. 135–8, 9 May 1900.

107 *Commandant's Report, 1897*, p. 56.

108 *British Whig*, 25 June 1900.

109 *Ibid.*, 28 June 1900.

110 Minto Papers, vol. 21, pp. 139–43, 10 July 1900.

111 House of Commons, *Debates*, 1900, I, 595.

112 Hutton Papers, p. 341, 17 May 1898.

113 RMC Club, *Proceedings*, 1898, pp. 14–17.

114 Bridger, "The Third Decade," p. 35, says that eighty-three graduates

and ex-cadets served in South Africa. *Canadians in Khaki: South Africa 1899–1900* ... (nd, np) supplies the names of sixty-seven who had served there by some time in 1900. The *Canadian Annual Review for 1901*, p. 295, states that 102 RMC graduates were in South Africa on 1 April 1900. Files at RMC records show that the total during the war was 113 out of a little more than four hundred cadets who had passed through the college. By that time many graduates had died and many more were in the armed forces in Canada, India, Britain, or elsewhere.

115 E. W. B. Morrison, *With the Guns in South Africa* (Hamilton: *Spectator*, 1901), p. 101.

116 *Times*, 12 Jan. 1901.

CHAPTER 8, PAGES 179 - 210

1 CO 42/881, pp. 16–18, Minto, telegram, 3 Jan. 1901.
2 *Ibid.*, pp. 37–8, Minto, telegram, 6 Jan. 1901.
3 Laurier Papers, nos. 52242–53, 5 Jan. 1901.
4 CO 42/881, pp. 16–18, Minto, telegram, 3 Jan. 1901.
5 *Ibid.*, p. 37, Minto, telegram, 6 Jan. 1901.
6 CO 42/879, pp. 625–7, WO to CO, 12 Dec. 1900.
7 CO 42/881, pp. 16–18, 41, Minto, telegram, 3 Jan. 1901.
8 *Ibid.*, pp. 390–2, 574–8; CO 42/886, pp. 223–6.
9 *Commandant's Report, 1901*, pp. 63–4; *1902*, p. 43; *1904*, p. 59.
10 *Ibid.*, *1900*, p. 56; *1901*, pp. 64–5; *1902*, p. 45.
11 House of Commons, *Debates*, 1901, II, 3784.
12 *GOC's Report, 1901*, p. 34.
13 Great Britain, Parliamentary Papers, XLI (1904), *Report of the Commissioners to Inquire into ... the War in South Africa, Cd. 1790*, paras. 8466–78.
14 House of Commons, *Debates*, 1902, II, 2562–3.
15 PAC, Grey Papers, MG 27, II B 2, vol. 12, no. 3, 8 April 1905.
16 *Commandant's Report, 1902*, p. 44; Grey Papers, vol. 12, no. 1, 22 Dec. 1904.
17 RMC Club, *Proceedings*, 1903, p. 68.
18 Douglas Library, Dundonald Papers, Dundonald to Borden, 11 Feb. 1904.
19 Bridger, "The Third Decade," pp. 35, 37–8.
20 DM 22913, 12 May 1903.
21 RMC Club, *Proceedings*, 1903, p. 47.
22 Laurier Papers, 215776, 29 June 1905.
23 *Commandant's Report, 1904*, p. 60.
24 Laurier Papers, nos. 96702–3, 19 April 1905.
25 *Ibid.*, no. 215776, 29 June 1905.
26 *Commandant's Report, 1905*, p. 60.
27 Australia, Parliamentary Papers, 1905/77 (in PRO, Cab. 11/27).
28 *Commandant's Report, 1906*, p. 53.
29 House of Commons, *Debates*, 1906, IV, 7182.
30 *Board of Visitors' Report, 1908*, p. 38.
31 PAC, Militia and Defence HQ [post-1922 papers], 74–37–1, vol. 1,

pp. 9–10, 22–3, 66, 68, 76; RG 9 II A 2, vols. 24–32, *Minutes of the Militia Council,* I (2nd meeting, 29 Nov. 1904), n.p.

32 House of Commons, *Debates,* 1905, IV, 6970–5.

33 Bridger, "The Third Decade," pp. 39, 42; Bridger, "The Fourth Decade and the Great War," *R.M.C. Review,* XXV (Dec. 1944), 51.

34 Grey Papers, vol. 12, no. 30, 8 April 1905.

35 CO 42/901, Grey, Confidential, 27 Aug. 1905. Unfortunately this report cannot now be located.

36 House of Commons, *Debates,* 1902, I, 443.

37 Canada, House of Commons, *Sessional Papers,* vol. XLV 1911, no. 35a, *Report of General Sir John French upon ... the Canadian Military Forces,* p. 19.

38 Research by T. L. Brock.

39 Brock ms, "Autobiographical notes of No. 338 Alfred La Rocque."

40 Minutes of the Militia Council, I (14 March 1905), paras. 647–8, I (28 March 1905), para. 766.

41 Bridger, "The Fourth Decade," p. 54.

42 Laurier Papers, no. 72312, 19 April 1903.

43 Bridger, "The Fourth Decade," p. 55.

44 RMC Club, *Proceedings,* 1903, pp. 122–4.

45 House of Commons, *Debates,* 1905, V, 7000–2.

46 RMC Club, *Proceedings,* 22 June 1905, p. 21; Bridger, "The Fourth Decade," p. 39.

47 CO 42/904, pp. 366–70.

48 *Times,* 8 March 1922.

49 House of Commons, *Debates,* 1906, III, 4247–8.

50 Minutes of the Militia Council, IV, 1908, paras. 39–40.

51 House of Commons, *Debates,* 1909–1910, III, 5790.

52 DND, HQ C417, "Board of Visitors' Report, 21 Feb. 1906," pp. 3–5.

53 Canada, House of Commons, *Sessional Papers,* vol. XLII (1907–1908), no. 17, *Report of the Militia Council, March 31, 1907,* appendix C; *Board of Visitors' Report, 1907,* pp. 22–8.

54 Minutes of the Militia Council, II, 1906, pp. 7–9, para. 672.

55 *Commandant's Report, 1906,* p. 52.

56 *Board of Visitors' Report, 27 May 1908,* p. 41.

57 Brock ms, No. 870, Eric de Lotbinière Greenwood.

58 Massey Library, "B" Company Order Book.

59 William Arthur Bishop, *The Courage of the Early Morning: a son's biography of a famous father* (Toronto, 1965), pp. 16–17.

60 *Ibid.,* p. 17.

61 Information given to the author.

62 House of Commons, *Debates,* 1907–1908, I, 1018–33; Bridger, "The Fourth Decade," p. 53.

63 Laurier Papers, pp. 135407–8, 22 Jan. 1908.

64 *Ibid.,* pp. 135430–3, 20 Jan. 1908.

65 *Ibid.,* p. 135434, 22 Jan. 1908.

66 House of Commons, *Debates,* 1909–1910, III, 5789.

67 *Board of Visitors' Report, 27 May 1903,* p. 2 (in DM 14266, 26 May 1902).

68 House of Commons, *Debates*, 1907–1908, IV, 7702.

69 *Ibid.*, 1909, I, 1732.

70 *Board of Visitors' Report, 3 May 1909*, p. 49.

71 RG 7, G 21, no. 251, vol. 1, Conference of CGS with Borden and Lake, 7 Oct. 1907.

72 *Commandant's Report, 1910*, p. 54.

73 RG 7, G 21, no. 384, vol. 2a–b, Deputy Minister to Governor-General, 28 June 1910.

74 *Board of Visitors' Report, 3 May, 1909*, p. 50.

75 *Ibid., June 1910*, p. 61.

76 Militia and Defence, HQ 74–24–7, 5 March 1907.

77 *Commandant's Report, 1910*, p. 55.

78 House of Commons, *Debates*, 1909–1910, III, 5785.

79 *Board of Visitors' Report, 1910*, pp. 58–9, 63–7.

80 Militia and Defence, HQ 74–1–71, MGO, 18 June 1910.

81 French, *Report*, pp. 18–20.

82 Canada, *Sessional Papers*, XLV, 1911, no. 35b, Major-General Sir P. H. N. Lake, *Report upon ... the Recommendations of General Sir John French*, pp. 12–13.

83 Militia and Defence, HQ 74–1–75, "Memo ... showing the cost of enlarging R.M.C.," 20 Dec. [19] 10.

84 *Board of Visitors' Report, 1910*, p. 63.

85 Bridger, "The Fourth Decade," pp. 55–63.

86 House of Commons, *Debates*, 1900, III, 9888.

87 Militia and Defence HQ 15–2–2, vol. 2.

88 *GOC's Report, 1903*, p. 40.

89 Bridger, "The Third Decade," p. 42; "The Fourth Decade," pp. 55–6, 63; *Commandant's Report, 1909–10*, p. 55; *1911*, p. 56.

90 French, *Report*, 1910, p. 18.

91 Bridger, "The Fourth Decade," p. 55.

92 *Ibid.*, p. 64, quoting Montreal *Star*, 1 March 1913.

93 Bridger, "The Third Decade," p. 39; "The Fourth Decade," pp. 55, 60.

94 *Canadian Magazine*, IV (1894–1895), 433.

95 Bridger, "The Third Decade," p. 42.

96 Bridger, "The Fourth Decade," p. 51.

97 *Ibid.*, pp. 59–60.

98 *Ibid.*, p. 56.

99 *Ibid.*, p. 63.

100 Militia and Defence HQ 74–11–9.

101 RG 7, G 21, no. 384, vol. 2.

102 Commonwealth Archives Office, Canberra, Australia, MP 84 81–26A.

103 Massey Library, Bridges' diary.

104 Lieutenant-Colonel W. Hamilton Merritt, *Australian Military and Naval Annual* (Melbourne, 1912), pp. 73–7.

105 Melbourne *Argus*, 30 April 1910; Joseph E. Lee, *Duntroon: The Royal Military College of Australia, 1911–1941* (Canberra, 1952), *passim*.

106 Sir Arthur P. Douglas, *The Dominion of New Zealand* (London, 1910), p. 278; *Army Review* (Oct. 1912), IV, 331.

107 Information collated from *Commandants' Reports, 1911*, pp. 57–8;

1912, pp. 64–5; *1913*, pp. 66–7; *1914*, pp. 66–7; *Militia Council Reports, 1911*, p. 17; *1912*, p. 19; *1913*, p. 27; *1914*, p. 25.

108 Militia and Defence HQ 74–24–7.

109 Information collated from RMC Registers. The social pattern did not change much until 1948.

110 *Board of Visitors' Report, 1912*, p. 70.

111 John S. Moir, *History of the Royal Canadian Corps of Signals 1903–1961* (Ottawa, 1962), pp. 1–7.

112 S. T. Wood, "High Endeavour," *R.M.C. Review*, XXVI (1945), pp. 19–33.

113 Militia and Defence HQ 74–38–3.

114 RG 7, G 21, no. 384, vol. 2a–b, War Office to Governor-General, 13 June 1912.

115 Brock ms, Greenwood to Brock.

CHAPTER 9, PAGES 211 - 25

1 G. W. L. Nicholson, *Canadian Expeditionary Force, 1914–1919* (Ottawa, 1962), pp. 14–19.

2 K. C. Eyre, "Staff and Command in the Canadian Corps: The Canadian Militia, 1896–1914, as a source of Senior Officers" (unpublished MA thesis, Duke University, 1967), p. 163.

3 *Ibid.*, p. 120.

4 *Ibid.*, p. 147.

5 *Ibid.*, pp. 147–63.

6 B. H. Liddell Hart, *The Real War, 1914–1918* (Boston, 1930), p. 435.

7 *Commandant's Report, 1915*, p. 32; *Board of Visitors' Report, 1915*, p. 38.

8 *Commandant's Report, 1914*, p. 66; *1915*, p. 38.

9 House of Commons, *Debates*, 1915 (March 25), II, 1519; information from G. G. M. Carr-Harris.

10 *Commandant's Report, 1915*, p. 31.

11 House of Commons, *Debates*, 1915 (March 25), II, 1519; *Commandant's Report, 1915*, p. 32.

12 Information from John H. Price.

13 *Commandant's Report, 1915*, p. 32.

14 *Commandant's Report, 1916*, p. 27.

15 Information from John H. Price and G. G. M. Carr-Harris.

16 RG 7, G 21, no. 384, vol. 2a–b, 25 February 1915.

17 RG 7, G 21, no. 384, vol. 3b, 30 December 1918; vol. 3a, July 1919.

18 *Commandant's Report, 1915*, p. 33.

19 *Commandant's Report, 1916*, p. 26.

20 RG 7, G 21, no. 384, vol. 3b, 17 July 1917; 19 September 1917; 10 December 1917; 19 February 1918.

21 *Commandant's Report, 1917*, p. 28.

22 *Ibid., 1918*, p. 25.

23 Information from John H. Price.

24 *British Whig*, 11 September 1913.

25 *Board of Visitors' Report, 1914*, pp. 70-1.

26 *Ibid., 1915*, p. 39.

27 *Commandant's Report, 1917*, pp. 30–1; *Board of Visitors' Report, 1917*, pp. 34–5.

28 *Board of Visitors' Report, 1915*, p. 39.

29 Bridger, "The Fourth Decade," p. 71.

30 House of Commons, *Debates*, 1915, II, 1599–622.

31 *Board of Visitors' Report, 1915*, p. 45.

32 House of Commons, *Debates*, 1917, VI, 5310.

33 *Commandant's Report, 1915*, p. 33.

34 *Commandant's Report, 1917*, pp. 32, 36.

35 MG 26, H 1(a), vol. 243, Lord Shaughnessy to Borden, 28 August 1918.

36 Bridger, "The Fourth Decade," p. 72.

37 Ex-cadet, "The Royal Military College of Canada," *Canadian Defence Quarterly*, II (1924–5), 244.

38 *Ibid.*, pp. 244–6.

39 Bishop, *The Courage of the Early Morning*, p. vi.

40 *R.M.C. Review*, XXV (1944), 72; *Commandant's Report, 1919, p. 25.*

41 C.W.R.-R.B., "Memoir: Brig.-General Duncan Sayre MacInnes, C.M.G., D.S.O., Royal Engineers," offprint from the *Royal Engineers' Journal* (July 1918).

42 Herbert Fairlie Wood, *Vimy!* (Toronto, 1967), p. 68.

43 Lieutenant-General Baron von Freytag-Loringhoven, *Deductions from the World War* (London, 1918), p. 143.

44 *Ibid.*, p. 156.

CHAPTER 10, PAGES 226 - 56

1 RG 9, II B 3, Militia General Order 7, 1920; Department of National Defence Headquarters (NDHQ) HQ 74–26–6, 28 June, 9 Aug. 1917, 7 March 1918.

2 *Commandant's Report, 1920*, p. 52.

3 MG 27, I D 3, vol. 94, no. 9410.

4 Information from Colonel T. F. Gelley; A. E. Kennedy-Carefoot, "Lieutenant-General Archibald Cameron Macdonell, K.C.B., C.M.G., D.S.O., etc." (unpublished mss loaned by Lieutenant-Colonel H. M. Wallis), p. 184.

5 Kennedy-Carefoot, "Macdonell," p. 185.

6 MG 30, G 24, vol. 3, "RMC," Macdonell to General MacBrien, 24 July 1920.

7 *Commandant's Report, 1920*, p. 75; *ibid., 1921*, p. 97; *ibid., 1922*, p. 101.

8 Information from Colonel T. F. Gelley.

9 Kingston Historical Society Minute Book, *passim*.

10 *Ibid.*, 13 January 1925.

11 Crusader (pseud.), "The Knight of the Old Red Patch," *Canadian Defence Quarterly*, II (1923), 344.

12 *Commandant's Report, 1922*, p. 92.

13 *Ibid., 1920*, p. 57, 73; NDHQ, 74–34–2, vol. II, 5, 6, 29 Oct. 1919.

14 Militia and Defence HQ 74–26–4, 23 April 1920; 1 May 1920; *R.M.C. Review*, II (May 1921), 73.

15 *Commandant's Report, 1922*, p. 90.
16 *R.M.C. Review*, XXVI (June 1945), 49.
17 *Commandant's Report, 1921*, p. 91.
18 *Ibid.*, p. 90.
19 House of Commons, *Debates*, 1920, IV, 3153.
20 *Ibid.*, 1921, III, 2805–6.
21 *Commandant's Report, 1922*, p. 100.
22 Canada, *Report of the Department of National Defence (DND Report)*, *1923*, p. 54.
23 *Commandant's Report, 1921*, p. 92.
24 *Ibid.*, p. 93.
25 *Ibid., 1922*, p. 100.
26 *DND Report, 1923*, pp. 53–4.
27 NDHQ 74–11–24, Macdonell, 9 June 1922.
28 *Commandant's Report, 1921*, p. 83.
29 *Ibid., 1922*, p. 98.
30 *Ibid., 1921*, p. 87.
31 House of Commons, *Debates*, 1921, III, 2803.
32 MG 30, G 24, vol. 3, Macdonell to MacBrien, 15 November 1920.
33 *Commandant's Report, 1920*, p. 57.
34 *Ibid.*, p. 71; *ibid., 1922*, p. 98; *Board of Visitors' Report, 1920*, pp. 79–80.
35 *Commandant's Report, 1920*, p. 64.
36 *Board of Visitors' Report, 1921*, p. 98.
37 *Advisory Board Report, 1922*, p. 106.
38 *Commandant's Report, 1920*, p. 62.
39 NDHQ 74–11–25.
40 NDHQ 74–15–74, Colonel, Director of Personal Services to Director of Military Training and Staff Duties, Canada, nd.
41 *Ibid.*, 74–26–4, [?] to Macdonell, 25 July 1923.
42 *Commandant's Report, 1921*, p. 82.
43 The Royal Military College of Canada, *Prospectus* (1928), p. 2; W. E. McNeil to Macdonell, 22 February 1924, in *R.M.C. Review*, V (May 1924), 19.
44 *Commandant's Report, 1921*, pp. 80–1.
45 *Ibid.*, p. 88.
46 *Kerry and McDill, The History of the Corps of Royal Canadian Engineers*, I, 295.
47 *Commandant's Report, 1922*, pp. 102–5, appendix, Report of the Director of Studies.
48 NDHQ 74–11–24, appendix to Commandant's Report (1922); *ibid.*, Macdonell to [CGS], 9 June 1922; *ibid.*, A. McNaughton to CGS, 16 June 1922.
49 PAC, Diary of General Sir A. C. Macdonell, 8 July 1921.
50 Massey Library, Arnold Case, RMC Court of Inquiry, 27 February 1924, exhibit "B."
51 *Ibid.*, evidence of BSM (UO) E. J. Crowe; F. G. Arnold to Macdonell, 3 March 1924. The RMC cadet ranks were renamed about this time and Crowe's rank is given in both styles in the testimony.
52 *Ibid.*, evidence of UO V. C. Hamilton.
53 *Ibid.*, 24 Feb. 1924, exhibit "A" [Greenwood's lecture to senior cadets].

54 *Ibid.*, supplement "c" to Second Court of Inquiry, 12 March 1924.
55 *Ibid.*, Court of Inquiry, 24 Feb. 1924, evidence of Major Cock.
56 *Ibid.*, F. G. Arnold to Macdonell, 18 Feb. 1924.
57 *Ibid.*
58 *Ibid.*, telegram, Macdonell to F. G. Arnold, 20 Feb. 1924.
59 *Ibid.*, Macdonell to Deputy Minister, 21 Feb. 1924.
60 *Ibid.*, W. F. Nickle to Macdonell, 22 Feb. 1924.
61 *Ibid.*, Major-General Panet to Commandant, 25 Feb. 1924.
62 *Ibid.*, Proceedings, 24 June 1924.
63 *Ibid.*, Arnold to the Commandant, 27 Feb. 1924.
64 *Ibid.*, Proceedings, 27 Feb. 1924.
65 *Ibid.*, F. G. Arnold to Macdonell, 3 March 1924.
66 *Ibid.*, 4 March 1924.
67 *Ibid.*, Macdonell to F. G. Arnold, 4 March 1924.
68 *Ibid.*, Macdonell to General MacBrien, 5 March 1924.
69 *Ibid.*, Macdonell to F. G. Arnold, 7 March 1924.
70 *Ibid.*, F. G. Arnold to Macdonell, 7 March 1924.
71 *Ibid.*, Order for a Court of Inquiry, 8 March 1924.
72 *Ibid.*, Macdonell to the Deputy Minister, 15 March 1924.
73 *Ibid.*, "Punishments awarded ... Cadet seniority lists."
74 *Ibid.*, F. G. Arnold to Macdonell, 24 June 1924.
75 Information from Brigadier D. R. Agnew.
76 Logan, "Notes," p. 55.
77 Information received from several members of the RMC staff and from ex-cadets.
78 T. L. Brock, *"Fight the Good Fight"*: *Looking in on the Recruit Class at the Royal Military College of Canada during a week in February, 1931* (Montreal, 1964; privately printed), p. 1. Written by a senior a few months after his graduation in 1934, this is a full and unvarnished account of recruiting practices.
79 Kennedy-Carefoot, "Macdonell," p. 197.
80 Ex-Cadet, "The Royal Military College of Canada." pp. 242–4.
81 Brock, *Fight the Good Fight*, p. 1.
82 Ex-Cadet, "The Royal Military College of Canada, p. 244.
83 House of Commons, *Debates*, 1924, v, 4809–4814.
84 D. Hist. 171.013 (D3), "Commandant's Report, 1924–25," pp. 6–7; *ibid.*, Director of Studies, "Report," p. 10. The only file on RMC commandants' and Advisory Boards' reports in the 1920s and 1930s is in the Directorate of History, Canadian Armed Forces Headquarters.
85 NDHQ 74–20–77, Colonel A. McNaughton, deputy chief of Staff to Constantine, 7 Nov. 1925.
86 NDHQ 74–20–77.
87 "Commandant's Report, 1925–26," p. 11; *R.M.C. Review*, XXVII (1946), 55.
88 *DND Report, 1929*, p. 51.
89 *Ibid., 1928*, p. 52.
90 "Commandant's Report, 1925–1926," p. 16.
91 D. Hist. 171.013(D3), "Advisory Board Report, 1927" (agenda and disposal sheet).
92 *R.M.C. Review*, X (June 1929), 96–8; *ibid.*, XXVII (1946), 56–7; D. Hist.

113.1009, General Staff memo, 21 April 1932; Everett Bristol, *R.M.C. Review*, VIII (Dec. 1927), 55.

93 *R.M.C. Review*, X (June 1929), 96–8; D. Hist., 113.1009; NDHQ 74–4–28, 5 July 1929.

94 *Advisory Board Report, 1929*, p. 3; HQ 74–26–4, vol. 2, memo, Royal Military College, 28 April 1937; extracts from "Commandant's Report, 1931," p. 52.

95 *R.M.C. Review*, XI (Dec. 1930), 21.

96 MG 26, H 1(d), vol. 282, folder 221, A. McNaughton to Borden, 23 Sept. 1929.

97 Ex-Cadet, "Royal Military College of Canada," p. 239; *Report of the Indian Sandhurst Committee* (1925–26), para. 38.

98 P. C. Fair, "R.M.C. Cadets at Camp Borden," *R.M.C. Review*, V (Nov. 1924), 36.

99 NDHQ 74–37–1, vol. 2.

100 Fair, "R.M.C. Cadets at Camp Borden," p.36.

101 NDHQ 74–37–22, vols. 1 and 2.

102 *R.M.C. Review*, XI (Dec. 1930), 41; *ibid.*, XVI (June 1935), 15.

103. *Ibid.*, II (May 1921), 17.

104 *Ibid.*, III (May 1922), 21; *ibid.*, IV (May 1923), 47; *ibid.*, VIII (June 1927), 28.

105 DND, C 4852, War Office to Adjutant-General, August 1924.

106 *R.M.C. Review*, IX (June 1928), 9.

CHAPTER 11, PAGES 257 - 84

1 House of Commons, *Debates*, 1928, I, 345–55; *ibid.*, 1931, III, 2905.

2 NDHQ, 74–1–19, vol. 2, 10 April 1935.

3 D. Hist. 171.013(D3), vol. 17, "Advisory Board Report," 1931, para 4; "Commandant's Report," 1930–35, para 9.

4 *DND Report, 1932*, p. 51; *R.M.C. Review*, XXVII (1946), 58, 61.

5 *R.M.C. Review*, XVI (Dec. 1933), 35.

6 *Ibid.*, XIV (June 1933), 12.

7 D. Hist. 171.013, vol. 23, "Commandant's Report," 1936–37, para 23 (x).

8 D. Hist. 171.013(D3), vol. 25, "Advisory Board's Report," 1939, para 3; NDHQ, 74–1–184; G. M. Lefresne, " 'The Royal Twenty Centers': The Department of National Defence and Federal Unemployment Relief 1932–1935," RMC, unpublished BA thesis, 1962, p. 205.

9 *DND Report, 1932*, p. 50.

10 T. L. Brock, "The College Under the New System of Organization," *R.M.C. Review*, XV (June 1934), 57–8.

11 D. Hist. 171.03, vol. 20, "Commandant's Report," 1933–34, pp. 3–5.

12 *DND Report, 1934*, p. 92; *ibid., 1935*, p. 86.

13 D. Hist. 171.013, vol. 18, "Outline of Discussion of New Entrance Requirements," "Advisory Board's Report," 1932.

14 *Ibid.*, vol. 20, "Advisory Board's Report," 1934, para. 6.

15 *Ibid.*, vol. 22, "Advisory Board's Report," 1936, para 6 (c).

16 *Ibid.*, vol. 23, Report of subcommittee, 13 May 1937, "Advisory Board's Report," 1937, para 10.

17 NDHQ, 74–34–2, vol. 2, 138, "Statement showing representation ... compared to ... the Population of the Provinces."

18 D. Hist. 171.013, vol. 25, "Commandant's Report," 1938–1939, para 5 (b) (i).

19 NDHQ, 74–34–2, vol. 11.

20 Schmidlin, "Length of the Course at the Royal Military College of Canada," *R.M.C. Review*, XVII (June 1936), 43–8.

21 D. Hist. 114–1, H. H. Matthews to Schmidlin, 22 Jan. 1936.

22 D. Hist. 171.013, vol. 22, "Advisory Board's Report," 1936, para. 6(c).

23 *Ibid.*, "Advisory Board's Report," 1936, para 3 and Report of the subcommittee.

24 NDHQ, 74–34–2, vol. 2.

25 *Ibid.*, 74–26–4, vol. 2.

26 *Ibid.*, 74–26–4, vol. 2, memo, "The Royal Military College of Canada, April 20, 1937."

27 D. Hist. 113.1009.

28 Memo, "The Royal Military College of Canada, April 20, 1937."

29 D. Hist. 113.1009, McNaughton to Matthews, 13 May 1937.

30 House of Commons, *Debates*, 1937, II, 1135.

31 *R.M.C. Review*, XIX (Dec. 1938), 17.

32 NDHQ, 74–24–2, 30 Oct. 1937.

33 D. Hist., 114.1, "Revision of the RMC Diploma, 1938."

34 J. Fergus Grant, "RMC Revisited: Random Reflections," *R.M.C. Review*, XIX (Dec. 1938), 29.

35 D. Hist. 113.1009, RMC 2–1–46, circular letter, 6 Aug. 1937.

36 *R.M.C. Calendar, 1939–40*, pp. 21–2.

37 *Ibid.*, pp. 26–9; "Commandant's Report," 1939, in *R.M.C. Review*, XX (Dec. 1939), 18; *Ibid.*, XXVIII (1947), 35.

38 D. Hist. 171.013, vol. 25, "Commandant's Report," 1939, para 5 (b) ii, and appendix C.

39 *Ibid.*, "Commandant's Report," 1939, para 5.

40 NDHQ, 74–37–22, vol. 1, 15 Dec. 1925.

41 B. H. Darwin, "Petawawa Summer," *R.M.C. Review*, XV (June 1934), 59.

42 T. L. Brock, "The College at Petawawa, June 1933," *R.M.C. Review*, XIV (Dec. 1933), 28–31.

43 NDHQ, 74–37–22, vol. 2.

44 "The Naval Course at Halifax," *R.M.C. Review*, XIII (Dec. 1932), 42–5.

45 DM&D, HQ, 74–20–34, [Anon] to the [R.M.C.] Adjutant, 26 Nov. 1932.

46 T. L. Brock, *Fight the Good Fight*.

47 John Windsor, *Blind Date* (Sidney, BC, 1962), p. 13.

48 *Ibid.*, p. 10.

49 *Ibid.*

50 NDHQ, 74–25–34, [Anon] to Staff Adjutant, 26 Nov. 1932.

51 *Ibid.*, 74–20–34, Adjutant-General to CGS, 7 Nov. 1933.

52 "Diary of T. L. Brock, 1933–34," in the possession of its author.

53 Brock, *Fight the Good Fight*, p. 8.

54 D. Hist., Crerar Papers, [Matthews], "Notes for talk with B.S.M. and C.S.M.S ... ."

55 *Ibid.*, K. Stuart, "Lecture to the Senior Class," n.d.

56 Windsor, *Blind Date*, p. 11.

57 Brock ms, Crerar to T. L. Brock, Nov. 1964, in the possession of T. L. Brock.

58 House of Commons, *Debates*, 1938, III, 2889–90.

59 NDHQ, 74–24–2, 24 Oct. 1938.

60 *D.N.D. Report, 1932*, p. 51.

61 NDHQ, 74–20–87, "Flying Royal Military College Cadets."

62 *Ibid.*, 74–26–4, vol. 3, 16 May 1939.

63 J. Fergus Grant, *R.M.C. Review*, XIX (Dec. 1938), p. 32.

64 *British Whig*, 21 Feb. 1924.

65 House of Commons, *Debates*, 1931, III, 2908.

66 *Ibid.*, 1937, II, 1135.

67 RMC 3645–14, vol. 1 (now RMC 4920–9, vol. 1), H. D. G. Crerar to Mrs. R. P. Monk, 23 June 1939.

CHAPTER 12, PAGES 285 - 304

1 Windsor, *Blind Date*, p. 7.

2 C. P. Stacey, *Six Years of War. The Army in Canada, Britain, and the Pacific: Official History of the Canadian Army in the Second World War*, (3 vols., Ottawa, 1955), I, 42; *R.M.C. Review*, XX (Dec. 1939), 11.

3 Stacey, *Six Years of War*, I, 61.

4 NDHQ, s 7698, Mobilization Instructions for the Canadian Militia, 1937, Section IX, 41 (d), quoted in Crerar to DND, 28 Sept. 1938.

5 *Ibid.*, Crerar to Secretary, DND, 28 Sept. 1938.

6 *Ibid.*, E.S. [Col. E. W. Sansom] to Major G. A. McCarter, RCA, GSO War Office, 12 Oct. 1938.

7 *Ibid.*, Anderson, memo, 21 Sept. 1939.

8 *Ibid.*, NDHQ Diary (copy), 27 Sept. 1939.

9 *R.M.C. Review*, XX (Dec. 1939), 25–6.

10 *Ibid.*, pp. 86–7.

11 NDHQ, s 7698, memo of a meeting of the RMC Club executive, 4 Oct. 1939.

12 Brock mss., RMC Club, memorandum, May 1940.

13 Douglas Library, Norman Rogers Papers, McNaughton memorandum, 4 Oct. 1939, with minutes by Rogers.

14 Brock mss., memorandum, May 1940.

15 *Ibid.*, A. M. Mitchell to Rogers, 10 Oct. 1939.

16 *R.M.C. Review*, XXVIII (1947), 35.

17 Kerry and McDill, *History of the Corps of Royal Canadian Engineers* II, 22.

18 *R.M.C. Review*, XXI (June 1940), 42; XXVIII (1947), 37.

19 NDHQ, s 7698, Anderson to Rogers, 13 March 1940.

20 *R.M.C. Review*, XXVIII (1947), 38.

21 NDHQ, s 7698, Stuart to Secretary DND, 5 Nov. 1939.

22 *Ibid.*, Stuart to Secretary DND, 30 Jan. 1940.

23 *Ibid.*, Anderson to Rogers, 13 March 1940.
24 *Ibid.*, Stuart to Secretary DND, 11 March 1940.
25 *Ibid.*, Anderson to Rogers, 13 March 1940.
26 *Ibid.*, Anderson to Rogers, 4 April 1940.
27 *R.M.C. Review*, xx (June 1940), 43, 91.
28 *Ibid.*, xx (Dec. 1940), 15.
29 NDHQ, s 7698, Director Naval Service to CGS, 27 Sept. 1939.
30 *R.M.C. Review*, xxviii (1947), 39–40.
31 Stacey, *Six Years of War*, I, 237.
32 NDHQ, s 7698, Defensor to Canmilitary, telegram, 29 Nov. 1940.
33 D. Hist. 321.009, Browne, 21 Dec. 1940.
34 NDHQ, s 7698, extract from personal letter of Crerar to president RMC [Club], 15 April 1941.
35 *R.M.C. Review*, xxviii (1947), 40–1.
36 *Ibid.*, pp. 37, 39.
37 *Ibid.*, pp. 41–3.
38 Stacey, *Six Years of War*, I, 140–1; *R.M.C. Review*, xxviii (1947),
39 Stacey, *Six Years of War*, I, 113.
40 *R.M.C. Review*, xxviii (1947), 39, 41, 132–3.
41 C. P. Stacey, *The Canadian Army 1939–45* (Ottawa, 1948), p. 309; *R.M.C. Review*, xxviii (1947), 132–3; information from Canadian War Service Records.
42 *R.M.C. Review*, xxviii (1947), 133.
43 *Ibid.*, xxvi (1945), 71.
44 Stacey, *Six Years of War*, I, 51–2.
45 Stacey, *The Canadian Army*, p. 128.
46 *R.M.C. Review*, xxvii (1946), 109–23; xviii (1947), 132–47; xxix (1948), 66.
47 *R.M.C. Review*, xxvi (1945), 87.
48 *Ibid.*, xxvii (1946), 79.
49 *Ibid.*, xxvi (1945), 83.
50 *Ibid.*, p. 135.
51 Stacey, *Six Years of War*, III, pp. 219–20.
52 Terence Robertson, *The Shame and the Glory: Dieppe* (Toronto, 1962), p. 3.
53 Stacey, *Six Years of War*, I, 373–4.
54 *Crerar Papers*, GOC in C/6–9/H, Hertzberg to Crerar, 26 Oct. 1942.
55 *R.M.C. Review*, xxvi (1945), 124.
56 *Ibid.*, p. 63.
57 *Ibid.*, xxvii (1946), 178; xxvi (1945), 107; RMC *Club News Letter.*
58 *R.M.C. Review*, xxvi (1945), 112.
59 *Ibid.*, p. 122.
60 *Ibid.*, xxvii (1946), 49–52.
61 *Ibid.*, xxvi (1945), 89.
62 *Ibid.*, pp. 180–1.
63 *Ibid.*, xxvii (1946), 21.
64 Stacey, *Six Years of War*, I, 282.
65 *R.M.C. Review*, xxvi (1945), 148.
66 *Ibid.*, p. 92.

67 *Ibid.*

68 *Ibid.*, xxvii (1946), 105.

69 Published by Gale and Polden, London, 1942, and frequently reprinted even after the war.

70 *R.M.C. Review*, xxvii (1946), 96–102.

71 *Ibid.*, xxviii (1947), 63.

CHAPTER 13, PAGES 305 - 31

1 Brock mss, Mitchell to Young, 2 April 1941; *ibid.*, Young to Mitchell, 5 April 1941.

2 *R.M.C. Review*, xxiii (June 1942), 13.

3 Brock mss, Mitchell to Stuart, 17 Nov. 1943.

4 *Ibid.*, Mitchell to W. H. O'Reilly, 31 Jan. 1944.

5 *Ibid.*, Bristol to Mitchell, 15 Feb. 1944.

6 *Ibid.*, Mitchell to Bristol, 7 March 1944.

7 NDHQ, S 7698, O'Reilly to Ralston, 20 March 1944.

8 *Massey Library* [H. L. Guy], "Report of the Committee on Technical Organization and Training in the Army" [1944], paras. 25, 34.

9 D. Hist. 112.21009, Young to Minister (through CGS) 14 Feb. 1945.

10 H. F. Wood, *Strange Battleground* (Ottawa, 1966), p. 17.

11 NDHQ, 74–33–16, Foulkes to Deputy Minister, 13 Sept. 1945.

12 Colonel S. H. Dobell, "The Re-Opening of the College," *R.M.C. Review*, xxviii (1947), 20; Massey Library, Clark Papers, HQS 29–5 FD22 (Trg.), CGS to CNS and CAS, 1 Oct 1945.

13 D. Hist., 112.21009.

14 Clark Papers [Chesley Committee Papers], BDF-DCGS(b), 1–1–1.

15 D. Hist. 112.21009, Foulkes to Chesley, 28 Nov. 1945.

16 *Ibid.*, "Report of the Committee on Provision of Officers for the Post-War Active Force" (Chesley Committee, Dec. 1946).

17 Clark Papers, BDF.DCGS(B) 1–1–1, Chesley to DCGS(B), 15 Feb. 1946.

18 *Ibid.*, CGS to the Minister, 28 Feb. 1946.

19 *R.M.C. Review*, xxvi (1945), 177.

20 D. Hist. 112.21109, Foulkes to Chesley, 28 Nov. 1945.

21 *R.M.C. Review*, xxvii (1946), 140.

22 *Ibid.*, pp. 145–6.

23 Kingston *Whig-Standard*, 23 Feb. 1946.

24 RMC Club, Kingston branch, minutes, 5 March 1946.

25 Dobell, "The Re-Opening of the College," pp. 20–8.

26 Clark Papers, RMC "Club brief presented to the Committee ... for the training and provision of officers for Canada's Army [1947]," appendix A.

27 *R.M.C. Review*, xxviii (1947), 24.

28 Clark Papers, Club brief, section 13, paragraph 1.

29 *Ibid.*, paragraphs 5, 6.

30 *Ibid.*, *passim.*

31 D. Hist. 324.009, Report of the Committee on Provision of Officers for the Post-War Army (Lett Committee, June 1946).

32 Dobell, "Re-Opening of the College," pp. 27–8.

33 Brock mss, Claxton to Mitchell, 15 April 1947.

34 NDHQ [Navy], NSC 1700–121/2, vol. 1, 28 Aug. 1940.

35 *Ibid.*

36 1700—121/2, vol. 1, p. 39, H. T. W. Grant to Director Canadian Naval Service (DCNS), 19 March 1941.

37 *Ibid.*, vol. 1, p. 40, H. T. W. Grant to DCNS, 5 April 1941.

38 *Ibid.*, vol. 6 [10 Oct. 1952].

39 *Ibid.*, vol. 1, p. 60.

40 *Ibid.*, vol. 2, syllabus 1943.

41 *Ibid.*, vol. 1, PC 27/9600, 77.

42 *Ibid.*, vol. 3, Leckie to Jones, 31 Jan. 1946.

43 *Ibid.*, Captain J. M. Grant to CNP, reporting on an RCN–RCAF conference, 1 May 1946.

44 *Ibid.*, vol. 3, DCNS to CAS, 13 March 1946.

45 NDHQ [RCAF] 895–70/1, vol. 1, CAS to A/C Orr, 28 March 1946.

46 *Ibid.*, "Supporting Data for Air Members of Air Council," 21 May 1946.

47 [Navy] NSC 1700–121/2, vol. 4, CO Royal Roads to Naval Secretary, 29 April 1946.

48 *Ibid.*, DNE, 29 April 1946.

49 [RCAF] 895–70/1, vol. 1, Campbell to CAS, 23 March 1946.

50 *Ibid.*, "Brief on Policy of RCAF Training at Royal Roads," 15 Nov. 1946.

51 NSC 1700–121/2, vol. 5, Lowe to CNP, 13 Jan. 1947.

52 *Ibid.*, vol. 4, Claxton to cabinet, 4900–67.

53 *Ibid.*, vol. 5, Claxton to CAS, CNS, 21 March 1946; Clark Papers, Claxton to Stedman, 30 May 1947.

54 Clark Papers, Claxton to Stedman, 30 May 1947.

55 *Ibid.*, Claxton to Stedman (tel.), 22 June 1947.

56 *Ibid.*, Stedman Committee, Interim Report, 26 June 1947.

57 *Ibid.*, Foulkes to Claxton, 28 June 1947.

58 *Ibid.*, Stedman Committee minutes, 20 June 1947.

59 [Curtis], "Plan for the Opening of R.M.C. ..." 18 July 1948.

60 Clark Papers, Stedman Committee minutes, 8 October 1947.

61 [RCAF], 895–70/1, vol. 2, W. M. Ogle [RCAF Enquiries re.] University Recognition of RCN College Course 1942–7, 28 April 1947.

62 *Ibid.*, vol. 3, CAS's Staff Conference no. 14, Minutes, 24 Sept. 1947.

63 *Ibid.*, vol. 4, Stedman Committee Report, 20 Nov. 1947.

64 *Ibid.*, CAS Conference no. 29, 9 Feb. 1948.

65 [NSC] 1700–121/0, vol. 1, RMC 80–4–1, submission to the cabinet, 3 March 1948.

66 *Ibid.*, Brigadier W. J. Megill, army member Canadian Services College Co-ordinating Committee to Chairman, 6 April, 1948; *ibid.*, précis, 421st Military Chiefs of Staff Committee, April 27, 1948.

67 *Ibid.*, vol. 1, Foulkes to Secretary, Chiefs of Staff Committee, 19 April 1948.

68 Clark Papers, Curtis sub-committee, 18 July 1947.

69 Massey Library, Agnew Papers, Simonds to Agnew, 2 Dec. 1947.

70 *Ibid.*, Simonds to Agnew, 2 Dec. 1947.

CHAPTER 14, PAGES 332 - 49

1 T. F. G[elley], "The Reopening of the Royal Military College of Canada," *R.M.C. Review*, xxx (1949), 15.

2 W. R. Sawyer, "The Present Four-Year Course at the Royal Military College of Canada," *ibid.*, xxxII (1951), 123–6.

3 John W. Spurr, "The Library, 1949–1951," *ibid.*, 127–31.

4 Sawyer, "The Present Four-Year Course ...", *ibid.*, p. 125.

5 J. I. B. W[illiamson], "R.R.-R.M.C. Classes United," *ibid.* (1951), 4–5.

6 NDHQ[RCAF] 895–70/1, vol. 4, Defence Council Minutes, 49, 11 April 1949.

7 NSC 1799–121/2, vol. 6, Defence Council Minutes, 21 April 1949; *ibid.*, Rayner to CNP, 27 April 1949; *ibid.*, H. G. DeWolf to Naval Secretary, 12 May 1949; *ibid.*, Defence Council Minutes, 16 June 1949.

8 [RCAF] 895–70/1, vol. 5, Millward to CAS, 10 Jan. 1950.

9 *Report on certain "Incidents"* ... *on board H.M.C. Ships* Crescent, *and* Magnificent ... (Mainguy Report) (Ottawa 1949), pp. 37, 45, 51; D. J. Goodspeed, *The Armed Forces of Canada, 1867–1967* (Ottawa, 1967), p. 231.

10 [RCAF] 895–70/1, vol. 5, Foulkes to CAS, 20 April 1950.

11 NDHQ [Army] 2001–82/3, vol. 1, CGS to the Minister, 26 May 1952.

12 HQ2–497–82/0 DM Sec't. 241–1300–1, Blatchford Secretary (PMC to Commandant RMC, 15 April 1954. The exceptions were negligible.

13 Percy Lowe, "Is R.O.T.P. a Failure?" *R.M.C. Review*, xxxIX (1958), 187–96.

14 [Army] 2001–82/3, vol. 1, Lieutenant-Colonel W. S. Hunt, D. Org. to VCGS, 16 April 1952.

15 *Ibid.*, Brigadier M. P. Bogert, DGMT to VCGS, 27 March 1952.

16 *Ibid.*, CGS *to the Minister*, 26 May 1952.

17 *Ibid.*, Claxton to Deputy Minister, 13 June 1952.

18 NDHQ [DM] 2–170–82/3, vol. 1, statement by Brooke Claxton, 12 June 1952.

19 *Ibid.*, C. P. Stacey, "Short Note on the Military History of St. John (St. Jean)."

20 [DM], 2–170–82/3, vol. 2, JSUCC & RMC minutes of special meeting, 23, 24 Nov. 1954.

21 *R.M.C. Review*, xxx (1954), 186–192.

22 [DM] 2–490–82/0–1, vol. 1, Bradshaw to Chief Secretary, DND, 23 Nov. 1954.

Appendices

1 / AN ACT TO ESTABLISH A MILITARY COLLEGE IN ONE OF THE GARRISON TOWNS OF CANADA.

[Assented to 26th May, 1874.]

Whereas it is expedient to make further provision for the education of Cadets and Officers of Militia in military knowledge and scientific pursuits connected with the military profession: Therefore Her Majesty, by and with the advice and consent of the Senate and House of Commons of Canada, enacts as follows:—

1 An institution shall be established for the purpose of imparting a complete education in all branches of military tactics, fortification, engineering and general scientific knowledge in subjects connected with and necessary to a thorough knowledge of the military profession and for qualifying officers for command and for staff appointments. Such institution to be known as the Military College, and to be located in some one of the garrison towns of Canada.

2 The College shall be conducted under the superintendence of a military officer having special qualifications with regard to the instruction to be given and discipline, whose title or designation shall be that of Commandant. There shall also be two other professors or instructors, and such other assistants as may be found necessary and as may be authorized by Parliament. The salary of the Commandant to be not more than three thousand dollars, and the salaries of the other professors to be not more than two thousand dollars each. All the staff of the College to be appointed by the Governor in Council and to hold office during pleasure.

3 The College shall be governed and its affairs administered under and according to regulations to be made from time to time and approved by the Governor in Council, such regulations to be published in the *Canada Gazette*, and after such publication to have the force of law as fully as if they were contained in this Act, of which they shall be deemed to form a part.

4 A Board of Examiners shall be appointed by the Governor in Council, in each military district, consisting of three or more members, one of whom shall, when practicable, be an officer of the militia staff, who shall be authorized to examine candidates for admission to the College as cadets, and give certificates (in form to be provided), to such as are able to qualify according to the regulations which may be adopted. Meetings of such Boards shall be held when directed by the Department of Militia and Defence.

5 All candidates for admission to the College as students shall be required to pass an examination before the Examiners as provided in the next preceding section, from whom a certificate must be obtained, that they are proficient in the subjects to be prescribed. They will also be required to pass a medical examination and produce evidence of good moral character. No candidate will be accepted who is under fifteen or over twenty years of age.

6 The Examiners shall transmit to the Department of Militia and Defence a report of the names of all candidates who succeed in obtaining certificates, for the information of the Governor in Council, with a report of each meeting, which report may embody any particular circumstances connected with the examination or any special recommendation.

7 The number of cadets with which the College may be opened shall not exceed twenty-two. And thereafter, for the first two years, the annual admission shall not exceed three from each military district, and after the third year shall not be more than two in each year from each military district. The selection shall be made by the Governor in Council from the list of names forwarded by the Boards of Examiners, having reference to the order of merit in which the applicants pass their preliminary examinations. The collegiate term shall be four years.

8 In the event of there being no names forwarded as provided from one or more of the military districts, either on account of there being no applicants for examination or a failure in obtaining a certificate, then the Governor in Council may select the required number from candidates who have passed an examination in any of the other districts.

9 The Governor in Council may, for special reasons in the interests of the service, admit for a limited time, officers of the Active Militia, although over the age of twenty years, who shall have obtained a first-class certificate under the provisions of the thirty-third section of "*An Act respecting the Militia and Defence of the Dominion of Canada,*" (thirty-first Victoria, chapter forty,) such admissions to be under such regulations as the Governor in Council may approve, and in addition to the number provided for in section seven of this Act, but at no time to exceed ten in number.

10 Each cadet will be required to furnish himself with a mattress and bedding, books and such apparatus as may not be supplied by the Government, and to pay a contribution in aid of the expense of procuring mess room table furniture.

To meet the ordinary expenses of living, and procuring uniform, a sum not exceeding the rate of three hundred dollars per annum, and such allowances as may, from time to time, be authorized by the Governor in Council, may be paid for each cadet during such period as he may remain at the college.

11 Every person entering upon a course of instruction in the College shall sign a roll of entry, and be thenceforward, for the period of his pupilage, subject to the Queen's rules and regulations, the mutiny act, the rules and articles of war, and to such other rules and regulations as Her Majesty's troops are subjected to.

2 / COMMANDANTS OF THE ROYAL MILITARY COLLEGE OF CANADA

1875–86	Colonel E. O. Hewett, C.M.G.
1886–8	Major-General J. R. Oliver
1888–96	Major-General D. R. Cameron, C.M.G.
1896–1900	Colonel G. C. Kitson
1901–5	Colonel R. N. R. Reade
1905–9	Colonel E. T. Taylor (college no. 45)
1909–13	Colonel J. H. V. Crowe
1913–14	Colonel L. R. Carleton, D.S.O.
1915–19	Brigadier-General C. N. Perreau, C.M.G.
1919–25	Lieutenant-General Sir A. C. Macdonnell, K.C.B., C.M.G., D.S.O., LL.D. (college no. 151)
1925–30	Brigadier C. F. Constantine, D.S.O. (college no. 621)
1930–5	Brigadier W. H. P. Elkins, D.S.O. (college no. 624)
1935–8	Brigadier H. H. Matthews, C.M.G., D.S.O.
1938–9	Brigadier H. D. G. Crerar, D.S.O. (college no. 749)
1939–40	Brigadier K. Stuart, D.S.O., M.C. (college no. 816)
1940–4	Major-General H. F. H. Hertzberg, C.M.G., D.S.O., M.C. (college no. H-2727)
1944–5	Briagdier D. G. Cunningham, D.S.O., E.D. (college no. 1841)
1945–6	Brigadier J. D. B. Smith, C.B.E., D.S.O. (college no. 2120)
1947	Major-General J. F. M. Whiteley, C.B., C.B.E., M.C.
1947–54	Brigadier D. R. Agnew, C.B.E., CD, LL.D. (college no. 1137)
1954–7	Air Commodore D. A. R. Bradshaw, D.F.C., CD (college no. 2140)
1957–60	Commodore D. W. Piers, D.S.C., CD (college no. 2184)
1960–2	Brigadier W. A. B. Anderson, O.B.E., CD (college no. 2265)
1962–3	Brigadier G. H. Spencer, O.B.E., CD (college no. 2424)
1963–7	Air Commodore L. J. Birchall, O.B.E., D.F.C., CD, ADC (college no. 2364)
1967–	Commodore W. P. Hayes, CD (college no. 2576)

3 / DIRECTORS OF STUDIES AND REGISTRARS

SENIOR PROFESSORS

1917–22   Director of Studies
             Professor I. E. Martin, M.A.

1922–6   Director of Studies
             Colonel H. J. Dawson, C.M.G., D.S.O., M.A.

1926–33   Senior Professor
             Lieutenant-Colonel E. J. C. Schmidlin, M.C., RMC, SME

1933–4   Senior Professor

             Professor F. H. Day, B.A., M.SC.
1934–41   Senior Professor

             Professor L. N. Richardson, M.A., M.SC.
1941–2   Senior Professor

             Professor H. H. Lawson, RMC, B.SC., M.E.I.C.

(RMC *closed as cadet college 1942–8*)

1948–67   Vice-Commandant and
             Director of Studies
                Colonel W. R. Sawyer, O.B.E., E.D., P.S.C., RMC,
                B.SC., M.SC., PH.D., LL.D., D.SC.MIL., F.C.I.C.

1967   Director of Studies
             Dean J. R. Dacey, M.B.E., B.SC., M.SC.,
             PH.D., F.C.I.C.

REGISTRARS

1948–63   Lieutenant-Colonel T. F. Gelley, M.A., LL.D.

1963   R. E. Jones, M.A., PH.D.

4 / STAFF-ADJUTANTS

Captain of Cadets   23 March 1876 to 26 January 1882
Staff Adjutant   1 July 1883 to 17 June 1965
Director of Cadets and Military Training   18 June 1965—

1876–82	Captain of Cadets	Captain J. B. Ridout
1883–1900	Staff-Adjutant	Major S. C. McGill
1901–5	Staff-Adjutant	Lieutenant-Colonel H. A. Panet, D.S.O.
1905–8	Staff-Adjutant	Captain F. D. Lafferty
1908–11	Staff-Adjutant	Captain H. A. Kaulback
1911–16	Staff-Adjutant	Major C. N. Perreau
1916–19	Staff-Adjutant	Major H. C. Wotherspoon
1919–24	Staff-Adjutant	Major E. de L. Greenwood
1924–8	Staff-Adjutant	Major R. L. Fortt
1928–32	Staff-Adjutant	Major K. M. Holloway
1932–6	Staff-Adjutant	Major H. M. Logan
1936–40	Staff-Adjutant	Lieutenant-Colonel C. R. S. Stein
1940–2	Staff-Adjutant	Major C. H. Walker
1942	Staff-Adjutant	Major G. Reed Blaikie, M.B.E., E.D.
1948–50	Staff-Adjutant	Major E. G. Brooks, D.S.O.
1950–1	Staff-Adjutant	Wing-Commander H. C. Vinnicombe, CD
1951–4	Staff-Adjutant	Major P. T. Nation, CD
1954–8	Staff-Adjutant	Squadron-Leader A. C. Golab, CD
1958–61	Staff-Adjutant	LCDR J. G. Mills, CD
1961–4	Staff-Adjutant	Lieutenant-Colonel J. G. Gardner, CD
1964–5	Staff-Adjutant	Lieutenant-Colonel J. M. Brownlee, CD
1965–7	Director of Cadets and Military Training	Lieutenant-Colonel J. M. Brownlee, CD
1967	Director of Cadets and Military Training	Wing-Commander A. Pickering, CD

5 / BATTALION SERGEANT-MAJORS

1878–1923	BATTALION SERGEANT-MAJOR (BSM)
1924–33	SENIOR UNDER OFFICER (SUO)
1934–42	BATTALION SERGEANT-MAJOR (BSM)
1952	CADET WING-COMMANDER (CWC)

1878–80	BSM H. L. Irving
1880	BSM H. W. Keefer
1880	BSM A. B. Ross
1880–1	BSM H. M. Campbell
1881–2	BSM E. T. Taylor
1882–3	BSM J. I. Lang-Hyde
1883–4	BSM W. A. F. Von Iffland
1884–5	BSM J. A. Moren
1885–6	BSM W. G. Yorkston
1886–7	BSM A. L. P. Davis
1887–8	BSM W. B. Lesslie
1888–9	BSM W. A. H. Kerr
1889–90	BSM B. E. Leckie
1890–1	BSM D. S. MacInnes
1891–2	BSM W. C. Dumble
1892–3	BSM B. H. O. Armstrong
1893–4	BSM F. C. Heneker
1894–5	BSM G. S. Wilkes
1895–6	BSM A. S. Evans
1896–7	BSM J. A. Stairs
1897–8	BSM F. F. Hunter
1898–9	BSM E. D. C. Harris
1899–1900	BSM W. R. McConkey
1900–1	BSM G. B. Hughes
1901–2	BSM D. K. Edgar
1902	BSM V. J. Kent
1902–3	BSM F. T. Lucas
1903–4	BSM F. H. Peters
1904–5	BSM E. J. C. Schmidlin
1905–6	BSM A. T. Powell
1906–7	BSM G. D. Rhodes
1907–8	BSM C. F. Carson
1908–9	BSM A. E. Grasett
1909–10	BSM E. O. Wheeler
1910–11	BSM W. L. I. Gordon
1911–12	BSM S. F. C. Sweeny
1912–13	BSM E. H. de L. Greenwood

1913–14	BSM H. S. Mathews
1914	BSM C. B. R. MacDonald
1914	BSM A. S. L. Bishop
1914	BSM E. A. F. Hale
1914	BSM W. F. Clarke
1914–15	BSM M. H. S. Penhale
1915–16	BSM D. L. Savage
1916	BSM H. D. Warren
1916	BSM F. A. Warren
1916–17	BSM F. H. Jones
1917–18	BSM N. H. Clarke
1918–20	BSM G. D. S. Adami
1920–1	BSM H. A. MacKenzie
1921–2	BSM C. D. T. Mundell
1922–3	BSM H. A. Richardson
1923–4	SUO E. W. Crowe
1924–5	SUO H. C. Fair
1925–6	SUO H. A. Davis
1926–7	SUO B. M. Archibald
1927–8	SUO J. C. Cushing
1928–9	SUO S. S. T. Cantlee
1929–30	SUO G. D. de S. Wotherspoon
1930–1	SUO C. R. Archibald
1931–2	SUO J. G. Carr
1932–3	SUO C. M. Drury
1933	BSM P. H. Riordon
1933–4	BSM H. M. Millar
1934–5	BSM R. M. Powell
1935–6	BSM W. A. B. Anderson
1936–7	BSM J. D. Young
1937–8	BSM C. H. Drury
1938–9	BSM M. D. MacBrien
1939	BSM A. C. Hull
1939	BSM A. E. McMurtry
1940	BSM T. L. Bennett
1940–1	BSM W. D. C. Holmes
1941–2	BSM N. B. Corbett

(*No cadets enrolled 1942–8*)

1951–2	cwc	J. I. B. Williamson	1959–60	cwc	R. B. Morris
1952–3	cwc	A. Hampson	1960–1	cwc	R. D. Byford
1953–4	cwc	J. A. Marshall	1961–2	cwc	J. G. Allen
1954–5	cwc	G. M. Kirby	1962–3	cwc	T. B. Winfield
1955–6	cwc	P. D. Manson	1963–4	cwc	R. B. Harrison
1956–7	cwc	B. L. Rochester	1964–5	cwc	J. D. S. Harries
1957–8	cwc	P. P. M. Meincke	1965–6	cwc	R. S. J. Cohen
1958–9	cwc	G. F. Williamson	1966–7	cwc	J. M. P. Goineau
			1967–8	cwc	D. O. C. Brown

Founded 1884, following organizational meetings on 13 and 23 February, 8 and 15 March, 1884.

PRESIDENTS

Year elected	College number	Name	Year elected	College number	Name
1884–5	7	L. Homfray Irving	1926	631	A. B. Gillies
1886–7	18	Duncan MacPherson	1927	623	S. B. Coristine
			1928	555	R. R. Carr-Harris
1888	4	William Davies	1929	667	E. G. Hanson
1889–90	6	S. J. A. Denison	1930–1	1119	J. H. Price
1891	10	V. B. Rivers	1932	472	A. R. Chipman
1892	86	R. W. Leonard	1933–4	805	C. W. G. Gibson
1893–4	37	E. H. Drury	1935	727	D. A. White
1895–6	15	F. J. Dixon	1936–7	877	G. L. Magann
1897	48	A. K. Kirkpatrick	1938–9	1003	A. M. Mitchell
1898	57	H. S. Greenwood	1940–1	803	J. V. Young
1899	14	J. B. Cochrane	1942–3	1141	W. H. O'Reilly
1900	41	Robert Cartwright	1944	698	Everett Bristol
1901	154	F. M. Gaudet	1945	982	D. W. MacKeen
1902	47	E. F. Wurtele	1946	1841	D. G. Cunningham
1903	21	A. E. Doucet	1947	1230	S. H. Dobell
1904	82	W. B. Carruthers	1948	1855	Ian S. Johnston
1905	188	W. A. H. Kerr	1949	1625	J. D. Watt
1906	186	V. A. S. Williams	1950	1542	E. W. Crowe
1907	139	C. R. F. Coutlee	1951	1860	Nicol Kingsmill
1908	232	John Houliston	1952	1828	G. E. Beament
1909	91	J. D. Gibson	1953	1620	R. R. Labatt
1910	63	George Hooper	1954	1766	K. H. Tremain
1911	255	H. A. Panet	1955	1474	de L. H. M. Panet
1912	246	H. E. Burstall	1956	2034	Paul Y. Davoud
1913	268	H. R. V. Count de Bury et de Bocarme	1957	1954	W. P. Carr
			1929–30	suo	G.D. deS. Wotherspoon
1914	299	H. J. Lamb	1960	1379	H. A. Mackenzie
			1961	2157	J. H. R. Gagnon
(Meetings interrupted during war years)			1962	2183	James E. Pepall
			1963	2336	J. H. Moore
1919	299	H. J. Lamb	1964	2351	Guy Savard
1920	293	C. J. Armstrong	1965	2749	James B. Cronyn
1920–2	392	W. B. Kingsmill	1966	2601	J. Fergus Maclaren
1923	337	A. C. Caldwell			
1924	140	G. S. Cartwright	1967	2791	Jean P. W. Ostiguy
1925	499	E. de B. Panet	1968–9	RCNC 90	John F. Frank

SECRETARY-TREASURERS

Year elected	College number	Name
1884	6	S. J. A. Denison
1885	78	H. J. C. Nanton
1886–91	115	F. W. White
1892–1918	47	E. F. Wurtele
1919–20	667	E. G. Hanson
1921–34	H5225	R. D. Williams
1935–9	1860	Nicol Kingsmill
1940–56	H5225	R. D. Williams
1957–68	H6888	T. F. Gelley

George R. I.

George the Fifth *by the Grace of God of the United Kingdom of Great Britain and Ireland and of the British Dominions beyond the Seas King, Defender of the Faith, Emperor of India. To our Right Trusty and Well-beloved Counsellor Sir Edmund Bernard Talbot (commonly called Lord Edmund Bernard Talbot), Knight Grand Cross of our Royal Victorian Order, Companion of our Distinguished Service Order, and Deputy to our Right Trusty and Right Entirely Beloved Cousin Bernard Marmaduke, Duke of Norfolk, Earl Marshall and our Hereditary Marshall of England, Greeting:*

Whereas *for the greater honour and distinction of our Royal Military College of Canada We are desirous that Armorial Ensigns should be assigned for that College:*

Know ye *therefore that We of Our Princely Grace and Special Favour have granted and assigned and by these Presents do grant and assign the following Armorial Ensigns for Our said Royal Military College of Canada that is to say: Per pale Azure and Gules on the Dexter side a Scaling Ladder Argent ensigned by a Mural Crown Or and on the Sinister side two Swords in saltire of the third points upward, on a Chief of the fourth three grenades of the first fired proper, an Inescutcheon charged with the Union Badge and for the Crest on a Wreath of the Colours An Arm in armour embowed gauntletted and holding a Sprig of three Maple Leaves and ensigned by the Imperial Crown all proper, as the same are in the painting hereunto annexed more plainly depicted to be borne by our said Royal Military College of Canada on Seals, Shields, Banners, Flags or otherwise according to the Laws of Arms.*

Our will and Pleasure therefore is that you Sir Edmund Bernard Talbot (commonly called Lord Edmund Bernard Talbot) Deputy to our said Earl Marshall, to whom the cognizance of matters of this nature doth properly belong do require and demand that this our Concession and Declaration be recorded in our College of Arms in order that our Officers of Arms and all other Public Functionaries, whom it may concern, may take full notice and have knowledge thereof in their several and respective departments. And for so doing this shall be your Warrant.

Given *at our Court at St. James's this thirty-first day of July, 1920, in the eleventh year of Our Reign.*

By His Majesty's Command
Milner

I hereby certify that the foregoing copy of the Royal Warrant assigning Armorial Ensigns for the Royal Military College of Canada is faithfully extracted from the Records of the College of Arms, London.
As witness my hand at the said College this sixteenth day of September, 1920.
Keith M. Murray.
Portcullis

Copy of Warrant Granting Armorial Ensigns.

TRUTH·DUTY·VALOUR

RMC teams, drawn from an enrolment that rarely exceeded two hundred between 1876 and 1950, were entered generally in the Canadian Intercollegiate Athletic Union, Intermediate Division. In 1950 RMC became a charter member of the Ottawa–St. Lawrence Intercollegiate Athletic Conference, but it continued to take in other intercollegiate competitions. Divisions other than intermediate are indicated.

1899 CI Football
1903 CI Hockey
1904 CI Hockey
1904 CI Football
1905 CI Football
1906 CI Football
1906 CI Hockey
1909 CI Tennis (senior)
1909 CI Football
1910 CI Football
1910 Dominion Champions, Football
1911 CL Football
1911 Dominion Champions, Football
1911 CI Tennis (senior)
1912 CI Football
1912 CI Hockey
1913 CI Hockey
1914 CI Hockey
1915 CI Hockey
(1914–18 *War Years*)
1920 CI Hockey
1921 CI Hockey
1922 CI Football
1923 CI Football
1923 Dominion Champions, Football
1924 CI Harriers (senior)
1924 CI Hockey
1926 CI Football
1926 Dominion Champions, Football
1926 CI Hockey
1928 CI Harriers (senior)
1929 CI Football
1930 CI Football
1930 Dominion Champions, Football
1931 Ontario Hockey Association
1931 Eastern Ontario Basketball

1931 CI Football
1935 CI Hockey
1935 Eastern Ontario Basketball
1937 CI Soccer (senior)
1937 CI Dinghy Regatta (senior)
1938 CI Soccer (senior)
1938 CI Track & Field
(1939–45 *War Years*)
(1942–8 *college closed*)
1951 OSL Track & Field
1951 Quebec Provincial Harriers (open)
1952 Eastern Ontario Basketball (junior)
1952 OSL Track & Field
1952 CI Harriers (senior)
1952 Quebec Provincial Harriers (open)
1953 OSL Swimming
1953 Eastern Ontario Basketball (junior)
1953 Quebec Provincial Harriers (open)
1953 CI Soccer (tie) (senior)
1954 OSL Harriers
1955 OSL Track & Field
1955 OSL Football
1955 OSL Skiing
1955 OSL Basketball
1956 OSL Football
1956 OSL Track & Field
1956 OSL Skiing
1957 OSL Football
1957 OSL Track & Field
1957 OSL Skiing
1958 OSL Track & Field
1959 OSL Track & Field
1959 OSL Harriers
1961 CI Regatta (senior)
1961 OSL Harriers
1962 CI Boxing (senior)

1962 osl Harriers
1962 osl Water Polo
1963 osl Rifle
1963 osl Gymnastics
1964 osl Gymnastics
1964 osl Track & Field
1964 osl Harriers

1964 osl Nordic Ski
1965 osl Fencing
1965 osl Gymnastics
1965 osl Track & Field
1965 osl Harriers
1965 osl Nordic Ski
1965 ci Boxing (tie) (senior)

9 / AN ACT RESPECTING THE ROYAL MILITARY COLLEGE OF CANADA*

Assented to March 26th, 1959
Session Prorogued March 26th, 1959

Whereas the Royal Military College of Canada by its petition has represented that it was created by *An Act to establish a Military College in one of the Garrison Towns of Canada*, being chapter 36 of the Statutes of Canada, 1874, to be an institution for the purpose of imparting a complete education in all branches of military tactics, fortification, engineering and general scientific knowledge in subjects connected with and necessary to a thorough knowledge of the military profession and for qualifying officers for command and for staff appointments; and whereas, under authority of section 46 of *The National Defence Act* (Canada), being chapter 43 of the Statutes of Canada, 1950, the Governor in Council by P.C. 2512, dated the 19th day of May, 1950, entitled "Regulations for the Canadian Services Colleges", designated the College as one of the Canadian Services Colleges for the purpose of the education and training of officer cadets for the Royal Canadian Navy, the Canadian Army and the Royal Canadian Air Force, with the government, conduct, management and control of the College and of its work, affairs and business being vested in the Minister of National Defence; and whereas the College by virtue of the *National Defence Act* (Canada)[1] is now governed and administered according to the Queen's Regulations for the Canadian Services Colleges, P.C. 20/848 and P.C. 2/971, 1957, and is thereby empowered to grant diplomas, certificates and awards; and whereas the College has prayed for power to grant university degrees; and whereas it is expedient to grant the prayer of petition;

Therefore, Her Majesty, by and with the advice and consent of the Legislative Assembly of the Province of Ontario, enacts as follows:

1 In this Act,

(*a*) "Chairmen of the Academic Divisions" means the members of the Teaching Staff appointed to head the academic divisions of the College, which are at present the Divisions of Arts, Science, Engineering and Graduate Studies;

(*b*) "Chancellor" means the Chancellor of the College;

(*c*) "College" means the Royal Military College of Canada;

(*d*) "Commandant" means the Commandant of the College;

(*e*) "Director of Studies" means the Director of Studies of the College;

(*f*) "President" means the President of the College;

(*g*) "Registrar" means the Registrar of the College;

(*h*) "Senate" means the Senate of the College and consists of the President, the Commandant, the Director of Studies, the Chairmen of the Academic Divisions, and the Registrar as Secretary;

(*i*) "Teaching Staff" includes the professors, associate professors, assistant professors, lecturers, and all other officers of instruction at the College.

*Statutes of Ontario, 1959, c. 131.
[1]R.S.C. 1952, c. 184.

2 (a) The Senate shall have the power to grant degrees and honorary degrees in arts, science and engineering.

(b) The Senate may also confer degrees in arts or science upon any person who successfully completed the curriculum in arts or science at the College during the period from the 1st day of September, 1948, to the 1st day of January, 1959.

3 The Chancellor, or in his absence, the President or the Commandant shall have the power to confer degrees and honorary degrees upon candidates to whom such degrees have been granted by the Senate.

4 This Act shall be deemed to have come into force on the 1st day of January, 1959.

5 This Act may be cited as *The Royal Military College of Canada Degrees Act, 1959.*

INDEX